ROBERT PERSONS

Robert Persons, S.J. From a small contemporary portrait
in Stonyhurst College, Lancashire

FRANCIS EDWARDS, S.J.

ROBERT PERSONS

The Biography
of an Elizabethan Jesuit
1546–1610

THE INSTITUTE OF JESUIT SOURCES
St. Louis, Missouri

Number 10 in Series 3: Original Studies Composed in English

© The Institute of Jesuit Sources
3700 West Pine Boulevard
Saint Louis, MO 63108
Tel: [314] 977-7257
Fax: [314] 977-7263

Library of Congress Catalogue Card Number 95-76346
ISBN 1-880810-10-7 (hard cover)
ISBN 1-880810-11-5 (paperback)

CONTENTS

CHAPTER

ILLUSTRATIONS

Following page 204

1. Nether Stowey Church, Somerset. View taken before 1939(?)

2. Balliol College. From *Oxonia Illustrata,* 1675

3. Persons's original entry in the novices' register, formerly kept in the Roman novitiate at Sant'Andrea

4. Pope Gregory XIII (1572–1585). From a portrait bust in the German College, Rome

5. Stonor Park, near Henley on Thames

6. Title page of *A Brief Discours . . . why Catholiques Refuse to Goe to Church . . .* , 1580

7. Claudio Aquaviva, S.J., general from 1581 until 1615

8. Pope Clement VIII (1592–1605). From the funerary monument in S. Maria Maggiore, Rome

9. The "Pigskin Library" in the English College, Valladolid, in part of an original house incorporated into the new building in Persons's time

10. Saint Omer's College. Overall view from an engraving

11. Pope Paul V (1605–1621). Contemporary engraving

12. Robert Persons, S.J. Title page of *A Briefe Apologie . . .* , 1601

13. Contemporary portrait in oils of Thomas Firzherbert. From Stonyhurst College, Lancashire

14. Robert Persons, S.J. Title page of *The Christian Directory . . .* , edition of 1607

15. White marble memorial tablet in the chapel of St. Thomas, in the Venerable English College, Rome, contemporary with Persons

Preface ═══

A life of Robert Persons, the Elizabethan Jesuit, has long been overdue. The task is challenging. Indeed, it is unlikely that anyone could write so controversial a life in a way to please everyone. Can a Jesuit approaching the subject be expected to show objectivity and impartiality? But could anyone else be expected to show a proper understanding of the subject? Perhaps it takes a Jesuit to understand a Jesuit. Certainly, it must be difficult for anyone raised in the prevailing atmosphere of post-Christian secularism to understand, still less sympathize with, the main object of Persons's whole existence—the preservation of a Church. The nub of the difficulty lies in the fact that he was at the center of a controversy still with us, one which still stirs deep emotions and touches heartfelt convictions. He was a wholehearted protagonist of a firmly Rome-based Catholicism. Such an attitude must repel many Christians as well as nonbelievers, and contemporary Catholics may well find some of his attitudes more an embarrassment that anything else. Persons failed in his main endeavor, which was to win England back to Rome. For some who believe, this failure will be a sure sign that Providence was not with him. For unbelievers this might be proof that his world outlook was alien to the progress of a great nation as it has evolved up to the present time.

Like Oliver Cromwell, Persons was a man who did battle for righteousness. Few such can be dismissed out of hand as villains, even if enthusiasm and circumstances led them sometimes to adopt methods not commonly associated with sanctity. Persons will be forever classified with the villains by some well-meaning critics, since for much of his time he was undeniably, by generally accepted political standards, a traitor. From 1582 until the end of the century, he was fully supportive of schemes to invade England and overthrow the existing regime. He could hardly have intended anything less than the deposition of Queen Elizabeth, but there is no evidence that he ever worked for her assassination. In fact, although assassination theory could be discussed in Jesuit lecture rooms until 1614, it was never for the Jesuits a practical ploy.

But even treason is a term which enjoys its relativities. "Treason never prospers. What's the reason . . . ?" Sir John Harington answers his question thus: "For if it prosper, none dare call it treason." Persons's might have been a treason which prospered—like that of

1688, which overthrew a monarch and a regime, so that no one now could call it treason—without a kind of disloyalty, not to say treachery!

Persons and his colleagues are open to criticism on another count. Obliged by the circumstances of persecution, he adopted methods of deception to protect various kinds of truth from a ruthless enemy. He came to England in 1580, not openly as a priest, but disguised as a captain returning from the wars in Flanders. He supported the use of amphibology and equivocation, amounting to denial of the plain truth, to make it possible to escape detection by pursuivants and to avoid betraying his companions. Those who supported the Queen in all her claims, religious as well as civil, and had no particular reason for practicing equivocation were able to adopt, and did, a tone of high moral superiority. Nothing was easier than to dismiss Persons and his colleagues as liars as well as traitors. Not until the end of the eighteenth century would Catholics be on a par with Protestants in their ability to share the same political loyalties and profess on all occasions the same love of truth undisguised. One cannot deny the skill of the Elizabethan government in placing their opponents at this disadvantage; but should one presume to blame Persons and others too heartily for endeavoring to escape the nets thrown over them by their enemies, using such means and expedients as they could devise without violating the moral law as they understood it? Let this be the last word in any attempt to apologize for the subject. The object throughout is to represent the man, his work, and his beliefs as objectively as possible. The reader may be left to judge, if he is so inclined.

No attempt to box into a few hundred pages the life of a man so multifariously active as Robert Persons can be more than partially satisfactory. One could have occupied all the space in considering his books and writings. Nothing will be easier than to detect sins of omission. For this is the story of a community and the history of a period as seen through the life of one man. He and his cause did not succeed, but neither did it fail entirely. The survival of British Catholicism owed much to Persons and his close friend and colleague, William Allen.

Persons's contribution will be variously assessed, but certainly his influence in founding and protecting the fledgling seminaries overseas was considerable if not decisive. These corners of more than one foreign field produced the priests who ensured the survival of their faith and ancient tradition in the face of opposition ranging from savage persecution to the most humiliating kind of ostracism.

The majority of Persons's countrymen in his own day had no sympathy with what he was trying to do. As time passed, a growing number of Catholics came to regard him, and even his seminaries, as more an embarrassment than an aid to the faith. When Persons began his mission in England, it seemed that the old faith might still prevail. Militants everywhere, especially the Huguenots in France, considered that it might be necessary to have recourse to force of arms. By the end of his life, militancy was over. The best the papists could hope for was that by keeping their heads down they would no longer be noticed, that they might be allowed to practice their faith in obscurity, not from a spirit of tolerance, but because it was evident they were no longer worth bothering about.

Whatever we think of his cause, it emerges from Persons's letters and writings that we are dealing with a man not only of rare conviction but of extraordinary intelligence and personal gifts. A man must be judged by what others—and not only his friends—say about him: *nemo sui ipsius judex*. He must also be judged by what he himself says and does and writes, and not only in his own defence. Persons was one of the ablest controversialists of his day, with a flair for his native tongue that, in contrast with some of his coevals, makes his writing seem almost as modern as our own. He was remarkably well informed in many fields, even if his memory often failed him on details, especially dates. Character is revealed in letters, especially to friends and colleagues. Many of Persons's letters survive, although at times only in the form of mid-seventeenth-century transcripts and summaries made by Christopher Grene, S.J. Persons's correspondence with friend and foe constitute the basis of the present work, with supplementation from his books and other writings and the published and unpublished comments of others, mainly of his own generation, whether friendly or not.

Every student of the period knows that its controversies, especially in the related fields of religion and politics, tend to be interminable. Perhaps the limited publishing facilities of these days is an advantage, at least in sparing the patience of the reader, since few can be allowed to write interminably. Selection of facts and evidence to fill the space allowed does, however, inevitably involve an arbitrary personal element. This author can only offer by way of defence that he has omitted nothing from the available evidence, especially original sources, with any intention of bending or hiding evidence from which more important issues may be analyzed, if not finally resolved.

As nearly always in a historical inquiry of this kind, one finds great unevenness in the evidence available. There is an almost overabundant supply in some areas, often the less interesting and significant, and a corresponding dearth in others, frequently the more crucial. To a considerable extent, the present writer is only a Scott— and perhaps even this sounds too pretentious—to more than one indefatigable Waverley who helped to amass the transcripts of letters and other documents in the archives of the British Province of the Society of Jesus, a process which has taken something like a century. Some of them are used or published here, it seems, for the first time.

One cannot mention every name that could, and perhaps should, occur in this context: J. H. Pollen, Leo Hicks, and Basil Fitz-gibbon, and more recently Philip Caraman, A. J. Loomie, Tom Clancy, and Tom McCoog—all Jesuits who have made notable contributions to the subject. Miss Penelope Renold deserves special mention for the assistance she gave to Leo Hicks and for the precious research tools she donated to the British Province archives.

Special thanks are due to those who were my fellow archivists, and also to the librarians in a number of countries and cities who showed me that courtesy and attention which one expects from profes-sionals of this kind, but which one must not take for granted. A special debt of gratitude I owe to the staff of the Vatican Library and of the Archivio Segreto, in particular, Monsignor Charles Burns; the Archivi di Stato in Rome, Turin, and Florence; the municipal archives at Palermo; the Rijksarchiv at The Hague; the Archives nationales and the Bibliothque nationale in Paris; the Archives du Royaume in Brus-sels; the Archivo nacional at Simancas. Memorable was Monsignor Greenstock's kindly welcome to the English College, Valladolid. On these shores, I am indebted more particularly to the staff of the Na-tional Library in Edinburgh, the Bodleian in Oxford, the library of the university in Cambridge, and the Berkshire Record Office, Reading. In London, I must acknowledge especially the staff at the British Library, the Public Record Office both at Chancery Lane and Kew and at the Lambeth Palace Library. Miss Elizabeth Poyser at the Archives of the Archbishop of Westminster, Mrs. Clare Grant in the library of the Most Honorable the Marquess of Salisbury, and Dr. Anthony Kenny, for-merly Master of Balliol, gave me much assistance and, indeed, hospital-ity on the occasion of my visits. I am grateful to all those who read the original script and offered valuable comment.

Francis Edwards, S.J., F.S.A., F.R.Hist.S.

114 Mount Street

London, W1Y 6AH

Abbreviations Used in the Notes

a.l.s.	Autograph letter signed
Arch.	Archivio
Barb.	Barberini
Borgh.	Borghese
BL	British Library
CRS	Catholic Record Society
Cod.	Codex
DNB	Dictionary of National Biography (For the most part, the compact edition of 1975 was used.)
EHR	English Historical Review
Endd.	Endorsed
F, Fa.	Fr., Father
f.	folio
Fo.	Fondo
F.G.	Fondo Gesuitico
HMC	Historical Manuscripts Commission
Holog.	Holograph
Hol.	Holograph
Lat.	Latin *(Latinus, a, um)*
N.F.	No foliation
N.D.	No date
N. di	Nunziatura di
O.P.	Order of Preachers
O.S.	Old Style
O.S.B.	Order of Saint Benedict
Rep.	Report
RHE	Révue d'Histoire Ecclesiastique
RP	Robert Persons
s.	same (=*idem*)
S.D.	Same date
SHS	Scottish Historical Society
SP	State Papers (indicating that the author of this book quoted from the original document)
STCA	*Short-title catalogue of books printed in England, Scotland, and Ireland, and of English books printed abroad 1475–1640.* London, 1948 (reprographic edition)
S.J.	Society of Jesus
Vat.	Vatican *(Vaticanus, a, um)*
VEC	Venerable English College, Rome

Key to Archives References

(I) Stonyhurst manuscripts

(II) Stonyhurst MS, Christopher Grene, *Collectanea P*

(III) Archives of the Archbishop of Westminster

(IV) Archivio Segreto del Vaticano

(V) Biblioteca del Vaticano

(VI) Archives of the Society of Jesus, Borgo Santo Spirito 5, Rome

(VII) Public Record Office, London

(VIII) Archivo nacional de Simancas, Spain

(IX) Archives of the English College, Valladolid

(X) Milton House Collection: Berkshire Record Office, Reading, Q.9. This collection was dispersed after auction in 1984.

(XI) Inner Temple Library and Archives, London; Petyt MSS

(XII) Lambeth Palace Library

(XIII) British Library (British Museum)

(XIV) Archives of the British Province of the Society of Jesus, 114 Mount Street, London

(XV) Archives of the VEC

(XVI) Archives du Royaume, Brussels, Belgium

(XVII) Archivio di Stato, Florence, Italy

(XVIII) Archivio di Stato, Turin, Italy

Key to More Often Used Printed Sources

(1) CRS, Vol. 2. *Miscellanea* II. 1906.

(2) CRS, Vol. 39. *Letters and Memorials of Fr. Robert Persons, S.J.* Vol. I (to 1588). Ed. L. Hicks, S.J. London, 1942.

(3) Paul L. Hughes and James F. Larkin, C.S.V. *Tudor Royal Proclamations.* Vol. 2 (1553–1587) and Vol. 3 (1588–1603). New Haven and London, 1969.

(4) Sir F. Maurice Powicke and E. B. Fryde, eds. *Handbook of British Chronology.* Royal Historical Society: London, 1961.

(5) *The Penal Laws against Papists and Popish Recusants, Non-conformists and Non-jurors . . . from the first year of Queen Elizabeth down to the present year.* Printed for R. Gosling in the Savoy, 1723.

(6) George Oliver. *Collections towards Illustrating the Biography of the Scotch, English and Irish Members S.J.* Exeter, 1838.

(7) Anthony Wood. *Athenæ Oxonienses.* 4 vols. 3rd ed. by Philip Bliss. London, 1813-20.

(8) Henry Foulis. *The History of Romish Treasons and Usurpations.* . . . 2nd ed. London, 1681.

(9) T. F. Knox, ed. *The Letters and Memorials of William Cardinal Allen, 1553-94.* London, 1882.

(10) *Biographical Studies (1951-56); Recusant History (1957 to present).*

(11) M. A. Tierney, *Dodd's Church History of England.* Vols. 2 to 5. London, 1839-43.

(12) Henry Foley, S.J. *Records of the English Province of the Society of Jesus.* 7 vols. (Vol. 7 in 2 parts.) London, 1877-83.

(13) James F. Larkin and Paul L. Hughes. *Stuart Royal Proclamations.* Oxford, 1973.

(14) *HMC Calendar of the MSS of the Most Hon. the Marquis of Salisbury.* . . . Vols. 1–24. London, 1883-1976.

(15) D. H. Willson. *King James VI and I.* London, 1956.

(16) Henry More, S.J. *Historia Provinciæ Anglicanæ S.J.* . . . Saint Omer, 1660. The Elizabethan matter translated and edited by F. Edwards as *The Elizabethan Jesuits.* London and Chichester, 1981.

(17) Peter Guilday. *The English Catholic Refugees on the Continent, 1559-1795.* London, 1914.

(18) Godfrey Anstruther, O.P. *The Seminary Priests.* 4 vols., 1968-77. Vol. 1 (1558-1603), Ushaw; Vol. 2 (1603-59), Great Wakering.

(19) A. Allison and D. Rogers. *A Catalogue of Catholic Books in English Printed Abroad or Secretly in England, 1558-1640.* (10), Vol. 3. 1956.

(20) CRS, Vol. 41. *Letters of Thomas Fitzherbert 1608-10.* Ed. L. Hicks, S.J. 1948.

(21) CRS, Vol. 4. *Miscellanea IV.* 1907.

(22) J. R. Dasent. *Acts of the Privy Council of England.* New Series. Vol. 7 (1558-1570) to Vol. 32 (1601-4). London, 1893-1907.

(23) See (2).

(24) T. F. Knox, ed. *The First and Second Diaries of the English College, Douai.* . . . London, 1878.

(25) Martin A. S. Hume, ed. *Calendar of Letters and State Papers Relating to English Affairs Preserved Principally in the Archives of Simancas.* 4 vols. for Elizabeth I. London, 1892-99.

(26) L. Hicks, S.J. *An Elizabethan Problem: Some Aspects of the Careers of Two Exile-Adventurers.* Fordham University: New York, 1964.

(27) T. G. Law. *A Historical Sketch of the Conflicts between Jesuits and Secular Priests in the Reign of Queen Elizabeth.* . . . London, 1889.

(28) *Calendar of the State Papers Relating to Scotland (and Mary, Queen of Scots) . . . in the Public Record Office . . . and Elsewhere.* Various

editors. Vols. 1 to 13 (1509-1603). London and Edinburgh, 1858 to 1969.

(29) *Calendar of State Papers, Domestic.* . . . HM Public Record Office. Details of individual volumes are given in notes to the text.

(30) John Morris, S.J. *The Troubles of Our Catholic Forefathers Related by Themselves.* 1st, 2nd, and 3rd series. London, 1872, 1875, and 1877.

(31) A. O. Meyer. *England und die katholische Kirche unter Elisabeth.* Rome, 1911; English trans. (*England and the Catholic Church under Elizabeth*) by Fr. J. R. McKee of the London Oratory. London, 1916.

(32) *The Month.* Published by the Society of Jesus from Farm Street/ Mount Street, London, 1864–.

(33) CRS, Vol. 9. *Miscellanea* VII. 1911; Section 2, correspondence of Cardinal Allen, pp. 12–105.

(34) Prince Alexander Labanoff, ed. *Lettres, Instructions et Mémoires de Marie Stuart, Reine d'Ecosse.* . . . 7 vols. London, 1844.

(35) Joseph Gillow. *Bibliographical Dictionary of the English Catholics.* 5 vols. London, 1885-1903.

(36) J. B. Black. *The Reign of Elizabeth, 1558-1603.* 2nd ed. Oxford, 1959.

(37) L. von Pastor. *Geschichte der Päpste seit dem Ausgang des Mittelalters.* 13 vols. Freiburg, 1891-1929. English translation by F. I. Antrobus and R. F. Kerr. London, 1891-1933.

(38) W. V. Bangert, S.J. *A History of the Society of Jesus.* St. Louis, 1972.

(39) CRS, Vol. 14. *Miscellanea* IX. London, 1914.

(40) E. P. Cheney. *A History of England from the Defeat of the Armada to the Death of Elizabeth.* 2 vols. London, 1926.

(41) A. W. Pollard and G. R. Redgrave. *A Short-Title Catalogue of English Books Printed in England, Scotland and Ireland and of English Books Printed Abroad, 1475-1640.* London, 1948. An earlier edition was published in 1926.

(42) T. G. Law. *The Archpriest Controversy, Documents Relating to the Dissensions of the Roman Catholic Clergy, 1597-1602.* 2 vols. London, 1896 and 1898.

(43) *Archivum Historicum Societatis Iesu.* Historical Institute of the Society of Jesus: Rome.

(44) Lon van der Essen, ed. *Correspondence d'Ottavio Mirto Frangipani, premier Nonce de Flandre, 1596-1600.* Tome I, Lettres (1596-98) et Annexes; Tomes II and III (2 parts), Lettres (1597-1606) et Annexes. Rome/Brussels/Paris, 1924-42.

(45) F. Edwards, S.J. "Vatican Historical Sources, 1600-1604." Manuscript available at 114 Mount Street, London.

(46) J. H. Pollen, S.J. *The Institution of the Archpriest Blackwell.* . . . London, 1916.

(47) Antonio Astráin, S.J. *Historia della Compañía de Jesús en la Asistencia de España.* Madrid, 1909. Tomo 3, Mercurian to Aquaviva, primera parte (1573-1615).

(48) HMC. *Guide to the Reports of the Royal Commission on Historical MSS., 1911-57.* Part 2, Index of persons. 3 vols.

(49) J. H. Pollen, S.J. *The English Catholics in the Reign of Queen Elizabeth . . . , 1558-80.* London, 1920.

(50) John Strype. *Annals of the Reformation and Establishment of Religion.* . . . 4 vols. London, 1709-31.

(51) William Murdin. *A Collection of State Papers Relating to Affairs, 1571 to 1596.* . . . London, 1759.

(52) W. Mazire Brady. *The Episcopal Succession in England, Scotland and Ireland, 1400 to 1875.* 3 vols. Rome, 1876.

(53) Thomas Thomson, ed. *The History of the Kirk of Scotland by Mr. David Calderwood.* 8 vols. Edinburgh, 1842-49.

(54) *Calendar of State Papers, Foreign Series, of the Reign of Elizabeth to 1589.* PRO. London, series continues.

(55) *The Correspondence of Robert Bowes of Aske.* Surtees Society: London, 1842.

(56) P. Pius Boniface Gams, O.S.B. *Series Episcoporum Ecclesiæ Catholicæ.* . . . Ratisbon, 1873.

(57) Alfred Poncelet. *Histoire de la Compagnie de Jésus dans les anciens Pays-Bas.* 2 parts. Brussels, 1927.

(58) Aidan Cardinal Gasquet. *A History of the Venerable English College in Rome.* London, 1920.

(59) A. J. Loomie, S.J. *The Spanish Elizabethans: The English Exiles at the Court of Philip II.* Fordham University: New York, 1963.

(60) Martin P. Harney, S.J. *The Jesuits in History.* Chicago, 1962.

(61) Francesco Sacchino, S.J. *Historiæ Societatis Iesu.* Pars 3ª, sive Borgia, Rome, 1649; Pars 4ª, sive Everardus, Lille, 1661; Pars 5ª, sive Claudius, Tomus prior, Rome, 1661.

(62) Hubert Chadwick, S.J. *St. Omers to Stonyhurst.* London, 1962.

(63) Pedro de Ribadeneira, S.J. *Historias de la Contrariforma.* Biblioteca de Autores Cristianos. Madrid, 1945.

(64) Sir Ralph Winwood. *Memorials of Affairs of State of Queen Elizabeth and King James I.* Compiled and ed. Edmund Sawyer. 3 vols. London, 1725.

(65) *Bulletin of the Institute of Historical Research.* London.

(66) T. W. Moody, F. X. Martin, and F. J. Byrne. *A New History of Ireland.* Vol. 3, 1534-1691. Oxford, 1976.

(67) Humphrey Ely. *Certaine Briefe Notes upon a Briefe Apologie set out under the name of the Priestes united to the Archpriest.* Paris, [1602].

(68) CRS, Vol. 30. Canon Edwin Henson, ed. *Registers of the English College.* Valladolid, 1589-1862; London, 1930.

(69) Peter Milward, S.J. *Religious Controversies of the Elizabethan Age: A Survey of Printed Sources.* London, 1977.

(70) P. Milward, S.J. *Religious Controversies of the Jacobean Age: A Survey of Printed Sources.* London, 1978.

(71) Rev. M. E. Williams. *The Venerable English College, Rome: A History, 1579-1979.* London, 1979.

(72) David Lunn. *The English Benedictines, 1540-1688.* London, 1980.

(73) Christopher Haigh. *The English Reformation Revised.* Cambridge, 1987.

(74) Michael E. Williams. *St Alban's College, Valladolid.* London/New York, 1986.

(75) A. J. Loomie, S.J. *Spain and the Jacobean Catholics.* Vol. 1, 1603–12. CRS, Vol. 64. 1973.

(76) A. G. Petti. *Recusant Documents from the Ellesmere Manuscripts.* CRS. Vol. 60, 1968.

(77) Arnold Pritchard. *Catholic Loyalism in Elizabethan England.* London (England) and the University of North Carolina Press, 1979.

(78) D. Andrew Penny. *Freewill or Predestination: The Battle over Saving Grace in Mid-Tudor England.* Woodbridge (England) and Rochester (N.Y.), 1993)

(79) Alexandra Walsham. *Church Papists: Catholicism, Conformity and Confessional Polemic in Early Modern England.* Woodbridge (England) and Rochester (N.Y.), 1993

(80) Mark H. Curtis. *Oxford and Cambridge in Transition, 1558–1642.* Oxford, 1959.

(81) Alan Haynes. *Invisible Power.* Stroud (England) and Wolteboro Falls (N.H.), 1992.

It is an ordinary course of Almightie God that when He will sett on foote any greate worke to His glory by help of man He alwayes multipliethe the difficulties, thereby bothe to encrease as well the dignity and meritte of the thinge itselfe, as also to make His servantes to distruste in their own forces and leane unto Him.

— Robert Persons, S.J.
A Storie of Domesticall Difficulties

Robert Persons[1] was born at Nether Stowey in Somerset on St. John Baptist's day, June 24, 1546. He described his father and mother, Henry, and Christina, as of "humble worldly condition but honourable and of somewhat better rank than their neighbours around, likewise catholics in religion." According to Foulis[2] his father was a blacksmith. A note prepared by the Jesuit historian claims his father was "occupied in agriculture," presumably a farmer.[3] The two ideas are not, of course, incompatible.

For most of his adult life, Robert was a figure of controversy. Indeed, this began even before he was born. Enemies later claimed that his birth was illegitimate. The charge seems to have come to the fore in 1601 at the time of the archpriest controversy. Henry Garnet, a fellow Jesuit, defended his reputation—or, more correctly, that of his parents—in a letter of May 20, 1601. It is significant that he was obliged to defend him against a well-known priest and critic of the Jesuits, John Mush, who included the slur in his *Declaratio Motuum*.[4] As might have been expected, some of Persons's Protestant critics, reacting in the spirit of the times, felt obliged to improve on this. Thomas Bell and Thomas James, for example, in books published respectively in 1603 and 1612 claimed that his real father was the parish priest of Stogursey. This flavorsome piece of scandal was taken up by Matthew Sutcliffe, dean of Exeter, who when challenged defended himself by pointing out—correctly—that the charge was one made by Persons's fellow priests.[5] John, Robert's brother, flew to his defence—not out of fraternal affection but to save the honor of their parents. Indeed, John

---

[1] This spelling of Persons is adopted throughout as the form he invariably used. His contemporaries likewise usually signed themselves uniformly, e.g., Burghley, William Waad, Thomas Wintour in his authentic signatures. Others spelled them as they wished.

[2] (8) 500; (1) 18.

[3] (VI) Anglia.38.I, f.125a.

[4] (II) f.596a; (1) 37. Cf. s. to the prefect of the English mission, 16.viii.1601; (II) f.538a and (1) 37.

[5] (1) 45, 46.

had no use for his brother's religion; on one occasion he declared, "There is not anyone more pernicious to our religion and state than is Persons the Jesuit."[6] John's most telling point was that "Vicar Hayward," the main rival for the distinction of Robert's paternity, came to Nether Stowey some three years after Robert's birth there. Certainly there was no scandal in the district regarding the origins of Robert or of the other children. As always, people tended to believe as they preferred rather than as the evidence pointed, once doubt had entered. The priests William Watson, Christopher Bagshaw, and John Mush were joined in a raucous chorus by Anthony Copley, a layman.[7] Robert himself appealed to the local register of baptisms. True, the registers disappeared probably during the civil war, but it is unlikely that Persons would have made his appeal to so reliable and public a witness unless he was very sure of himself.[8]

Robert was the sixth son of eleven children, though perhaps not all survived. John Hayward, canon regular and still "a pious catholic," had charge of the church at Nether Stowey in which the child was baptised. "He was pleased with Robert's disposition, and somewhat also moved" by the fact that Robert was the first child he baptised after coming into the parish.[9] Hayward maintained his interest. "This man lived there for thirty years together until . . . Persons's departure out of England, who having been his master in the Latin tongue, and liking his forwardness in learning, did ever afterward bear a special affection towards him."[10] The family background was seemingly happy, although the religious divisions of the Reformation had their effect on the Persons clan also. Still, John, the Anglican minister, reported of the parents that they "lived together man and wife most comfortably above fifty years."[11]

---

[6] J. Persons to T. Somaster, 31.v.1602; (1) 40–46; from (I) Anglia.A.III, No. 14.

[7] See W. Watson (C. Bagshaw?), A sparing discoverie . . . (1601), pp. 41–42; J. Mush, Declaratio motuum . . . (1601), p. 23. A. Copley, Answer to a letter of a Jesuited gentleman . . . (1601), pp. 6, 13, 32, 36, et passim.

[8] H. Foulis could not find them ((8) 500). N.B.: No dispensation for illegitimacy was required at Persons's entry into the Society of Jesus or for his ordination. See also (1) 37, 44, and especially p. 13 n. "An enquiry was made into the slander . . . by the protestant earl of Bath, the most powerful nobleman in the neighbourhood of Nether Stowey, and the charge was pronounced 'a lewd slander.'"

[9] (1) 18. See A manifestation of the great folly . . . ([Antwerp], 1602), sig.Z1–2/pp. 89f.

[10] (1) 46.

[11] (1) 41. For the overall religious situation in England at this time, see (73). But this plays down the persecution of seminary priests and Jesuits in the period. See also (77) and (79).

A good deal less comfortable but normal for the times was the experience of the sixteenth-century education mill, at least for Robert. "Scarcely was he out of childhood" when he was put to work with "an elder brother, a merchant, to learn business." Unfortunately for the man if not for Robert, "this brother lost nearly the whole of his fortune and sent Robert back home to his parents."

John Hayward came to the rescue. At his persuasion, Robert and John were sent to the local grammar school at Stogursey.[12] Hayward also promised to help with fees and expenses, but he seems to have died within the year. To continue their schooling the boys were now obliged to attend "a free scolle" in Taunton. Robert, if not John, was obliged to endure for about a year a master who was "very sharp and cruel to his scholars." The master later admitted, according to John, that he treated Robert more harshly because "he found my brother to have a good wit and could do well." But a point was reached when Robert could endure this blend of sadism and zeal no longer. He wrote a letter to his father, complaining of his master's cruelty and his own unfitness to be a scholar. Henry was moved by the letter. So was Christina. She "presently took horse, it being seven miles off, and when she came thither went and told his master all what he had written, and made him to whip him well. And afterwards did so chide and threaten him that if he came home, she would tie him to a post and whip him; and yet that should not serve his turn; for she would presently send him back to his master again." The schoolmaster was a Catholic and eventually lost his post for his convictions.

Young Robert bowed—and bent—to the inevitable. Indeed, "he fell to his book very heartily and became the best in the school, and so continued as long as he was there." He even came to admire his master cum tormentor, observing "his great goodness of life and other things which did him good afterward." At all events, this fearsome dominie contributed much to Robert's further progress because, convinced of the lad's "good wit," he persuaded his father to send him to Oxford, further prophesying that "he would prove a rare man."[13]

No clear record is known of Robert's first entry into Oxford. Neither is the date of his matriculation recorded. As he remembered it, he was eighteen when he began studies at the university in 1564.[14] After studies in logic at St. Mary's Hall, he moved to Balliol in 1566.

---

[12] (1) 19.

[13] Ibid. and Richard Persons to Edward Coffin, S.J., n.d., (1) 38–40 from (I) Anglia.A.VII, No. 43. Another brother, Thomas, was also at Oxford with Robert and John. Richard and George remained or became Catholics ((1) 38, note at (B)).

[14] (1) 19. Anthony à Wood puts it at the end of 1563 ((7) II, col.64). See (1) 38.

The first clear record of his Oxford career is his receiving the Bachelor of Arts degree on May 31, 1568. Soon afterwards he was enrolled as a probationer fellow of Balliol.[15] To obtain his degree Persons subscribed to the oath of supremacy of 1559. "Accordingly, wicked and ambitious youth that I was, not to lose my degree, I twice pronounced . . . that abominable oath though at heart I detested it."[16] Edmund Campion, proctor that year for the university, shared his doubts and unease. Persons dealt with him through his friends to get himself excused from the oath. Campion would have complied but he was already regarded with suspicion by "a companion in office who watched all his proceedings." The oath had to be taken publicly, so Persons could not be excused. Campion as proctor was also obliged to preside in Congregation and witness to the oath. However, it seems unlikely that after the probationary period Persons, as à Wood claims, accepted holy order as a chaplain-fellow.[17]

Persons soon distinguished himself as a tutor, exercising the kind of influence indicated by the subsequent careers of some of his students: Alexander Briant, Richard Yeomans, and Simon Fenell, for example, all of whom became priests and one a martyr.[18] After the uncomfortable experience of the oath taking, the new Fellow of Balliol did not seem to have allowed the religious question to weigh heavily upon him. Nevertheless, a harder-line Protestantism was now extending its influence at the university.

In 1569 "the ringleaders of the heretics in London," well aware that much of Oxford had adopted a foot-dragging attitude towards the Reform, decided to move in on the Catholics. Bigotry was everywhere in the atmosphere of Europe in those days, but nowhere more so than in Spain and England. A Puritanical group at Oxford now set up a seemingly unofficial but effective "inquisition tribunal against Catholics." One of its first victims was Richard Garnet, a personal friend of Persons and also a Fellow of Balliol. He was seized and imprisoned. He was the first to take his stand for the old faith and "subsequently suffered much at the hands of the heretics."[19] Persons felt the force of his example, but not yet to the point of wanting to follow it. All the same, he withdrew to his native Somerset for a time, where he managed to drum up financial support from friends and

---

[15] J. Foster, *Alumni Oxonienses, 1500–1714* (Oxford, 1891), p. [1123].

[16] (1) 19.

[17] (7) II, col.65. A. Kenny suspects the idea arose from confusing Robert Benson with RP in the Balliol register.

[18] (1) 19.

[19] See (1) 16 and 20.

patrons, especially one John Stone, a relative and "a rich man of Bristol," indeed, the mayor of Bristol that year. He required the money to keep him while he studied common law in London. The Inns of Court were not less Catholic in sympathy than Oxford but under less pressure from the Puritanical element. While in London Persons successfully avoided the twin "danger," as he later described it, "of marrying a wife as also of obtaining an ecclesiastical benefice." He returned to Oxford and to relative peace—but not for long.

So far his was a tale of progress. Tutor to the sons of noblemen, he soon came to enjoy the trust and friendship of their parents. On December 3, 1572, he became a Master of Arts and soon afterwards received his appointment as bursar of Balliol College.[20] It is not likely that a man who combined dangerous opinions with notable acuteness would do less than tread warily in a task in which he was succeeeding so well. But his very success probably contributed to the hatred of rising enemies. One of them, Christopher Bagshaw, now enters the scene in the role he would fill for a lifetime, a Perrin to Persons's Traill, in a hatred and rivalry that would prove implacable to the end. Persons attempted to make peace throughout his life but with no success, although Bagshaw followed him into the Church and even into the priesthood. The rivalry began in 1573, possibly 1572; and from this time the historian must wrestle with the familiar, fascinating, and difficult task of trying to decide, where the evidence is contradictory, who is telling the truth. It is certainly a worldly point in Persons's favor that so far he had been anxious to avoid controversial situations. A well-trained and pliable conscience helped him through moments of moral challenge. But it is difficult to believe that an academic entirely taken up with success in his own field was so lacking in judgment, to say nothing of integrity, as to commit the egregious error of deliberate peculation, above all in a trivial matter. This could be a prejudiced judgment which depends on what Persons became rather than on what he was when certain accusations were made. Certainly, his enemies then seemed intent on discrediting him at all costs. Finding nothing more serious, they contrived to make the most of an accusation of minor peculation, suggesting to this observer a lack of scruple which, however incongruously, can characterize the deeper dislikes even of men religiously inclined.

Writing somewhat later,[21] Archbishop George Abbot described the origins of a feud among the Balliol dons which led to Persons's

---

[20] J. Foster, *Alumni Oxonienses*, ibid.

[21] See P. A. Welsby, *George Abbot—the Unwanted Archbishop* (London, 1962). He lived from 1562 to 1633 and was archbishop from 1611 to 1633.

undoing in the university. To offer some justification for his antagonists, it could well be that Persons, perhaps driven by an uneasy conscience and rising moral frustration, too freely gave vent to a wit that was always shrewd and sometimes mordant. Unable to repay him in his own coin and quite ungrateful for his generous alms of home truths, they minted a currency in baser metal to settle their accounts. A series of incidents in 1573 added up to an episode.

Bursar from October 18, 1572, and "joined in office with one Stancliff, a very simple fellow," Persons traded on his colleague's weakness and falsified the accounts "much to the damage of the college; as also deeply polling the commoners' names . . . and . . . not sparing his own scholars, . . . it was thought that he had purloined 100 marks."[22] The office was changed on the feast of St. Luke, and on October 18, 1573, one Hyde succeeded Persons. With Hyde's approval if not at his instigation, and with questionable purity of motive, "there were some that between that and February 1573/4 scanned over the books" in response to "secret complaints" from some of their scholars. They found, or thought they found, evidence of irregularity. More significant in some respects, they established from other sources, at least to their own satisfaction, that Persons was a bastard. Since it was required by statute that every Fellow should be *legitimo thoro natus*, they went on to have him expelled. Abbot recorded a further piece of gossip. "Persons was not of the best fame concerning incontinency, as I have heard some say who lived in Oxon at that time." Abbot had the grace to admit, "Whether that were then objected against him, I have not heard." If there had been any plausible foundation for the slur, doubtless Persons's enemies would have made the most of it.

Another incident at this time suggests anything but moral laxity.[23] Persons went up to London on business at Christmas 1573,

---

[22] G. Abbot to Dr. Hussaye, 1.ii.1601, (8) 501.

[23] I am indebted to Sir Anthony Kenny for permission to study the accounts and other material at Balliol College. See Henry Savage, Master, *Balliofergus or a commentary upon the foundation, founders and affaires of Balliol Colledge, gathered out of the records thereof and other antiquities* . . . (Oxford, 1668), p. (111), (Jesson Library 88.d.10). "Robert Persons was Socius Sacerdos of this colledge, commonly called Chaplain-Fellow; and consequently entered into Holy Orders when but Bachelor of Arts, for so tis required of everyone that is to be chosen Chaplain Fellow. He resigned his fellowship Anno 1573, Feb.13, with dispensation . . . to keep his chamber and scholars as long as he pleased; and his commons to be allowed him till Easter following" (pp. 112f). Persons's resignation in his own hand, not without obscurity, is in the Balliol College Register, 1514–1682, at p. 125. The "Bursars Computi 1568–1591" should provide evidence of Persons's carefulness as bursar or otherwise but dates on the earlier pages are sometimes badly damaged. Two leaves covering a period after 1569 have been torn out. Dates are clear from 7.vii.1572. After the "communia servientium post 7m diem Julii 1572," one reads as follows: "Quoniam collegium nostrum injuria negligentia et morte quorundam custodum

staying as the guest of the father of a boy, James Hawley, whom he was tutoring. In his absence, Persons's rivals took the lad, "a handsome boy," to a theatrical performance, first warning him to keep the matter from his tutor lest he be punished for it. Young James, to make assurance doubly sure, avoided his tutor altogether on his return. He took up residence with Christopher Bagshaw, who was to be "the conspirators' chief actor in the plot" or their principal tool.[24] Adam Squire, master of Balliol, and Thomas Hyde, bursar—"heretics," as Persons later dubbed them—seem to have been the main inspiration. Bagshaw probably wanted to become the boy's tutor himself, but as Persons was dean that year it was well within his prerogative to compel Bagshaw to return the lad. Unwilling to provoke a scene, Persons chose the quieter way of bringing the matter to the master's notice and then before a College Meeting where the "conspiracy . . . burst into light."

---

sociorum, bursariorum, et cohabitantium ante actae aetatis ad paupertatem misere redactum est, ita ut aere alieno plurimum laboraret ut hoc malo ac infamia collegii inde enata istius nos nostrumque donum uberemque placuit magistro et omnibus sociis solvere pro cubic[ulis?] suis per unius anni spatium id proximum sequentis 20 Octob.-1572." This was signed by Adam Squier, Joannes Tunckis, Robertus Persons, Joannes Wilson, Thomas Hyde, James Stanclyff. A list of arrearages follows for 1559, 1563–65 and 1570. Lists of payments "e cubiculis" vary from ten to two shillings, Persons paying on average 3s 4d. This source produced in all £4 13s a quarter(?) while the "summa totius lateris" amounted to £54 5s 4d. So it seems that a serious attempt at restoring college finances began after Persons came on the scene, which is consonant with his later interest and competence in the finances of the seminaries. After an account of expenses from 7.vii.1572 to 7.vii.1573 occurs the following: "Computo inceptoris Rob. Persons et domini Jacobi Stancklif bursariorum collegii de Baliolo Oxon diligenti examinatione considerato, quaedam visa sunt magistro et omnibus sociis negligentia omisa quaedam temere et inconsiderate gesta, et nonnulla superflua petiserunt in detrementi [1 word?] et ante hoc in nostro collegii inauditis quorum detrimentorum summa est XVII lib. XIXs. ob.9 quorum nulla sit causa (allocatis omnibus allocandis) cur detrimenta excederent summa 4 admaximum. . . ." (The reference is to pounds.) In conscience, the Master and Fellows could not "exonerare praedictos bursarios summa XI lib . . . quaeque per neglegentiam et incuriam bursariorum contingeret." This was signed by Squier, Tunckis, Wilson, and Hyde. Any evidence on RP offered by Squier must be accepted with reserve; but, if RP and Stanclyff, in the course of bringing order to the college finances, were only out by eleven pounds, this was not a great sum even in those days. One may note the further comment of a Catholic imprisoned for debt. After saying that RP left Oxford to avoid Squier's pressure to make him accept Anglican ordination, he further observed, "Those who understand the ways of Oxford can well consider the fact that bursars receive a percentage on every pound, and it is the custom for them to receive some gratuity from trademen" ((VI) Anglia 38.II.f.181, Italian copy). If so, there was ample room here for Squier's hardly disinterested misinterpretation. Savage's rough notes (Balliol MS 429, with pp. 145–51 of MS 255) do not allude to the peculation charge, while regretting that of bastardy, since "noe man is eligible into our society [Balliol] but one that is legitime thoro natus." See below and A. Kenny, *Balliol Studies* 2.

[24] (1) 21 and 17.

This action of Bagshaw's was probably in the nature of a revenge. He was, as Abbot described him, "a smart young man . . . who thought his penny good silver." Notwithstanding the fact that he was already a Bachelor of Arts, he was for some offence "swinged by Persons being Dean of the College." In a word, this proud and vulnerable man, hypersensitive to any affront to his dignity, had to submit to a birching, seemingly by Persons himself. He cherished his resentment "and afterward coming to be Fellow was most hot in persecution against Persons."[25] Dr. Squire was happy to encourage him, since he "thought himself to have been much bitten by vile libels" and presumed Persons to be the author—not without reason, perhaps, since Persons was reported to be "wonderfully given to scoffing, and that with bitterness, which also was the cause that none of the company loved him." Squire and Bagshaw were natural allies in making the most of the fraud charge. Meanwhile Persons "stood in the act" celebrated on October 12, 1573.[26] Richard Persons gave another reason for friction between his brother and Squire. Robert "told him sometimes of his evil life" which none knew better than he; but Squire "could not abide to hear of it." An example of his "evil life" was some device by which Squire managed to con a few Somersetshire men out of their modest possessions, lands, and money. They lodged a formal complaint with a justice of the peace at Nether Stowey, who passed the case to Persons in Oxford. If Squire thought Persons would cover up for a fellow don, he was to be severely disillusioned. Indeed, Persons pursued the matter so vigorously that Squire was obliged to pay the men full compensation. Only influence, it seems, saved Squire from losing the college mastership and perhaps further disgrace.[27]

Revenge was not to be long delayed, for Robert had now made up his mind to become a Catholic. Squire procured a meeting in the college chapel which found "ways sufficient concurring to expel" him "in truth no man standing for him."[28] Persons remembered Squire's enmity, later claiming that he was never involved in controversy with the university but only with one man there, namely, Adam Squire, afterwards son-in-law to the Bishop of London. He dismissed Squire as "a man of known infirmities—to say no worse."[29]

---

[25] G. Abbot to Dr. Hussaye, 1.ii.1601; (8) 501f. See (7) II, cols. 65f: à Wood gives "prosecution" for "persecution." Hussaye wanted to know "what is on record any way against Mr Persons."

[26] (7) II, col.65.

[27] (1) 39.

[28] (8) 501.

[29] RP, *A briefe apologie* . . . (1602), 194.

After the college meeting, Persons was offered the alternatives, approved by a majority of five or six, to resign the fellowship or be expelled. If he resigned, he could stay on a few months to settle his affairs. If he opted for expulsion, it had to be that very night. Persons elected to resign on the understanding he could have a few months in the college "to live there after his own fashion." This was guaranteed by a "private oath" of the Fellows, and the Latin record gives him a stay until Easter of 1574.[30] "But this last decree was presently after cancell'd or cross'd and so remains in their register-book."[31]

Persons was by no means content to live out his time quietly. On the contrary, he roundly rebuked eaters of meat during Lent in the college bounds for thus violating the statutes. Some had not only eaten meat in their own chambers but had drawn their scholars to it and found ways of penalizing those who did not join them.[32] With his friend Dr. Martin Culpeper, recently promoted Warden of New College, he discussed ways of getting them punished.

Culpeper was prepared to support Persons if adequate evidence was at hand and even to "lay them in prison." When it became known that Persons was collecting the evidence, the miscreants appealed to Squire, at that time in London. He had immediate recourse to the Earl of Leicester, High Chancellor of Oxford. Leicester wrote a sufficiently sharp letter to Culpeper, now vice-commissary, telling him to desist from helping "an attempt or meaning of one evil affected in religion towards others that were good Protestants for a trifle of eating a little flesh."[33]

Understandably, Culpeper was not prepared to brave Leicester even to please Persons, so the latter had to accept defeat. Squire and his allies made the most of their victory. "Against their oaths," they put

---

[30] (8) 502: Easter 1573/74 fell on March 22.

[31] The canceled passage is in the Balliol College Register, 1514–1682, p. 125. RP's resignation is as follows, "Ego Robertus Persons socius Collegii de Balliolo dne meam inc titulum et clamen quae habeo vel habere potero societatis meae dicto Collegio quod quidem facio sponte et[crossed through] coactus die decimo tertio mensis februarii Ao . . . 1573. Per me Rob. Persons." Savage commented, "That he wrote his resignation sponte et coactus but afterwards some friend of his wrote (non) overhead, and made it sponte non coactus. Answ. This "non" was written with the same hand as the "et" under it was written with, and therefore writing his resignation with a running hand, he mistook: upon a review whereof, he blotted out the "et" and wrote "non" over it immediately; and that he should of purpose write such a contradiction as "sponte et coactus" cannot be incident to a wise man and a scholar. If any say twas a jest I believe he would not "jocari in re tam seria. . . ." Further, "had he been expelled the house, this expulsion and the cause would have been registered."

[32] *A briefe apologie . . .* , 196.

[33] Ibid., 197.

it about that Persons was no longer a Fellow of Balliol. They even went to St. Mary Magdalen's, the parish church, "and rang the bells backward as if fire had been in town." They explained to the people "that a great papist was fired out of Balliol College that day."[34] Always a man of dogged courage and determination, Persons nevertheless refused to go. His senior colleagues had the decency not to press him further before the time appointed. Culpeper, James Hawley, and others testified to the fact that he stayed on. Indeed, "after he had been some months in London he returned . . . to visit friends in the university, which did utterly condemn so barbarous and boyish a fact as the ringing of the bells."[35] But Squire found another opportunity to humiliate Persons and speed his departure.

As dean, Person had to preside over "corrections"—birchings—"in the hall on Saturdays." About the time of his exclusion, Squire ordered him on one such occasion "to call the book and roll." Squire then came in and exhorted him to have a good care to the discipline of the youth in the college for the rest of his time in office. But the advice was given in a spirit of mockery, as was obvious enough both to the onlookers and to Persons himself. He decided, no doubt wisely, that enough was enough. Continued antagonism between himself and the master could bring good to none; and so he "got him away to London."[36]

But Persons made friends at this time as well as enemies. In London he became acquainted with Lord Buckhurst, afterwards Treasurer, "who loved him exceedingly well, and kept him some two or three months with him and would never willingly have him out of his company."[37] Furthermore, Sir Richard Baker, whose son he had tutored, of his own accord offered Persons a lease of certain lands in Somerset which had just come to his eldest son. Persons, building up his resources, accepted the offer and sold the lands for £100 to James Clark, secretary to Sir John Popham, Solicitor General. It is probable

---

[34] Ibid. According to Foulis, Bagshaw was the principal instigator of the bell-ringing episode ((8) 501). According to Savage (Balliol MS 529), RP "was rung out of the College by Magdalene bells. There was great want of candlesticks (the usual instruments of ringing on such occasions) so that they were fain to make use of Mag. parish bells."

[35] *A briefe apologie* . . . , ibid. Facsimile reproduction of RP's resignation "sponte et coactus" in (1) facing p. 22. See also (7) II, 67 n.(*); (24) 363. J. Mush, *Declaratio motuum* . . . , 57, says RP was expelled for sedition and faction; C. Bagshaw and H. Ely sing harmoniously in this choir.

[36] (8) 502. The above narrative of events, compiled from several MS accounts, tries to put them in logical sequence, correcting Abbot's account especially. (See (1) 39). Some doubt evidently remains.

[37] (1) 39.

that Persons made several visits to London at this time, if only to get away from the unfriendly atmosphere of Squire's Balliol.

Persons was certainly back in London after Easter 1574, where he still enjoyed the protection of Lord Buckhurst, an acquaintance made "by means of the Culpepers and Sidneys," two or three of whose sons Persons had likewise tutored.[38] Nevertheless, not even Buckhurst, still some distance from the height of his own career, could do much in the new religious climate for a man of Persons's growing convictions. In fact, it was Buckhurst, according to one account, who persuaded Persons to go to Padua to study medicine at the university there, which enjoyed a high international reputation in that field. In metaphysical matters the atmosphere of Padua was remarkably liberal. It is probable that Buckhurst was hoping that, once away from the unhealthy antagonisms then prevailing at Oxford, Persons might lose the edge of a zeal which was more a reaction than a spontaneous enthusiasm for the popish cause. He could then return to England to spend his life in something genuinely useful. At all events, Robert betook himself to Padua in the company of "Mr Lane of Corpus Christi," also M.A., Oxon.[39]

Persons left England in May or June 1574. He put all his property "in confidence" with Buckhurst, who "dealt honourably" with him even after he knew that he had entered religion in Italy, handing over his property faithfully to Persons's assigns.[40] Already Robert intended to effect a formal reconciliation with Rome but not yet to become a priest. Indeed, he was altogether taken by the idea of studying medicine in the university of Vessalius, Fallopius, and Acquapendente, the founders of modern anatomical science. Thanks to the Venetian preoccupation with trade and the arts and its contact with the world of Islam, it was not excessively preoccupied with questions of strict Catholic orthodoxy.[41] The way to Padua lay through Calais, Antwerp, and Louvain, where Robert waited for a group forming up to visit the Frankfurt Fair. He now had as companions John Yates and William Slade, who both became priests; Yates became a Jesuit missionary in Brazil as well.

It was in Louvain that Persons underwent the spiritual experience that determined the principal direction of his life. He went

---

[38] (1) 23.

[39] See (1) 39.

[40] (1) 23.

[41] See Prof. P. van Kessel, "Prosecution of German Students in Padua During the Counter-Reformation," a paper read at the International Colloquium of the Ecclesiastical History Society (Oxford, 1974).

through eight days of the Spiritual Exercises of St. Ignatius under the evidently competent direction of Fr. William Good, S.J. At the end of it, he already wished to change his studies "of physick into divinity." It was the human soul rather than the body that would become his main preoccupation. Practical as always, however, he kept in sight the fact that he had forwarded his money to Venice and must travel there to recover it, taking in Padua on the way.

From Antwerp to Frankfurt and thence to Padua, his travel companions were George Lewkenor, later a medical doctor, and Luke Astlow, who was destined to meet an early death in Padua the year after their arrival. Even now, Adam Squire was not quite left behind. In response to a letter from his brother John describing "how impudently" Squire had charged them both "with stealing away college writings," Persons wrote to Squire himself. The contents of the letter are unknown, but Archdeacon Somaster of Totnes described it as a libel, indicating that it was at least a piece of plain speaking.[42] We would expect no less of the writer. Persons and company reached Padua in September 1574, but they were all drawn irresistibly to the great lodestone, Rome. Robert looked forward to meeting again his "great friend" John Lane, who had arrived shortly before together with Owen Lewis, later bishop of Cassano. Persons reached Rome in time for Pope Gregory's opening of the Holy Door at the beginning of the jubilee year 1575. But the attention of the classical scholar was powerfully deflected by the still-splendid sights of antiquity. "God knoweth, I carried little devotion out of Rome with me, for I had attended more to see profane monuments of Caesar, Cicero and other such like than to places of devotion."[43]

All the same, Persons was soon on the road back to Padua together with Lane and Astlow. Money was not in short supply and in Padua they were able to afford "a very commodious house." Persons now applied himself to medicine and his two housemates to law. Time to reflect brought with it certain scruples. Persons remembered that he had left Rome without "taking the commodity of the jubilee" indulgence. He had not even gone to confession there. He decided that he must repair both omissions but feared his friends would laugh at him for his scruples. However, these did not extend to telling them the simple truth. He told them he was going to Parma on instructions from Buckhurst to settle some business of his. Lane and Astlow at the end of May accompanied him on the road as far as Venice. He then set off on his own as if for Parma but soon changed direction and

---

[42] See J. Persons to T. Somaster, 31.v.1602; (1) 44.

[43] (1) 24.

proceeded to Rome on foot. This was not from necessity but to make his progress a penance for his former negligence. He arrived in Rome about the end of May 1575. After a few more weeks there, he made a great decision. On July 4, 1575, he applied for admission to the Jesuit novitiate as a postulant, and was accepted as a novice on the feast of St. James, July 25.[44] The ambience could not have been all that strange, for with him were Henry Garnet, William Weston, and William Holt, all kindred spirits from Oxford. For the next three years Persons was happy in having and making no history except of a purely spiritual kind.

---

[44] (1) 25 and n. (*). In his memoirs RP relied excessively on memory for dates. He put the date of his entry into the Society of Jesus in June 1575. Nathaniel Southwell (Catalogus primorum patrum, (I) A.iv.3)) relying on the Procurators' Book in Rome, no longer extant, made it July 4. The beginning of postulancy is the beginning of life as a Jesuit. (See (16) 44 and (XIV) 46/10/5). Astlow and Lane decided to follow RP's example, but Astlow died before leaving Padua and Lane only survived until 1578.

Chapter Two
The Venerable English College, Rome
1578–1579

Persons completed his early training in the Society up to sacerdotal ordination in record time. "After almost three years . . . I was made priest while I studied my course of divinity in the Roman College." As a priest, he "supplied the place of the English penitentiary in St. Peter's for some space." He also took charge of the second-year novices, and so continued until 1580.[1] During this time he became involved in the development of the English College, soon to become "venerable."

A hospice for English priests had been founded in the eleventh century. Dr. William Allen, founder of the English College, Douai, in 1568, persuaded Gregory XIII to develop the role of the Roman institution, which had virtually become a shelter for elderly priests and dons in exile, an ecclesiastical Sleepy Hollow.[2] After his return to Douai from Rome on July 30, 1576, Allen dispatched four students to Rome on August 16 to form the nucleus of a new college. The hospice, which enjoyed an annual income of 1,450 crowns, would alleviate Douai's problem of overcrowding and limited funds. Little enough of this money was now spent on pilgrims, few of whom came from Protestant England. The resident chaplains could easily afford to share their income with the students, although there would now be less available for improving the property or relieving English exiles in the city. The principle was unexceptionable, but one could not expect those who would be the losers to do anything but complain.

Some of Allen's students who had lived outside moved into the hospice in 1577, being joined by six more, and six more again in 1578. From 1574 Allen was fully supported in his efforts by Owen Lewis, archdeacon of Hainault, who was busy in Rome about the affairs of the

---

[1] (1)25. The exact date of RP's ordination is unknown. It was probably near the end of July.

[2] For the history of the earlier foundation, see (17) 63; A. Gasquet, *A History of the VEC* (Rome/London, 1920); Anthony Kenny, "From Hospice to College," four articles in *The Venerabile* (the college journal) vols. 19 and 20; Michael E. Williams, *The Venerable English College, Rome* (London, 1979).

Archbishop of Cambrai. Indeed, he may have suggested this new development in the first place. Certainly he saw the advantage of adding the hospice income to that of Douai, for this institution received only 1,200 crowns a year from the Pope to support some hundred students. In view of his founding influence, inevitably Lewis had much to do with new appointments to the staff of the hospice.

Like most members of smaller nations, Lewis tended to favor his own countrymen before others. Through his influence Maurice Clynnog, a Welshman, was appointed the first superior. As Persons put it, hardly concealing his own bias, between "Welshmen and true Englishmen dissensions easily arise from memory of their ancient rivalry, they being of the stock of different peoples."[3] While the English—even a man of Persons's sophistication—regarded the Welsh as roughly of the same clay but somewhat spoilt in the firing, misunderstanding was always round the corner no matter what happened.

Maurice Clynnog was first elected custos, or warden, of the hospice in 1565 and held various offices after it. It was not remarkable, then, that he was again chosen warden on May 26, 1576, or that Owen Lewis should have favored his advancement to superior of the new student body when Cardinal Morone's decree of February 4, 1577, formally brought the college into existence.[4] The change in atmosphere was almost violent. Sir Richard Shelley once complained that the hospice had become "the exclusive preserve of Oxford men of plebeian origin" who were mere "benefice hunters."[5] Certainly, a memorial of 1568 claimed that the *confratres* spent their days in card playing, drinking, and even more disreputable pastimes. Gregory Martin reported to Edmund Campion in a letter of May 26, 1578, that there were now twenty-six students living in the hospice and in an adjoining building which communicated with it internally. There was no special seclusion from the other occupants, although the chaplains were forbidden to interfere in the scholar's affairs.[6]

It soon became necessary to determine more exactly whether the institution was primarily hospice or seminary. The chaplains took

---

[3] (1) 95 n.(*). For a brief sketch of Lewis's career see Kenny, "From Hospice to College," 20, pp. 2f.

[4] Gasquet, *A History of the VEC*, 63 and 66. Friction in the college between some of the resident priests and Clynnog predated the latest troubles by at least twelve years: see Kenny, 19, 6f, 480–85.

[5] Quoted Kenny, "From Hospice to College," 19, 483f.

[6] (24) appendix, p. 316; see Catholic Encyclopedia (1909), art. on English College, Rome. The warden of the hospice was also the nominal rector of the students. See Morone's rules, Kenny, "From Hospice to College," 90.

an initiative of their own in electing Henry Henshaw as warden on May 17, 1578, with apparently no reference to Cardinal Morone. This was interpreted by some as a move to protect their vested interests against the new foundation.[7] Morone now stepped in, separating the government of the college from that of the hospice. Clynnog was appointed rector of the scholars.[8] Allen was not happy with Clynnog's appointment, but for a time all went well, as Persons reported to Campion on November 28, 1578.[9] From the autumn of 1578, at the special request of the Pope and Protector Morone, two Jesuits were appointed to assist Clynnog in managing the students, who now numbered forty.[10] Dr. Clynnog, an elderly man, faced the task with courage but without previous experience other than having been a professor of law—not divinity. At Christmas of 1578, the Pope eased his task in one important respect. He ordered all the old chaplains to depart within fifteen days and assigned all the rents of the hospice to the seminary.[11]

The principal engineer of all this under the Pope and the Datary was Owen Lewis,[12] while Clynnog, as rector, had the unenviable task of sending forth his former fellow chaplains, he alone remaining under the new dispensation. It was not to be expected that the "honest and virtuous priests" who saw themselves expelled as "malefactors without any provision" would go like lambs dumb to the slaughter. They resented Clynnog's managing to stay on while some darkly wondered if "Mr. Archdeacon's intent and drift" was less to advance the seminary than his friends.[13]

Clynnog, like Shylock in Venice turning to the Jews, looked to his fellow Welshmen, few though they were, for support and solace rather than to the Englishmen, as was only natural. An able man, he had once been nominated to the See of Bangor,[14] but his studies of jurisprudence do not seem to have extended to equity. At all events, some were soon complaining "that many of the priests and others of the best-born English went all this winter with naked thighs and full of

[7] Gasquet, *A History of the VEC*, 66.

[8] Kenny, "From Hospice to College," vol. 20, p. 100.

[9] (23) 1f.

[10] (41) 67.

[11] Ibid., p. 68, quoting Persons.

[12] (1) 192f.

[13] (1) 144. According to H. Ely, "the 8 priests" were "by violence almost put out because they would not obey to the pope's commandment" ((67) 73).

[14] (1) 87 "Domesticall difficulties"; see (1) 45.

the best-born English went all this winter with naked thighs and full of lice, and all the Welshmen double apparelled."[15] The English now numbered about thirty-two with some eight Welshmen.[16]

Clearly a struggle was developing as to whether the new college should be known as the British, Welsh, or English College. In view of the relative numbers involved, perhaps the result was a foregone conclusion. But the victory would be Pyrrhic.

The Jesuits were by no means enthusiastic about their enforced participation in the affairs of the college. They knew they would be sharing the odium for a situation in which they had no measure of control or real responsibility. The two Fathers, to whom a third was added later in 1578, tried to mediate between Clynnog and his Welshmen and the English. Their success was not notable, but they did prevent the discontented from trying "to seek redress otherwise."[17] Clynnog was content to stress his authority by publishing at Christmas the papal brief of appointment.[18]

Apart from the English students, there were other English observers of the scene, including some twenty-four English Jesuits in Rome in various stages of formation.[19] Among these was Persons, who, although he could not yet do much about it, confessed that "we Englishmen were loath that our Fathers should go thither to see the nakedness of our nation and the impossibility to redress it."[20] His first chance to do something came when he was residing in the Roman College and received a deputation of English students from the newest seminary. They included Ralph Sherwin, George Haydock, and Martin Array, names later distinguished, two as martyrs. Already their presence, perhaps, commanded respect. Nevertheless, Persons proceeded cautiously, as became a former tutor and dean of Balliol and one well acquainted with the ways of students. He listened sympathetically and sent them away.[21]

Thirty-four of them then petitioned Owen Lewis to procure Clynnog's removal on the grounds that he was "not acquainted with

---

[15] (1) 144; (23) 10f.

[16] (67) 73f.

[17] (1) 144; (23) 10; Kenny, "From Hospice to College," 20, 175.

[18] (23) 10, n.(10) gives further details of Clynnog's appointment. It is likely that Morone followed Lewis's advice in this.

[19] See RP to E. Campion, 28.xi.1578, Rome, (23) 1f and nn.(5)–(7). Holt was a student of the college and later became one of its first rectors.

[20] (1) 144.

[21] (1) 45 and 87.

such a charge."[22] Lewis temporized, did nothing, and the English and Welsh polarized finally into rival factions. Persons kept in touch with the situation but otherwise trod warily. He reported the developments to Allen, adding the witness of his own eyes when the students came to see him "being very evil provided for necessaries, sometimes going all ragged, and in worse case."[23] The root cause of the difficulty was, no doubt, that 2,000 crowns a year was not enough for growing numbers. But racialism was rearing its ugly head. "Who can stay young men, or old either, once incensed on both sides by national contentions? You know what passeth in Oxford on like occasions." Meanwhile Persons did his best to persuade the students to come to terms with Lewis and Clynnog.[24]

The men in charge were not forthcoming, so the students began to agitate for the replacement of Clynnog by a Jesuit. Persons learned of this in an interview seemingly arranged with him by Clynnog and Lewis. "Mr Maurice before me inferred that we had either suborned or comforted them in this their request."[25] All too aware of the danger of the charge of being saddled with a Jesuit "intrigue," Persons now withdrew. "I retired myself and would meddle no more."[26] Clynnog, while uncertain of the real cause of the trouble, was unable to see any fault in himself. No doubt the root cause was lack of funds. During the winter of 1578–79, the Pope gave three hundred crowns to buy clothing and bedding. But as A. Kenny justly observed, "the sum was insufficient, and paltry in comparison with the 50,000 crowns he had thrown away on Stukeley's antics."[27]

The students now approached Morone directly, but he felt bound in loyalty to uphold Lewis and Clynnog. Promising redress, he did nothing. Navarola, the Jesuit spiritual director in the college, was due for transfer to Siena, but the General of the Society was not anxious to get further involved, because the rumor was now going round Rome that the Jesuits "desired this government."[28] A full account of the battle of wills that followed would take long in the

---

[22] (1) 193.

[23] RP to Allen, 30.iii.1579; (1) 136; (23) 3; (67) 74.

[24] (1) 124.

[25] (1) 145; (23) 11.

[26] (1) contains many documents on the continuing student quarrel.

[27] Kenny, "From Hospice to College," 20, 176. Thomas Stukely/Stucley was an adventurer apparently with an understanding with Sir William Cecil. See F. Edwards, *The Marvellous Chance* (London, 1968), chap. 5. Kenny's handling of Stucley does not belie this view. See also (1) 161f.

[28] (1) 146; (23) 12.

telling.[29] Meanwhile Persons and Thomas Darbishire, S.J., slipped easily into the role of whipping boys and scapegoats for the general confusion.[30]

Since Morone failed to give the students satisfaction, they betook themselves to the Pope. By January 28, 1579, memorials had been addressed to him and to the Bishop of St. Asaph and Sir Richard Shelley, English prior of the Order of St. John.[31] While the students pleaded for Jesuit control, Benedict Palmio, the Italian assistant, and other Jesuits, perhaps with prophetic foresight, begged Morone "to get our Fathers from the seminary." Significantly, Lewis opposed this, declaring that "if they went away the matters would go much worse, and the seminary not be able to stand three days." Persons agreed with him.[32]

After receiving the students in audience, the Pope ordered Morone to give way. The former accepted Morone's resignation, probably on Sunday, February 17, 1579, and even gave the students "leave to choose a new governor."[33] Owen Lewis was furious and protested to the Jesuit general against a takeover. He found allies in Como, cardinal secretary of State, and Morone, who for all his earlier acquiescence resented the direct appeal to the Pope as an affront to his own dignity and authority. The Pope gave way. On February 28 Morone informed a deputation of four of the student leaders that not only could they not have the Jesuits but must accept having Clynnog reinstated as rector. The protector even spoke of imprisonment and whipping for recalcitrants. He allowed them a day in which to decide whether to submit or depart. In the event only ten signed a form accepting Clynnog's rule. A further misunderstanding over the document of appointment almost caused a riot when it was read out at supper. According to Persons, "if our Fathers had not been there some evil perhaps had been committed."[34] As it was, the English contingent decided on Shrove Monday, March 1, to leave in a body, including "little Christopher Owen," who rose from a sickbed to make sure he would not be left behind.[35]

---

[29] (1) 193; for the later stages of the quarrel, see Anthony Munday, *The English Romayne life* (London, 1582). Munday arrived in Rome on 2.ii.1578. His account is partial but firsthand.

[30] (1) 148; (23) 14.

[31] The various memorials are in (1) 102–35.

[32] (1) 148f; (23) 14f.

[33] Ibid. See Kenny, "From Hospice to College," 186.

[34] (1) 150; (23) 17.

[35] (1) 151; see ibid., 98; (23) 18; Kenny, "From Hospice to College," 19f.

It is perhaps a pity that it occurred to no one at this time, not even Persons, to suggest the foundation of some kind of Welsh college. The fact that Welshmen had been primarily concerned with the launching of the new college gave them some moral right in the matter and manner of its further development. Unfortunately, they came to regard the English, in spite of their superior numbers, as unwanted interlopers rather than as guests to be honored, so that a situation developed which could not endure. The Welsh had their supporters: Spetiano, secretary of the Sacred Congregation of Bishops; Morone, a longstanding friend of Clynnog's; and even the Jesuit general, Mercurian, insofar as he felt himself "already oppressed by the burden of many seminaries" and had no desire to take on more.[36] The papal *camerlengo*, Ludovico Bianchetti, favored the English and saw to it that their frequent petitions came to the Pope's notice.

On Shrove Tuesday, March 2, the scholars went to the Pope "betimes" with a "supplication" tabulating their grievances, asking to go with his favor and "to kiss his foot at their departure."[37] The prospect of thirty-three high-spirited young missionaries, "all divines and philosophers," being thus thrown out and away was more than Persons could bear. He spent much of March 2 with Mercurian and with Fr. Oliver Manare, having "a pull of weeping with each of them."[38] Further tears were later shed with his colleagues Holt, Darbishire, "and others." However, the tears were less from sorrow than for joy "that God had sent to our country such youths of such conscience, patience in adversity and other like virtues."

On Ash Wednesday, Mr. Creed, an Englishman, received the departing students into his home, where they organized a kind of seminary, cooking for themselves and living from a common purse. Money came from various sources, including Thomas Goldwell, bishop of St. Asaph, and Alfonso Agazzari, S.J., who diverted to their use thirty crowns previously earmarked for "the poor college at Siena." They also begged on the streets of Rome and received sympathy, which in the short run was not less useful than the alms. It all produced a reaction against Lewis and his friends. From being the upholder of legitimate authority against student insubordination, he became the cruel tyrant persecuting holy innocents.

Pope Gregory caught the new mood. While not tempted, perhaps, like an earlier Gregory to exclaim, "Non Angli sed angeli," he

---

[36] (1) 98.

[37] (1) 151; (23) 18. The "supplication" is in (1) 121, being presented on March 3; (23) 18, n.(22).

[38] (1) 152; (23) 19.

was aware of the scandalous implications of seeming to drive away future martyrs and heroes of the faith. Perhaps he also remembered that Lewis had scarcely picked a winner in promoting his late ally, Thomas Stucley. A man who is wrong once can be wrong again. That same afternoon, Ash Wednesday, the Pope sent for the students and gave them an audience lasting nearly an hour. The tears flowed once again, with the Holy Father watering the scene as lustily as the rest. The college *commedianti* had even remembered to bring their gowns, which they now offered to lay at the Pope's feet before departing for ever. "At which the good old man put his hand to his breast and shook his head."[39] As a fitting climax, one of the chamberlains escorted them back to the seminary "with great honour and solemnity," their way lying "through the city in the sight of all; and so replaced them in their college with the benediction and protection of the pope."

Of course, they did not live happily ever after. Indeed, they soon realized their immediate gain was small. Persons was also happy at the outcome, but when the tears of joy had dried he too was left with reservations. They had certainly aroused "a wonderful opinion" of Dr. Allen's foundation and of what men "who had shown themselves so invincible here"[40] would one day do in England. Not until March 19, however, after a further exchange of memorials from all sides, was an important decision reached. Morone sent for Mercurian and "in the pope's name told him that His Holiness commanded him expressly to take the whole charge of the seminary upon him in all respects, as he had charge of the German College."[41]

Far from jubilant at a new triumph for the Society, Mercurian tried to persuade Morone to get the order rescinded. But Morone stood by the papal instruction. This included setting up a college initially for fifty students. Morone called in the two Jesuits already working there to discuss the situation. There was some return to the earlier arrangement allowing the presence of visitors and pilgrims but placing the accent on its work as a seminary. Only students should live in the original building. Those not connected directly with this work would live outside.[42] Expectations were that proper allocation of place and space could provide rooms for two hundred scholars. The cost of

---

[39] (1) 154; (23) 22; see (11) II, ccclvii–ccclviii.

[40] (1) 159; (23) 28.

[41] (1) 157, see 87; (23) 25.

[42] (1) 158; (23) 26. The final settlement was incorporated in Gregory XIII's bull for the foundation of the college, which was back-dated some months afterwards to 23.iv.1579; (11) II, App. cccxxxvii. Morone's draft arrangements for the college government are in (31) 481. Owen Lewis eventually secured pensions for the displaced chaplains; (23) 10, n.(11).

alterations to the premises and "provision for such a multitude" would
be borne by the Pope. Clynnog became custos for the pilgrims, while
others, including Bishop Goldwell, were given proper accommodation
in the vicinity. Morone allowed the important point that the Jesuit
administration should only have to deal with himself or the Pope.[43]

Once the papal decision had been made, the Jesuits, true to
the spirit of that generation, hastened to obey cheerfully. It meant, as
Persons thought, that there could now be no question of Jesuits going
to work in England. Suitable men would be fully taken up with work
in the growing college. The latest development had also made the
Jesuits more enemies, and not only in Rome, although the decision
had been none of theirs. "While consultation was being held about
some suitable person for rector," Persons himself filled in. "He took up
the office willingly and worked hard at adapting the house to scholastic
purposes until . . . Alphonsus Agazzari of Siena" was appointed.[44] The
latter filled the post for the first seven crucial years. According to
Persons, Agazzari not only put the administration on a sound footing
but extended the buildings and increased the revenues. Besides the
three hundred gold crowns which Gregory XIII paid over from the
papal treasury as long as he lived, he also assigned to the use of the
college the principal revenues of the abbey of Santa Sabina in Piacenza,
which amounted to some three thousand ducats annually.[45]

Another important innovation at this time of renewal was the
"commissioners," who would examine every student individually for
seriousness of purpose "to see who were fit to stay there and who were
not, and that an oath might be proposed to know who had intention
. . . to return into their country to teach and preach Catholic
religion."[46] The dilettante days were over. Morone, acting in the papal
name, appointed and sent them. Most of the students, as Persons

---

[43] (1) 158; (23) 26f.

[44] (1) 100. Agazzari was certainly installed by May 1579. See *Annual Letters of the
College*, (12) VI, 67, and list of rectors, 123. RP refers to his own period of rule as "a
matter of days"; (1) 93.

[45] (1) 94.

[46] (1) 193; see 87. The form of the oath is in the *Liber ruber* (annals of the
college); (1) 131. This register gives details, including name and nationality, of scholars
who took the oath. See also (11) II, app. cccxliii. Dr. W. Kelly published the *Liber* for the
CRS, vol. I, 1579–1630, as vol. 37 in 1940, and vol. 2, 1631–1783, as vol. 40 in 1943. See
also *Responsa*, edited by A. Kenny, part I, 1598–1621 (CRS 54, 1962) and part II,
1622–85 (CRS 55, 1963). Of forty-two scholars three—two Welshmen and an Englishman—refused the mission oath later in 1579; (23) 11, n.(12). "Weary of Rome," Clynnog
went to Rouen and soon afterwards to Spain ((1) 162). He was drowned on the way in a
mishap at sea in 1579 or 1580.

claimed, took the oath "with great alacrity and resolution." It provided a precedent for all the English seminaries abroad run by Jesuits.

Owen Lewis, already discredited in Rome by reason of his former association with Thomas Stucley, retired to Milan to become vicar general to Archbishop Carlo Borromeo. Unfortunately, he left behind him a nephew, Hugh Griffith, one of those restless spirits who, like Iago, seem born to stir up trouble. He was taken to be the man who at least maintained his uncle's suspicion, to put it no more strongly, against the English contingent. He had been sent to Rome from Douai partly because people there found him "insupportable."[47] From Rome he wrote to Allen that "the Jesuits have been and shall be proved the . . . counsellors of all these tumults; and that they would not have our priests to go to England, but to tarry longer in Rome and take their temporal commodity."[48] He was opposed to the idea of the Jesuits themselves going to England. Allen warned Lewis in a letter of May 12, 1579, "You must temper your cousin [*sic*] Hugh's tongue and behaviour who is of a bitter and incompatible nature." In Rome "his disordered humours" had been "a great cause of hatred and all these garboils."[49] Not surprisingly, Alfonso Agazzari was obliged to get Morone to expel him from the college. One wonders if, without Owen's patronage, he could or would have followed an ecclesiastical career. At all events he followed his uncle as Provost of Cambrai. Two more of his faction, also protected by Lewis, were William and Gilbert Gifford, "two young men of good family and rare talents" who "subsequently came to Rheims and contributed much to the formation of a faction among the scholars."[50]

Allen did his best to disabuse Lewis of the idea that he was the object of either his own or Jesuit hostility. He hoped that the recent "sinister accident" would not be allowed to prejudice a work so happily begun, and that all the students would be content "with so honest a thing as to have the Fathers for their governors."[51] But Persons fully realized that *omnes quærunt quæ sua sunt.*[52]

Persons no less than Allen had forebodings for the future. Between the aggrieved Owen Lewis, a man also devoted to the cause, and the English there loomed already a gulf that none could bridge. Persons lost no time in trying to effect a reconciliation, but all in vain.

---

[47] Allen to Lewis, 12.v.1579; (11) II, App. ccclxvi and ccclxviii–ccclxix.

[48] Ibid., ccclxx.

[49] (9) 80.

[50] (21) 68f.

[51] Allen to O. Lewis, Paris, 12.v.1579; (11) II, App. ccclxvi.

[52] (1) 160; (23) 26f.

Allen concluded that it had been a mistake to appoint Clynnog in the first place. At all events, now that the students had obtained what they wanted, they should be discouraged from following up any fatal taste for politicking which they might have acquired. They were there to study and prepare for work on the English mission.[53]

But centers of opposition to Jesuit influence were building up in several parts of Europe. In Rome Nicholas Fitzherbert, a gentleman who had lived in the city for some years, was soon joined by Solomon Aldred, formerly a tailor in Lyons, who came to Rome with his wife on a papal pension. He struck up a friendship with Owen Lewis before the latter's departure from the city, continued to serve his interests, and was to take up others a good deal more sinister from the Catholic viewpoint.[54]

---

[53] (11) II, App. ccclxx.

[54] See (1) 88.

Chapter Three
The Great Experiment: 1579–1580

P ersons left no surviving record of when his thoughts first turned to a Jesuit mission in England. During his theological studies he compiled a "compendium of all the controversies" from Latin sources, which he used later on the mission. He also made a special study of "the particular cases for England," that is, of moral theology. This also stood him in good stead.[1] But when he appealed to Allen to come to Rome in the spring of 1579, he was thinking of the need to have at hand someone of the prestige necessary to overawe the racial divisions in the college, which were by no means exorcized by a change of regime, especially since Allen was "a great friend" of Owen Lewis. Typically, Persons got Agazzari to persuade the Pope to summon Allen, so that his presence would not depend on the Jesuit's persuasiveness alone. Persons wrote to Allen himself on March 30, 1579,[2] a long letter describing recent quarrels but ending optimistically on the ensuing advantages "which perhaps would not have ensued—or at least not so soon."[3]

Persons hoped for closer relations between Douai—transferred perforce to Rheims in 1578—and the college in Rome. He also hoped that Allen could persuade the Jesuit general to allow his men to start a mission in England. There were enough English Jesuits who were eager to go, while the faithful were reported as eager to receive them. Persons was ready to go with the rest. "Seeing I have offered myself a good while ago to the mission of the Indies and cannot obtain it, it may be God's will to have me go to this other."[4]

---

[1] (1) 25; *Controversiæ nostræ temporis in Epitomen redactæ,* copy in Bodleian Library, MS Rawlinson C.588, ff.1–122, and in Balliol College, E.14.9: Douay MS 484, ff.1–406b., ff.408–26 "Quæstiones pertinentes ad Baptismum . . ." (eighty-five questions in eleven sections). Controversia 3, Quaestio 3, established the date, 1579; see (1) 25, n., and for J. Reynold's censura of 1611; see also *The Month,* vii. 1900; P. J. Holmes, "Elizabethan Casuistry," *CRS* 67(1981) based on the "Douai Rheims" and the "Allen Persons" documents.

[2] (9) 74, RP to Allen, 30.iii.1579; see (1) 135–37.

[3] (1) 135.

[4] Ibid., 137; see (9) 74, from (II) f.381.

Allen arrived in Rome on October 10, 1579,[5] together with his brother, Gabriel, Dr. Worthington, and Roger Baynes, with the intention of wintering in Rome.[6] Not only the Pope, but the Cardinal of Como and Cardinals Morone and Paliotto wished to see Allen.[7] The visit failed to reconcile "the two nations" in the college. "Good words were given on both sides, yet was it . . . from the teeth outward, as afterward appeared."[8] At the same time, closer cooperation was guaranteed between Rheims and Rome. The Jesuits used their influence with the Pope to get the Rheims pension increased by fifty crowns a month, not to mention "sundry indulgences and benedictions" in the spiritual order.[9] Persons had hoped that Allen would be named a cardinal, but in spite of such pressure as Sir Francis Englefield, Count Olivares, the Spanish ambassador, and others could apply, Gregory would not be moved.[10] Perhaps the additional fifty gold crowns a month to Rheims were a kind of compensation.[11]

A very significant result of the Allen visit was the setting up of a Jesuit mission for England. This would work alongside the secular priests, as Allen wished. Some hundred secular priests emerged from Rome alone by the end of the century, while nineteen more became Jesuits,[12] a fact which properly understood indicates the essential harmony between them. After Allen's departure on Ash Wednesday, February 16, 1580, Persons proceeded to execute plans for the new mission.[13] He would go to England as superior with Edmund Campion, then teaching happily in Prague. It would be necessary to recruit from English Jesuits already working in different regions of the world, but Persons foresaw a ready response once the mission was actually established.[14] Though representing religious generally, the Jesuits, being a new order, "could pretend the recovery of no temporal possessions from any man," whereas members of older orders, even if they

---

[5] (1) 101.

[6] RP to Allen, 30.iii.1579; (1) 137.

[7] See (9) 398, from (1) 384 and 140, n.1.

[8] (1) 137.

[9] (1) 194; see A. Agazzari to Allen, Rome, 13.vi.1579, Latin; ibid., 138–40. The Roman foundation depended mainly on students from Rheims.

[10] (1) 138.

[11] (1) 100, 137.

[12] (1) 101.

[13] See RP to William Good, n.d.: ibid., 140–60. Good was then working as a missionary in Sweden; and (1) 137. The letter to Good is the main source used here.

[14] See (1) 142.

claimed nothing, were bound to rub the consciences of those who had gained by their dispossession.[15]

Mercurian and his assistants were aware of the physical dangers of the English mission, but even more so of the spiritual. In mission countries supposedly more barbaric, the Catholic missionary rarely needed to conceal his purpose or identity. Protestant England, however, was much less indulgent. The Jesuits would need to live "in secular men's houses, in secular apparel, diet, conversation and the like," so that the "conservation of religious spirit" would put to the test even the most saintly.[16] But Pope Gregory wanted the mission and that was that. Claudio Aquaviva, Roman provincial, volunteered to go; but on February 19, 1581, he was elected general. So the new mission had at least the support of the highest-ranking Jesuit.

Urged by letters from Allen and Persons and commanded by the General, Campion, good Jesuit that he was, accepted what was "both sudden and strange news to him." He could have been under no illusion as to what the future might hold in store, and it hardly needed "a certain virtuous young man of the Society" from Silesia to scrawl over his door "Campianus Martyr." The youth received a good penance.

Campion arrived in Rome during Holy Week of 1580.[17] He had little more than a fortnight in which to prepare for the English journey. He spent most of his time in "devotion and visiting the churches leaving all other cares to Fr Persons, his companion . . . and superior."[18] On April 10, Low Sunday, a party of thirteen, including Ralph Emerson, Jesuit lay brother, Bishop Goldwell, and Dr. Nicholas Norton, his friend, set off for England.[19] The Pope carefully made it clear that the expedition was intended as a gesture of goodwill and reconciliation, not of aggression. He begged them "to consider well their personal danger, as also by their public going they should not exasperate overmuch the State against themselves and others; and that for this respect they should go very privately and before the rest, and no further than Rheims where Dr Allen was, and there expect the

---

[15] (1) 194. See David Lunn, *The English Benedictines 1540–1688* (London, 1980), especially chaps. 3 and 4.

[16] (1) 195.

[17] (1) 26.

[18] (1) 160, 195.

[19] The other priests were Dr. Edward Bromberg or Bromborne, William Giblet, Thomas Crane, and William Kemp, who "had bin chaplens of the Hospital," and Ralph Sherwin, Luke Kirby, and Edward Rishton. Thomas Brisco and John Paschal were described as "two scholars." Dr. Henshaw, also an "ould chapline," seems to have joined the party later; (24) 172, following Grene, who quotes from the *Vita Campiani;* and (1) 162. RP's "Third Memoir" included Dr. Bavin.

other mission."[20] Then would be the time to decide whether to go on or return to Rome.

Elizabeth I may have been a renegade, but the Pope had no desire to antagonize her unnecessarily or force her into persecution. In any case, the sinner could always turn from her wickedness and live. So he prescribed that "in all matters pertaining to the secular State they should regard her as lawful queen and accord her the outward form of honour including those of speech until such time as the Apostolic See should make a further decision in the matter."[21] This resolution was sought and obtained at the last audience with the Pope on April 14, 1580, before the party set out for England. In fact the Pope granted more than the petitioners sought, in that they had asked only that the bull oblige the queen but not themselves as things then stood, and themselves only "in future when the public execution of the bull [could] be made."[22]

Nineteen questions were put to the Pope at this audience, fourteen relating to the excommunication of 1570 and five more to *communicatio in sacris*—the participation of papists in Protestant religious functions.[23] The concessions were large, considering the times and the danger to the Catholic faith to be avoided. "The Lord Prior Shelley" was retired to Venice "for more perfect ending of contentions."[24] We may, if we will, see all this as mere cunning, a ruse to make the Queen lower her guard so that she could be struck more effectively. We may also see it as a genuine step towards peace and reconciliation, the expression of a hope that England would return peaceably and willingly to the Catholic fold. That the missionaries saw it this way is evident in their conduct throughout the journey, which went forward in a state of almost unseeing euphoria.[25]

Their progress through Italy anticipated an easy triumph, with no attempt to conceal their purpose. Bystanders were generous with their admiration. Sympathy seemed almost out of place. In other

---

[20] (1) 196.

[21] RP or Richard Walpole to Clement VIII, 1602; (II) 466; "Apology" for R. Southwell's *Libellus supplex* of 1587, Latin; see (49) 293–98.

[22] (49) 293; see EHR VII, 84–88 and (31) 113, n.2.

[23] (49) 294, n. 1; EHR VII, 31–38; from (IV) Arm. 64, vol. 28, ff.176r—9v.

[24] (1) 163.

[25] Before priests can exercise their function, at least licitly and sometimes validly, they need authorization, known as "faculties," from higher authority. The extent of these depends on rank and sometimes privilege, the most extensive being given to ordained cardinals and bishops. Ordinary priests may receive unusually extensive faculties as a privilege. The faculties of Campion and Persons were dated 14.iv.1580; text in (31) 422–25.

respects, because it was made on foot, this was not an easy journey, although for the weak or elderly there were three or four horses. They kept to their prayers, examens, and spiritual conferences, at least on these occasions facing the prospect of martyrdom and "assuring themselves that they should find nothing but extremity of persecution in England."[26] Indeed, they exhorted one another to "humility, patience and Christian fortitude" to face the suffering before them. They had a foretaste of this on the journey itself. They were obliged to stop for periods of rest and recuperation, staying a whole week at Bologna to allow for a swelling in Persons's leg to go down. Cardinal Paliotti received them with a father's loving kindness. All the same, he made them work, "causing them to make . . . spiritual conferences in Latin before him after dinner together with his doctors and learned men." Campion and Sherwin gave distinguished performances.

From Milan they traveled on to Turin and thence to Geneva to avoid the Spanish soldiery overrunning Savoy; in Geneva they were arrested by the city guards, who apparently took them for Spaniards and haled them before the local magistrates and ministers for examination.[27] "They all answered briefly that they were Englishmen and all Catholics, and the most of them priests" on their way to Rheims. The magistrate was surprised to see so many English Catholics. He observed, "'Your queen is of our religion.' Whereto they answered that they held themselves not bound to be of the Queen's religion, what religion soever she was of." When the magistrate was satisfied they were not connected with the Spanish forces, he allowed them the "ordinary liberty" of the city, which allowed "all kind of men" to stay for two or three days. He had them escorted to their inn, "The Sign of Geneva," by an officer "and willed them to be well used."[28] Far different would be their reception by the ruling Protestants of their own country! While in Geneva they managed to visit the celebrated Théodore Béza.[29] His reception was likewise benign, although they did not tell him they were Jesuits or missionaries. But he seemed anxious to avoid serious controversy, although he became suspicious and aloof when his visitors began to display their erudition.[30]

---

[26] (1) 197 ("Third Memoir"). The litanies were probably *Litaniæ Deiparæ Virginis Mariæ ex Patribus et script[oribus] collectæ a RRPP Edmondo Campiano . . . et Laurentio Maggio, Soc. Jesu sacerdotibus et ab iisdem per singulas hebdomadas distributæ.* Reprinted at Rouen in 1887 from a Paris printing of 1633.

[27] (1) 197.

[28] Ibid.

[29] (1) 198.

[30] Ibid.

The rest of the journey to Rheims was relatively uneventful. After consultation with Allen the party split up as a tardy concession to security. Campion, Persons, and Emerson went to St. Omer, Sherwin to a priest-uncle at Rouen. Morton and Goldwell were put on the road back to Rome, "lest their entry at this time put suspicions in the head of the State of greater matters than were meant." One could not blame Elizabeth's government for getting it wrong. "At this very time Dr Sanders," with the approval of the papal nuncio in Spain, where he resided, led a farcical and abortive expedition to Ireland. It did succeed, however, in making "the whole cause of the priests that were sent in mission to England more odious."[31] In fact the prospect was so unfavorable that the Jesuits at St. Omer advised Persons to call off the expedition at least for a time.[32]

Their sublime disregard for security along the way meant that the English authorities knew all about them well in advance. The ports were "laid for them with spies," and it was even claimed "that their pictures were drawn and sent to the ports."[33] But Persons and Campion had come too far to be put off. They went ahead "considering the greater their perils were, the more likely that . . . Divine Providence would assist them." Somebody remembered that St. Augustine made his way to England by way of St. Omer. Surely this was a good omen?

In fact, the entry into England succeeded better than common sense could have expected. Persons, as superior, entered first on June 12 by the Dover-Calais route. He went disguised as "a captain returned from the Low Countries." Wearing a proper air of braggadocio and bluster, he deceived completely the watchers at the port. The role of a soldier probably fitted him as well as that of priest, and on many subsequent occasions he showed himself at least as much the one as the other. Even so there were close calls with merchants "that were earnest Protestants and with the searchers of . . . Dover and Gravesend."

---

[31] (1) 199. The story of the papal "Irish expedition" under San Giuseppe, a fitting ally and protégé of Thomas Stucley, remains to be told. It belongs to the libretti of comic opera rather than to military history. See *A New History of Ireland*, ed. T. W. Moody, F. X. Martin, and F. J. Byrne, vol. III, 1534–1691 (Oxford, 1976), 107f; and A. Kenny, *The Venerabile*, 20, 91–98, 101–3, 171–75. There is much seemingly unexplored material in (IV) Segreteria di Stato, Inghilterra 30/ Irlanda 1; and Lettere di Particolari, 3; Inghilterra 1 and 2.

[32] (1) 162; (35) vols. II, V; Goldwell died in Rome in 1585 and Morton some two years later.

[33] (1) 200. Sled the spy's report of 1580 indicates the scope and accuracy of the English government's information; CRS 53 (1960/61), 193–245 from Brit.Lib. Yelverton MSS, Add. 48029, ff.121–30; see (29) Addenda 1580–1625, p. 4, No. 11. Sled included a special list of those coming from Rome on 25.ii.1579/80, "among whom are the names of Campion and Persons"; CRS 53, 209.

Indeed, on the way to London from Gravesend "in the tilt-boat by night" he found himself among the Queen's musicians returning from Kent. Worse still, "arriving on foot without horse" in London, "he could get no lodging and was forced with great danger of being discovered to go up and down half a day from place to place . . . from the break of day until noon." But his nerve did not fail him. He went to the Marshalsea Prison and asked for Thomas Pound, a Catholic prisoner there. Persons dined in his chamber and "was singularly comforted with the sight not only of him but of many confessors of Christ that suffered there." Whatever he owed to the angels, Persons after dinner certainly met one "good angel."

George Gilbert, a wealthy young landowner, converted to Catholicism under the influence of Darbishire in Paris and Persons in Rome. He had been to Italy "to prosecute the learning of such gentlemanlike exercises as men of his quality are wont to learn in Italy as riding, fencing, vaulting and the like." Back in England, he assisted priests and tried to convert his friends. On the principle that the safest place in the vicinity of a cocked and loaded gun is under the barrel, Gilbert and his friends lodged "in the chief pursuivant's house" in Chancery Lane, who was also a friend of the bishop. Ironically enough, they were also protected by Adam Squire, the bishop's son-in-law, "whom they fee'd"—bribed. In this way they were "protected for diverse years and had access of priests unto them, and sundry Masses daily said in their house until the Jesuits came in."[34]

While Persons's meeting with Gilbert may have been providential, it was not entirely a matter of chance. Friend as well as foe had been aware of the mission on the way to England, and Gilbert had been keeping a lookout for it. He had intended to make a vow not to marry, but Persons persuaded him instead to vow chastity only "so long as Catholic religion should not return publicly into England."[35] Evidently Persons believed not only in the success but in the imminent success of his mission. He believed overmuch in reason, perhaps. Torn from the bosom of the universal Church by politics, economics, and plain misunderstanding, England would surely be brought back by careful argument from Scripture and tradition. Could the factors which had kept the country faithful to the Roman connection for so many centuries fail to win out over a separatist sect which had been in existence only for two decades?

Left to free and public debate, the outcome of the issue was at least doubtful. Sir William Cecil and Sir Francis Walsingham, however,

---

[34] (1) 201.

[35] Ibid.

were determined that there should be no such thing. The Queen must be retained in her present way of thinking by all means available. One way to ensure this was to equate the old religion with treason. Certain events of the previous ten years had been easy to interpret thus. The excommunication of 1570 closely followed by the Ridolfi plot seemed to provide more than superficial justification for the generalization that papists were traitors. In fact, the events of these years were much manipulated by Cecil and Walsingham. If Rome produced the bull of excommunication, its promulgation and therefore effectiveness had much to do with Ridolfi. He had an understanding with Walsingham, who in turn was controled by Cecil, as became a man who owed his entire career to Sir William.[36] This is an area of deep controversy, but the reader must remember that the evidence for the authenticity of the plots until and including that of 1605 is no more convincing than that against; and some would say much less. As an eminent Protestant historian, Martin Hume, observed, "the accusations that have been repeated by nearly every English historian from Elizabeth's time to our own, of widespread and numerous plots by Catholics to assassinate the Queen at this period, are to a large extent unsupported by serious evidence. . . . In accordance with the usual practice, it was the policy of the English government at the time to blacken the character and methods of the national enemy as much as possible."[37] Certainly, the most probable explanation of the Ridolfi plot is that it was a contrivance mainly by Cecil to destroy not so much enemies of the State as his own rivals.

Undoubtedly, Cecil's masterstroke was to identify so completely with the Protestant Reformation that to cast doubt on the one seemed to cast doubt on the other: a ploy for papists and eccentrics, surely? His true religious convictions—if he had any, one is inclined to add—remain matter for debate. But his decisive influence on the

---

[36] The second question raised in "Ad consolationem et instructionem . . ." ((IV) Arm.64, vol. 28, ff.176r–9v) was "whether catholics in England may with a safe conscience contradict [repudiate] the said Bull, either because it was not sent there by Pius V and actually executed but only conveyed there by a private person; or else because catholics in England are not sufficiently clear as to the mind of the pope, since it was posted up on the doors by a private gentleman. And whether it should not suffice for the catholics that some of them have undergone most cruel death." The Roman answer to this was, "If anyone should teach that the obligation of this Bull has ceased, he would not contradict it, since this is certainly consistent with the mind and intention of the legislator; and in a word it may be said that the catholics, in regard to it, are only bound by the law in general [jure communi] and not by any new obligation."

[37] M. Hume, *Treason and Plot* (London, 1901), 113. For Ridolfi, see F. Edwards, *The Dangerous Queen* (London, 1964), and *The Marvellous Chance* (London, 1968). The "need" for plots to discredit the Catholics becomes evident from (73). The "Reform" had many enemies and doubters. See also (77) and (79).

legislation of 1559 which effected the religious revolution cannot be denied. Certainly the religious climate to which he arguably made the largest contribution had great relevance to the work and career of Persons. Those who refused the oath of supremacy could not hold public office or be admitted to university degrees. Anyone who maintained "the power or jurisdiction of any foreign prelate or potentate within these realms" forfeited goods and chattels at the first offence, incurred a praemunire[38] at the second, and on a third was guilty of high treason. A law of 1563 made a first offence incur praemunire and a second, high treason, albeit without corruption of blood or involvement of the heirs. Handling or printing books upholding papal authority incurred the same penalties. If a man heard Mass "but once in his lifetime, upon a second refusal of this oath," he was guilty of high treason. Not even the monarch could "dispense with a member of the house of commons taking the oath of supremacy." It is obvious how essentially absurd as well as unjust this claim is when one considers that, for the previous thousand years since England converted to the Roman faith, there had never been a conflict of loyalties remotely amounting to treason in spite of differences concerning temporalities and jurisdiction.

Following the Ridolfi plot, an act of 1571 penalized any who brought in or executed papal bulls, designating this too high treason. Even importing and distributing "Agnus Deis, crosses, pictures or beads" incurred a praemunire.[39] All this was the legal background to the new Jesuit enterprise. Severe on the statute book, however, this law was still being applied with caution. Neither Elizabeth nor Cecil wished to make martyrs, or even create a new wave of exiles. The hope was that Catholicism, synonymous with death for any honorable career, would be driven into quiet corners, there to atrophy and die. It would come to an end with the death of the last Marian priests, who meanwhile might be left to make their pathetic gesture of defiance. The incoming Jesuits and seminary priests represented an alarming sign of contradiction, the challenge of which was fully perceived and accepted. Persons had to admit that "times grew to be much more exasperated."[40]

Soon after their reunion in London about the end of June 1580, Persons and Campion organized a meeting of priests to discuss emerging problems. It took place near St. Mary Overy's in Southwark—in the vicinity of the Clink. George Blackwell and Nicholas

---

[38] (5) 1–10. See article on "Praemunire" in the Encyclopedia Britannica, 11th edition.

[39] (1) 201.

[40] See (49) 335.

Tyrwhitt were prominent among the priests. Laymen were also present.[41] The worst hindrances to the mission obviously came from the civil authorities, but some difficulties were created by the Catholic community itself. The three main problems concerned "going to church, the second about fasts and days of abstinence, and the third about the persecution newly raised or increased by their coming in."[42] The problem of fast days was fairly easily solved by leaving it to individual consciences to observe the more rigorous practices laid down by older English custom or else the more lenient discipline prevailing on the continent.

Persecution was the most serious problem. The Jesuit arrival was taken by government not as an olive branch but as a gesture of defiance that called forth a swift reaction. Proclamations were read out everywhere against them. Many gentlemen and even noblemen suspected to be Catholic were summoned to London and committed to prison for their "doing with Jesuits."[43] Some Catholics swiftly concluded that the best thing the Society could do for the Catholic cause would be to leave England forthwith. Indeed, Willson, "a very grave and ancient priest," expressed this view to Persons himself. Others hoped that he would "never yield to any such fearful motion." Persons reminded his hearers that the Jesuits were there not to please themselves but because they had been sent in by the Pope and he alone could call them out again. As for the persecution, it would eventually die away. "Where God has his hand that is stronger than all." In any case, the Jesuits would only go to those who invited them. Meanwhile, they would serve the Catholics "though it were with danger to their lives." Willson "as a very pious man" accepted this. The majority were

---

[41] (1) 176.

[42] (1) 177. As 1580 wore on, pressure on recusants increased considerably. See [Walsingham] to Huntingdon, 7.vi., "The queen, hearing of the backwardness of her Lancashire subjects to embrace religion, has sent an ecclesiastical commission to the Bishop of Chester, Lord Derby, yourself and others, to bring them to more dutiful minds . . ." (29) Addenda 1580–1625, p. 7. A memo from Burghley of June(?) ordered that "the deprived ecclesiastical papists in England be collected and sent to castles, as Wisbech and Banbury; that lay recusants on bond be sent for by the commissioners and bestowed under some guard in London; that their armour be seized. That all such as will not come to church be fined and imprisoned, by virtue of the ecclesiastical commission" (ibid., 8). William Chaderton, bishop of Chester, reported to the Earl of Leicester the progress of the anti-recusant campaign by August 8 (ibid., p. 11); see also "Form of the recognizance taken by the High Commissioners at their sessions in Yorkshire" of December(?) (ibid., p. 27); and "touching certain recusants in Essex, Norfolk, Suffolk and Cambridge"; BL, Cotton MS Titus B.iii, f.60.

[43] (1) 178.

ready to deal "most confidently with the Fathers, even in the middest of the persecution."[44]

The thorniest problem concerned attendance at Anglican churches. Before the arrival of the Jesuits and seminary priests, it had been tacitly accepted by their clergy that Catholics could attend churches of the Establishment. The civil power was content with this, knowing that force of habit and continued contact with new ways gradually growing older and more respectable would wean the Catholics away from allegiance to Rome. The new priests, well aware of this danger, brought with them a sterner doctrine. The authorities lost no time in showing what it might cost. "The Council . . . put in prison presently upon their arrival in England divers men of account, as the Lord Paget, Sir John Arundell, Thomas Tresham, Mr William Catesby, Sir Thomas Throgmorton," and others, threatening sharp legislation if they took the Roman line.[45] Persons refused to believe that Elizabeth and her council were implacably opposed to reconciliation. The mission was late but surely not too late. He was wrong. Queen and council interpreted "all such recusancy to come of obstinate and rebellious meaning."[46] So the Southwark conference took place in circumstances of great danger.

Robert Johnson, priest, and Henry Orton, layman, were arrested by Sledd, a notorious pursuivant, on their way to the meeting.[47]

---

[44] (1) 177. See (5) 10–15 for the legislation of 1581. The £20 monthly fine began this year. Persecution for recusancy increased greatly after the 1580 mission arrived but did not begin with it. See (VII) SP 12, vol. 130, No. 43. "The warden of the Fleetes certificate of prisoners under his custodye for not conformynge themselves in causes of relligion 31 July 1580," a list of recusants committed mainly by the Bishop of London and held for part or whole of the period April 1577 to April 1579. The seventeen persons included two women. A further nine were listed as "remayninge in the Flete for disobedience in causes of religion committed by the LL of the privie counsell and others the high commissioners." They included the redoubtable Francis Tregian. Some forty-nine persons had been summoned before "the comissioners for causes ecclesiasticall" and allowed "to remain abroade upon bondes." By 8.iv.1580, "theis persons remayne in the severalle prisons." Two more added by Burghley brought the total to fifty-one (Brit.Lib., Harleian MS 360, Nos. 30, 31). Certificates of about 31.vii.-1580 from the keepers of various London prisons are extant in SP 12, vol. 140, Nos. 36–40 and ibid., 141 No. 1 (22.viii.1580); see (29) Eliz.I, 1547–80). On 22.viii.1580 Archbishop Sandys instructed John Wickliffe, "keeper of his house at Battersey . . . to deliver up that house to the Lords of the Council to be a prison for obstinate papists"; (20) Eliz. I, 1547–80, p. 672. See also V. Burke, (10) 14, 71–77, "The economic consequences of recusancy fines in Elizabethan Worcestershire" (1581–1605).

[45] (1) 178.

[46] Ibid., 179.

[47] CRS 1, 67. Both were committed to the Gatehouse on 12.viii.1580 "upon my Lord Mayor his commandment by John Smithe, Officer." They were examined and the

Persons took it as "a marvaile" that he, Blackwell, and the rest were not taken. Forced to admit that the government meant business, Persons left London with Campion on or about July 18, retiring to Hoxton, then a pleasant country village, where the Treshams had a house. There they probably stayed.[48] Here the two Jesuits settled to composing apologias intended not for immediate publication but for presentation to the Privy Council, and for wider dissemination in case they were captured. These would counteract false or misleading statements which the government, considering the precedents, could be expected to publish for their discredit.[49] Campion gave Thomas Pound his production, to be known as *The Challenge* or "brag," addressed to the "Lords for her Majesty's Privy Council," while keeping a copy for himself. Pound did not scruple to read it or to decide that the time for publication had arrived. When Persons returned to London about the end of September, "infinite copies had been taken thereof."[50]

Persons's manifesto, produced at the same time as Campion's, was delivered sealed to a friend still unknown. He respected the writer's wish that this "confession of faith for the London magistrates," seemingly first composed in Latin like Campion's *Decem rationes,* should not be divulged until Persons's arrest.[51] It therefore remained unknown at the time. Apart from the purely religious content, Persons condemned the attempt to make Catholicism synonymous with treason, in order to save its claim that religion and conscience were free. Truth was shamelessly doctored.

> Anyone . . . imprisoned was not only refused permission to speak again, but even the words and arguments he had used previously were all suppressed, or reproduced in a form entirely changed, his sayings being artfully quoted in a distorted sense, or even monstrous crimes being falsely attributed to him, such as conspiracy, rebellion, high treason and suchlike.[52]

In anticipation of misrepresentation, he pleaded,

---

findings sent to the privy council.

[48] This was also the scene, presumably, of the reading of the "Monteagle letter" at the time of the Gunpowder Plot. For the date of the missionaries' departure from London, see RP to Agazzari, 5.viii.1580; (23) 28f, n.1, 41–46.

[49] RP to Agazzari, 17.xi.1580; (23) 49, see 57.

[50] RP, "Life of Campion," 62; see (32) CXV, 57. The text of "The Challenge . . . ," the only surviving piece of his prose in his "golden period," is in J. H. Pollen's *Ten Reasons* (London, 1914), 7–11.

[51] Contemporary Latin copy (translation?); (VI) Anglia 30.I, f.151v; (23) 28–34; translation on 35–41.

[52] (23) 29, see 35.

I hope your worships will never forget that however I may differ from you in my view of . . . the true religion, and be unable to make my conscience agree with yours, nevertheless I am a Christian and . . . an Englishman to whom a measure of humanity [should] be granted as equity itself dictates.

He acknowledged himself, priest and Jesuit, a hater of tyranny, and one rejecting "all the congregations and sects of the Puritans." He was firmly convinced that "there can no more be a new faith or religion than there can be some kind of new God."[53] He explained the world-wide evangelizing mission of the Society of Jesus, vehemently repudiated any intention of stirring up "rebellion and I know not what unholy plots in our peaceful kingdom." The Roman authorities had "banned all conversation . . . about politics and [had] been unwilling to listen to any who made mention of them."[54] As for the Queen and her subjects, "that obedience which they owe to their sovereign we inculcate not less but truly much more than does any of the protestants."

Persons's document, unlike Campion's, was unpolished; but its main points were cogent. He assured his enemies in government, "We incline the people to patience in all things, and counsel them to endure without resentment any punishment" which may be inflicted.[55] But he ended with a challenge. "Your ignorant ministers have never dared to submit to the test of disputation. I therefore beg that here or elsewhere, I may, at your pleasure, join issue with some of your ministers or prelates in disputation."[56] He begged them not to suppose that this was prompted by arrogance or obstinacy, but only by the obligations of obedience and conscience.

Inevitably, Campion and Persons turned the matter over together before putting pen to paper, and each re-echoes the other in the more important passages. "You are persecuting a corporation that will never die. Sooner will your hearts and hands, sated with blood, fail you than men will fail" to respond to the call of sacrifice and even martyrdom.[57] Already he foresaw that religious toleration, a new and dangerous idea, would need to be accepted as part of the system of every civilized state in the future. He saw how illogical it was to beg toleration for the papists while refusing it to others. He also recognized

---

[53] (23) 37, see 31.

[54] (23) 32, 38f. See RP's "Instructions," ibid., 18. The irenic nature of Catholicism at this time is clear from P. Holmes, *Resistance and Compromise* (Cambridge, 1982), 1–89.

[55] (23) 33; see 39.

[56] Ibid.

[57] (23) 34; see 40; see Campion's "Challenge"; "Ten Reasons," 1914 edition (London, 1914), 10.

that Catholic countries gave no good example in this. For himself, however, regarding "this kindly consideration towards those . . . of a different religion, just as I have wished to find it always in others, so according to the slight opportunities I have had, I have frequently practised." He claimed to have protected Protestant Englishmen in Catholic lands persecuted by law.[58] There is no reason to doubt Persons's sincerity. He did much in later years to help British prisoners in Spanish galleys and elsewhere. Bitter experience and recurring disappointments did not change his mind. Indeed, his most mature thought on this subject is contained in *The treatise tending to mitigation* . . . of 1607.

Elizabeth I had been raised in a hard school, and her ablest ministers were men more concerned with maintaining their own influence, power, and prosperity than with new theories in civics. Cecil understood his own purpose perfectly, which was the manipulation of the sovereign, his peers, and people to ensure the establishment of a new order of things for all foreseeable time, one essentially and immovably Protestant and secular in outlook. Persons was challenging him to raise his mind to a plane completely alien to him and perhaps to most others. The Queen might have been moved to comply, but it was easy to persuade her that these men were not to be trusted. In any case, the premature dissemination of Campion's "Brag" through Pound's indiscretion afforded some excuse for responding harshly towards what could be seen as an act of plain defiance. Furthermore, the Anglican Church at that time had no champions to put in the field against men of the caliber of Campion and Persons. There seems to be little contemporary doubt about the paucity of intellect and spirituality in the ministers of religion at this time. Cecil and the council could not afford to accept the challenge.[59] Like every movement of the kind, the Reformation by no means signified for all the simple advent of peace and light. As Strype put it, "frequent wrongs had been done unto cathedral churches, colleges, hospitals, the companies in London and other religious foundations, by means of commissions for concealed lands and possessions obtained of her Majesty by men that showed themselves greedy of getting what they could . . . whosoever suffered by it."[60] Halfhearted attempts had been made to remedy the evils but with little visible result. Strange Protestant sects had also arisen, so that, as Christopher Haigh observed, "the Reformation did not pro-

---

[58] Ibid.

[59] See (11) II, 141–43; for the higher clergy and scholars deprived by 1561, see (50) I, London 1709, 240–45.

[60] (50) II, London 1725, 601.

duce a Protestant England . . . [but] a divided England."[61] All these tributaries, with the latest Roman contribution, threatened to swell to a torrent of dangerous proportions for Cecil's new England.

Certainly the missionaries found much dry ground thirsty for the irrigation of their teaching. Beginning at Hoxton, one Gardener, a former devotee of Foxe the martyrologist, became a Catholic. Other converts included Lord Compton, Sir Thomas Tresham, Sir William Catesby, and his uncle Dymock. The Council responded with "sundry terrible proclamations . . . against Jesuits."[62] Gentlemen and even noblemen were summoned to London and imprisoned, including the Lords Paget, Compton, and Vaux; the knights Tresham, Catesby, and John Arundell; and Ralph Sheldon and Thomas Throckmorton. Sherwin, the priest, was taken later in the year.[63] Some attempt was made to bring the prisoners over by persuasion but there was no question of public debate.[64]

After completing the "apologies" at Hoxton, Persons and Campion separated, not only to keep one move ahead of the pursuivants but also to bring their message to a wider audience. Persons probably went through Gloucester, Hereford, Worcester, even reaching Derbyshire; Campion through Berkshire, Oxfordshire, and Northamptonshire, although doubt remains because for obvious reasons no one, least of all the Jesuits, mentioned by name the places through which they passed, certainly not at the time.

Persons kept in touch with Rome. He wrote to Agazzari from the country on August 5,[65] having already written to Mercurian on leaving London. Two copies of the letter were sent by different routes to Rome in the hope that at least one would arrive. He and Campion would spend two or three months on tour before meeting again in London. Autumn was a good time for this since most of the gentry then resided on their estates.[66] George Gilbert provided them with all

---

[61] See ibid., 593–600, and (73) 209.

[62] The first of these in fact seems to have been of 10.i.1581. See (3) II, No. 655 (pp. 481–84); T. McCoog, S.J., "The Establishment of the English Province of the Society of Jesus," (10) 17, 121–79, especially 121–27 for the spirit of the mission.

[63] Committed to the Fleet on 9.xi.1580, later transferred to the Tower; (VII) SP12, CXLIX, No. 83; (12) III, 290; (22) XII, 264; see (1) 29.

[64] (1) 29. The Anglican side had competent controversialists; see (50) II, 159. "A catalogue of all the English popish books writ against the Reformation of the Church of England" 1558–80, "with the names of such learned divines as answered them."

[65] (23) 41–44, Italian; 44–46, translation. Mercurian died on 15.viii.1580; see (23) 41, n.(1).

[66] (23) 41, see 44.

necessaries for the journey.[67] Although persecution had intensified, above all in London,[68] Persons wanted more Jesuits to come to the harvest field. Wherever he went he formed groups of faithful ready to receive them and advise them about work and survival. James Bosgrave, S.J., provided some embarassment when he came to England for *health* reasons; unaware of what was involved, he agreed to go to the Anglican service. The delighted authorities put it about that he was about to abjure Catholicism publicly in a ceremony in St. Paul's Cathedral. When Bosgrave realized what he had done, he informed the privy council and the Catholics as well of his true intentions. He was subjected forthwith to a very harsh imprisonment.[69]

An important factor was the attitude of the Catholic embassies in London. Bernardino de Mendoza, the Spanish ambassador, was most friendly. On his return to London, Persons spent a long evening with him on October 19. He was to be an important link in the communications chain. Letters for Persons from Europe were to be directed in the first instance to the Flemish Jesuit rector at St. Omer, who would send them on as opportunity offered.

Thus far, the government policy of crude heavy-handedness, instead of terrorizing the Catholics, or the best of them, only drew them closer to one another. The prestige of the Jesuits stood high and many secular priests wished to join them. This result was unforeseen and Persons needed instructions.[70] Meanwhile, by mid-November Persons and Campion had established something like a chain of reception points to which newly arrived priests could report for work and information without the risk of initially fending for themselves.[71] George Birkhead, a priest with a special future in this history, arrived on November 17, 1580.[72]

By the end of 1580, the persecution could be described as ferocious. "Everywhere . . . men, women and even children are being dragged to prison. They are bound in iron chains, stripped of their possessions, deprived even of light, and in proclamations, harangues and sermons their reputations are destroyed . . . as traitors and re-

[67] (23) 44 and 41, n.(4).

[68] (23) 45.

[69] RP to Mannaerts, 20.x.1580; (VI) F.G.651/640, f.59, a.l.s.; P. S. Czynski, "Elsinore 1580: John Rogers and James Bosgrave," (10) 16, 1–16.

[70] RP to Mannaerts, 20.x.1580.

[71] RP to Agazzari, London, 17.xi.1580; (23) 46–56, Latin, English translation, 56–62. How far these centers were completely new and how far already used by Marian priests is matter for (difficult) research.

[72] See (23) 47, nn.(5), (6), (7).

bels."[73] Events in Ireland and Scotland and the breakdown of the proposed Anjou match for Elizabeth contributed to the fears of government,[74] as did the Spanish acquisition of Portugal. The arrival of the Jesuits and seminaries provided the last straw.[75] Of all the threats to Elizabeth, the papal expedition to Ireland was no doubt the least significant, but its propaganda value was incalculable. While Burghley had little to laugh at, surely he could not have repressed a smile however grim when he learned the truth of this ludicrous affair.[76]

In the autumn of 1580, Persons embarked on an activity that was to occupy much of his working life, the apostolate of the pen. The first secret printing press in England was set up at Greenstreet, East Ham, some time before Parliament reassembled on January 16, 1581.[77] Composed and printed by Persons himself, the first work was *A brief discourse contayning reasons why Catholiques refuse to goe to church. . . .* It appeared, with an epistle dedicatory, claiming as its author I. Howlet and bearing the false imprint of John Lyon of Douai. Persons insisted it was not a spirit of rebellion but conscience alone that prevented Catholics from going to Protestant services.[78] It aimed to counteract a more comfortable doctrine circulating in a manuscript attributed to William Clytheroe, later a priest,[79] but probably by Alban Langdale, Viscount Montague's chaplain no less.[80] Understandably, many were "glad to have such a cushion put under their elbows to ease their pressures."[81] Such included the Lords Paget, Compton, and Sheldon and Sir William Catesby.

It was Francis Browne, Lord Montague's brother, who let Persons set up his press in his Greenstreet house. Stephen Brinkley and seven assistants, all dressed like gentlemen to put the pursuivants off the scent, did the actual printing. Here were printed also, it seems,

---

[73] (23) 48, see 56.

[74] See Conyers Read, *Mr. Secretary Walsingham* (Oxford, 1925), II, 117ff; *Lord Burghley and Queen Elizabeth* (London, 1960), chap. 12.

[75] For a competent Protestant account, see Conyers Read, *Lord Burghley and Queen Elizabeth* (v. supra), chap. 13, 235–55. The first edition of *The execution . . .* carried on its titlepage the date 17.xii.1583. See R. M. Kingdon edition (New York: Cornell University Press, 1965), pp. xvii and 7.

[76] The author has a fuller study of this event in preparation. See above n.31.

[77] This was the Parliament which first met on 8.v.1572. See (4) 536.

[78] (21) 3; see (1) 179. Several editions survive in the BL (first of 1580, 1599, 1601); reprinted by the Scolar Press in 1972 from the 1580 edition at Ushaw. See (19) 115, printed "apparently before November 6, 1580"; (23) 76, n.14.

[79] (1) 179f; (21) 5, n.

[80] See (35) IV, 115–18 and DNB.

[81] (1) 179f; (21) 5f. See (79), chap.3.

A brief censure uppon two bookes written in answere to M. Edmonde Campions offer of disputation, again with the John Lyon imprint. *A discoverie of I. Nichols minister* . . . without imprint, was more likely printed at Stonor Park, which succeeded the Greenstreet press. Both were printed in 1581.[82]

The "brief discourse" against going to Anglican churches tried to be altogether conciliatory in tone. The dedicatory preface was "to the most highe and mightie Princess Elizabeth by the grace of God, Queene of England, France and Ireland"—even Ireland, the papal fief! She is addressed as "most excellent and souverayne dread ladye and princesse." Neither she, the lords of her council, nor anyone else could complain of anything in the writer save his religion, which was still "the common received religion of universal Christendom."[83] He compared unfavorably the relative freedom allowed the sectaries and the persecution of the Catholics.[84] Even before the draconian legislation of 1581, he could protest against "the extreme penalties" laid on the latter for following the religion of Elizabeth's ancestors.[85]

The author rejected as "intolerable . . . the giving out publicly that all Catholics are enemies and traitors to [her] royal majesty." On the contrary, they would be ready to defend "with the utmost drop of their blood" her throne and realm.[86] All they wanted in return was "some favourable toleration . . . in religion." Even the Turks allowed their subjects to follow their own religion. Nor did Christian princes ever force their non-Christian subjects to embrace their own faith. But he did not deny that the Church had always allowed civil magistrates to recall to the unity of the Church heretics who attempted to depart from it and corrupt others. It was the Protestants who had rejected Church unity, not the Catholics, and so the latter could not reasonably be persecuted.[87] In any case, the Catholics had a right to debate and reflection before being deprived of the religion which England had held for a thousand years. Public debate by whatever method, scholastic or otherwise, was all that Persons desired. Her Majesty's word would suffice as a safe-conduct, just as "the Council of Trent made the safe-conduct to our adversaries, which they notwithstanding refused to

---

[82] Leona Rostenberg, *The Minority Press and the English Crown, 1558–1625* (New York, 1971), 23 (not always accurate in detail); (19) 114–21 passim; C. A. Newdigate's notes, XIV 46/5/2/2; D. M. Rogers, "English Catholicism and the Printing Press, at Home and Abroad, 1558–1640," D.Phil. thesis Oxon, 1952.

[83] RP, "A brief discours . . . ," sig.iir.

[84] See J. Crehan, S.J., "The Prose of Robert Persons"; (32) May 1940, 366–76.

[85] RP, "A brief discours . . . ," sig. ++ iiiir.

[86] Ibid., sig. ++++ iiv.

[87] Ibid., sig. ++++ iiii r/v.

accept." If debate were refused by their adversaries, it would indicate "too much distrust in their own cause." He addressed the Queen as "sovereign princess and mother. . . . Whither then should children run in their afflictions but unto the love and tender care of their dear mother," especially one with so much power "to relieve them in all points."

In the main text, it was emphasized that Catholics were convinced their religion was the true one, so that to go to Protestant services would be as illogical as for a Protestant to attend Catholic functions.[88] If toleration were refused, the Catholics, unlike the "sectaries," must still wait upon the sovereign's good pleasure for redress. There could be no question of rebellion.[89]

Not less than the problem of printing was that of distributing printed books. "All the books are brought together to London without any being issued and, after being distributed . . . [to] . . . the priests in parcels of a hundred or fifty, are issued at exactly the same time to all parts of the kingdom." The pursuivants usually followed this up next day with a search of Catholic houses. But "there are plenty of young men of breeding ready to introduce them by night into the houses of the heretics, into workshops as well as palaces, scattering them in the court also, and about the streets so that it may not be Catholics only who are accused."[90] It seems that thus early in English history there were those who may not have agreed with what Persons had to say, but were prepared at some risk to defend his right to say it. He may have been the first to articulate in English the idea of toleration, but his grain was not thrown on ground unreceptive.[91] It is not true, then, that "the Jesuits were inexorably wedded to the principle of coercion."[92] What is true is that the fragmentation of Christendom at the Reformation introduced a spirit of mistrust and mutual defensiveness that would not be bridged for centuries. Cecil, Walsingham, Leicester, and their allies fostered this spirit of alienation and hostility to protect the Church Established, and it is usually assumed they had no choice

---

[88] Ibid., p. 3.

[89] Ibid., p. 68. Cf P. Holmes, *Resistance and Compromise*, 33–46.

[90] See RP to Agazzari, August 1581; (23) 85.

[91] *A treatise tending to mitigation towardes Catholicke subjectes in England. Wherein is declared, that it is not impossible for subjects of different religion . . . to live together in dutifull obedience and subjection, under the government of his Majesty of Great Brittany. Against the seditious wrytings of Thomas Morton . . . and some others to the contrary . . .* ([Saint Omer], 1607).

[92] W. K. Jordan, *The Development of Religious Toleration in England 1558–1603* (London, 1932), vol. 1, chap. 6, especially 382–94.

against the Jesuit threat; but a question should open up for the historians of this generation.[93]

Already, Persons's health was far from robust. He was obliged to leave undone a second and third part of the treatise against church going "partly by evil disposition of body," but even more by reason of "sudden business." This was the imminent discovery by the pursuivants of the Greenstreet press, which had to be moved to Stonor Park.[94] The intensity of the persecution caused not only disappointment and dismay in Rome but led to the encouragement of an assassination attempt on Elizabeth, who now seemed confirmed in the role of a false Jezabel. The nuncio Sega informed the Cardinal of Como in mid-November of a report by Dr. Humphrey Ely, delivered in great secrecy on behalf of "certain English noblemen" and the Jesuit Fathers, that they would try to kill the Queen. They wanted the prior approval of the Pope, at least verbal, that no sin would be committed, knowing that they might lose their lives in the attempt. Sega gave them his opinion that Pius V's bull of excommunication gave all the Queen's subjects the right "to take up arms against the Queen with impunity."[95] Como replied to Sega on December 12, 1580, conveying the pope's "santa benedizione" for Sega and approval in general terms for the attempt.[96] Since Elizabeth was responsible for the loss of "so many millions of souls," her assassination would be a meritorious act.

The principle of tyrannicide was everywhere accepted, at least since the days of John of Salisbury. Protestants and Catholics at this time only disagreed in identifying the tyrant.[97] By the autumn of 1580, Rome was aware that as a gesture of goodwill the Persons-Campion mission was a failure. Elizabeth's uncompromising edict of July 15 left no room for maneuver[98] Gregory XIII, much like the Queen, was not one to ignore a challenge. Ely's sources are unknown, but Jesuit policy was always opposed to

---

[93] See William Haugaard, *Elizabeth and the English Reformation: The Struggle for a Stable Settlement of Religion* (Cambridge, 1968).

[94] See "A brief discours . . . ," 68 r/v.

[95] Sega to the Cardinal of Como, Madrid, 14.xi.1580, Italian; (31) 426f.

[96] The phrase is peculiar, but A. O. Meyer's transcript of this correspondence ((31) 426–28) is altogether accurate. A.O.M. was unable to consult the original volumes since they were mislaid at the time. I have examined them in Segreteria di Stato, Spagna, 25 and 27. There is no reason to doubt their authenticity.

[97] See Junius Brutus (Du Plessis Mornay), *A Defence of Liberty Against Tyrants* (*Vindiciæ contra tyrannos*), ed. and trans. Harold Laski (London, 1924).

[98] W. Allen to Como, 12.ix.1580; (9) 89–91; he reported the main content and effect of the edict; (3) II, 469–71.

assassination as a practical solution, although it might be defended in theory. Persons himself, certainly, never swerved from his rejection of this alternative. One would therefore want better evidence to believe that any Jesuit was genuinely involved in this strange attempt.

The dissemination of Campion's "Challenge," and perhaps of Persons's "Confession of Faith" flicked the authorities on the raw, not only for its confession of faith but also because it revealed the methods used to discredit the papists.[99] The Jesuit insistence on their purely spiritual motives and intentions likewise spoiled the image of the scheming Jesuit. Indeed, Persons claimed that already some fifty thousand now refused to go to the Anglican services, a number too great for the pursuivants to cope with, in spite of their increased numbers and extended prisons.[100] Some imprisoned gentlemen were assured that, if they went to church once a year only, not for religion but simply to please the Queen, it would suffice. They still refused. Morale was high and no signs of division had yet appeared. "The secular priests cooperate with us; or rather I should say obey us in all things with the greatest goodwill." The reputation of the Society of Jesus was everywhere high. Persons feared it was too high for the Jesuits to live up to. But they came close to the ideal. Their giving did not count the cost, their fighting did not heed the wounds, their toiling found little rest; for they were under constant pursuit from faithful and pursuivants alike. Certainly there was no reward in human terms if much in the spiritual. This paradoxically happy situation was not destined to endure.

Not only did Persons call for more Jesuits but also for enlarged faculties to deal with the moral problems arising. In view of later accusations, one plea is significant. "There is crying need of a bishop . . . to supply us with holy oil for baptism and extreme unction. For lack of this we find ourselves in grave difficulties. Unless His Holiness grants speedy relief we shall soon be completely at a loss."[101] Persons was now sorry that Bishop Goldwell had turned back. Meanwhile, Ralph Sherwin, Luke Kirby, Robert Johnson, and John Hart, secular priests, sent greetings to their brethren in Rome—from prison—and by way of Persons's letter of

---

[99] (23) 57.

[100] (23) 51, see 58.

[101] (23) 52; see 59.

November 17 from London.[102] Campion left for Lancashire on November 16.

There were by now many places in London where Persons could stay, but he stayed nowhere more than two days to avoid the hyperactive pursuivants. During the daytime he kept on the move from early morning till late at night. His time was spent in preaching, saying Mass, sometimes twice a day, dealing with the moral problems of individuals, directing other priests to suitable places and ministries, reconciling schismatics, writing letters, and arranging help for those in prison and in want.[103] But not even the myriad problems of the English mission engaged his whole attention. He was now looking towards Scotland. He claimed that it was at Queen Mary's request that he thought of converting young James VI, something close to the heart of Allen, Sir Francis Englefield, and other leading exiles.[104] In the next decade, at least partly by his inspiration, "many missions" were to have Scotland as their goal.[105]

---

[102] See RP to Agazzari, Rome, 17.xi.1580; (23) 47–56.

[103] (23) 54; see 61.

[104] (II) 444. Rivers was seemingly "socius" or secretary to Henry Garnet, S.J., superior of the Jesuit mission in England from the summer of 1586 until his execution in connection with the Gunpowder Plot in 1606. He has now been identified as Henry Floyd, S.J. See *Notes and Queries* 239 (March 1994): 62–63.

[105] (1) 213.

Chapter Four

Strategic Withdrawal: 1581   ═══

I t was as supporting innovation as well as treason that the Privy
Council attacked the mission from Rome. After ten years of undog-
matic slumber, save in the point of the papal supremacy, the
Church by Law Established seemed to many to represent orthodoxy.
All the same, the best Anglican apologists were still in the future.
Meanwhile, the accusation of treason, not wholly new, since it had first
been mooted by Henry VIII, could be plausibly supported by indis-
criminately associating all papists with what had happened in Ireland,
as well as with plots dark and doubtful elsewhere, but all supported by
the men in the Vatican. The best argument, perhaps, was place, favor,
and possibly power if one went along with the accusations but persecution, dispossession, and even loss of liberty and life if one did not.

A proclamation of January 10, 1581, ordered the return of
children, seminarians, and dependents from overseas and also the
arrest of Jesuits. Elizabeth felt it her duty as a Christian prince to make
sure her subjects were raised "in the true Christian religion" unadul-
terated by "men's fancies and vain traditions."[1] From this time forth
none "of any degree or quality whatever" could travel abroad without
the royal license. Punishment awaited those who sheltered Jesuits and
seminarians, and reward lay ahead for those who denounced them.
Parliament, which reassembled on January 16 and sat till March 18,[2]
followed this up with the harsh act of 23 Elizabeth, cap.1. This made it
high treason to absolve any from obedience to the Queen in order to
make Catholics of them, likewise to be reconciled or absolved. A priest
saying Mass was to be fined two hundred marks with a year's imprisonment. Hearing Mass brought a fine of one hundred marks and
likewise a year's imprisonment. Absence from church as defined in the
statute of 1559[3] now carried a fine of £20 for every lunar month's

---

[1] (3) II, 482.

[2] This Parliament was originally elected in the spring of 1572; (4) 536. For the
effect of the fines on Worcestershire, see V. Burke, chap. 3 above, n.44.

[3] 1 Eliz. Cap. 2.

defection. Further penalties fell on absence from church for more than a year and on keeping a schoolmaster who stayed away from church.[4]

Undeterred, Persons continued the fight with his own weapons, not least the printing press. He aimed "to ensure that the heretics should not be able to publish anything without its being almost immediately attacked most vigorously." William Charke produced *An answere to a seditious pamphlet by a Jesuite in 1580* to answer Campion's "brag." This was reissued in 1581[5] and, along with it about the same time, Meredith Hanmer's *The great bragge and challenge of M. Champion, a Jesuite.*[6] The books in question attacked the Jesuits and in particular the founder, St. Ignatius. Persons had an answer out within ten days showing up "so many lies" that the authors were "mightily ashamed"— or should have been![7] *A brief censure uppon two bookes written in answere to M. Edmonde Campion's offer of disputation* was printed secretly by Stephen Brinkley.[8] Charke came back with *A replie to a censure written against the two answeres to a Jesuites seditious pamphlets,* also published by Christopher Barker in 1581.[9] Hanmer brought out about the same time *The Jesuites banner,* a book commendable for the brevity of its title if not for the soul of wit.[10] The tournament continued with Persons's *A defence of the censure given upon two bookes of William Charke and Meredith Hanmer, mynisters, whiche they wrote against M. Edmonde Campion.* By this time he had rolled his guns back to Rouen, where the book was printed in 1582.[11] Charke seemingly launched the last salvo in this engagement with his *An answere for the time unto that defence of the censure of 1583.*[12] Also about this time appeared Allen's *An apologie and true declaration of the institution and endeavours of the two English colleges. . . .*[13]

Of more lasting interest than all these was Campion's *Decem rationes,* an answer to the charges of the edict of July 15, 1580, which

---

[4] See (5) 9–14.

[5] See STC 5005, 5006 and RP to Agazzari, 16.vi. (V. infra, n.7.)

[6] See STC 12745.

[7] RP to Agazzari, 16.vi.1581; (23) 72–83 Latin, 83–90 English translation, especially 75 and nn.(8) and (9).

[8] Greenstreet Press, 1581, but with the imprint of "John Lyon at Doway." See (19) 115; (69) chap. 3.

[9] See STC, p. (110).

[10] See ibid., p. (283).

[11] (19) 117.

[12] STC 5008.

[13] Allen's book was printed at "Mounts in Henault" (Mons), 1581; see (27) 75, n.(11).

appeared in the summer of 1581.[14] Although Campion considered Persons's replies to Charke and Hanmer adequate, Persons wanted an eloquent enlargement of the reasons for seeking a public disputation.[15] Campion, then evangelizing Lancashire, sent his book to Persons in London to prepare for the press. Campion arrived at Stonor about the end of April 1581 at Persons's request, to supervise the first impression. A secular priest, William Maurice, gave invaluable help in locating Stonor, then unoccupied and buried in the middle of a wood, and in reassembling the press. Stephen Brinkley was brought from London at some risk and expense to oversee the actual printing, in which Campion also helped.[16] Maurice had the most delicate task of procuring paper, ink, and other essentials.[17]

Once Campion was settled at Stonor, Persons left for Lyford Grange, leaving his colleague to see that the books were sent to Oxford when ready. While at Stonor Persons just escaped a descent by the pursuivants on his house "near to Bridewell church in London" about mid-April. His books, rosaries, and other items were all seized. Apparently he had been betrayed by a servant of Roland Jenks of Oxford, their bookseller.[18]

By June 14, when Persons wrote a report for the Pope and the French commissioners for the Anjou match returned to France empty-handed, the Privy Council had already issued instructions to every part of the realm for an inquisition into the numbers of "recusant Catholics."[19] It was time to apply the law 23 Elizabeth, cap.1, with rigor. Few could pay the huge fine, so most had to look forward to an imprisonment which might be perpetual. A spate of "books, sermons, ballads, libels," and plays now appeared to bring the papists into popular discredit. Torture was now used freely, especially on captured priests suspected of having contact with Jesuits. But there were still many who did not shrink from a "bitter fight," including George Gilbert, who had been the saving of the mission at its inception.[20] Aware of the brutal revenge which the government would wreak upon him if caught,

---

[14] *Rationes decem: quibus fretus certamen adversariis obtulit in causa fidei, Edmundus Campianus . . . allegatæ ad clarissimos viros, nostrates academicos* (Stonor Park, 1581).

[15] See reprint in English translation (London, 1914), with frontispiece and title page from the Latin copy at Stonyhurst; see (21) 26f.

[16] (21) 16f; (1) 29.

[17] See J. Morris and J. H. Pollen, *The Month*, vii.1889 and i.1905.

[18] (21) 16, 17; (1) 182.

[19] RP uses the word "mandatum"; if it was a proclamation, however, it is not in (3).

[20] (23) 65, 67, and 65 n.(5) for sources on Gilbert.

Persons persuaded him to go abroad, and urged the Pope to show him special favor.[21]

The worst enemies of the Catholics were those who had changed sides. Sledd, Slade, or Slaydon, a former servant in the English College, Rome, returned to England about 1580 and offered his services to the government.[22] Persons reported to Agazzari on June 16, 1581, that Sledd had authority from the Privy Council to break into houses and search at will.[23] It was a profitable undertaking. The almost frantic reaction by the authorities was as much as anything an answer to the effect of the clandestine books. Officials had exerted great efforts, including the use of torture, to uncover the printers, but so far without success.[24] Nevertheless, the danger had not cowed seminarians or Jesuits into retirement. In their different areas Campion and Persons both followed a similar routine: preaching in the morning, riding and meditating in the afternoon, and exercising the quill. After supper they heard confessions or discussed problems with visitors. They changed their abode frequently to lower the risk of capture; but, in view of the numbers who flocked to them and found out where they were, their continued avoidance of capture was astonishing. There were many narrow escapes for both of them, and on three occasions Persons attributed his escape to a miracle. But the miracle was not repeated for all. Although Persons made a signal escape on one occasion by accidentally missing a house where the pursuivants were waiting for him, the priest Rishton and six others were hauled off to prison. When his London house near Bridewell church was raided, he had already transferred his more important possessions elsewhere; but unfortunately Alexander Bryant had to bear the revenge intended for Persons. He was stretched on the rack "a whole foot longer than nature made him."[25] It was not, perhaps, surprising, considering the earnestness with which Burghley was founding his commonwealth, that papists were "treated more inhumanly than any other kind of miscreant, even thieves and murderers."[26]

---

[21] RP wrote similarly to the Cardinal of San Sisto, Gregory XIII's nephew; (23) 68.

[22] For Sled (Sledd), see (23) 68, n.(1).

[23] Ibid., 68f.

[24] See RP to Aquaviva, 16.vi.1581, (VI) F.G.651, ff.284r–5v; a paragraph from this letter is in (23) 69 from D. Bartoli, Inghilterra, p. 66 Italian, English translation, (12) III, 610.

[25] See (18), and (23) 88. Bryant was also tortured by needles thrust under his fingernails, still "an unheard of kind of cruelty"; see (23) 88 and 81 n.(31). It is a defect of (73) and other contemporary writing that torture is played down.

[26] (VI) F.G.651, ff.284r–5v.

About the end of June 1581, Persons and Campion after another meeting agreed to separate. Campion took the road to Norfolk while Persons returned to London. With Persons's approval, Campion turned off to visit Lyford, home of the Yates family, although Yates himself was in prison for his convictions. Campion stayed only a day before leaving with Brother Emerson, but he turned back at the request of several gentlemen, including some from Oxford University.[27] This time disaster struck. Campion was captured and brought to London on July 22 to be incarcerated in the Tower.[28] The French in England for the Anjou match showed little enough interest in the Catholic recusants.[29] Jean Bodin told Persons baldly by way of Edward Gratley, priest, that he was in England "not to treat of religious matters but matrimony."[30] In any case, he disapproved of the Jesuits and their mission. Anjou made no gesture even to save Campion, Bryant, and Sherwin, who were done to death on December 1, 1581.[31]

It is significant that the point of Catholic faith for which the recusants were willing to die was one not solemnly defined until centuries later, namely, the spiritual and even temporal power of the pope and his function as head of Christendom. This was the crucial point interpreted by Elizabeth and her government as a matter of treason. Everard Hanse, priest, questioned in open court as to the head of the Church of England *(Ecclesiæ Anglicanæ)*, boldly declared, "the Roman Pontiff." For this he was judged guilty of treason and executed on July 31. Some wanted to see papists, especially Jesuits, burned for heresy, but the privy council realized that it was more plausible to execute them for treason.

The act of March 1581 was now rigorously applied with no need, after the departure of the French mission, to observe even perfunctory moderation in the persecution of the Catholics. Lives as well as property were now sought. Evidently, the Council hoped that a short, sharp terror with public bloodshed on the gallows would bring the papists to their senses and frighten off the rest. It was not to be so simple. Persons revealed more than his own spirit when he declared,

---

[27] See (21) 18f.

[28] (23) 91, n.(1).

[29] J. B. Black, *The Reign of Elizabeth*, 2nd ed. (Oxford, 1959), 349.

[30] (21) 24, 25; see (1) 183.

[31] (21) 34, 35. See P. McGrath, "The Bloody Question Reconsidered," (10) 20, 305–19. For an account of the working of the treason laws, see G. de Parmiter, "Plowden, Englefield and Sandford, 1585–1609," (10) 13, 159–77, and 14, 9–25. See also Mildmay's speech in Star Chamber on 15.xi.1581; CRS 60 (1968), 9–13.

"Our help is in the name of the Lord who is stronger than all."[32] Disaster struck again on August 4. An order was issued to search Stonor Park.[33] Not only the press itself but Brinkley and his four assistants were taken.[34] John Stonor and William Hartley, priest, were also seized.[35] Persons escaped just in time and took up residence at Henley Park, a house belonging to Francis Browne.[36] Soon afterwards he moved to Mitchelgrove, home of the Shelleys, in Hampshire. Shelley also was in prison. His house was close to the sea and Persons immediately recognised the great opportunity.

It seemed high time to make a firsthand report to the authorities abroad, especially Allen, on the state of the mission, and also to arrange for books to be printed on the continent, since the operation was too hazardous in England.[37] For Persons there could be no question of surrender but recent disasters might tempt others. Certainly, plain brutality and the example of false brethren and apostates were having their effect. The average man, and even more than average, is not built for martyrdom, certainly not the kind that Burghley and Walsingham could inflict. John Pasquale, a young Kentish gentleman, gave way under pressure from Sir Owen Hopton, lieutenant of the Tower, and judges assembled in Guildhall, although he later rallied. On the other hand, John Nichols, a Protestant preacher from Wales who went to study in Rome in 1579, returned to England and renounced Catholicism after only a brief experience of Hopton's Tower. He became a prison spy, a profession sometimes followed by men of genuine talent and education who were temporarily or chronically down on their luck.[38] As such, Nichols "wrote a most spiteful booke against the Jesuits and other priests, telling a hundred false tales . . . to make them odious."[39] While in the Tower, Hopton even managed to persuade Nichols to claim that he had been a Jesuit himself and had reached a high level of confidence even with the Pope and the cardi-

---

[32] (21) 34, 35: notes of another letter from RP to unknown of 30.viii. in (23) 93f.

[33] (1) 30; see (22) XIII, 151, J. Hart, *Diarium Turris*.

[34] (1) 183.

[35] (1) 30; Sander, *De Schismate* . . . (1628), 355.

[36] (1) 183; (21) 26, 27.

[37] (21) 26, 27.

[38] See L. Stone, *An Elizabethan: Sir Horatio Palavicino* (Oxford, 1956), chap. 6, especially 236; Edwards, *The Marvellous Chance*, chap. 1.

[39] (1) 182; (21) 7–13; also RP to Agazzari, viii.1581. (23) 85 and 76 n.(15). Nichols's book was probably *A declaration of the recantation of John Nichols (for the space almost of two yeares the Pope's Scholer in the English seminarie or Colledge at Rome) which desireth to be reconciled and received as a member into the true Church of Christ in England* (London: Christopher Barker), 14.ii.1581. See also (21) 7.

nals. Thus he was now in a position to publish to the world their guilty secrets. This took the form first of all of a sermon to his fellow prisoners in the Tower, delivered on February 5, 1581. It was published on February 14.[40] Persons replied forthwith in *A discoverie of I. Nichols, minister, misreported a Jesuite, lately recanted in the Tower of London.* . . . This was the last work printed at Stonor. Its main point was that Nichols had been dismissed from the English College after little more than a year on the grounds of total unsuitability.[41] The Jesuits themselves did not always survive the test; for example, Thomas Langdale and Christopher Perkins, who was later knighted by Elizabeth and sent on embassy to Germany.[42]

In 1581 yet another lifelong enemy of Persons appears. It all began when a quarrel developed between the Earl of Southampton and Lord Montague, both Catholics. The earl put away his wife, Montague's daughter, "as suspected of incontinency." Persons believed that Charles Paget, another Iago in the play, had some hand in the misunderstanding, as also in that between Lord Paget and his wife, and between the Earls of Arundel and Northumberland. This year Charles Paget went to live in Paris, becoming a firm associate of Thomas Morgan, a Welshman who had been in the service of the Archbishop of York. At his death Morgan took a post in the household of the Earl of Shrewsbury, Mary, Queen of Scots', keeper. Morgan won her confidence and went to work as her agent in France. Paget and Morgan were in close contact with Nau and Curle, her secretaries, "and ruled all about her and had the sceptre in their hands."[43] The four managed all Mary's affairs until her execution, when "the said two secretaries were pardoned and let go."[44]

Towards the end of the summer, George Gilbert took the advice of Persons and others to retire into France.[45] Persons's first intention on leaving Mitchelgrove was to return to London,[46] but he heard of a group of priests and others who were going to France "on

---

[40] (21) 6, n.; see "A sermon preached by a Jesuit in the Tower on Sundaie the 5th daie of februaire. . . ." See Arber, *Register of the Stationers's Company*, II, 177; (1) 28, n.

[41] (21) 7; (69) 52–54.

[42] See (1) 182.

[43] (1) 183–84.

[44] For the dubious role of C. Paget and T. Morgan in Mary's story, see L. Hicks, S.J., *An Elizabethan Problem* (New York, 1964). Persons enlarges in (1) 184 on the curious activities of Paget and Morgan in Paris, who secretly undermined her confidence in her ambassador, the Archbishop of Glasgow, and used the thirty thousand crowns a year of her dower lands "to pleasure much there frendes and hinder there adversaries."

[45] (1) 183; (21) 13, 27.

[46] (21) 27.

private business." They offered to take Persons with them.[47] He did not jump at the idea. He might not be able to return easily or even at all. His enemies would represent it as cowardly desertion. He might also "lose the opportunity . . . of dying for the faith." Haunted by televisionary dreams of comfort, this is not something we can easily understand; but it is a factor essential to the understanding of Persons and his contemporaries. At all events, after an almost sleepless night grappling with the problem, Persons opted for the voyage to France.

Perhaps it was the prospect of setting up a new press which finally moved him to his decision.[48] Another book against Charke and Hanmer was called for, also a Latin book on the English persecution for the enlightenment of educated Europe. The ordinary English Catholics needed a practical handbook of instruction in their faith—if any English Catholic just then could be described as ordinary! Persons also had by him one thousand gold crowns towards the expenses of translating the New Testament into English. The scholars at Douai would do this. He also wished to confer with the Archbishop of Glasgow, Queen Mary's exiled ambassador in Paris, and with Edmund Hay and William Crichton, two renowned Scottish Jesuits, with the object of opening up a mission to Scotland. This depended on the prior approval of Allen and Mercurian.

The passage to France was not accomplished without further complication. Adverse winds unexpectedly forced the party to hole up perilously in a barn for three days, waiting for "God to send them a favourable wind." Persons was at least fortunate in that Robert Alfield, who was destined to become a pursuivant, was still loyal. Although his brother was a priest and, indeed, recommended him to Persons, his earlier exploits had included robbery. They were the sons of a Protestant divine. The party left some time between August 13 and 21. On arrival at Rouen, Persons wrote to his two Jesuit colleagues still at liberty in England.[49] Persons could not have known that he would never see England again.[50]

---

[47] Ibid.

[48] RP to Aquaviva, 21.x.1581; (23) 107; (21) 28, 29.

[49] (21) 28–31 and n. Persons believed that Alfield betrayed his own brother, but this does not appear from PRO, SP12, 248, No. 29.

[50] See (23) 95, n.(3) and (21) 26, 27 n.

Chapter Five

The Forceful Solution, First Phase
1581–1582

T he life of Robert Persons from now until the end of his life presents to the outside observer something of a mystery, even a contradiction. With no more than the authority of superior of the Jesuit mission to England and subject to provincials wherever he resides, he becomes the adviser and confidant of princes and ambassadors, and the point of liaison for high political schemes taking him through most of western Europe except Germany. A remarkable feature of the Jesuits was that, in an age which revered rank and precedence more than most, they enjoyed influence at top levels without special trappings of title and office. Place hunting and the pursuit of wealth that went with it had become an abuse in the Church and made Ignatius of Loyola determined to combat them by the force of contrary example. By the time Persons left England, most in authority in Catholic Europe accepted and even respected this Jesuit exercise of humility, at least as a pardonable idiosyncrasy in men who were otherwise useful for their intelligence, integrity, learning, and readiness to serve, qualities not often found in the same man in any era. These were also the days of personal rule everywhere, so that anyone by the force of personality and the prestige of the institution which promoted him could exercise influence at the top and bypass bureaucracy at many levels. Of the latter there was no lack in Europe, especially in Rome and Spain. Persons had the dynamism required to win the confidence of the Pope and the Spanish king, for most of his career, at least. That he was only a man in black was therefore overlooked. It was important that the Society of Jesus, not yet a century old, still enjoyed a certain spontaneity in spirit and organization. The older orders had often grown tired; worse still, they had suffered demoralizing defections when some of the leaders of the Protestant Reformation emerged from their ranks. Luther, Coverdale, Peter Martyr, and Bucer had all been monks.[1] The Jesuits set out with a tabula rasa, shedding features of the older orders that seemed likely to impede a contemporary

---

[1] See T. H. Clancy, S.J., "An Introduction to Jesuit Life: The Constitutions and History Through 435 Years" (St. Louis, 1976), especially 17, 98, 115.

apostolate. There was no office in choir, for example. It was only with reluctance that the founder agreed to rules at all, believing that the inspiration of the Holy Spirit should be a sufficient rule of life. All the same, he insisted on obedience to superiors. His was an army, the first "salvation army." Nevertheless, the government aimed to be paternal, not military. The general acted on advice and after discussion. Persons fitted into the system perfectly. Although he used his discretion, at no time, it seems, did he disobey any order from his general or even lesser superiors.

Undoubtedly, the brilliant, apparently free-lance work of Persons in the sphere of politics had its dangers. As Clancy observes, "It was Jesuit magnanimity . . . which led the Society into politics. They were at the service of the pope and the pope had many diplomatic and political errands and missions that he sent them on."[2] The Jesuits themselves, for example, Olivier Mannaerts (Manare) realized the danger of being accused of interfering in the affairs of princes. This could cause scandal even if its real motive was often jealousy. A factor operating in Persons's favor was that the Society at this time was a small and elitist body. The Fourth General Congregation, which met in February 1581 to elect the new general, Claudio Aquaviva, numbered only fifty-seven professed Fathers. There were only one thousand Jesuits in all, including the spiritual coadjutors. Smallness bred intimacy and trust and encouraged individual initiative. Persons had no difficulty in establishing a good relationship with the new general, a kindred spirit in enthusiasm, dedication, and readiness to consider new ideas. One of Persons's new ideas was to establish the equivalent of an English province in exile. Not all foreign Jesuits saw the need. Indeed, the idea of an English colony abroad, so to speak, including a novitiate, colleges for training, and a tertianship, was not the obvious solution it later seemed by reason of long familiarity. Indeed, it appeared chauvinistic to many foreign Jesuits, implying insufficiency in their preparation, which was quite good enough for every other part of the world, even the most remote. In any case, Persons's organization developed empirically as need seemed to demand. If he had the blueprint of it all in his mind at the outset, he left no written indication of it.

After a successful crossing to France, Persons proceeded to Rouen, where he took immediate steps to ensure the continuance of the mission he had left behind. Writing from Rouen, Persons appointed Jasper Heywood, who was John Donne's uncle, superior of the Jesuit mission in his absence. He and William Holt arrived in England

---

[2] Ibid.

shortly after Campion's arrest. Heywood had to deal with a generation-gap problem, in that the newly arrived priests were promoting the relaxed fasting laws in use on the continent against the more rigorous English customs. Many of the laity were scandalized rather than consoled.[3]

Accompanied by George Gilbert, Persons went to confer with Allen at Rheims. He also wrote to Aquaviva to explain the reasons for his return to the mainland and to give an account of the printing venture.[4] This began again in Rouen when Persons persuaded George Flinton, an English merchant, to start up a press. He succeeded well until his death some years later. His first effort was probably *A defence of the censure gyven upon two bookes of William Charke and Meredith Hanmer, mynysters, whiche they wrote against M. Edmond Campion*, published in 1582. Stephen Brinkley was still in the Tower but obtained his release through friends some time before September 1583.[5]

Staying in Rouen with Archdeacon Michael de Monsi, a cardinal's nephew and city councilor, Persons spent the winter of 1581 and 1582 organizing the press and writing to various people.[6] By about October 21, 1581, news arrived that Campion had been twice subjected to ruthless racking in the Tower. In this state he was at last cynically allowed the privilege of the desired disputation with Protestant divines; this took place between August 31 and September 27.[7] Without doubt, the terrible news of this treatment meted out to an intimate friend and colleague radically altered Persons's attitude towards the English queen and government. Conciliatory approaches were time wasted and only invited return gestures of contempt. Perhaps Persons the soldier now prevailed over Persons the priest. It is tempting, with the cheap wisdom of hindsight, to criticize the Catholic powers abroad and the exiles for all the time, trouble, and money which were to be poured out on abortive efforts to solve the English problem by force of arms. The

---

[3] (1) 177.

[4] The explanatory letter to Aquaviva seems to be lost. But see (16) 113–21 for a letter of 26.ix.1581. See (21) 30f and 31n.

[5] (21) 30n. and (12) VI 554; (69) 55f.

[6] See RP to Aquaviva, 21.x.1581; (23) 95–106, in Latin; English translation, 107–15. The date is conjectural from the source printed here, but a full version in Latin though not(?) in Persons's hand is in (VI) F.G.651, n.f. This MS is endorsed in RP's hand, "literæ P. Personii 21 8.bris 1581." But it is evident that this long report was written over a period beginning not later than 26.ix., since this date was given at the end of what was probably one letter before Watts's letter, which was given verbatim; (23) 100, see 109f. This copy(?) has no signature, seal, address, or indication of place of origin, although it was clearly written in Rouen.

[7] See RP to Aquaviva [21.x.1581], (23) 95 and n.2.

effort would have been better spent on other things, such as enlarging
the facilities of the colleges abroad. But this was by no means evident
at the end of 1581. A short, sharp military solution is always a temptation and, if it succeeds, needs no further justification. But the Protestant victory of 1688 was not to be anticipated by the Catholics in
1582—or even in 1588.

In fact the best hope for English Catholics at this point in 1581
seemed to lie through converting Scotland and bringing pressure on
Queen and council by foreign ambassadors. Persons made these points
in his letter to Aquaviva of October 21(?). A good promise was the
succession of Mary, Queen of Scots, to the English throne "after the
death of this woman who now reigns." The execution of James Douglas, earl of Morton, on June 2, 1581,[8] succeeded as regent by the Sieur
d'Aubigny, duke of Lennox, also seemed a promise of better things.
Lennox was a "politique" but a Catholic and enjoyed the support of
the Earl of Arran, Lord James Stuart, captain of the King's Guard, and
of Lord Seaton and other friends and seeming friends of the Scottish
queen. King James was still a minor and a cipher in the affairs of his
kingdom. At any rate, those who governed the northern kingdom were
not closed to Catholic influences, unlike those in the south.

Persons now persuaded a Welsh secular priest from Menevia,
William Watts, to work first of all in the north of England to explore
the possibilities of a passage and mission into Scotland. He was "short
of stature and thick, his beard yellow and thick, his face white and the
tip of his nose going downward like unto a hawk's bill."[9] Imprisoned
in York in 1579, he managed to escape. Much was to be hoped from
the Scots, a people of an "open-handed and generous disposition."
Support was also expected from Ambassador Beaton in Paris, who
could "discover means whereby the King of France could be roused to
intervene with the Queen [Elizabeth] on behalf of the Catholics" at
least to get their crushing fines reduced.[10] The French king was not
forthcoming. Incidentally, so far no one in authority knew of Persons's
presence in France apart from de Monsi, with whom he lodged, and
Allen.[11]

---

[8] (23) 109.

[9] (18) 374.

[10] (23) 107; see 96, n.(5).

[11] RP to Aquaviva, 21.x.1581; (23) 107 gives "Sens" but the text is probably
corrupt. See ibid., 98 n.(10). Monsi was the nephew seemingly of Charles, cardinal de
Bourbon, archbishop of Rouen. After Henri III's death, he was declared King of France
by the League in opposition to Henry of Navarre; (23) 97 n.(9). See Aquaviva to Monsi,
23.xii.1581, ibid.

On October 21 Persons received "two large bundles of letters" from England urging him to return. Heywood and William Holt were active in the north but there was no Jesuit in the south. The secular priests, however, were carrying on the task with no less zeal. Before leaving England, Persons sent some into Wales, a place "not so hostile to the Catholic religion," although, thanks to lack of priests, sunk into "a state of deep ignorance." One priest was inserted into Cambridge University, an "entirely heretical institution," as "a scholar or gentleman desirous of study."[12] The Protestant ploy of infiltration was now to be adopted by the Catholics.

At this time, Watts reported favorably on converting the North and also on passing into Scotland. Persons urged him to the latter course without delay, making contact with the nobility and, if possible, the young king himself. James might at least offer asylum to Catholics fleeing from persecution in England, even if he could not become formally their protector in England itself. The Catholics would support his eventual succession to the English throne. For the present, he was to be reminded of his friendship with Catholic princes, the religion of his mother, and the death of his father at the hands of heretics, albeit in battle. Certain plots against his young life had been frustrated by the efforts of Catholics.[13] With all this in mind, Watts crossed the Scottish border about August 26, 1581.

In a letter carried by a servant who had hoped to find Persons in London, Watts reported very favorably on the prospects of a Scottish mission. The servant had very confidential matters to impart which could not be put in writing.[14] Meanwhile Persons had much to occupy him in the written account of Watts's Caledonian odyssey among the lairds and nobles who had not altogether forgotten their Catholicism[15] —and certainly not their manners.

Watts's "Certain animadversions for Father Redman [Persons]," probably in a letter of September 15,[16] made various suggestions, most of them fairly obvious, for the mission. Overlooking completely the circumstances of Mary, Queen of Scots', imprisonment and the close surveillance of her correspondence, he seemed surprised that she had

---

[12] (23) 108. See (80).

[13] See (23) xlii.

[14] (23) 109 and 99 n.(15). RP received Watts's letter on 15.ix.1581; (23) 112.

[15] (23) 110–12.

[16] See Watts to RP, n.d., (23) 100–102, Latin, 110–12 English translation; addressed to "Redman," RP's alias. Part of this letter, not known elsewhere, is in (VI) F.G.651, n.f., 21.x.1581, and headed "Animadversions pro D. Redman," occurring in this text at end of para. III, 102.

not done more to influence her son from England. Meanwhile, the central figure for a Catholic mission, to whom missionaries should refer themselves by way of beginning, was Baron Seaton, whose principal residence, conveniently enough, was near Edinburgh.[17] Persons lost no time in getting in touch with Lord Seaton and trying to establish contact with the Scottish queen "by whatever means were available." Watts was asked to remain in the border country to await further word, receiving, meanwhile, the financial help he asked for from England.[18]

Persons now sought the General's advice and approval before proceeding further. For at least two years any work would have to be done by English priests, since no Scots were available. At all events, there were "no laws made against us, and we have a common language with the Scots."[19] If anything, the need for books seemed greater in Scotland than in England, and it was the absence of Catholic literature that had enabled heresy to triumph. Money would have to come from outside—perhaps from the Pope. For the Scots were poor, and so far lacked "that zeal for the Catholic cause which would make them willing to spend any money on it." Although Persons did not say so, the fact was that much of the interest professed in the Catholic cause came from the prospect of money that people outside might be prepared to pay over to supporters, ostensible as well as real. Persons had laid out one thousand crowns on the project; but the English Catholics, being bled white in their own country, could not be expected to pay for this new mission. Persons wanted the Pope to spare four hundred crowns a year for two or three years to pay for clothing, horses, and minimum equipment. Aquaviva considered it inopportune to ask the Pope even for so little at this time, but he raised a loan of two hundred crowns himself and forwarded it to Monsi in Rouen.[20]

Persecution was having its effect, but the English government now began to look for subtler means to discredit the papist cause. An attempt was made towards the end of 1581 to represent Catholicism as the religion of the Jesuits. Decrees issued to the two universities urged everyone to see if "they knew or suspected anyone who favoured the Jesuits or the Jesuits' religion."[21] As if in defiance, about this time Persons sent in "two young merchants"—learned men—one for Eng-

---

[17] (VI) F.G.651, n.f., 21.x.1581.

[18] (23) 112.

[19] (23) 113.

[20] Aquaviva to RP, 19.iii.1582; (23) 104, n.(24) acknowledging RP's receipt of the money and thanks.

[21] (23) 114.

land, one for Scotland to sell "certain merchandise" and take in books and letters.[22]

Two matters called for immediate attention. There was a considerable demand for the Office of the Blessed Virgin to be reprinted in English, since not all could follow Latin. Translations had been permitted in the past, but a fresh permission seemed called for. It had been available in French from the time of Queen Mary. More pressing, perhaps, was the need for extended faculties.[23] In a letter of October 14, Aquaviva informed Allen of his success with the Pope. However, Gregory was not prepared to grant dispensation from a vow of chastity except to women. "If men, through lack of religious orders, could not keep that vow in England, they could do so out of England." Those in wedlock received more indulgence. Dispensations for affinity and consanguinity up to the second degree had long been granted—to Heywood for example when he was in Germany—and this was renewed. But for dispensation in the second degree *in foro externo* the Pope delegated no one.[24] Persons also wanted authority for himself, Heywood, and Holt to communicate their faculties to all other priests on the mission—to Scots, if any, as well as English.[25]

Persons in Rouen soon became a liaison for the Catholic exiles and their brethren in England and also for the exiles and continental rulers who might assist them. He was also a source of news—another Richard Verstegan or Hugh Owen. Highly significant was his role as Allen's right-hand man. He had a swift, intuitive ability to appraise an administrative problem and find a practicable solution. But he was also a man of deep and sensitive spirituality and a writer of note, even if he

---

[22] Ibid. What follows is based on a passage in (VI) F.G. not occurring in other printed sources of the 21.x. letter.

[23] (23) 105, see 115. The alternative ending to this letter of 21.x. in (VI) F.G.651 suggests Antonio Baranticollo as the Italian Jesuit who would tutor James VI in his language. Fr. Ferdinando Capretio could be used in England. If the archdeacon was absent from Rouen when the pair arrived, they should contact George Flinton or the "deacon" of the English living there. Letters for RP should be addressed to the archdeacon.

[24] (33) 83. Aquaviva replied direct to RP on 17.ii.1582, telling him the faculties for the Anglo-Latin Office and Fasts had been granted; that the Paris nuncio might be the ordinary for England; and that he could dispense from matrimonial nondiriment impediments; (23) 106 n.(31). Seemingly in a letter of 22.xi.1581, a great part of which is lost; (23) 118f. Regarding the concessions sought from the Pope, see Aquaviva to RP, Rome, 23.xii.1581 (infra). Aquaviva mentioned again the faculties required for printing the "Little Office" and matters concerning the Paris nuncio. A *libellus supplex* had been sent to the Pope concerning the faculties sought by Allen. They were expected shortly and would be sent as soon as obtained. There is much on the question of faculties in (VI) Anglia.9.II.2.

[25] (VI) F.G.651/640, n.f.1, 2nd addition.

lacked the elegance and flourish of Campion. It is significant that his best-known work, one which received the compliment of plagiarism from the Protestants, was *The Christian directory guiding men to their eternal salvation*. In an intensely political age, many grew tired of politics and turned again to spirituality. Persons produced a work to fulfill their need. The answer, besides prayer, to the most urgent practical religious problem, toleration, had to be met by Protestant or Catholic through the tortuous ways of politics. Persons never shrank from its necessity, but he made it clear in more places than one that this was not his first choice. He became a politician by necessity. His primary vocation was that of priest; his avocation, politics. However, it cannot be denied that he entered into his avocation with rare zest and with no obvious signs of reluctance. A welter of political activity now began which was to occupy not only the next few years but most of his life. It made him enemies among Catholics as well as Protestants, which one would expect. Not only would force be met with force, but equivocation in the spoken word would contribute to concealment. However much it might be justified, the use of amphibology undoubtedly helped the enemies of the Jesuits to believe the worst of them; and sometimes even made their friends doubt. But while the truth that lay behind denials may have countenanced recourse to arms and invasion, there is no reason to suppose that Persons or any other Jesuit ever intended or plotted assassination.

Still wielding a pen no less mighty than the sword, by October 21 Persons completed a symposium of translations from the works of Luis de Granada and others.[26] To help with manpower, assigning foreign Jesuits to serve in England was debated, but Aquaviva felt that in the prevailing circumstances of hot persecution, it would be sacrificing men for nothing. At all events, he agreed to approach the Pope and the Cardinal of Como for money.[27] As a modest example of equivocation, Agazzari received a letter from Persons addressed as from London on November 22, 1581.[28] The unhappy example of John Nichols and Lawrence Caddy, spoiled products of the English College, Rome, led Persons to urge caution on Agazzari in dismissing students, even those who were unsatisfactory.[29] Agazzari clearly expected more

---

[26] The main work was seemingly Gaspar Loarte's *The Exercise of a Christian Life;* (69) 73f.

[27] 14.x.1581, from Rome, Latin with English translation; (33) 85.

[28] RP to Agazzari, 22.xi.1581, London (actually Rouen); (23) 115–17, Italian, 117f, English. See also 116 n.(4). RP explored equivocation in *A Treatise Tending to Mitigation* . . . (1607).

[29] RP to Agazzari, 22.xi.1581.

sympathy for his handling of a difficult situation, and relations between the English College and Rouen cooled for a time.[30]

Persons now decided to send Watts on a return visit to Scotland, this time accompanied by Holt, the Jesuit.[31] Longer-term arrangements proceeded in Europe as the Scottish Jesuits, especially William Crichton, became interested in the mission.[32] Crichton wrote encouragingly to Anselmo Dandino, papal nuncio in Paris, in April 1581.[33] Beaton wrote to spur Aquaviva on, who was able to convey to him in December the Pope's favorable reaction. William Crichton and Edmund Hay, experienced men, would be the spearhead of the new effort.[34] These, along with Beaton and Persons, would settle the time of entry.[35] As for new recruits, any who wished to join the Society should do a noviceship first.[36] The whole affair should be kept secret, even from other Jesuits.[37] Hay was designated the leader of the pair and received fuller instructions than Crichton.[38] Persons, however, under

---

[30] (23) 118 and 117 n.(5).

[31] See Mendoza to Philip II, 9.ii.1582; (25) 286. For a discussion of the chronology and errors arising, see (23) 125, n.(2); RP to Agazzari, 3.ii.1582, ibid., 126.

[32] Crichton was born about 1530 and joined the Society of Jesus in 1561 in Rome. Of "average health," he studied previously at St. Andrews, Paris, Rome, Leipzig, and Louvain. As a Jesuit he studied philosophy in Rome (the catalogue says also "in Scotland," but this might be erroneous) and theology under Toledo. He was rector of several colleges over the years and vice-provincial of Aquitaine under Everard Mercurian (d.1.viii.1580). Aquaviva turned his attention to the missions. Ordained priest in 1563, he was professed of the four vows on 28.viii.1568; (VI) Flandro-Belg.9, catalogi triennales 1584–1603, entries for 1593, f.26. The records do not always tally, especially with regard to his age (e.g., ibid., 1597, f.2). See also DNB. He was of the Ruthven clan (see (27) 257).

[33] HMC 15th Rep., App. II (Eliot Hodgkin MSS), 263.

[34] Hay was related to Crichton ((XIV) 46/22/5, No. 268, Chadwick notes) and a lifetime associate. Born about 1534 in "Albany," an ill-defined area north of the Forth, of noble parentage. He gained his Bachelor of Arts degree at St. Andrews, probably with W. Crichton on 25.viii.1553; *Early records of the University of St. Andrews, 1413–1579*, SHS, 3rd series, 8, (Edinburgh, 1920). He entered the Society of Jesus with Crichton on 5.xii.1562; (VI) Rom.170, 117. He befriended Fr. de Gouda at Louvain in April 1562 and offered to go with him to Scotland on legation. Present at the Third General Congregation of the Society of Jesus in 1573 as provincial of the Province of France, became the first rector of the new college at Pont-à-Mousson on 27.x.1574; P. Nicolas Abram, S.J., "L'Université de Pont-à-Mousson, 1572–1650," in *Documents inédits*, A. Carayon, vol. 22 (Poitiers, 1870). He held the post until xi.1581, when he was awaiting or preparing a journey to Scotland.

[35] Aquaviva to Beaton, Rome, 22.xii.1581; (VI) Francia I, f.114r/v, Latin draft.

[36] Aquaviva to RP, Rome, 23.xii.1581; (VI) ibid., f.115v, Latin draft.

[37] Aquaviva to E. Hay, Rome, 23.xii.1581; ibid., f.114v, Latin. Hay was asked to work out a letter cipher and give the General a copy.

[38] Aquaviva to Crichton, Rome, 23.xii.1581; ibid., Gen. ad Aquitaine Prov.,

the General, was to give directions to the other two; this he did to Crichton at Rouen, giving him Emerson as companion.[39]

From Scotland, Watts sent Holt back to London about January 31, 1582, where he interviewed the Spanish ambassador, Mendoza. Holt carried the assurance that the leading Catholics, especially Lennox, Huntly, Eglinton, Argyll, and Caithness, would do everything consistent with the dignity of kingship to convert King James. He might even be deposed to await the arrival in Scotland of the Scottish queen! But this was to be no simple peace mission as previously in England. Some two thousand foreign troops would be needed to overawe the Scottish Protestants and neutralize the danger of an English invasion. The Pope and Philip II might manage this between them.[40] After sending Holt back to Scotland, Mendoza wrote to Mary, asking her to consent to whatever measures might be necessary for the conversion of her son and Scotland. He also wrote to Philip, weighing up the pros and cons of the scheme, and to Allen, who forwarded his letter to Rome.[41]

Back in Edinburgh about March 7, 1582, Holt rejoined Watts and learned that Crichton and Hay were already in conference with Lennox and his friends. Crichton and Hay were sent back to France with a new scheme which called not for two thousand but for twenty thousand men to be recruited from six nations including England! Catholicism was to be reestablished by force of arms not only in Scotland but also in Ireland and England itself. Queen Mary would be freed but nothing was said as to whether she would rule or where. Sixteen further proposals included twenty thousand crowns which Lennox might draw on in Paris for immediate expenses.[42] In England, violence on any large scale was by this time a state monopoly. In Scotland it was still freely adopted by any noble faction for political ends. Not even the monarch was safe from kidnapping and manipulation. The intervention of the Scottish Jesuits merely turned the politico-religious problem towards the lines of a solution fully in keeping with their own national tradition. Persons was perhaps swept along in a current too strong for him to resist, but he was probably not inclined to resist overstrenuously. Priest killing was becoming a habit in

---

f.98v. Latin draft.

[39] (1) 30.

[40] (23) pp. l–li.

[41] Ibid.

[42] J. <Kretzschmar, *Die Invasionsprojekte der Katholischen Mächte gegen England zur Zeit Elisabeths* (Leipsig, 1892). Lennox's proposals, Dalkeith, 7.iii.1582, 124–28. Guise's modifications on 128f.

England: Everard Hanse, seminary priest, died on July 31, followed by the culling of December 1, 1581; many others would follow as the reign proceeded. Evidently, the legal treason involved in merely being a priest was now acccompanied by the real thing in those who followed these aggressive policies. But Persons felt no compunction in attempting to overthrow a regime founded on wrong thinking and believing, and one which had taken the initiative in violence.

Persons was busy with writing in the winter of 1581/82;[43] he attempted as well to solve a problem regarding the education of Catholic boys, especially because any with a vocation would need a sufficiency of Latin not available to them in England. The answer was a school in exile. It was founded at Eu in Normandy, on the demesne of the Duke of Guise, who helped with an endowment of £100 per annum. He had already built a new house for the French Jesuits, so their original house in the town was redundant. Claude Mathieu, the French provincial, was happy to admit the new tenants.[44]

It was now time for fence mending with the English College, Rome. When Agazzari was asked not to send unsuitable men to the English mission, he pointed out to Persons that at the end of their studies his students were under oath to go there; there was nothing else for them to do in Rome, where, in any case, they did not wish to stay.[45] Replying, Persons admitted fully Agazzari's position and apologized for his hastiness in attributing blame. But he added, "You, too, I know, if you were here, would feel the same distress . . . seeing scandals and finding no remedy."[46] He undertook to send, as far as he could, only suitable subjects; but men were unpredictable, especially in the extraordinary circumstances of persecution. One man was doing well. "Your scholar, Edward Gratley, salutes you with reverence and much affection . . . and is behaving very well." Before long, he was to become a most effective betrayer of his erstwhile cause.

Elizabeth's council could not have been surprised to learn that a reign of terror is only effective if everyone is properly terrorized. Those who defied it to the point of martyrdom brought a backlash. As Persons reported, Walsingham "lately declared" it would have been

---

[43] (23) 97, n.(6).

[44] (21) 36, 37; see (1) 30; RP stated that it only lasted until the assassination of Guise in 1588, but in fact it persisted until after the opening of St. Omers, i.e., until about 1594; (1) 31 and n.1; (II) f.500; *Stonyhurst Magazine* 1 (1883): 284. The school had some twenty pupils by the time it was forced to flee from France.

[45] (21) 38, 39.

[46] RP to Agazzari, 3.ii.1582; (21) 40, 41; see (23) 124f, Latin; 125f English translation.

better for the Queen to have spent forty thousand gold pieces—he did not say on what—rather than kill those priests in public. "We find nearly all the more moderate Protestants very well-disposed to us." They were impressed by Catholic readiness not only to die for their faith, but to defend it, and did not fail to note the reluctance of their own divines to engage in disputation.[47] "Never were Masses in London so frequent, so abundant, so devout, as now they are celebrated in almost every corner" even in prison. Campion's gaoler in the Tower had been converted, while Baron Howard of Effingham had prevented Campion's executioner from cutting him down before he was dead.[48]

While Fr. Robert may have told the truth, undoubtedly he was purveying material designed to boost the morale of Agazzari's students, who would shortly be facing the same perils themselves.[49] England's Protestantism was at this time only skin-deep, as is evident from the writings of her greatest contemporary poet.[50] Nevertheless, the council's victories were significant and gained in unexpected places. Persons's servant, Robert Alfield, now decided he had enough. He had been well treated. [51]When Persons discovered his treachery through reading the correspondence of the man he already distrusted, Alfield was put in a Roman prison for a time.[52] George Gilbert's former servant, Rogers, also became a spy for Walsingham under the name of Nicholas Berden.[53] Fortunately, one man stayed firm. When Brother Emerson returned from Sotland with Crichton about mid-March 1582, Persons sent him back to England to help out the shorthanded Jasper Heywood. Emerson, of course, in accompanying Persons had come to know well the houses and families which could be expected to extend shelter to the incoming missionaries.[54]

---

[47] (21) 42–45; see RP to Agazzari, 1.iii.1582; (23) 126–32, Latin; 132–36 English.

[48] (21) 46, 47.

[49] RP reported eleven priests executed under the new treason laws before the end of May 1582; (21) 38f. A nobleman returning from one of these scenes of carnage was reported to have told the Queen of their death protesting innocence of the crimes laid to their charge. Furthermore, they had prayed for Elizabeth. "'Is that so?' said the queen when she heard it. 'Well, that is nothing to us. Let them look to it who condemned them'"; ibid., 44f.

[50] See P. Milward, S.J., *Shakespeare's Religious Background* (London, 1973); and (73).

[51] RP to Agazzari, 12.iii.1582; (23) 136–39, Latin; 139–41 English translation.

[52] Ibid., 140f and 138, nn.(6), (7); see (21) 48–49.

[53] (21) 54f.

[54] Ibid.

English papists everywhere now turned their eyes towards Mary, Queen of Scots, as Elizabeth's most obvious successor. Those in England were content to await the end of her natural term. Those in exile were not always inclined to be so patient. The Queen herself was still allowed to receive once a year the French officials who ran her French estates as *la reine douairière*. At Mary's instance, according to Persons, Henri Samerie, a French Jesuit, was deputed to join them at the end of 1582 as a physician. He managed to conceal his priestly identity for a year or two, after which the Queen was obliged to send him away.[55]

Meanwhile Persons continued to be busy with his pen. He published a modest treatise in English and Latin on the persecution and a letter addressed to the Privy Council.[56] Another important work in English was *On resolution.* The first part gave reasons for "resolution," the second demolished the obstacles to it. There was also a reply to Charke's latest effusion[57] and several more small works. Just as important as the books themselves was a system of distribution. By this time Persons had devised a system for "smuggling in Catholic books, holy oils, vestments and letters, and for distributing them throughout the kingdom. Places, times, occasions, and trustworthy men to look after it all have been appointed, and everything else needed. . . . We lacked all this hitherto."[58]

While Persons may have been the brain behind it all, evidently there were men and, no doubt, women in England of equal resource to support him. The best that the Privy Council could do for the time being was to continue persecution. John Payne was executed at Chelmsford on April 2, 1582. Before he died he asked the executioner to convey his appeal to the Queen that she desist "from this shedding of the blood of innocent men."[59] Edward Osborne, however, who had

---

[55] (21) 54–57. According to J. H. Pollen, his place was taken by a French priest, Camille de Préau, who remained with her till her death. Mary referred to Samerie in her letters as La Rue and Hieronymo Martelli. See ibid., 56 n.

[56] The book in question was a reissue ("Parisiis apud Thomam Brumennium" in 1582) of "De persecutione Anglicana, epistola. Qua explicantur afflictiones . . . & . . . martyria quae catholici nunc Angli, ob fidem patiuntur." By RP, it was publishd as at Bologna: "Bononiae apud Jo. Baptistam Algazarium," 1581. For details of further editions and translations of 1582, see the BL catalogue and (69) 65.

[57] See n.5 above.

[58] RP to Aquaviva, 11.iv.1582 [Rouen]; (VI) F.G.651/640, Latin holograph, n.f., a.l.s., signed "Euseb." The true date of this lettter seems to be May rather than April. See (19) III under Persons for bibliographical details of these works. The Marian priests are rarely if ever mentioned. It is likely that, being less subject to persecution, they rather kept themselves apart from the "forward" elements.

[59] RP to Agazzari, 6.iv.1582; (23) 141f, Latin, 142f, English; see (VI) F.G.651, s.

been dismissed from the English College, Rome, and who left the Franciscan Order after less than two months, was arrested and broke down under pressure. He revealed houses and hosts and thus presented Persons with a new problem, because a diminishing number of layfolk could be expected to run this risk of betrayal. Osborne eventually repented and returned to Europe, where he died in 1600.[60] But the damage was done.

To return to Scotland, Crichton and Hay now had their situational report ready.[61] The Jesuits were mainly in favor of concentrating on the conversion of the young king, but much would depend on Guise for a final decision. The two Jesuits were by this time too well known not only to the Scots but also to the English, from whom little was hidden. A new team was called for, men acceptable not only to James but also to Lennox and Huntley, his principal advisers.[62] By the end of April 1582, Aquaviva was eager to see the report or, better, Crichton himself.[63] Persons was about to leave for England when a messenger arrived from Hay and Crichton about April 11, asking him to await their imminent arrival.[64] Soon afterwards Emerson arrived. On this day, Persons saw Elizabeth's edict of April 1, "declaring Jesuits and non-returning seminarians traitors."[65] Crichton and Hay, on their arrival, confirmed the favorable answer from Lennox and James[66] and also brought news of the Jesuits' meeting with Guise in Normandy concerning the advancement of the Catholic cause and the release of the Queen of Scots.[67] It is noticeable that Hay quietly dropped out of the negotiations from this time forward. It is likely that he was unwilling to be associated with the use of armed force. He may also have been aware that the Scottish Protestants were preparing a countercoup.

---

to s., 11.iv.1582, n.f. See chap 1, p. 1, n.4.

[60] Sources and more details in (23) 141, n.(2).

[61] See J. B. de Tassis to Philip II, Paris, 18.v.1582; (25) III, 370–73.

[62] "De missione in Scotiam pro conversione Regis"; (VI) Anglia 42, f.216, Latin, n.d. but delivered after 30.iv. (See Aquaviva to Claude Mathieu, provincial, 30.iv.) No indication of author, but the document is in Crichton's hand. Aquaviva rejected the idea of sending a "Fr Lorazeno" to Scotland, seemingly Beaton's suggestion. Aquaviva is awaiting a letter from Crichton or Crichton in person.

[63] Aquaviva to C. Mathieu, Rome, 30.iv.1582; (VI) Francia.I, Ep.Gen., f.135v, Latin draft. Also a draft to Beaton, same date.

[64] RP to Aquaviva, 11.iv.[1582], v. supra, names deciphered; see (23) xlix.

[65] RP to Aquaviva, ibid. See (3) II, No. 660.

[66] Mendoza reported the arrival of Crichton and Holt in France as on 14.iv.-1582; see Mendoza to Philip II, 15.v.1582; (25) III, 362.

[67] (1) 30.

A pamphlet appeared in which Morton, the late regent, figured as a martyr for their persuasion.[68]

The Lennox scheme brought back by Crichton was discussed by Glasgow, Guise, and Allen in several conferences in Paris lasting till the first week in May. A stumbling block was likely to be the participation of the Spaniards, who could hardly be kept out of it. Glasgow kept de Tassis, the Spanish ambassador, in the picture, while Guise informed the nuncio, a somewhat unexpected reversal of roles. Persons kept a low profile—doubtless he was much occupied with his press, which in the event would make a far more significant contribution to the cause. But his main support at this time was from the French. "It must not be known, whatever happens, that I am in negotiation with the Spaniard."[69] Had something like the Bourbon family compact of two centuries later existed at this time, how different the history of Europe and England would have been! All the same, Persons was in Paris by mid-May to confer with the three leaders, who considered his presence vital.[70]

It was decided at Paris that Persons should report to Philip II, while Crichton would go to Rome to report to the Pope and, of course, Aquaviva. While in Paris Persons renewed his vows according to pious Jesuit custom, before setting out for Lisbon to find the King of Spain. It was all supposed to be completely secret.[71] The companion for his journey was William Tresham, brother of Sir Thomas of Rushton. Recovering from a fever, Persons could not move quickly. Crichton left Paris soon after May 22, with the nuncio's recommendation to the Cardinal of Como.[72] Leaving Paris on May 28, Persons reached Lisbon on June 15. The nuncio, meanwhile, forwarded to Como a memorial, apparently by Persons,[73] and a longer one, reminiscent of Lennox's, probably modified by Persons or Crichton or both together.[74] Persons seemed to think that six thousand infantry would suffice to deal with Scotland and afterwards march into England. Nuncio Castelli reason-

---

[68] "The confession of James, Earl of Mortoun. . . ." See Pitcairn, *Bannatyne's Memorials* (1835), 317–32.

[69] See RP to Aquaviva, 11.iv.1582 (v. supra).

[70] Castelli to Como, 22.v.1582; Kretzschmar, *Die Invasionsprojekte*, 131; see (23) liii.

[71] RP to Aquaviva, 11.iv.1582, (v. supra).

[72] (23) 166, n.(1).

[73] G. B. Castelli to Cardinal of Como, 22.v.1582; (IV) 15, ff.498 et seq.; (23) 142–48 and 143 n.

[74] (23) 148f, n.(1). Some doubt remains as to how far this is Persons's, but without doubt he endorsed its proposals.

ably doubted if Guise would accept an estimate so optimistic.[75] The sole aim of the project was the restoration of the Catholic faith in Scotland and England, the liberation of the Scottish queen, and the preservation of the young king from the further influence of heresy.[76] It would also mean peace for neighboring countries which had been so long troubled "by the malice of these heretics."[77] The moment was ripe, James willing, good ports readily available, and no lack of friends very willing to show the army "the way to England." This at least was plausible. Not only the Catholics and Catholic nobility but also many Protestants would be ready to fall in behind Lennox. The ministers of religion were generally disliked for their "wicked lives and extreme avarice and tyranny."

The English Catholics longed for their liberation, fully recognized Mary's right to the crown, and saw no other hope for themselves. During the past year "the heretics" had begun to tear children, especially of distinguished families, away from their parents to bring them up as Protestants. Elizabeth's proclamation of April 1, 1582, regarded all Catholics as "deadly enemies of the state and of her person, and traitors to their country."[78] So they had nothing more to lose in prospects or reputation by taking up arms. But this they could not do without foreign help. They would have the support of many Protestants "partly because of the coarse and wicked life led by the Queen who has earned universal hatred," and partly because of the unworthiness of her ministers, men of low or no rank who had ousted the nobility and men of true stature.[79] The courtiers would soon turn against her if the opposition was effective.[80] The war should not last more than a month. The English were used to upheavals of this kind throughout their history. The latest most successful coup was that of Henry VII, the founder of the dynasty.[81] The present one called for eight thousand foreign infantry with money to recruit eight thousand more in Scotland. A beginning should be made not later than October 1582.

The reason for taking up arms in Scotland lay in the intention of Huntingdon, Leicester—curiously Burghley is not mentioned—and their friends to deprive James not only of his right to the English

[75] Kretzschmar, *Die Invasionsprojekte*, 131.

[76] (23) 148–57, Italian, 158–66, English translation from (IV) Inghilterra, 1, f.51.

[77] (23) 158.

[78] (23) 160.

[79] (23) 153; see 161.

[80] (21) 153, see 162.

[81] Ibid.

throne but even of life itself.[82] When the allies reached England, they could give out as a second reason the intention to execute the papal bull of excommunication against Elizabeth. In an attempt to turn the tables, since Elizabeth was not rightful queen, all who took up arms in her behalf would be declared guilty of high treason, forfeiting not only their lives but also their possessions and claims by inheritance. These would go to the nearest in blood who made due submission.[83]

Rome should extend no more olive branches. In view of Elizabeth's contumacy, the Pope should renew the bull of excommunication. No longer would Catholics regard her as queen.[84] Persons the writer foresaw the need of books ready for distribution explaining and justifying the latest turn of events. These would emphasize the Scottish queen's present right to the throne. The plan should be executed now while the advantage of surprise was still to hand. Even a year's delay might doom the plan. Lennox and the Catholics had the upper hand, but they might soon lose it. In this at least Persons and his friends were prophetic.[85]

The whole scheme was no worse than others of the kind which began ostensibly with Ridolfi and were to continue until 1604 and the peace with Spain. It was no worse, but neither was it better. Its naivetés and easy assumptions suggest the work of enemies drawing unsuspecting feet into a quagmire rather than a genuine project aiming at a quick and effective remedy. But we can hardly doubt Persons's sincerity. He could only have countenanced it as a desperate remedy for a desperate situation, a fear that, after all, persecution might prevail and prevail soon, overthrowing the Catholic cause in both countries.

It was misleading to say that, even in their present plight, the English Catholics would have rushed to help a foreign invasion. Nor did priests working in England, Jesuits or others, favor this method. No doubt, popular historians have vastly overestimated the goodness of Queen Bess and the merriness of England under her rule. Nevertheless, the country could not plausibly be represented at this time as yearning to throw over her yoke. The contrary was sufficiently proved when an *empresa*—an "enterprise"—was at last attempted in 1588. Most of the Catholics wished to prove their loyalty to their queen and a country that was at least nominally Protestant rather than to a country that was foreign, even if it was wholly orthodox. It is interesting to speculate on the fortunes of the English Catholics if they had adopted

---

[82] (21) 164.

[83] (21) 162; see 164.

[84] (21) 165.

[85] (21) 157; see 165.

the openly militant attitude of the Protestants of France, which undoubtedly paid off. In fact, the English papists never did so after the hesitant and halfhearted feudal gesture of 1569. In any case, they had no one possessing the birth, training, or inclination to lead them in such enterprises.

In view of the distinction of his associates, Persons could only have been a contributor, cooperator, or approver rather than one who instigated the scheme, such as it was. More certainly from his hand was a shorter memorial about this time.[86] This omitted all personal reference to Queen Elizabeth and the problem of her successor but brought in the Welsh. It was more concerned with the ecclesiastical establishment to follow, Allen being proposed for bishop of Durham. His presence in England would be worth some thousands of soldiers![87] Owen Lewis could go to Scotland, where he would find surroundings more congenial than England for his Celtic temperament. Glasgow likewise should find a place in Scotland. The whole document is in the nature of a supplement or modification of the first[88]—perhaps Persons's personal contribution.

Guise, Allen, and Persons met at Castelli's nunciature to hear read out the document which would go to Rome and Lisbon.[89] Guise had scruples about bringing in Spaniards, although Lennox was willing to go to France to raise an army if Mary agreed to the whole scheme and consented to the continued reign of her son.[90] Mary herself apparently conveyed letters to Mendoza dated April 6 and 8, largely repudiating the project.[91] Whatever later propaganda was to claim, it is sufficiently unlikely that Mary would have consented to any plot to remove Elizabeth from her throne. Her consistent wish for her own lifetime was to reoccupy the throne of Scotland and establish her right to the English succession. Nothing else, in any case, made intelligent

---

[86] Copy with the nuncio's letter of 22.v. (See n.70, above.) "Empresa" (Spanish) and "impresa" (Italian) are both used in this work.

[87] Castelli to Como, 22.v.1582 (v. supra).

[88] See (23) 148 n.(1). The long memorial is not in RP's hand but a deciphered text like Castelli's letter (Kretzschmar, *Die Invasionsprojekte*, 131). It was received at Rome as coming from the Duke of Guise (see ibid., p. 146). RP was not of sufficient weight to originate such a project, even if some of his suggestions were adopted.

[89] Castelli to Como, 22.v.1582, cipher; (23) 148.

[90] Lennox to Mary, Queen of Scots, 7.iii.1582; (25) III, 333.

[91] (25) III (1580–86), 330. Mendoza received her(?) letters on 26.iv. See Mendoza to Philip II; ibid., 349. A large question hangs over the authenticity of Mary's letters at this time, especially those in cipher.

sense for one in her position; and, whatever her enemies tried to make out, the Scottish queen was not a fool.[92]

The Mendoza letters strongly suggest forgery. That of April 6 orders Glasgow not to deal with de Tassis but only with Mendoza. This meant a correspondence which could be spied on or intercepted, increasing also complications for Guise. Mary was scathing about the Jesuits, who in fact were among the busiest people working for her cause. She disapproved of anyone being sent to negotiate on her behalf with the Pope or King Philip. Lennox must stay in Scotland and no forces must be raised in France. She must be associated with her son "in the crown of Scotland." While not disapproving in round terms of a relief force for Scotland, she attached so many conditions as to make it practicably impossible. Cecil and Walsingham as masters of statecraft and espionage would have been altogether capable of producing such a letter.

Nevertheless, it must be admitted that Mary's friends abroad discerned no inherent contradiction in all this. If Mendoza did not find her attitude absurd, Cardinal de Granvelle thought she showed "much good sense."[93] Indeed, there was some "very intelligent person near her" to write her letters, which showed very clearly "the lines upon which the affair should be conducted."[94] But as if to confirm our suspicion, Mendoza reported to Philip on April 11 that the French ambassador had asked the English queen for permission to send a gentleman to Scotland who would renounce all the claims of Mary in favor of her son.[95] There is evidence here, surely, of an attempt to set Spanish and French diplomacy at cross-purposes.

Philip himself was decidedly doubtful as to the usefulness of using force at this stage.[96] Philip was against the idea of deposing James, at least until the arrival of his mother and unless he became Catholic. This would be impolitic and also "against their oath" of loyalty. James and the Catholic leaders should stay in Scotland; meanwhile, they should "dissemble and wait on God." Mendoza must keep them all on the leash "until the affair be ripe." This could not be before the pacification of Flanders. Mendoza must also keep in touch with Mary, at the same time encouraging the missionaries who were to receive immediately two thousand crowns in aid. Contact with the Scots must be maintained through persons and not letters, which could

---

[92] See Edwards, *The Dangerous Queen,* 359–421.

[93] See 6 and 8.iv.1582, v. supra; (25) III, 330–33.

[94] Cardinal de Granvelle to Philip II, Madrid, 4.vii.1582; (25) III, 382.

[95] Ibid., 383.

[96] Philip II to Mendoza, 23.iv.1582, St. Ubes; (25) III, 343.

go astray, causing "suspicion to the French and others who might undermine the business."[97]

Mendoza, meanwhile, was nettled by Crichton's independent action with no reference to himself, especially his promise to Lennox, as it was reported, of fifteen thousand men for Scotland. Mary had certainly not authorized it. Mendoza was unblissfully unaware of Guise's responsibility in all this, thinking that Crichton was simply acting on his own. Priests could only be trusted with "matters of state," he concluded, when they were "taught word for word" what to say. In any case, Spain and the papacy could not mount a major campaign without alarming the French, who might be frightened off altogether and into the arms of Queen Elizabeth. Crichton and Holt had by-passed Mendoza on the way to France, so he was under the impression they were still in Scotland. In any case, he wanted Persons, as the abler man, to replace them in the northern kingdom, to which Glasgow was urged to return.[98]

Already the division and mistrust between the major Catholic powers was worth many soldiers to Elizabeth. But she and Cecil, who was sufficiently aware of something afoot, were not content to stand idly by. As Mendoza reported, four days previously the Queen sent the Earl of Angus "to the border with a quantity of money, chains and other jewels, to buy over some of the Scots, the sole object being to get possession of the King of Scotland and stir up civil war there."[99] Mendoza was well aware of the perils of divided counsels. He regarded the priests as largely responsible: dangerous amateurs who were impeding the work of the professionals, conducting affairs "differently from what the Queen of Scotland and I desire."[100] Not until mid-May did he learn of the decisions reached at Paris between Glasgow, Persons, Allen, and Guise. Mendoza was asked to approach Philip and provide Persons with a letter of introduction; this he did by way of de Tassis in Paris. But foreseeably, he was not happy in his work. "There is nothing apart from my salvation which I desire so much as to leave England."[101] He felt more usefully employed in all this time in suing for compensation for "Drake's robbery."[102]

---

[97] Ibid., 343f.

[98] Mendoza to Philip II, London, 26.iv.1582, 4.v.1582; (25) III, 49–52; see s. to s., 20.v. ibid., 373.

[99] Ibid., 352; s. to s. 4.v.1582; ibid., 355f.

[100] Mendoza to Philip II, London, 15.v.1582; see (25) III, 362. The above seems closer to the original Spanish than M. Hume's.

[101] Ibid., 364. See J. B. de Tassis to Philip II, 18.v.1582; ibid., 370.

[102] Ibid., 365.

Whatever Burghley knew about developments before mid-May, doubtless he was considerably more enlightened after the interception of Mendoza's dispatch to Philip of May 15, 1582, sent by special courier. The pretext for this violation of diplomatic immunity was the fact that "his passport was only signed by a counsellor," so they conveniently took it to be forged. Mendoza fondly imagined that his packet had not been tampered with.[103] In fact, such interception had been practiced at least as early as 1579, when Sir Henry Cobham, ambassador in France, showed clear knowledge of information contained in letters from Morgan to Glasgow.[104]

Persons arrived in Lisbon about June 15, where Philip was still consolidating his acquisition of Portugal in 1580.[105] It was not the best moment to broach the allied plan. The resistance of Terceira under Don Antonio, coupled with an attack of gout, was sufficient to divert the King's attention from northern affairs. Juan de Idiaquez, secretary of state, managed the first interview.[106] Persons gave it as his and Crichton's view that Guise and the Pope could not conduct an effective crusade on their own. Men and ships could best be assembled in Portugal, or perhaps in a northeastern port, Bremen, Hamburg, or elsewhere, coming together in the Ems for the final descent on England.[107] Philip was touched by Persons's zeal but was dismayed, as well he might be, by the communication of the plan to so many people. Indeed, he had done his best to discourage, without actually forbidding, Persons's coming to Lisbon.[108] Many others, including Englefield, had seen the danger of having so many cooks stirring the broth. But all agreed that the Pope could not be left out, for his support gave it the aura of a crusade; if he were not brought in, he might be tempted to leave it all to Spain.[109] Englefield thought Glasgow the most unreliable of the confederates, as a man principally devoted to his own interests and quite capable of revealing all to the French.[110] What possible chance of success had a project in which so few of the planners trusted one another?

---

[103] Mendoza to Philip II, London, 21.v.1582; (25) III, 375.

[104] (51) 343.

[105] (1) 30. RP's memory was far from perfect on dates of this kind. See (23) iv–v.

[106] G. B. de Tassis to Philip II, Paris, 18.v.1582; (25) III, 373; and s. to s., 29.v.1582, ibid., 378.

[107] Ibid., 379.

[108] Philip II to G. B. de Tassis, Lisbon, 11.vi.1582; ibid., 379.

[109] De Granvelle to Philip II, 4.vii.1582; (25) III, 383f.

[110] Ibid., 384.

Another strange letter purporting to come from the Queen of Scots reached Mendoza at the end of July.[111] She was all for multiplying "means of communication now that the irons are becoming hot and the wind blows stronger." She only knew what was going on in France through Glasgow's letter to Mendoza, and nothing about the Jesuits' part in it. She had not wanted de Tassis brought in; this was Guise's doing. Further observations of the kind made the letter an ideal means for spreading confusion and misunderstanding among her friends. She consistently played down the part which France should play, a strange conceit for *la reine douairière*! The most suspicious passage, however, against all her declared intentions in more authentic letters in her own hand, came near the end. "I have resolved not to enter into any sort of agreement with this queen. . . . I will not on any account pledge myself to her on the conditions she demands of me in this place." Knowing that her correspondence was watched, quite apart from the fact that there is little to suggest duplicity in her genuine letters, it is surely impossible to believe she would have written this. At the same time, there is just sufficient in the letter to make it plausible and to prove that, if it was an alien concoction, it was done with no little skill. We would not expect less from Walsingham's office. Consistently, she showed deep concern for money to fortify "the strong places in Scotland" and to win her friends in her own land.[112]

Although Persons allowed himself to be carried away by his hopes and enthusiasm, those who needed to be convinced rather held back. True, de Granvelle gave a kind of cool support, agreeing with Persons that, if the plan were taken up, it should not be later than October.[113] The Pope was eventually prodded by Castelli in Paris, and he in turn by Persons, into giving some support, but was unwilling to open his coffers until Spain showed positive signs of action.[114] As the King made clear in his letters to Mendoza, quite apart from his preoccupation with Terceira, he thought that the scheme had little-enough substance. The entry of Guise and the French, moreover, provided a factor outside his control and therefore a real risk of failure. And

---

[111] Mary to Mendoza, 29.vii.1582; (25) III, 392–94. She acknowledged receipt on 12.vii. of Mendoza's letters of 26.iv. and 1.vii. and letters from Glasgow and Englefield.

[112] Ibid., 393f.

[113] (25) III, 382; see RP to Beaton, Lisbon, 2.vii.1582; (23) 166f.

[114] RP (alias Gerardo Bentivoglio) to Castelli, Lisbon, 16.vii.1582; (23) 167, summary.

would the Pope be prepared to lay out money in sufficient quantity?[115] Spanish resources, with so many commitments, were not limitless.[116]

On July 6, Santa Cruz gained a decisive naval victory over Don Antonio's forces under Strozzi at the Azores, in which the latter was killed.[117] This was the moment for the Jesuits to press their apparent advantage from the victory at the courts of Rome and Lisbon. At least King James and Lennox should be subsidized so that they could maintain an adequate guard.[118] Philip in fact provided twelve thousand crowns, while the Pope, prevailed upon by Crichton, agreed to send four thousand.[119] The money was actually sent! By this time, however, the superior cohesion and unity of the Protestant force was in place for an effective strike. As early as March 7, 1580, Burghley hinted less than darkly to Robert Bowes, the ambassador, that the "disease" had reached the point where "no remedies will prevail but such as are violent."[120] That was the time when Esmé Stuart, sieur d'Aubigny, was created Earl of Lennox as the prelude to becoming virtual head of state.[121] Apart from stirring up the Kirk to hostile preaching, Burghley worked to get him excommunicated, which would have made him ineligible for office.[122] Angus was given a pension of four thousand crowns a year to work for his expulsion and overthrow if they could not "succeed in killing him." Other earls were prepared to join the hunt for four thousand crowns each, while a number of barons were available at two thousand. All the same, understanding well the stuff of politics, they wanted something better than Elizabeth's word as guarantee, nothing less than a document under the Great Seal of England. Or so it was plausibly reported by Holt to Mendoza on July 12, 1582. Holt was now working on his own. It was mooted that he might leave with

---

[115] See (23) p. lv.

[116] (23) lvi; see Castelli to Como, 30.x.1582; (23) 169–71. The Pope offered 50,000 crowns towards an expedition costing 400,000.

[117] R. Trevor-Davies, *The Golden Century of Spain* (London, 1937), 192f. See Castelli to Como, Paris, 16.viii.1582; R. Toupin, S.J., *Correspondence du nonce en France, Giovanni Battista Castelli, 1581–1583* (Rome, 1967), 380.

[118] (21) 60f; see (1) 31. RP left Paris on 28.v. See Hosack, *Mary, Queen of Scots* II, 557.

[119] This is probably the ten thousand crowns referred to in Castelli to Como, 30.x.1582; (23) 169–71.

[120] (51) 343.

[121] Bowes to Burghley, 29.iii.1579; (55) 15.

[122] Mendoza to Philip II, London, 25.vii.1582; (25) III, 387. See Read, *Lord Burghley*, 280–84.

Lennox and the young king, but Mendoza opposed it.[123] This may well have been a bad mistake.

On August 22 the carefully planned Ruthven raid took place when a Protestant hunting party caught something better than a stag, nothing less than the King himself. The elaborate house of cards set up by Guise, Allen, Persons, and the rest collapsed completely when the King was deftly flicked from under the pack. Lennox and his party could not, of course, continue a legitimate government without James.[124] As soon as news of the success arrived, Sir George Carey was sent to Scotland with letters from Elizabeth for the young king and his new masters. Bowes was instructed to do everything possible to strengthen Gowrie and the new ruling faction.[125] Lennox, with no practicable alternative, agreed to surrender Dumbarton and quit the country within twelve days. It was all a matter of money. Bowes assured his queen she could "have them all at her devotion" provided she paid them.

Lennox left Scotland at the end of December, making his way back to France by way of London.[126] He had an audience with the Queen on January 14, during which she "rattled him up." This was mild compared with the farewell issuing from the new rulers in Scotland, who assured the King that, "if he did not cause the duke to depart, he should not be the longest liver of them all!"—duke, King or both? Once the Queen felt assured of her victory, she was amicable enough; but Lennox did not escape a final going over by Walsingham. "It is curious to observe by what low devices and with what complete success the English secretary became possessed of Lennox's most secret feelings and opinions."[127] Gladly he escaped to France.

William Holt was arrested in Scotland soon after receiving a letter from Persons writing as William Gibbs to William Brereton.[128] Even by August 26, Persons was not yet appraised of the new situation and wrote to Holt in hopeful terms of the forthcoming empresa. He

[123] (25) III, 388.

[124] (21) 62f; see (1) 31. RP erroneously gave the date of the raid as 23.viii.

[125] P. F. Tytler, *History of Scotland* (Edinburgh, 1866), VIII, 111f.

[126] (1) 31; (23) lviii.

[127] Tytler, *History of Scotland*, 126f.

[128] The letter of 26.viii.1582 was taken from Holt and filed in due course with the state papers, Spain (PRO, SP94, 1, f.103); (23) 167f, English, endorsed "Copy of the lettre discyphered and founde with William Holt. This was sent from William Gibbe in Spayne to William Brereton alias Wattes as William Holt affirmeth." Holt was no doubt trying to lead his questioners astray, but both men may have passed by the name of Brereton at different times and even shared the same correspondence. See also (23) 168, n.(1).

felt worn out in body and mind by his efforts, having suffered "infinite overthwarts of late"; but "good success" must come shortly.[129] Certainly Philip would not have approved of any attempt to abduct James from Scotland. Such a blow would reap "singular inconvenience."[130] Persons was actually in audience with King Philip when news of the latest Scottish coup arrived. There was nothing to do but await the further turn of events; and Scotland being Scotland, turn they surely must. Perhaps the Jesuit's disappointment was so evident that almost then and there Philip agreed to add two thousand annual crowns to the Pope's two thousand for the Rheims seminary,[131] promising also to support Allen's candidature for the cardinalate.[132]

The strain of the negotiation and the disappointing sequel brought on Persons's first serious breakdown in health. Nevertheless, he struggled back to Madrid, following the King's instructions, to leave a report with the nuncio, Taberna. In the presence of failure, the nuncio was hardly sympathetic. Indeed, he told Como that Persons's report contained "a much exaggerated account of the present plight of the Catholics . . . and of the great ruin that will result from it."[133] On the way back to France, Persons fell seriously ill at Bilbao. Indeed, the absence of news prompted Allen to tell Agazzari in a letter of December 29 that he was dead.[134] In fact, he was staying with lay friends to recover. This he might have done in a short time, but an incompetent doctor failed in his remedies and he contracted jaundice. William Tresham, no doubt thinking he could do no more, left him at this point. Persons probably owed his life to his fellow Jesuit, Gil González Dávila, who, learning of his plight, sent a lay brother to look after him. The brother brought him to the Jesuit house at Oñate on January 11, 1583, whence Dávila reported to the General five days later.[135] Although Persons stayed here until the spring, he did not allow himself a sufficiently long convalescence. From this time, though not complaining, he refers in his letters fairly frequently to fevers and indispositions. Crichton, meanwhile, left Rome for Chambéry, and in 1584 returned to Scotland.

---

[129] "William Gibbe" (RP) to unnamed, 26.viii.1582; (VII) SP94,1,f.103 decipher; (23)166f. Hicks took the correspondent to be Watts or Holt.

[130] (23) 168.

[131] (21) 62f; (23) lvi; (1) 31.

[132] (1) 31.

[133] Taberna to Como, 30.x.1582; (23) 170f.

[134] (21) 62f; (9) 173 with correct date 30.xii.

[135] RP to ?; (VI) Anglia. 38.II, f.21; (23) 171f and 171, n.(2). See CRS 9, 100; (21) 62f; (1) 31.

Inevitably, the 1582 fiasco greatly strengthened the voice of those Catholics who were against the "forward" policy of seminaries and Jesuits. Elizabeth's government should be humored rather than opposed. Let the faith be whispered in attics and cellars and not shouted from the housetops. The idea seemed realistic and greatly attracted the vast majority of men who are not built for martyrdom, Catholic or not. Many had admired the panache of Campion's almost open preaching and the daring of Persons's clandestine presse, but more began to wonder, with the prospect ahead of unrelenting persecution, whether such things should not be sacrificed if it meant more of the quiet life for more of the faithful. Was there any point in a heroism which really achieved nothing? Certainly Providence was not favoring the way of force.

Robert Persons and his associates saw things differently and accurately, in view of the unremitting determination of Burghley and Elizabeth to wipe Catholicism off the face of England if they could not manage the whole earth. Weaning the papists from the Roman allegiance could only be a matter of time. Sons would not be so steadfast as their fathers, especially when the regime learned to divide and confuse by blandishing those prepared to offer even the tiniest pinch of incense to Caesar. Buoyed by false optimism and desiring to justify their spirit of compromise, many persuaded themselves that there would soon be a positive response from the government to a certain readiness to be "reasonable." Such readiness might mean giving information against fellow papists, who would thus soon cease to be fellows. But might not treachery effect more for the cause than treason? What did these terms now mean?

Persons was a man of considerable understanding; but he could hardly be expected to appreciate any purity of motive in those who from now on strenuously opposed everything he tried to create, and who attempted to make him the cause of everything that went wrong. The instinct of self-preservation was usually uppermost in the mind of those who chose the sheltered path. What began as a measure of cooperation could end not infrequently in complete capitulation.

The cleavage between the two positions could be dated, as Persons saw it, from the time of the Paris conferences in 1582. Hell may have no fury like a woman scorned, but there are many runners-up. Some of these now were men of influence who had been left out of these conferences or allowed only minor roles because they were not trusted. Charles Paget and Thomas Morgan were initially omitted, not on any plea of Persons's, but because Guise and Glasgow feared they would reveal all to Elizabeth's government. Doubtless they would have; for these were the protagonists of appeasement and would have easily justified their action by their own principles. Paget agreed effectively with Mendoza that politics was not a proper occupation for the clergy. In view of the highly visible part played by Crichton and Persons in the recent fiasco, it was tempting to make them scapegoats for the total failure, including the latest events in Scotland. From this time, certainly, Paget became a confirmed enemy of Persons.[136] There was, no doubt, an element of jealousy and frustrated ambition in all this. In due course he came to collaborate fully with the English government. By his own importunity, Paget was eventually admitted to the later conferences, urging Guise to a course which afterwards he himself censured. He volunteered to go to England. There he acted in a contrary sense to what was agreed and he returned empty-handed.[137] There is something in the Paget story that suggests a pathological lack of balance. When the two Jesuits were sent to negotiate in capacities which Morgan and Paget no doubt coveted for themselves, insult seemed added to injury. Incipient dislike became implacable enmity.

Mary, Queen of Scots, like many good people, sometimes believed too readily in the goodness of others. She placed too much trust, it seems, in Paget and Morgan, her agents in Paris, and in Nau, a Frenchman, and Curle, a Scot who put her English letters into cipher. Fr. Samerie, S.J., found out that the four sometimes managed the correspondence "in opposition to the duke and archbishop," so that "the poor queen was estranged from her best friends." Paget and Morgan in 1582 set up a lay group formally opposed to Allen and the priests, convinced that politics was a lay affair and preferably one for noblemen. True or not, it was dangerously plausible. The council recognized the chance of dividing the hated cause.[138] Paget disliked Allen more than Persons at this time, regarding him as the real leader. But he had as yet only a small following. Charles Arundell, William Tresham, Thomas Fitzherbert, and others still thought with Persons. "If priests beside . . . or with their breviaries, or by their credit in . . . princes' courts, where breviary men were esteemed, could help . . . and serve you gentlemen . . . towards the reduction of our country, why . . . not use their labours . . . without emulation?"[139] Was Persons's question a trifle naive?

Not all was disappointing this year. The persecution, as can happen, moved some of the most idealistic, and some of the youngest

---

[136] See L. Hicks, S.J., *An Elizabethan Problem* (Fordham, 1964).

[137] (23) lvii, n.(119).

[138] (21) 64f.

[139] RP to C. Paget, Rome, 30.xii.1597; (II) f.452; partly printed in (9) 391.

of them in the universities, to go to study under Dr. Allen.[140] The Pope was begging money around the courts,[141] so by the end of 1582 twenty more students came to Rheims.[142] Soon afterwards, Persons sent from Spain two thousand ducats, with a promise of the same every year.[143]

---

[140] (21) 70f; for a letter on the persecution, see ibid., 74f; (23) 126–36.

[141] (11) II, 247 and cccxxxv; (24) 340–45.

[142] Allen to Agazzari, 5.xi.1582; (9) 168.

[143] (21) 72f.

Chapter Six

The First Invasion Plan, Second Phase: 1583 ═══

E ven with the reversal of fortunes in Scotland and the death of Lennox on May 26, 1583, the idea of an empresa was by no means abandoned. Persons certainly had something to do with keeping it alive after his arrival in Paris near the end of May.[1] The obstacles were formidable. The Anglophile party in Scotland was taking all precautions to ensure that their opponents should not emulate them in a successful countercoup. The French ambassador de Mainville's correspondence was closely watched, as he himself was well aware. He complained to Robert Bowes and William Davison, the English agents; but this, of course, made no difference. His correspondence had certainly been intercepted in March 1582, although it was returned to him with the seals unbroken.[2] Walsingham had a technique for this. More effective was Bowes's corruption of Rosco Benetti, who conveyed de Mainville's letters to de Mauvissière, French ambassador in London.[3] The interception of letters, even in cipher, afforded the further possibility of forging letters to cause confusion and provoke further replies. When Holt was captured in early March of 1583, they took at least one cipher from him "confessed to have been given forth by the Scottish queen." This with the copies of "all the ciphers taken with him" was sent to the jubilant Walsingham.[4] At least from this time,

---

[1] See Castelli to Como, 30.v.1583; (IV) Segreteria di Stato, Francia. 17, f.165, cipher deciphered.

[2] R[obert] B[owes] and W[illiam] D[avison] to Sir Francis Walsingham, 16.iii.-1582/83; *The Correspondence of Robert Bowes . . .* , Surtees Society (London/Edinburgh, 1842), 382f. Summarized in (27) VI, No. 356. Arthur Gregory was apparently an expert in breaking and remaking sealed letters. His skill as a forger is revealed in a letter to Sir Robert Cecil where he refers to "secret services which none but myself hath done before; to write in another man's hand, and, discovering the secret writing being in blank, to abuse a most cunning villain in his own subtlety, leaving the same in blank again. Wherin, though there be difficulty their answers show they have no suspicion"; A.G. to Salisbury, n.d., PRO SP14/24/38. Elsewhere Gregory claims he has always and only "on the sudden executed that which has been commanded by authority"; PRO, SP12/260/49, n.d.; J. H. Pollen, *Fr Henry Garnet and the Gunpowder Plot* (London, 1888), 29; John Gerard, *Contributions Towards a Life of Fr. Henry Garnet, S.J.* (London, 1898), 76.

[3] [R.Bowes] to F. Walsingham, 28.iii.1583, "private"; (55) 390–92.

[4] ? to Walsingham, 28.iii.1583; ibid., 393–97.

then, we have good reason for treating the Scottish queen's correspondence with the greatest reserve. There was some connivance in the capture of Holt and probably some duplicity on the part of his captors to make him hand over the ciphers. Certainly, he was "entertained secretly" by Lord Seaton before his seizure.[5]

In mid-March, then, Bowes and Davison were able to report to London not only the fact that an invasion scheme was still alive but even some of the details, although these smack of embellishment. In the summer three armies of fifteen thousand men each would invade England by way of Berwick. It was presupposed that by this time the King would be in other hands. The main object was to liberate the Queen of Scots. The signal to begin would be an attempt on the life of Elizabeth or one of her ministers. This information was supposed to come from "persons of good credit and judgment."[6]

Jasper Heywood, meanwhile, still held a lonely fort in England. It now emerged that Bowes had tried to gain control of Holt after his capture but had been thwarted by de Mainville. Indeed, Bowes had urged the use of torture to open the Jesuit's mouth, but James assured the French king by letter on April 27 that he would not "damage" Holt, neither would he let him be sent to England. After breaking free from the Ruthven raiders, James passed Holt over to the French on July 20. He made his way to Rome by way of France.[7]

After three months' convalescence at Oñate, which ended about mid-April, Persons's best course seemed to be to return to England.[8] Allen certainly wanted this, since reports on Heywood's lieutenancy were not reassuring. Persons paid a call on the King before leaving Madrid on April 30, 1583. Philip assured him the Anglo-Scottish enterprise would begin that year. It helped that the Pope was prepared to pay a quarter of the expenses.[9]

Guise and Maine now sponsored a more sinister solution of the English problem. On May 2 Castelli reported to Como a meeting with the dukes, who informed him that a member of the Queen's entourage was ready to undertake her assassination. His motive was anger at the death of a relative in her persecution. He had already approached the Scottish queen, who would have nothing to do with it. This at least was

---

[5] W. Davison to s., Edinburgh, 4.iii.1582/3; (28) VI, 316.

[6] R. Bowes and W. Davison to Walsingham, 18.iii. 1582/3; (55) 389f.

[7] (23) 202f, n.(5); (21) 92f and n.; Tytler, *History of Scotland*, 138; James VI to Guise, 19.viii.1583 (25) 503.

[8] Allen to Aquaviva, 29.iii.1583; (21) 88f.

[9] Castelli to Como, Paris, 30.v.1583; (IV) Segreteria di Stato, Francia 17, f.165, cipher deciphered; Kretzschmar, *Die Invasionsprojecte*, 163.

credible. Paris was more receptive. A substantial sum lodged with Glasgow would be paid over when the deed was done. This would be the signal for invasion. Castelli, as he told Guise, was reluctant to tell the Pope. Although he could be glad enough to see Elizabeth out of the way, "it is not appropriate that [God's] vicar should bring it about by such means." Guise insisted that such a deed would make everything easier—and cheaper. "Would to God that with such small sums"—100,000 crowns—"a kingdom so important could be won."[10] In the event, the Holy Father had no more scruples than Guise in ridding the world as directly as possible of an irreformable tyrant. Castelli got the go-ahead by way of Como on May 23. The Pope would contribute his levy of twenty thousand crowns. "God grant," sighed Como, referring to the original offer, "that this be not another of those promises that are never kept."[11]

Regarding a new attempt at invasion, Guise and Castelli understood that Mary and Seaton were in favor at least as it touched Scotland.[12] This was the scene in Paris on which Persons arrived about the end of May.[13] He hastened to assure the nuncio of Philip's continued interest; and, if any allusion was made to assassination, it remained unrecorded. While the Jesuit had little regard left for Elizabeth, the murderess of esteemed and innocent colleagues, and fully supported military intervention to set the record straight, at no time did he approve of assassination attempts. Theory might justify them, but he realized one edge of this double-edged weapon is always turned towards the wielder. He rejected even the theory. In his *Watchword* Sir Francis Hastings charged the Jesuits with a readiness to kill princes. This Persons repudiated in *A temperate wardword* . . . of 1599, giving ample chapter and verse.[14] He roundly declared, "He was never consenting, witting, willing, inducing, yielding, nor privy to any such personal attempt against her Majesty in his life." Furthermore, he had

---

[10] S. to s., 2.v.1583; (IV), ibid., f.142, cipher deciphered; Kretzschmar, *Die Invasionsprojekte*, 161f.

[11] Como to Castelli, 23.v.1583; (IV) ibid., f.165; Kretzschmar, *Die Invasionsprojekte*, 163.

[12] Castelli to Como, 30.v.1583; Kretzschmar, *Die Invasionsprojekte*, 164–66. There is no satisfactory evidence for the idea that Mary favored more than an expedition to free Scotland and herself. In her authentic correspondence in her own hand, she shunned any thought of dethroning Elizabeth or succeeding her save by legal inheritance after her (unassisted) death. See de Tassis to Philip II, 24.vi.1583; (25) 479.

[13] Ibid., see (1) 32n.

[14] RP, *A temperate ward-word to the turbulent and seditious watch-word of Sir Francis Hastinges knight, who indevoreth to slaunder the whole catholique cause and all professors thereof, both at home and abrode*, printed by "N.D." (Antwerp, 1599); Scolar Press reprint 1970, 66–72.

discouraged those who had such things in mind, especially one man unnamed. Was this the man who put himself forward in 1583? In any case, he was well aware that "English Catholics themselves desired not to be delivered from their miseries by any such attempt." Persons was ready to be a soldier but not an assassin.

Guise, de Tassis, de Mainville, Beaton, and Claude Mathieu met at the nuncio's in Paris in June to discuss the invasion project. Although Allen was then in the capital and Persons at St. Cloud, neither was called to this first meeting. The loss of the Scottish base meant the attempt would have to begin with England. Would Allen and Persons go along with this? But there were deeper reasons. "Everybody trusts Mathieu," wrote Castelli pointedly enough in his dispatch to Rome. Guise gave a copy of his plan in French to the Spanish ambassador and in Italian to the nuncio. They then dispersed to reflect and consult further with one another on an individual basis. Success would now cost a good deal more than eighty thousand crowns, and neither de Tassis nor Castelli thought it possible to mount a campaign by September. Mary was reported as wanting the release of her son and the strengthening of her party before anything else was attempted. So the laird of Fentry, Glasgow's nephew, was sent off to Scotland to see what or whom he could buy with a few thousand crowns.[15]

The latest scheme, although Persons had nothing to do with its concoction, would involve him deeply.[16] De Mainville was to return to Scotland, influence the King, and buy a party, much as England had done. An army of twelve thousand Germans, Italians, and Spaniards would invade Scotland. After it had landed, a French army would disembark in Sussex. Exploiting civil and religious discontent along their separate ways, the two armies would eventually meet. There would also be a diversionary landing in Ireland. The English exiles, Catholic or not, including Allen and Persons, were now under suspicion. To avoid the danger of betrayal, they should not be allowed home before the armies arrived.[17] Mathieu would hold the money collected for the enterprise. Allen was informed, however, and although he had reservations wisely thought it best not to try to teach the soldiers their business.

While Guise was eager to begin, however, Philip held back, rather to his disgust. The cost of 100,000 crowns or so was not prohibi-

---

[15] Castelli to Como, Paris, 10.vi.1583; Kretzschmar, *Die Invasionsprojekte,* 168.

[16] Kretzschmar, *Die Invasionsprojekte,* 168–71; Castelli sent it to Como on 10/20.vi.1583.

[17] Ibid., 170. N.B.: From now the difference between old- and new-style dating begins.

tive and could be spread over a period.[18] Guise in his eagerness was even ready to nominate Allen as the bishop of Durham and *nuntio per la guerra*.[19] Philip had a keener sense of the realities: "the small foundation that can normally be laid on the assurances of exiles and malcontents"; the fact that the English Catholics were unarmed; and the impossibility of raising and paying an army of ten thousand men in England without betraying all to the Queen, who would resist strenuously.[20] By September 24, Philip's negative response to the project was conveyed to Castelli via de Granvelle.[21]

Persons could not and did not blame the leaders for this new reserve in their attitude towards the exiles. The "faction" begun in 1582 by Paget and Morgan against Allen and the Jesuits was now "much increased." It had coalesced with that of certain English and Welsh in Rome and had even spread to Rheims. Students discontented for whatever reason "took sides with that faction in order to strengthen themselves against the Fathers and then immediately received favours from outside."[22] Allen and Persons saw clearly that the English voice would never be heard in continental politics, even those concerning England, unless it spoke clearly and without contradicting itself. But if, for the sake of peace, Allen's party took the others into its confidence, it was almost certain to be betrayed to the English queen. If it did not, the breach would grow ever wider. Faced with this dilemma, Persons and Allen decided to try the path of trust.[23]

In the early summer of 1583, Allen and Persons went "to stay with them in Paris for a few days," Allen in the same house with Paget "to show him more confidence."[24] Lord Paget and Sir Charles Arundell also came from England at this time, and to them no less Allen and Persons strained themselves to "yield satisfaction." They shared all their "affairs and secrets" with Charles, and he in turn with Paget and Morgan. They shared their confidences with William Parry, who came to Paris in December 1583. In January 1584 he crossed to England and revealed all to the Queen's government. Persons did not know or claim that this was done by commission from the rival pair.[25] Still in

---

[18] Como to Castelli, 20.vi.1583 and 15.viii.; Kretzschmar, *Die Invasionsprojekte,* 172–74.

[19] S. to s., 15.viii.1583; ibid., 174.

[20] Taberna to Como, 12.ix.1583, Madrid; ibid., 175f.

[21] S. to s., 24.ix.1583; ibid., 178f.

[22] (21) 95.

[23] (21) 97; see (1) 32.

[24] Ibid.

[25] RP to Paget, Rome, 20.xii.1597; (II) 452; partly printed in (9) 391.

the summer of 1583, Persons tried to persuade Lord Paget to "overrule or temperate" his brother, but in the event he and Arundell both strove for opposites.[26] Glasgow, Guise, and "other persons of quality" were enlisted to use their good influence, but without avail. In any case, there was always Owen Lewis, who corresponded with his nephew, Hugh Griffiths, and with Paget and Morgan, to weigh down the opposite pan of the scale.[27]

The Scottish kaleidoscope soon presented the world with another new pattern. Although de Mainville returned to France soon after the Ruthven raid,[28] it was not before he had skillfully prepared the ground for James's escape from his captors, effected on June 27 at Falkland. Nevertheless, by means of one Fowler and Rocio Bandelli, de Mainville's "confidential servant," the English court got to know all that was going on from his correspondence with de Mauvissière.[29] As for England, Persons went to Paris about July 3 to confer with Allen.[30] He left for Rome with Stephen Brinkley about the beginning of September to discuss with Aquaviva all the matters at issue.[31] They arrived about September 17.[32] At all events, Persons still enjoyed the confidence of the Spanish, the Prince of Parma being instructed by Madrid to call him to the conference.[33]

By the end of the summer, Persons had recovered, if he had previously lost, the confidence of Guise, who sent him to the Pope with the latest plan of the "enterprise" which the duke had drawn up and dated August 22, 1583.[34] An important point was to provide James immediately with money for an adequate bodyguard, since Queen Elizabeth was "busy promoting her faction in Scotland." This might soon snatch the King once again. The Pope should leave the execution of the plan to Philip II and Guise in a combined Franco-Spanish

---

[26] (1) 33.

[27] (1) 32 and n. Hicks claims, "Thomas Morgan and Charles Paget were now admitted to the confidence of the party . . . and it seems that Guise, Beaton and Castelli now took them fully into their confidence concerning the invasion attempt." See Guise's Instructions for Paget, 28.viii.1583; (25) 1580–86, 505; (26) 21.

[28] (23) lviii.

[29] Tytler, *History of Scotland,* 136f; (26) 20, n.62.

[30] RP to Aquaviva, 11.vii.1583; (23) 172; CRS 9, 102; see (33) 102.

[31] RP to Agazzari, Paris, 2.viii.1583; (23) 172–82: mainly a report on English affairs. See (23) 183–85.

[32] No reference found to RP's arrival. Brinkley stayed in the VEC for ten days beginning 17.ix.; The Pilgrim Book, (12) VI, 554. Christopher Bagshaw arrived on 21.ix. and stayed eight days.

[33] (1) 33.

[34] (25) III, 503–5; see (23) 182, n.(1).

operation involving first of all a landing from Flanders. Parma would hold the seas round Dunkirk to allow the passage of troops. There would be much indigenous support in England. "The Earls of Rutland, Shrewsbury, Worcester, Arundel," and others were blithely represented as rushing to the cause the moment it appeared on the horizon. The Pope should encourage them by issuing indulgences, renewing the bull of excommunication and censuring all who rallied to the Queen's support. Allen would become bishop of Durham.

Unfortunately Castelli died about this time.[35] It is difficult to believe that if he had lived he would have favored sending Charles Paget, alias Mopo, to England as agent for Guise's arm of the enterprise. Mopo's task was to prepare the English to receive the French, assure them that the only purpose was to restore Catholicism and "place the Queen of Scotland peacefully on the throne of England." All foreigners would leave when the task was done.[36] There is no reason to suppose Mary knew anything of all this. Indeed, she had been invited elsewhere in the negotiation, it seems, to abandon all claim to England![37]

Influenced by Allen's support, Pope Gregory gave his own approval.[38] He drew up briefs on September 24, one renewing the excommunication and others appointing Allen bishop of Durham and papal nuncio for the expedition, as requested.[39] He also gave Persons a bill of exchange for four thousand gold crowns to provide James with his bodyguard.[40] While in Rome, Persons had an important interview with Aquaviva. With his usual optimism, Fr. Robert assured him that the present unhappy situation in his country could only be temporary. He looked forward himself to returning to England when the fury of persecution had subsided, but for the moment it would be foolhardy for one so well known to cross the Channel. Meanwhile, John Currey, a novice-priest in the Society, should go to England to work, among other things, for a reconciliation between Heywood and those he had alienated before he retired from the scene.[41] Persons would go to meet Heywood himself in Rouen. Another man destined for the mission at this time was William Weston. The cause suffered a considerable blow

---

[35] (25) III, 503–5.

[36] Ibid., 505f.

[37] Ibid.

[38] See (9) 206.

[39] See (23) 182f, n.(1).

[40] (21) 110, 111.

[41] Ibid.

with the death of George Gilbert on October 6.[42] Indeed, without him
it might never have got off the ground.[43]

Charles Paget and Sir Charles Arundell went to England in
September.[44] Their object was to procure the adhesion of Henry Percy,
eighth earl of Northumberland, William Shelley of Mitchelgrove, and
others to the Guise plan for liberating the Scottish queen, putting her
on the throne of England, which was her right, and restoring "the old
faith."[45] Percy, a Catholic, believed that Elizabeth hated him, basing his
opinion on a phrase she had dropped to Simier while in England. He
passed it to Guise and he to the earl. Percy now feared meeting the
fate of the late Duke of Norfolk[46] and sent his agent, Pullen, to France
ostensibly to see how his four sons were faring, who were being educated in Paris, but more particularly to consult Allen and Persons as to
what he should do. Elizabeth wanted his sons back in England, but the
two priests agreed that the best way for the earl to secure himself, not
to speak of his succession, was to keep one or two of his eldest sons
abroad.[47] Percy received this reply but decided that the last word
should lie with Paget, since the boys were "entrusted in some sort" to
his care. Following his recommendation, they all returned to England.
In the event, they lost all their "good inclinations" towards Catholicism
and the earl was put in the Tower. There he died a violent death in
1585, "the heretics declaring that he killed himself while others say
that he was murdered by them."[48] Persons thought the sons should
have been sent to Italy for their education whether their father wanted
it or not. In any case, while he was in England, far from promoting
Percy's collaboration with Guise, Paget did precisely the opposite.[49]
However he went about it, it is difficult to condemn Paget for rejecting
an attempt which meant not merely the release of the Scottish queen
but also the dethronement of the Queen of England. Such were the times.

[42] From RP to Agazzari, 28.x., "When I had written as far as this, your Reverence's letter arrived giving me an account of the death of . . . George," i.e., George
Gilbert, RP's "best friend"; (23) 184f.

[43] Ibid., 112f: see Agazzari to Aquaviva, (I) Anglia.A.VII; (12) III, 680–701.

[44] (1) 33.

[45] (26) 21 and 25.

[46] See Edwards, *The Marvellous Chance.*

[47] (21) 99.

[48] Ibid. See E. B. de Fonblanque, *Annals of the House of Percy* (London, 1887),
II, 152–76.

[49] RP to J. de Idiaquez, Rome, 3.vii.1597; (III) VI, Nos. 41, 42, Spanish,
Quoted and translated, (26) 22f.

Persons left Rome at the beginning of October and was back in Paris on the 19th.[50] He met Paget and received his account of the unfavorable reaction the enterprise had met with in England. The priest William Watts told Guise, Mathieu, and Persons that Paget had deliberately engineered the unfavorable response. Furthermore, as a result of his visit, William Shelley and Northumberland were both ruined. Watts claimed that Paget told him while "walking upon the . . . seaside" and waiting for a sail to England, that he could destroy in a few days all that the Jesuit had planned for so long.[51] Persons also learned from Samerie[52] and others that Paget and Morgan by their letters had alienated the Queen of Scots from the plan and caused her to write to Percy "to be sure not to associate himself with the Duke of Guise or the Spaniards in this project."[53] If so, Mary surely acted with wisdom and, if Paget and Morgan gave her this advice, they did well. But Pasquier, her master of the wardrobe, recounting the matter later, implied that Mary had not been given the true account of what was intended. She knew of a design to release her and reestablish Catholicism in England, but she understood also that she was required to renounce her right to the English succession. This she refused to do even after being promised a revenue of 100,000 crowns and her domain in France. There was never any question of her working for Elizabeth's deposition. As regards England, an invasion scheme was so "full of difficulties" it could not be done without hazarding the lives of many English friends. But if such a scheme were devised for Scotland, she would do her best to win over her son and the Scottish nobility.[54]

After this, it is easy to see why Paget and Persons never again trusted one another, although Persons later made several attempts at reconciliation for the sake of restoring some unity to the cause. Throughout, Mary was consistent in her claim to the English succession but only after the English queen completed her natural life span and provided she died without legitimate issue. This was clear in a document of January 15, 1581, which Mary wished to bring to Elizabeth's attention, and through her to the English Parliament.[55] She had

---

[50] RP to Agazzari, Paris, 28.x.1583; (23) 183f, Italian, 184f, English.

[51] (1) 32.

[52] Henri Samerie/Samier, a French Jesuit, visited Mary in disguise on three occasions in 1582, 1583, and 1584 using the aliases of La Rue and Hieronymo Martelli; (27) vii and viii passim; arts. by J. H. Pollen in (32) 1.ii.1911; Fouqueray, *Histoire de la C.ie de Jésus en France*, II, 112–19; (26) 22f, n.68; Toupin, *Correspondence du nonce*, 438, but Samerie is not here named.

[53] RP to Juan de Idiaquez, 3.vii.1597; quoted (26) 23.

[54] (26) 24; quoted from Pasquier's answers of 2.ix.1586; (27) viii, 659.

[55] Sheffield Castle, 16.i.1580/81; (51) 366–70.

always been careful by proper behavior "to merit the good grace and amity of the said queen." She was aware that she was accused of something far different, but Elizabeth could prove the truth of her utterances by a simple investigation of the facts. She repudiated the recent descent on Ireland, also the idea that religion could be established "by force of arms."[56] This remonstrance never reached Queen or Parliament.[57] Burghley and the council could be trusted to see to that.

Since the Queen of Scots touched Persons's life at many points, it seems relevant to say something of the very limited way in which he, or any others for that matter, could communicate with her. Her letters from abroad came by way of ambassadors who handed her packets to Secretary Walsingham, a man possessing no discernible scruples, who would redirect them. Secretary Thomas Wilson told Shrewsbury, her jailer, in a letter of January 31, 1581, "The French ambassador hath sent unto me a packet for your charge, wherein I think there is no matter of moment; and I think he would hardly trust me with any dangerous matter."[58] It is equally unlikely that Mary would have confided dangerous matter to such a perilous channel of communication, or even believed in any possible alternative that could be trusted.[59] Henry Samerie's testimony to Mary's rejection of schemes aimed at Elizabeth's overthrow seems unimpeachable, and it was confirmed by Pasquier in an examination of September 2, 1586, when he swore that he had never been acquainted with any practice prejudicial to the Queen of England.[60]

Persons and Paget continued to follow the logic of their divergent ways. Soon after returning to Paris, Paget visited the new ambassador, Sir Edward Stafford. On October 27 he reported Paget's offer of "all the services that might be" with an assurance "he never did or would do anything against the Queen or his country." Stafford demanded some proof of his goodwill, "especially in discovering some practice against the state, which he, being of that religion he was, haunting with them that were papists of state and not of religion, he might easily do without prejudice to his conscience."[61] Such was every man's duty. Stafford summed up neatly the dilemma now facing

---

[56] (51) 370.

[57] See J. D. Leader, *Mary, Queen of Scots in Captivity* (Sheffield, 1890), 455, n.2.

[58] Ibid.

[59] Walsingham's facilities regarding forgery and falsification are well set out in Thomas Harison's confession. He worked for a time in the secretariat; (28) Q IX, 530. The date of this document is uncertain but undoubtedly not earlier than 1587.

[60] (26) 23. See (77).

[61] (26) 24.

English Catholics: cooperate with the government as good subjects or else be accounted traitors. Cooperation meant informing on fellow Catholics. "Traitors" could not hope for toleration. As for loyal subjects—which meant those ready to spy on the rest—Elizabeth's government made no promises, but it allowed them to hope. The only alternative to Persons's policy of relying on force from abroad was to rely on the goodwill of the government at home—a cruel dilemma.

It was part of the tragedy of the time that Paget's hopes were doomed to be disappointed and deceived and that, while Allen and Persons were right in their assessment of the government's real motives, their acceptance of the challenge could not but cause great suffering to those they wanted to help. But the persecution that increased in consequence was Elizabeth's and not theirs. Perhaps they could hardly have done otherwise without loss of integrity or without trusting a regime in which no trust was to be placed. Ironically, another lesson to be learned was that no trust could be placed in Catholic governments abroad to apply the swift and relatively easy remedy of invasion and conquest, a tactic which, as the exiles had to learn, could be neither swift nor easy. Philip II is often blamed for procrastination, but his closer contact with political realities meant that his decisions were responsible and his delay often statesmanlike. Meanwhile if Charles Paget felt any inclination to waver, his noble brother was at hand to remind him of his duty. The latter wrote to him from London, telling him that his stay in Rouen was much misliked, "considering the company there." He threatened to disown him as a brother if he forgot his duty to England.[62]

Persons wrote to Como at the end of October to tell him that all was in readiness and Guise only awaited the order from Philip.[63] The order never came. Meanwhile, the secular priests, John Mush and John Cornelius, coming from Rome on their way to England, called on Persons, who found them "true servants of Christ." He rebuked poor Agazzari for "great niggardliness" in supplying their journey money. Their complaints could alienate people from the Society.[64]

In the late autumn of 1583, Persons met William Weston to brief him as successor to Heywood in England. John Currey would assist him. Hopefully between them they could calm the teacup storm over fasting.[65] The controversy virtually ended when Heywood was

---

[62] (29) 1581–90, 125; from PRO, SP12, 163, No. 18.

[63] Richard Millinus [alias RP] to Como, Paris, 31.x.1583, copy?; (23) 185f, Latin, 186f English; especially nn.(3) & (4).

[64] RP to Agazzari, Paris, 28.x.1583; (23) 183f, Italian, 184f, English.

[65] (21) 112f.

captured on his way to France, being forced back to England by contrary winds. He was kept in prison till 1585 and then sent into exile. If 1583 was not a good year for the Catholics, neither was it for the Anglicans. Edward Grindal, archbishop of Canterbury, after being deprived of spiritual jurisdiction for his strong stand over "prophesyings," died in July.[66] His successor, John Whitgift, formerly bishop of Worcester, came to Canterbury in September. He lost no time in harrying the Catholics, but also the Puritans. This brought him into collision with Burghley, who wished to play the puppeteer over men who had no desire to be puppets. However, three more Catholics were martyred in October and November,[67] so that there was some consolation for both men.

In spite of persecution or because of it, fifty young men from Oxford, Cambridge, "and other colleges" arrived at Rheims within the month.[68] They included not only graduates but sons of noblemen and heirs to considerable estates. A partial motive was "contempt . . . for the scanty learning and bad teaching of the heretics."[69] Many wanted the better education they thought they would get at Rome or elsewhere on the continent. But there were complications. The system had been devised for young men aged from eighteen to twenty-four, still malleable and teachable; but older men were now applying who could hardly be expected to bend themselves, sometimes literally, to the discipline intended for boys and youths. Cardinal Filippo Buoncompagno, protector of England, with Italian optimism, thought that older men should be admitted to Roman studies. Having given a guarantee to observe college discipline, thirteen were admitted. But in a matter of months, when the novelty had worn off, predictably they declared the system more fit for children "than for men of their state and judgment."[70] Their protest was not unreasonable. They could be corrected like schoolboys or undergraduates with the rod and other humiliating forms of punishment, although it is not on record, it seems, that older men were treated in this way. It was Christopher Bagshaw who came to Rome in 1583 "as the leader of this band of scholars,"[71] a circumstance which could bode no good for Persons.

---

[66] See Claire Cross, *The Royal Supremacy in the Elizabethan Church* (London, 1969), 62–75; Patrick Collinson, *Archbishop Grindal* (London, 1979), passim.

[67] (21) 114f. One of them, Edward Arden, was accused of involvement in John Somerville's treason. For a general dictum on alleged plots, see M. Hume, *Treason and Plot* (London, 1901), 88f, 113.

[68] Allen to Agazzari, 8.viii.1583, Rheims; (9) 203.

[69] (21) 116f.

[70] Ibid.

[71] Barrett referred to this "band" in his letter to Agazzari of 17.viii.1583; ibid.

Dr. Barrett, prefect of studies at Rheims, warned Agazzari of the trouble he could expect from Master Christopher. "He has good talent, fit enough for studies, but is very passionate and difficult and restless." He seems to have begun with good intentions towards the Society of Jesus, opposing such as loved it "less than they ought." But his character had a fatal flaw: "He could not bear the least word that had any note of reprehension or admonition."[72] Bagshaw possessed a highly critical tongue and pen; and since, as Thackeray observed, the world is a looking glass which gives back to every man the reflection of his own face, it frequently happened that Bagshaw was given an image of himself he could only resent. Persons, too, could be critical with tongue and pen. Perhaps it was inevitable that Bagshaw, "thinking his penny good silver," in Squire's phrase, should remain what he had already become at Balliol, a bitter enemy of Persons, and transfer his hatred to the Society of Jesus, in which Persons seemed to have so much influence.[73] As his surviving books and letters show, Bagshaw was by no means Persons's intellectual equal. Nevertheless, he was not to be lightly regarded, nor would he forgive anyone who appeared to do so.

Serious problems arose this year inside the ranks of the English Jesuits themselves. Christopher Perkins, a priest of great ability, was dismissed from the Society. He had been designated for the English mission; but, revealing little of the Jesuit virtue of obedience as Jesuits understood it, he required as a condition of his going a "dispensation from the Pope . . . to go to protestant churches and to take in a good sense the oath of the Queen's ecclesiastical supremacy and other like things."[74] Allen and Persons took this as an indication of ignorance of the English scene which time and experience would correct. But before this could come about, Perkins was expelled for "bad conduct." His was the kind of love, such as it was, that turns readily to hatred. He went to England, apostatized, and, being the kind of man Elizabeth's government was looking for, enjoyed favor and promotion, including a knighthood. He did not hesitate to harry his former coreligionists.

Thomas Langdale was another Jesuit who apostatized this year. His case, in Persons's phrase, was "a very strange one." Apparently on sudden impulse, in spite of the fact that he was an old man and had enjoyed positions of trust, he went to England and made immediate

---

[72] (21) 118f.

[73] See above, chap. 1, p. 6.

[74] (21) 100f. For others who left the Jesuits, see (VI) F.G., 685A, *De disertoribus,* from 1563.

contact with the Privy Council. The council gave out that he had offered to go to Protestant churches and urged others to do the same. "He had leave to go through the whole kingdom, saying Mass where he liked and without danger."[75] Although the Catholics avoided him, knowing he would betray them, he tried to win acceptance through Jasper Heywood.[76] The original permission was not due to any magnanimity on the part of the authorities, of course, but because he was likely as a Jesuit "to do more harm to the Catholic religion than all the tortures and gibbets of our adversaries." Allen and Persons did their best to put the record straight with the Catholics, but the scandal could not be hidden.[77] Eventually he was absorbed into his family circle, good Catholics, and gave no more trouble. His antics may have arisen from senility.

Although there was no question of infidelity in Heywood's case, he had shown too little sensitivity, it seems, towards the Marian priests and others who preferred older ways, especially in the matter of fasting.[78] In any case, Heywood's attitude contravened an agreement accepted when the new priests first entered the country, that the "usual fast of England should be peacefully observed." Persons, in view of his known political activities, could not now return to England to settle matters without danger not only to himself but to any who sheltered him. Such would be subject to the death penalty.[79] Aquaviva therefore refused to allow his return or even a visit to Scotland in 1584.[80]

Another danger to the cause this year was provided by the spy and agent provocateur William Parry. Parry came to Paris in November 1583 to "find credit with Allen and Persons."[81] He thought to advantage himself with the recommendation of Charles Paget and Thomas Morgan. Allen interviewed him, but Persons refused to have anything at all to do with him. Parry then decided to offer his services to the Pope by letter and by way of the Paris nuncio, Girolamo Ragazzoni. Strangely, he begged "a plenary indulgence for his sins when he had effected his designs" for a great service to the Church in

---

[75] (21) 102f.

[76] See Jasper Heywood to Allen, 16.iv.1583; (21) 102–4.

[77] Ibid., 104f.

[78] Ibid., 106f.

[79] Aquaviva to RP, 8.xi.1582; (VI), Francia I, f.142v; and s. to s. 19.iii.1582; ibid., f.134v; (23) 172, n.(1).

[80] Aquaviva to RP, 3.vii.1584; (VI) Francia. I, ff.197–8r; (23) 172.

[81] (21) 120–23.

England.[82] This service, as he later declared, though it was not indicated in his letter, was the assassination, no less, of Queen Elizabeth. Thomas Morgan, Parry's compatriot and "infinite friend," took him to the nuncio. Ragazzoni sent Parry's original letter to Como in his dispatch of December 18, 1583, but with a warning that he was not to be trusted.[83] The warning may have come from Morgan, who had intercepted, as he said, two letters in Paris.[84] These also Ragazzoni sent to Rome. Parry took a copy of his letter with him to England in January 1584 to make an impression on the council. He met Watts on the way at Rouen, who somehow got out of him the admission that he was going to England "to oppose the Jesuits."[85] In this he had been encouraged, as he credibly said, by Paget and Morgan.[86] With Cecil's permission, following an assurance of important matter to reveal, Parry went to England to confer with Burghley and the Queen, claiming that he had been sent with papal approval by friends of the Scottish queen, the Jesuits, and others to kill the English queen, who would be replaced on the throne by Mary. Como meanwhile sent an answer by way of Morgan to Parry's letter to Rome.[87] Parry showed the letter to the Queen. It was only in general terms to what had been a general proposition of service and approved as such by the Pope. Parry himself, however, supplied lurid details. Burghley and Elizabeth had no difficulty in believing him.[88] Parry received no "office or dignity" such as he had hoped for, but the Queen granted him a liberal pension; and he was returned as member of Parliament for Queenborough, Kent, in November 1584.[89] There for the moment we may leave him.

[82] (21) 122f.

[83] Ragazzoni to Como, Paris, 18.xii.1583; (IV) Segreteria di Stato, Francia 17, ff.264f, original: Parry's letter on f.265; P. Blet, S.J., *Girolamo Ragazzoni évèque de Bergame, nonce en France, Correspondence . . . 1583–1586* (Rome and Paris, 1962), 170. For a critical examination of the Parry plot, see L. Hicks, "The Strange Case of Dr William Parry," *Studies*, vol. 37 (1948); copy (original?) of Como to Parry, 30.i.1584 in BL, Lansdowne MS 96, f.48r.

[84] Blet, *Girolamo Ragazzoni,* 167.

[85] (21) 122f.

[86] (1) 32f. J. H. Pollen thought RP was unfair to Paget at this point. See (1) 32, n., and (26) 21–29.

[87] Ibid. RP gives January (1584) as the month of Parry's crossing to England in (1) 33.

[88] (21) 124f. Persons consistently avoided the topic of assassination, of which he clearly disapproved. It is possible that Castelli, distrusting exiles, did not raise the subject with him at the conferences, but it is less easy to believe that Guise did not. William Crichton altogether repudiated the idea of tyrannicide or assassination as applicable to Elizabeth when Parry approached him in Lyons; (26) 62.

[89] See art. by L. Hicks in *Studies,* vol. 37; see n.83 above.

Chapter Seven

The First Invasion Plan, Third Phase
1584–1585

Persons spent the winter of 1584 with the Prince of Parma and Olivier Mannaerts (Manare), S.J., in Tournai. This was the closed season for war but Persons was busy. He helped obtain a captaincy for William Tresham and chaplaincies for Pullen and William Watts. Watts died "soon after."[1] As Leo Hicks pointed out, the negotiations of 1583 "terminated his activity as a political negotiator" in the sense that he never again acted as an envoy.[2] Nevertheless, he continued to operate as a deus ex machina and liaison, moving easily in the company of the great and influential. He could persuade and deter, mar if not make all; but the circumstances were never quite right for him to become another Anthony Possevino, even if the ability was there.

Persons met Allen in Paris on January 12, the first of a series of meetings for consultation on the affairs of the mission.[3] A letter from London dated December 24 told of the alarm and fury of the government reflected in bitter persecution and propaganda. The threat of the empresa was now common knowledge and, not surprisingly, England was in the throes of plot mania. Thanks to Parry and perhaps others, rumors of attempts on the life of Elizabeth circulated freely. These were not absurd, since Pope Gregory and Como were short of a Judith rather than the will. It is hardly likely they thought they had found the man in Parry, who had been a government spy for years previously.[4]

---

[1] (1) 33. RP says "both died," i.e., Pullen also; but this seems a *lapsus memoriae;* v. infra, "Scrittura data dal P.re Personio."

[2] (23) lxi.

[3] See RP to Aquaviva, 12.i.1584, Paris; (23) 187–91, Latin, 191–93, English, from a "contemporary copy."

[4] A letter in Italian from Como to W. Parry of 30.i.1584, on Italian paper with an Italian watermark, appears to be genuine. It praises without mentioning some work which Parry has in hand, and grants him "plenaria Indulgenza et remissione di tutti i peccati," as he had requested. It closes with, "Metta dunque ad effetto li suoi Sancti et honorati pensieri, et attenda a star sana . . ."; BL, Lansdowne MS, 96, ff.48r–9v. In this context, it is reasonable to suppose that the work in hand was assassination. For the Parry plot, see (26) 61–73.

But they had not rejected him outright. The Holofernes theme was not confined to the canvases of the artists; and a little later in the day certain figures of Elizabeth's government were to toy with her remedy as a solution for their own problem centered in Mary.

Inevitably, Persons's name was linked with Parry's as a potential assassin, but the Jesuits never countenanced this way out of the dilemma. In any case, Parry was well-known to them as one of Cecil's agents.[5] While there might have been plots against the life of Elizabeth, in fact there seem to be none that stand up to critical examination, certainly none in which agents provocateurs were not somewhere involved. But the council took full advantage of the atmosphere of suspicion and credulity abroad as an instrument in their war on influential Catholic families. Knowing that they could not have been guilty, the council found it effective policy to claim that they were. So it was that Francis Throckmorton, "a wealthy young man of very good birth," was arrested on the flimsiest of evidence and tortured "very cruelly on the rack three times" to make him confess to conspiracy. "He is reported to have uttered no other word at the height of his sufferings but this only: "O God be merciful to me, a sinner."[6] He was racked four times in all. Nevertheless, a letter from Tournai of March 8 claimed not only that Throckmorton had been informed by Mendoza of the "enterprise" but that he had also made damaging admissions under torture.[7] One useful result of all this confusion from the council's viewpoint was to leave Mendoza himself less certain concerning the wisdom of an empresa, considering the people he had to deal with.

Undeniably, the easy victory so far of the Elizabethan regime over all attempts to overthrow it made the value of any further attempt problematic, or perhaps worse than useless, since failure could only provoke and justify a more intense persecution. Solutions by force seemed discredited. Mendoza was expelled when his part in the invasion scheme was discovered. William Carter was hanged, drawn, and quartered on January 11, 1584, for printing his *Treatise of schism.* . . .[8] Five priests from the new foundations at Rheims and Rome followed

---

[5] "A catholic to a monk at Liège," Brussels, 14.vii.1599; PRO, SP12/271, No. 74, quoted, (26) 63, n.178.

[6] (23) 198f, Latin, 199f, English. Hicks thought this letter came originally from RP because he wintered (1583–84) at Tournai, but he admitted an element of doubt; ibid., 198, n.(1) bis.

[7] See (26), chap. 2.

[8] Not to be confused with the Jesuit Thomas Lister's treatise, *Contra factiosos* . . . of 1595, which circulated in MS and was sometimes known by this title. See (27) App. D, 143–45.

him to the scaffold on February 12. Only the papists could still see this as other than an ordinary act of justice.

Small wonder if what appeared to be the more moderate party of the Pagets and Morgan should win more general support among Catholics. Even the militant Gregory XIII had second thoughts. As for the restless in the Catholic ranks, if they failed to get a pension from anywhere, or if they were discontented in the seminaries, "or were given to faction and nationality between English, Welsh, Irish and Scots," they joined the Paget division.[9] Tangled allegiances and wavering loyalties made it easy for the English council to find informers who could not simply be called spies, and men who sought reconciliation with the regime who could not simply be dismissed as "traitors" save by partisans of the other side.

It was Thomas Throckmorton, son of Sir John and another member of the Paget group, who had managed to get his elder brother, Francis, appointed go-between for Mary and Bernardino de Mendoza. Juan Battista de Tassis, Spanish ambassador in France, combined loyalty to his sovereign with adherence to the Paget group. To them belonged William and Gilbert Gifford in Rheims, Edward Gratley in Paris, William Clitheroe and his friends in Rouen, Owen Lewis and his nephew, Hugh Griffith, and Nicholas Fitzherbert in Rome. Thomas Fitzherbert, Richard Hopton, and Stephen Brinkley, however, stood by Persons in Paris; but he was prepared to name even Sir Charles Arundell among his friends, a man of most dubious allegiance.[10] Sir Francis Englefield in Spain was a man, undoubtedly, after Persons's own heart.

Allen and Persons attempted reconciliation with the Paget party, visiting Paris frequently for the purpose, but they could offer no real success for their own policies by way of bait. Inevitably, seeing their division, the English council "fostered the same greedily, sending over diverse spies to that effect."[11] The Jesuits tried to counteract division by getting pensions for the exiles, especially for the more articulate. Agazzari used his influence with the Pope to help in this; but the result was emulation and complaint rather than satisfaction, so that Allen advised him to pass this invidious task to a layman. Even this became the cause of new conflict over the person chosen.[12] Since the English could not agree, Agazzari eventually chose an Italian. Allen

---

[9] (1) 35.

[10] (1) 36; (26) loc. cit., and 39, 128, 207.

[11] (1) 38. RP's autobiography ends with 1584.

[12] RP refers to them simply as "the factions"; (21) 130, see 131; see also RP to Agazzari, 12.i.1584; (23) 197f; Allen to s., 3.i.1584, (9) 220; Agazzari to Allen, 17.ii.1584, ibid., 225.

wrote Agazzari a letter apologizing for his countrymen who seemed "never to be content however well things go with them, and to bear ingratitude to friends and helpers."[13] Allen put it down substantially, to coin an anachronistic phrase, to exiles' neurosis.

Foreseeably, as a result of the militant exiles' failed policy so far, the screw of persecution in England tightened by several turns. The ports were closely watched. Leicester, "head and front of the puritans," Elizabeth's favorite, was leading a new assault on papists.[14] Lord Paget and Charles Arundell, at the spectacle of Throckmorton's fate, fled abroad "to enjoy liberty of conscience."[15] Northumberland, who did not escape, was put in the Tower in January, only to leave as a corpse after his death on June 20, 1585. His murder, arranged by Sir Christopher Hatton, was reasonably suspected.[16] Philip Howard was put under house arrest on December 20, 1583, but freed in April 1584, since no connection could be proved with Francis Throckmorton or Charles Paget.[17]

Parma's main concern in calling Persons to Flanders this winter was to ask his advice regarding the Catholic exiles, "who were there in great numbers."[18] He left France towards the end of January, leaving behind much unfinished business.[19] So many of the exiles were serving in the duke's army that a separate regiment was formed under the Earl of Westmorland. Parma wanted Persons's advice as to the appointment of suitable chaplains.[20] Oliver Cromwell was by no means the first in English history to want the closer association of the military life with Christian principles. Pullen, their tutor, became a priest after the earl's sons returned to England, and he and William Watts were appointed chaplains of the new ideal through Persons's agency.

In contemporary phrase, the exiles had the wolf by the ears. There was no hope now of toleration, and in fact there never had been, so pressing on with the empresa seemed to be the only hope. It was believed that King Philip only waited on word from the Pope to proceed. Allen and Persons therefore drew up in mid-January a memorial to encourage him. A copy for Rome was handed to the

---

[13] (21) 130f.

[14] (23) 193.

[15] (23) 189, n.(3); (VII) SP12/164, Nos. 5, 6; see CRS 21, 121.

[16] (23) 192, 189 nn.(4), (5); Lingard, *History of England,* 1849 ed., vi, 390–94.

[17] See Fonblanque, *Annals of the House of Percy* II, 153–76.

[18] (21) 125.

[19] According to RP it was "towards the end of the year" (1583); (23) 125: but a letter to Aquaviva was dated from Paris, 12.i.1584; (23) 187.

[20] (21) 125.

nuncio.[21] Not until the autumn did Persons realize how much Elizabeth had known all along of what was afoot. He put down the primary cause of leakage to bungling by Mendoza.[22] This memorial of January 16, 1584, was full of naive optimism no doubt calculated to move Philip to action, since doing anything seemed better than doing nothing. Arundel, Northumberland, and Rutland were to be the leaders of the uprising, although they were all in captivity. If not these then others! Guise added his own plea for a speedy decision. This was directed to the Pope and the Spanish king.[23] There was about it all an air of near desperation.

Certainly, at this time the English situation seemed hopeless enough from Persons's viewpoint. By the beginning of 1584, James Bosgrave and Thomas Mettam, Jesuits, were in prison. Jasper Heywood soon joined them.[24] On February 8 he was transferred from the Clink to the darker Tower.[25] By this time trouble was also brewing in the English College, Rome. Christopher Bagshaw was the storm center. After resigning his Balliol fellowship in 1582, he went to Rheims to be ordained priest in 1583. Destined originally for the English mission, he set out for Rome on August 13 to pursue further studies in theology. After his arrival "such trouble ensued therein as had never been seen before,"[26] as Persons described it. This time Agazzari had all Persons's sympathy: "You are suffering . . . gratuitously at their hands and are having stones cast at you for numerous good deeds."[27] He urged him to stand firm and in fact Agazzari did so. Meanwhile, some of the students recently arrived in Paris from Rome were "infecting the greater part of the young men who came from England with unfavourable opinions of our Society."[28] Maurice Clynnog and Owen Lewis must have felt that at last the whirligig of time was bringing in its revenges.

More cheering for the exiles was the news from Scotland in the spring of 1584. For once the other side bungled. An attempt to snatch James yet again, concocted by Rothes, Angus, and Mar in the fore-

---

[21] "Scrittura data dal Padre Alano et dal Padre Roberto a 16 Gen[na]io [1584] perché si mandasse a N.Signore"; (23) 193–95 Italian, 196–97 English; (IV) Seg.ria di Stato, Francia 17, f.285. See also (23) 194, nn.(1) and (2).

[22] (23) lxii and n.(134).

[23] Allen and RP, Memorial to Gregory XIII, 16.i.1584; (23) 197.

[24] See (23) 190, n.(6).

[25] Ibid. He was tried and condemned to death but sent into exile in January 1585.

[26] (21) 117.

[27] RP to Agazzari, Tournai, 24.iii.1584; (23) 200, Italian, 201, English.

[28] S. to s., Paris, 10.vii.1584; (23) 215, Italian, 216, English.

ground, Gowrie in middle ground, and Bowes and Walsingham in the shadows, was scotched by the Earl of Arran, James's closest adviser, who had foreknowledge of the plot. Gowrie was taken on April 16, although his three confederates managed to flee across the southern border. Gowrie paid for his treachery with his life. William Holt, the Jesuit, was now "labouring fruitfully in that vineyard once again."[29] The Kirk, moreover, could not this time sit back and watch in safety and complacency the aftermath of changes it had failed to effect. "The preachers fled with the rest"; but if Elizabeth killed priests, Arran "was very capable of doing what Morton said needed to be done to preachers."[30] As everyone knew, the party was by no means over. Walsingham met the fugitive rebels before they penetrated far into England and ordered them back to fight another day with the promise of English support. Persons's reaction to all this was to urge Aquaviva to send more money into Scotland, the most effective means in the material order for counteracting English influence.[31]

After the latest turn of events in Scotland, a law was passed putting the ministers of the Kirk under the authority of bishops, while lifting the excommunication of the Archbishop of Glasgow pronounced two years before.[32] Protection was to be extended secretly to English Catholics fleeing to Scotland. Even in England the ministers did not escape criticism. One who presumed to preach on the theme of obedience was told by a hearer that, if he had practised the virtue in Scotland, he would have found no need to flee.[33] In fact, the Scottish ministers had drawn up twenty-one articles against the King's government, one calling it heresy for him to declare himself head of the Church, another saying he could be excommunicated and deposed if he misgoverned, and another claiming that the authority of bishops was against the Word of God. Béza in Geneva was their ultimate court of appeal. Persons took it all as a hopeful sign that a kingdom divided against itself could not stand.[34] Glasgow meanwhile, Mary's ambassador, addressed an appeal to the Pope and Jesuit general for more men to be sent into Scotland.[35]

---

[29] (21) 134–35. The quotation about Elizabeth is from A. Lang, *History of Scotland* (Edinburgh/London, 1902), 297.

[30] Ibid.

[31] RP to Aquaviva, Paris, 29.v.1584; (VI) FG. 651/640, n.f., a.l.s., Italian.

[32] Not Beaton, Mary's ambassador in Paris, of course.

[33] RP to Aquaviva, Paris, 10.vii.1584; (VI) F.G.651/640 n.f., a.l.s., Italian.

[34] Ibid.

[35] Ibid.

Persons expected to remain in Flanders for a matter of months and begged the services of the faithful Emerson then in Rouen. Since he was so close to the Spanish authorities, Aquaviva asked Persons to intercede for the maintenance of "our nuns." It was not a bad moment, since the war was going well for Spain. Ypres fell on March 22 and the relief of Ghent seemed near, so that efforts could soon concentrate on Antwerp. But in England five priests had been martyred, seventeen more condemned to death, including Jasper Heywood and Arthur Pitts, while Arundel and Northumberland were confined more closely than ever. Five priests were obliged to escape to France, and others would be forced to follow them to escape starvation. The best hope for the Catholics at home—those who could afford it—was flight abroad.

Persons left Flanders for Paris on May 2. His business in Tournai had gone reasonably well. He had successfully enlisted Parma's active interest in getting pensions for the exiles. A gentleman had been dispatched to plead their cause in Spain. Fr. Robert also managed to persuade Parma to overhaul Sir William Stanley's English regiment that had surrendered at Deventer in 1583. Morale was low, some of the men returning to England every day. Parma thought little of them or the other English who came to serve, since their discipline was poor. Persons carried his point that chaplains were needed to boost morale, and also that the regiment would provide excellent employment for the many Catholics who were still coming over to escape persecution. So Parma decided to increase it from its original seven companies of infantry by some five or six more. A priest was already working among them with good results, providing the justification for more. The men seemed very receptive. With typical optimism, Persons opined, "The Queen of England will fear a few English Catholic soldiers more than a host from any other nation, and in consequence will be less eager to persecute the Catholics remaining at home."[36]

---

[36] RP to Aquaviva, Tournai, 2.v.1584; (VI) ibid. The best sources for English and other foreigners serving the archdukes are the Archives du Royaume, Brussels, Secrétairerie d'Etat et de Guerre, Régistres de patentes, titres, ordres et depesches concernant les troupes. . . . The first twenty-five volumes, covering roughly a year a volume, tell the story to 1613. Much was digested and published for Irish history in Brendan Jennings, O.F.M., *Wild Geese in Spanish Flanders 1582–1700* (Dublin, 1964); but there are a number of English references. See also L. Willaert, "Négociations politico-religieuses entre l'Angleterre et les Pays Bas Catholiques 1598–1625 d'après les papiers d'État et de l'audience . . ." *RHE* (Louvain), tome vi, 1905; Robert Lechat, S.J., *Les refugiés anglais dans les Pays-Bas espagnols durant le règne d'Elisabeth 1558–1603* (Louvain, 1914); Geoffrey Parker, *The Army of Flanders and the Spanish Road 1567–1659* (Cambridge, 1972), and *The Dutch Revolt* (London, 1977).

Somewhere along the line, perhaps in his school days when he learned to flee mother and schoolmaster alike, Persons became an excellent horseman. He needed his skill. On the way to Paris, somewhere between Ghent and Oudenarde, it seems, Fr. Robert and Hugh Owen, Parma's liaison, nearly fell into the hands of English soldiery from Mechlin. Fortunately, they were both good horsemen and well mounted, so they managed to fly a little ahead of their pursuers. It was not Persons's first experience of the kind. Between Louvain and Beveren "where all our carts and convoy were taken, . . . I escaped by the benefit of a good horse."[37] He was back in Paris about mid-May.[38] After another routine discussion of mission business with Allen, he went to reside in the Jesuit house of St. Louis. He was received "with great warmth and kindness" by Claude Mathieu and by "the holy man, Ralph, in whose worth and straightforward goodness" Robert found great support. Even here he found trouble in the importunities of the unfortunate exiles who were trying to exist between frying pan and fire. But a greater challenge now promised or threatened. Mathieu and Crichton both felt it needed a man of his caliber to go to Scotland to exploit the possibilities clearly indicated in Holt's latest letters.[39]

Persons was quite willing to go, although his eyes were open to the perils. He wanted a command "so that if I am taken, I shall know . . . that it is God's providence that wishes me to suffer for His name, and not to be separated from my colleagues who have gone so gloriously before."[40] Aquaviva was not prepared to risk the loss of Persons, but he acceded to his and Mathieu's request to send in more men. Allen and Persons now consulted with Mathieu in Paris on English affairs, because Odo Pigenat, the provincial, was often absent and showed no great interest. Indeed, on one occasion he inadvertently kept a letter from the General for Persons some five months before he thought of passing it on!

The anti-Jesuit movement, for reasons we have seen, continued to make progress in Paris and elsewhere. Thomas Bourchier, an English Franciscan, was now added to the number, as well as an Anglo-Flemish member of the Order, Bateson. Bateson had a brother who had been dismissed from the Society of Jesus for unbecoming conduct. He became an ally of Solomon Aldred, a layman, who, while enjoying a pension from the Holy See, became a spy for Sir Christopher Hatton

---

[37] (1) 33.

[38] Ibid. and n. See (IV) Segr.ria di Stato, Francia. 17, f.397; (23) lxiii, n.(138).

[39] These were included with RP to Aquaviva, Paris, 29.v.1584; (VI) FG 651, ibid., Latin.

[40] Ibid.

and Walsingham.[41] Aldred hoped that if Allen and Persons could be persuaded or commanded to abandon their writing, English Catholics might get toleration. Sixtus V, a Franciscan who succeeded Gregory XIII in 1585, seemed more inclined to abandon the hard line. Bateson even reported that Queen Elizabeth was ready "to hear a Mass privately in her chamber"![42] So influential for a time did the Aldred-Bateson axis become that it succeeded in getting Roger Baines, Allen's secretary, imprisoned by the Inquisition "for a year and more," while even Allen and Persons lay for a time under the threat of penalty.[43] Worse still, William of Orange was assassinated on July 11, 1584, so that the threat of reprisal hung heavy on the sultry air. Edmund Hay reported on October 29 that Persons—no easy man to scare—had left Paris in fear of his life.[44]

Midsummer 1584 actually brought the English mission within sight of closure. Aquaviva was ready to declare Elizabeth the victor, recall his men from England, and even Holt from Scotland. Even Allen seemed prepared to acquiesce, while Pigenat and other Jesuits positively favored it.[45] Persons wrote a letter of earnest protest to the General on June 11.[46] In the event, Persons was the man he listened to. The English mission stayed in business.[47]

In Scotland the latest reaction proceeded apace. The Catholic laird of Fentry and the Master of Gray both received words of sympathy from the young king.[48] In fact, James, at the tender age of seventeen, had already learned to face all ways, the next best thing to having eyes in the back of his head. He had learned to say whatever the hour demanded, being fully aware that before the end of the day he would probably have to contradict himself. Elizabeth, or rather Burghley, never at a loss, now sent Mauvissière, the French ambassador, into Scotland, with Henri III's consent, to see if he could reconcile James and his rebels, so that they could live to fight another day—for the advantage of England, needless to say. She even thought of reopening

---

[41] RP to Aquaviva, Paris, 23.vii.1584; (23) 223f. See L. Hicks, S.J., "An Elizabethan Propagandist: Solomon Aldred," (32) 1945, 181.

[42] (1) 34f. For R. Bateson, see (VI) FG, Dimissi, f.20. His dismissal was "in forma communi." Also, (21) 126f.

[43] (1) 34f.

[44] (1) 35 and n.

[45] (23) 201, nn.(4), (5).

[46] RP to Aquaviva, Paris, 11.vi.1584; (23) 201–4 Italian, 204f English. For the date of this letter, see 201, n.(1).

[47] (23) 201f, n.(4).

[48] (21) 139; (23) 209, 213.

negotiations with Mary so as to use her "to intervene and reconcile her son to his rebellious subjects, promising her liberty if she prevail" with him.[49] Meanwhile the pressure on English Catholics continued. Nine more were executed before the year was out. Five—relatively fortunate—were publicly whipped at Winchester, but everywhere indignities at least were heaped on those who remained faithful to the Roman connection.[50]

On June 4, Aquaviva told Mathieu and, through him, Pigenat that Persons was to take formal charge of the Scottish mission.[51] The provincial, replying on August 20, pointed out the difficulties of making one man responsible for both missions, in view of the ancient enmity of the two nations. Furthermore, the Scottish Jesuits, older in years and in their experience of the Society, might not relish the appointment of a younger man. Aquaviva pointed out in turn that the religious affairs of the two nations were inextricably bound up together, and in any case, the Scots had petitioned this appointment. William Holt's example showed that Englishmen could be perfectly acceptable in Scotland[52] and this was how Crichton secured his further deployment there.[53] Holt, however, thought that Persons should not be removed from Rouen, where he was doing excellent work for both nations.[54] Persons himself was not anxious to assume the double responsibility.[55] He found England quite enough. But much would depend on good relations with Lord Seaton; and Crichton, as he confided later to Nicholas Faunt, found in him "neither capacity, secrecy, or any other good government."[56] Certainly, Persons could not relish becoming the paymaster, or at least attorney, for the money-hungry lairds and politicians of Caledonia. But Aquaviva insisted, even against Pigenat's support of Persons's plea,[57] since no one else was so likely to win James's confidence.[58]

---

[49] (23) 217 n.(4).

[50] RP to Aquaviva, Paris, 23.vii.1584; (23) 222.

[51] (VI) Francia. I, ff.194r–5r, Italian.

[52] (23) 221, n.(21).

[53] RP to Aquaviva, Paris, 11.vi.1584; (23) 201–5; (21) 142f; and s. to s. Paris, 23.vii.1584, (23) 217–24.

[54] (21) 144f.

[55] Ibid. See s. to s., 23.viii.; (23) 224.

[56] N. Fante to F. Walsingham, London, 14.ix.1584; (VII) SP12/173, No. 14. See (29) 1581–90, 201.

[57] O. Pigenat to Aquaviva, 20.viii.1584; (VI) Epp.Gall.14, f.59. Aquaviva to Pigenat, 22.ix.1584; ibid., f.58v; mentioned in (23) lxiv, nn.(140), (141).

[58] (23) 222.

In the sequel, Crichton and James Gordon of the Huntley clan were sent to join Holt. But it was not to be. They were captured on the journey.[59] It was the Dutch who intercepted them early in August. They allowed Gordon to go free, retaining Crichton and Patrick Addy, secular priest, who were handed over to the English government soon afterwards.[60] After confinement and examination in Walsingham's house in the beginning of September, both were sent to the Tower on September 16, where Crichton remained until May 1587.[61] According to Persons, Crichton managed to clear himself of suspicion especially in connection with Parry's plot, so that he was later allowed to proceed to France. For ordinary recusancy they could not condemn him to death, "for their laws against priests and Jesuits were only applicable to the English."[62]

Walsingham was keeping an unblinking eye all this time on Mary's correspondence. Thomas Phelippes, his principal decipherer, copied a letter apparently coming from Persons in July. The letter revealed little enough. He is clearly aware of the emulation between Mendoza, Parma, and de Tassis. The Spaniards promised much and performed little, so that the French and Scots were more than some-what disillusioned.[63] They were no longer so ready to leave the initiative to Philip even if the Pope would not move without him. Guise had left the French court about July 20, having caught wind of an attempt on his life.[64] All the same, there were considerable offers of men, money, and munitions from France so that Guise might take the initiative.[65] It is scarcely authentic Persons, and one is instinctively suspicious of anything that might come from Walsingham's workshop.

---

[59] (21) 146f. See "The examination of two Scottish . . . William Creychton and Patrick Addie taken on board a ship coming from Dieppe," 3.ix.1584; (29) 1581–90, 200. "Substance of the discourse in Italian found about Creychton . . . relative to the plot for the establishing of the Romish religion, and liberating the Queen of Scots, being part of the same enterprise whereunto Throckmorton and Charles Paget were privy"; ibid.

[60] (23) lxiv and n.(143).

[61] Sources for this episode and Crichton's life are given in (23) 253 n.(2).

[62] (21) 147. "Deposition of William Creychtoun as to his knowledge of Dr Parry, against whom he had been cautioned as a spy for the Queen of England"; (29) ibid., 227, No. 54 (15.ii.1585).

[63] RP(?) to Sir Francis Englefield, Paris, 24.vii.1584; (23) 224–26, English. A passage seems missing after "the French and Scott are now" (p. 225), presumably Phelippes's haplography. No signature: "You knowe by whome."

[64] Ibid., 225.

[65] RP and Englefield are both referred to in the third person so that the correspondents are either two different persons, or else the letter is merely Phelippes's resumé or paraphrase. Endorsement: "24 July 1584. Letters decifered of Father Persons to Sir Frances Englefield."

Persons was quite aware of some of the consequences of the close surveillance of Mary's correspondence by Walsingham. If she was slow in answering a letter of Sir Francis Englefield's, it could only be because it had not been delivered. Persons noted that, while he had only received one or two letters from her in nine or ten months, and those containing only a few lines apiece, Morgan received several letters a month. He did not complain, as he said, since this left him free for other business.[66] Mary herself was beginning to hope for more than anything Persons had to offer. While Elizabeth, and certainly her ministers, had no intention, one may believe, of bringing matters to a concrete conclusion, negotiations had now ostensibly begun for a treaty between her and Mary. Robert Beale, clerk of the Council, arrived at Sheffield on May 13, 1584. To prove her sincerity towards Elizabeth, Mary penned her a long letter retailing the Countess of Shrewsbury's indiscreet observations on the English queen's private life and morals.[67] Needless to say, it never reached her. Likewise needless to say, her motives were interpreted altogether adversely in offering this information.

A charge frequently made against the Jesuits, especially from 1595, when the opposition became vociferous, was that they drew off vast sums in alms. So it is interesting to read what Persons had to say on the subject before there was any serious charge or controversy. He claims that in the three years he had been trying to get help for the mission, "I have not received a farthing in alms . . . except 500 scudi from Mr George [Gilbert] and 200 crowns from Fr General: other sums of money I have received from people to pay for journeys." However, he had managed to provide "chalices, vestments, missals, breviaries, "little office" books, catechisms and books of devotion and controversy to the value of more than 4,000 crowns." Sometimes he was reimbursed, but such transactions involved "great uncertainty" and "much loss and danger. . . . It is not forty days since I spent upwards of eighty-eight crowns just in gifts to needy priests."[68]

Persons tried to believe, or at least make others believe, lest they despair altogether of success, that "the heretics were beginning to relax, having little hope of succeeding by cruelty."[69] It was even being said that no more would be put to death for religion. So now was the

---

[66] Ibid., 226. See Mary to Mendoza, 28.ii.1583; (25) 447.

[67] See Leader, *Mary, Queen of Scots in Captivity*, 552–57. A discussion of the date of this letter follows on 557–60.

[68] RP to Agazzari, Paris, 23.vii.1584; (23) 216, Italian and English.

[69] (21) 145–47. See RP to Aquaviva, 23.vii.1584, Paris; (II) f.175; (23) 217–21, Italian, 221–24, English.

time to advance.[70] In fact, the policy of merciless persecution was paying off extremely well for Elizabeth. But there was still strong resistance. By no means all wished the Jesuits and their friends off the scene. George Birkhead, seminary priest and later archpriest, and one whom Persons came to regard as "showing but little favour towards the Society," now made a fulsome acknowledgement to Agazzari of the Jesuit contribution to the mission. He thanked the latter for the benefits he bestowed "by constantly sending such eminently prudent and holy men to convert it." His compliments were not only for Campion but also Persons, begging him to send others of the same religious order "as soon as possible."[71] As for the Catholics, "quite incredible is the fervor and consolation amid such miseries which our . . . God gives them." Of no small help to them was the translation from the Latin Vulgate done at Rheims in 1582.[72] Birkhead had to admit that this very fervor drove their enemies to even greater bursts of ferocity, but the best acknowledged that "by no other way is the cause of God so honourably promoted or the neck of heresy so soon broken."[73] Persons should not be allowed to retire to Rome but be sent back to England, where his return was ardently awaited. Meanwhile all were looking forward to the second part of his *Book of Resolution*. In view of this kind of encouragement, Aquaviva could no longer delay a reinforcement in the person of William Weston, a man "very learned and singularly virtuous and prudent."[74] Born at Maidstone in Kent in 1550, he was another of the Oxford converts, joining the Douai community in 1572. On November 5, 1575, he entered the Society of Jesus in Rome.[75] His prospects now on English soil in human terms were bleak enough. Everyone's fear of torture after capture was real: "Truly to be hanged," wrote Persons, "is child's play in comparison with being tortured." He hoped that there would now be less of it. True, Lord Burghley was as completely emancipated as any from human feelings in the matter, but he was aware that it did not improve his reputation abroad, at least in Catholic countries. He therefore had printed in English, Latin, French, German, and Italian—Spanish was notably omitted—*The execution of justice in England,* which played down the role of torture in pushing the new religious policy. An answer to it had been produced in English

---

[70] S. to s., 23.vii.; ibid., 223.

[71] (21) 150–53.

[72] See (19) 104. P. Milward, *Religious Controversies of the Elizabethan Age* (London, 1977), 46.

[73] (21) 154f.

[74] Ibid., 156f; (23) 227.

[75] See (30) II, London, 1875, 1–284. New translation by P. Caraman, S.J., *An Autobiography from the Jesuit Underground . . .* (New York, 1955), 22.

and the printing was almost finished. A Latin translation was in preparation for Rome.[76]

Aquaviva's definitive orders for England and Scotland reached Persons in a letter of July 29. Allen, Persons and Weston conferred together towards the end of August before Weston left for England. Emerson, who had been on the coast until August 20 finding out new ways of getting over since the old ones were blocked, now joined them. Two routes had been found by which four or five priests and some eight hundred books in English had already passed over. The journey was expensive because of the risk.[77] Persons replied to Agazzari on August 7, enclosing a copy of Allen's *True, sincere and modest defence* . . ., with a promise of the same to follow in Latin.[78] Persons wanted Mannaerts to send Fr. Marshal after Weston, who would go in first with Emerson. The latter would give Weston the necessary guiding and briefing until he was sufficiently acquainted with the hostile environment to fend for himself. Emerson was also adept in the perilous task of book distribution. Claude Mathieu was due to go to Rome to represent his province in a forthcoming meeting of Jesuit procurators. He would be able to give the General an accurate and sympathetic picture of English affairs. With a thought for Paget and Morgan, Persons urged the General to warn Pigenat "not to believe everyone who talks to him about our mission without conferring with those who have handled it from the very beginning."[79]

Weston's passage into England was well organized beforehand, Persons arranging a "special boat" to land at a point on the coast owned by a Catholic gentleman. He would put them on the road to London, "where there are many houses equipped to receive them."[80] Thomas Marshal came to Rouen with Weston; but, although he seemed "a good priest," he did not square up to Persons's expectations for a missioner.[81] Accompanied by Ralph Emerson as planned, Weston

---

[76] RP to Aquaviva, 23.vii.1584 (v. supra). The Catholic work was Allen's *A True, Sincere and Modest Defence of English Catholics*. The Latin translation was incorporated in the *Concertatio* (Trèves, 1588). Both works edited and translated into English by R. M. Kingdon (New York: Cornell University, 1965); P. Milward, *Religious Controversies*, 69f.

[77] RP to Aquaviva, Paris, 20.viii.1584; (VI) F.G.651/640, n.f., a.l.s., Italian.

[78] RP to Agazzari, Paris, 7.viii.1584; (23) 226, Italian, 226f, English.

[79] RP to Aquaviva, 20.viii.1584 (v. supra).

[80] See s. to s., 15.ix.1584, Paris; (23) 240–2, Italian, 242–3, English; see ibid., 241, n.(6).

[81] Thomas Marshall entered the Society of Jesus 1574–75, aged 29; another Marshall was Robert Southwell's fellow novice in Rome, who died on 13.ii.1581. See (23), 241, n.(8), and 245. Neither are to be confused with John Martial, cofounder with Allen of the VEC in 1568.

embarked at Dieppe for England on September 12.[82] For all his experience, Emerson was captured and began an imprisonment which lasted twenty years. He was not helped by the fact that his consignment of books, which was also seized, included *Leicester's Commonwealth*, the best-known *chronique scandaleuse* of the whole period.[83]

By September 10 Persons knew that the General wanted him to stay in France. He therefore set up a modest establishment at Rouen, "a most convenient town on account of its nearness to the sea." Here he could organize crossings to England and arrange for the import of books, Bibles, holy oils, chalices, and vestments.[84] Conditions there were never worse and money was scarce. Even so, there were some three hundred priests managing to work and survive albeit as homeless wanderers. There were now nearly two hundred in the college at Rheims, with about the same number "living precariously outside the seminaries." Many recusants were in prison, especially in London, York, and Hull. The laity were only allowed to receive visitors after midday to prevent Mass somehow being said, while priests were not permitted visitors at all, so as to prevent recourse to the sacraments. Anyone bringing alms was haled before the magistrate. Some complaint was made to the Bishop of London, who held "first place among the inquisition." He was reported to have said, "Let the papists feed on their own excrements."[85] Small wonder if some preferred death to imprisonment.

Perhaps there was exaggeration in some of the stories reaching Rouen, but the government was much concerned to whip up maximum hatred against the recusants, making the most of propaganda arising out of the Parry-Throckmorton plots. The consequences could only be dire in an age which entertained no qualms about cruelty. Allen's sister was among those who fled to Rheims. Even children, as in the case of Worthington's sons, were subjected to whipping and other torments to make them inform against their parents.[86] Francis Throckmorton was executed on July 10, although he had been assured his life

[82] (21) 156–59; RP's notes on the mission end with an extract from Weston's autobiography; (30) II, 66 et seq. See (23) lxvi.

[83] Authorship is still disputed. P. Holmes, *Resistance and Compromise* (1982), attributes it to RP but see (23) lxvi and L. Hicks, "The Growth of a Myth: Fr Persons and *Leicester's Commonwealth*," *Studies*, Spring 1957, 91–105. See RP to Ribadeneira, 10.ix.1584, Rouen; (23) 227–40; for a discussion of the date and text of this letter, see ibid., n.(1), 227–29.

[84] (23) 236.

[85] Ibid., 237.

[86] Ibid., 239.

would be spared.[87] Persons saw this as an act of revenge for the murder of the Prince of Orange.[88]

Persons's harrowing account of the English scene addressed to Ribadeneira on September 10 was no doubt intended to unlock the treasure chests of Europe as well as wring all hearts. He spent some time in Paris in September but returned to Rouen at the end of the month to escape the plague.[89] By October Allen and Persons had agreed to abandon all thought of strong-arm tactics, at least for the time being.[90] From now on, they would be content to wield the sword of the spirit.[91] A cipher letter of Persons's at this time, not only urging Mary to escape but also trying to keep alive Parma's interest in the *empresa*, contradicts this, but its authenticity seems unlikely.

Not surprisingly, there was a dearth of reliable news from England. Had Weston arrived safely? By the end of November there had been no word of Holt for three months. Heywood was more closely guarded than ever, and there was a strong likelihood he would soon be joining the martyrs. News arrived on November 23 of the Queen's triumph in capturing Crichton. Persons felt obliged to leave Rouen for Paris to escape another death threat. Certainly, Hay, Pigenat, and Aquaviva all referred to some danger of the kind.[92] It was believed, quite reasonably, that it all had to do with the discovery of *Leicester's Commonwealth* in Emerson's luggage and the conjecture that Persons was the author. At all events, Aquaviva suggested he come to Rome. Certainly, Elizabeth and her council had some reason for anxiety in spite of their success with the persecution and in getting the *empresa* scotched. Anjou died on June 10, Orange was murdered at Delft on July 10, and Parma began the siege of Antwerp in August. Brussels and Mechlin were also being invested.[93] In October, by way of some response, an "association" of English nobles and gentlemen was formed to ensure "her Majesty's defence and safety" against all who

---

[87] RP to Agazzari, 7.viii.1584, Paris; (23) 226, Italian, 226f, English. The original description has been lost. Only Grene's summary survives (II) f.460.

[88] RP to Aquaviva, 12.i.1584, v. supra. (23) 188, n.(1).

[89] RP to Agazzari, 30.ix.1584, Rouen; (23) 245, Latin and English translation of Grene's summary. Bassett died at Rheims about the end of November. See ibid., n.(1).

[90] RP to Mary, Queen of Scots, 10.[x].1584; (23) 246–52 and n.(1), English decipher. The Queen's letter which drew forth this reply is no longer extant and there is reason to believe it was at least edited in F. Walsingham's workshop.

[91] (23) 246, and n.(1). Again, her answer is a decipher in Phelippes's hand and so doubtful evidence. We believe it if we want to.

[92] RP to Aquaviva, 25.xi.1584, Paris; (23) 260–62, Latin, 262f, and 260, n.(1).

[93] See P. Geyl, *The Revolt of the Netherlands, 1555–1609* (London, 1932), 192–95.

might attempt to take her life. Persons was an obvious target.[94] It is more likely, however, that Burghley and Walsingham were interested rather in a kidnap attempt along the lines of Dr. Story's experience in August 1570 and the attempt made against Hugh Owen in 1608.[95] Certainly, Rouen was on a waterway and Paris was on the Seine, so that it would have been quite possible to snatch the Jesuit, batten him under hatches, and take him to England for an ordeal far worse than assassination.

In spite of the depressing picture of persecution, by the end of 1584 the Catholic resistance in England was forcing the government to think again. The sight of good men dying for a faith which had nothing to do with politics, as far as the martyrs were concerned, was infectious. Nor did persecution make a favorable impression abroad. The council, therefore, now leaned to a policy of sending priests and others into exile rather than to the gallows after binding them to an oath not to return in the Queen's lifetime.[96] But they were by no means eager to go. Europe was a dubious refuge. Many of the exiles, even the important ones, had died, "and for the most part from sheer starvation."[97] Most of the younger and more intelligent found their way to Rheims, where they tried to continue or take up studies. Some, as we have seen, joined Parma's army. But Rome, by this time, was coming under the Paget spell. Rheims should be restricted rather than enlarged. Access should be limited, so that there was no danger of it becoming an all-purpose hostel for emigrés.[98] These were Allen's instructions, and he incurred some blame for not executing his orders more exactly. Replying to the charges, Allen pointed out that the exiles were usually men of social standing and that, if they were turned away from Rheims, they would flock to Rome, increasing problems for that city.[99] Persons continued to insist that the heretics were flagging and victory was just round the corner. The Earl of Huntingdon in the north and Leicester everywhere had the reputation of being the most cruel of the persecutors.[100] Scotland provided the best hope. True, Crichton was in the Tower of London, but Gordon was still at large

[94] Burghley to Cobham, 27.x.1584; (14) III, 72.

[95] A. Loomie, *The Spanish Elizabethans* (New York, 1963), 90f. For Storey, see (29) Eliz., 27 and 389–415 passim.

[96] RP to Aquaviva, 25.xi.1584 (supra), 261, n.(3). The first batch of prisoners was exiled in January 1585. By September 70 were expelled.

[97] Ibid., 263.

[98] Como to Ragazzoni, 8.x.1583–86 (Rome/Paris); P. Blet, *Girolamo Ragazzoni . . . Correspondance . . . 183–86* (Rome/Paris, 1962), 217. See (9) 242 and (23) 262, n.(4).

[99] Allen to Como, 16.i.1585; (9) 244–46, Latin.

[100] RP to Agazzari, 6.xii.1584, Rouen; (23) 264–66.

and active. All in Paris were agreed that the Scottish mission should not be interrupted.[101] Even those in the Tower or elsewhere—Crichton, Patrick Addy, Emerson, a novice brother, and Heywood—were all giving an edifying example, thus pushing the government towards a new law making exile rather than death the penalty.[102]

Persons left Paris for Rouen about the end of October.[103] Here he stayed with Brinkley, who "translated Loartes' book under the name of James Sanker, and Mr Flinton, an honest merchant," who helped Persons with the "second edition of the book of resolution much augmented."[104] He was set back by shortage of funds, and in mid-January by "pains in the chest" which were severe enough to prevent his writing letters. News from Rome was exasperating thanks mainly to the continuing antics of Mr. Bagshaw. Mindful of the remedy so often applied to himself in his younger days, Persons thought, unwisely we may believe, that Bagshaw even now was by no means too old for a whipping, and in public. His real need was to be taken down a peg. It was important that his kind should not be allowed to leave their superiors looking "fearful and therefore contemptible."[105] Persons, the sixteenth-century army officer, is dealing with insubordination in the ranks.

The Parliament which began its session on November 23, 1585, and ended on March 29, 1586, was also in a militant mood. Much moved by the plot scares of 1584, it enacted that any priest ordained overseas by papal authority who returned to England was guilty of high treason. On September 2, 1584, Mary, the eye of the potential storm, was moved from Sheffield to Wingfield Manor and the custody of Sir Ralph Sadler and John Somers.[106] Persons knew of the

---

[101] S. to s., 13.xii.1584; (23) 266–68.

[102] RP to Aquaviva, 25.xi.1584; (23) 262. RP also wrote to Agazzari on 25.xi. See s. to s., 13,xii.1584; (VI) F.G.651/640 for question of transferring the title to the Crown to the King of Denmark to block the Catholic succession of Mary, Queen of Scots.

[103] Edmund Hay wrote on 29.x.1584 that RP had left Paris fearing for his life; (1) 35, n.

[104] (1) 35. Gaspar Loarte: born at Medina del Campo, joined the Society of Jesus in 1552, lived mostly in Italy, rector of Jesuit houses in Genoa and Messina before returning to Spain. He died at Valencia on 8.x.1578. Loarte's book referred to appeared in Spanish in 1574, Italian (Venice) in 1575. Brinkley's translation appeared in 1582 as *The first booke of the Christian exercise appertayning to resolution. Wherein are layed downe the causes and reasons that should move a man to resolve hym selfe to the service of God: and all the impedimentes removed which may lett the same*, by "S.I." The preface was signed "R.P."—presumbly Robert Persons. For further editions, translations, and discussion of this work, see de Backer and Sommervogel.

[105] RP to Agazzari, 17.1.1585; (VI) F.G.651/640, ff.14r–15v, a.l.s., Italian.

[106] (23) 268, n.(1).

move some time before December 22.[107] By this time he could no more withdraw from politics than could a walnut shell from a whirlpool. But again we must wonder if a letter to the Scottish queen of February 15, 1585, was really his.[108] One would expect Persons to show a better understanding of the closeness of her imprisonment. Instead, he almost rebukes her for not replying to his earlier letters of October 10 and 12, 1584.[109] This could indicate that Mary herself was suspicious of the true origin of these letters. These could, of course, have come from Walsingham's office with the intention of trapping her into indiscretion. Few things could be more compromising to one in her situation than a correspondence with Persons, as she must have realized. Persons tells her he is at Rouen, still hoping she may effect her escape or be released, although the hope seems to be fading.[110] If this was government bait, wisely, she does not seem to have risen to it.

Persons's lasting contribution to the recusant cause was undoubtedly his writing, and in this area the most lasting of all was his spiritual writing. He had been engaged for some two years already on a systematic treatise of Christian ascetical practice designed for the educated laity, working it in between other commitments. He planned to distribute the material through three books. "The first was about resolution, the second about how to make a good beginning, the third was about means to perseverance." The first book had been finished, albeit more sketchily than he could have wished, but he had managed to print 2,500 copies, a large undertaking for those times. It was bought up at once, by Protestants as well as Catholics, "thanks to the novelty of the subject" and because Protestants "know nothing of devotional matters and do not write about them."[111] Indeed, "our heretics" had prevailed upon the Queen to let it be printed at home albeit with the expurgation deemed appropriate. Another man who scented a best-seller was a certain barber of Rouen who arranged for a second printing without the author's knowledge, a misdemeanor easily forgiven, if not by the author, in the days before formal copyright procedures had been established. Unfortunately, his text was much corrupted.

---

[107] RP to Agazzari, 22.xii.1584, Rouen; (23) 269.

[108] All that survives is a copy, presumably Thomas Phelippes's decipher or alleged decipher; PRO, *Mary, Q. of Scots,* 15, No. 21; see (23) 269.

[109] See (23) 269, n.(2); and Allen to Mary, Queen of Scots, 5.ii.1585; (9) 247f.

[110] RP to Aquaviva, 12.ii.1584/5, [Rouen?]; (VI) F.G.651/640, n.f. The key persons referred to were in cipher in the original.

[111] Ibid. This refers to *The first booke of the Christian exercise* . . . (v. supra, n.104) of 1582. *A Christian directorie* . . . was printed in August, 1585; (69) 74f.

In February 1585 there seemed to be a lull in affairs such as might allow Persons to go to Rome to spend from eight to ten months at Sant'Andrea, where he could do his tertianship and pursue his literary interests in the calmer atmosphere of the novitiate. Allen, the active administrator, had little sympathy for Persons's bookish tendencies, however, and desired him to remain in Rouen. He was under some pressure from Mannaerts to go to Flanders but was reluctant to become an attorney for the exiles. Certainly, Paris in mid-February held out little attraction, since envoys were awaited from England who would discuss with representatives from the Low Countries, in the presence of the French king, measures to help the Dutch insurgents fighting Parma.[112] Persons's next movements, however, were determined by yet another turn of fortune. Twenty-six Catholics were waiting on the shores of England to be shipped to France as exiles. The Jesuit felt bound to assist them as far as he could. In any case, since heresy had appeared in the pages of the local literary pirate's version of his book, it was imperative to produce a corrected version forthwith and also to prepare the two volumes to follow. He admitted to "small ability and knowledge in spiritual matters" and still hoped to enjoy the Roman experience at the end of the summer. "I think this would help me to make bread to feed me for the rest of my life; for I am aware of the enervating effect of this daily contact with worldly affairs." But all depended on permission from Aquaviva.[113]

The Jesuits Heywood, Bosgrave, and John Hart were among the exiles awaited at Rouen. Crichton was expected to join their number shortly. Persons, with Pigenat's approval, was ready to offer them hospitality until Aquaviva decided where to send them. Holt in Scotland was still doing well, but the Master of Gray, recently on embassy to England, seemed untrustworthy.[114] About the end of March, Persons visited Allen in Rheims. He persuaded the Jesuit to change his plans completely and go to Flanders after all, staying in a Jesuit college near the sea so as to make it reasonably easy to stay in contact with events in England.[115] In the meantime, Persons's brother, George, had become a Catholic. He had been well received in Rome by Agazzari and the General, but Robert was sensitive on the issue of nepotism. He advised

[112] RP to Aquaviva, 12.ii.1584/5 (v. supra, n.110). (VI) F.G.651/640 contains forty-seven unbound letters of RP not used in (23).

[113] Ibid., Postscript. For E. Bunny's Anglican edition of *A book of Christian exercise* . . . of 1584, see (69) 74.

[114] Ibid.

[115] RP to Agazzari, 30.iii.1585, Rheims; (VI)F.G.651/640, f..22, a.l.s.

George, all the same, to come to Flanders where he might be able to secure him a modest competence in return for service, but no more.[116]

It was in February 1585 that Lord Paget made an unexpected advance to Fr. Robert through Agazzari in Rome, urging reconciliation with his brother Charles and with Thomas Morgan. Owen Lewis wrote in similar vein to Allen. This party, too, saw clearly the threat to any influence the English might exert in Rome or elsewhere while they remained disunited. Persons wished for harmony but found it impossible in conscience to promote a reconciliation which involved surrender of his own convictions. He prayed for them daily and remembered them at Mass, but he realized that there was no real possibility of compromise. What they wanted from him was not reconciliation but capitulation. The others could have said the same. In the end, they must all agree to differ, as charitably as they might, which was not much.[117]

Persons left Rouen at about the end of March but reached Louvain only in mid-April, staying there some three weeks. He was already exploring the possibility of opening a new way into England by the ports of Flanders, since those of France were now insecure by reason of the religious wars. The Flemish provincial agreed that St. Omer would be the best base of operations until Antwerp was relieved. St. Omer was near three ports, Dunkirk, Gravelines, and Calais. With the backing of Guise and Parma, they would hardly experience difficulties with the port authorities.[118]

Pope Gregory XIII died on April 10, 1585, an event inserting a comma rather than a period in the history of the times. In May, however, Persons almost reached the conclusion of his own career. "Travelling from Brussels to Termonde, I lost everything I carried when our convoy was attacked and broken by the soldiery. Many were carried off prisoner [to Mechlin]."[119] Once again, Persons's horsemanship and his eye for horseflesh saved him as he "only escaped by the goodness of the horse." But there was a larger victory on May 26 involving the destruction of some two thousand of the enemy and the capture of thirty-two large ships; this brought the fall of Antwerp that much nearer.[120] Persons, no pacifist, reveled in the victory. "War is

---

[116] Ibid. Postscript.

[117] RP to Agazzari, 3.iv.1585, (VI) ibid., ff.24f, a.l.s. From Masière on the Franco-Flemish frontier; impossible to identify with certainty.

[118] RP to Aquaviva, 10.v.1585; (VI) ibid., a.l.s., Italian; see (23) 270.

[119] Or Dendermonde in East Flanders, twenty-six kilometers east of Ghent.

[120] RP to Agazzari, 28.v.1585; (VI) ibid., f.17, a.l.s.; See RP to Aquaviva, same date, infra.

lawful and expedient in divers cases." No Norman bishop or Knight Templar could have combined more readily than Fr. Robert the roles of priest and warrior.[121]

Persons had his permission to go to Rome in a letter of April 9, although he could hardly take advantage of it for some months.[122] On the way to St. Omer, which he reached about July 12, there was yet another narrow escape. He was evidently spending time with the soldiers in the camp. The enemy "attacked us between Ghent and Oudenarde and captured one of the lancers who was our escort, wounding two merchants. But by God's mercy, I escaped with the loss of only my cloak. Had they taken me, I would have gone without delay to pay a visit to good Fr Crichton."[123] In addition he still had health problems. He was under a doctor's care for an inflammation in one eye and, though he had been bled three times that summer, he did "not feel any better yet."

About this time an agitation commenced, especially among the exiles of the Paget group in Paris, for the appointment of bishops in England. Persons, changing his earlier opinion, thought it inopportune in present circumstances. A greater problem was the growth of anti-English feeling, as Elizabeth began to assume a more direct role in the war in the Netherlands. On July 24, "all the English merchants in [St. Omer] were arrested and put in prison."[124] Worst of all, perhaps, in mid-August, "Allen lay at death's door having been unable to pass water for three days." Allen himself, Barrett, and others begged Persons to come at once to Rheims. On his arrival, Persons found that Allen had departed six days before for the baths at Spa leaving orders that the former should follow him.[125] The journey took Persons some five days on horseback.

While still at Rheims, Gilbert Gifford, one of the Paget party, paid Persons a visit making "great protestation of affection" and expressing a desire to make an Ignatian retreat in a Jesuit house.[126] Gifford was, of course, acting the spy on Persons, hoping that he would trust him with letters to post. Persons was no mean practitioner himself when it came to espionage. While he had been preparing his Italian journey at St. Omer, to get "true and reliable information" on preparations against Parma in England, Persons, through a Protestant

---

[121] RP, *The Christian Directory . . .* , Part I, chap. 2.

[122] RP to Aquaviva, 28.v.1585, [Louvain]; (VI) ibid., f.44 r/v, a.l.s.

[123] RP to Agazzari, 12.vii.1585, St. Omer; (23) 270f.

[124] S. to s., 25.vii.1585, St. Omer; (23) 272.

[125] S. to s., 12.viii.1585; (VI) ff.35–36, a.l.s.

[126] RP to Agazzari, 12 and 16.viii. (v. supra). PS.

captain, found an agent to send posthaste to England on the pretext of bringing back a couple of horses. He not only got the horses, together with Leicester's passport, "but was very well received in the court and allowed to take part in their day-to-day deliberations." On his return, Persons sent his information by way of two messengers, one to the camp and one to Rheims. The man who went to the camp was captured and all his letters carried back to England. However, Persons was confident they could not damage any Catholic or prejudice any business in hand. It was the man who went to Rheims who brought back news of Allen's illness.[127]

By this time, the students in the English College, Rome, had discovered new cause for complaint: the Jesuits were finding vocations among them for their own order. As a countergesture, they began to recruit among themselves for other orders, especially the Dominicans, who were taken to be the Jesuits' greatest rivals. Unfortunately, the college authorities do not seem to have shown the humor or resourcefulness that the occasion demanded. Seven or eight students left on their own initiative to join the Dominicans, although once the demonstration had served its turn, they returned to the world, as the phrase is. While the Jesuits showed less than the savoir faire one might have expected in handling the situation, skilled English government agents were doubtless at work, as one would expect.[128]

So serious did the trouble stirred up for the Jesuit regime in the English College, Rome, become this year that Sixtus V sent two bishops, of Piacenza and Castro respectively, to report. They found no fault with the regime, but they deemed it prudent to transfer Agazzari to the Jesuit college in his native Siena. Allen was urged to come to Rome to see the problem at first hand.[129] Bagshaw had clearly emerged as the storm center. Perhaps Persons was right in thinking that Bagshaw had been dealt with too gently. Certainly, Agazzari had tried "by every means of charity and courtesy" to soften the blow of his being sent away as a necessary condition of peace. "He procured not only that he should be ordained for Mass, but also that a good viaticum be granted him, and besides the viaticum a good number of crowns." The latter he used, it seems, to buy himself a doctorate at Padua on the way home. Allen was angry because it was done without

---

[127] Ibid.

[128] See L. Hicks, "An Elizabethan Propagandist: The Career of Solomon Aldred"; (32) 181 (5.vi.1945) pp. 181–91; (58) 88.

[129] See (58) 89 and (9) lxxxiii. For his account of VEC events, RP used from the archives "Scritture dei secolari, bundle 29" and "Lib.304" ("Memorabilia exhibita . . . contra Archidiaconum Camaracensem et D. Mauritium 1579") RP relied too much on memory. The register is the most reliable document for dates. See (1) 101f, n.

his superiors' consent and after he had studied theology for only a year in Rome. Allen therefore refused to keep him in Rheims, as he wanted, and sent him into England.[130] Bagshaw never apostatized or repudiated Catholicism, but he became so choked with resentment, frustrated ambition, and a desire for revenge on the Jesuits, whom he took to be mainly responsible for his troubles, that he soon found himself sympathizing and even collaborating with the regime in England that hated all things Catholic. On more than one occasion, he did the work of an informer for Elizabeth's council. Very likely he was influenced subconsciously by the fact that for a papist to hate Hispanophiles and Jesuits was the way to a quieter life, if not formal toleration.

Brinkley was now proposed as holder of a watching brief in Paris for England, Scotland, and France, while Robert's brother George did a similar service in St. Omer.[131] Allen and Persons left Rheims for Rome on September 23, moving by slow stages because Allen was still convalescent.[132] They arrived on November 4.[133]

---

[130] (21) 118f. Sega's report of viii.1585; (31) 428–54.

[131] RP to Cosimo Massi (Parma's secretary), 20.ix.1585, Rheims; (23) 272f, Italian, 273f, English.

[132] They were not summoned by Sixtus V in connection with the "enterprise," certainly not RP. See (23) lxxi, n.3.

[133] See (58) 89; (9) lxxxvii; (23) lxxi–lxxii. From now there is little biographical material for RP until he left Rome again and resumed business by letter. See (23) lxxii.

Chapter Eight

The Failure of the Empresa: 1586–1588

E arly in April 1586, Allen and Persons visited the Prince of Parma's son, then in Rome for his devotions and tourism, to enlist his support for two projects, namely, the empresa and Allen's promotion to cardinal. The young man was not particularly interested in either.[1] Martyrdoms seemed likely to continue in England, and on May 8 Persons accompanied two future martyrs, Henry Garnet and Robert Southwell, to the Milvian Bridge on their way to the mission.[2] Even Persons was beginning to abandon hope of the enterprise which might have made martyrs unnecessary; but he went on working for it all the same. The tide in the affairs of men which should have been taken at the flood seemed already past—but perhaps not.[3] Persons had raised the connected subject of Allen's promotion with Idiaquez during his visit to Lisbon in 1582.[4] Philip II had promised to move in the matter, but to date he had left the promise unfulfilled. He too was a busy man, as Persons well knew. However, the chance of giving him a timely reminder on both counts was offered by Miguel Hernandez, a Spanish chaplain from Flanders who was on his way to Spain. Along with a letter, he took with him a copy of Sander's *De schismate* recently edited with notes by Persons himself.[5]

About mid-August 1586, the Duke of Guise had two visitors from Scotland. One was sent on to Spain forthwith, the other to Rome with letters from Huntley, Morton, and Lord Claud Hamilton.[6] These had a plan to free James from the Anglophile regime. The best course would be to divert Elizabeth's attention and resources by war, but otherwise the conversion of Scotland could be effected by two or three thousand crowns a month for the hiring of soldiery. Persons was not

---

[1] RP to Massi, Rome, 6.iv.1586 (v. supra).

[2] (16) 168.

[3] RP to J. de Idiaquez, Rome, 20.v.1586; (23) 276–78, Italian, 278–80, English.

[4] (23) 277, n.(2).

[5] See (23) 278, n.(3). Hernandez was a pioneer chaplain to the Catholic forces in Flanders. (57) 406f.

[6] RP to Card. Farnese, Rome, 22.viii.1586; (23) 280–82, Italian, 283–85, English. See 280, n.(2).

persuaded by this naive suggestion; but if the original was sent on he may have believed that he received a letter from Mary, Queen of Scots, on May 31, 1586. This letter is only known to us in a cipher copy in the hand of Thomas Phelippes. This means at least that Burghley was well aware of the letter and its contents. Part of the latter at least suggests another of Walsingham's contrivances, a link in the chain of "evidence" which would drive the Scottish queen under the axe at Fotheringhay. The letter came from Chartley, from which close prison one cannot believe that Mary was able to smuggle out any genuine missive, especially at this time.[7] She assures Persons of her "immense consolation" in knowing that King Philip has entrusted her deliverance to Parma. She also "begs earnestly" that no account be made of "any danger to her life" but all should go forward "for the restoration of God's honour in that realm."[8] The enigma of Mary's letters need not further detain us.

Clearer by far is the account of Persons's dealings with the seminaries. As always, the most deserving works of the Lord were on a shoestring. The Rheims college had already produced "more than forty martyrs and nearly five hundred priests," but it was experiencing "great and present need." There were "two hundred or more" mouths to feed and "the travelling and other expenses of thirty or forty men who are sent to England every year." Persons had urged the cardinal-protector to persuade the Pope to increase his allowance, but he "could not be made to realize matters at that time"—August 1586. An appeal was made to Farnese, one of the wealthiest cardinals, since the present pension was only "150 crowns a month and does not amount to a fifth part of the necessary expenditure."[9] Pope Sixtus V was usually too much occupied with the problems of his own see and realm to have much attention or money to spare for shoring up the crumbling furthest frontiers of the Church.

Persons was able to take some comfort in good news from the fighting front. Neuss, near Düsseldorf, fell to the all-conquering Parma in July. "And we trust in God that one day we shall see the same thing happen in London. . . . Day by day they make fresh martyrs in that realm."[10] In the event, there was consolation also from the Holy See. Thanks to Farnese, following Persons's plea, the Pope issued the brief

---

[7] RP's memory or record may have been at fault. The true date of this letter was 25.v.(?). (23) 281, n.(3).

[8] Ibid.

[9] RP to Farnese, VEC, 22.viii.1586; (23) 280–82, Italian, 283–85, English.

[10] (23) 284f.

Afflictæ et crudeliter vexatæ on September 3.[11] Striking the hot iron again, it was probably about now that Persons presented Farnese with a memorandum urging the creation of the English cardinal without delay—that is, without waiting for an answer from Spain.[12] His most cogent reason was the need for a rallying point with authority above parties to decide policy and settle disputes. He might also have the persuasive power required to push Philip to the empresa. Some of the impoverished gentlemen could also be supported as members of his entourage, presuming that he would be in receipt of a pension proportionate to his status.[13]

William Holt left Scotland in March or April 1586, arriving in Paris on June 23.[14] Investigating the troubles in the English College, Rome, the Pope wisely decided that a rector of the same race was needed to deal with the peculiar temperament of the English, which was more than Italians could cope with. He accepted Allen's suggestion that Holt be appointed to restore some measure of happiness to the members of the happy breed in that place. His appointment was finalized on October 24.[15] Restlessness in the college subsided for some years under the direction of a man who had known the difficulties of the mission at very close quarters. Persons left the college early in October to become Latin secretary to the General for some six months.

By mid-March 1587 Count Olivares, Spanish ambassador in Rome, was authorized to support Allen's promotion. This was effected in the consistory of August 7.[16] Meanwhile, on March 18 Allen and Persons produced a joint memorandum on the future occupant of the English throne. In the background was a Spanish claim.[17] The Pope should not be brought into any of it, since the Roman sense of security and secrecy was virtually nil.[18] Rome was a place of parties and factions where no secrets were hid, certainly not for long. The succession question should be held over, since it was bound to be controversial. Certainly, the Guise party in France and the Scots and their queen would not be supportive of a Spanish claimant. Neither would the English, Catholic or not. Better present the world first of all with the fait accompli of a successful "enterprise." Then would be time to

---

[11] (23) lxxiii and n.(132).

[12] (23) 285f, Italian, 286f, English, a.l.s., RP's hand. See 285, n.(1).

[13] (23) 286 and 285, n.1.

[14] (23) 303, n.(2).

[15] See (35) III, 363.

[16] See (23) 285, n.(1).

[17] (23) 289–92, Italian, 292–94, English.

[18] See (23) 289, n.(1).

decide. The only declared Spanish intention at the outset should be "to revive the Catholic faith and avenge the intolerable injuries" inflicted on King and Church. True, Mary might be killed in the course of the action, and then the Spanish candidate would be the most obvious one. Cardinal Allen would determine the matter finally through Parliament. True again, the will of Parliament depended on who packed it. And so the "would be's" and "must be's" ran on.[19] Olivares referred to the memorandum in his letter of March 23, 1587, to Philip. Whatever the hazards, the Pope would have to be convinced of the legitimacy of Philip's claim to the English crown.[20] About this time, Allen and Persons drew up a formal memorandum for Philip "concerning the English succession and the expedition against England."[21]

The situation was simplified to some extent by the execution of the Scottish queen, news of which arrived in Rome on March 24. Before this somber event, Persons was already researching the descent of the house of Lancaster to bolster Philip's claim. Even if this had been perfectly clear, he could hardly have vindicated his right without recourse to arms, as Persons thought. It was not perfectly clear, for it derived from events some two centuries old; but might could and should make it right.[22] Moreover, Mary's killing provided a perfect and sufficient motive on the emotional level. "Vengeance due for the blood of the Queen of Scotland" and her last will and testament "written in his favour," as it was claimed, were sufficient title in themselves, to say nothing of the insult and injury he had received from Elizabeth.[23]

William Holt needed a successor in Scotland to hold the lords in loyalty "to his Catholic Majesty."[24] It was Holt before his departure who persuaded them to send a representative to Spain. The disastrous choice was Robert Bruce, a spy in the pay of the English government. He reached Spain about the early autumn of 1586, and returned in May 1587, with a gift of money from the people he was about to betray.[25] True to his own cause and vocation, however, Persons was admitted to final vows in the Society of Jesus in Rome on May 9.[26] Unaware of Bruce's real loyalty, Persons still wanted Holt to return to

---

[19] (23) 294.

[20] (23) 289, n.(1).

[21] (23) 295–99, Italian, 299–303, English. See Olivares to Philip II, 27.iii.1587; ibid., 303, n.(1).

[22] *A treatise touching the right of Marie of Scotland* (Rouen, 1584).

[23] Allen and RP, Memorandum, 23.iii.1587; (23) 295–303.

[24] "Alcuni casi . . . ," (23) 303–9.

[25] See (23) 304, nn.(3) and (4).

[26] (23) lxxiii.

a scene where he had done much good and won much trust. Persons still envisaged Scotland as the springboard for any attempt on England, and it was vital to have a liaison who was altogether reliable. With his instinct for the power of the pen, he saw that a book was needed "to announce and justify the enterprise," put out in Latin, English, and French at least. It would point out "the multiple bastardy of this Queen Elizabeth, her wicked mode of life, the injuries she has done to all Christendom," especially King Philip, and not least "her excommunication and deposition by the common law and by the bulls of various pontiffs." Philip was invited to comment before the book was put in press. It would not be disseminated before the invasion had actually begun.[27]

From the less than sublime to the not really ridiculous, a question arose in the English College about midsummer as to the desirability or otherwise of continuing the study of polyphonic music. This too engaged some at least of Persons's attention. There was more to the question than met the ear. As far as the ear was concerned, Persons favored Doric rather than Ionic modes, a Platonic reaction. But there was more. "In order to continue the choir, we must necessarily keep in the house besides the chapel-master some boys to sing soprano; and these boys are wicked for the most part owing to their evil behaviour with other choristers."[28] A late twentieth-century readership will hardly need footnotes to explain what are scarcely obscure references.

The consistory of August 7, 1587, which promoted Allen to Cardinal of S. Martinus in Montibus,[29] witnessed sharp speeches from the Pope against Philip II. All the same, Allen's promotion, as something pleasing to the Spaniards, was taken to mean more than the speeches and to be a sign of goodwill, albeit grudging. Mary's death made some gesture towards the English Catholics almost obligatory. Otherwise, while "that most wicked Jezebel continued to reign," the Catholics might give way completely to despair.[30] Undoubtedly, the influence of Parma and to a lesser degree Farnese had been important if not decisive in Allen's promotion, and Persons wrote his acknowledgement to Parma.[31]

So imminent did the invasion of England now seem in February 1588 and so unlikely its failure that Persons in a letter to Parma's

---

[27] (23) 309.

[28] RP to Hoffaeus, Assistant, 6.vi.1587, Rome; (23) 309f Italian, 311f English.

[29] (35) I, 19.

[30] Ibid.

[31] RP to D. of Parma, 20.viii.1587, Rome; (23) 312, Italian, 313, English.

secretary expressed his hope that William Holt and Joseph Creswell, Jesuits, then on the way to Flanders, would actually find him in England.[32] The two Jesuits in question left Rome on February 18 at Allen's request, to be in readiness for the Armada.[33] Persons took Holt's place in the English College as rector by way of temporary measure. He hoped soon to follow them on the road to England.[34] Holt and Creswell received "special instructions" dated February 24 from Aquaviva, although their inspiration and source of information was Persons.[35] They were to put themselves at Parma's disposal, following Allen's directions. They were not to "obtrude themselves in affairs of state." They were to speak for the most part only when spoken to and concentrate on spiritual matters. Holt was superior, Creswell his "consultor," while Weston was over them both. They should be careful what they did, especially when dressed as Jesuits, for if they went "without need to public hostelries in places where we have colleagues, no doubt they would expose themselves to considerable comment."

Success for the total venture was not helped by the diverse aims and interests of the allies. If Philip II regarded the Armada as a costly distraction thrust upon him by circumstances, the Pope saw it as an expensive and almost unnecessary distraction from his mainly Mediterranean interests. He was content that the Catholic powers should use their resources against "the enemies of the faith," but this did not include England, which was not nearly so "harmful to Christian souls" as the pirates of Algiers. Philip had disappointed him in 1585 when he wanted an alliance against the pirates; but the King of Spain was more concerned to revenge the ravages of Drake against Cadiz and Lisbon, and the aid given by Elizabeth to the rebels of Flanders. All the same, Sixtus and Olivares signed an agreement in July 1586 to begin an English expedition in September. Instead of which there had been endless foot dragging and waste of resources.[36]

Sixtus entertained no personal dislike of Elizabeth, although she encouraged the Turks against the Spaniards. It was only her religion, as he said, which prevented her from being his favorite princess; and, even though she was a heretic, he could not be blind to her

---

[32] RP to Massi, 24.ii.1588; (23) 313f, Italian, 314, English.

[33] See (23) lxxiii and 313, n.(1). See Borja de Medina, S.J., "Jesuitas en la Armada contro Inglaterra (1588) . . ."; (43) LVIII (1989), 3–43.

[34] (23) 314.

[35] (23) 361f, Latin, 362f, English; from (VI) *Instructiones, 1577–96.*

[36] See Matteo Brumano, bishop of Mantua, to the D. of Mantua, 27.viii.1588, Rome; (37) X, 604f.

qualities as a ruler.[37] Doubtful of the sincerity of Henry of Navarre's conversion, he thought that Elizabeth might truly be won. Without the influence of Burghley and other courtiers, perhaps she might have been. Certainly, Sixtus repudiated all idea of assassination and made several attempts at reconciliation.[38] Indeed, part of Crichton's mission may have been to establish an understanding.[39] The Pope, then, only assented to the Armada in 1588 as a last resort. The Spaniards felt he was less than generous in helping to foot the bills. Perhaps; but he granted so-called crusade bulls from which considerable sums could be raised.[40] He also seems to have permitted the reissue of Elizabeth's excommunication, although the connected document as it emerged was written in English, in the third person, and undated. William Gifford, avowed enemy of the Jesuits, later claimed it for Persons, but a document so important could plausibly only have come from Allen.[41] No evidence has so far come to light in the Vatican for any formal renewal of the 1570 bull.[42] Olivares certainly named Allen as the author of a manifesto, forwarded to Parma for approval in April 1588, who allowed its publication.[43] This was for distribution after a Spanish landing. On March 30 the Pope launched a great jubilee indulgence throughout Italy, while Allen further contributed to the cause with an opuscule attacking Elizabeth for the scandal of her life public and private.

The fate of the Armada was determined on the night of July 28, 1588, although the saga dragged on till the end of August. In a sense it was the end of the road for Allen. He was left 2,500 crowns in debt; and, although Olivares helped him with a subsidy of 3,000 crowns, he could go "neither backwards nor forwards."[44] Sixtus, whose mood was almost one of "I told you so," was not prepared to help further. Let the Spaniards get on with it. For the rest, good soldiers do not run away; they only make strategic withdrawals. The first intention now was that Allen and Persons, with Spanish connivance, withdraw discreetly to Flanders.[45] In the event, Allen stayed in Rome and Persons went to Spain.

---

[37] Ibid., 299.
[38] Ibid., 300.
[39] Ibid., and Fouqueray, II, 108 et seq.
[40] (37) 312f.
[41] See (31) 277 and n.(2); English ed., n.323.
[42] Ibid., 278; English edition, 324.
[43] Ibid.
[44] Olivares to Philip II, 3.x.1588, Rome; (9) 306f, Spanish.
[45] S. to s., 9.x.1588, Rome; ibid., 308.

The situation for the Catholic English cause generally and for the colleges in particular was now everywhere parlous. Allen informed Como that unless money were forthcoming Rheims could hardly continue.[46] Spain was still the great hope. The precise circumstances of Persons's departure for Spain are difficult to determine. Like King Philip, however, struck though not stricken by one disaster, he was not the man to wait for the second blow, which might prove fatal. He evidently decided, with Aquaviva's permission, to go to the country which might still support the cause now that the reaction in Rome to the latest turn of events had so much stifled interest that it might be left to die. Once again, his vision and refusal to accept defeat produced lasting results. The ensuing nine years produced a memorial to his name in several new colleges overseas, one of which, Valladolid, still flourishes.

Persons left for Spain on November 6, 1588.[47] While on the journey, Henri, duc de Guise, and his brother, the cardinal, were assassinated on the order of Henri III, a circumstance which lent point to Fr. Robert's journey, because they had been the principal support of the Rheims seminary. It was expected that Elizabeth would do her best to follow up this latest success with an attempt to get the seminary suppressed. Unlike the English papists, the French Huguenots were always unashamedly militant in approaching the problem of survival. But in July, to guarantee their own survival, the seminary students joined the citizens to help defend Rheims against a threatening Huguenot army. This had the approval of Dr. Richard Barrett, Allen's successor as president since October 31, 1588.[48] Part of his task was to restore "discipline which had collapsed" perhaps partly as a result of the students having to join the equivalent of a "home guard."[49]

Persons had detailed instructions for his Spanish sojourn, dated from Rome, October 31, 1588. He was to discuss with the King, and such of his ministers as he saw fit, the Society's work for the good of souls and its fidelity in serving His Majesty. An order of the Inquisition forbidding Jesuits in Philip's dominions from going to northern regions must be rescinded. It was a notable irony that a wish so dear to the heart of Lord Burghley should be endorsed by the Spanish Inqui-

---

[46] See Allen to Como, 27.ix.1584, Rheims; (9) 240–42; L. Hicks, "Fr Persons . . . and the seminaries in Spain"; (32) i–vi.1931, 193–204.

[47] L. Hicks, "Fr Persons and the seminaries . . . ," part II, ibid., 410–18.

[48] (9) 310f.

[49] RP's letter of introduction to Fr. Gonzalo de Avila from Aquaviva is dated 6.xi.1588. He is "going to the court to conduct certain business for God's service as you may learn in detail from himself"; (VI) Ep.Gen.Toletan. 5.I, f.29v., Spanish draft. A like letter was addressed to Philip II; ibid.

sition. In any case, it did not apply to others, lay or ecclesiastical, so why to Jesuits? Significantly, Persons was ordered to handle matters "in accordance with our institute, without any intervention in military matters."

Without excessive digression, it seems necessary to explain briefly a complex situation in order to render Persons's work and difficulties in Spain somewhat more comprehensible.[50] From 1586 the Jesuits were undergoing severe internal dissension while still struggling to survive the aftermath of a gruelling dispute with the Order of Preachers—Dominicans—over theological questions concerning the workings of divine grace.[51] The Spanish Jesuits, with easy access to court and society, were often under superiors who were more taken up with external works than with their own communities. This led to a certain laxity in the observance of the Jesuit Constitutions. When the General insisted on more exact observance, some Jesuits concluded that his powers were excessive. Demands were therefore made for a vice-general for Spain, a proposition greatly fostered by the distrust of many Spaniards for anything emanating from Rome.[52]

In March 1586, following some complaint by a Jesuit, Diego Hernandez, several Spanish Jesuits, including a provincial, were arrested by the Inquisition. The latter had three main grounds for concern. Why did the Society accept "new Christians"—those dubiously converted or of Moorish descent—into its ranks? Why were such promoted to positions of responsibility—rectors, provincials, visitors? Why did Jesuits, alone of religious, refuse to accept office under the Inquisition as consultors or examiners—*calificadores*?[53] Aquaviva appealed to the Pope. The Inquisition in Spain provocatively ignored the papal letter seeking further information, and further ordered the Jesuits to surrender all printed copies of papal bulls confirming their privileges. In consequence, Sixtus V, a Franciscan and not otherwise a warm supporter of the Jesuits, sprang to their defence.[54]

---

[50] The question of political involvement by Jesuits was aired in the Fifth General Congregation of 1593; v. infra. For RP's instructions, see Aquaviva to RP, 31.x.1588, Rome; (VI) Tolet.4, f.41.

[51] See (47) III, Madrid, 1909, chap. 3–7, 250–346.

[52] (60) 159. For the larger treatment, see (47) III, 347–504.

[53] (47) III, 369. The main sources on the problems of the period are (VI) Hisp.143, "Perturbationes in Hispania 1580–1606." This volume includes Instructions for RP dated 1589 and the visitation of the professed house and English College, Valladolid, in 1592: also Hisp.144, "Persec.Fratr. 1576–1608," dealing with the cases of Cani, Avendogni, Bagnii, and others. For the general congregations, especially the Fifth of 1593, see (VI) Cong. 1, 1A, 20B, 43–50.

[54] (47) III, 453–75.

As regards its internal problems, it is likely the Society would have been left to settle them in its own way but for the continuing agitation of a small but vociferous body within the order who were ready to appeal to the Inquisition to get their way. Through the Inquisition, the Jesuits Dionisio Vasquez and Enrique Enriquez got an order from the King curbing the freedom of provincials in sending their subjects outside Spain, even those being sent to the normal, triennial meetings of Jesuit "procurators" in Rome. Once again, the Pope intervened to protect the freedom of the Society in observing its own established procedures.[55] As if in reply, the Supreme Council of the Inquisition in a decree of July 4, 1587, forebade Catholics to go to missions or heretical countries without its permission.[56] In August, acting upon directives from the Pope, the nuncio sharply rebuked Cardinal Quiroga, head of the Inquisition, for at least acquiescing in restricting the recourse of the faithful to Rome. Quiroga was now obliged to restore to the Jesuits by way of the nuncio the bulls which had previously been confiscated, an operation only completed by mid-September of 1587.[57]

Aquaviva well knew that, at least from 1586 until well into 1588, the Jesuit dissidents had been sending memorials to King and Inquisition petitioning changes in the Institute. These authorities, however, kept matters to themselves. In fact, the Valladolid inquisitors solicited the Jesuits for memorials, which they passed on to Philip through the cardinal of Toledo.[58] Jesuit superiors were not previously approached even if they knew of it. Information and complaints went to the Pope, however, who passed on a resumé to Aquaviva some time in 1588.[59] From 1587 the Jesuit dissidents agitated for a visitation of the Society in Spain. De Villalba, provincial of Castile, the seat of unrest, tried to appease them by appointing them to office, but Aquaviva was not slow to point out his mistake.[60] There was also a movement for a general congregation, but this was rejected by the "procurators'" congregation which met in Rome on September 1, 1587. Meanwhile Gil González Dávila replaced Villalba early in 1588.[61] By this time, Quiroga and Diego de Chaves, the royal confessor, had persuaded the King to ask the Pope to withdraw certain of the Society's privileges. All was conducted with the usual Spanish secrecy, so neither

---

[55] (60) 160.

[56] (47) III, 397.

[57] Ibid., 398f.

[58] Ibid., 409.

[59] Ibid., 410, 417–20, and notes on sources.

[60] Ibid., 426, 429.

[61] Ibid., 432f.

General nor Spanish provincials knew what was going on.[62] Sixtus agreed to a visitation, to be organized by the nuncio, however, not Quiroga. On November 14, 1587, Philip further insisted in a letter to Olivares on the necessity of such a visitation, because there had been so many complaints. Aquaviva and the nuncio were both foreigners, so they could not be trusted with it. Eventually Pope and Grand Inquisitor agreed on Jeronimo Manrique, bishop of Cartagena, as the man to head it. He admitted to a Jesuit that he had come to court to reform them.[63] Porres, the first Jesuit to get wind of a visitation, and Dávila tried to persuade Manrique not to accept the task and warned him of opposition. Manrique took this as a threat and informed Philip. Porres at the same time submitted a memorial to the King setting out Jesuit objections, mainly that changes in the Institute could only be made by the Holy See and a secular priest, even a bishop, was not the best man to understand the problems of religious. In any case, what the dissidents described as the tyranny of superiors was no more than their ordinary effort to uphold standard discipline.

A tussle now developed between Pope and nuncio, King and Inquisition, the Society and its dissident Spaniards. A solution came nearer when Philip, with no little forbearance, agreed in a letter to Sixtus of December 9, 1588, to leave the final solution to him. At the same time, if there was no visitation, he would "adopt the remedy for [his] realms that seemed most in order to deal with the evils . . . feared."[64] The Pope had given substantial support to Jesuit authorities, but he was by no means happy with the Society, as he made clear to Aquaviva. Even the title seemed presumptuous, while the departures from the norms of monastic life introduced by St. Ignatius could not recommend themselves to those trained in older traditions. On November 10 the Holy Office was ordered to examine the Jesuit Constitutions for errors calling for correction, but all was to be done secretly lest the honor of the order be impugned.[65] In the summer of 1589, Aquaviva heard that the Pope wished to introduce capitular government and election, which would considerably curtail the powers of the general. The system worked well enough for other orders but would have changed the nature of the Society so radically that Aquaviva felt bound to battle on for preservation. First he submitted to the cardinals of the Holy Office a long and persuasive apology for the way things were. Fortunately he gained the sympathetic ear of Cardinal Marcanto-

---

[62] Ibid., 436.

[63] Ibid., 438f.

[64] Ibid., 441.

[65] Ibid., 456.

nio Colonna, who had the ear of the Pope. Aquaviva also mustered support from the north, Emperor Rudolph and Sigismund of Poland being doughty defenders, although even more energetic was Duke William of Bavaria.[66] Sixtus now declared himself content to confine his reforming zeal to certain individual Jesuits who had interfered more than was fitting in matters of state.

In order to stave off what yet might prove a fatal blow, Aquaviva decided to make his own visitation of Jesuit houses in Spain. The idea had come to him first in 1586. He sent José de Acosta, sixteen years a missionary in Peru, six of them as provincial, to Spain early in 1589 to placate King and Inquisition, especially Quiroga, and calm the storm among the Jesuits themselves. The King should be invited to approve the visitors. He requested no exemption from the jurisdiction of the Inquisition, but asked that the Jesuit libraries should not be impounded. The Society as well as the Inquisition had the right to keep prohibited books.[67] It is highly significant that de Acosta was instructed to work with Robert Persons, who would exercise his influence with Philip on behalf of the Spanish provinces and the whole Society, as well as of the English mission.

De Acosta had a certain precedence. He would interview the King first, but it was Persons after him who would present Aquaviva's letter of introduction. De Acosta also had the list of men from whom Philip was invited to choose the visitor in the General's name for the Jesuit provinces of Castile and Toledo. The General's preferences were stated but the King had first choice. Persons would give the General's letter to the Toledo provincial. When Persons had finished his task in Madrid, he was to go to Flanders with a commission appointing him superior of the English Jesuit chaplains as well as superior of the Jesuits in England. The King was to be urged to accept reform in the sense desired by the conforming Jesuit majority. That is, the superiors must be allowed to govern freely and enforce observance.[68] Aquaviva, as a prudent realist, was genuinely anxious to do all he could to fall in with the royal wishes regarding himself and the Society.

It seems no exaggeration to say that Persons now assumed the most important role of his entire career—nothing less than preserver of the Society of Jesus in the form laid down by the founder. Had he failed to convince the King of the rightness of so preserving it, as the vast majority of Jesuits inside as well as outside Spain wished, the Society would have become something very different, something much

---

[66] Ibid., 461.

[67] Ibid., 479f.

[68] See RP's Instructions, (VI) Instit., 188, ff.293–97.

less than a worldwide organization in which the general, acting on papal orders or with papal permission, could work untrammeled anywhere on the globe in accordance with the needs of the Church as they occurred at any moment.

The failure of the Armada marked a watershed in English religio-political history, including that of the Church Established, as well as of the English Catholics. The price Persons paid for his alliance with Spain, as still the only potentially effective friend of the recusants abroad, was the alienation of a growing body of English Catholic opinion at home and in Europe. This included not only influential laymen who resented any kind of clerical incursion into what they took to be their privileged territory, but also a growing number of secular and, later, other priests. It would be unjust to attribute lay resentment merely to jealousy or the prospect of losing influence and therefore income to sacerdotal interlopers. The question could be fairly asked, Was it the business of priests not only to take part in politics but to promote invasion and political change on an international scale? Should they not keep closer to the sacristy? Persons replied in effect that the future of the Catholic cause in England lay by the political path as much as by any other. He was a man of prayer, but militancy was also called for, a circumstance always well understood by continental Protestants, especially the Huguenots.

As we have seen, when the Jesuits first arrived in England, they were looked up to by papist clergy and laity alike as the example to be followed in everything. By this time, however, it seemed to many that the Jesuits had backed a loser and were no longer to be trusted. The Society founded by a Spanish soldier-saint had hitched itself disastrously to the Spanish war machine. True, Jesuits in England were careful to stay out of politics. Their role was spiritual and their undiscriminating treatment as traitors by English law was altogether unjust. Nevertheless, their connection with those on the continent such as Persons, who made no secret of their reliance on Spanish power, gave the English state a pretext, which many could see as a reason, for pursuing all Jesuits everywhere, including those papists, for that matter, who still saw the Society as an object of admiration.

After the Armada, many English Catholics, especially in England, felt the only way forward was by rapprochement with their government. Many Catholics offered their services to the English state to help repel the Armada. They had been contemptuously refused. But the effort to get through to Queen and council must not be abandoned. Many others, however, fully realized that, if there had been no concessions to their faith when the government seemed weaker, there would certainly be no concessions now that its position was almost impregnable. The only concessions would be minor indulgences for those who promised by their hostile attitude to the Hispanophiles to promote division and therefore weakness in the cause. Such would be used. They would not be loved or trusted.

The beginning of a serious rift between Jesuits and secular clergy, or rather some of them, is usually seen in Wisbeach in the mid-1590s. But a truer beginning seems discernible in Spain about 1590 with a secular priest, still a student with the Jesuits, a man of considerable intelligence, resourcefulness, and decided independence of mind. A good politician, he learned early to dissemble and bide his time till the moment seemed ripe for an overture to the English council. Master John Cecil it was who articulated a new trend of thought among the secular clergy on the subject of the Jesuits. Like all such trends, it began as a small trickle; but by the end of the century, finding a channel prepared by the history of the times, it became a flood which threatened to sweep away nearly all that Persons had worked and striven for. Unfortunately, John Cecil's approach involved not so much negotiation as capitulation.

Chapter Nine ≡≡≡
Persons in Spain: 1589–1592 ≡≡≡

José de Acosta and Persons reached the Spanish court early in 1589. Against Persons's instructions and the feeling of the Spanish Jesuits, the King interviewed Fr. Robert first on February 6 for about two hours.[1] After treating of English affairs, Persons took up the matter of Spanish Jesuits going to evangelize in northern countries, something so far forbidden by the Inquisition, lest their faith be defiled by contact with alien pitch. Philip listened sympathetically as Persons broached the main subject, namely, the visitation. The Jesuit Institute should not be changed. Neither should the Spanish provinces be cut off from Rome, as would happen if an independent vice-general was appointed. Such a move would cause those of other nations to dislike the Spanish Jesuits. Nevertheless, Jesuits everywhere revered the King of Spain whatever their nationality.[2] Unfortunately, in Spain rebels were in control in the Society and superiors lacked heart or courage to touch or teach them, thanks to the support they found in the Inquisition. Aquaviva suffered much over this division, although there was no one more devoted to the King of Spain and his interests. Nothing had hurt him more than to hear that the King was not pleased with him, although he knew no reason for his discontent.[3]

The King listened sympathetically and sent Persons to Juan de Idiaquez, his secretary, to expound it all again. De Acosta, having offered the proposed list of visitors and recounted the other points of his instructions, was told to await a reply. The decision given on January 16 was that Philip did not wish to come between Aquaviva and his order and he would allow him to appoint the visitors.[4] Aquviva returned thanks immediately. De Acosta published the names already on his list in the hope of royal approval: one each for Portugal, Castile with Toledo, and Andalusia with Aragon, this latter taken by de Acosta. On March 20 and 30, Persons wrote to the General giving the good

---

[1] (47) III, 480; see L. Hicks, "Fr Persons and the Seminaries in Spain," part 2; v. supra, p. 413.

[2] (47) III, 481f.

[3] Ibid., 482. No report has survived. Astráin relied on (61) Pt. V, l.9, No. 168.

[4] Ibid., 483.

news of a self-operated reform.[5] The latter no doubt rightly saw Persons as the principal architect of this happy result.

Probably at a meeting with the King on February 6, Persons brought up the subject of financial assistance for Douai. It was not a good moment, since the kingdom was on the verge of bankruptcy. However, Philip was somewhat reassured, because he believed that the English Catholics did not favor his cause, an impression strengthened by a forged letter from Burghley which came to Mendoza, Spanish ambassador in Paris at this time, purporting to originate with an English Catholic.[6] So Persons had to exercise all his skill and powers of persuasion to get an immediate grant for Douai of three thousand ducats.[7] But it is doubtful whether it was ever paid, considering the state of the treasury.

The Acosta-Persons interview of February 6 notwithstanding, a letter from the secretary of the Spanish embassy in Rome reported that two or three bishops were to be appointed for the visitation of the Jesuits. Aquaviva warned the Madrid Jesuits. Once again, Persons came to the rescue.[8] Philip gave assurances and the Jesuits went ahead with their own inquiry. Aquaviva made it clear that he wanted no cover-up. The strain of all this had taken its toll of Persons's health.[9] About the end of March, he was obliged to retire to a Jesuit house near Alcalá to recover from exhaustion. Wisely, the General did not hurry him. Persons had it in mind to visit Portugal and Andalusia, but Aquaviva insisted on his staying near the court, although he was allowed a pilgrimage to Guadalupe later in the summer.[10] He still had to wait for the lifting of the Inquisition's prohibition against Jesuits going to northern countries.[11] Meanwhile, preparations were already in hand to retrieve the disaster of the 1588 Armada.

It was Persons who gave Philip another letter from the General assuring him of the Society's support and goodwill in all his un-

[5] They have not survived. See Aquaviva to RP, 11.v.1589; (VI) Generals' letters, Tolet.4, ff.52r–3v, Italian, arrived 2.v.

[6] Hicks, "Fr Persons and the Seminaries," II; v. supra, 413; J. H. Pollen, (32) iii and v, 1911.

[7] Fabricius Como to ?, 4.iii.1589; Hicks, "Fr Persons and the Seminaries," v. supra, 413 n.(1) and 414 n.(1).

[8] (47) III, 484.

[9] Aquaviva to RP, 17.iv.1589, Italian draft; (VI) Tolet.5.I, f.58.

[10] (II) f.479; see CRS 14, 18. For the two new visitors, see *Annales Societatis*, Par.5.1.c.9 and Sacchini, *Historia S.J.*, vol. V, 1561, 458. See Aquaviva to RP, 11.v.1589; v. supra.

[11] Aquaviva to RP, 11.v.1589; v. supra.

dertakings.[12] Aquaviva also warned Gonzalo de Avila, one of the visitors, against the danger of overloading their willing English donkey.[13] Persons was to have a companion and secretary, since the doctor forbade him to write himself.[14] Two brothers and a priest were sent from Rome to help de Avila with his manpower problems. However he obeyed the doctor's orders, Persons somehow found time to research in the contemporary archives of the Escorial, looking for the raw stuff of history. He found "an eloquent oration of Fr. Campion's" of which he sent a copy to Joseph Creswell with orders to get from Prague copies of Campion's writings, including plays, with a view to producing a life in Latin. Luis de Granada had already produced a life in Spanish.[15]

On May 8, 1589, three students set out for Valladolid on a virtually secret mission from Rheims. The murder of the Guises[16] had removed the principal patrons and protectors of the seminary, and it was thought not impossible that the ever-militant Huguenots, after the manner of the times, might attack the seminary and massacre the students. The only safe place for an alternative foundation was somewhere in the Spanish dominions. Persons took the initiative in inviting the seminary authorities to send three men apt for a task not only difficult but probably dangerous. Henry Floyd, John Blackfan, and John Boswell were still theological students when they set off for Spain.[17] Thanks to the civil war raging in France, they were stopped and robbed seven times by roving bands of soldiers. Even so, they reached Spain by the end of the month; but they had still not found safety. Drake and John Norris had been ravaging the Spanish coast. Corunna and Lisbon had been attacked between mid-April and May 25, while Vigo was captured and burned on June 19. The three English students were arrested at Burgos the day after their arrival on suspicion of being spies for Drake.

---

[12] Ibid. See Aquaviva to Gonzalez de Avila, 15.v.1589; v. infra.

[13] Aquaviva to G. de Avila, 15.v.1589; (VI) Tolet. 5.I, f.59v, Spanish draft.

[14] See Aquaviva to RP, 11.v.1589; v. supra.

[15] RP to Rector of the VEC, 28.v.1589, el Escorial; (II) f.299. See also s. to s., 7.i.1590, Madrid; ibid., f.498; CRS 14, 21.

[16] John Blackfan, S.J., *Annales Collegii Sancti Albani in oppido Valesoleti* (Roehampton: Manresa Press, 1899), 33. Probably written c.1620, in five different hands. Blackfan only wrote the last three paragraphs, according to Canon Edward Henson; (68) viii. Henson's narrative of these events (ibid., xii–xiii) is controversial.

[17] Blackfan is quite clear about the names of the first three students, but Henson assumed that William Cowling, Gerard Cliburn, and Francis Lockwood—clearly indicated in the Douai Diary ((24) 221) as going to England on 10.xi.1588—were in fact the first three students to go to Spain.

Fortunately, Emmanuele Lopez, Jesuit rector of the college of St. Ambrose, was able to explain their true mission to the authorities of the Inquisition, since they had letters of introduction to him from Paris. They were then freed and allowed to pass to Valladolid. As it seemed a good town and a center suitable for study, they decided to stay there. Meeting by chance two more English students, they installed themselves in a hospice attached to the monastery of Santa Clara and began to attend lectures at the university and the Jesuit college. Everyone received them in kindly fashion, especially Fr. Antonio de Padilla, formerly a count. They also experienced great generosity from wealthy benefactors in the locality, especially Alfonso de Quiñones, who "never refused anything that was asked of him" until his death in April 1592.[18]

Persons first put down in writing his intention to found a Spanish seminary, it seems, in a letter to Creswell of June 24. He suggested that Creswell send him "all or the principal" scholars at the end of the summer. There were four more in Sicily whom Creswell should put on the road for Andalusia. If Creswell needed further explanation, Allen would provide it.[19] Persons duly reported the arrival of "our friends" in Madrid on July 22 and in "perfect health." The King gave him a "very gracious audience" on July 13 and granted him "letters in favor of the new seminary to be founded in Valladolid."[20] Other noblemen, following the royal lead, showed themselves favourable.[21] These included Sir Francis Englefield and the Duchess of Feria, an Englishwoman.[22] Persons left Madrid with his companion and helper, Brother Fabricio, to arrive in Valladolid about mid-August. He

---

[18] Blackfan, *Annales Collegii Sancti Albani,* 37; CRS 30, xiii. Henson seemed to think, on no proffered authority, that the students came from Rheims and joined together at Valladolid with no clear idea of what they were trying to do. This is a possible interpretation of a passage in Blackfan, who suggests further that they met two more students by merest chance. Henson's idea was that all was going well until the Jesuits intervened. "This little community was living quietly and unmolested when Fr Persons appeared on the scene and trouble began." Reliable evidence suggests that Allen, Persons, and Aquaviva were behind a new foundation from the start, though not necessarily by the Jesuits. For obvious reasons, the subject was kept out of general correspondence until the project seemed certain of success. See Blackfan, 34f; (68) xiii. Blackfan certainly suggests that an element of choice as regards place was left to the students.

[19] From el Escorial(?); (II) f.479; CRS 14, 19. The king is referred to in cipher not deciphered as "101." The context makes his identity clear.

[20] Philip was probably influenced by the surrender to Parma of Geertruydenberg by English mutineers, opening a gateway for an attack on Holland. See P. Geyl, *The Revolt,* 217.

[21] RP to Creswell, 22.vii.1589, Madrid; (II) ff.479, 481; CRS 14, 19.

[22] Blackfan, *Annales Collegii Sancti Albani,* 37.

found the English students badly lodged in attics that were like furnaces in the summer heat, and at once "gave orders" for a more commodious lodging to be found. There were now seven in this informal community: the three from Rheims, two more "who had scarcely imbibed the rudiments of grammar," and two priests from Lisbon, William Collins and Francis Lockwood. They were all "marvellously cheered by the arrival of Fr Persons."[23] But others, especially some in the lower echelons, were by no means cheered by the arrival of this man of driving energy. As always, he began at the top. This meant Don Alfonso de Mendoza, abbot-president, though he was not a monk, of the collegiate church at Valladolid. Suspicious at first, he soon became a friend of the college. The chief Inquisitor, Juan de Quiñones, as might have been foreseen, was positively hostile, as was the local prefect, seeing the newcomers only as nationals of the great enemy of Spain. Needless to say, Persons was not abashed. In addition to his powers of persuasion, he had an order from the King, bearing his seal and signed by members of his council, commanding whomever it might concern to favor and protect them and grant them leave to beg alms for their aid and maintenance. They were to live together in the hospital of St. Cosmas.[24] Thus Persons procured proper recognition for an organization which previously had only been a fortuitous group of students living uncomfortably together under one roof.[25]

In August 1589 Henri III, in accordance with a justice having little that was poetic about it, succumbed to the assassin's dagger. The Huguenot Henry of Navarre succeeded him; and, with the rout of the Catholic League at Ivry in March 1590, it seemed that the Catholic cause in France had little to hope for. All the wiser, therefore, seemed Persons's foresight in laying his new foundation at Valladolid. But as he reported in August 1589, the growing pains were sharp. The Brethren at the Hospital of St. Cosmas were by no means happy with their guests. The "abbot" was kind enough, but the community resented a royal order which might eventually oblige them to share their revenues with the newcomers. Persons could well understand a situation in which money was short and hastened to reassure the Brethren that they wanted none of their ducats, only a place to stay. Their hosts were not convinced, and it was the "abbot" who advised Persons to report the state of affairs to the King.[26] A house was subsequently rented

---

[23] Ibid.

[24] CRS 30, xiv–xv; Blackfan, 37–40.

[25] For an anti-Jesuit view, see John Southcote's notebook for John Cecil's comment; CRS 1, 111.

[26] RP to Don Juan Ruiz de Velasco, 5.viii.1589; (VIII) 85, f.134, Spanish holog.

which became the permanent home of the college. A further condition was that the inmates should not beg in the locality.[27] The students now put on a uniform and began to live according to an order of the day if not exactly a rule. Once again Persons resorted to his pen, this time to bring the new seminary to the notice of a wider public also expected to be generous. All was in position by Michaelmas of 1589.[28]

By the end of April 1589, the immediate threat hanging over the Society of Jesus had lifted. De Acosta proved competent and prudent in managing the visitation. Pope and King were content not to change the Institute, so that critics were either reconciled or forced to bide their time in relative silence. Aquaviva wisely decided not to punish the malcontents but simply to transfer them elsewhere.[29] He continued to rely heavily on Persons's rapport with Philip to keep him in a benevolent mood. On September 15 Persons left Valladolid for Madrid to report on progress to King and superiors, returning to Valladolid on October 25 with the new rector, Fr. Bartolomé de Sicilia, who was succeeded on November 26 by Fr. Pedro de Guzman. At the end of the year, the lease of the house was converted into a freehold, and Fr. Richard Gibbons became prefect of studies with Fr. William Flack for "minister" to manage temporal affairs.[30] On September 1 John Cecil, another convert graduate from Oxford, arrived at the seminary, followed on October 1 by John Fisher or Fixer, likewise from the university. Already priests, they were destined to provide Persons with many an opportunity for practising heroic patience. Whatever else he failed to discern in them, he noted already their talent for meeting people and making friends. So they were sent through the country "to win goodwill and stir up devotion in the people" towards the latest enterprise.[31] Certainly the good citizens of Valladolid did not lack curiosity regarding this latest phenomenon.[32] By the end of 1589, the seminary had already grown to some twenty persons, although with "no laws or constitutions as yet." Persons wanted its "head government," like that of any English teaching institution abroad, to be vested in Cardinal Allen.[33]

---

[27] CRS 30, xvi.

[28] The *Liber alumnorum* makes September 1 the foundation date, while the earliest extant account book gives July as the first month of its existence. See CRS 30, xvii; Blackfan, 38.

[29] Aquaviva to RP, 12.vi.1589; (VI) Tolet.4, ff.53v–4r, Italian draft.

[30] CRS 30, xvii.

[31] Ibid., 4, 7; Blackfan, 39.

[32] Blackfan, 38.

[33] RP to J. Creswell, Toledo, 9.xii.1589; (II) f.498; CRS 14, 20.

Aquaviva fully supported the Valladolid venture but wanted Persons to spend as much time as possible in Madrid, where his work was not only for England but for the whole Society. It was all the more desirable at the end of November 1589, when the "visitors" were about to present their report to His Majesty. Persons was to check this so that all would be "according to the truth." It was essential to have someone at the court to counterbalance the influence of Don Francisco de Avila, the Inquisitor, no friend of the Society, who would be only too pleased to support the voice of the Jesuit malcontents.[34] One such was raised in 1590, that of Bautista Carrillo, a young priest only ordained in 1586 but already a noted preacher. He had been associated with one of the memorials presented to the King in September attacking the current form of the Jesuit Institute. Aquaviva feared that Philip might be tempted to bring pressure to bear on the provincial congregations soon to meet to choose representatives or "procurators" for the forth-coming congregation in Rome, a triennial affair. De Acosta's report, putting an end to the dreadful interim, was expected by April 1590.[35]

The regime at Valladolid was now beginning to crystalize. Aquaviva, supported by Persons, rejected out of hand a suggestion that the students be arrayed in violet or purple, colors far too lordly and triumphalist. Neither should "sons of heretics" be admitted, lest the sensitive nose of the Inquisition be offended.[36] Doubtless, Persons brought up the subject of the seminary in an audience with the King on May 26, 1590. Fortunately, the visitor was entirely in favor of the institution and promised the General he would leave the seminary properly settled before he returned to his own province of Toledo. With the help of Alfonso de Quiñones, Persons bought an adjoining house and joined the two into one; he also constructed a small chapel near the entrance.[37] But it promised to be only the end of the begin-ning, since more students arrived from Rheims in the autumn with the promise of even further recruits to come. Philip was now persuaded to make a grant of 140 ducats a month towards the upkeep of fourteen English priests and students, to begin on June 1. When and whether it arrived remains a question.[38]

---

[34] Aquaviva to RP, 27.xi.1589; (VI) Tolet.5.I, f.101v, Spanish draft.

[35] S. to s., 20.iii.1590; (VI) Tolet.5.I. f.118.

[36] S. to s., 24.iii.1590, Rome(?); (VI) Tolet.4, ff.61v–2r. The letter deals with individual appointments and mainly Spanish matters. See also, s. to s., 9.vi; ibid., 5.I, f.128v.

[37] CRS 30, xvii; Blackfan, 41.

[38] Ibid.

Persons returned to the house himself on June 15 "after a most painful winter past in Madrid."[39] Even at Valladolid he was a man trying to rest in his workshop. There was still building going on; the Jesuit staff also needed some direction, since the rector was a man "hardly suitable."[40] Already there was pressure for yet another seminary at Seville, but even Persons found it "impossible to attend to so many things together." In any case, the present maintenance of Valladolid would amount to 2,500 scudi, so they could hardly afford another foundation.[41] This summer he was expecting no less than twenty or thirty students from Rheims and Eu. Fortunately, Juan Lopez de Manzano was available to succeed the rector, with Roderico Cabredo as confessor and spiritual director, two men who had Fr. Robert's entire approval. Already he was looking forward to a flourishing household of some fifty,[42] a prospect improved by a generous donation from the Bishop of Jaen, which promised to become annual.[43] In September Aquaviva wrote in recognition of all Persons's efforts and also announced the death of Pope Sixtus. "I hope in the Lord that by the time you receive this, He will have given us a successor who will protect us with readier goodwill than the other . . . so that trouble-makers will not enjoy quite so much licence to upset religious discipline."[44]

Persons left Valladolid about September 7. After spending some time at the Escorial, he was writing from Madrid on November 4 to declare his intention of visiting Seville with Charles Tankard and four other English priests bound for England.[45] Eight in all had this destination, including John Cecil and John Fixer. They had faculties from "Rome and Rheims, given them either by . . . Allen or by [Dr. Barrett] at their departure."[46] Persons had only good to say of any of them. Their year in Valladolid had been most useful for them, since they were able "to revive their books and learn both the language and the manners of this nation." They had been a source of great edification. Persons intended to show off at least some of them to the King and other "great personages, chapters and the like," no doubt to

---

[39] RP to Creswell, 24.vi.1590, Valladolid; (II) f.498. (CRS 30, 17 gives 1.vi. as the day of RP's return [an error?]).

[40] Ibid.; CRS 14, 21. The VEC archives originally contained some nineteen letters dealing with Valladolid affairs. (II) f.477 gives dates and notes of addresses; CRS 14, 21.

[41] S. to s., 22.vii.1590, Valladolid; (II) 500 CRS 14, 21.

[42] S. to s., 23.vii.1590, Valladolid; ibid.

[43] S. to s., 20.viii.1590, Vallad.; CRS 14, 22.

[44] Aquaviva to RP, 4.ix.1590, Rome(?); (VI) Tolet.5.I, f.150r.

[45] S. to s., 2.x.1590, Rome(?); ibid., f.153v.

[46] RP to Barrett, 7.xi.1590, Valladolid; Salisbury MSS, see (14) part 4, 69f.

console them for past generosity and to encourage more for the future. The intention now was that three or four should come to Valladolid from Rome every year, where Persons would look after them at least for some months before sending them on to England. However, they had to be of good life and learning, coming by direction and not "without order from superiors as some . . . before."[47] Otherwise they would not be received.

A letter from Persons of November 7 and two more of November 11, presumably to Allen, found their way into English official archives. One must assume that they were handed over by the two priests deputed to carry them, in particular, John Cecil. He had been a shrewd observer of the Spanish scene, possessing strong political proclivities which he no doubt believed placed him beyond the scope of ordinary loyalties. He had evidently decided that there was no way forward in England for the papists along the lines of Persons's policies, which presupposed the implacable hostility of Queen and council. The alternative to sharing the husks, and not many of those, with the swine on foreign soil was to return home cap in hand to what would not be an enthusiastic welcome but might be grudging acceptance—if previous conditions were agreed to. These must preclude all dealings with Spain and the Jesuits, unless as spies; this meant also revealing names, places, and plans of fellow Catholics who adhered to the other side. It was a hard choice but it now seemed to a growing number the only alternative to total extinction. It was the easier alternative to spoliation and perhaps martyrdom, which could not be a majority preference. It meant that Persons—the thought of Allen was always carefully avoided—and his friends must be seen, not as heroic warriors for the beleaguered faith, but as traitors even to the cause of their own religion, as well as men working for the interests of the archenemy of England. This was a view which would take a few years to develop. Meanwhile, in 1590 the cloud seemed no bigger than a man's hand, and Persons's was still large enough to cover it.

Ten students from Rome arrived at Valladolid in mid-October, soon reduced to nine after the death of Matthew Bedingfeld from "flux."[48] Persons managed to be with him at the end.[49] Ten more who

---

[47] Ibid. At the end RP asks to be remembered to "Mr Webb, Mr D Worthington, Mr D Gifford and Kellynson and the rest"; RP wrote another letter on 7.xi. to Allen(?), also intercepted; PRO, SP Dom. Eliz. Addenda, 31, No. 161.

[48] RP to Humphrey Shelton in Rome, 7.xi.1590, Valladolid(?), contemporary hand with PS in RP's hand, "I have not comoditie to wryt with myne owne hand," intercepted with the previous two. It acknowledged a letter from Shelton of 26.ix. brought "by one of those ten which arrived heare"; PRO, ibid., No. 160.

[49] Ibid. For M. Bedingfeld see CRS 14, 22, note.

came from Rheims were thrice despoiled by Vendome's soldiery "and so came hither all naked." Several priests were now destined for England including John Cecil, who was deputed to find a ship in Seville.[50] Persons, suspecting nothing of his future role, deputed Cecil to find a house in London to which letters could be forwarded from a Dutch address. Until the new intelligence path was established, Persons was careful but not careful enough. A letter to John Cecil included the names of two trusty Catholics in London. This he handed over to the authorities in England on his arrival as a pledge of faith unfaithful keeping him falsely true.[51]

Persons, meanwhile, was taking an interest in a much-neglected class of person, the English galley slaves kept in penal establishments in Seville. Too literally whipping boys for the sins of their countrymen, Fr. Robert took up their cause with enthusiasm, reporting to Juan de Idiaquez from Seville on March 3, 1591, the conversion of ninety men and some eighteen boys.[52] He took the opportunity to tell the secretary how "shocked" he was "at the coolness" with which the Spaniards received the "goodwill offered by the English with such love and with great risk and loss to themselves." Had he ever heard of Sir John Hawkins's sophisticated duplicity, one wonders, manifested exactly twenty years before? Something which the Spaniards would not have forgotten.[53] But Persons insisted that a great obstacle to progress was "the lack of confidence in the English, even though Catholics, which hitherto has been shown on all occasions." At the time of the Armada, as a notable example, the King had given no trust to "any living person of our nation either within or outside the kingdom, though there were many who could have helped." Many of the English had been deeply grieved by this.[54] Almost while Persons was writing, John Cecil was on his way to a fresh demonstration of English reliability. Persons, while pleading for a greater degree of confidence in his countrymen, shown by granting them promotions, was careful to

---

[50] RP to J. Creswell,12.xi.1590, Vallad.; (II) 500; CRS 14, 22.

[51] RP to Swinborn, 20.ii.1591, Seville; (VII) SP Dom. Eliz., 241, No. 41, holog.

[52] RP to J. de Idiaquez, 4.iv.1591, Seville; (II) f.246, Spanish copy; (9) 329. Further brief references to this and other letters of 1591 in (II) f.477. This seems to be the mass conversion indicated in RP's "Annales seminarii . . . hispalensis ab anno 1595" (CRS 14 (1914) p. 3) of 1590 among the prisoners at Puerto S. Maria, twenty-five miles from Seville. Once again, RP's memory for dates is fallible.

[53] To get the release of some of his men from the Seville prisons, Hawkins pretended to be ready to place his fleet at the king's disposal. They were released, and at the intercession of the Queen of Scots. See Edwards, *The Marvellous Chance*, 287–91; J. A. Williamson, *Hawkins of Plymouth* (London, 1949).

[54] RP to J. de Idiaquez, 4.iv.1591, v. supra.

emphasize his devotion and theirs to the King. He recognized the need for security. Finally, he still hoped for success by invasion. This was in the event to be attempted again in 1596, 1597, and 1601 but with no success.[55] A man who might still be a key figure in such a venture was Sir William Stanley, who should now be allowed to return to the fighting front in France or Flanders. Keeping him idle in Spain was to "inflict a thousand deaths on him."[56]

About Eastertide Persons was overtaken by an illness which sounds very much like nervous exhaustion.[57] He told Cardinal Sfondrato how deflated he felt when he witnessed the "dilatory methods" around him "and the great opportunities lost whereby all could have been remedied with ease."[58] Even now he could not put completely on one side the great works going forward at Valladolid and Seville.[59] But in mid-April 1591 he was still unable to write letters, although he was getting them written for him. Cecil and Fixer wrote to him on April 5 to elicit information which might ingratiate them yet further with the chief enemies of the papists in England. Persons, all unsuspecting, obliged them with news about the movements of two priests, Warford and Oliver Almond, information most useful to the priest catchers. Cecil included cryptic references to Lord Strange and his possible title to the crown on the Queen's death. This letter, too, found its way to Lord Burghley.[60] Did he inspire the references to Strange to coax out of Persons comments to embarrass Strange and make his elimination in the succession stakes that much easier? At all events, the Jesuit's reply on May 13 to the unblest pair of sirens seems to be the first extant indication that he was now turning to Elizabeth's successor as much as invasion to answer the Catholic problem. Persons gave Cecil and Fixer the appropriately foxy task of sniffing out the attitude of the Earl of Derby and of his son, Lord Strange, to the Catholic faith. In replying, the priests would avoid direct reference to the noble lords, using cryptic references to shield them from danger.

---

[55] A. J. Loomie, S.J., "The Armadas and the Catholics of England," *Catholic historical review* 59:390.

[56] RP to J. de Idiaquez, 4.iv.1591 (v. supra).

[57] RP to J. Cecil and J. Fixer, 13.iv.1591, Seville(?); Salisbury MSS, 168, No. 13. The letter to Cowling has probably not survived.

[58] RP to the Cardinal of Santa Cecilia, 18.iv.1591, Seville(?); (IV) Segreteria di Stato, Spagna 38, f.420, holog., Italian.

[59] Grene commented with exasperating brevity, "from Seville 8 April, 1591, and the same year divers other letters from Valladolid about the seminaries and little else"; (II) f.305.

[60] RP to J. Cecil and J. Fixer, 13.iv.1591, v. supra; (14) IV, 104f.

Even from Elizabeth's viewpoint, it should not have seemed in itself sinister that Persons was taking this interest in her successor. She was without an heir or hope of providing one, being well advanced in years. However, she wished even talk on the topic to be regarded as treasonable. The Cecils of Theobalds were not minded to discourage her as far as the generality of her subjects went. Whatever the contribution of John Cecil, if any, Ferdinando Stanley, Lord Strange, who succeeded to the Derby title in 1593, died in suspicious circumstances the following year—yet another redundant nobleman like the fourth Duke of Norfolk and the eighth Earl of Northumberland. Whatever the involvement of the Cecils in their deaths—and one could argue that there was none—their own prospects were undoubtedly safer after their demise.

When it became known in the Catholic community that priests like John Cecil were ready to sell them to the authorities, a new element of doubt and distrust entered to divide and weaken. John Cecil's betrayal and that of others who were to follow his dubious example achieved nothing for the Catholics, only a grudging toleration for himself and his friends, so that they could continue their work of espionage. John Cecil, working under the name of John Snowden, made his first statement for Burghley on May 21. It gave the names and described the movements of the latest batch of priests from Valladolid, including himself and Fixer.[61] Persons's desire was that they should convince the Catholics there was no question of a Spanish occupation of England, only another reformation of religion. Cecil was required by Fr. Robert to do more than make a list of all who would help the Spaniards. "Howsoever I found them affected . . . I should make the Spaniards believe that the number of their favourers was great," and only too ready to help "where they should see an army on foot to stand with them." Snowden also supplied names and positions of Persons's correspondents in Europe. An important task was to contact Lord Strange and persuade him to contact Allen. Fixer handed in a similar report.[62] Snowden gave up the names of three Jesuits in England still at liberty, Southwell, Garnet, and Curry. He also furnished details of pensioners and pensions. Perhaps it was from this time that Fr. Robert took his place in the estimate of the regime as Public Enemy No. 1. "Persons doth prevail with them all, and in fine nothing is done there in English affairs but what he will."[63] It was a field day for the great Lord Burghley.

[61] John Cecil, first(?) deposition, 21.v.1591; (VII) SP12, 238, No. 160.

[62] (29) 1591–94, 40; PRO, ibid., No. 162.

[63] PRO ibid, No. 161. T. Wilson's deposition of 22.v. gave more on Sir William Stanley; ibid., No. 163.

It was not difficult for Cecil and Fixer to justify themselves in the eyes of many papists, not to speak of the average good patriot. As Fixer, who adopted the alias of Thomas Wilson, put it, "The principal motive of my return into this realm was upon the natural love and affection which each man hath to his native soil to prevent as far as I might . . . the invasion and spoil of the same by foreigners." He was relying heavily on Burghley's avowed intention to "persecute or trouble no man for matters of conscience where it [was] not intermeddled with matters of state." But he was aware he would have to earn immunity by working as a government informer. He was willing to do it but "upon condition that it be done with such secrecy that Catholics suspect not that I have intelligence with your Honour."[64] At the same time, he was hoping, "as other priests," to be "sufficiently . . . maintained by such Catholics" as would receive him and give him "entertainment in their houses." Thus entered on the scene the phenomenon of the desperate man who wanted to have it both ways with little or no regard for consistency or honor.

It has to be admitted, however, that from the mid-1590s the situation at Valladolid and even at Seville was hardly calculated to enhance the prestige of the Jesuits or foster the loyalty of their students. Generous in the main principle of allowing aliens in their midst, the Spaniards could show pettiness, selfishness, and worse in day-to-day dealings with them. The English seminaries and their income, managed by less than the best of the Jesuits, became a goose that was squeezed to provide golden eggs and also plucked to feather the nests of others hardly worthy. When this process began seems impossible to say; but it seems to have begun early enough to scandalize Cecil and Fixer, so that they had some excuse for betraying Persons and putting their trust in an English government which never intended to keep faith—and never said that it would. Far from the English scene, it may well have seemed better in a dilemma to hold out the begging bowl to an unfriendly government at home rather than to foreigners who in spite of the common religion seemed basically unsympathetic. Saints can live easily with saints whatever their nation but saints are always in short supply. Persons was right in judging that from Spain there was something to hope for, but from the ruling regime in England, nothing. Cecil and Fixer, and many who were to follow them, tried to keep faith, perhaps, in their own way, but as far as possible from martyrdom.

Snowden frankly admitted in a letter to Burghley that it was impossible for a Spanish invasion to get under way or to succeed. He

---

[64] Endd. by Burghley, "May 1591. Thomas Wilson alias Fixer: Answers to certain articles"; SP12, ibid., No. 166. Snowden and Fixer were examined by Burghley on a number of subsequent occasions; see Cal. SP Dom. Eliz.

rejected Persons's idea that even if it did reach England some three or four thousand Catholics would flock to it, an idea included in a recent book published by the Jesuit in Amsterdam.[65] However, Snowden admitted that, even though many disliked it, they still saw no alternative. Most would profit by it if it succeeded, do nothing to help it to begin, condemn it if it failed, and repudiate any previous sympathy and connection with it—an attitude compatible with popular political wisdom.[66] Snowden was soon asking for a passport to take him back to a mining operation beneath the seminaries which Persons had erected so painfully. No one really likes or trusts a spy and the ruling Cecils were not exceptions. They made it clear to John that his plausibility had not disarmed their critical faculty. In any case, he had not gone far enough to win real confidence. He still considered himself a papist and a priest.[67]

Persons returned to Madrid from the new colleges probably about the end of June 1591. Whatever the misgivings of Cecil and Fixer, the new foundations in their material aspect were going well. The Andalusian provincial helped much in Seville, while the house in Valladolid, after agreement with Gil González Dávila, the Castile provincial, was to get William Holt from Flanders as rector.[68] Joseph Creswell would come to assist Persons.[69] The chapel and another range of buildings had been completed at Valladolid.[70] Persons not only controlled the building operation but was mainly instrumental in raising funds, an exhausting and time-consuming operation in itself.[71] By this time the community numbered nearly sixty. Persons left Madrid on July 17 to return to it.[72]

Creswell, meanwhile, was having trouble with the students in the English College, Rome. Persons was willing to believe that much of the unrest came from the "ungrateful youths" themselves, but it is evident from his advice to Creswell that he was considered at least partly to blame in treating the students more like children or even prisoners than responsible adults. "All signs of diffidence make Eng-

---

[65] J. Cecil/Snowden deposition, 25.v.1591; (VII) SP12, ibid., No. 180. No. 181 lists in two factions the Catholic exiles abroad adhering to Allen and Persons, and to Paget and friends.

[66] Ibid., No. 181.

[67] See Snowden to Sir Robert Cecil, 20.vi.1591; (VII) ibid., 239, No. 46.

[68] See Aquaviva to RP, 9.vii.1591; (VI) Tolet.5.I, f.195r, Spanish draft.

[69] S. to s., 9.vii.1591; (VI) Hisp.74, Soli di Hispania, f.31.

[70] Blackfan, 43.

[71] Ibid., 44; CRS 30, xiii.

[72] RP to Creswell, 17.vii.1591, Escorial; (II) f.300; CRS 14, 22.

lishmen more distrusters and canvassers, as you know." He was advised to let "pass all things already done"; "many defects must be winked at and not pursued in a multitude; and for spyeries and sentinels . . . [this] is the way to mar all."[73]

Soon after Persons returned to Valladolid in July, a severe and rather mysterious epidemic struck the college and most of the students. Eleven died. The rector fell ill and withdrew to the professed house; Persons had to withdraw to the College of St. Ambrose. Almost no one was left with sufficient health to care for the rest.[74] An even more ominous threat was looming in England, thanks primarily to the efforts of John Cecil and Fixer to alert the reigning Cecil to the threat of the seminaries. A royal proclamation was drawn up against them on October 18. Its language, calculated to dismay all but the most stalwart, was offensive in the extreme to Catholic sentiment. The Pope, a Milanese, was Philip II's servant and vassal, "hanging at his girdle." The seminarists were "a multitude of dissolute young men" who, partly for "lack of living, partly for crimes committed," became fugitives, rebels, and traitors. The seminaries in Rome and Spain trained them in sedition and sent them back as Spanish agents intent to overthrow the kingdom. None could now deny that the law operated "against such traitors for mere treasons, and not for any point of religion as their fautors would colour falsely their actions."[75] In fact, those who were arraigned refused to answer how they would react to a Spanish or papal invasion. This was reasonable. For by this principle, on a truthful answer to a hypothetical question as to what a man would do in any given circumstances, anyone could be hanged.[76] The whole atmosphere was now overcharged with emotion. The imposition of the £20 per month fine was represented as clemency, since those who rejected the Queen's religion deserved the reward of treason. Allen and Persons were mentioned by name as principal instigators of the system and, more particularly, of another invasion attempt to be launched this year. In consequence, the English Inquisition was to extend its activities, commissions being set up in the main centers of recusancy—Durham, Oxford, Hampshire, Surrey, and Dorset—to counteract the Jesuited missionaries. The commissioners would "enquire by all good means what persons are by their behaviours or otherwise worthy to be suspected." Not only householders but lodging-house keepers were

---

[73] S. to s., 27.vii.1591; (II) f.305 and ibid.

[74] Blackfan, 44.

[75] Proclamation from Richmond, 18.x.1591; (3) III, 86–93; the decree was promulgated on 29.xi.1591, OS.

[76] Numerous examples in R. Challoner's *Memoirs of Missionary Priests* (London, 1924). See also P. McGrath, "The Bloody Question Reconsidered," (10) 20, 305–20.

responsible for watching their guests, whose names were to be kept in "a register or calendar" liable to inspection.[77]

One cannot blame the Queen or her ministers for taking due precautions against any who were ready to assist a Spanish invasion, but there was no attempt to distinguish between recusants who acknowledged only the spiritual authority of the Pope and reserved the right to reject his temporal policies, and those who, like Allen and Persons, were prepared to countenance even foreign invasion to bring relief to their fellow papists. But Persons's intransigence, if that is the word for it, arose only from the intransigence of William Cecil and his like-minded friends. Since Burghley refused, behind flimsy appearances to the contrary, to negotiate or distinguish, Allen and Persons were left with no alternative but to continue the struggle on grounds and with weapons which were in effect thrust upon them by their adversaries. It is ironical at first sight that Burghley should have imported an inquisition into England, but he was an admirer, in private if not in public, of Spanish success and greatness and attributed much of this to unity of religion. This is evident from his treatise "An antidote against Jesuitism . . ." of 158(3?).[78] Allen and Persons received further justification from the fact that when the papists, persecuted as they were, rallied to Elizabeth's cause in 1588, yet received no kind of recognition but only contempt. Nor did the white flag now raised by John Cecil and Fixer provoke any better response.

In the sequel, the proclamation of 1591 produced an equal and opposite reaction. If many were cowed into outward conformity, others were spurred to take action. This year proved the turning point for Valladolid. The Spanish court, stung by Her Majesty's insults, rallied to the support of the college.[79] New arrivals at Valladolid from England admitted that "the late proclamation set out by the Queen in November last against this seminary did first of all give them notice thereof, as also appetite to see the place."[80] By the year's end, however, if Persons had reason for satisfaction, he had none for complacency. Rodrigo de Cabredo, a well-qualified man, became rector in Septem-

---

[77] Read, *Lord Burghley and Queen Elizabeth* (London, 1960), 468.

[78] Inner Temple, Petyt MSS, series 538, Vol. 37, ff.177 and seq., final draft; ibid., Vol. 43, ff.304–14, earlier draft in W. Cecil's hand, 15[83?]; Somers' Tracts, I (London, 1809), 164–70. Spedding wrongly ascribed this document to F. Bacon. See C. Devlin, S.J., *Life of Robert Southwell* (London, 1956), 330–32.

[79] (59) 190.

[80] *A relation of the King of Spaine's receiving in Valliodolid, and in the Inglish College of the same towne in August last past of this yeare, 1592. Wryten by an Inglishe priest of the same college to a gentleman and his wyf in Flanders . . . MDXCII*, Scolar reprint 351 (1977), p. 12; quoted ibid., 190. V. infra.

ber, but expenditure was outstripping income to an alarming degree. Nor was the news from Rome encouraging. Creswell, unable to cope with the situation in the college, was confirmed as assistant to Persons in Spain. But it proved difficult to find a substitute, since Holt was now considered too valuable to leave Flanders.[81]

The beginning of 1592 found Persons in Madrid and much improved in health. Philip was persuaded to petition the Pope for a formal instrument putting Valladolid under direct control of the Holy See, thus avoiding potential friction between Rome and Madrid in the manner of its procurement. He obtained the instrument, dated April 25, 1592, without much difficulty.[82] The rector was parish priest as well as head of the college, which was empowered to grant degrees in the arts and theology equivalent to those of Oxford and Cambridge. The students could also be ordained by rector's license without dimissorial letters from the ordinary. As at Rome, the students were obliged by oath to work on the English mission, the time of their return being fixed by rector and provincial. The rector granted sacramental faculties for students going to Ireland and Scotland, as well as England. He was also empowered to nominate judges to settle civil, criminal, or mixed legal cases in which the college was involved. His appointment was by the Jesuit general but with Cardinal Allen as protector. In temporal affairs the college was directly under the aegis of the King of Spain and his council of state.

Not the least of Persons's competencies was his persuasiveness as a beggar. Even from an archbishop of Toledo who was no lover of Jesuits he managed to get an annual endowment in his will of one thousand crowns per annum for Valladolid.[83] He even obtained a license from the King to import English cloth, in spite of the fact the two nations were at war.[84] Living quarters were enlarged and a villa house and garden acquired for the students' recreation.[85] Aquaviva had also been urging the Spanish brethren to greater efforts and interest on Persons's behalf, and by the spring of 1592 results were beginning to show.[86] Meanwhile in Rome, Mutio Vitelleschi, a future general, was appointed to succeed Creswell, some indication of the size of the

---

[81] See Aquaviva to RP, 28.x.1591, Rome; (VI) Castell.6, f.105, Spanish draft. See O. Mannaerts to Aquaviva, Tournai, 8.xi.1591, Latin; (VI) Germ. 169, f.319r/v.

[82] Printed in the Bullarium as of 3.x.1592. CRS 30, 246–51, Latin text: see xviii & n.(*).

[83] Blackfan, 47.

[84] CRS 30, xviii.

[85] Ibid. and Blackfan, 48.

[86] Aquaviva to RP, 20.i.1592; (VI) Castell.6, f.119r, Spanish draft.

problem and the importance Aquaviva attached to the English College.[87]

The General was more aware than Persons, perhaps, of the financial difficulties in which Spain found itself—there had been several fleet disasters this year.[88] He therefore asked Persons to reflect that it might be better to put off the foundation at Seville for a time.[89] But Fr. Robert was now looking even further than Seville. The English merchant community at San Lucar de Barrameda had since 1517 possessed a house downriver from Seville. From 1591 Allen appointed chaplains with Persons as visitor, an arrangement completed on April 29, 1591. The competent John Cecil had helped in the negotiations before his departure for England.[90] The church of St. George and the adjoining residence had become very dilapidated by the time Persons took over. He therefore used his considerable influence with the King, and also with the Duke of Medina Sidonia, whose domain included both port and house, to provide funds for a complete restoration. Persons also appointed four chaplains with a view to future developments, no doubt.[91]

On August 3, 1592, King Philip, the infante, and Princess Clara Eugenia paid a ceremonial visit to the college at Valladolid. The building was still incomplete; but everything was done to make the occasion memorable with flowers, decorations, silk-covered walls, prayers, and a solemn Te Deum in the presence of the Archbishop of Compostela, who graciously showed the royal guests to their places. The students gave welcome addresses in ten languages. All filed up at the end to kiss the King's hand, but brushing this aside, he embraced them instead.[92] Inevitably perhaps, some of the brickbats contained in

---

[87] Ibid.

[88] CRS 30, xvii–xviii, n.(*).

[89] Aquaviva to RP, 8.vi.1592; (VI) Castell.6, f.124, Spanish draft.

[90] J. Cecil's account is *A discoverye of the errors committed and injuryes done to his Ma. of Scotlande and nobilitye off the same realme, and John Cecyll, priest and D. of divinitye, by a malitious mythologie titled an Apologie and compiled by William Criton, priest and professed Jesuite, whose habit and behaviour, whose cote and conditions are as suitable as Esau his handes and Jacob his voice* (Paris[?], 1599), 19. J. Cecil "with characteristic vainglory claims the lion's share in the foundation not only of the residence of St Lucar, but also of all the seminaries of Spain," J. H. Pollen, *CRS* 14 (1914), 4 and n.(+).

[91] *CRS* 14, 6. The chaplains were Thomas Stillington, Martin Array, George Ambler, and William Seburne.

[92] Blackfan (p. 45) puts the royal visit in the summer of 1591, but Henson was doubtless correct in placing this event in 1592, when more building had been completed (CRS 30, xviii). Nor could such a visit have been reconciled with an epidemic raging in the college. Moreover, Fray Diego de Yepes in his *Historia particular de la persecucion de Inglaterra* (Madrid, 1599), follows a work printed in 1592, *Relacion de un sacerdote Ingles*

Elizabeth's proclamation were returned on this occasion. Philip was likened to good King Abdias, who, when the wicked Queen Jezebel persecuted the prophets of God, saved 150 of them by hiding them in caves and feeding them, if only on bread and water.[93]

The more effective reply to the November proclamation was Persons's edition, with answers to its various charges, under the pseudonym of Andreas Philopater.[94] Persons did not blame Elizabeth for such things, "but the wicked deceit and importunity of some in her entourage who extort them from her."[95] She herself was not "greatly moved to hatred or love of any religion or sect," being goaded chiefly to excess by Burghley, "a man of long and most evil days."

The royal visit to Valladolid of August 3 was probably exploited by Persons to obtain letters from the King and his ministers authorizing the setting up of a seminary in Seville. Within two months he had a working community established. Benefactors were solicited from among the clergy and nobility alike.[96] Paradoxically, Burghley's proclamation put a favorable wind behind the sails at Seville, as it had done at Valladolid. The King wrote encouragement to the cardinal of the city and to the Duke of Medina Sidonia.[97] Aquaviva furthered Persons's plans by sending Henry Walpole to Valladolid, so that Holt could continue in Flanders.[98] He also wrote to the provincial to allay the fears of the Spanish college in Seville at the prospect of a rival English institution next door to drain alms and interest away from itself.[99] The General had received letters from Spanish Jesuits asking him to hold up the English foundation since there was already so much begging going on. Aquaviva indicated his desire to be

---

. . . *de la venida de su Majestad . . . al collegio de los Yngleses* (see ibid., ix). Gillow reasonably attributes authorship to RP, for although it was issued anonymously the writer refers to the building operations "wherein presentlie I have some charge and exercise in this place to overlooke the builders." See also *A relation of the King of Spaine's receiving. . . .*

[93] Loomie, *The Spanish Elizabethans*, 191.

[94] This was a pseudonym of Joseph Creswell's (see (19)) but RP seems to have been the author of the present work. Published at Antwerp by Arnout Conincx in 1592 not at "Augustæ" of the imprint: several editions of the work under the title *Elizabethæ, Angliæ Reginæ hæresim Calvinianam propugnantis sævissimum in catholicos sui Regni edictum, quod in alios quoque Reipub. Christianæ Principes contumelias continet indignissimas: promulgatum Londinii 29 Novemb. 1591. Cum responsione ad singula capita: qua non tantum sævitia, & impietas tam iniqui edicti, sed mendacia quoque, et fraudes ac imposturæ detegantur, & confutantur. Per D. Andream Philopatrum presbyterum ac Theologum Romanum, ex Anglis olim oriundum.* . . .

[95] *Edictum . . . Augustæ* (1592), 10. From the Latin.

[96] CRS 14, 8f.

[97] Quoted Loomie, *The Spanish Elizabethans*, 192.

[98] Aquaviva to RP, 31.viii.1592, Rome; (VI) Castell.6, f.130r, Spanish draft.

[99] Aquaviva to Bartolomé Perez de Nueros, 28.ix.1592, Rome; (VI) Boetica 3, f.84r.

informed if opposition from the Spanish Fathers continued.[100] Fortunately, the General and Persons had the full support of the provincial, Bartolomé Perez.[101]

On the night of June 25/26, the Jesuits in England received a severe blow when Robert Southwell was arrested at Uxenden.[102] The effect on Persons was to encourage Aquaviva to send in more men. This should now be easier, since Seville was relatively near the coast and offered a more direct line of communication with England.[103] In Rome three short-lived popes were succeeded by Clement VIII, who as Cardinal Aldobrandino had been protector of the English nation. Persons therefore allowed himself to hope for good support, especially for the new seminaries. Creswell was preparing a report on them for the Vatican. Meanwhile, Clement was asked to encourage the Archbishop of Seville to be benevolent to the strangers at his gate.[104]

The Seville foundation had its official opening on St. Catherine's Day, 1592. Fr. Francis Peralta was the first rector, a man who served the English exiles many ways before his death in 1622. Fr. Charles Tankard was minister. Persons and Creswell also took up residence with the first students—four in all. In January 1593 a more ample building was taken on the Plaza Santa Magdalena. On the feast of St. Thomas of Canterbury, December 29, an open day was held, so that the local people could come and see the college to which they contributed generously, poor as well as rich. Seminaries only began with the Council of Trent and such institutions were still a novelty. The first in Spain, at Tarragona, was as recent as 1570. Persons's new foundation was still only the seventh in the whole of Spain.[105] The Cardinal Archbishop of Seville presided at the inauguration. Fr. John Worthington preached in Latin while, after the Mass, four of the students took the college oath to return to England after ordination. All proceeded more or less as at Valladolid. Persons was glad to spend money on something which encouraged everyone. And this was, after all, the land of fiesta.

---

[100] S. to Frs. at Seville, 26.x.1592, Rome; (VI) ibid., f.85r. See s. to Bartol. Perez, provincial of Andalusia, 26.x.1592; ibid., ff.84f.

[101] CRS 14, 3, n.(*).

[102] Devlin, *The Life of R. Southwell,* 280f, chapters 19–21.

[103] RP to Aquaviva, n.d., Valladolid(?); (VI) Hisp.(Soli), 139, f.126r, not RP's hand, Spanish. Hicks thought it was written after 15.iii.1593.

[104] RP to Clement VIII, 1.xii.1592, Seville; (IV) F.B.III, 124.G.2, f.3r/v. RP drew up a memo on the early history of Seville and four other foundations from 1589 to 1595, entitled "Annales seminarii seu collegii Anglorum Hispalensis ab anno 1591." Written between 1.iii.1610 and 16.iv., when he died. It is known only from a copy ((II) f.344 et seq.). See CRS 14, 1–3.

[105] Kirchenlexikon XI, 42; CRS 144, 8.

Chapter Ten ═══
Seville and St. Omers: 1593 ═══

B
y an act of 1585, any student studying in a seminary abroad who failed to return to England within six months and to apostatize was ipso facto a traitor. The edict of 1591 developed this idea but failed to stop the flow overseas. Indeed, recusancy was growing, especially in Cheshire and Lancashire. Local authorities, often sympathetic, connived by not applying the law, and the adoption of aliases made it difficult to keep track of individuals. The battle of wills between London and the provinces continued when in 1593 Parliament enacted that all convicted recusants over sixteen years of age should be confined within five miles of their homes under threat of forfeiture of all goods, lands, and annuities during life. A clause not actually passed, reflecting an idea of Burghley's, would have removed children of Catholic parents from the age of seven to be brought up at their parents' expense in the houses of bona fide Protestants according to their religion. A report on the bill, including this clause, came to Persons's notice in Spain some time before the opening of Parliament on February 19, 1593. He warned Aquaviva immediately and typically proposed the remedy: a school to be founded in the Low Countries for Catholic boys.[1]

At Seville, meanwhile, two exceptional students, Richard Walpole and Henry Floyd, defended theses successfully before a learned and critical audience, including Jesuits who had not hitherto been friendly. Perhaps his success persuaded Walpole to join the Society three days later.[2] In Madrid Persons managed to get "without further procrastination" 4,000 scudi for Valladolid, "a rent of 300 scudi" for Seville, and an allowance of 1,720 scudi to start up a college for boys at St. Omer in Flanders. This was intended to maintain sixteen persons for a beginning, with a promise of more as the number grew. The city

---

[1] (62) 10–12. Aquaviva to RP at Seville, 15.ii.1593 ((VI) Boetica 3, f.100r) is very satisfied with news of the new seminary. Wm. Baldwin left for Flanders, and H. Walpole likewise(?) to assist him.

[2] CRS 14, 9f. Aquaviva to RP, 12.iv.15935, acknowledges two letters of 16 and 27.ii. and congratulates him on the happy outcome of the Madrid journey. The St. Omer Jesuits would feel overburdened if they had charge of the seminary. Aquaviva has sought Mannaerts's advice in this.

of St. Omer was not enthusiastic, since it was on the frontier; but reconciled itself to boys between ten and eighteen with Jesuits in charge, more particularly since the Spanish court was solidly behind it. Fr. William Flack, minister at Valladolid for some years, was to head the school after some study of the seminary at Seville. Although the Flemish provincial had been asked to provide staff, Henry Bury would be minister and Nicholas Smith prefect of studies. Holt in Brussels would provide the connection with the court. To him Persons donated five hundred scudi collected in the Spanish court, with a promise to pay further expenses until the golden stream from Spain began to flow. The boys coming from England would also bring money with them. When they reached sufficient maturity, they could pass to other seminaries. The latter might even contribute to their support as the hope of the future. Aquaviva was called upon to help and to enlist the aid of Vitelleschi, rector in Rome.[3]

The latest foundation was another success and continues to this day as Stonyhurst College. Nevertheless, the initial labors put a great strain on Persons's health. Fortunately, in Cabredo, rector at Valladolid, Fr. Robert had a staunch helper in persuading King and court to stand by their promises. But the Spanish brethren were rarely overjoyed to witness the miracle of blood coming from a stone which they took to be at their own expense. They were motivated not by jealousy but by the crying needs of their own good works. Nor was Persons himself notably happy in this work. "I feel such repugnance to visiting Madrid that I go there as if to purgatory; this for many reasons, especially because I have to see the hopeless want and misery of the poor Englishmen who are there, and hear the clamours of those who write to me in such numbers immediately they know I have arrived." At all events, by way of compensation, Cabredo at Valladolid and Francis Peralta at Seville were proving highly competent.

Persons was due at this time to visit Andalusia and possibly Castile to participate in the provincial congregations which would draw up the agenda for the international meeting in Rome. There were still fears that disaffected Jesuits and others would wish to see fundamental changes in the structure of the Society. Persons turned to the King, asking him to be their defender, and received the promise that "his help would not be wanting."[4] Many of the problems arising during

---

[3] RP to Aquaviva, 22.iii.1593, Toledo; (VI) Hispania 135, f.147, Italian. The "first royal answer giving a pension of 1920 crowns bore date" 13.iii.1593; CRS 14, 12, n.(*); (62), chap. 1. For a register of boys educated there, see Geoffrey Holt, S.J., *St. Omers and Bruges Colleges 1593–1773: A biographical dictionary*, CRS 69 (1979).

[4] RP to Aquaviva, 19.iv.1593; (VI) Hispania 135, f.187, Italian. Aquaviva to RP of 10.v.1593 describes RP as writing from Toledo on the way to Seville (v. infra).

Aquaviva's generalate from 1581 to 1615 arose from the sheer increase in numbers and works; from some five thousand members in 1581 to nearly thirteen thousand in 1615 with thirty-two provinces at the end as against twenty-one at the beginning. The 144 schools of 1581 numbered 372 in 1615; the residences grew from 33 to 123. The problem was to move with the times and grow without losing the necessarily elitist concept of the Society. Some, especially in Spain, felt the General's charge was now too much for one man. His power should be curtailed, with provincial chapters to make local appointments of rectors and provincials.[5] As so often, the would-be reformers showed more zeal than discretion, more energy than genuine understanding of the problems to be solved. Or so the majority, including Persons and the General himself, saw it.

The leader of the "reforming" movement was none other than José de Acosta, one of the General's recent "visitors." His ability and experience were sufficient to prove that the movement was no student romp. He went to Rome, arriving on December 2, 1592; and at an audience with the Pope, of which Aquaviva knew nothing, he claimed that unrest among the Spanish Jesuits was due to the worldliness of superiors and the excessive power of the General. Acting on his advice, Clement ordered Aquaviva to summon a general congregation—an altogether more solemn affair than the congregation of procurators. In the event, the Jesuits as a body stood firmly behind the General in aiming to preserve intact an institution which had proved itself by so much success. Even in Spain, "in the provincial congregations not one of the alienated group was chosen" as its representative for Rome.[6] De Acosta, not to be outdone, then struck up an alliance less than holy, perhaps, with Francisco de Toledo, an eminent Spanish Jesuit theologian resident in Rome, to maneuver himself into the position of organizer of the congregation. Aquaviva, by superior tact and tactics managed to outflank him; but something was owing to Clement's preference for the French rather than the Spanish, especially after the conversion of Henri IV.

The Fifth General Congregation opened in Rome on November 3, 1593. Persons, needless to say, was very much involved and interested in the threatening crisis. He entirely favored Aquaviva and the established order of things, and these internal troubles caused him more grief "than anything else in this life." In March, perhaps, Persons had discussed matters directly with de Acosta, who urged him to approach the General, as if on his own initiative, to urge him to call

---

[5] (38) 98.

[6] (38) 100; (60) 161f; (47) chaps. 15–17.

the general congregation. Certainly something needed to be done. In Madrid, for example, the Jesuits were much divided, "nearly all being in opposition to the rector."[7] Never shy about going to the summit, Persons wrote to the Pope albeit by way of Aquaviva, who gave the letter to Allen to be presented. First of all, he was properly grateful for the brief setting up the school at Seville. As for the general congregation, His Holiness would know well enough how "the devil would like to bring confusion under various pretexts of reforms and of the public good." He concluded of the malcontents, "there is usually very little piety in these schemers, and little evidence of religious life." Some were merely ambitious, showing "unconcealed envy of the Italians." There was also "obvious dislike of being subject to the orders of Rome." He asked Clement to ensure that the congregation would be held in an atmosphere of liberty and free discussion, with no "schemes and plots from outside."[8]

Elsewhere the Society was keeping its head above the waves. Garnet in England wished to receive some dozen candidates for the Society. Aquaviva told him to send them to Flanders for distribution through the provinces.[9] The Jesuits at Seville were encouraged to help the English seminary.[10] By April there were forty-six in residence; but in spite of a large outlay—some 2,400 ducats in four months—they were less than 200 ducats in debt. The house, adapted to receive eighty, had the finest position "in the whole town." The staff was performing well. William Flack left San Lucar on April 8 to take up his post in Flanders.[11] With a certain wry humor, perhaps, the King decided that the 1,720 ducats per annum for St. Omers were to be levied on English merchandise. Meanwhile, present needs were met by "devoted persons." As in Spain, it was essential to enlist local sympathy, as far as possible, and to have in particular the favor of the provincial, Oliver Mannaerts.[12]

Asked by the Jesuit provincial of Castile to take part in the congregation at Medina del Campo, Persons hurried up his business at Seville so as to leave about April 20. Not only Richard Walpole but two

---

[7] RP to Aquaviva, n.d., "soli" not in RP's hand; (VI) F.G.651/640, n.f.

[8] RP to Clement VIII, 15.iv.1593, Seville; (II) f.327, Italian. RP sent this letter and Creswell's for the Pope to Aquaviva to deliver or not as he saw fit. See RP to Aquaviva 19.iv.1593, Seville (v. supra).

[9] RP to Aquaviva, 7.vi.1593, Rome; (VI) Boetica. 3, f.119, Spanish draft.

[10] S. to s., 19.iv.1593. V. supra.

[11] CRS 14, 12 and RP to Aquaviva, 19.iv.

[12] Ibid. Aquaviva replied to the letter and enclosure of 19.iv. on 7.vi; (VI) Boetica. 3, f.119, Spanish draft.

lay brothers from England had come to swell the Jesuit community, and more were expected. This creaming-off of vocations to the Society was to become yet another bone of contention.[13] Persons got back to Valladolid by way of Lisbon and Seville about June 15 to find a daunting heap of letters awaiting his reply. It took him two days to read them before ever he could think of replying. They mainly told of persecution and harassment in England, enough to deprive him of a night's sleep, as he confessed to Aquaviva. However, both Garnet in England and Mannaerts in Flanders were interested in St. Omers. Garnet assured him there would be "no lack of boys . . . to fill it." Someone in Flanders wanted the school to be located at Courtrai but Persons insisted to Aquaviva that this would be too far from a seaport. Already Fr. Robert saw it also as a place where Jesuits from Seville might come for rest and change.[14]

By midyear, yet a further interesting development seemed possible, this time in Lisbon. San Roque was a house for English priests and a chaplaincy for English residents in the city. It was attached to the Jesuit house, which had the right to nominate the chaplain. Someone was needed who spoke French and Spanish, so Fr. William Coulins filled the vacancy.[15] Persons saw the house as yet another staging post for priests on the way to England. If he had any idea at this point of founding another college, he kept it to himself. Even the cooperative Aquaviva must not be pushed too hard or far. There were some who were best kept out of England, as Persons saw it. These were the exiles in Flanders who, weary of their hard lot, now thought of returning to England and throwing themselves on the mercy of the "heretics." If only to prevent a further negative influence on the morale of the recusants at home, he asked Philip to be generous.[16] Meanwhile there was no word of approval from Allen for the St. Omer foundation; this was taken to mean that another letter had been lost.[17]

---

[13] RP to Aquaviva, 19.iv.1593; v. supra.

[14] S. to s., 16.vi.1593, Valladolid; (VI) Hispania 135, f.306, Holog., Spanish.

[15] Ibid. See also Canon W. Croft, *Historical Account of Lisbon College* (London, 1902). This account is very sketchy, especially regarding dates. It claims, "The design of establishing a college at Lisbon . . . originated with a priest named Nicholas Ashton," p. 2 (Aston in the Register, p. 171). He studied at Seville from its inception in 1592; he came to Lisbon in April 1597, where he "became rector of the English residence, projected the foundation of a college, purchased a house for the purpose, and dying, bequeathed it to Ralph Sleighford, alias William Newman."

[16] RP to Philip II, n.d., Valladolid(?); (II) f.500. This was a very difficult year for the exiles. See CRS 52 (1959), A. Petti's edition of *The Letters and Dispatches of Richard Verstegan*, passim.

[17] RP to Aquaviva, 15.vii.1593, Valladolid; (VI) Hispania 135, f.372, Spanish holog.

Thus far William Holt had lived a charmed life, it would seem, in avoiding trouble. But now there was some "small unpleasantness" between him "and some soldiers and gentlemen of his nation." Perhaps he was losing patience with their importunity. It did not help that he did not know how to speak Spanish or to "deal with the ministers of the Spanish nation." Clearly, he was a man growing tired. He had become "very depressed and anxious to get away after so many long years of work." All the same, he made it clear that, as became a good Jesuit, he was ready to make the decisions of the General and Persons his own.[18] Holt recommended Creswell as his successor in Flanders for reasons sufficiently obvious. Certainly, it seemed to Persons time for the King, Philip, and Creswell to discuss a plan to ensure the support not only of the seminaries but also of private individuals, "and this without any expense to his Majesty"(!). After this, Creswell could go to Flanders and Holt come to Spain.[19]

Affairs at Valladolid were reportedly going well. Persons was somewhat dismayed by the size of the bills, but even after building expenses had been paid there were still nearly one thousand escudos in hand. The total community now numbered fifty-four.[20] Flack was proving a happy choice as rector of St. Omers.[21] A further hindrance to business was removed when Aquaviva gave Persons permission to make quick decisions when it seemed necessary without recourse to Rome. On the strength of this, he sent Henry Walpole to England, something he had wanted "for a long time"; Garnet had been clamoring for some competent support. By this time, Allen had caught up with the St. Omers project; but although he wanted it to be set up in Douai, Persons brought him round to his own view. In any case, this was Philip's choice, or so Persons could consistently plead.[22] The absence of the more effective Spanish Fathers in Rome for the congregation left a void at the court which Aquaviva asked Persons to fill. This meant that the oversight of the new foundations had to be conducted by the remote control of letter.[23]

Even now Persons had not abandoned all idea of an empresa. Towards the end of August, he received a long and detailed report of affairs in Scotland. He passed his information to Juan de Idiaquez,

---

[18] William Holt to Aquaviva, 16.xii.1593, Brussels; (VI) Germ. 171, f.7, Latin holog.

[19] RP to Aquaviva, 15.vii.1593; v. supra.

[20] S. to s., 11.viii.1593, Valladolid; (VI) Hispania 136, f.14, Italian holog.

[21] Aquaviva to RP, 27.ix.1593, Rome; (VI) Castell.6, f.164, Spanish draft.

[22] RP to Aquaviva, 11.viii; v. supra.

[23] Aquaviva to RP, 30.viii.1593, Rome; (VI) Castell.6, f.163, Spanish draft.

using a messenger "in his dress a soldier but by calling a priest."[24] This was none other than John Cecil, William Cecil's informer, who was left to make his own relation to the Spanish secretary. Persons recommended him as "a man of trust" who had risked his life to gather and deliver his findings. His own letter stressed once again the importance of the Scottish dimension in English affairs. John Cecil—Snowden—was negotiating on behalf of certain Scottish lords matters which "might yield very great advantage to both kingdoms." They were not strong enough to act on their own. John Cecil purveyed a plan whereby an invasion could be effected through "a port in an accessible but safe part of the country whereby aid could reach them from elsewhere without the English queen being able to prevent it." There were many lords who had been converted to Catholicism and who would rally to its support. If Philip refused to help them, they would leave Scotland, adding thus to the number of unproductive mouths to be fed by the overburdened Spanish state. Persons added his own encouragement, pointing out the close proximity of England and Scotland. If it all seemed doubtful, someone could be sent back with "this priest" to test the truth of his utterances and gain further information. At all events, Idiaquez should keep the Scottish lords in tow and encourage them with a speedy reply. Secrecy was essential, explaining why John Cecil came disguised as a soldier. He had brought with him three English students—three more spies?—and, be it noted, his funds were exhausted. Persons would find a man to accompany him back to Scotland.[25]

So it was that Persons became involved in the obscure aftermath of the affair of the Spanish Blanks. James VI's main preoccupation was to avoid becoming a puppet either of the Scottish Kirk or of the English Crown. This obliged him to play off one interest against another, and to use the Catholics to counterbalance the combined weight of English and Scottish Protestantism. After James's Protestant league of 1590, uniting Scotland, England, Denmark, and Henri IV, the Catholic earls of Scotland instinctively drew closer to Spain as their only support abroad. It is, of course, highly significant that Elizabeth's government, thanks to a Catholic priest if not to others, was fully aware of these negotiations between the Scottish Catholics and Spain.[26] From 1592 the organizing leaders of the Catholics were Lords Belgarys and Graham of Fentry. George Ker, Lord Newbottle's brother, was sent to Spain as their envoy, carrying letters of recommendation, with

---

[24] RP to Juan de Idiaquez, 31.viii.1593, Valladolid; (VIII) Estado 839, f.76, Spanish holog.

[25] Ibid.

[26] See Hume, *Treason and Plot,* 25.

a further project simply committed to memory for Spanish assistance to the Catholics in their struggle against the Kirk. The project was to be written down on paper only when he was safely in Spain. The paper was provided: as it was claimed, a number of blank sheets signed and sealed by various Catholic nobles and gentlemen of whom the most significant were the Earls of Huntley, Errol, and Angus.

Apart from the obvious intervention of the English council and the presumed presence of spies, it is impossible to accept without considerable reservation the story of 1593 in view of a similar device, proved to be a deception, adopted in 1586. This 1593 project was for three thousand Spanish soldiers, with arms for a like number of Scots, to rescue James from his Protestant enclave and to reestablish Catholicism in Scotland and subsequently in England. "Rescue" appears to be the correct word, since James was a party to the plan.[27] A principal obstacle to credibility is that its truth depends on the veracity of George Ker under threat of torture. He was arrested by one of those suspicious strokes of providence or "marvellous chance," too common at this time to be in the aggregate universally plausible, just as he was on the point of embarking for Spain. This was on December 7, 1592. "All his letters [were] captured"—careless man!—and sent to England. The Queen—or, more correctly, Burghley, of course—used this as a reason for sending money and men to James "with orders from him to prosecute rigorously all who were concerned or suspected."[28] Ker, threatened with torture, told all, or all that he was told to tell, producing a "secret paper" purporting to be "a copy of the Scottish king's instructions to Spain." These should have been sent by Pury Ogilvie, "but thereafter were concredit to Mr George Ker, and withdrawn at his taking for the safety of his Majesty's honour."[29]

It is sufficiently unlikely that James, already wise beyond his years in such matters, would have handed over or authorized such a document as the above, so conveniently and damningly labeled. The Catholic earls, though warned by previous experience, made over, seemingly, signed and sealed blank sheets. Hume noticed the peculiar resemblances in James's alleged production to Burghley's style in drawing up pros and cons in statements of the kind. Scholars since his time have denounced the whole affair as a typical Cecilian fraud.[30]

---

[27] (25) IV, 603–6, 603 n.(*); Hume, 26f.

[28] Hume, ibid., 27 and n.2.

[29] Ibid., 28.

[30] See the Marquis of Huntley, *Memorials of Aboyne*. Hume contended that his discovery of "the original document" ((25) IV, 603) proves the authenticity of the plot. But this was not an original document connected with Ker in 1592 but only the relation of events brought to Spain by John Cecil in the summer of 1593, as RP's correspondence

Certainly, for Burghley all worked out well. Sir David Graham, baron of Fentry, was taken and beheaded, while the three earls were obliged to flee northwards. James had been sharply warned of the dangers of flirting with the papists. Indeed, under threat of being turned off the throne by Elizabeth if he failed, he "persecuted the said earls and the Catholics all he could."[31]

If, wise in his generation, the King gave way for a time, he did not allow himself to be blown before the English storm beyond Whitsun of 1593. He then adopted a "dour attitude towards the Protestants who had discovered the conspiracy."[32] Hence the need for yet another ruse, this time with John Cecil as the spy/catspaw, to force the young king back to more acceptable policies. We need not suppose that Elizabeth herself had any hand in these nefarious transactions, nor was it necessary for her to do so with so consummate a master in such matters at her elbow. Another "plot" might at least bring a few more Fentrys under the axe and warn off the rest. Snowden's plot, as he confessed it, was a copy of the other. The Catholic lords sent an English priest to Spain to commit their plans to King Philip. "But as they dared not send their signatures so soon after the other affair"—which meant there was no proof against them—"they sent the priest with a token to Fr Robert Persons . . . to whom he was already well known."[33] As Hume observed, "the Catholic lords had been detected on each occasion that they had sent either written communication or blanks to Spain. Robert Bruce [in 1586] had played them false and betrayed their secrets." So did John Cecil/Snowden.[34] Such was the sorry foundation of Persons's hopes for gaining control in Scotland by some sudden and secret coup. If Jesuitry has anything to do with cunning, it could be admitted, William Cecil was a far better Jesuit than Robert Persons!

A letter of Fr. Richard Gibbons to Aquaviva early in October asked him to bring pressure to bear on Persons to write the life of the martyred Edmund Campion.[35] His letter gives interesting sidelights on

makes clear. Hume admitted Cecil was the bearer, and "seems to have been afterwards a spy in the service of Sir Robert Cecil" (ibid., 606, n.). The entire episode stands in need of further critical study.

[31] (25) IV, 603. Hume admitted, "This would appear to be almost literally true. Elizabeth sent Lord Borrough as a special envoy to urge James to severity. . . ."

[32] Hume, *Treason and Plot,* 29.

[33] (25) IV, 603. John Cecil's report on 604f. The demands of the Catholics on which RP commented in the above letter to Idiaquez are on 605f. See "John Cecil's statement," 607f.

[34] Hume, *Treason and Plot,* 41f.

[35] R. Gibbons to Aquaviva, 6.x.1593, Valladolid; (VI) Hispania 136, f.93 r/v.

Persons as one of his brethren saw him: "always so ready to help everybody and sing their praises if they deserve any." "He is a man who flees from praise" and, unless the General gave the order, he would "never produce anything." Although Aquaviva must have known the pressures on his subject, he agreed that Campion's life should be written and Persons was the man to do it. "Let all be done with completeness and fidelity." All the same, it was foreseen that there might be items included which the censors would see fit to omit.[36]

Early in November, Persons asked the General for permission to put "Fr Oswald," Tesimond, in Valladolid, whose name would become only too familiar in connection with the Gunpowder Plot. It was essential to have a certain number of English Fathers in the seminaries, a point which the Spaniards fully accepted.[37] The seminaries were still "growing every day to the general satisfaction." Persons left the one at Valladolid, which now had accommodation for a hundred persons, "in excellent condition" both temporally and spiritually. Rodrigo de Cabredo was not only efficient but "much liked by all the scholars." Not quite so notable was the performance of the rector at Seville, but he "carries out his duties well." Some truth between the lines was conveyed in the fact that at Seville "a number of laymen who had known Fr Charles Tankard when he was attached to the governor of the province were wont to seek out his company in the English college." The best way of putting a stop to this was to "summon the said father to Valladolid."[38] Persons was not so much afraid of corruption by the dolce vita as that some of his priests might drop indiscreet remarks in the hearing of English spies, who were not in short supply. It was ironic that Persons himself should have been so completely fooled in this respect—admittedly by one of the best. In any case, the idea that toleration at home might be won for abandoning support for Spain was spreading even to the occasional Jesuit. Such a one was Thomas Wright, who was brought to Valladolid to lecture, appropriately enough, on controversies. Difficult subjects such as Wright were

Latin holog. RG says he has written to the rector of Prague for Campion's letters and MSS, and the reminiscences of others. RG had been consultor and admonitor to the rector at Valladolid. Was it about now that RP began a life of Campion in Latin? ((1), Anglia.A.II, 14, in RP's hand). RP wrote to Aquaviva on 8.ix. 1593 describing the satisfactory progress of the seminaries. See Aquaviva to RP, 28.x. 1593; (VI) Castell.6, f.167, Spanish draft.

[36] Aquaviva to RP, 22.xi.1593, Rome; (VI) Tolet.5.I, f.?23, Spanish draft.

[37] RP to Aquaviva, 2.xi.1593, Valladolid; (VI) Hispania 136, f.107r, Italian holog. Two letters from Aquaviva of 30.viii. reached RP about the end of October.

[38] S. to s., 4.xii.1593, Madrid; (VI) ibid., f.163, Italian holog. Reply to Aquaviva's of 28.xi.

usually treated with remarkable forbearance by the General, Persons,
and superiors in general. There was always a fear, no doubt, that if
they were driven to change sides completely, they could do considerable damage—as some did.

Certainly, although subjects were bound to obedience, they
were normally put to work in occupations fitting their talents and
temperament. Such as might break under the strain or too quickly
were not sent into England. Any other policy would, of course, have
been self-defeating.

The best news at the end of 1593 came from St. Omers. Flack
and Walpole already had a community of twenty, including fourteen
scholars—"very fine little boys." One hundred were expected within
the year. A number of English papists had written to say they valued
this seminary above the rest. More important, they guaranteed a
supply of pupils. The Spaniards also contributed generously with
money, so that there were already two thousand crowns to keep the
new institution afloat, a considerable sum even taking the prevalent
inflation into account. Inevitably, not all the Flemish Jesuits, thinking
of their own needs, rejoiced in the success of this alien growth. Some
thought the seminary should not have the status of an independent
college but should have a superior under the rector of their own
college in the place. This was one more problem for Aquaviva to solve.
To complicate matters, Philip II had in his first letters-patent inserted,
at Persons's own suggestion, a proviso that the royal allowance be paid
to the rector of the Flemish college if only until the English college had
its own rector. Flack might have to be sacrificed as the man in charge,
although he was the most competent "to keep the account of monies
with Spain" and also to maintain contact with the boys' parents and
relatives in England.[39]

---

[39] Ibid.

On Philip's instructions Persons prepared "dispatches" for Rheims, St. Omers, and also the nuns of Syon, all dated February 24, 1594. They were mainly to do with finance and royal promises connected therewith. Money already owed to Rheims for two years was to be paid. The Bridgettine nuns of Syon, after various migrations, reached Lisbon on May 19, 1594. Persons was instrumental in getting them a royal annuity.[1] He had previously taken their cause to Rome when the archbishop refused to receive them, so that Clement VIII put them under the immediate jurisdiction of the Holy See, a privilege retained until their return to England in 1861. The original 1720 ducats for St. Omers, levied "upon uncertain licenses," was now transmuted to "2,000 crowns of gold" derived from merchandise coming into Gravelines, a source considered good for more than 10,000 crowns a year. The King also wrote to the bishop, governor, and magistracy of St. Omer to recommend the English foundation "as a thing principally esteemed and loved by his Majesty."[2] There was now no limit on the number of students to be admitted, subject to the discretion of the Fathers as to what funds would allow. Finally, Persons received a royal warrant on a bank in Antwerp for four thousand crowns to be paid to Rheims, the arrears in the royal alms of some two years. Aquaviva was informed of all this in a letter of March 10.[3]

At St. Omer the local authorities were unhappy about an independent establishment for English boys and still more at the raising of any restriction on the original sixteen allowed. Thus the King's authority was necessary to oblige them to leave such decisions to the Jesuits themselves. At the same time, the latter were responsible to

---

[1] RP Memorandum; (II) f.248. Grene has omitted several lines in copying the original, so it is not clear how the nuns stood in this. On f.477, "Anno 1594. Nullam epistolam invenio præterquam quod habes fol.248.d." See Benedict Williamson, *The Bridgettine Order, its Foundress, History and Spirit* (London, 1921), 45.

[2] (II) f.248.

[3] RP to Aquaviva, 10.iii.1594, Madrid; (VI) Hispania 136, f.245, Italian. The financial details repeated in s. to s., 20.iii. from Cordoba, lest the earlier letter should be lost or intercepted; ibid., f.249, holog.

the magistracy for the proper running of the place.[4] There was a question as to whether Allen should exchange Rome for Flanders, a move which would certainly have added weight to the English side of any future dispute.[5]

The problem of Elizabeth's successor was becoming more acute as the Queen's life drew noticeably closer to its end. Among bona fide papists, as distinct from agents provocateurs, there was never any question of assassinating the Queen, even if few admired her and many on the continent were prepared to countenance foreign invasion to bring about improvement. Nevertheless, it seems that it was not until 1597 that official Spanish policy formally excluded any "attempt to use violence against the person of the queen."[6] However she left the scene, all Catholics were agreed that they should do something to provide for her successor and not leave the last word to their enemies. Inevitably, Persons was among those who took a great interest in the question. True to form, he had already produced a work on the subject and promised Aquaviva on March 10 "the portion of the *Book of Succession of England* which is in course of being translated."[7] This was the celebrated work, soon to be notorious in some quarters, in which Persons had considerable part and interest, but not the simple claim of authorship.[8]

On February 6 Persons enjoyed "a long and very agreeable audience" with Philip "about the affairs of the Society." Although the King was amenable enough to leaving the Society to manage its own affairs, especially in the congregation in session in Rome, some of his officials seemed too willing to interfere. Philip, as usual, promised Persons his support.[9] In Rome the Jesuits had made significant surrender of some of their privileges under pressure from one at least of the Spaniards. The thirty-second decree allowed that, out of deference to the tribunal of the Inquisition, "essential for Catholic faith and the peace of the kingdom," the Jesuits should waive certain privileges when operating in Iberia. The Inquisition disliked the Jesuit privilege of reading books on the *Index prohibitorum* and of absolving from heresy

---

[4] S. to s., 10.iii.1594; v. supra.

[5] See s. to s. 20.iii.1594; v. supra.

[6] See Loomie, "The Armadas," 400. Francisco de Borja de Medina, S.J., "Jesuitas en la Armada contra Inglaterra (1588): notas para un centenario," (43) LVIII (1989), 3–42.

[7] (VI) Hispania 136, f.245r; v. supra.

[8] See L. Hicks, S.J., "Fr Robert Persons and the Book of Succession," (10) 4 (1957), 104–37, especially 126–28.

[9] RP to Aquaviva, 20.iii.; v. supra.

in foro conscientiæ, that is, in the confessional without public process or acknowledgement; it also objected that a Jesuit needed permission of his superior to be promoted to office, even the highest, whether ecclesiastical or secular. Aquaviva sent a papal brief acquiescing in the first two demands. The General himself had granted the third in letters patent of March 20, 1589. For the rest the Society in Spain was urged "seriously and gravely" to bow to the demands of the Inquisition at all times, while the King was to confirm it all by his authority.[10]

With two letters of recommendation from the King for the governor and municipality respectively, Persons came to Seville on March 22.[11] He was agreeably surprised by the council's response. At a meeting with them, he "found in all of them such willingness to help on this work that it really seems to be the hand of God." Rarely did a proposition meet with unanimity in the Council of Seville, "but in this case there was not a single vote against us." In fact, when Persons asked for another two hundred escudos a year, added to their three hundred, they made it three hundred extra. This was sufficient "to rent any big house in Seville." However, it could not be too far from St. Hermenegild, where the students heard their lectures. One residence seemed especially suitable; but the King's help would be necessary to set aside an entail. Furthermore, "the high constable of the court here" wanted it, but the King would be prepared to order him aside, or so Persons understood. The house was "very large and spacious and in a beautiful position, quite close to the Society's college, the river and open country." But Fr. Robert's main ambition was to produce "a very select body of men," the ripe fruit "of those splendid saplings from St Omers'." So far there were none of the "evil humours" that were causing division in Rome and Rheims; on the contrary, "the greatest spirit of union and of respect and deep affection for the Society" prevailed. Indeed, the best might feel drawn to join the Jesuits "in due course."[12]

Joseph Creswell fell ill about this time.[13] Persons left Seville for Madrid on May 11, taking Creswell with him and also an Englishman, Brother Arthur. The provinces of Seville, Castile, Toledo, and Andalusia all received English members about this time. Meanwhile, the disturbing news arrived from England of Henry Walpole's capture

---

[10] *Decreta, canones, censuræ et præcepta congregationum generalium S.J.* . . . . Tomus I.us (Avenione [Avignon], 1830), 323–25.

[11] RP to Aquaviva, 20.iii.; v. supra. Tesimond is named in s. to s. 12.v.1594; v. infra.

[12] S. to s., 18.iv.1594, Seville; (VI) Hisp.136, f.204, Spanish holog.

[13] Ibid.

almost as soon as he arrived. It was as well that he went "with a great desire of martyrdom and the dispositions likely to merit this favour from our Lord." In spite of the loss, Persons wrote to England asking for Robert Southwell or William Weston, promising another in exchange. For the rest, he refused to be dismayed. In a short time there would be "men sufficient to supply and maintain the mission against all the forces of the heretics. . . . The number of those captured, and still more those martyred, is very limited considering the sizeable number of men sent there and the many more who are anxious to go." These included Henry Walpole's three brothers already waiting in the slips. Garnet had the General's permission to receive another twelve into the Society, of whom four had been sent to Flanders "in the last few days." Seventeen Jesuits were now working in England with the prospect of good vocations to follow from the seminaries.[14] Of these Seville was not only free of debt but had one thousand ducats in hand in spite of the six thousand spent in the seventeen months of its existence.[15]

William Holt now had Aquaviva's leave to proceed to Spain. "Although he is of a somewhat unsociable disposition, he is a man of tried virtue and good intelligence, and . . . well able to accommodate himself to other people's views." Creswell had proved rather less accommodating, although he too was a "conscientious religious, with good address and intelligence." Meanwhile, it seemed high time for Holt to quit Flanders. A rift was growing between him and William Crichton, formerly "very good friends." Colonel Semple, a Scot in Madrid, showed Persons a letter in which Crichton complained about setting up "a seminary for poor and undistinguished boys from England" while the King had so far done nothing for "boys from Scotland of noble lineage." Persons did not defend himself on anachronistic principles of democracy but on Crichton's error as to fact. The majority of pupils at St. Omers were "the sons of gentlemen of very good position." Another report claimed that when the Bishop of St. Omer asked how it was that the English had so many seminaries and the Scots none, Crichton replied that this was because "the English were more persistent and went begging far and wide, while the Scots were of a more reserved and aristocratic temperament unsullied by this vulgar trait," with further comments of the kind. Persons refuted with feeling the further charge that he had not helped Crichton's "business

---

[14] S. to s., 10.v.1594, Seville; (VI) ibid., f.316, Spanish holog.

[15] S. to s., 12.v.1594, Marchena; (VI) ibid., f.318, Spanish holog. This contains much of the information in the letter of 18.iv. Creswell wrote to Edmund Harewood at the VEC about this time. The rent contribution by the Seville municipality was now given as 586 ducats per annum. On 15.v., Clement VIII had letters apostolic drawn up confirming the privileges of the college; CRS 14, 12.

here in Spain." In fact he had put at his disposal "money, labour, advice and everything else." In any case, his schemes "for curing the ills of Scotland . . . were not well-founded and, indeed, impracticable." Crichton was urged to abandon them and found instead "a good seminary for Scotsmen in Flanders." The Spaniards would have been very ready to help, but Crichton only presented a memorial on the subject just before he departed. "And then he was too impatient to wait for the answer or even to draw his travelling expenses, and so he left with neither." He then tried to negotiate by letter, "a very feeble way of proceeding. . . . And because he does not get what he wants, he gets annoyed and starts complaining of others."[16]

The decrees of the Fifth General Congregation reached Spain by late spring of 1594. Persons concluded, "they all make a good impression except the third about the Hebrew race." This aimed to exclude any of Jewish descent from entering the Society. "It is scarcely decent to exclude any race of Christians from a means which our Lord left for their salvation, namely, the religious life, if they are incurring danger in the world." Many felt the decree would stir up discord within the Society, even in Spain. Admittedly, some of the royal ministers had spoken to Persons on occasion, intimating that such a decree would be a good thing. Persons brought forward many reasons against it. Nevertheless, a good Jesuit was expected to conform his own ideas to those of the Society. "Now we will turn over a new leaf and seek the best arguments we can to defend what our mother has decided."

The twelfth decree touched Persons more closely and required further elucidation. "Let no one on any account," it ran, "be involved in the public or secular affairs of princes which pertain to matters of state." Persons wished to observe it to the letter; but in the English situation, where religion and politics were inextricably entwined, how could this be done? Everything attempted there for the "service of religion" was opposed to law and government. The problem was all the more pressing in view of Elizabeth's death, which some believed imminent. Indeed, an English spy reported to Thomas Phelippes from Liège, "the Queen of England is dead."[17] Persons wanted advice, dispensation, or instruction from the General.

All this time Persons was translating the *Book of Succession* for Aquaviva. The latter foresaw the reaction of the hornet's nest to this provocation and could not be encouraging. A positively discouraging letter of his dated March 30 reached Persons on June 4. In any case,

---

[16] Ibid.

[17] Robert Robinson/Saint Main/Sterell to John Morice/Phelippes, 28.v.1592, Liège; (29) 1591–94, 225. Previously quoted, RP to Aquaviva, 12.v.; v. supra.

orders had been given to the agent in Flanders to hold up and keep secret the English version until further notice. Allen at least must have time to consider and decide. A Spanish version, or at least that part which dealt with the various pretenders, was already in the hands of Juan de Idiaquez. Persons could not take it back, but the Spaniards would keep it secret except from the Pope and their ambassador in Rome, "or so they have assured me." Had Persons foreseen the General's desire to call a halt, he would have held it up himself. "However the matter did not depend simply on me but on at least three or four others who also had a share in it. They are men of notable importance, experienced and well-qualified to judge in matters which concern the whole nation." These thought not only that no harm could come of it but that it would "help the cause considerably."[18]

The Spanish translation for Aquaviva left for Rome by one of the King's galleys early in June. The English version was held back "since it would not be understood"—or too readily misunderstood? It had been penned "with all courtesy and impartiality with prejudice to none." The first of its two books insisted that the principle of heredity alone should not be the determining factor. Religion was the vital consideration. Mistakenly, the Catholics overlooked this at the death of Mary I. The second book dealt with the claims of five royal houses and ten or eleven individuals. No claimant was preferred to another, and the claims were those made by the claimant, no one else. The heretics wanted to forbid all discussion so that they could saddle the country with a monarch of their own choice. Nothing was said against the King of Scots except that he was a Protestant, but his claims were considered with the same objectivity as those of the Spanish. The latter, indeed, found no cause for enthusiasm in the book and Philip found nothing in it to hasten him towards naming a successor.[19] Persons did not see how the book could give "just cause for offence" to anybody; but he was ready to stand by the General's decision.[20]

To Persons's relief, Aquaviva thought the book "good and necessary." But while he felt that laymen could go on working on it, it would be better for Jesuits to have nothing to do with its publication. One could not hope for secrecy in such matters. The General's more

[18] RP to Aquaviva, 4.vi.1594, Madrid; (VI) ibid., f.362, Spanish holog. For the authorship question, see L. Hicks's art. in (10) 4, 104–37; v. supra. This letter is given in toto on 110–12 except for a postscript.

[19] See Loomie, "The Armadas," 394, 400.

[20] RP to Aquaviva, 4.vi.; v. supra. The contents of this letter were sent "by an extra post on the 4th of this month." Observations on the English foundations virtually repeated the substance of former letters. The supplement to this letter was dated 16.vi. For the attitude of James VI, see Hicks, "Fr Persons and the Book of Succession," 119f.

enthusuastic support was given to St. Omers precisely as an institution independent of others in the city.[21] By about June 20 Mannaerts had concluded that it should be allowed to have Mass and vespers in its own chapel, although without music, until the provincial had inspected the premises for himself. He also should have the last word in determining the number of pupils, which would depend on financial resources. The rector would be independent of the rector of the Flemish college but subject to the provincial and the advice of his own consultors. The advice of externs could only be sought with the provincial's approval. As the boys were of "noble or decidedly worthy parents" and were exiles for religion, they should not be treated like servants and only beaten for exceptional offences.[22] In its administration the school should resemble those already operating in Rome and Spain, since it was expected that many of the boys would proceed eventually to one of these places for further study.[23]

By mid-June, the Rheims seminary had moved back to Douai, its city of origin. Credibly, the management was "much consoled" to find waiting for it "the warrant for 4,000 crowns" sent from Spain.[24] Not all was consoling elsewhere. On July 12 Persons wrote two letters to the General, one evidently intended for wider dissemination and full of optimism. "Peace and contentment reigned" at Valladolid, where all were in good health and heart. At Seville so complete had been the cooperation of the Spanish Fathers that Peralta asked the General to send them a special letter of thanks. As for the feared effects of rivalry, the professed house had "been more prosperous in one year after the English college was established than for two or three years previously." No less than seven thousand ducats had been received this year in alms.[25] The second letter, while not belying the first, admitted certain personality clashes among the English members, notably Gibbons, Tankard, and Thomas Wright, which Persons found irritating. Such things in an enclosed, academic society are perhaps inevitable even with the grace of God. Gibbons suffered from "fits of anger"; but Persons, by his own account, treated him with great patience and even

---

[21] Aquaviva to RP, 1.viii.1594, Rome; (VI) Castell.6, f.183.

[22] For his high reputation see (57) 346–51. Although no longer provincial, "il est sans cesse consulté et, dans les affaires les plus épineuses nous verrons les provinciaux, non seulement prendre son avis, mais lui abandonner la direction"; op. cit., 350.

[23] "Primæ determinationes RP Oliverii Manarei pro seminario Andomarensi," 19.vi.1594; (VI) Germania 177, f.313r/v; see (62) 30.

[24] RP to Aquaviva, supplement of 16.vi to letter of 4.vi.; v. supra.

[25] S. to s., 12.vii.1594, Valladolid; (VI) Hispania 137, f.24, with a second letter on f.26, less optimistic, for private viewing?

indulgence, allowing him the use of his rooms and books in his absence, "holding back only some secret papers."

By the summer of 1594 the college of St. Ambrose, Valladolid, was having problems. It stood to the English seminary in the relation of "mother and child or master and pupil."[26] For some years, as he claimed, Persons had watched the college "go into decline and discontent both as regards its administration and its studies." The Spanish, no less than the English, Jesuits were embarrassed that the English students should witness division among them caused by two members of the staff, one of whom was excessively out of touch and the other too often engaged elsewhere. Persons used his influence with the General to bring about amendment. This influence, however, could itself raise further questions. Persons's position was altogether anomalous. One could hardly blame the authorities at St. Omer, for example, for wanting to know precisely what "orders or authority" he had from the General "to discuss the affairs of the seminary with them." Persons suggested to Aquaviva what his function should be. "I would like them to be told . . . that you want them to listen to what I have to say to help that seminary and keep it in step with the seminaries here."[27]

If only because Aquaviva wished it, Persons now threw himself energetically into the task of founding, or helping to found, a Scottish seminary. By the beginning of September, he had already made a start in discussion with Bartolomé Perez. Anxious to dispel the idea that his own nationality would make him do less for the Scots, he assured Perez that he was only hesitant to take on the further task because he was so much taken up with the English; but in fact a Scottish seminary deserved to be taken up "even more than the other." He would do all he could for both.[28]

A Scots college was already in existence at Douai but was not exactly flourishing when Persons began to take a more direct interest. John Leslie, bishop of Ross, exiled in 1574, founded a Scots college in Paris. Transferred to Pont à Mousson in 1581, it closed its doors in August 1590 for the usual reason, lack of funds. It was reerected at Douai in April 1593 by William Crichton under the name of "Arthur Gordon," aided by James Tyrie, another Scottish Jesuit. The twelve students included four who had joined at Douai in 1593. On April 5, Clement VIII formally recognized by brief the transfer to Douai, confirming its rights and privileges and putting it under Jesuit direction.

---

[26] S. to s., 12.vii., second letter; v. supra.

[27] S. to s., 7.ix.1594, Valladolid; (VI) ibid., f.164, Spanish holog.

[28] Ibid. Gibbons's departure for Rome from Valladolid on 1.viii is referred to in RP. to Aq. 10.viii.1594; (VI) ibid., f.118r.

The reasons for the move were given as the bad climate from the Scottish viewpoint, the frequency of war, and the distance of the Lorraine location from Scotland.[29] Crichton asked Aquaviva to put the government in the hands of the Flanders provincial. He offered no name for superior, perhaps having himself in mind. There were Scottish ecclesiastics at Tournai and St. Quentin, but none with any desire to take on the college, as Crichton claimed. He thought, reasonably enough, that a competent Belgian would be preferable as superior to a less competent Scot; less reasonably, perhaps, he thought that this superior should not be a Jesuit, even though he was under the control of the provincial and rector of the local Flemish college. Three from the seminary had already applied to join the Society, although two more priests who wished to be admitted to theological studies were rejected "propter infirmitates." Crichton no less than Persons was aware of the background problem created by "the multitude of spies and traitors" in the area.[30] In 1595 the seminary moved to Louvain.[31]

At the beginning of October 1594, Persons went back to Seville. The move was dictated by reasons of health as well as by further expected developments in the city. Contracting a "quartan ague" on September 13, he expected another attack on October 2. Fever or no fever, the work went on as Creswell came to visit him to discuss the more complete report to the General which Persons could not then carry out. His personal attention was also required at a time when the college was about to acquire another house. Thomas Wright as a problem was now passing from the chronic to the acute stage. According to Persons, he behaved well at Valladolid up to some three months previously, living "peaceably and without giving offence" if not evidently overendowed "with spirituality and interior life."[32] But now he had conceived a desire which would not be thwarted to visit England "for reasons of health." Persons, Tankard, and Creswell all failed to convince him that England was not the best place at that time for any Jesuit's health.

---

[29] Based on H. Chadwick, S.J.'s, notes; (XIV) 46/22/5.

[30] W. Crichton to Aquaviva, 12.xi.1594, Antwerp; (VI) Ep.Gen.33, f.70, a.l.s; (XIV) 46/3/13/6, transcript.

[31] H. Chadwick, notes on Scotland; (XIV) 46/22/5.

[32] See RP to Aquaviva, 2.x.1594; (VI) Hispania 137, f.201, Spanish holog.

N ot before the third week in February 1595 did Persons recover
sufficiently to deal with a new and unusual dilemma.[1] William
Cardinal Allen died on October 16, 1594, leaving behind him
another succession problem. The vacuum created set up currents
strong enough to disturb the smooth course of several men fitted by
nature, grace, and favor to assume his mantle. Robert Persons was
among them.

He had the required intelligence, dedication, and gift for
leadership and practical affairs; and he enjoyed the trust of men in
authority, especially Philip II. True, the Vatican now leaned towards
Henri IV and most things French but was not unaware of Persons's
achievement, especially in connection with the seminaries. His devotion
to the English cause was plain to see—much too plain for some. Jesuits
were obliged by their institute to shun honors and titles but could not
refuse a direct commission from the pope. Cardinal Toledo, for example, formerly a Jesuit, was invested in the purple in 1593.[2] Some of
Persons's Spanish friends were already referring to him as "illustrissi-
mus"; but, although he was aware of it, he considered it indelicate to
advert to the fact until he received letters of protest from Mannaerts
and Richard Gibbons. Mannaerts exhorted him in a letter of November 24, 1594, to prove his "integrity and sincerity" by standing aside in
favor of Owen Lewis, bishop of Cassano. In any case, the bishop already had the income required; Persons had not. The writer was
aware that the Duke of Feria and leading Catholics, including cardinals, had put Persons's case to the Pope. But it was as a "plain religious" that Persons could serve best, dealing freely with all and begging for good causes. As a cardinal he could certainly not go begging
and would furthermore be obliged to give his whole attention to
"church politics, financial affairs and [his] own establishment."[3]

---

[1] See RP to Aquaviva, 20.ii.1595, Seville; (VI) Hispania 138, f.142, 2 letters,
Latin and Spanish, the Latin in (16) VI, par. 4. RP sent a copy of Mannaerts's letter of
24.xi.1594? to Aquaviva with the two letters of 20.ii. (v. infra).

[2] See (16) VI, par. 3.

[3] Ibid.

Mannaerts's arguments were not all that cogent and one suspects a trace of jealousy in his anxiety to discourage. But Persons himself seems genuinely to have preferred to continue as an *éminence noire* rather than don the purple. He addressed Aquaviva on the subject in two letters of February 20, 1595, having previously discouraged his Spanish confrères from raising the subject at court.[4] While assuring the General that he had no wish to take a step which would have ended his career as a Jesuit, he had to avoid the subject as far as possible, "lest, as the saying is, while trying to stifle the smoke [he] seemed willing to blow the flame." Sir Francis Englefield handled the topic which was amply answered on May 10.[5]

Persons was altogether correct by Jesuit principles in resisting any attempt to bring about his elevation. To have acted otherwise could have been taken for ambition, a grave fault for Jesuits. But one may doubt the wisdom of his friends who advised against his promotion. Much subsequent misunderstanding might have been avoided had he been promoted to an office which, if it finished his career as a religious, would have given him the authority he tended to exercise anyway by force of personality, understanding, and experience. As time passed, the secular priests, growing in numbers and experience themselves, hoped for organization on hierarchic lines accepted as the pattern in the Catholic Church since apostolic times. Had Persons been given a rank which gave him unequivocal authority, none could have blamed him for using it. As it was, his influence, that of a priest otherwise unadorned, could be easily represented as the efforts of a man constantly rising above himself and assuming over others, especially the secular priests, an authority which he did not have. Persons could scarcely by this time have opted out of a position of almost unique influence, since there was no one to replace him. However, by continuing to exploit his opportunities, even if it was always for the good of the cause as he saw it, he appeared to many, and not merely the malevolent, as a man behaving ambitiously while hypocritically denying it.

Writing from Seville on February 20 to Aquaviva, Persons expected to leave that city soon. Meanwhile, seven thousand ducats had been spent on buying the new house, although three thousand more were needed for restoration. By this time the King had set aside the entail to favor the Jesuits. The achievement was real; but one speculates on the feelings of the nobleman who was forced to stand aside for the advantage of a handful of foreign exiles. Meanwhile, at Valladolid it was admitted that Thomas Wright was "doing no good in

---

[4] RP to Aquaviva, 20.ii.1595 (v. supra).

[5] (16) VI, p. 232.

that house." Persons urged the General to prepare letters of dismissal; but it was doubtful that Wright would bother to stay on to receive them.[6] Creswell at Madrid was carrying on "the business of the two seminaries" but not with Persons's success. He had not found the provincial helpful. The position of the English Jesuits in exile was altogether anomalous and would remain so until the formation of an English province in 1623. Persons tried to get Creswell recognized as a de facto procurator or treasurer for the new foundations, but it was difficult to get him taken seriously as a quasi-independent official. Hard put to it to find suitable men for important posts, the Castilian provincial now sent Gonzalez del Rio to Valladolid as rector of the English college. He was described to Persons as "a very suitable person"; the latter observed laconically, "Time will show." Fortunately, the continuing generosity of the good people of Seville made up for disappointments elsewhere.[7] And in England came good news from Garnet that Richard Blount, former student of the English College, Rome, after two years of the Spanish experience, wished to join the Society.[8]

Two months later, time was already showing where Gonzalez del Rio was heading. The new broom at Valladolid began to introduce reforms which were not so much sweeping as devastating. Thanks to illness, Persons had not been able to discuss matters with him before he took up his new post. The previous rector, Cabredo, had also been transferred before the new man came on, so that he could not impart the wisdom of experience. It would probably have made no difference. Del Rio soon reached the unshakable conviction that he knew better than either of his consultors—men, significantly, who had known no disagreement with Cabredo or Persons. Colleges elsewhere in the Society had suffered much from the recklessness of new rectors. If del Rio took advice, it was from Fathers outside the house who could know nothing of its needs.[9] Some of his arrangements threatened to divide the community into Spanish and English sections, too readily becoming factions. Persons always foresaw the danger of racial division. It was pardonable, maybe, that del Rio caused a better kind of bread to be baked, although even this increase in expenditure brought a threat to the college finances. More grave to the point of being unforgivable was his waste of resources on lavish entertainments given to extern guests. Indeed, the house was almost used as a hotel, which gave

---

[6] RP to Aquaviva, 19.iii.1595, Seville; (VI) Hisp.138, f.184, Spanish holog.

[7] (39) 13.

[8] RP to Aquaviva, 19.iii. (V. supra.)

[9] RP to Gonzalez del Rio, 12.v.1595, Seville; (IX) Serie II, Legajo 1, Spanish contemporary.

justifiable scandal to those who contributed in alms to its upkeep. The General, Cabredo, and Persons had agreed that putting up even one guest was an extravagance hard to justify.[10] Swift reform was called for.

A welcome sight for Persons was the safe arrival of the Spanish Plate fleet from the West Indies in Seville harbor. "Our harvest also depends on when this one is gathered in." A severe storm had broken up the convoy, thus making it more vulnerable to English pirates. Meanwhile the human harvest promised well with students arriving from Douai and St. Omers about the end of April. The latter contingent had been obliged to walk three hundred miles on foot, since their money had run out halfway.[11] Unfortunately, two parties destined for Seville had been "captured and carried off by the heretics," English, in the Queen's ships. "One of the thirteen taken in Ireland, carted off to London loaded with chains, subsequently escaped from prison" and still made his way to Seville. The worst loss involved six boys from St. Omers and Fr. William Baldwin, who was captured with them. Not even this shook Fr. Robert's faith in divine providence. "It is the Lord. Let him do what is good in His eyes. In so many other things He consoles and helps us; and if we accept good from His hand, why not evil also?" A thought straight out of Job, but not the easiest pabulum for meditation.[12]

By this time Persons had recovered from his "quartan ague" but was still left with pain and swelling in his legs. This was taken as a disguised blessing which let him off another journey to Madrid urged upon him by two Scottish gentlemen and John Cecil alias Snowden. He helped them by letter and "in other ways," but he feared that "the dilatory methods of this court, for our sins, must bring everything to ruin."[13] Snowden and his friends or dupes were acting ostensibly on behalf of the Scottish Earls of Angus, Errol, and Mar. Persons still had no inkling of Snowden's true role. In any case, his thoughts were mainly where his truer interest lay. At Seville some eighteen thousand ducats had now been laid out on the building, which when finished would be worth more than thirty thousand. "It will be the finest college for many a league and have room for over 150 persons." Here the rector's performance was exemplary. Persons, brooding somewhat over the loss of Cabredo at Valladolid, tried to convince Aquaviva the Society had "no work on its hands in Spain of greater importance than

---

[10] Ibid.

[11] Ibid. and RP to Aquaviva, 15.v.1595, Seville; (VI) Hisp.138, f.264, Spanish holog.

[12] RP to Aquaviva, 15.v.1595 (v. supra).

[13] Ibid.

the seminaries."[14] The house at San Lucar de Barrameda was also doing well. The church had been restored, and shops on the exterior were expected to bring in five hundred ducats per annum for the support of the chaplains. The Duke of Medina Sidonia was taking a personal interest. He not only contributed to the table but also guaranteed an adequate apportionment of water.[15] Persons's temperament was able to work with the Spaniards, so that, although he usually left it to Peralta to deal with the provincial of Andalusia, sometimes the latter preferred to deal with him directly.[16]

By midyear the prospect of a cardinal's hat had receded. Aquaviva approved of letters sent in various directions to divert attention from his candidature.[17] Persons himself asked Idiaquez to use his influence with the King against it. A greater threat to Persons's unhindered progress, however, came from nearer home. The Spanish Jesuits, for the most part, accepted with good grace the presence among them of foreigners as proud as themselves and as conscious of their nationhood, men who did not always appreciate the favor conceded not only in allowing them to remain but to remain as rivals for the same limited sources of alms. Or so it could seem. The fact that all were, if not Jesuits, then at least fellow students and priests of the same religion, no doubt helped to prevent any major crisis or confrontation. Persons well understood the situation and behaved at all times with reticence and courtesy towards his hosts. Not all understood the finer nuances of Spanish punctilio, however, and mutual irritations could arise which ended in the Spaniards sometimes opposing the strangers in their midst and all their works. However much he understood the motives, Persons felt called upon to make a heartfelt protest to the General in a letter of June 12. His greatest difficulties arose, not from "the enemy without" or from "the maintenance and government of the seminarists," but from obstacles created by "members of our Society." Persons claimed that he had always been careful not to beg from those who were already contributing to the works of the Spanish Jesuits. Bartolomé Perez, a former provincial, had understood this, and without him the work could not have started. His successor was less enthusiastic, and the latest innovations had given rise to complaints from

---

[14] Ibid.

[15] Ibid.

[16] See RP to Provincial Mendez, 20.v.1595, Seville; (VI) ibid., f.281, Spanish copy.

[17] See RP to Aquaviva, 12.vi.1595, Seville; (VI) ibid., f.299, Spanish holog. The phrase used was "en Roma, Francia y Flandes," which suggests that RP did not write them himself or even through a secretary.

and about Valladolid, all of which had a boomerang effect on the morale of the house.[18]

The importance of character and temperament in dealing with the Spanish, and the singular success of Persons, was underlined by Creswell's relative failure in his attempt to fill in for his colleague. Creswell confessed in a letter from Madrid that he was "distressed and worn out by the difficulties" and the small favor shown him, so that he was thoroughly discouraged. Admittedly, supervising the four seminaries, two in Flanders, two in Spain, and handling the affairs of England, Scotland, and even Ireland in the court were no light task. Aquaviva had allowed Creswell to have an assistant paid for by the seminaries, but he had recently been sent away. Creswell's duties should in any case be reduced to those of procurator. Even in this his success seemed uncertain. He had "not got one ducat for the seminaries" since he had been in Madrid but had cost them "more than a hundred." Creswell was given another assistant, who turned out to be a Spaniard with whom he could not get on and who had "no sense or discretion about the business transacted."[19]

Persons allowed himself to believe, at least when he wrote to the General and others with influence and authority, that the conversion of England was only a matter of time and little time at that.[20] There was some cause for optimism. By July some of Persons's former critics were viewing his work more favorably. Vernal, rector of the professed house in Seville, came with twelve more Fathers to visit the English house on June 20. Shortly before, a similar party came from St. Hermenegild. Some of the Jesuits at Madrid still muttered, and Creswell could not prevent it. They felt that money could be better spent than on the chimerical "conversion of kingdoms." Another setback was provided by the death of the Bishop of Jaen, who had contributed one thousand ducats annually to the English seminaries. Apart from the abiding problem of del Rio, a mild fracas had broken out at Valladolid between the rector and Antonio de Padilla, supported by the English Fathers, over a theological thesis defended by one of the student priests. Persons suspected del Rio's friendship with José de Acosta as an underlying cause.[21]

Inevitably, the most impressive example was provided by those struggling with persecution rather than by those pursuing studies and

---

[18] Ibid.

[19] Ibid.

[20] S. to s., 10.vii.1595; (VI) ibid., f.339, Spanish holog.

[21] Ibid. S. to s., 9.xii., dealt with the above and with using Fr. de Sicilia and a problem concerning the French Jesuits; ibid., f.122.

politics, or even careers, in relative peace abroad. Henry Garnet had been running with the hare for some nine years, a success few expected. A very recent escape had been "almost by a miracle." Now that Baldwin and Jones had arrived on the English scene, it seemed time to give Garnet a rest, perhaps in Spain. In the event, he had another ten years to run before a martyrdom curiously mixed with glory and shame.[22]

By this time Garnet's England was showing considerable if concealed interest in the Queen's successor. In the summer of 1595, Sir Anthony Standen wrote to Persons to draw him out on the forbidden topic. Standen had been a spy for the English Council in Spain and Flanders. After a chequered career he returned to England in June 1593 and to an eclipse which he was determined should not be total or final. Distrusted by the Cecils, he was taken up by Essex and Anthony Bacon. It was probably as a piece of service for them that he now wrote to Persons with particular reference to the succession of James VI, a cause they had much at heart.[23]

Persons's reply to Standen virtually summarized the main argument of "Dolman's book." The succession of James seemed unlikely. Parliament had cut off Mary's title "by the oath and statute of association," which affected the son. He was a Puritan. Few wanted the union of both kingdoms, even the Scots and English. The Catholics found James unacceptable not only for his religion but also for his "extreme ingrate and unnatural dealing towards his mother." Indeed, his conduct was usually seen abroad as amounting to betrayal, making him a man not to be trusted. Persons was not excessively concerned with the principle of heredity. "Howsoever these matters of titles go . . . it is enough for a Catholic sober man to have any prince admitted by the body of his realm and allowed by the authority of God's Catholic Church . . . that will defend the religion of his old, noble ancestors." Genealogy was not enough. By the other test, certainly, James failed.[24]

High summer in Madrid: among the topics of an audience with Philip II was an invasion of England projected for the autumn. Sir John Hawkins and Sir Francis Drake were absent on expeditions against the Spaniards. Sir John Norris, reputedly the best soldier, was in Ireland, so that England was denuded of its ablest defenders. Scotland and Ireland were both in revolt. Henri IV was still too busy establishing himself in France to have time or attention for adventures

---

[22] RP to Aquaviva, 10.vii. (V. supra).

[23] For Standen's earlier career, see L. Hicks, S.J., "The Embassy of Sir Anthony Standen in 1603," part 1, (10) 5, 91–127. See (81) passim.

[24] RP to Standen, 8.ix.1595; (II) f.310.

abroad. Philip's army was ready in Flanders and his ships in all the ports of Iberia. The descent on Britain should be made in the winter, when the Queen least expected it, and with an army of moderate size rather than a vast machine that would give out too noisy a warning of its approach. The point of entry could be by Scotland, Kent, or Milford Haven, Henry VII's original choice. "There is no sort of difficulty whatever," wrote Persons in his enthusiasm. Wise in this at least, he offered no suggestion for a leader of the expedition.[25] As for Elizabeth's successor, the English Catholics would be happy to leave the choice to Philip. It was only "a certain faction" led by Charles Paget, Thomas Morgan, and Thomas Throckmorton who were opposed to such a scheme, as was Owen Lewis, but he died on October 14 of this year.

Presupposing easy success, in England itself, the succession issue should be handled delicately. Restoring Catholic religion was the principal object. The other question should be handled in a "provisional parliament" made up of Catholics which would choose subject to Philip's approval. He would also nominate the first bishops "in accordance with the privilege of the Kings of England." And so the scheme ran naively on.[26] Persons could only have supported it as a desperation measure, being keenly aware that every week's delay might mean another martyr, something glorious for the individual but for the cause the loss of one more precious workman. He was oversanguine in his estimate of the popular support such an invasion would receive even from the Catholics; but historians have tended to exaggerate the general approval given to the regime, especially its religious policies.[27] Undoubtedly there was unrest. A food shortage in London caused some two thousand apprentices and others to take up arms against the Lord Mayor. Order was restored only when four or five of the leading spirits were hanged, drawn, and quartered as traitors. The papist problem was complicated by the fact that Henri IV was now using his

---

[25] RP to Philip II, memo, n.d.; (VIII) Estado 2851, n.f., unendorsed Spanish holog.

[26] Ibid.

[27] The problem is interestingly discussed from the Protestant viewpoint in *Church and Society in England: Henry VIII to James I*, ed. F. Heal and R. O'Day (London, 1977). A Spanish attack was expected in England about now, a landing in Cornwall being reported on 26.vii. as having destroyed Penzance. (See G. B. Harrison, *A Second Elizabethan Journal 1595–1598* [London, 1931], 39f). On 7.viii. the preparation of a new armada was reported from Lisbon: some forty ships and ten thousand men; ibid., 40: and on 22.viii. "There is a most certain expectation of the enemy attempting us next year, either directly here at home or by the way of Scotland"; ibid., 41. It was expected to be much larger than the attempt of 1588. On 13.xii. the navy was ordered to put to sea as soon as possible with victuals for twelve thousand men for five months; ibid., 65.

influence on their behalf, so that many "were let out of prison, giving sureties that they would not flee abroad." Sir John Norris and his brother had been seriously wounded in the Irish war. Perhaps it did all add up to a moment auspicious enough for the Spaniards to mount an attack.[28]

Persons did not stay long in Madrid, although he expected to return soon to take an active part in any preparations for invasion. Creswell was sorry to see him go, but Fr. Robert was very much tied to his work at Seville. There were now sixty mouths to feed with the number "growing every day." The church was consecrated on October 8, although the congregation was smaller because five students had recently died. Their last words were reported as conveying their great sorrow not to survive to be "cut in pieces for their Lord's sake." However, they were soon replaced by others no less heroic from persecuted families in England.[29] One of the newcomers brought Persons "notes from various prisons, which he concealed in buttons, shoes and other more secret places." Others had been captured before they left England.[30]

Persons left Seville "in reasonably good condition" to arrive in Madrid by mid-November. A like optimistic judgment could not be passed on Valladolid, where the English Fathers were now at such odds with the rector that nothing less than Persons's presence was deemed sufficient to bring remedy. It was considered undesirable to replace del Rio before he finished his normal term of office.[31] But this problem had to wait while Persons took up the cudgels on behalf of the French Jesuits.

They had been in a difficult position, ironically enough, since Henri IV's conversion to Catholicism. News of the event traveled to Rome and messages back again too slowly to prevent the red tape from tying itself in knots. An excommunication originally launched by Sixtus V in 1585 against Henri, duc de Vendôme, as a relapsed heretic, was still technically in force when in March 1594 Aquaviva ordered the French Jesuits, out of deference to the Holy See, to take no oath of

---

[28] RP to Creswell, 28.x.1595, Seville; (IX) Serie II, Leg.1, contemporary Spanish copy. For rioting in London on 4.vii. see G. B. Harrison, *A Second Elizabethan Journal*, 32–34, 39; food shortage and rising prices, 39, 50, 51–53.

[29] It seems impossible to identify these boys. Unfortunately, the remaining Seville records are fragmentary. See "A register of the students of St Gregory's College at Seville, 1591–1605," (10) 9, 163–70. The list in CRS 14, 13–18, stops at vii.1595. The only brothers in the Henson/Loomie list who seem to fit are Brian and William Huddlestone; "A register . . . ," p. 167. But this is not a Dorset Catholic name (see Rachel Lloyd, *Dorset Elizabethans* [London, 1967]); could it be an alias?

[30] RP to Creswell, 28.x. (V. supra.)

[31] RP to Aquaviva, 2.xii.1595, Madrid; (VI) Hispania 139, f.122, Spanish holog.

allegiance to the converted king until the censure had been lifted. However, when the Parisian clergy, the professors of the Sorbonne, and the papal legate, no less, took the oath, the French provincial gave his Jesuits leave to do likewise. Aquaviva reacted by declaring their "offer to take the oath as a dishonour to the Society." The Jesuits shrugged and obeyed the General. This was the signal for a campaign to get them expelled from France. Jean Châtel's attempt on the King's life on December 27, 1594, brought crisis nearer. He had attended lectures at the Jesuits' Clermont College at some time in his life, so that only the worst could be supposed. It made no difference that he denied, even under torture, having accomplices. On January 7, 1595, Parlement ordered the Society to quit Paris.

Effort was now needed to save the rest of Jesuit endeavor in France; the colleges at Périgueux and Auch, for example, opened in 1592 and 1593 respectively. The Jesuit visitor in Spain, Alarçon, told Persons a tale of muddle and delay. Since the Spanish provincial when approached for help "gave no sign of any enthusiasm," Alarçon came to Persons. The latter took it up with his usual persistence and aplomb. Taking advantage once again of his confidential relationship with the King, he bearded him in the Pardo palace "very plainly, after dinner" on November 27. The audience lasted "over an hour and a quarter, a very gracious one and quite private." Persons had a memorial ready, anticipating that he would be asked for one. He was referred to Francis Idiaquez who "promised to use all his influence, and held out very great hopes." Although Persons had evidently mastered the techniques of approach and comportment required in the Spanish court, this was one affair in which he accomplished very little.[32]

Even at this interview, however, Persons achieved something for his seminaries. "Although the Fathers here do not know it, nor is it well they should on account of the massive suspicion now rife, [the King] has promised me a grant of 7,000 ducats from an impost at Seville to distribute among the seminaries and houses for paying their debts." If the Spanish Fathers had known this, they would have regarded it as alms taken from them, but Persons was confident that the money would not have been given to them in any case. Nevertheless, Persons had good friends among the Spanish Jesuits, something he was very willing to acknowledge. "I can truthfully say that I have never in my life found greater love and friendship than in these realms." He took it as the divine will that there were "men of all sorts for the common trial of all." The Spaniards, living in their imperial age, had a

---

[32] Ibid. El Pardo was a small town near Madrid where Charles V built a hunting lodge in 1543 which came to be used as a royal retreat.

tendency to regard the rest of the world as inferior, a trait soon to be shared by the English if they did not have it already. Persons was a man of international outlook. He thought it would be an advantage if at least a dozen Spanish students were sent to Rome to acquire the cosmopolitan outlook of the Eternal City. Significantly, the Spaniards who most favored Persons, Gil González, Perez, Cabredo, Duarte, Ribadeneira, had all done some of their studies in Rome.[33] Meanwhile, Creswell in Madrid and Holt in Flanders had to continue begging even at the cost of irritating their colleagues, who felt forced into the position of rivals.[34]

Whatever the educational advantages of other institutions in Rome, those in the English College were at low ebb. News arriving from various sources described a situation which was tempting Aquaviva "to give up the government of it." Persons was dismayed but hardly surprised. "The Society has got nothing but trouble from it so far and the ingratitude of those who have benefited from it." But to relinquish it would be disastrous. "The English nation does not possess secular priests of the calibre required for such government." That is, there were none of the qualities needed left over from Douai or the English mission. So to withdraw the Jesuits would be fatal. Handing it over to others would do nothing to allay the rebels' thirst for trouble but rather whet their appetite for more. Would it be better to revert to the idea of a hospice and distribute the income among the other seminaries? There was something in the atmosphere of Rome, it was said, highly inconducive to student endeavor. Contact with great personages was too easy, while hobnobbing with English layfolk in the city caused the students to become excessively brash and forward, so that they were almost unemployable later.[35]

Persons in reply pleaded for reform not destruction. The rector should be a resolute man who would rule with "sweetness and mildness" but also know how to "chastise the bad." Persons's further comments on the ideal no doubt indicate the pattern to which he tried to conform himself. He should not be "too intimate and friendly" nor yet "pernickety in taking notice of trifles." Certainly, the students should be cut off "from all familiarity with people outside, and even from those in the college itself who were known to be turbulent. Ready to punish, and expel in the last resort, he should not be "too hard-

[33] Ibid.

[34] Ibid. and T. Covert to Aquaviva, 11.viii.1595, Antwerp; (VI) Ep.Gen.34, f.272; (XIV) 46/3/13/6, transcript. There was tension among the English Jesuits. A serious quarrel broke out between William Holt and Thomas Covert. (See ibid.)

[35] RP to Aquaviva, 9.xii.1595; (VI) Hisp.139, f.122, Spanish holog. This letter really continued that of 2.xii.

hearted to forgive and forget where there [was] amendment." There should be no question of the students electing prefects or household officials. These should be appointed by the rector and on merit alone, not popularity. A foreign rector needed "two or three English Fathers" who would know how to "smooth over a thousand difficulties." The college tutors, by giving way too easily to the demands of the students, had seemed to justify the trouble makers and made the rest petulant and even contemptuous. An abysmal mistake had been to appoint a faction leader as priest in charge.[36] Philip of Spain also took an interest in the problem. Indeed, he sent a letter to Aquaviva to be enclosed in Persons's own, another tribute to the latter's influence in that quarter. He also instructed his ambassador to cooperate fully with Pope and General in any reform they might see fit to initiate.

But if one house was falling apart, another was knitting together. It was time to petition papal confirmation for the "conveyances made by the English merchants" regarding the foundation at San Lucar de Barrameda. Persons also wanted faculties "to make rules and ordinances for the good conduct of the priests in charge." The matter was put into the hands of Roger Baines and John Cecil to be brought to a successful conclusion under Aquaviva's direction. Presumably William Cecil was also kept in the picture.[37]

A memorial forwarded to Rome at this time asked for some definition of the status of English Jesuit institutions in exile. Persons often acted with a kind of authority, but his position as "prefect of the missions in the English seminaries" needed closer definition. Nor were foreign Jesuits alone in thinking so. While he accomplished much by force of personality, persuasiveness, and his influence in the Spanish court, he might disappear from the scene at any moment, so that an office was required for continuity, rather than merely an ill-defined official. Persons submitted a schedule of notes and rules for setting up and carrying out such an office, on which he invited the General's further comments and decision.[38] This, too, went to Rome with Roger Baines, formerly Allen's secretary. In spite of his association with Snowden/Cecil, Baines seems to have been loyal to Persons, although in an "information" for Burghley, Snowden put him among those who were "no favourers of the Spaniards and withal no friend to our state."[39]

It was not in letters to Aquaviva but to Juan de Idiaquez that Persons revealed the depth of his anxiety regarding the English Col-

---

[36] Ibid.

[37] Ibid.

[38] Ibid.

[39] Of 26.v.1591; (VII) SP12, 238, No. 181.

lege, Rome. The night of December 5 passed in a waking nightmare. "It has deprived me of sleep and upset my brain so much that I am not fit to leave the house." Hence Creswell, still unwell himself, was sent to discuss the matter with the Spanish secretary. Aquaviva's letter to Persons of October 29 had announced his decision, approved by the assistants, to give up the government of the college in Rome. The last straw came with the knowledge that the rebel students not only had influence with the English exiles but with the Pope and cardinals. Andrew Wise, an Irishman with the title of Grand Prior of England, had assumed Owen Lewis's mantle of opposition to Persons and the Society. Supported by the Paget-Morgan group and claiming to be the leader of the English nation, he had the ear of the Vatican. As Persons saw it, if the Jesuits gave up, the college would become "a seedbed of license, dissensions and opposition to all things Spanish including the King." In this way, the cause would lose its best friend abroad. After bringing the Roman seminary to ruin, they would turn on the Spanish foundations. Only the combined influence of General and King could avert disaster.[40] Reforms already indicated by Persons must be instituted forthwith. The Spanish ambassador in Rome must persuade the Pope to listen to the Fathers who were trying to run the college and to "good and peaceable men outside." Baines and Richard Haddock were named. So also was John Cecil, "whom his Majesty sent to Rome last summer" from Madrid. Much depended on Idiaquez, who must now persuade Philip to write to his ambassador in Rome forthwith. Fortunately, Aquaviva had put off the final decision regarding closure until he knew the reaction of Persons and Creswell.[41] Persons was consoled in this dark hour by his close understanding with Creswell. "I find in myself . . . goodwill and heartfelt friendship. . . . So clear . . . is your trust and loyalty. . . . May God prosper you always!"[42]

---

[40] RP to [Juan de Idiaquez?] 6.xii.1595, Madrid; (VIII) Estado 965, Spanish a.l.s. RP offered to enclose any reply for Aquaviva prompted by this letter with his own to go to Rome by "the trusty man."

[41] Ibid.

[42] RP to Creswell, 24.xii.1595; (I) A.V.9, No. 28.

Another Attempt at Invasion: 1596

Persons returned to the English College at Valladolid some time before Christmas 1595. On December 20 the provincial, Gonzálo Dávila, made his second visitation. The college was found to be saddled with a debt of 1,943 reales. Accounting had been slipshod from the beginning, receipts and payments being recorded without detailed entries. Only totals were put down, with no mention of the source of income. Dávila saw to it that the books from now on would be kept more professionally.[1] On January 15, 1596, del Rio departed for Segovia. "If he had remained till the end of his three years, he would undoubtedly have ruined the college completely." He did not leave willingly. Indeed, he tried to ingratiate himself with staff and Jesuit community to lengthen his time, but none of the latter, at all events, took his side. "The end he seems to have set himself was to play lord and master, entertain his friends, and stroll about with a following of students like a retinue of honour. . . . He had even begun to make accusations against us to Father General."[2] Aquaviva ordered him to defer to Persons, who was directed to report fully to Rome. It was his experience of del Rio which led Persons to promote the appointment of a "prefect of the mission," someone to have full authority even over rectors. He was justifiably annoyed that the hard-won money intended to further the mission in England should be poured out on table delicacies for superiors and their friends in Spain. "It is incredible how ambitious they are to rule at their own discretion."

Persons brushed off somewhat tersely about this time an approach from Roger Baines on the subject of the cardinal's hat.[3] Persons made it clear he wanted no further mention of it. Nevertheless, a letter and memorial of March 26 to the King pleaded for Persons's promotion as much as anything to forestall the elevation of a man from the faction opposed to Spain and Spanish interests. This meant also some-

---

[1] CRS 30 (1930), p. xix.

[2] RP to Creswell, 16.i.1596, Valladolid; (I) A.V.9, ff.254, 259. From Creswell's "Responsio ad calumnias." Grene gives a list of RP's letters of 1596 in (II) f.488.

[3] RP to Roger Baines, 24.i.1596, Seville; (VI) Anglia.38.II. f.195 (Grene's synopsis).

one in favor of the succession to the English throne of James VI, who was taken to be anti-Spanish. One member of the Morgan-Paget faction had stolen a march on their rivals by getting "in an underhand way from a printer at Antwerp the original manuscript of the *Book of Succession*. Before its publication they passed on a prejudicial summary not only to the Pope through the Brussels nuncio, Malvasia, but also to friends in England."[4]

The result of William Gifford's premature disclosure was to prejudice minds against a work which set out to be an impartial examination of all the claims and claimants. It was made to appear a partisan broadside for the Spanish claim alone. In accordance with the logic of the developing rift, Paget's party now aimed "to sow discords and divisions between the Fathers of the Society and the secular priests of English nationality in England and Flanders; and also in the college in Rome. The aim was to exclude [Jesuits] from all government and authority over the English clergy and students both inside and outside the kingdom." In fact, no Jesuit, including Persons, ever claimed authority over any of the secular clergy in England.

The astute government of Elizabeth I had not failed to use its opportunity in the burgeoning quarrel. It helped the Paget, pro-Scottish, faction against the Hispanophiles by tolerating secular priests who supported the former and persecuting Jesuits and other priests who did not. The Paget faction was winning support for what seemed to many the moderate and realistic view. Some seven or eight gentlemen in Flanders—Spanish pensioners at that—were claimed to have signed a petition to the Pope expressly denouncing others of their countrymen, if not by name, for misleading the Spanish king and his viceroy and council in Flanders. This was now a quarrel which could not be settled by compromise, but only by a surrender which neither side could begin to envisage.

The Hispanophiles learned the truth of the situation from intercepted or discovered letters written by William Gifford and Charles Paget to the late Bishop of Cassano, and seemingly from others addressed to Thomas Throckmorton. Philip was urged to arrest Paget and Morgan forthwith and sift their papers, as had been done to Thomas Morgan, who was banished in the Duke of Parma's time. The King was further advised to drop all idea of founding a Scots college in Louvain, since this could only advance his enemies. He should also press for the creation of an English cardinal who would have the caliber required to offer the enemy effective resistance. While awaiting

---

[4] Dr. William Gifford was responsible. See Hicks, "Robert Persons and the Book of Succession," (10) 4, 104–37, especially 107.

Elizabeth's demise, his forces should occupy Ireland, taking full advantage of "the hatred and ill-will between the educated and savage members of this race [which] is no less great than that which they both bear to the English." The more sophisticated were to be found in the towns and ports, while "the savage and uncouth elements filled the countryside," even if the latter alone had so far taken up arms against the occupying power. The Earl of Tyrone, then in rebellion, should be helped and not left to his fate like an earlier earl of Desmond and more recently the Scottish lords who had surrendered to King James.[5]

In early May, Creswell, Persons, and Englefield drew up yet another memorial of the kind with which Philip was now only too familiar. The progress of the seminaries and the *Book of Succession* had opened the eyes of Catholics, and for that matter Protestants, to the real problem, leaving the former hopeful and the latter apprehensive. James VI was toying with the idea of conversion, but the Catholics leaned to the infanta, especially if she married the Cardinal Archduke of Austria. But the Scottish claim was making progress, even in Rome. The worst that could be said about James was that he was not a Catholic. Meanwhile, the best way for Philip to make sure of his own claim would be to invade England as soon as possible. Circumstances were favorable but they would not endure indefinitely.[6]

It would be a grave error to make a simple division between the Jesuits and the secular priests at this time. By no means all British Jesuits were Hispanophile in the succession question. William Crichton, the Scottish Jesuit, actively promoted the cause of James VI. He clarified his stance in a letter to Persons of January 20 from Louvain. Intending to do for the Scots in the matter of founding colleges what Persons had done so successfully for the English, he used his own initiative too little and relied excessively, it seems, on his confrère. Persons showed some irritation, pointing out the burden of two seminaries, each of which maintained some seventy souls. It was a pity Crichton had not pressed harder for himself when he was in Spain. Now he might still enlist the help of the cardinal in Louvain. But Persons did not wish to appear lukewarm. He suggested that Crichton should send "six Scottish youths of good character" who had "no objection to living with Englishmen" to the English seminaries in Spain. Creswell would do what he could and Persons would put his

---

[5] RP(?) to J. de Idiaquez, 26.iii.1596, Madrid, with enclosure s.d. for Philip II; (IX) Serie II, Leg.1.

[6] "Lo que se ha sacado tocante el estado presente de las cosas de Inglaterra de diversas cartas escritas tanto de Inglaterra misma como de Flandes i Roma a las personas infrascritas en estos ultimos meses passados de Março, Abril i Mayo 1596," Spanish, Creswell's hand and signed by him, RP, and Francis Englefield; (VIII) Estado 967, n.f.

own shoulder to the wheel when he arrived shortly in Madrid.[7] This could be the first step to a Scottish seminary as such.

The main difference between Crichton and Persons concerned the English succession. The Scot not only favored James's candidature but thought Persons was positively hostile to it. Persons was at pains to demur. "I would much prefer that the kingdom of heaven and not any earthly kingdom were the subject of our discussion"; however, "the iniquity of the times" and "the extreme misfortune that has befallen our country" made it not only imperative to take part in politics but, in order to "procure its salvation," see to it that a Catholic succeeded to the throne. The missions to Scotland of William Watts, William Holt, and Crichton himself, all contrived by Persons, and the promise of 24,000 gold pieces from Philip and 4,000 more to James himself from Pope Gregory before the latter's death, were facts sufficient to prove that he entertained no prejudice against James. But Crichton himself was witness to the fact that James persisted in his heresy, and "some years later" he had to admit that there was no hope of the King's conversion. "As things are, the interests of the state and of religion are so intertwined that one cannot treat of the restoration of the the the one without the other, nor of the restoration of the Catholic religion except by means of a Catholic prince. . . . For the rest, let him be of any nation, any race, any tongue under heaven." Hereditary right was a subsidiary issue, and in any case James's right was only "on a par with that of others." Conversion from expediency was problematic and uncertain. "Foolish then . . . we should surely be if, after sustaining so many labours, encountering so many dangers and enduring so many martyrdoms, we were again to hand over all our interests and those of God and of the State to an heretical king or one suspected to be such." Persons's last wish was that Crichton would take all he had said in a friendly spirit.[8]

Recent dramatic news from England told of Drake's death at Nombre de Dios—Sir John Hawkins had died the previous year—and the stiffening of Spanish resistance to English piracy in the West Indies; but Persons could still spare a thought for "the old woman"—his mother, who had wielded her rod to such good effect all those years ago.[9] Nearer the point was a letter from Crichton in reply to his, which agreed substantially with him on Scottish affairs but complained

---

[7] RP to Crichton, 10.v.1596, Seville; (II) f.316; Salisbury MSS, 42, 43; (14), 122, Latin.

[8] Ibid.

[9] RP to "his loving brother Mr Henry Garth, fishmonger &c." [sic], 12.v.1596, [Seville?]; (III) Anglia.A.IX, No. 50, formerly in (I). There are several cipher references undeciphered.

that the publication of the *Book of Succession* had been premature. "There is a French proverb: you don't catch a hare by a drum. Ministers are now beating it in the pulpits of England and Scotland both."[10] But drums beaten in the summer of 1596 were more than a metaphor when Essex and Raleigh made their descent on Cadiz in June and July. Even the patient and cautious Philip was galvanized into sudden action. The second Armada, talked about for years, was "organised, equipped and sent to sea within a few weeks in the autumn months of 1596."[11] Persons, elated, prepared yet another long memorandum for Don Martin de Idiaquez. Martialed in seventeen sections, the document reiterated the writer's main thoughts on the subject as they had been contained in previous efforts of the kind. Philip must not appear to be conquering England, let alone annexing the English crown to Spain. There should be diversions through Scotland and Ireland. A new idea was that raids on the coasts of England from small boats should be carried out throughout the summer by the exiles in Flanders. The excommunication of Elizabeth should be renewed and Allen's address of 1588, never yet published, should be printed and distributed.[12] Sir William Stanley should be treated as a key figure in making contact with the English nobility and gentry. Dr. Stapleton should eventually be the new cardinal for England and meanwhile given legatine authority such as Allen had received in 1583. Various others, churchmen and laymen, were proposed for key roles in the invasion and subsequent settlement. Much attention should be paid to the organization of intelligence, something well understood by Parma and Don John of Austria but much reduced in quality in recent years. Queen Elizabeth did it better, keeping Chateau-Martin as a spy in San Juan de Luz for a hundred ducats a month and a percentage on all English merchandise coming in. Surprisingly, Persons claimed that Garnet had assured him by letter that there were reliable men who could get information from the source in the English council chamber. In Europe Hugh Owen and Richard Verstegan were at hand to do good service.[13]

Detailed instructions were drawn up for Charles Tankard, S.J., "and his companions at their setting out for the King's fleet." They were taking part in a holy crusade, nothing less, so they must impress on officers and men alike that there must be no "thefts and robberies

---

[10] W. Crichton to RP, 20.viii.1596, [Louvain?]; (II) f.318, Latin.

[11] (40) II, 93.

[12] "Puntos principales para facilitar la empresa de Ynglaterra"; (VIII) Estado 839, ff.126–28, Spanish; (25) IV, No. 648.

[13] Sterell was an English spy: see (26); for Chateau-Martin see (14) IV.

and suchlike oppressions of the poor; for on account of these crimes
. . . God is wont to throw into ruinous rout the troops engaged in
war." The priests must give a good example at all times and assure
those about to be liberated that the aim was to help "the downtrodden,
restore the Catholic faith and do hurt to no one who does not offer
resistance." Above all, they must convince their hearers of the King of
Spain's good intentions and counteract "the false opinions instilled in
them by the heretics." The Jesuits on the expedition must obey Tankard. The seminary priests were exhorted to accept his advice.[14] In this
last, if in no other respect, Persons was surely living in the past.

It was further proposed about this time that a committee
should be set up in Flanders under the viceroy to deal specifically with
the English and their affairs. One object was to work for a general
acceptance of the infanta's succession after Elizabeth's death. Opposition was expected from Charles Paget, William Gifford, William Tresham (who were then in Flanders), and from Hugh Griffith, Thomas
Hesketh, and Nicholas Fitzherbert in Rome. However, the new committee would screen future exiles and advise on dispensing patronage.
The English would be "employed according to their social status and
talents in suitable tasks so that they would not live in idleness as at
present." This was the root cause of faction and discontent. The committee would also keep careful track of Elizabeth's spies working in
Flanders, follow her example in fomenting trouble in her own realm,
and organize espionage in England. The overriding aim was to "put
some life and spirit into the Catholic cause which up till now remains
almost inert because it is no one's business to mobilise and direct it."
Not only Colonel Stanley and Hugh Owen should be included but also
some Spaniards to ensure coordination and cooperation at all levels.
William Holt should participate in matters of greater moment.[15]

By the end of August preparations were well under way for an
Irish expedition under Don Martin de Padilla, admiral of Castile and
formerly captain-general of the galleys at Lepanto. He had defended
the entrance to the Tagus against Drake in 1589. By October a fleet of
some 150 ships was ready, as many as in the Armada of 1588 or the
English fleet sent against Portugal in 1589 and that against Cadiz this
year. But its quality was inferior. The English Council was well-in-
formed on all details by mid-October.[16]

---

[14] "RP in the name of the Visitor and his own, *Instructiones pro Patre Carolo
Tancardo SJ et sociis . . . ,*" 30.viii.1596; (VIII) E.839, f.143.

[15] "Las razones por las quales conviene que aya alguna Consulta particular en
Flandes cabo la persona del Governador para las cosas de Ynglaterra . . . ," 1596; (VIII)
E.839, f.129, Spanish; (25) IV, No. 647, pp. 628–33.

[16] (40) II, 94–97.

At the beginning of September, Persons was still at Valladolid mopping up after del Rio. He was ordered to San Lorenzo, but before departing drew up a report for Philip's secretary on the state of the college. He was also engaged in a translation into Latin of the *Book of Succession* for the Pope and in drawing up a memorial for the Duchess of Feria "and others of our nation" concerning the infanta's succession. It had a wise word for the French. Henri IV's interests would be better served if she rather than the King of Scotland had England, especially if she renounced all claim to Brittany, Aquitaine, Anjou, and Normandy, another point made in the *Book of Succession*. She might also be brought to renounce the traditional English claim to the throne of France.[17]

Persons had asked to be summoned to Rome at the beginning of the year, but it was not the problem of the succession but of the English College that drew him. A fresh tumult had broken out. The whirligig of time was still bringing in Maurice Clynnog's revenges. But Persons felt he could deal with the situation even if it had defeated all before him, a point made clear in a letter of January 31, 1596, to Roger Baines.[18] Meanwhile the soldier manqué continued to ply the Spanish secretariat with notes and memos.[19] Nevertheless, the King and still more his professional men at arms were reluctant to take Persons fully into their counsels. Perhaps they felt it was not his business to advise them on war any more than it was theirs to tell him how to administer the sacraments. In any case, Persons had now been absent from England for some sixteen years, long enough for the total scene to have changed considerably. While Persons and his immediate circle might be reliable enough, the same might not be true of his friends. He was evidently wrong in trusting John Cecil. But he continued unabashed to be free with his advice.[20]

By this time, the easy financial situation of the Spanish seminaries as it had existed on paper and in promise, at all events, a few months earlier was now reversed. They were "too loaded with debt" to make further progress. Creswell in Madrid was achieving little, so that Idiaquez was asked to unblock the channel and start negotiations for a firm settlement. Persons could not leave Valladolid for Rome before this was in prospect. Not that he cherished any illusions as to the task before him in the Eternal City. It is significant, perhaps, that he looked to support from the Spanish court rather than the Roman authorities

---

[17] RP to Juan de Idiaquez, 2.ix.1596, Valladolid; (VIII) ibid., f.138, Spanish a.l.s.

[18] (VI) Anglia.38.II, f.195 (Grene).

[19] RP to J. de Idiaquez, 2.ix.1596; v. supra.

[20] Ibid.

in the coming crisis.[21] Certainly, the Paget party had been busy. They were encouraging the college students in letters full of crusading zeal to push the cause against Spaniards and Jesuits alike. A letter of September 19, 1596, accused the Jesuits of sowing discord among princes, attacking the Scottish claim in the *Book of Succession,* and working to turn England into a Spanish colony.[22] Perhaps their influence not only caused the Vatican to draw back from naming a succesor but made even the Spanish authorities hesitant. Certainly, the French influence in Rome was growing. If Persons did not underestimate the force of anti-Spanish feeling, he almost refused to take cognizance of it in his political attitudes. Certainly, the French would never countenance a Hispanophile succession in England, least of all the accession of a Spanish princess. From the spiritual viewpoint, however inevitable, the interaction of religion and politics was now frequently exerting a disastrous effect on those who set out originally simply to convert England to Catholicism. As Persons put it, speaking for his own side, "many young men who leave England with good intentions fall into the hands of these seditious men and imbibe impressions which they can never afterwards shake off until they are eventually ruined." Many were so disillusioned as to become "enemies, spies, apostates and heretics." The Spanish authorities could be astonishingly indulgent. Not a few of their enemies went on living on Spanish pensions, to Persons's considerable disgust. Until their sources of supply were cut off, there could be "no end to the business" begun in the English College, which was now threatening the whole cause with disaster.[23]

Early in November Persons was in Madrid. He dealt roundly with another letter from William Crichton which was mainly taken up with an attack on the *Book of Succession.* As for catching hares with a drum, "the drum was not intended for the catching of hares but rather to keep off the wolf that desires to creep in by night." The "law of the heretics" making it high treason even to discuss the issue was simply a ploy to take advantage of the general ignorance "and foist on us one of their own to succeed. It is this that the noise of the drum exposes." The Pope needed the information no less than other Christian princes

[21] Ibid. See RP to [Martin de Idiaquez ?] n.d. [1596]; (VIII) ibid., f.125, a.l.s.; (25) IV, p. 649.

[22] RP, "Que la parcialidad de Carlos Pagetto y Tomas Morgano aya sido y sea muy preiudicial al servicio de su Magestad para las cosas de Ynglaterra," 30.vi.1597, Rome; (III) Old Series VI, No. 41, p. 153; see (II) f.463; (9) 386; (11) III, App. p.lix, enclosed in s. to s., 3.vii.1597; (III) ibid., No. 42, p. 157. RP also wrote to Thomas Covert on 31.v.1597 urging reconciliation with W. Holt, S.J., in Flanders; (III) ibid., No. 37, p. 139, contemporary copy.

[23] RP, Memo on Paget and Morgan, 30.vi.; v. supra.

and Catholics generally, in order to assess the rights and prospects of individual candidates.[24] To refute Crichton, Persons could produce witness from England that the book had been found most useful. As for causing an increase of persecution, after its appearance the Catholics had been "treated much more mildly." Two Jesuits had recently been freed in Scotland. Lord Fentry had been executed before the appearance of the book, no one after it. Persons repeated his intention to work strenuously for a wholehearted Catholic to succeed. The Catholics made a mistake "at the death of Queen Mary when they chose this present Queen Elizabeth for the sole reason she was an Englishwoman . . . and rejected Mary, the queen of France, a Catholic, because Scotland was her native land." They saw their mistake too late. It should not be repeated. "The pope must finally determine what is best for us and for Christendom, for the greater glory of God."[25]

By the beginning of November, the sorry result of the second Armada was known in Spain. De Padilla set out with his fleet from the Tagus on October 13. Once again, the weather proved staunchly Protestant. On October 17 an equinoctial gale from the southwest struck the fleet off Cape Finisterre and scattered the ships like nutshells. Some forty, including no few of the best, were wrecked on the shores of Cantabria. Perhaps five thousand men were drowned, among whom were a number of Irish exiles. Fewer than fifty vessels reassembled at Corunna. Many of the crews who reached shore deserted, while those who remained were largely struck down by disease. A new expedition was planned almost immediately for the following year, but more in the hope of saving face and what little was left of morale rather than with any hope of retrieving the disaster of the two previous attempts. Once again Queen Elizabeth had triumphed. But if Persons's cause seemed for the moment overwhelmed, it was by no means crushed. Only with death would the Jesuit abandon his struggle.[26]

---

[24] RP to Crichton, 2.xi.1596, Madrid; (II) f.318. RP wrote to H. Walpole on 14.xi.; ibid., f.488. Alas, Grene's summary confines itself to "an et quousque liceat Anglis Catholicis bellare pro haereticis contra Hispanos."

[25] RP to Crichton, 2.xi. (V. supra.)

[26] See (40) II, 101–3.

Chapter Fourteen

Return to Rome and Problems
of Church Government: 1597

At the beginning of 1597, Persons, all unknowing, bade farewell to Spain for ever.He was called to Rome to quell new disturbances in that local Vesuvius, the Venerable English College. The smoke of scandal was billowing again from a crater which had never ceased to smolder since Persons knelt before the Pontiff with his Latin translation of the *Book of Succession.* The Jesuit could not be surprised by a reception that was little more than correct and certainly far from cordial. An acrid smoke cloud was drifting across Europe from Spain and Flanders to blur the vision of Roman authority, sometimes bringing sharp and genuine tears of grief. About now a serious difference developed between Persons and a Flemish Jesuit of much distinction. It was a good indication of the strength which the anti-Spanish party had attained and the plausibility at least of its principal contentions that a man of the caliber of Olivier Mannaerts (Manare) should have felt obliged to reject the considered view of one of his own order. Mannaerts might have been elected general in 1581 had he not been suspected of *ambitus,* a grave sin in a Jesuit of those times. He had apparently taken steps to bring about his own election. As T. Clancy saw it, by 1597 he was "another of the intimates of St. Ignatius who lived too long."[1] At all events, he was acting provincial in Flanders when Persons wrote to him from Barcelona while awaiting a galley bound for Italy.[2] Grand old man in his own province, as Clancy observed, "when he was seventy he wandered out of his depth in the murky waters of English politics and gave a good deal of unwanted advice to superiors in Rome and England. His letters to Aquaviva betray a keen sense of disappointment that his age and experience were not given greater deference. The General had to tell him firmly

---

[1] Clancy, "An Introduction to Jesuit Life," 136.

[2] Strictly speaking, Mannaerts fulfilled this function only from 22.ii.1597 until 20.vii.1598, while the former provincial Duras was appointed an assistant and before a regular provincial was named.

to leave delicate political negotiations to wiser and younger heads."[3] Mannaerts revealed active opposition to the English Jesuits when he wrote to Persons on October 3, 1596, to say he believed that the Flemish situation would be much improved by the removal of William Holt, S.J. Holt was certainly willing to go and, as Persons admitted, the seminaries in Spain would have been glad to have him. Creswell might take Holt's place. All the same, Persons understood the nature of the opposition too well to think that substituting one individual for another would bring about a lasting settlement.[4]

As we have seen, the troubles in Flanders and Rome were intimately connected. In the English College the Jesuit confessor, Edmund Harewood, had been removed to please the students, but this was followed by even worse disturbance. Holt in Flanders had friends in high places, including the Duke of Feria and Stephen de Ibarra. Before leaving Brussels for Spain, Ibarra urged the archduke to make Holt his special confidant on English affairs. But the fact that Holt's best friends were Spanish did not help him in Rome. Dr. Barrett, rector of Douai, learned from Pope Clement himself that Holt's detractors had the whole Society in their sights, claiming that the Jesuits aimed at dominating the rest of the clergy. The latest upheaval in the English College was as much a triumph of enemies outside the college as of student power. It was they who stirred the students to subscribe memorials demanding the withdrawal of the Jesuits from England. Persons countered vigorously, pointing out that the Society served the interests of all the exiles, including the ingrates who attacked them. Holt, who was now the special object of their attack, had often pleaded their individual causes in letters to the court of Spain.[5] However vociferous, the opponents of Jesuit aims were only a minority united in nothing save their opposition to Holt and men like him. The achievements of the others spoke for themselves: new seminaries, 600 priests, 130 martyrs, 200 confessors, conversions numberless, and many published books. Finding the English Jesuits united so far among themselves, they tried to make headway against them through their foreign confrères. They had succeeded at least with Mannaerts, who had asked for Holt's transfer. Not that Persons was blind to the faults of his brethren. He agreed that Holt might be reproved for his brusqueness.[6]

---

[3] Clancy, "An Introduction to Jesuit Life," ibid.

[4] RP to Oliver Mannaerts, 10.i.1597; (III) Old Series VI, 4, p. 13; (11) IV, lxxxiv.

[5] Ibid.

[6] Ibid.

Four months lay between Persons's departure from Madrid and his arrival at Villafranca near Genoa early in March. He fell ill twice on the journey and "twice passed blood from [his] bowels," having left Spain in a fever. He asked Agazzari, rector of the English College, to meet him near Civitavecchia, doubtless to brief him before he came to Rome.[7] Persons expected only a short stay in the city to settle questions concerning the succession, seminaries, and the mission in general before returning to Spain. He was aware that he must not appear too Hispanophile or too antagonistic to James VI. Indeed, he had done that king "many good offices" at least "while there was any hope of his becoming a Catholic," but he did not deny that he preferred the infanta to succeed.[8]

The most complete account of the latest troubles in the English College were contained in Cardinal Sega's report of March 14, 1596.[9] A year after Sega's attempted reform, the outlook was as dark as ever. Persons made a report of his own, perhaps for King Philip, in May 1597.[10] According to M. E. Williams, "the real roots of the trouble would seem to be, as Kenny suggests, the faulty system. The superiors felt it was impossible to expel a student since he might apostatise and inform against the college and the missions in England."[11] Whether or not "there were bound to be tensions" in a seminary for secular clergy run by regulars, it is undeniable that "the students either admired their superiors and were tempted to join the Society or they hated them and indulged in open revolt." Persons's analysis of 1597 is penetrating. "The immediate cause of trouble was the papal grant to Cardinal Allen to allocate faculties, according to individual talent and desert, to priests going on the English mission." After Allen's death in 1594, Owen Lewis, bishop of Cassano, claimed this right as the principal ecclesiastic of English nationality." The Italian rector of the college, who "knew little about English affairs or English people," agreed too readily to the students' petitioning the Pope on Lewis's behalf. Cajetan, the protector, took this as a personal affront. Staging a demonstration

---

[7] RP to Roger Baines, 4.iii.1597, Villa Franca; (VI) Anglia 38.II, f.197r.

[8] RP to W. Holt, 15.iii.1597, Genoa; (III) Old Series VI, No. 17; see (11) III, App. lvii, Italian, copy of a cipher letter intercepted and deciphered, presumably by a member of the Paget faction. It was used later as ammunition by the appellants against the Jesuits.

[9] See (12) VI, 1–66, see 118–20; (VI) Ottoboni 2473, f.185 et seq.

[10] RP, "Relacion del principio progresso y fin de la turbacion del Collegio Yngles en Roma que duro mas que dos años y medio, y redondo en prejuicio y peligro de la causa universal de todos los Catolicos de Ynglaterra," 22.v.1597, Rome; (IX) Serie II, Legajo 1, contemporary copy; (III) Old Series VI, No. 36, p. 131.

[11] (71) 19.

with the encouragement of conationals outside the college, the students turned it into a protest against Jesuits and Hispanophiles generally. In spite of "some very unruly and scandalous conduct," the Pope was prevailed upon to take no decisive action even against the ringleaders, with a foreseeable effect on discipline. Soon after, Sega made his visitation and produced the report of 1596, although he died before his work was completed.

Cardinal Toledo succeeded to the vice-protectorship and the task of visitation. Jesuit before he became a cardinal and thinking, no doubt, to proceed with fine objectivity, he promised the "rebels" a change of government in the college at Rheims as well as Rome and the removal of the Jesuits from England. A confessor was appointed from among the students in revolt, in fact the leader of the rebellion. "Like a tribune of the people," he "was to have regular audience with the protector every Thursday to lay before him the grievances and complaints of the discontented." Commenting with restraint, Persons thought this "tended to increase the discord." Certainly, there were now two factions: twenty-eight "rebels" against twenty-six "loyalists." The rival groups would not "eat at the same table" or even "hear Mass in the same church." Rather than the Jesuits, the dissidents preferred the "heretics of England," saying "they expected greater charity from them than from the Jesuits." They hated all things Spanish, including their theologians. But while one party refused to raise their hats to the Spanish ambassador when they met him on the street, the others made him an obeisance all the more profound.[12]

Two Roman priest-students, Richard Button and Sylvester Norris, went to England in October 1596 to found an anti-Spanish party. Charles Paget was informed by letter, together with a postscript from Dr. Gifford, dean of Lille, and further invited to circularize his friends. The letter was later intercepted by the other side and sent to Rome via Flanders. The party did not conceal its intention to cooperate with the English State to the limit of the acceptable, regarding the Jesuits and Spaniards as enemies and fully upholding "the existing temporal state of the Queen." Thus they hoped to avoid not only martyrdom but even persecution. At his first meeting with the students, Persons managed to persuade some to change their minds, but others "took it to be a sign of their predestination to be unyielding in this quarrel."[13]

---

[12] Ibid. *(Relacion . . .)* A long list of grievances was drawn up about now, if not at Sega's visitation. "Quomodo sæculares a Patribus Societatis in Anglia degentibus opprimuntur deque Patrum dominandorum desiderio in Anglos et Anglicanum Clerum"; (III) Old Series V, 113, f.427 et seq. See R. Fisher on VEC affairs; ibid., No. 114.

[13] Ibid. *(Relacion . . .)*

Arriving in Rome about the end of March 1597, Persons presumably stayed with the General at the Gesù. He found the papal curia almost uniformly hostile to the *Book of Succession*, taking it simply as a boost for Spain at the expense of the King of Scotland. He lost no time in airing his Latin translation of the original work. This had the desired effect. The book was now accepted as an impartial treatise on the rights of the nine or ten possible candidates. It was seen as a device to perpetuate the ruling junta that English law should make it treason even to discuss the subject.[14] But the English situation was still viewed in Rome, as Persons saw it, through a glass darkly. William Gifford had succeeded in winning to his views Innocenzo Malvasia, nuncio in Brussels from September 1594 to the spring of 1596.[15] Gifford in turn relied on Ralph Liggons, William Tresham, and others "of that faction." Gifford had been mainly instrumental, it seems, in creating a disturbance among the Roman students intended to counterbalance the weight on the other side of the seminaries in Spain. It had not been easy, since the assistance given to the recusant cause by Spain was plain for all to see. But "once the passions of these perverted youths . . . had been aroused and fed by men of influence . . . [they] flared up to . . . an intensity" that Persons found well-nigh incredible. Students who had accompanied him from Spain exerted a most effective influence, in Persons's view. These told the others how much kindness they had received there, so that some at least "found themselves put to shame and confusion."[16]

Pope Clement, seeing now more clearly the other side of the question, sent Persons to live in the English College for what was hoped would be the few days necessary to clear up the mess. Toledo had complicated the situation further, although his intention had been to give English Catholicism a less Iberian look, so that English Protestants might identify it less with the national enemy and thus incline more readily towards toleration. But his death in 1595 eliminated a serious obstacle for Persons. "God our Lord was very good in removing him . . . before he found himself overwhelmed and worn out by the task."[17]

Persons's first act towards pacification was to deliver on April 3 a long address to the assembled students. It was a straight appeal to

[14] See (36) 219, 442–49.

[15] According to Mgr. D. Conway, he was "not generally considered as permanent nuncio," *Archivum Hibernicum*, 23 (Maynooth, 1960): 16.

[16] RP to J. de Idiaquez, 1.v.1597, Rome; (III) Old Series, VI, No. 32, holog.; (I) Anglia II, No. 26; also (II) f.463, note, "Lo que halle en Roma acerca de las cosas de Inglaterra desde el primo de Abril hasta el p.o de Mayo 1597."

[17] Ibid.

the fundamental idealism and generosity of youth. He called on the instinct of gratitude in reminding them of the contribution made by the Spaniards to the survival of English Catholicism. San Lucar and Lisbon catered to old as well as young; they lodged priests on their way to England, clothed them, and gave them fifty crowns as journey money at their departure.[18] The seminaries in Spain helped not only students but English Protestants who were often handed over by the Inquisition to be looked after and perhaps brought by kindness to conversion to the faith. This was especially true of younger men. True, some may have seen this merely as a step to liberty; but with more priests going into England, Scotland, and Ireland—forty in the last six or seven years— there was a better chance of following up the converted. The English houses in Spain maintained a hundred by the year. King Philip had been encouraged by the results to continue his two thousand crowns per annum to Douai. It was difficult to collect, but it was collected and would continue unless the divisions among the English, especially in Flanders, drove the Spaniards to terminate their bounty.[19]

Meanwhile, the strife in Rome had caused some to dismiss the English Catholics as "a stubborn and heady people that cannot be quiet within their country where they might live in peace if they would." Their martyrdom was only the effect of obstinacy. Their ingratitude was shown by their treatment of the foreign Jesuits who had been the "readiest . . . in all countries to help us; their houses have been our houses, their friends our friends, their credit our credit." So far the English government had not prevailed, but they still might if present contentions continued. The Catholic laity, of course, were scandalized by all this. There were "national rivalries . . . as between English and Welsh, Scottish and English, Irish and British"; and differences of status and occupation "as between seminaries and soldiers, priests and laymen, secular churchmen and religious orders and of one order against another."

Persons was careful to name no present individuals involved, although he underlined the existence in the larger world of two irreconcilable groups. One side had produced martyrs, conversions, many youths "saved that otherwise might have been lost," "many books written and much prestige gotten to our nation, and union made everywhere." The others had produced no kind of positive result. Persons understood matters too well not to see plausibility in the stand

---

[18] RP, Speech to the English scholars at Rome, 3.iv.1597; (I) Collectanea N.II, p. 125: Grene's note, "A better copy is in the English College," and "Vigilia Paschasii" p. [3] Apr. 1597.

[19] Ibid.

of his opponents, although this was not an aspect to stress in a public homily designed to restore unity of purpose. Presumably, the other party did not intend to hinder. But in fact they had been responsible for the ruin of the Queen of Scots and the "fourteen English gentlemen that died with her and for her entrapped by the rash . . . treaty of Ballard, wherein, I can assure you, the right hand had neither part nor knowledge."[20] Sir Francis Walsingham and Gilbert Gifford had engineered "the division and emulation agreed upon at that time to be prosecuted between priests and Jesuits." Division had spread from Flanders to Rome but the situation was by no means irremediable. These in Rome were small quarrels but they wasted energy, and he appealed to the students to learn from his own expensively acquired experience.[21] There should be no recrimination but only a resolution to return "to our old comfort and quietness again." As an Englishman and a Jesuit, he hoped to reconcile the English to the Society of Jesus since Jesuits loved both Englishman and England. His last word was an offer of service. "In fine, I am wholly yours. Use me to your best commodity."

Persons's speech showed insight into human nature, but there was more to it than the cleverness of an able politician. It was the sincere appeal of a man who had given up everything for a cause and was convinced that he was talking to men who had done likewise. No pulpit eloquence could resolve real grievances. He therefore held "seven or eight conferences" with the students, including the disaffected, to search to the bottom of their discontent. Persons knew how to listen as well as talk. At the end of it, they seemed so genuinely converted that even Persons found "cause for astonishment." Outside influences were still at work, more especially that of Owen Lewis, although he died in 1595. St. Charles Borromeo of Milan, no less, had appointed him vicar-general, so that it is unrealistic to dismiss him as someone simply unworthy. All the same, he never forgave the takeover of the English College by the Jesuits. Edward Bennet, fellow Welshman, by permission of the Jesuits had been able to continue Lewis's influence in the college as confessor to the students. He also kept the students' money and allocated it to them for spending. He had even received Toledo's leave to write and receive letters without showing them to the rector, and to give the same leave to others. Once a week he had audience with the protector, during which he presented the

---

[20] Not listed in (19) or (41) and not printed (?). One was against the "Cardinal's epistle for the deliverye of Deventrye [Deventer], and the other against the fathers of the Societye." Even "Walsingham hymself was ashaymed to lett them be printed."

[21] See *Relacion del principio* . . . , 22.v.1597. V. supra.

Nether Stowey Church, Somerset. View taken before 1939(?)

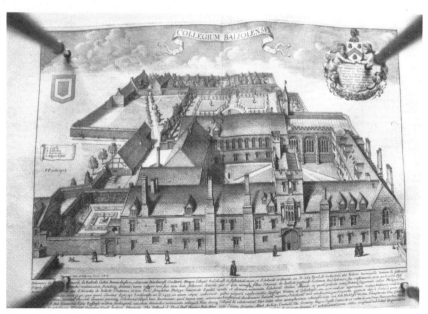

Balliol College. From *Oxonia Illustrata,* 1675

Persons's original entry in the
novices' register, formerly kept
in the Roman novitiate at Sant'And

Pope Gregory XIII (1572-1585).
From a portrait bust in the
German College, Rome

**Stonor Park, near Henley
on Thames**

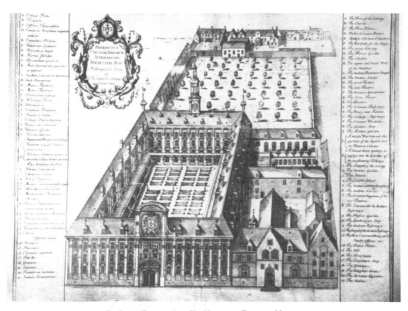

**Saint Omer's College. Overall
view from an engraving**

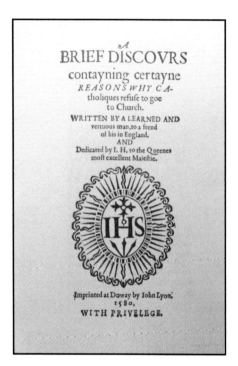

Title page of *A Brief Discours . . . why Catholiques Refuse to Goe to Church . . .*, 1580

Claudio Aquaviva, S.J., general from 1581 until 1615

Pope Clement VIII (1592–
1605). From the funerary
monument in S. Maria
Maggiore, Rome

The "Pigskin Library" in the
English College, Valladolid, in
part of an original house
incorporated into the new
building in Persons's time

Pope Paul V (1605–1621).
Contemporary engraving

Robert Persons, S.J. Title page
of *A Briefe Apologie . . .* , 1601

A BRIEFE
APOLOGIE,
OR DEFENCE OF THE CA-
tholike Ecclefiaftical Hierarchie, & fubordination in England , erected thefe later yeares by
our holy Father Pope Clement the eyght; and impugned by certayne libels printed & publi-
fhed of late both in Latyn & Englifh; by
forme vnquiet perfons vnder the
name of Priefts of the
Seminaries.

*VVritten and fet forth for the true information and
ftay of all good Catholikes , by Priefts vnited in
due fubordination to the Right Reuerend Arch-
prieft, and other their Superiors.*

Hebr. 13. verf. 17.
Obedite præpofitis veftris, & fubiacete eis, &c.
Obey your Superiors , and fubmit your felues vnto
them.

1. Theff. 5.
Rogamus vos fratres, corripite inquietos.
We befeech yow brethren repreffe thofe that are vn-
quiet amongft yow.

Permiffu Superiorum.

Contemporary portrait in oils
of Thomas Firzherbert.
From Stonyhurst College,
Lancashire

Robert Persons, S.J. Title page
of *The Christian Directory* . . . ,
edition of 1607

THE
CHRISTIAN
DIRECTORY

Guiding men to eternall saluation,

Deuided into three Bookes.

The Fɪʀsᴛ vvherof teacheth hovv tᴄ makᴇ
a good Resolution. The Sᴇᴄᴏɴᴅ, hovv
to begin vvell. The Tʜɪʀᴅ, hovv ᴛᴏ per-
seuere ᴀɴᴅ end happily.

In this volume is onely conteyned the first booke,
consisting of tvvo Partes, vvherof the former lay-
eth doope the motiues to Resolution, and the other
removeth the impediments : both of them hauing
byn lately reviewed, corrected, and not a litle al-
tered by the Author himselfe, for the greater com-
modity and vtility of the reader.

Matth. 16. verf. 26.
What auaileth it a man if he could gaine the
whole world by loosing his soule? Or what ex_
change will a man giue for his ovvne soule?

One thing is necessary. *Luc. 10. v. 42.*

Superiorum permissu. 1607.

D · O · M ·

PATRI ROBERTO PERSONIO ANGLO SOMERSETANO
SOCIETATIS IESV
SACERDOTI INTEGERRIMO ATQVE DOCTISSIMO
ET HVIVSCE COLLEGII OPTIMO MODERATORI
QVI AD ANIMI CVLTVM AD STVDIVM PIETATIS
AD ANGLIAE CONVERSIONEM COLLEGIORVM
DOMICILIIS AC DIVERSORIIS PER OPPORTVNA
LOCA QVA PER IPSVM EX INTEGRO
CONSTITVTIS QVA COLLOCVPLETATIS
AB IPSO MAGNAE SPEI CONVOCAVIT MAGNIS
LABORIBVS INSTITVIT IVVENTVTEM HISPALI
VALLISOLETI GADIBVS VLISSIPONE DVACI
AVDOMARI ROMAE QVO DVCE ET SOCIO PATER
EDMVNDVS CAMPIANVS CATHOLICAE REIPVBLICAE
PROPVGNATOR ACERRIMVS IN ANGLIAM PRIMVS
EX SOCIETATE TRAIECIT QVOQVE VINDICE
ET PATRONO VERITATIS HOSTIVM PASSIM EXAGITATA
TEMERITAS LIBRIS SCRIPTIS SERMONIBVS LITERIS
EXEMPLIS DEFENSA RELIGIO RECREATA SANCTITAS
CVM INTER HAEC IPSE NVLLAM CAPERET PARTEM
CONCESSAE QVIETIS NVLLVM A SVO CAPITE RECVSARET
DISCRIMEN HONESTISSIMAE DEFENSIONIS
SEMPER PARATVS SEMPER ERECTVS
SEMPER IN MEDIAM FLAMMAM PERICVLOSISSIMAE
CONCERTATIONIS IRRVMPENS ANIMAE MAGNAE
PRODIGVS OMNINO VIR LXIIII EXPLEVIT ANNOS
EX QVEIS SEX ET TRIGINTA IN SOC IESV
PER OMNIA VIRTVTIS
EXEMPLA TRANSEGIT
OBIIT XV · APRILIS
MDCX ·

White marble memorial tablet in the chapel of St. Thomas,
in the Venerable English College, Rome,
contemporary with Persons

memorials of the dissident students and their complaints against the rector.[22]

At least by the end of April 1597, Persons was aware of the strenuous propaganda being leveled against Spain and the Jesuits by Button and Norris in England. Even in Rome Persons was not able to prevail with some five students due to leave in the autumn, but even these were forced to wear a mask of compliance. Persons was not deceived and suggested their return to England be held up for a time.[23]

But apart from the death of Lewis, Toledo, and Thomas Throckmorton in the autumn of 1595, other leaders of the opposition had spiked their own guns. Friar Sacheverell in Rome became involved in an unsavory public scandal leading to imprisonment. He escaped to London and by April 1597 was the guest of the Lord Treasurer. Hugh Griffith became involved with a married woman, so that he had to withdraw to the safety of his benefice at Cambrai. One of his last acts before leaving Rome was to exhort Edward Bennet never to make peace with the Jesuits; but in the event Edward came under the influence of his brother John from Spain, so that he became a valuable source of information for Persons to assess the aims and motives of the "rebels."

Having analyzed causes to his satisfaction, Persons passed to remedies. Using letters from England and Flanders, he showed that there was no significant division among the Catholics, as was claimed by Paget and his company. Most were aware of the services rendered to the Catholic exiles by Philip II, and the posturing of the anti-Spanish element in Rome only caused scandal. Persons claimed to be supported by the written testimony of some eight hundred Catholics. Nor should anyone think that Dr. Stapleton, in line to succeed Allen, sided with the dissidents. The Pope and cardinals now realized that the English Catholic cause could not survive without the support of Spain.[24]

Under the weight of much logic and facts they were not in a position to dispute, the students could only give way. Cardinal Borghese came to the college to seal the pacification on May 7.[25] Persons insisted on no recrimination, and six of the formerly discontented wrote to Aquaviva "promising all obedience and quietness for the time to come." They asked pardon and even wrote to William Gifford,

---

[22] RP, "A brief ragguaglio of the stirs . . . ," 18.x.1597 [Rome]; (II) ff.352, 307, noted by Grene as "out of F. Persons own handwriting."

[23] RP to J. de Idiaquez, 1.v.1597. V. supra.

[24] See "A brief ragguaglio. . . ." V. supra.

[25] For an exact date, see ibid.

Hugh Griffith, and other partisans in Flanders to abandon the quarrel. Supporters in Rome showed "a great change of heart," or at least felt obliged to hide their feelings for the time being. Mora and Malvasia recognized their error, and the Pope was delighted at the return of peace. Persons's reputation never stood higher in the Vatican. Nor was it, perhaps, ever to stand so high again.

The reconciliation of May 7 came in time to check a serious rift among the Jesuits in Flanders. Persons replied on April 12 to a critical letter of Mannaerts dated as recently as March 22. Persons's tone was conciliatory, but he was sad to think the Belgian had sided with those who attacked William Holt. Mannaerts had allowed himself to be too readily overawed by the English who insisted on their "nobility." Holt, Owen, and the rest were not men of "mean birth," while the pedigree of Sir William Stanley, Sir Francis Englefield, and Thomas Fitzherbert shone forth in their names, to say nothing of the "high ecclesiastical dignitaries" associated with them.[26] Mannaerts had only known the Paget group for some four months, Persons for some fifteen years. The Fleming should not let his laudable desire for peace serve a cause which was stirring strife in Rome. Meanwhile Holt would stay on in Flanders for his experience.[27]

As part of establishing good relations with the Vatican, Persons now cultivated the cardinal-nephew, Aldobrandino. He sent him by Roger Baines a full report on English affairs, hoping for a "speedy and favorable issue" so that he could get back to Spain.[28] In a letter to Holt, Persons admitted that there had been "errors on both sides, saltem in modo agendi," in the English College. Ignoring any deeper causes of the rift, he put it down to men of different race failing to understand one another.[29] Not very helpfully, the Spanish ambassador, Sessa, presented his own report to the Vatican in mid-May, in which he asked not only that Dr. Thomas Stapleton but also William Gifford be allowed to come to Rome. This was in connection with finding a successor to Allen. Persons was not against the idea in principle but thought none suitable at that time. Stapleton, certainly, a man of weak health, died on October 12, 1598. Nor did Persons wish himself to be

[26] RP to Mannaerts, 12.iv.1597, Rome; (III) Old Series, VI, No. 24, Latin holog.; (11) III, App. lxxxvi.

[27] RP to Mannaerts, 10.i.1597, Barcelona; (III) ibid., VI, No. 4, Latin holog.; (11) IV, lxxxiv.

[28] RP to Card. Aldobrandino, 2.v.1597, Rome; (IV) F.Borgh. III, 124.G.2, f.5, a.l.s.

[29] RP to W. Holt, S.J., 5.v.1597, Rome; (III) ibid., No. 106, f.491; (11) III, App. lxxviii.

considered, although his name was hinted at, as he understood it, in the list of Sessa's candidates.[30]

Throughout June Persons was troubled with some affliction in his knees, but managed to keep the protector, Cajetan, informed of English affairs, as the Pope wished, using Baines as go-between.[31] Meanwhile, the peace restored at the English College proved very short-lived—not more than a month in fact. A new conflagration began with a small spark: an extra vineyard promised but not provided and matters of like triviality. In August, one priest "having overeaten and overdrunk himself at a tavern, came home sick." This was not all. Some "went very frequently to taverns," giving themselves out to be German. When the Germans got to hear of it, they responded in kind. Cardinal Madruccio, their protector, informed Cajetan on September 28. While he was reading the letter, a captain of the *sbirri* came in to say that two groups of German students had been arrested, saying they were English. An English secular priest, Middleton, was also arrested in a brothel where he "had a chamber." The cardinal informed Persons, who went immediately to prevent their delivery to gaol before he had spoken with the cardinal.[32] When the Pope got to hear of it, he was inclined at first to look on the Anglo-German rivalry as something of a joke, but not the Middleton affair. However, the English behaved arrogantly and so they went before a court. After an eighteen-day examination, six were sent away to Douai—not a heavy sentence.[33]

All this was the symptom of a deep malaise in the college. The Jesuits were not the only order experiencing difficulty at this time. The Dominicans, too, were having trouble with certain enfants terribles who, when they became disillusioned and disgruntled, likewise turned to the Paget faction for support.[34] But Persons now had the ear of Aldobrandino, papal secretary of state, Cajetan, and Peña, official of the Rota and confidant of the Duke of Sessa.[35] All the same, the opposition in England was growing. Richard Button and Sylvester Norris were joined by Friar William Sacheverell, O.P., and Robert Fisher from the English College, one of the more forward of Persons's enemies.

---

[30] RP to Pedro Ximenes de Murillo (Sassa's secretary), 18.v.1597, VEC; (III) ibid., No. 35; (II) f.463; (24) I, 393.

[31] RP to Cajetan, 1.vii.1597, Rome; (IV) F.Borgh. II, 448.AB, f.426, Italian holog.

[32] RP, "A brief ragguaglio of the stirs. . . ." V. supra.

[33] Ibid.

[34] RP to J. de Idiaquez, 3.vii.1597, Rome; (III) Old Series VI, No. 42, f.157. This letter accompanied the report on the "parcialidad" of Thomas Morgan and Charles Paget of 30.vi.1597. V. supra.

[35] RP to de Peña, 11.vii.1597; (V) Vat.Lat.6227, f.165, a.l.s.

These two told Sir William Waad, secretary to the English Council, of thirty English student-priests who preferred to leave Rome "rather than be of the Spanish faction along with the Jesuits."

Connected with the reaction against the Jesuits but not simply caused by it was a movement among the abler secular priests to attempt some kind of structured organization. In spite of adversity, numbers were growing, so that it no longer seemed satisfactory to rely on help from outside their own ranks, whether Jesuits or others, in disposing of priests and their work. Two loose associations began about this time, one for the north, especially Lancashire, and the other for the south. Some of the priests from both corresponded with the anti-Jesuit party in Rome, fanning no doubt the dying embers of revolt among the students but also offering them the interesting prospect of a more effective church organization and union among themselves. Persons was mainly concerned with "the potential harm and confusion" it threatened to any harmonious working among priests of all allegiances, no doubt fearing its anti-Roman propensities.[36]

While Persons was convinced that a show of firmness was all or most that was required to bring the recalcitrant to heel, the Spanish authorities preferred the way of appeasement. Instead of a hard face presented to the leaders in Flanders, they were receiving "favour and largess." Lip service was enough to win reward so that "the good lose courage and patience and the unruly go from strength to strength." Philip was unwilling to accept the fact that he could not retain the goodwill of all parties among the Catholics. Persons looked forward to a return to Spain, when he could explain the true state of things, as he saw them, to the King's Majesty in person.[37]

In a discussion with Aldobrandino on July 11, Persons referred oratorically to "the most important business that has been undertaken in the Christian commonwealth for many centuries," namely, the English succession. The matter should be gone over with the French by some "capable and discreet man" who, after briefing by Persons, might be able to overcome the objections and suspicions of Henri IV. The Spaniards should also be kept in the picture. Whatever Aldobrandino thought of Persons's advice, he compensated him for his trouble with "a magnificent present of wine."[38] And whatever the secretary of

---

[36] RP to J. de Idiaquez, 12.vii.1597, Rome; (V) ibid., f.34, Spanish copy: another copy on f.166.

[37] Ibid.

[38] RP to Aldobrandino, 12.vii.1597, Rome; (IV) F.Borgh. III, 124.G.2, f.13, a.l.s.

state thought of keeping the Spaniards informed, Persons did his best on his own account through Sessa and Peña.[39]

In August 1597 Persons gained the impression that bishops would be appointed for England. He was much in favor of the idea. He told Peña and Aldobrandino that the only way "to prevent the entrance of those seditious men into England" was to appoint two bishops.[40] For some months the Pope had been in consultation with the cardinals of the Inquisition about setting up "a subordination" in England. It was considered important that nothing should be done to exasperate the State against the Catholics. Enquiries were instituted in England which did not ignore the "unquiet" even if they did not fuss over them. Dr. Haddock, Martin Array, James Standish, Thomas Allen, the cardinal's nephew, William Baldwin, and finally Persons all agreed that "some subordination" was imperative.[41] Towards the end of August, Persons asked Aldobrandino to bring to the Pope's attention the three main points of a memorial from "the English Catholics."[42] The first request was for a brief exhorting them "and especially the priests, to patience, long-suffering and union among themselves." Further, they wanted two bishops, one to stay in England assisted by six or seven archpriests chosen from the "graver and wiser," the other to stay in Flanders with a like body to rule the English priests abroad. Persons also requested that none be allowed to take a doctorate without leave of superiors and the second bishop and his advisers. Four years of further study should normally be required. All should be decided before the heretics got to hear of the Roman decisions.[43]

Secrecy and speed were two qualities usually conspicuous by their absence on the Roman scene, and Persons now fervently recommended both; he also recommended Cardinals Tarugi and Madrucci as advisers, since these had experience of Protestantism in their provinces. For the rest, "if a difficulty occurs I am sure I could resolve it

---

[39] RP to de Peña, n.d. (viii.1597?), Rome; (V) ibid., f.183, Spanish, a.l.s.

[40] S. to s., n.d.(viii.1597?), Rome; (V) ibid., f.184, Spanish, a.l.s. See s. to s., ibid., f.186. This also reports an interview in which he promised to raise with the Pope "on Monday next" the subject of two bishops.

[41] RP, *A briefe apologie, or defence of the catholike ecclesiastical hierarchie, and subordination in England* . . . (Antwerp, 1601), ff.98r–9v.

[42] See "Rationes pro episcopis duobus Anglicanis" [16.viii.1597]; (III) ibid., No. 80; (V) ibid., ff.26f; (IV) F.Borgh. III, 124C, ff. 134f; (11) III, App. cxvii–cxix; (V) ibid., ff.7r–26v, *Relacion sobre la conservacion i buen progreso de las cosas de Inglaterra.*

[43] RP to Aldobrandino, n.d.[viii.1597], [Rome]; (IV) F.Borgh. III, 124.G.2, f.23, Italian, signed; (11) III, App. cxvii, No. xxi. A list of "graver and wiser" priests was included. See *Relacion sobre la conservacion i buen progreso.* . . . V. supra, especially ff.16r–18v.

with ease, if they would deign to hear me."[44] Unfortunately, since he was a simple priest, they might not. This was the other side of the coin in rejecting the cardinal's hat. His unadorned status also made him vulnerable to charges of interference by those less inclined to see his intervention as merely a desire to help. But if spirit was as willing as ever, the flesh was still weak. "A bad attack of flatulence" prevented him from sending to Spain and Flanders by way of de Peña translations of important documents concerning the infanta's succession claim and the reasons for creating bishops. No one could be trusted to observe the proper secrecy in doing the work, so they were delivered as they were by Roger Baines on August 15.[45]

By this time Persons was sufficiently recovered to begin the round of the cardinals, starting with Alessandro and Paravicini.[46] The latter agreed that Nicholas Fitzherbert should be transferred to Spain "on the pretext of business of some sort."[47] Persons still maintained a direct interest in the students and altered other appointments so that he could be present on August 18, when one of them defended a thesis.[48] This in spite of incoming letters and outgoing memoranda on the principal subjects at issue.[49] At a papal audience on September 16, Persons learned that Stapleton would not be coming to Rome, so as "not to inconvenience the University of Louvain."[50] On the nineteenth, the Pope issued two briefs, not vital but significant. The first met Persons's wishes about priests taking higher degrees, although it was not published before 1601. Humphrey Ely was probably correct in supposing that it was prompted by the actions of Christopher Bagshaw and Sylvester Norris, "who going from the college took their degrees by the way" and used them subsequently without much subtlety as a lever on superiors, or so their critics concluded. Ely was furious. "By this buggy bull all hope of promotion and preferment is taken away hereafter from us poor Englishmen."[51]

---

[44] RP to Clement VIII, 13.viii.1597, Rome; (II) f.355 "ex autographo," presumably a draft; probably accompanying the "Rationes pro episcopis . . ." V. supra. See (11) III, App. cxvii–xix; RP, *A briefe apologie . . .* , p. 102.

[45] RP to de Peña, 14.viii.1597, Rome; (V) ibid., f.185, Spanish, a.l.s.

[46] S. to s., 15.viii.1597, Rome; ibid., f.188.

[47] S. to s., 16.viii.1597, Rome; ibid., f.187. See s. to s., 16. viii; ibid., f.189.

[48] This was at the Gregorian University, the former "Roman College" as such, now occupied by a state school.

[49] S. to s., 17.viii.1597; (V) ibid., f.190.

[50] S. to s., 17.ix.1597, Rome; ibid., f.30, Spanish, a.l.s. See also s. to s., 19,20.ix.; ibid., f.195.

[51] See (11) III, App. cii: RP "A briefe ragguaglio of the stirs . . ." V. supra; H. Ely, *Certaine briefe notes . . .* , 89–94.

On August 16 John and Edward Bennet set forth for England. Chambers and Standish followed them soon afterwards. They left behind many sick in the city, from the Pope, who was "sick of his gout," to the Jesuit Edward Harewood, formerly minister at the English College, dying at Sant'Andrea. These were the days when much of Rome was malarial swamp.[52] Meanwhile, Msgr. Malvasia had been busy in Stapleton's cause. As Persons drily observed, "it is strange to see an Italian so labour for an Englishman as this good prelate doth without interest, as it seemeth, except the hope that the good doctor will concur with him . . . to gain England to the Catholic religion by driving Jesuits from thence."[53] Well aware that his opponents had been heard at least for their much speaking, even to the point of repetition, which was not quite pointless, Persons sent two further statements to the Pope, one describing the "conditions of things during the time of the disturbances" and urging that the ax be laid to the root and the poisonous growth cut off.[54]

Persons's presence in the English College was not enough to fortify the rector, Mutio Vitelleschi, in his struggle with the malcontents, in spite of previous experience of the post in 1592. His ability was attested by the fact that he was elected general in 1615. Nevertheless, by the autumn of 1597 the situation had so deteriorated that the rector could no longer give an exhortation "because they mock at everything that bears on spirituality and virtue." The immediate remedy was to send ten or eleven to Douai, where, it was hoped, in a college run by the secular clergy, they would feel more at home. "Forty . . . good" were retained. Persons was careful to keep in close touch with Cardinals Cajetan and Borghese. On September 28 two students were arrested, from whose examination it was hoped that the names of accomplices and further circumstances would emerge.[55] In consequence, Persons called for the formal transfer of six students. They were not badly treated. Each received twenty-five crowns for viaticum and "suitable clothing" for the road to Douai. Otherwise they had to depart without viaticum. Open letters which went with them exhorted the rector to treat them well. Cajetan was also asked to receive them before they left but to be firm, allowing no "accusation,

[52] RP to Edward and John Bennet, 20.ix.1597, Rome; (X) Section 7.D/E.Bt.Q.9. See s. to [T. Fitzherbert ?] 26.ix.; (II) f.315.

[53] RP to T. Fitzherbert (?), 26.ix.1597. V. supra.

[54] RP to Clement VIII, 28.ix.1597, Rome; (II) f.358, Latin.

[55] Ibid. But see RP to H. Garnet, 12.vii.1598; (II) f.438 (v. infra) where RP says the date of the arrest was the morning of Sunday 27.ix. This was the first open sign of trouble that came to RP's notice, it seems, since the pacification of Ascension Day, 7.v. In fact 27.ix. was a Saturday (NS).

appeal or delay."[56] Protector and vice-protector fully complied. The letters for transfer were signed by mid-October.[57] The fact that the six were transferred and not dismissed is sufficient indication that their faults were not considered incompatible with a vocation. The case of some who remained was otherwise. "One host and his servants testify that within eight days they had been of late six times at his tavern, seven, six, four, three and two at a time." There had been "many embracings and other scandalous behaviour, and commonly their drink was vinum græcum . . . wherewith some have been so merry as they have gone forth singing of Sellengers rounds throughout the streets."[58] The further fact emerged at their trial that they went "banqueting continually in Englishmen's homes." This explains where they found the money. Some of these Englishmen, at least, were almost certainly English spies.[59]

One sympathizes with students who were expected to study and concentrate on spiritual matters in the midst of an unavoidable and continuing political conflict from which, in spite of Persons's best efforts, they could not be isolated. Was there some slight excuse even for Tempest, Hill, and Benson, whose behavior in the taverns was reported as the worst?[60] It was "noted by the judges that . . . none of the quiet scholars that obeyed the Fathers . . . are accused for any of these disorders." Edmund Harewood, who supplied Persons with useful information on the college, died on September 21.[61]

By mid-October it was clear that, much to Malvasia's annoyance, Stapleton would not be leaving Flanders. He was no more anxious than Persons for the highest honor but his failing health had the last word.[62] By the end of October some thirteen scholars had departed for other seminaries, most to Douai, some to Spain. They left

---

[56] "Forma quædam dimissionis, nisi aliquid severius addendum videatur de delictis etc." [sic], x.1597; (I) Anglia II.31, a.l.s. For Card. Cajetan, RP's hand; copy in (III) Old series VI, No. 64, f.229.

[57] "Literæ patentes illustrissimorum cardinalium Cajetano et Borghesio ad Rectorem Collegii Duaceni pro sex alumnis dimittendis," 14.x. 1597; (I) Anglia II.31; ibid., V.A.60, f.935, copy; (III) ibid., No. 63, f.227.

[58] See "Sellinger's round" in Brewer's *Dictionary of Phrase and Fable.*

[59] See L. Hicks, S.J., "The strange case of Dr William Parry," *Studies,* vol. 37 (Dublin, 1948); "An Elizabethan propagandist: Solomon Aldred," (32) 181 (1945).

[60] RP to John Bennet, 18.x.1597; (X), Section 7, D/E.Bt., Q9/2.

[61] RP "A brief ragguaglio of the stirs. . . ." V. supra. See Humphrey Ely, *Certaine briefe notes upon a briefe apologie* . . . (Paris, [1603]), 77, 82–83. Ely was in the college about this time. See RP to J. Bennet, 18.x.1597. V. supra.

[62] RP to de Peña, 15.x.1597, Rome; (V) Vat.Lat. 6227, f.191, Spanish, a.l.s. RP dated another "brief ragguaglio" of the "stirs" in the VEC 18.x.1597; (II) ff.352 and 307.

cheerfully. Even John Middleton, the chaplain-in-chief of the taverns, went off "with great demonstration of change and contentment of mind." All the same, before their departure, the Pope "made unto them a very sharp reprehension at their leave-taking."[63] Not surprisingly, for the college had come very close to shipwreck.

The Pope's "new orders" for the college were published there about October 20.[64] Retrospective references made it clear the Jesuits had almost reached the end of their tether, "overborn by the clamours and impudent accusations" of those "shameless companions that cared not what they affirmed of them." Some had begun to wonder whether after all theirs was the right cause. Not so Persons. He had no doubt that he was right. Undeniably, he spoke from much experience. In tackling the problems for the longer term, his soldierly qualities were again in evidence, though he described the ills of the college to the cardinals in medical terms. "A longfestered and grievous wound" called for someone to "appease the present pain" before applying "local medicines for . . . healing the wound itself." Recent expulsions had lanced the wound but the "remedies of disorders past" still remained.[65] Again, he rejects any thought of reprisal. Reconciliation must be the sole aim. And so he keeps in touch with the Bennet brothers, not only John but Edward also, the late ringleader of revolt; and Edward deigns to reply as well as John.[66]

By mid-November it seemed that a formula for success had been found, as he reported to Creswell. "All are exceeding quiet, merry and contented, and there is no memory of stirs past, but only a general detestation thereof." The nine or ten who had previously thrown in their lot with the "rebels" were now fully reconciled. Persons's principal reforms, approved by Pope and cardinals, consisted first of all in "cutting off" the baneful influence of English externs, although visits were allowed in the parlors to bona fide visitors. Internal amenities were also improved in that the students were divided into "chambers" or dormitories, each with its own student prefect to keep a benevolent eye on discipline. All was "much more pleasant than before, for now they are twelve or fifteen together only, or fewer, at a fire, where there is better conversation than when they were so many."[67]

---

[63] RP to H. Garnet, 12.vii.1598, Naples; (II) f.438.

[64] RP, "A brief ragguaglio of the stirs. . . ." V. supra.

[65] RP to T. Fitzherbert (?), 26.ix.1597, Rome; (II) f.315.

[66] RP to John Bennet, 18.x.1597, Rome. V. supra. Much of this letter deals with the cardinal's visitation of the VEC.

[67] RP to J. Creswell, 12.xi.1597, Rome; (IX) Serie II, Legajo 1, contemporary

The Jesuit teaching staff and students now mingled amicably. Jesuits made it normal practice "to go and sit amongst them and converse." This of itself tended "to check and remove any evil speech, or language tending to unquietness." The Sodality of our Lady, a pious and voluntary society, grew in numbers as spirituality re-emerged. With the death of politics, studies began to arouse lively interest once again. The students themselves even asked for Jesuit "repetitors" or tutors. Henry Tichborne and Thomas Owen, "a very grave, learned and spiritual man," were appointed to this task. Out-landishness in attitude had been accompanied by freakishness in hairstyles. So now, quite spontaneously, "every man began presently to cut his long beard . . . as also to lay aside all other signs of . . . singu-larity." Sallenger's rounds were heard no more on the street as the students proceeded to their school or elsewhere to the "good edifica-tion" of all. Persons was too old a hand to suppose that trouble could be over for ever, but he was grateful for the present respite. So was the Pope, who prepared a bull to "confirm all presently," adding "such further orders as shall be thought best."[68]

Persons never took the existence of enemies for granted or supposed that they could not be brought round to his own views. On September 20 he wrote to Paget in Flanders. Edward Bennet, who now referred to the Jesuits' "modest and discreet dealing" in resolving the college crisis, delivered the letter.[69] Paget replied in what Persons found to be a "very vehement" letter. He wrote to Paget again in December reaffirming "there wanted no love or desire to do them good."[70] But there could, of course, be no question of reconciliation of views so diametrically opposed. Paget seemed to insist that "informa-tions" given by Persons were tantamount to "wrongs and injuries" done to him personally. He was urged to modify his claim that he, Morgan, and Gifford represented quite simply "the English Catholic nobility and gentry." A long recapitulation of their differences and rivalry since 1583 followed.[71] Persons complained of a "most slander-ous memorial" given the Brussels nuncio in September 1597 for for-warding to Rome. It was an attack on the Jesuits who were struggling for the cause, while others lived "wasteling and wrangling." Paget

---

copy. See also RP(?), "A further declaration of the matters fallen out in Colledge in Rome and the cause of the desmission of some priests and schollers from thence," 16.xi.1597; (III) ibid., No. 68. This makes the cardinals primarily responsible for the pacification.

[68] RP to Creswell, 12.xi.1597. V. supra.

[69] RP may have been wrong as to the date. J. H. Pollen thought E. Bennet probably left Rome on September 16.

[70] RP to C. Paget, 20.xi.1597, Rome; (II) f.452; (9) 391, partly printed.

[71] Ibid.

wished to be the friend of the Jesuits, as he said, but only on his own impossible terms. He was exhorted instead to "join again with the body of all good Catholic English both at home and abroad" to "follow the selfsame course with them for the reduction of our country."[72] It was an appeal of the irresistible to the immovable. Persons saw his critics as sheep attempting to negotiate with the butcher. Paget saw Persons as a sheep trying to frighten the butcher with his wolf's clothing and only increasing his rage in consequence. While the true aims of Elizabeth's government seemed to offer the possibility of diverse interpretation, there could be no reconciliation between these divergent views. One can sympathize with Paget's yearning to live a quiet life and avoid martyrdom at almost all costs. Nevertheless, it was Persons who read the signs of the times aright and who realized correctly that there could be no acceptance of papists by the state while the regime of the Cecils endured. But this was a truth which would only emerge when state and other archives opened to general inspection centuries later.

---

[72] Ibid.

Chapter Fifteen

Jesuits Fall Out
Persons Goes to Naples: 1598

The winter of 1597 to 1598 passed quietly in consolidating reforms in the English College and dealing with routine mission
and other affairs. This allowed Persons more time to deal with
the archenemy. In mid-February he wrote rebuking Charles Paget for
his failure to see "that there had been the slightest fault in [his] conduct" at any time. Paget was prepared to engage in something like a
formal debate before arbitrators if not exactly judges, but not to concede the negotiation at a purely personal level, as the Jesuit wished.[1]
Persons, too, could be tortuous; but, consistent with his own view of
the English government, he never attempted to trade with the enemy
at this stage and certainly never traded what should have been confidences in the hope of toleration, as Paget's party did. But one could
not fairly accuse Paget of inconsistency, only of unrealism, perhaps. At
the same time, he could hardly have contradicted the plain truth of
Persons's conclusion. "We have become wearisome even to ourselves.
We have laid ourselves open to the ridicule of public enemies, and we
have saddened all bona fide Catholics both at home and overseas." It
was suggested that William Baldwin call on Paget in Flanders about
Easter on his way from Rome to England.[2]

Persons addressed himself also to William Gifford; and to Dr.
Pierse on February 20, asking him to use his influence in dissuading
the dissidents in Rome and elsewhere. It was a forlorn hope.[3] A further letter to Gifford of March 20 complained of his alliance with Paget
against the Jesuits.[4] But it was not that simple. Olivier Mannaerts still
largely rejected Persons's view of the issue and on February 14 wrote

---

[1] RP to C. Paget, 14.ii.1598, Rome; (VI) Anglia. 31.II, f.711, Latin from an
English original(?). Paget wrote again and RP replied on 8.iii.1598, apparently in terms
similar to the above; (II) f.361.

[2] Ibid.

[3] RP to Dr. Pierse, 20.ii.1598, Rome; (II) f.361.

[4] RP to W. Gifford, 20.iii.1598, Rome; (II) ibid. Grene's summary is very brief,
perhaps in view of the repetitive nature of the contents. RP had seen two of W.G.'s
letters.

him a letter which the latter found "somewhat harsh." Persons replied as respectfully as a junior should to a patriarch, but he made it clear he expected no more help from that quarter.[5] Indeed, when Mannaerts heard of the pacification in the English College, Rome, he not only disapproved of Persons's measures but offered him a "severe rebuke." Paget and Gifford had done their work so well that Mannaerts found Persons "impulsive and implacable." Indeed, the former pair had been considering some public gesture of humility, but it was Mannaerts on his return to Brussels who encouraged Paget to resume "something of his former attitude of hostility." Persons treated Mannaerts to a resumé of his sixteen years' experience of the Paget faction, an account which included an examination of all the charges against the Society contained in a recent memorial by Robert Fisher.[6]

Persons answered the charges fully in a statement to Pope and cardinals. "Nothing has happened during this pontificate to confirm the innocence of our Society so completely and its patience and immense charity towards these men by whom the charges have been preferred."[7] Baldwin was deputed to take the documentary evidence to Flanders for Mannaerts's perusal, and an answer likewise to the "same men who had originated" the charges. Holt and Barret also received copies to help them "induce Gifford to make some admission of his fault." The main object in all this was not so much to convert the unconvertible as to influence the prospective seminarians passing from England through Flanders to the Jesuit seminaries in Spain and Rome. All were reminded that Persons had the full backing of the Pope as well as of Cajetan and Borghese.

Even after considering the evidence, Mannaerts still found it impossible to believe that he could have been wrong. "Would there had not been such a conspiracy of the English Fathers of our Society, and that they had suffered themselves to be piously admonished by others and more correctly informed." Persons might well ask if Mannaerts really thought he knew more of English affairs and had "better information." Nor did Persons relish the category of partisanship in which his opposition to the others seemed to place him.

Undoubtedly, Mannaerts was influenced by considerations other than the reasons of the Paget faction. In letters to the General

---

[5] RP to O. Mannaerts, 20.iii.1598, Rome; from a transcript in (XIV) of MS in the Jesuit Archives, Loyola. See L. Hicke, *Collection of Robert Person's Letters*.

[6] Text of the Memorial; (III) Old Series VI, No. 57; abstract with RP's comments, No. 59; other abstracts in (XI) Petyt MS 38, No. 342, English, No. 344, Latin; see "A summary of charges against the Jesuits," endd. in (III) ibid., No. 69: main points are in (42) 7–61.

[7] RP to Mannaerts, 20.iii.1598. V. supra.

and others, he made it clear that he disliked the quasi independence of the English Jesuits in Flanders, particularly that of William Holt, whom he found secretive in his ways and not open with superiors.[8] He resented Holt's close understanding with the intelligencer, Hugh Owen; and, having more than an ordinary regard for claims of blood and title, he shuddered when Holt, a commoner, trounced Paget, Gifford, and others of quality in round terms. It was by "wicked accusations" that Holt, Owen, and their friends had tried to get their adversaries expelled from Flanders by public authority. Naively, Mannaerts supposed that all that was needed to restore harmony was a little goodwill on all sides. He accepted the view that the Jesuits should confine themselves to schoolroom and sacristy and leave politics to the well-born laity, though not, of course, to such as Sir William Stanley. Garrulous, glib, well-intentioned, and resentful of those who rejected his transparent wisdom, Mannaerts's letters never got to grips with the basic issues.[9] Nevertheless, his influence could not be ignored.

In a letter of August 2 to the General, Mannaerts claimed that the ruling archduke had induced him to try to reconcile the warring factions. Even if certain English noblemen had stirred up faction in Rome, as Persons claimed, this was only their reaction to being "pursued by so much contumely." As religious, the Jesuits should bear with them and heal their ills, "not drive them to extreme fury."[10] A letter of February 13 declared, "It is from the handling of affairs which do not belong to our simplicity that all these things flow."[11] It must be admitted that the Fifth General Congregation of 1593 discouraged Jesuits from playing any direct part in politics. Evidently, however, the English exiles with a vital interest in the next successor to the crown had a problem which their confrères living in Catholic countries could afford to overlook—and sometimes did. The misunderstanding between some of the Flemish Jesuits and the English was hardly less profound than the one existing between the latter and the Paget faction. Mannaerts was resentful that the English Jesuits always wrote to one another in English, whereas others always used Latin; this was made worse by the fact that "not all their matter is written with fitting prudence." Mannaerts was aware of some three hundred names sent to Rome as backing for Holt and Persons. "But those who signed were almost all

---

[8] O. Mannaerts to G. Duras, 12.vii.1597, Brussels; (VI) Germania 177, f.192 r/v, a.l.s.

[9] See s. to Aquaviva, 2.viii.1597; ibid., ff.216r–17v, Latin a.l.s.

[10] See s. to Duras, 13.i.1598, Douai; (VI) Germania 178, f.9; s. to RP, 13.i., Douai; ibid., 11r–12v. O.M. to Duras, 13.ii.; ibid., ff.53r–54r; s. to Aquaviva, 14.ii.; ibid., ff.51r–52v.

[11] (VI) ibid., ff.51r–2v, Latin a.l.s.

commoners, drawn from the common herd . . . soldiers . . . adolescents, students, serving men and maids etc. *[sic].*"[12]

Replying to all this, Persons pointed out that a conciliatory and appeasing spirit can sometimes do damage. Lutheranism had made headway thanks to those who encouraged it under the pretext of restoring harmony. In the present case, without Mannaerts's patronage, the opponents of the English Jesuits would long ago have made peace on "fair and easy conditions."[13] What Persons found chiefly galling was that Mannaerts had been content to take all his information from the English Jesuits' enemies and critics. In the end, Persons came near to losing patience. "Though I am most willing to profess myself your Reverence's son, yet am I not to be considered such a child in the cause of England after labouring in it for nearly twenty years that I can be repressed by mere abuse while the arguments I offer are treated with contempt."[14] In England "not one in a thousand" supported Paget and, however completely the other side reversed the statistics, not thirty priests disagreed with the policy of the Jesuits. All this time the others had promoted secret faction against the Society while denying this in letters to Persons and his colleagues.[15]

William Baldwin departed for Flanders on April 19, 1598, to carry out his errand of reconciliation. The General considered it politic to let him replace Holt. Meanwhile, "openly confessing that it was the calumnious letters of the sedition-mongers that had deceived them . . . some of the student leaders begged with great ardour and humility to enter our Society."[16] Only one was allowed to do so. For the rest, "never since the foundation of the college" had such "peace and harmony been witnessed there." Meanwhile, in Flanders Mannaerts reported on April 10 that Holt and Gifford had met at Frangipani's nunciature to attempt a reconciliation. The English were not the only ones experiencing this kind of difficulty. "The French nation was likewise at scandalous loggerheads." As for the English, agreement was reached on the authority of the archduke "that all writings and evidences should be burnt in the presence of representatives from both sides, with notary and witnesses, and should embrace and abjure the causes of the quarrels." Holt and Owen, however, were troubled at the proposed destruction of evidence and procedings in secrecy. They wanted an adequate vindication in open court. "So Holt and his

---

[12] Ibid. See O.M. to Duras, 27.iii.1598, Louvain; ibid., f.79 r/v. Latin a.l.s.

[13] See RP to Mannaerts, 20.iii.1598. V. supra.

[14] Ibid.

[15] RP to Richard Gibbons, S.J., 21.iii.1598; (II) f.362, Latin.

[16] RP to Mannaerts, 26.iv.1598, Rome; (II) f.324, Latin.

friends succeeded in getting the peace agreement overthrown." Mannaerts was acting with authority, since he was appointed to fill in for the provincial, George Duras, now German Assistant to the General. Mannaerts remained in office until the appointment of Bernard Olivier on July 20.[17] Piqued by defeat over the reconciliation, he refused to take Persons's side against the others.[18]

It was not the end of the affair. In Brussels Mannaerts found "all the nobles exasperated." He joined the chorus that blamed Persons for being one of those wicked animals that defend themselves—in his case, to the nuncio, the protector, the General, and the Pope himself. Mannaerts refused to believe the evidence of a shifty letter from Gifford submitted to him by Persons, apparently preferring to believe that the latter invented it.[19] He went on to enlist the support of Duras, now German assistant in Rome.[20] Aquaviva, however, put himself firmly on the side of Persons and the English Jesuits.[21] Cardinals Cajetan and Borghese wanted the articles calumniating the Society sent to Rome, and they also wished the authors to acknowledge or revoke them so that the truth could be known. There was no desire for vengeance or a continuation of a quarrel, but in view of past experience they realized that a show of friendliness on the part of the late antagonists could reasonably be taken as merely a tactical ploy.[22] Mannaerts, Jesuit or not, was unwilling to accept the General's final decision. The Belgian appealed to Aquaviva not to let himself be overcome "by the importunity of those who sent [him] false information."[23]

Some time after mid-March, Persons moved to Naples to take advantage of the famous mineral springs. However, the weather was "cold, damp and changeable," although the doctors, as was in their interest, held out hopes of a cure.[24] Persons found time to write an overdue letter to King Philip, urging him yet again to reach a decision

[17] Mannaerts to RP, 10.iv.1598, Antwerp; (VI) Ep.Gen.35, f.834 et seq.; Frangipani correspondence, 329–45, Latin.

[18] Ibid.

[19] "Responsum R.D. Guilielmi Giffordii, decani insulensis ill.mo D. Nuncio Apostolico Belgii exhibitum, mense Aprilis 1598 de calumniis Societatis Jesu illatis, cum brevibus ad ipsum scholiis," (III) ibid., No. 87, endd. by RP.

[20] See O.M. to G. Duras, 10.iv.1598, Antwerp; (VI) Germania 178, f.92, Latin a.l.s.

[21] Aquaviva to Mannaerts, 29.iv.1598, Rome; (VI) Flandro. Belg.1.II. ff.673r–74v, Latin register.

[22] Ibid.

[23] O. Mannaerts to Aquaviva, 2.v.1598; (VI) Germania 178, f.110r–11v, Latin a.l.s.

[24] RP to Card.Borghese, 31.v.1598, Naples; (IV) F.Borgh. III.124.G.2, f.16r/v.

with regard to the infanta's claim to the English succession.[25] He also found time to intervene with the viceroy, Count Olivares, on behalf of certain "unhappy Englishmen in the gallies." He asked not only that they be freed but also sent home, since they evinced a "desire and promise to live and die good Catholics." They were poor seafaring folk having nothing to do with piracy, even if their ship had been armed. This was for self-defence.[26] Even if Elizabeth's subjects came to Spain originally with hostile intent, they were usually treated very leniently if they saw the error of their ways and turned to Catholicism. Similarly, the English authorities, Persons claimed, acted with like consideration towards captured Spaniards. At all events, a letter to Spain of May 22 announced that Olivares had "granted liberty to the Englishmen at the instance of Father Persons."[27] In fact it was not so simple. Persons wrote to Garnet later, "We have had much ado these days about the delivery of thirty-four Englishmen whom we found here in the gallies, at the oar, in extreme misery." By July 12, certainly, they were all freed. One was a young gentleman whom Persons sent to Rome since God had "given him good desire to follow the life of the seminaries."[28]

The political event of prime international importance in 1598 was the signing on May 2 of the peace of Vervins between France and Spain. Persons was interested if only because "from the conditions of the treaty which have so far appeared, it must be concluded that the Queen of England will also be a party to it." He urged Aldobrandino to persuade Henri IV to bring in the cause of the English Catholic recusants. She might listen to him if to no one else. Certainly, persecution continued unabated, and Persons emphasized the point by mentioning the martyrdom of two priests "in the part of England bordering on Scotland."[29] He included for meditation in Rome on this theme "certain chapters" from a book lately printed with the approval of Queen and council.[30]

[25] RP to Philip II, 28.v.1598, Rome; (VIII) Estado, Cartas de Flandes, Leg.228-8, años 1598–1602, Spanish a.l.s.

[26] RP to Olivares, 21.v.1598, Rome; (VIII) E. 1095, f.218, Italian a.l.s.

[27] Olivares to [Philip II?], 22.v.1598, Naples; received on 27.vii.(!); (VIII) ibid., f.217.

[28] RP to H. Garnet, 12.vii.1598, Naples; (II) f.438, English.

[29] The earlier reference seemingly to the execution of the Ven. Christopher Robinson, secular priest, at Carlisle in March 1597; the second more difficult to identify. Five Catholics were excuted for religion in 1597 and seven in 1598, not all priests.

[30] RP to Aldobrandino, 31.v.1598, Naples; (IV) F.Borgh. III, ibid., f.15 r/v, Italian a.l.s. This letter was given to Card. Borghese to pass to the Cardinal Secretary. RP's letter of 31.v. to Borghese (v. supra, n.24) asked him to add his own influence to the plea of the English Catholics. Their detailed proposals to RP(?) apropos of a religious settlement were dated 13.vi.1598 (NS). They added up to a demand for the repeal of all

William Gifford, still far from acknowledging any fault in himself, wrote to Persons complaining of injuries done to him, declaring further "that there were as many lies in the articles brought against him as there were lines." To vindicate the good faith of those who delated Gifford, Persons now sent the internuncio, Frangipani, four of the dean's letters from Rome, faithfully copied and vouched for under oath before a public notary. Persons did not plead for retribution but requested only that Gifford be called before the internuncio, "put on oath, and pressed to answer in so many words whether those letters had been written by him or not." If he denied them, the original letters were extant in Rome to give him the lie. If he admitted the letters, Frangipani should "reprove him and insist on an end to the dispute."[31] Replying to Persons on May 16, Frangipani found Gifford "clearly reluctant either to acknowledge or repudiate those letters" and so far was not pressed to do so. He used "one manner of speech" to the nuncio while insisting to others that he was the victim of "barefaced calumnies and lies."

Frangipani was clearly embarrassed by it all. Upright enough himself and perhaps too much a lover of the quiet life on account of his poor health, he evidently found the tedious squabbles among the English more than he could cope with. Indeed, Persons was told that, "in accordance with his temperament," Frangipani was inclined to "have all the writings burnt." Persons could not, of course, allow himself to be treated like one of a pair of recalcitrant schoolboys. The truth or otherwise of the calumnies put out against the Society by Fisher and his allies must be shown once and for all to be false as the prelude to any kind of settlement or understanding.[32] Meanwhile, Gifford's original letters stayed in Rome while Persons stayed in Naples.

Persons followed the English scene in letters from Garnet of May 6 and 13, and direct to the protector. There was general acceptance of the "subordination" set up in England by Cajetan. Rule by archpriest rather than bishop was felt to be more appropriate in a persecution situation. Persons had envisaged the appointment of bishops, as we have seen, but in a letter to Garnet of mid-July he expressed satisfaction at the general acceptance of the archpriest. To silence the critics, the Pope declared truly that Jesuits had never "desired authority or jurisdiction over priests in England." All must now

anti-Catholic laws from the days of Henry VIII; (IV) Nunziature diverse, 264, ff.233 and seq.

[31] RP to Frangipani, 27.vi.1598, Naples; (I) Anglia.II, No. 38, Latin contemporary copy endd. by RP.

[32] Ibid.

accept this "sweet and moderate kind of subordination . . . for the time present." Before the critical spirits had time to recover, there was universal acceptance by the secular clergy of the new arrangement, or at least no open dissent. Furthermore, a "hearty union" between them and the Jesuits seemed sufficient to destroy the effects of "that slanderous libel written by Fisher" and subsequently confessed by himself to be such. A copy of Fisher's accusations had been sent to Garnet by Cajetan's order. Persons wanted this "suppressed or burnt" or kept to himself "for charity's sake," lest it come to "the enemy's hands who would make his advantage of it."[33]

But the specter of Fisher would not be laid. Neither would that of the late trouble in the English College, Rome, as Garnet made clear. Those who had come away with the anti-Jesuit view of life could not be easily quieted. Persons put the blame on the students rather than the staff.

> Coming hither very young, and finding themselves . . . provided for abundantly, and acquainted daily with sights and relations of popes, cardinals and princes' affairs, our youth that was bred up at home with much more simplicity, and kept more under by their parents and masters than the Italian education doth comport, forget easily themselves, and break out to liberty; I mean such as have run astray and lost respect to their superiors in Rome.[34]

But such were always a small minority. The English were not alone in this. Spaniards, Frenchmen, and others experienced the same temptation in the good-natured, easygoing atmosphere of Rome. Some only went to the city to see the sights or even to escape from poverty and difficulty at home.

The Catholic community in exile also offered peculiar problems. It included spies for the English government and those whose faith had not only died but lay rotting in the ground.[35] Their effect on the seminarians was disastrous. Baronius told Persons, "Our youth bragged much of martyrdom but they . . . had no part of martyrs' spirit which is in humility and obedience." Vexed by the college troubles, the Pope "would put his finger to his brain signifying that there stood their sickness." The remedy was not obvious. Overforceful purges could drive them to the heretics, and some had dared to threaten just this. It was a good sign, no doubt, that those sent away to other seminaries had thus far settled down well. Some who "had been deceived" now proved to be "the best and most contented youths of

---

[33] RP to H. Garnet, 12.vii.1598. V. supra, n.28.

[34] Ibid.

[35] Ibid.

the house."[36] The basic difficulty was that the students were necessarily affected by the controversy over the place of Spain in English recusant calculations. Men young enough and not hardened in their opinions followed those whose superior knowledge, experience, and more commanding personality virtually imposed acceptance and obedience. Foremost of these was Persons himself. Accused by critics even for his pacification, Persons was further charged with "tyrannicide" and accused of being "Turkish" and "machavilian." He was not unduly perturbed; rather, he was content "to expect his reward from God; and the less he [had] from men the better." Certainly, he had brought many to serve the Church as priests and could not be fairly accused of driving "any man from his good purposes."[37]

Certain priests in England, however, felt discouraged in their "good purposes" by the fact that some had larger "faculties" than themselves—spiritual authority, that is, to absolve from sin and censure, especially in the confessional. Some had been punished for alleged insubordination by having their faculties suspended or taken away altogether. The subject was to be an important bone of contention among the appellants. Faculties could be granted by several authorities in graduated order from the Pope, the cardinal protector, the rectors of the English colleges abroad, and the nuncios in Paris and Brussels. Persons was therefore no doubt telling the simple truth when he said he had no knowledge of "faculties taken away from some on the way towards England" nor of other priests "to whom greater [faculties] were given than the other sort had." In an atmosphere becoming increasingly charged with emotion, and in which partisans and trouble makers were eager to use any pretext for embarrassing the other side, every sort of rumor or report could be exploited to fan the flame of controversy. Persons "knew it to be false that any . . . extraordinary faculties have been given to any since this . . . reformation happened in Rome." As far as he knew, there had been no question of penalizing any who had dared to "speak or not speak . . . in this Roman action." Nor had any been threatened or bribed by the promise of extension or the threat of limitation of faculties. In any case, if they had been so deprived with the object of curbing their tongues, they "were like to speak the more for it as more displeased."

It eventually emerged that, when the Pope's fiscal examined the depositions made at the visitation of the college, he found three "more culpable than the rest who were departed before towards England." After consultation with the Pope, it was agreed that it was "no

---

[36] Ibid.

[37] Ibid.

way convenient that those persons should go and live in England in so holy a work until they had given better satisfaction." So the protector wrote to the Brussels nuncio not only to see they were prevented from passing further but also "to recall their faculties" until further notice. Neither Persons nor any Jesuit was involved. Any comfort for Persons could only be derived from Plutarch's dictum that "every virtuous man ought to hire somebody to be his enemy thereby to have a watchman over him for avoiding of faults."[38] It all boded ill for the future.

Refreshed by the thermal springs of Naples, although his companion, Martin Array, fell sick of an ague,[39] Persons looked forward to a return to Rome and delicate negotiations to get the Catholics somehow included in the peace of Vervins.[40] He needed to proceed carefully because, although he appreciated the importance of the French influence with Elizabeth, he did not wish to appear to Sessa or de Peña to be switching his main interest if not his allegiance from Spain. He therefore dealt with Cajetan, the protector, whose influence and authority were beyond suspicion. He always had to be careful not to appear to be commanding rather than persuading in dealing with the higher powers. "I am exerting considerable pressure on . . . Cardinal Aldobrandino, but if there is too much zeal, they will react in the completely opposite direction." Letters were always liable to be lost even when they were not actually intercepted. But in all this trafficking in high policy, Persons did not disdain the human side.

> I have memories of the little glasses of lagrime and Albano so refreshing last year, and of the competent carving knife of the good Juan Baptista. I greet him from my heart, and Juan, the waiter, and Lorenzo. I beg your Excellency to give the latter a glass of good, neat Albano for my sake. Give my hearty greetings to the doctor also, and to all in your house where even the cats are very dear to me for the sake of their master whom I love.[41]

Persons made it clear in his letter of August 7 to Sessa that he hoped to return to Spain, although he realized the obstacles in the way. Meanwhile, now that his knee had improved, he hoped to return to Rome "after the first rains in September." News from England was that Catholics were being "persecuted more than ever before as though in derision of the treaty with France and of his Holiness in whose name it was made." The papists were taunted with the ineffectiveness

---

[38] Ibid.

[39] Ibid.

[40] RP to Sessa, 7.viii.1598, Naples; (IV) Nunziature diverse, 264, ff.244r–45v, Spanish a.l.s. See s. to de Peña, 7.viii.; ibid., ff.246r–47v.

[41] RP to de Peña, 7.viii.1598. V. supra.

of their friends overseas. "How foolish you are to die and undergo torture for your pope when he himself despises you and makes no account of you; nay, does not even know you exist!" They were further apprehensive "because among all the articles of the peace just concluded there is none that speaks of religion although it was for this that the wars were waged in the first place." In spite of all, the faith was "making great progress thanks to the preaching and labours of the seminary priests and Fathers of the Society." But they were anxious for relief from persecution following some intervention by the Catholic princes.[42]

By some extraordinary circumstance, Persons came into the possession of three authentic papers relating to "the affair of Charles Paget in Flanders." They were to be read in a certain order. The first two had been procured "very secretly" in England by some who had "the means to read them and copy them word for word." They came under oath from "two persons of credit" who had on other occasions sent the original documents but this time had "the obligation of sending them back immediately to the state secretariat in England in view of the danger they would incur if they were discovered." They were for Cajetan's eye alone, as Persons implored, since others working in the Roman curia and curial offices were not to be trusted.[43] It is difficult to believe that Persons had a contact or contacts among the confidential clerks of the English privy council, in view of the proverbial efficiency and lynx-eyed carefulness of Sir Robert Cecil, principal secretary. Nevertheless, there was one man among his clerks who might have been willing to pass on information in this way. Simon Willis began his office as secretary in 1595, with Levinus Munck to share the work from 1596, and seemingly to assume seniority, until 1602, when Willis was dismissed. Cecil mentioned briefly the causes of Willis's dismissal in a letter to Sir Henry Wotton of March 29, 1608, disclosing "how basely he was used by one he had employed, and yet had no resentment to him further than the injurious effect it might have on his Majesty's service and the good of his country."[44] True, Willis had little good to say of Sir Robert during his travels in Europe in virtual exile, but this may have been part of a typically Cecilan ruse to plant yet another spy abroad among the Catholics in exile and to cause further dissension. At all events, in a "reply to charges of consorting with Catholics" of February 9, 1609, Willis claimed quite plausi-

---

[42] RP to Aldobrandino 7.viii.1598, Naples; (IV) Nunziature diverse, 264, ff.241r–42v, Italian a.l.s. Sent through Borghese, vice-protector.

[43] RP to Cajetan, 22.viii.1598, Naples; (IV) ibid., ff.229r–30v, Italian a.l.s.

[44] See A. Collins, *Letters and Memorials of State* . . . II (London, 1746), 326f. A. G. R. Smith, art. on the secretaries, EHR, VII (1968), 481–504.

bly, "My journey to Rome for which I suffer was not without his Majesty's leave, procured by such means as your Lordships have formerly heard." A certain Francis Mitchell noticed that in Lyons and Geneva he did not behave "like a Romanist . . . but frequented the exercises of those of the religion . . . and afterwards the ambassador's sermons at Paris for the most part every Sunday," where he also took the Anglican Communion in Mitchell's company.[45] All in all then, it is very likely that this was yet another of Sir Robert's brilliant ploys to keep the papists at perpetual loggerheads. Certainly, Cecil never liked or trusted Charles Paget. But then he liked and trusted very few.

The first of Persons's enclosures for Cajetan was one from Paget to his English agent of April 27, 1598. It was to be shown to the Queen so that Paget could be allowed to "cross over into her dominions with more security."[46] Weary of exile, he wished to return to England and his estates on almost any terms, although, as Persons noted, he was already enjoying more than the original value of his estates in his Spanish pension. Paget offered his help in the impending negotiations for peace with Spain, hoping to ingratiate himself further with the thought that he had it "on a very good authority" that Philip was "planning a foul deception." He was anxious that his dealings with the court, already suspected by his enemies, should not be known. His letters should be burned.

Persons's second enclosure to Cajetan—"litera B"— was a list of Paget's principal objections to the Jesuits. Persons, of course, received frequent and less-than-honorable mention for his politics. In France he wrote *Leicester's Commonwealth*—not named as such here— and sent it into England by a lay brother. He promoted the efforts of Parry and Savage to kill the Queen. Persons denied all this but made no comment on a scheme he was supposed to have shared with Claude Mathieu to invade England with five thousand men. He claimed more than plausibly that plots to kill the Queen were mere devices of her ministers to put her in fear and keep her in dependency on them. Alleged as the author of the *Book of Succession*, Persons was supposed to have bound by oath all priests entering England to uphold the exclusive right of the infanta. Certainly, he admitted writing another book on the reformation of England to be published when the time was ripe. Paget also charged the Jesuits with collecting money in England for the poor, which they spent on themselves and their "seditious books." They claimed a virtual monopoly of good works and wanted

---

[45] Simon Willis to the Privy Council, 1.ii.1609; Ellesmere MS, EL 2195, copy; CRS 60 (1968) No. 28, pp. 196–201.

[46] "Letter A," enclosure with RP to Cajetan, 22.viii.1598; (IV) Nunziature diverse, 264, f.234r, Latin copy or translation.

nothing less than the complete overthrow of nobility, laws, customs, and all the ancient order of the land.

It is remarkable how many of the charges against the Jesuits that persisted in popular historical tradition until very recent times are to be found in the polemic of Charles Paget. He was anxious throughout to vindicate his loyalty to Elizabeth, being opposed "to every manoeuvre . . . that could embarrass . . . her Majesty or the State." He desired "that all who share[d] the contrary and malevolent intent should be corrected and reformed." A large part of the remedy lay in getting the Jesuits out of England. They should also be removed from the seminaries, "so that young men would not feel drawn to an Order which launched them on a career of intrigue and sedition." The English Catholics would be glad to see them go if only because they were branded as *politique* and lukewarm if they refused to shelter them. Spanish influence alone stood in the way and restrained a Pope who was otherwise altogether convinced of their troublemaking.[47]

Even the enemies of the Society found Paget unsavory. Sir Robert Cecil wrote to Sir Henry Neville, ambassador in Paris, in September 1599,

> I see the queen is not minded to pardon him and restore him upon such merit as giving intelligences, which may be true and may be false. For we do know that he is out with the Jesuits' faction not out of love to the English, but out of other private ends, which do divide most of these fugitives only in this proportion, to emulate and supplant each other, but ever to convenire in tertium.

The Queen would hold out no hope to Paget until he effected "some matter of weight worthy the remission of his vile treasons." Meanwhile Neville should keep him dangling in hope. "Between these lines if you walk with him, the queen will allow it, and so if you make some use of him, he shall have some crowns."[48] So Paget was now well advanced on the road to becoming spy and informer, a creature despised while he was used.

Persons's third enclosure.[49] rebutting many charges detailed elsewhere, repudiated authorship of Leicester's *Commonwealth,* making Charles Arundell chiefly responsible, a commonly held view. Distancing himself from any part in the Babington conspiracy, Persons admitted

---

[47] "Calumniæ Caroli Pagetti contra Patres Societatis ad Reginam Angliae 1598"; (I) Anglia II, No. 46, ff.167r–69v, Latin copy in RP's hand. Another Latin copy in (IV) Nunziature diverse, 264, ff.237r–38v. English version in (VII) SP12/267, No. 67.

[48] R. Cecil to H. Neville, 25.ix.1599, Court at Nonesuch; (64) 112.

[49] "Responsum ad præcipuas Caroli Pagetti calumnias . . ." [22.viii.1598], v. supra; (IV) ibid., 264, ff.239r–40v, headed "Litera C," Latin.

some responsibility for the invasion attempt of 1584, but insisted that his role was insignificant enough compared with that of Guise, the papal nuncio, Allen, Claude Mathieu, and Archbishop Beaton. In any case, Paget himself had expressed enthusiastic support at the time, even if he subsequently worked against it, bringing to ruin the Earls of Arundel and Northumberland in the process.

In spite of widespread slander, the views of the Jesuits on assassination were scarcely ambiguous. "Fr Persons and other members of the Society never hitherto gave willing ear to the idea of laying violent hands on the person of the queen; not even when it was proposed as a matter of conscience by men of the highest integrity and reliability; and still less did they lend any such idea their approval." The idea of giving absolution for a murder before it was committed was equally absurd to anyone "who knew something about church doctrine and procedures."[50] This particular calumny, as Persons observed, sprang chiefly from Protestant critics. Certainly, Paget could only surmise maliciously what was said in the confessional.

Persons did not substantially deny Paget's charge of "compiling a book about the queen," but insisted that Allen was the senior partner in the project. He wrote it "with the authorisation of the supreme pontiff and in defence of the apostolic see." Paget was only guessing once again about this, since he was in France at the time, while Allen and Persons were in Rome. If it did reflect in any way on the Queen, it was because she had chosen to found her kingdom "on the oppression and destruction of the Catholic religion." As for Paget, he was critical of any idea of reforming England, for almost the whole of his family fortune had been founded "on the seizure of ecclesiastical property" and he feared any possible future restitution. So his accusation about the Jesuits' money collecting was a stone thrown in a glass house. In fact, according to Persons, the only collection made on his initiative was in 1581, when a thousand gold pieces were collected to help Allen and the college at Rheims.

In England about this time leading Catholics, not without difficulty and danger, contrived to hold a consultation to consider statutes to be repealed if the Queen were persuaded to grant toleration after peace with France and Spain. It was Persons's intention to pass the document to Cajetan, with copies of anything of special interest for

---

[50] Nevertheless, such charges were often made in connection with the plot stories used to discredit Catholics, especially priests. See (26) passim. RP's clear disapproval of tyrannicide as a practical expedient, as against John Hus and John Knox, comes in *The warn-word to Sir Francis Hastinges watchword: conteyning the issue of three former treateses* . . . ([Antwerp], 1602), part 2, 19f.

him to Sessa.[51] Persons was anxious not to weaken the Spanish connection, since the true feelings of Henri IV towards the English Catholics in general had yet to be proved in action. He could hardly have any objections to chasing the Jesuits out of England; but, as Persons saw it, "this would be more harmful" to the papist community "than not to have the said toleration."[52] Certainly, with men like Paget in the lead, they might well have found themselves praying to be saved from their friends. Persons was now looking forward to a return to Rome from Naples by a galley which had come from Sicily.

It was in September 1598 that Persons at last caught up with the dubious activities of John Cecil. Did his information come from Simon Willis? Typically, Persons made the approach direct to Cecil with a rebuke for dealing not only with the factious but also with the late William Baron Burghley, Lord Treasurer, who died on August 4. With Sir Robert Cecil to succeed him as virtual head of state, a man after and with his father's own heart, this death made less difference to the papist cause, perhaps, than the death of Philip II on September 13. Philip III, amiable enough, had nothing of his father's grip on public affairs. He was not expected to be a match for Henri IV, and whatever the hopes of John Cecil, Paget, and others from that direction, no match for Robert Cecil, a man no less astute and if anything even more devious than his gifted father. As John Chamberlain, a man close to affairs, wrote on July 2, 1612, soon after his death, "he juggled with religion, with the king, queen, their children, with nobility, parliament, with friends, foes and generally with all."[53]

With no real pause for fair trial, the new "subordination" for the secular priests in England soon had its critics. Persons reported to Clement VIII in October that two spokesmen, William Bishop and Robert Charnock, were coming to interview the Pope at Ferrara. They wanted to be reassured that the new arrangement was not simply a shift of the Jesuits to hold them in tutelage. Significantly, they went by way of Paris "to get letters of recommendation from the Most Christian King against the Fathers of the Society." Persons could not offer a favorable testimonial. "They are considered to be turbulent characters,

---

[51] De Peña passed on the Paget papers, received from RP with letters of 22.viii., to Sessa in a packet of 29.viii; (IV) ibid., 264, f.231r. Enclosure "A" was a copy of Paget to his agent, Gerard Burghert, alias Thomas Barnes. See letter of 27.iv.1598; (VII) SP12/266, No. 116; (29) Eliz., ibid., pp. 68f: also Paget to Burghert/Barnes, 8.v.1598; (29) ibid., p. 48. Thomas Barnes was a spy for the English government, writing as "Robert Tissue."

[52] RP to de Peña, 22.viii.1598, Naples; (IV) ibid., f.190r/v, Spanish.

[53] J. Chamberlain to Dudley Carleton, 2.vii.1612, London; (VII) SP14/70, No. 1; (29) 1611–18, p. 136. This passage is not indicated in the calendar.

accomplices of those who a short while ago upset the English College in Rome."[54] Clement was urged to delay the meeting for a Roman occasion when Persons would have the opportunity to reply to what would almost certainly be unfair charges against the Society. But the Pope could not so easily leave Ferrara, the latest papal acquisition and center of interest and politics. Persons therefore contrived to go northward with Holt, who was going to Spain. Thus they could be at hand to counteract the influence of Bishop and Charnock, who had probably arrived already. On October 24, Persons asked Bellarmine, not yet a cardinal but a man in the odor of sanctity and with influence, to give the Pope a letter from the archpriest and his assistants asking for papal ratification of their appointment. Cajetan was also given a copy, and with it news of an understanding reached in Flanders between William Gifford and the papal nuncio. Persons asked to see the nuncio's letter himself "to know if he tells the same story or a different one." He made a further plea for secrecy, but neither he nor the General supposed that this could be achieved.[55] Persons set off for Ferrara about November 2.

The problem of providing a more formal organization for the three hundred or so priests now working in England could hardly be settled without controversy. Perhaps the best summary of the pros and cons for setting up bishops was contained in a document of September 29, 1612, forwarded by the Brussels nuncio to the papal secretary of state.[56] The three main reasons applicable in the present context and pressed by those calling for bishops were the availability of the sacrament of confirmation, a head or heads of sufficient caliber to command general obedience and respect, and an authority to make frequent appeals to Rome unnecessary. Ireland already had bishops, so why not England? The main reasons against were that the presence of bishops would increase persecution for the laity who would have to host them. If they were captured and broke down under examination or even apostatized, the scandal would be considerable. If they escaped abroad, they would become yet another burden on the Holy See. Some suspected that the English government was interested in bishops, since they could become effective allies in the drive against Jesuits. If the Jesuits reacted, this could foment division to the point where the continuance of the papist cause became impossible. The men chosen for the honor might prove to be careerists rather than bona fide pastors.

---

[54] RP to Clement VIII, 24.x.1598, Rome(?); (IV) F.Borgh. III.124.G, f.56 r/v, a.l.s.

[55] RP to Cajetan, 25.x.1598, Rome; (IV) Lettere de' cardinali, I, f.154, Italian a.l.s.

[56] (IV) F.Borgh. II,23–24,ff.224r–41v. Nuncio's covering letter, 6.x.1612; ibid., f.224r, copy.

According to the nuncio's covering letter for the above, controversy really began after the death of Cardinal Allen in 1594. Before this there was no room for envy or emulation, since no one supposed that Persons, the man in black, was telling Allen what to do. After his death, however, many believed and others feared that Persons was the most outstanding character on the recusant stage. But as a Jesuit he could not be appointed to rule the secular clergy even if he were otherwise fitted, something that many denied vigorously. Cajetan's "constitutive letter" from Rome of March 7, 1598, set up George Blackwell as the first archpriest. The appointment was made on the advice of many people, Jesuits not excluded but certainly not exclusively. The problem was to find someone who would work in harmony with everyone else on the mission and be a figure universally respected. While not a man of outstanding gifts, Blackwell might well have succeeded; but his critics, moved by motives very mixed, were determined not to let him succeed. The small but able and articulate group hostile to Jesuit influence attacked him almost immediately as a creature of Persons. One motive for irritation was that some had already taken the first steps on native soil to work out a form of organization for which they no doubt hoped eventually to get Roman approval and ratification. Cutting across this local initiative, as it seemed, was the preemptive system of archpriest and assistants imposed by Rome. William Bishop, Robert Charnock, Anthony Champney, John Cecil, John Mush, and John Colleton were the ablest and most forward of the group involved. They resolved to challenge the new arrangement with as little delay as possible.

Unfortunately, as happens often in religious causes, the affair unfolded with few indications of Christian charity. A number of books produced by the "appellants" came off the press in the next few years, notably between 1601 and 1603, which varied only in their degree of vituperation and repetitiveness. Unwilling to attack the Vatican directly, they made Persons and the Jesuits its whipping boys for the error of setting up the system in the first place and blundering again by promoting Blackwell. Persons answered them to some extent in kind, but his style was pungent, not abusive, and written in English of a clarity exceptional in his age.

Perhaps the ablest of the secular priests who opposed the archpriest settlement was John Colleton. Like Persons he was a native of Somerset, born at Milverton. He tried his vocation with the Carthusians at Louvain, entering and leaving the order partly at least on the advice of Fr. Collum, a Jesuit. One motive for his entering was an impediment in his speech; one for his leaving was a tone-deafness which made him useless in choir.[57] In 1602 he published *A just defence of the slandered priests*. Repetitive and ill-arranged at times, it was still the work of a scholar with a considerable knowledge of canon law, considerable enough to overturn the idea that the appellants were simply a coterie of noisy rebels. Much of the material was regurgitated and republished in 1603 in Robert Charnock's *Reply to a notorious libel*. Inferior to Colleton's works in most respects, it had the advantage of coming from a man who took part in the first appeal. He also brought out more effectively a difference in the attitudes of Jesuits and others towards authority and obedience. Both works make unflattering references to the "blind obedient," a subtle criticism of Jesuit spirituality. Certainly, obedience as a virtue was developed by St. Ignatius. Poverty and chastity were not less regarded in the Society than in the older orders, but obedience was intended to be the principal hallmark of the Jesuit. Ignatius wrote a letter on obedience which was essential pabulum for all in training. The good Jesuit was like a stick in the hands of an old man—the founder's own metaphor, an instrument for the use of the superior, whose will must be seen as virtually God's. The concept was paramilitary in this first salvation army.

When the Pope, therefore, and even Cajetan, exercising his duly delegated authority, set up a form of government and appointed the governor, all should accept this decision with alacrity and without question as an expression of the Divine Will. As a formula for unity and working together, it explains in human terms a great deal of Jesuit success and effectiveness. Like ants or bees, all had their place in the hill or hive; cheerfully, and theoretically, without question, all did the work enjoined on them. Certainly, if all on the English mission had been able to accept this view of things, the history of the Church in England at this time would have come much closer to being a simple success story. But there was a significant minority which could not accept this mystical view of things. They could not feel bound to accept Cajetan's arrangement in a spirit of "blind obedience." Their reasons were convincingly set out in Colleton's book. He took the trouble to quote at length documents, letters, and replies, so that one was not obliged to follow the argument simply on the authority of his unsupported word.

The burden of Colleton's argument was that to set up a form of government without precedent in the Church required more than the authority of a cardinal; nothing less than papal authority would suffice, as he claimed, manifested in a brief or document which they could see and examine for themselves in notarial copy. So it could be

---

[57] (18) I, p. 83.

taken that the first appeal of 1598 was directed to finding out the authentic papal will. If this in fact corroborated Blackwell's archipres-biterate, all as loyal sons of the Church would hasten to obey. Meanwhile, our lusty dissidents refused to accept Blackwell's word for an arrangement which had apparently been set up simply on the word of a cardinal manipulated by the sinister Robert Persons. The attitude of the appellants was scarcely flattering to any concerned in the arrangement, notably the cardinal and the first archpriest, but not excluding those who had offered advice. Perhaps it was not surprising, then, that the authorities treated the first appeal as an act of insubordination and rebellion. Certainly, the attitude of the appellants contrasted ill with that of the Jesuits, who, although they were in favor of bishops, accepted the decision without demur. The minority was aware, however, that truth sometimes lay with minorities as in the case of St. Thomas of Canterbury, who had been one against Henry II and his court, yet came to be revered as a saint throughout Christendom.[58]

So William Bishop and Robert Charnock undertook their journey to Rome. Convinced of the reasonableness of their cause, they expected to be received with courtesy if not cordiality. Their critics, however, were much concerned to preserve a common front against the common foe, so much so that perhaps they overreacted in treating as insubordination what could have been taken as a perfectly legitimate expression of doubt and a desire for certainty. Unfortunately for the appellants, there was always in the background a fear on the part of the Catholic authorities that they were somehow, even in their legitimate aspirations, being made use of by the enemies of the Church, as well as of the Jesuits and, indeed, of everything Catholic, for their own purposes. And so, of course, they were. And as time advanced, the usefulness of the appellants to the enemies of the Church became ever more apparent and their exploitation more systematically thorough.

---

[58] John Colleton, *A Just Defence of the Slandered Priests*, 92f.

Willliam Holt left Rome about November 7, 1598, leaving Persons behind.[1] The death of Philip II on September 13 came as a considerable blow, but Persons lost no time in establishing contact with Philip III and in enlisting his interest for the English recusant cause. Furthermore, the "Queen of England and her heretics had not sought to partake in the peace now concluded; on the contrary, rather had she given his Majesty fresh reason for administering punishment in her latest acts of insolence."[2]

A movement to found a Benedictine community from among the English ladies, exiles in Flanders, began at this time. They included the daughter of the Earl of Northumberland, executed for his part in the northern rising. The Pope readily gave his permission and a blessing. Persons also supported the venture with enthusiasm. He wrote to the Empress hoping that the infanta Isabella, wife of the new governor due to arrive shortly, would take up "this work of piety" as her first concern in the new environment.[3] Persons did not look for thanks. "If I should respect men's words or thanks in this life, long ago I should have left off to deal" for Douai and for many others "that reap the benefit of my labour . . . [but] speak their pleasure of me . . . and talk at random." Mannaerts was not the only Jesuit who failed to see eye to eye with him. "The peace made by Fr Baldwin with Dr Gifford is scarce taken well by friends and laughed at by our adversaries." Frangipani had organized a reconciliation at which the copies of Gifford's letters attacking the Society were ceremonially burned. True, Gifford had on this occasion asked Baldwin's pardon on his knees for his attacks on the Jesuits, promising "never to intermeddle more." The nuncio described the scene to Cajetan and Persons in letters of September 27. The latter, knowing what was in the heart of man, was

---

[1] RP to Mannaerts, 7.xi.1598, Rome; (II) f.361.

[2] RP to Philip III, 10.xi.1598, Rome; (VIII) Estado 182, n.f., a.l.s.

[3] RP to Empress Maria, 10.xi.1598, Rome; (II) f.434, Spanish. Maria returned to Spain in 1581. Isabella Clara Eugenia, sister of Don Carlos and Philip III, married Albrecht, brother of Emperor Rudolf II and Matthias; see R. J. W. Evans, *Rudolf II and His World* . . . (Oxford, 1973), 59, genealogy, 311.

chiefly happy to reflect that the originals of the compromising letters were still in Rome.[4]

Like so many in Rome, Cajetan also suffered from bad health, which made it difficult for Persons to contact him even by letter when he wrote in October.[5] In mid-December he reported in his own fashion the arrival of William Bishop and Richard Charnock. "The two ambassadors of the disaffected priests in England have at least arrived. After reaching Rome, they came to the college for the eight days' hospitality which it is customary to give strangers. We received them with goodwill and charity." But "since they came without the order of their superior in England," they experienced no great cordiality on the part of staff or students. Persons could hardly be blamed, perhaps, for fearing that they would endeavor to stir up memories of old strife among the students for present purposes. So "no student goes to call on them apart from a few who do so for the sake of old acquaintance and who sing the same song." Even now, evidently, strife could break out again with little stirring.[6]

Fortunately for himself, the archpriest had agents in Rome to counteract the hostile and not always accurate propaganda of his adversaries. On December 12 Drs. Haddock and Martin, George Blackwell's men, much older priests than Charnock or Bishop, called on them and gave them, "albeit in a friendly spirit," a dressing-down lasting some two hours. They were left in no doubt that their out-of-hand rejection of Cajetan's arrangement was much resented in Rome. At the end of it, they were "slightly humbled" and promised to take no further step without Cajetan's "order and approval." The cardinal was still absent from Rome.[7]

This year occurred yet another of those strange contrivances, all too common during the joint reign of the Cecils, William and Robert, apparently aimed at killing the Queen but in reality a government ploy to push the papists yet further into the slough of discredit. Garnet wrote Persons a long account—alas, now lost—on June 28 of a plot named after Edward Squire. To this Persons replied in the new year.[8] Meanwhile, touching the problem of the archpriest, the Pope

---

[4] RP to Dr Barrett, 21.xi.1598, Rome; (II) f.435.

[5] RP to Cajetan, 25.x.1598. V. supra.

[6] S. to s., 13.xii.1598, Rome; (IV) Lettere a cardinali, I, f.159, a.l.s.

[7] Ibid. RP drew up on 1.xii.1598 "An observation of certain aparent judgments of Almighty God againste such as have been seditious in the English Catholique cause for these nine or ten yeares past," (I) Anglia.A.II, No. 44; (II) f.485; CRS 2, 202–11. Miss P. Renold believed the true date of this document to be 1601.

[8] RP to H. Garnet, 30.i.1599, Rome; (II) f.354. According to Grene, "he giveth

and Aldobrandino, evidently wishing to preserve impartiality, avoided any prior meeting with Persons, who tried several times in vain to get an audience ahead of the appellants.[9] He was clearly afraid that the Vatican would weaken and give way on the point of bishops. Not that Persons had any objection to episcopacy, as we have seen, but he feared the overall effect if it seemed to be given as a reward of disobedience and insubordination. One thing at least seemed clear. Pope and cardinals were anxious not to appear to be dominated by Persons's views on the English situation.

Charnock's examination before a papal commission comprising "the two cardinal protectors, Acaritius, the Pope's fiscal, and other parties" began on January 4, 1599; Bishop's began on January 10. The inquiry into matter and motives was thorough. On January 15, it emerged from Charnock's examination that of some three hundred clergy—probably an underestimate—only some fourteen or fifteen suppported the appellant cause. Bishop thought it was twelve. Charnock's interviews ended on February 4, Bishop's on January 25. Bagshaw, Bluet, Cope, Heborne, Watson, and Clarke were named among their supporters. After a report to the Pope, the cardinals and Acaritius went to the English College to read their *acta* before the parties themselves and get their further comments, and to elucidate matters still not yet clear, such as Bagshaw's insistence that the archpriest's authority be revoked. Persons commented, "Lo what a resolute lawmaker is here who recalleth the pope's subordinations in a word, and setteth up another of his own making with as great facility."[10]

It was, no doubt, well that Persons had been held at arm's length during these proceedings, since the outcome was almost all he wished. A brief of April 6, 1599, confirmed the protector's letters setting up the archpriest.[11] Furthermore, "the said messengers" were not allowed to return immediately to England, being "restrained" for a time in the English College; no great hardship, but they could not relish the fact that the Jesuits were their "jailers." Bishop and Charnock both promised for themselves and their friends never to "stir

a very good account of all that matter," but Grene did not transcribe this letter further. This is the only copy. There seems to be no extant account of the trial of Squire and the rest. See F. Edwards, S.J., "The Strange Case of the Poisoned Pommel: Richard Walpole S.J. and the Squire Plot 1597–8," (43) Vol. 56 (1987) 3–82.

[9] RP to Aldobrandino, 13.ii.1599, Rome; (IV) F.Borgh. 448.AB, f.327, a.l.s.

[10] RP, *A briefe apologie . . .* , p. 134b. Chapter 9 (pp. 119–40) covers the Bishop/Charnock episode. Numerous documents giving the Jesuit and appellant viewpoints in (42); J. Mush, *Declaratio motuum . . .* (London(?), 1601), for the appellant account.

[11] *A briefe apologie . . .* , 140b. On p. 143 RP says "the Breve beareth date of the 21" of April. But see (11) III, App. No. XXVII.

more in these affairs." They were then set at liberty. Persons, genuinely anxious for reconciliation and wishing to show goodwill, invited them to visit college and vineyard, but both smarted under what they took to be their humiliation at his hands. He was the enemy and his insidious influence had moved Pope and cardinals to their final verdict. As Persons commented, "it is an ordinary act of all malcontents . . . to lay their ill successes upon other men; and when they dare not do it unto princes or supreme magistrates . . . they accuse commonly such particular men as they imagine to have procured the same."[12]

On Good Friday, Persons wrote an appeal to John Colleton and John Mush, two able allies of Bishop and Charnock.[13] He appealed for unity, denying that he was "of another body, and therefore no great friend of theirs." His efforts for the seminaries were sufficient evidence of his genuine concern for the secular clergy. He hoped that before all else Blackwell and Garnet would strive to maintain peace on the mission.[14] Mush replied for both on May 28. It seemed to "many of good learning and timorous consciences" that there was sufficient reason for not accepting Cajetan's system of government. Now that the Pope himself had spoken, the matter could be regarded as finished. On receipt of the brief they would do their "best endeavour to pacify and unite all the rest." He had reached a good agreement with the Jesuit Holtby the Christmas before. Mush and Colleton, able and intelligent men, had been leading spirits in setting up the "associations" which preceded the establishment of the archpriest.[15]

Bishop and Charnock, sent to France and Lorraine respectively, were pursued by Persons—but only with what was meant as kindness. He wrote two letters of recommendation for Bishop early in May.[16] A letter of May 7 to the Cardinal of Burgundy recommended "his person, his cause, his virtue, his business and talents," corroborating what the protector had already written. The Burgundian cardinal was also thanked for the "signal favour" he had already shown "Dr John Cecil."[17] Showing equally rare persistence in the opposite direc-

---

[12] Ibid., 122a.

[13] H. Ely, *Certaine briefe notes* . . . , 105. Ely dilates on the theme with normal appellant exaggeration. "Never was there heard of such iniustice since good St Peter sate in that chaire" (p. 108). The turn of the screw was the "imprisonment" of Bishop and Charnock "under the custodie of their adversaries," i.e., the Jesuits at the VEC.

[14] RP to J. Colleton and J. Mush, 9.iv.1599; (II) f.488. Apart from this brief notice, there is an extract in *A briefe apologie*, 142f.

[15] J. Mush to RP, 28.v.1599, London; *A briefe apologie* . . . , 143f. RP wrote to Mush again on 27.vii.; ibid., 144b–45, pleading for an "oblivion of those affayres past."

[16] On 4 and 7.v.1599; (II) f.488.

[17] RP to the Cardinal of Burgundy, 7.v.1599, Rome; (II) f.352, Latin.

tion, Mannaerts continued to harangue the General on the English exiles in Flanders. Aquaviva replied in mid-June 1599 in crisp, well-chosen phrases. The fact that his English confrères were criticized did not mean they had given good cause for offence. Indeed, criticism could only be completely stifled by closing the English mission. Even Mannaerts should see that this was undesirable. The malevolence of Gifford and Paget towards the Society had been proved beyond doubt by intercepted letters. Nevertheless, the wily dean, even after the operatic scene in Frangipani's presence, refused to "acknowledge or confess his fault completely."[18] Persons the soldier wanted total victory.

Two significant allies of Persons died about this time: William Holt in Barcelona on May 25, 1599, and Dr. Barret, president of Douai, on May 30.[19] Cajetan took this as an auspicious moment to make a visitation, Dr. Richard Hall, canon of St. Omer, and John Wright, dean of Courtrai, being appointed visitors on July 1. Cajetan gave Persons among other items a copy of the latest ordinance for Douai.[20] Dr. Worthington was appointed with scant delay to succeed Barret.[21] The English College, Rome, was mainly taken up just now with an appeal concerning its property at Piacenza, settled favorably in mid-August.[22] The Valladolid college was also flourishing, but the death of Charles Tankard meant the loss of a man "who is not made but in many years." This effectively kept Creswell in Spain. Three students of promise had also died in Rome.[23] Otherwise, the college was "most blessed, quiet, content, studious and virtuous," as Persons reported.

Contrary to earlier, overoptimistic reports, the college at Valladolid was now entering a stormy phase. The trouble began with "some disorder grown . . . about entering into religion." Excellent in itself, this was now, it seems, being "taken in hand with levity, rashness or upon passion, discontentment, desire of liberty, novelty and other

---

[18] Aquaviva to O. Mannaerts, 12.vi.1599, Rome; (VI) Ep.Gen. 1586–99; Gallia 44, ff.56v–58r.

[19] RP to the doctors of Douai, 27.vi.1599, Rome; (II) f.488.

[20] "Letters of Card. Cajetan in Persons's hand," 1.vii.1599, Rome; (II) f.352. "There were other letters from the same cardinal to the doctors of Douai drawn up in Persons's hand."

[21] See RP to W. Gifford, 14.vii.1599, Rome; (II) f.488. This letter "exhorteth him to peace."

[22] RP to Alberto Pietra at Piacenza, 14.viii.1599, Rome; (I) Anglia. A.II, No. 54, signed.

[23] They died of dysentery. See RP to Aldobrandino, 20.x.1599, Rome; (IV) F.Borgh. III. 124.G.2, f.21r, Italian a.l.s. RP included with this "reliable reports" of Irish as well as English affairs.

such humours." It looked to Persons and to others like an outbreak of the Roman disease. Some having lost their first fervor, and unable to go on or back, hit upon life in a religious order on the continent as a decent alternative to the hard life of a priest on the English mission. The further removed from the likelihood, the less attractive to many seemed the glory of martyrdom. It was all very human. Some tried to join the "holy Order of St Bennet" but "gave so little contentment to the Fathers of that Order as now they desire no more of us." Persons was sorry for the youths themselves, but "God hath His secret judgments, and some he punisheth one way and some another." He was careful to insist that genuine vocations to the religious life should not be discouraged.[24]

After completion of the Douai visitation, Hall and Wright sent to Rome their report dated August 16. With it went a letter from Worthington to which Cajetan replied on September 13, a copy being given to Persons, since it is likely he had some hand in its contents.[25] A little earlier Persons replied to yet another of his critics. William Tresham, uncle of Francis, later involved in the Gunpowder Plot, was a soldier of fortune—declining fortune—in the archduke's army in the Netherlands. An ally of Charles Paget, he drew up a memorial against William Holt and other Jesuits, which he presented to Fr. Maggio, S.J., in Paris. Persons, showing an impressive grasp of facts and detail, answered the usual charges once again with practiced patience.[26] But it was a delicate matter to defend the detention of Charnock and Bishop in the English College until they had agreed to abide peacefully by the papal decisions. The appellants, now discernibly a party, endeavored to make it appear in word and writing that the gallant pair were the victims of outrageous injustice. Humphrey Ely led the field. Addressing himself directly to Bishop and his commiserators, Persons pointed out what was to be increasingly forgotten as time went on, namely, that the cool reception extended to the pair in Rome had nothing to do with their appeal proper but was a rebuke for the "manifold calumniations and odious exaggerations made . . . against the proceedings of their superiors."[27] Certainly, appellant tactics from now on explain why the Vatican became increasingly reluctant to concede the point of bishops. Diocesan organization presupposed a certain tranquility and civilized

[24] RP to John Blackfan and John Lloyd, 23.viii.1599, Rome; (IX) Serie II, Leg.1, signed.

[25] Cajetan to Dr. Worthington, 13.ix.1599, Rome; (II) f.488.

[26] RP to William Tresham, 30.viii.1599, Rome; (II) f.488.

[27] RP to "Mr Bishop and others," 9.x.1599, Rome; (II) f.306. Grene only mentions the letter, some four pages long: but see RP, *A briefe apologie . . .*, 127v–40r; *Copies of certaine discourses . . .* (Rome, 1601), 171 (See (28) cxxix–cxxx).

decency in which the bishop could operate. That this was lacking in England was mainly due to the English government. But the ill-natured conflict reflected in many books from now on made it painfully clear that the papists themselves, to the embarrassment of the best of them, were contributing no little to the general atmosphere of strife and chaos. Persons and the Jesuits could not but be scandalized by continued efforts to overthrow the papal ordering of things, since they were founded in special devotion to the Holy See. The appellants, while wishing to be Catholic and Roman, did not feel the obligation to the same degree. The first two appellants while in Rome behaved discreetly enough, desiring only that the Pope should "confirm this order already appointed."[28] Unfortunately for themselves, their cause was frequently to be taken out of their hands and developed by others whose real intentions could be taken as suspect.

Maggio, a distinguished Venetian Jesuit, unlike Mannaerts, had the grace to approach Persons himself on the subject of Tresham's charges. Persons replied to his letter of August 30 in mid-October 1599. He referred pungently to some who could be displeased when they did not get all they wanted whenever they wanted it, and who could be consumed with jealousy at what was given to others. Although Persons expressed "a special love" of many years' standing for Tresham, it is evident that he was yet another in exile who had turned selfishly sour. At one point he had even intended "to bring scandalous matters to light" unless he were "given satisfaction." Persons was still ready to help him "not because of any threat but out of charity and because this is our profession."[29] Perhaps one of Robert Cecil's spies, John Petit, came close to the truth when he described Tresham as "a vain fellow, full of wind," one who played "with both hands . . . to be trusted by neither side."[30] In a struggle for mere survival, a man could fall low indeed.

New orders for Douai were not received without "murmuration."[31] Perhaps this prompted Persons to formulate nine ordinances for the guidance of the seminaries run by the English Jesuits. They were issued as from the General to confirm ordinances already published on April 15, 1598. They were binding on the prefect—Persons for the time being—and vice-prefect of the mission as well as on pro-

---

[28] RP, *A briefe apologie* . . . , 130. RP wrote again at this time to J. Mush, W. Tresham, J. Colleton, M. Kellison, "and others"; (II) f.306.

[29] RP to Maggio, 18.x.1599, Rome; (II) f.353.

[30] (29) Elizabeth 1598–1601, pp. 343, 358f, 456. For W. Tresham see F. Edwards, *The Gunpowder Plot: The Narrative of Oswald Tesimond* (London: The Folio Society, 1973), App. 1. But note that WT was the uncle, not the brother, of Francis.

[31] RP to M. Kellison, 18.xii.1599, Rome; (II) f.488.

vincials and rectors. The vice-prefect was to receive a list of students from each seminary at the beginning of the year, with an indication of age, studies, and talents, as was done for Jesuit scholastics. He would then pass it to the prefect with his comments. A brief summary of the temporal and spiritual status of each house was also required. Every college would have a copy for its own files. Superiors were to provide at the beginning of each year a house history for the previous year. Their need of new students and the number of men suitable for work in England were to be submitted with appropriate details every year by November 1. The prefect's approval was required before any students could be sent from England or Flanders to Rome or Spain. His leave was also required before local superiors could summon or detain students, although they could express preferences. The intention was to avoid rivalry and contention among institutions and superiors. Traveling expenses of students must also be settled by the prefect or vice-prefect. Anyone who begged admission to a seminary without going through these preliminaries should not be admitted without the prefect's consent.[32]

By the end of 1599 matters were coming to a head at Valladolid. The Spaniards were having no better success in dealing with English subjects than the Italians had previously had in Rome. Persons from his own experience instinctively took the side of the superior. He should not appear to be afraid of his subjects. Although eight had been sent on the English mission—the largest number so far in one year—this might be taken to conceal failure of a kind. Certainly, it was not desirable that they be paid overgenerous traveling expenses.[33] After quitting the college they might "speak ill of everybody and say there was no reason for expelling them since they were sent away with presents."[34] Fr. Blackfan was advised to introduce the reforms which had succeeded in Rome in the matter of providing supervised recreation, spiritual counseling and the careful arrangement of recreation rooms and dormitories. Not only Persons but the Pope and Aquaviva were anxious to see these reforms introduced.

[32] RP, "Ordinationes aliquot reverendi Patris nostri pro seminariis Anglicanis dirigendis et in pace conservandis, manu P. Personii scriptæ et ab eo sine dubio compositæ," 14.i.1600, Rome; (II) f.418. RP wrote to the rector of the English College, Valladolid, on 15.1.1600, answering queries and giving "many resolutions for the government of that seminary," ibid., f.338, Spanish. Full text in (IX) Serie II, Leg. 1, contemporary copy. The rector's original "preguntas," 23.xi.1599.

[33] Blackfan, *Annales* . . . , 56–58.

[34] RP to rector at Valladolid, 15.i.1600, Rome; v. supra. This letter was accompanied by the General's instructions for all the English colleges in exile. V. supra.

The peace of a house, it was claimed, depended in large measure on the house confessor or spiritual father, who should develop sympathetic rapport with every student. However, a situation could develop where the rector would need to speak to a student "very plainly," imposing perhaps "a good penance." The extreme penalty was confinement to a room for a few days or enforced absence from lectures and recreation. In the last resort, a student should be sent from the house,

> dressing him only in the clothes he brought with him or other old ones, giving him no more than six or eight reals or a crown for alms. He should leave early in the morning before the others were up, orders being given to the porter not to let him reenter. The students should be forbidden to speak to him, even outside and in private without express permission.

After expulsion, the rector would explain the proceeding to the community "to avoid talk" and to remove any impression of the heroic in the rebel's stance. The rector must show himself neither soft nor unsympathetic, pointing out that what was done was demanded by "the common good of all and the cause of England in particular." A man "thrown out ill-clad and penniless" would not dare to create a scene with the local magistracy, nor in this state would he get much sympathy in Flanders or elsewhere.

If such precautions seem harsh, it is difficult to see any milder remedy that would avoid the politicking and party strife which almost destroyed the college in Rome. Persons worked as ever with a certain ruthless logic to ensure success. But his enemies were no less ruthless and their own logic not less unyielding. Without doubt, Persons succeeded, when he did, because he was never afraid to rule, but also because none could suppose that he had anything at heart but the good of the English mission which he served with selfless zeal.[35]

The *Book of Succession,* still sending out ripples, was taken by many in informed Scottish circles to signify Persons's hostility to James's accession in England. Persons wrote to the Earl of Angus in mid-year 1599; receiving no reply, he wrote again in January 1600 to put the record straight. He insisted on his "affection towards his Majesty of Scotland," proffering his "cares, endeavours, labours and dangers" on his behalf as sufficient evidence. From 1580, when he first set foot in England, Persons had regarded his well-being as a primary interest. James VI was then young "and in the hands of them that bought and sold him, lost and gained him, tossed and tumbled him up and down with such indignity and peril . . . as all the Christian world

---

[35] RP to Blackfan, 15.i.1600. V. supra.

took compassion of it." During this time Persons had labored much in the cause of the northern kingdom.[36] True, his efforts had gained him little admiration in certain quarters. But he had taken part in "matters of state" not from choice but only because circumstances following his father's murder and the "barbarous imprisonment" of his mother had forced him to it.

Persons again insisted that it was he who persuaded Philip of Spain to give James twelve thousand crowns a year disbursed at Paris in 1583 and 1584. Gregory XIII's four thousand crowns Persons himself "brought also and delivered in Paris." This might have continued had there been any encouraging sign from Scotland.[37] Persons still maintained his reservations concerning the King's cause. Unless and until he converted to Catholicism, which did not seem likely, the English Catholics could not be expected to regard his succession with enthusiasm.[38] As to the *Book of Succession,* "as I cannot set down . . . at this time who was the true author thereof—if anyone was—so can I assure you upon mine own knowledge before it was printed, it passed through the hands . . . of the wisest and gravest English Catholics living then in banishment," men with genuine regard for James and his mother, including Allen and Sir Francis Englefield. There was no injury offered to James, because his claim was set down first and assessed whether he became Catholic or not. Other Protestant claims were also considered. If more was said for the infanta or any other Catholic prince, it was because religion was "the first true ground of all right to Christian kingdoms." As for himself, Persons claimed not to have dealt in politics for many years, being concerned only with "mere ecclesiastical and spiritual functions," particularly the seminaries. If he was at fault in those earlier journeys and labors, "God knoweth it proceeded only of zeal to further His cause of religion and to preserve, help and advance his Majesty of Scotland."[39]

Persons was still ready to help James. "But I cannot run upon faction or flattery or worldly respects against my . . . conscience." He was lukewarm towards the principle of legitimism. "I am indifferent to any man living that shall have right thereunto of what nation, place or people soever he be so he be a Catholic." If he were not a Catholic, "as it belongeth not to my vocation to strive against him . . . so long as he

---

[36] RP to William Douglas, earl of Angus, 24.i.1600, Rome; (VII) SP Scotland, Elizabeth I, 66, No. 4, copy; (III) Old Series VI, No. 101, f.371, English copy. The rough draft of this letter in RP's hand is in (I) Anglia A.VI. No. 28; see (27) XIII (1597–1603), part 2, Edinburgh 1969, pp. 613–17

[37] Ibid.

[38] Ibid.

[39] Ibid.

is so, nothing under heaven can ever move my heart and will to favour his pretences." For the rest, Persons prayed daily for the King and Queen of Scotland, the young prince, Angus, and the whole nobility and realm. He also prayed for Elizabeth and England. "The happiest days that ever could shine to me in this life were to see both our realms united together under one Catholic governor and prince of our own blood." Otherwise, "any misery is less than the misery of heresy that destroyeth both soul and body." Signing himself "from Rome at the beginning of this new year and age," he hoped to see "the end of all sects and heresies," seeing that such are not commonly "daughters of many ages but do come and go as times do change and as fantasies of men do alter."[40]

New age or not, old problems persisted. The latest ploy of the Paget faction was to claim that there had been a rift between Allen and Persons. He was ready with his reply. "There are extant letters of his own hand written to Charles Paget and others calling them traitors to God and their country by their seditious dealings, and other letters of theirs whereby it is evident that they sought to disgrace him the most they could." Indeed, they sent one of their number to Spain to work for his discredit. Allen no more than Persons ever approved of their attempts to negotiate directly with the English government. Nor did Allen relent towards them before his death.[41]

Persons may have accepted a definition of politics which enabled him to say that he had not dealt in politics for some years. Certainly, he tried to intervene in the peace negotiations of 1599. In February 1600, urged thereto by letters from Flanders, as he claimed, he begged Clement VIII "to instruct the nuncios in Flanders and France to make urgent representations for liberty of conscience" in England while the treaty was being negotiated at Boulogne. "They say" the Queen and her council would grant it if pushed with determination. Some Catholics in Paris had already extracted a promise from the French king to use his influence with Elizabeth.[42]

The question now arose as to whether Persons should go to Flanders himself to be near the center of diplomatic operations. The initiative, it seems, came from the King of Spain. Persons had good reasons for not leaving Rome. The English College had been pacified, but only just; and there were those outside who were anxious for renewal of conflict. It was important to remain in contact with the

---

[40] Ibid.

[41] Ibid.

[42] RP to Clement VIII, 21.ii.1600, Rome; (II) f.418b, transcribed from an Italian a.l.s.

archpriest, which was easier through the well-established Roman line of communication. Furthermore, the English queen and council, who kept "a very sharp eye" on Persons's movements—as he well knew— "would think he was up to something"—as he would be. He might even succumb to assassination, since this was accepted by all schools of thought as a last resort. But there was a more prosaic threat to health. For two years he had suffered severe sciatic pain which prevented him "from going about on foot except short distances." It was still more difficult on horseback, so there could be no more hairbreadth escapes from tight corners. "In Flanders the loan of carriages would not be available to him as they are in Rome." Not of least importance, Persons the writer had an oeuvre in hand. The *Certamen Ecclesiæ Anglicanæ pro Fide Catholica,* "a very large work," not to say bulky, was to be a history of England from its first conversion, with special reference to times "since the fall of Henry VIII." To assist him Persons "had men and books brought to Rome from Germany and other places." Rome was now, in fact, the center of a web of activities which also included supervision of the English mission and its members in exile. It was the focal point of a considerable network of intelligence of which even Sir Francis Walsingham might not have been ashamed. Most important, since Rome has always been a place for the personal shopper, Persons had ready access to Pope, protector, and General. Peripheral Flanders, important as it was in many respects, offered no adequate substitute.[43]

All of this brought sharp criticism from the appellants and their friends. As Colleton expressed it, Persons's were

> professedly state books, and being writ in favour of the Spanish faction rather than any other, were the more likely to bring affliction upon Catholics—the Spaniards having given so oft attempt to invade our country. Fa. Persons, his dealings with the students in Spain to come in those armadas are evident proofs of his meaning, and consequently his books might be judged most hurtful to Catholics.[44]

It has to be admitted that Persons in the end gained little from Spain in the defence of English Catholics, although the colleges on Spanish soil helped to guarantee the continuity of an English Catholic tradition. On the other hand, the appellants gained nothing positive from the English State in the way of toleration, only permission

---

[43] RP, Memorandum "de la yda del padre Personio a Flandres [*sic*]," (II) f.432. Grene took it from an original in RP's hand dated from Rome, 24.iii.1600. See Job Simons, *Robert Persons, S.J., Certamen Ecclesiæ Anglicanæ* (Maestricht, 1965). Synopsis and illustrative passages from a four-volume Latin MS at Stonyhurst. Simons has an interesting chapter on RP as historian (VIII) and on "Persons versus Foxe" (IX), as well as on the sources of the *Certamen* itself.

[44] Colleton, *A just defence . . .*, 314.

to continue their own activities relatively unhampered in the hope that the division and dissension thus engendered would help to weaken Catholicism further. This undeniably it did. Whichever side in the struggle itself had the right of it, if one is inclined to decide such a thing, certainly the struggle itself brought positive advantage to the English government.

Chapter Seventeen

The New Appeal: 1600–1601

As we have seen, the concept of obedience meant different things for the Jesuits and the secular priests—or some of them. It was stretching any definition, however, when William Bishop acquired a doctorate from the Sorbonne about this time, ignoring the papal prohibition. He further used the occasion to write Persons a "most discourteous letter"; the latter tried to reply "civilly," as always.[1] In mid-April, Persons complained to Garnet of "the shameful impudence and ingratitude of several" and more especially of "the slanders" of Middleton and Murray.[2] By this time the rift among the Catholics seemed to be reaching a point of no return. The surviving correspondence becomes a dreary waste of charge and countercharge mainly over trivialities. But each cut, however shallow, was added to the previous wound, so that the surviving body of the papists seemed in danger of bleeding to death through wounds self-inflicted. Nevertheless, they were doing better than survive and apparently still grew, certainly if the number of incoming priests is anything to go by. Perhaps, after all, the wounds were largely superficial. Doubtless there was a tacit recognition of the fact that there was a better chance of survival if the government thought they could be left to themselves to destroy themselves without its having to employ the double-edged sword of persecution. Persecution there was, but not as severe as it might have been had it seemed that all papists worked in close harmony. So Persons and the Jesuits constituted a factor very useful if not essential to the survival of the secular clergy.

Certainly, Persons was constantly under fire from the less tractable spirits. He was able to stay on in Rome, but his very success and apparent influence made him the obvious cause for everything coming from Rome that was misliked. Persons was only human and some of the appellant charges against him may have had some ground. But much of the criticism reached the point of hysteria, so that at this distance in time one must ask oneself what it was really about. Surely

---

[1] RP to William Bishop, 28.v.1600, Rome; (II) f.338. The judgments quoted are Grene's.

[2] RP to H. Garnet(?), 14.iv.1600, Rome; ibid.

not over the question simply of whether there should be bishops and, if so, who they should be in a persecution situation.

Undoubtedly the manifested spirit of independence could border on a spirit of insubordination reminiscent of the worst moments in the seminaries. The habit of complaint becomes so ingrained that one wonders again where the true causes lie. The dissidents had sufficient experience of Rome to know that blaming the Jesuits would make no real difference to their relations with the Vatican. In any case, it happened often in this generation of diminished papal power that only those foolish enough to bend over were actually birched. Working within the appellants was a psychological mechanism which calculated with varying niceness the balance to be held between Catholic conviction and a ruthless inquisition in England determined to destroy it completely. One cannot begin to understand the Catholic community without constant reference to persecution.[3]

Robert Charnock, intelligent and energetic, developed early as an enfant terrible. On April 12 John Pitts informed Persons that contrary to the papal ruling Charnock had gone to England. The latter claimed in his *Reply to a notorious libel* . . . (p. 263) that neither Bishop nor himself was prohibited under oath. Pitts seemed to accept this. Persons, good Jesuit that he was, had no time for people who needed to be put under oath before they obeyed the wish of a legitimate superior. He rebuked Pitts roundly. In fact, from now on Charnock and his allies would see all unwelcome decisions from Rome as being substantially those of Persons, so that they were under an obligation to disobey rather than otherwise, vindicating thus their rightful independence. Persons did his best to put them right. "I had no other part . . . but to procure to mitigate the judges' decree against him, and to stay divers other matters that might and perhaps would have been argued."[4] It was not, of course, in the appellants' interest, real or imagined, to believe him; and Persons was too shrewd not to know this. He was content to tell Pitts and his friend Ely that the real issue was whether "a few malcontent spirits . . . broken from the body by various discontentments" should be allowed to prevail against those

[3] This is a possible objection to Prof. John Bossy's thesis in *The English Catholic Community 1570-1850* (London, 1975). See also A. D. Wright, "Catholic History, North and South," *Northern History*, 14 (1978): 126, 151; P. McGrath, "Elizabethan Catholicism: A Reconsideration," *Journal of Ecclesiastical History* 35, No. 3 (July 1984): 414-28. C. Haigh likewise tends to play down persecution (See (73)). English historians, it seems, do not sufficiently take into account letters from England in foreign archives, especially Rome.

[4] RP to John Pitts, 30.v.1600, Rome; (I) Anglia.A.II, No. 58, English copy.

who were "united by lawful subordination to his Holiness."[5] It is significant that Pitts, scholar, writer, and man of genuine learning, should have chosen to side against Persons on this issue, rather than with him.

Meanwhile, the English papists certainly seemed determined to destroy themselves by their internal dissensions. Persons wrote to John Colleton early in June to deplore "new complaints and fresh contentions . . . about things past" following the papal brief of April 6, 1599, setting up the archpriest.[6] Charnock claimed convincingly that the appellants had accepted wholeheartedly the papal decisions.[7] It was certain Jesuits, however, who were instrumental in continuing the strife. It was bad enough that before the brief appeared a Jesuit, Thomas Lister, should have produced a "treatise of schism," still circulating in manuscript, which saddled the appellants with this grave charge. Now, according to Colleton, another Jesuit, Robert Jones, was maintaining that anyone who thought the appellants were not schismatics before the arrival of the brief incurred ecclesiastical censure. Colleton protested to the archpriest but he stood by Jones. The brief had encouraged Blackwell to consult the Jesuits on important issues. He felt further obliged to support them in all contended matters. The Jesuits in turn, including Garnet, felt equally bound to uphold the archpriest. Colleton, smarting under the accusation, asked for a debate in Blackwell's presence with Garnet, Lister, and other Jesuits, opposed by three appellants. Colleton warned that the alternative was "either wittingly [to] suffer perpetual infamy to come upon us, or take our pens in hand and clear ourselves as we may."[8] He foresaw without relish that this could lead to a battle of books which could consume them all. Reasonably, he reminded Blackwell that he had commanded in writing with written witness "all parties to desist to . . . follow the note of schism against us." The charge should "lie buried in perpetual oblivion."[9]

Persons was clearly embarrassed by Lister's original treatise, which had been written "with somewhat more sharpness than many men's particular actions deserved." Certainly, the whole matter should

---

[5] Ibid. See J. Pitts, *Relationum historicarum de rebus anglicis* (Paris, 1619).

[6] RP to John Colleton, 3.vi.1600, Rome; (I) Anglia.A.II, No. 60, f.188, English copy. See (XI) 47, ff.231r–32v, copy. See RP, *A briefe apologie* . . . , 157b. T. Lister's "Adversus factiosos in Ecclesia" is here referred to. See also C. Bagshaw, *Relatio compendiosa turbarum.*

[7] R. Charnock, *A Reply to a notorious libel..*, 198.

[8] J. Colleton, *A just defence* . . . , 274.

[9] Ibid., 276.

now be laid to rest.[10] This was true but it did not answer Colleton's just objection. Blackwell now refused any debate and threatened suspension if they persisted in defending their former action. Colleton and company, inspired by St. Augustine's "He is cruel that neglecteth his good name upon the clearness of his conscience," then appealed to the University of Paris.[11] The Sorbonne upheld them on the main counts: they were not schismatics because they "deferred to admit" Cajetan's authority, nor was their appeal in any way sinful.[12] Blackwell reacted to all this with a decree of May 29, 1600, declaring the appellants had rebelled against his office, disobeyed the Holy See, and forbade defense of the contrary notion.[13]

By this time Persons was trying to paddle a leaky canoe through white water. His main preoccupation and that of his friends in England, still the large majority, was to maintain unity at all costs. The appellants' main concern was to secure what they hoped would be justice after a proper hearing of their case. The two causes were not incompatible but called for skill in handling, as well as a charity and goodwill which were notably absent at least from the surface of the recusant scene at this time. Persons was aware of his role of scapegoat. Bearing some of the responsibility for the unacceptable, he could be made responsible for all of it. If only as an effective man of action, his own conscience did not rebuke him, nor could such a man allow himself the luxury of self-doubt. To complicate matters further, a disquieting rumor, hardly of chance origin, was circulating in Flanders to the effect that some were to be "called out of England and punished" there. If this was untrue, the Pope might still be forced "to some such resolution" eventually. Meanwhile, Colleton was urged to give no "comfort to heretics and grief and scandal to Catholics" by helping the division to begin again. He should work for "an end of formal controversies and peace and union . . . for the time to come."[14]

The Jesuits themselves, alas, did not always provide the best example of fraternal unity. To disagreement between Mannaerts and the English Jesuits, the latter now added division among themselves. In Spain John Floyd fell out with Richard Walpole, and Joseph Creswell with Anthony Hoskins. Creswell was left to make the final decisions about Valladolid, but Persons intended to admonish Walpole

---

[10] RP to J. Colleton, 3.vi.1600. V. supra.

[11] Colleton, *A just defence*, 277–83.

[12] Ibid., 218.

[13] Ibid., 284.

[14] RP to Colleton, 3.vi.1600. V. supra.

himself.[15] It was not only seminary priests and students, then, who showed obstreperousness in foreign service. Persons told Creswell, "As Fr Peralta and others have often noted . . . these young English Fathers of ours, being quickly put into government after their noviceship and studies, run into dangers if they be not looked into. For they easily fall to banding and negotiating up and down against the rector." He knew three Fathers at Seville, Gibbons, Charles Tankard, and Henry Walpole, "to have made such a faction against Fr Cabredo as he was like to go out of his wits." Persons's solution was the same as for recalcitrant seminarians: the three hyperactive spirits were sent elsewhere. No more than seminarians should they be given the kid-gloved treatment. Aquaviva agreed that "it destroyeth young men in the Society to be complimented withal," although they should be treated "very courteously."

Firm and sure in handling men, Persons could be taken out of his depth in aesthetical matters. He discouraged overmuch interest in music at Valladolid. More wisely, we may believe, Creswell thought "that if it be moderately used it doth no hurt but rather good." One wonders if encouragement of music and even other arts in the colleges and seminaries would not have diverted to healthier channels much of the interest in politics domestic and international. "Recreation" seems to have been understood only as talking or conversation. Persons certainly demurred. "How you may assure yourself of that moderation especially where instruments be used, I know not. And divers men do doubt and write against it." But he was ready to listen to others. Certainly, the General was thinking of forbidding musical instruments in the seminary. Persons believed that after they were forbidden at Rome, there had been more "moderation, more spirit in the house." It is difficult, of course, to argue with experience. Creswell's did not always square with Persons's. Persons had doubts about the rector at Seville, but the provincial had not. A recent visitation showed the college was in "good state . . . temporally and spiritually," and he could only wonder that the rector had been able to achieve this "without rents so many years." No one else could want the appointment.[16]

Moved by the pleas of Persons and other exiles, the Pope addressed a brief to the Flanders nuncio on July 12, 1600, taking cognizance of the need for a Catholic successor to Elizabeth. Her death seemed, and was, imminent. A second brief, addressed directly to the English papists, exhorted them to unity and perseverance. A third to

---

[15] RP to [J. Creswell], 26.vi.1600, Rome; (I) Anglia.A.II, No. 61, English copy; (II) ff.338f, summary. Creswell wrote to RP on 4, 17 and 20.v. on a "varietie of matter."

[16] Ibid.

the archpriest, his assistants, and the clergy generally, exhorted them to unity and to do all in their power to ensure a Catholic succession. The nuncio was ordered to address the English Catholics to the same effect as soon as he heard of "the death of that wretched woman." There was, of course, no question of hastening it, not even of suggesting someone to succeed. It reflected the universal reluctance of Catholic sovereigns to declare themselves.[17] The draft of the instructions of July 20, 1600, for the nuncio was in Persons's hand, indicating clearly his considerable influence in their compilation.[18] A summary of the brief was immediately to be sent by trustworthy messenger to the archpriest, his assistants, and the Jesuits. These, in turn, would keep Frangipani informed of day-to-day events. The Catholic cause should be pushed hard meanwhile among nobility and men of influence. Persons insisted much on unity especially among the priests. Any who flouted the archpriest's authority should be coerced, if necessary, "by censures and church discipline."

By this time, the anti-Jesuit party among the English exiles in France was enjoying much the same success with the French provincial, Lorenzo Maggio, as were those in Flanders with Mannaerts. Persons told Aquaviva, "These trouble-makers are so crafty and malign that when they find one of our Fathers on his own and unable to inform himself of the truth, they act and talk flatteringly towards him . . . so as to set him against those whom they wish to bring into discredit."[19] Aquaviva, satisfied by his own assessment of the situation, ordered Persons to try to satisfy Maggio as he had formerly tried with Mannaerts. In spite of trouble with his eyes, Persons drew up a detailed reply and asked the General to send his own word of warning. Garnet now reported from England on June 14, as from Blackwell, Charnock's claim of harsh words coming from Maggio against the archpriest and his adherents. Blackwell took it as false, but Persons knew the truth only too well and proceeded at once to give Maggio better information.[20]

The Fifth General Congregation of 1593 had looked askance at Jesuit involvement in political issues, so that it was fairly easy for Charnock to get a sympathetic hearing from less discerning Jesuits

---

[17] Clement VIII to Frangipani, 12.vii.1600, Rome; (11) III, App. lxx–lxxi.

[18] "Instructiones quædam ad ea melius exequenda quæ tribus Brevibus apostolicis de rebus Anglicanis continentur," 20.vii.1600, Rome; (I) Anglia.A.II, No. 62, Latin, draft and alterations in RP's hand; (11) III, App. lxxi–lxxii. Tierney describes them as "Persons to the nuncio," which is misleading, since such instructions were issued from the secretariat of state.

[19] RP to Aquaviva, 22.vii.1600, Rome; (VI), F.G.651, ibid., n.f., Italian a.l.s.

[20] RP to Lorenzo Maggio, 22.vii.1600, Rome; (VI) ibid., Italian a.l.s.

when he averred with a kind of truth that some had taken part in "actions against their prince and country, and against Catholic priests" in accusing them of schism.[21] He also made Persons "a chief dealer in the sending of those armadoes [sic]" by Spain. Slipped in for good measure, "we have also certain intelligence that the Jesuits had devised a means to have had the Tower of London to hold in the Spaniards' name."[22] Fully committed to appeasement, Charnock and his friends found any attempt to influence the English succession as only a veiled attempt to turn England into a Spanish colony.[23] Charnock was moderate in comparison with William Watson, whose *Decacordon* . . . claimed that in "manners, government and order of life" the Jesuits were "more malicious against both the Church, commonwealth, prince and peers than the puritans." They were all the more dangerous for "having many singular fine wits among them."[24] In a work of rollicking invective, Watson concluded, "So long as there is one Jesuit left in England, there will be mutinies, treasons, conspiracies and factions, do what pope or prince or any other is able to do or say to the contrary."[25]

Persons was swift to point out to Maggio that appellants were as liable as any to rebellion, disobedience, and, for that matter, shiftiness. William Bishop went to Paris in defiance of an oath pronounced before the examining cardinals to stay away under pain of suspension *a divinis.*[26] Charnock, as we have seen, denied taking any oath.[27] However, he later admitted that oaths "were taken by Acarisius the fiscal when Mr Bishop was delivered out of prison; which acts of the fiscal were of none effect, as not having commission to do anything in that cause."[28] No Jesuit could have been more slippery. Persons could hardly have been mistaken on this, since he followed the original appeal closely in all its phases, nor on the further point that the English queen and her councillors fomented the division.[29]

The appellants were not unaware of the unfavorable reaction of many, probably most, papists to their good relations with the persecutor, and also to the remarkable leniency shown towards them by

---

[21] R. Charnock, *A Reply to a notorious libel*, 145.

[22] Ibid., 81.

[23] Ibid., 82.

[24] William Watson, *A decacordon of ten quodlibetical questions* ([London], 1602), 26.

[25] Ibid., 112.

[26] RP to Maggio, 22.vii.1600. V. supra.

[27] V. supra, chap. 17, p. 68.

[28] Charnock, *A reply* . . . , 99.

[29] RP to Maggio, 22.vii.1600. V. supra.

government as an apparent reward for their divisive role.[30] Colleton apologized, "The temporal magistrate doth not press the priests . . . since they have known the difference between priests and statists." Even more might be looked for when the Queen was finally convinced "of the priests their truth and loyalty to her person, crown, estate and dignity." He claimed further, "Yet have not the priests used this little favour which they have had to the afflicting [of] any of their Catholic brethren."[31] If Colleton was not lying, he must have been unaware of the activities of John Cecil, to name no others. This, of course, was possible.

Persons, anxious to vindicate the appearance and contents of the *Book of Succession,* denied that persecution had increased in consequence. In fact, it had declined, "thanks to the interest which many of the queen's own councillors take in the claims set out in the book." The kings of France and Scotland no longer misunderstood its purpose.[32] But all this turmoil and the pressure of work was taking its toll.

> "I can no longer rest in mind or body, and my health has broken down under the strain of maintaining these seminaries in temporalibus et spiritualibus, producing priests and sending them clothed and provided with journey-money and all other necessities into England. This I have done for all these trouble-makers as well as for many others. At the end of it all I am even reduced to offering apology . . . and to proving that I am not the cause of all the rebellions and storms, and this even to men of sober judgment like yourself" [Lorenzo Maggio].[33]

On July 21 a Catholic gentleman in England informed Persons of Charles Paget's latest achievement: a new tractate sent to William Waad, the Queen's attorney, mounting a systematic attack on the Jesuits. It was not printed or published, but John Cecil wrote and published a book highly critical of Fr. William Crichton.[34] Printed in Paris, where Paget had been active for some twenty years, it had its effect. At all events, it spurred Frangipani to contemplate doing something in the matter of the succession even if he scarcely knew what. Persons had no doubt in his answer to the nuncio's letter of August 19 that any who favored unconditionally the succession of James VI

---

[30] V. supra, chap. 17, p. 67.

[31] Colleton, *A just defence,* 326.

[32] RP to Maggio, 22.vii.1600. V. supra.

[33] Ibid.

[34] *A discoverye of the errors committed and injuryes don to his Ma: of Scotlande . . . by a malitious mythologie titled an apologie and compiled by William Criton pryest and professed Iesuite* ([Paris, 1599]). See (19) 170.

should be discouraged. Nor would they have the Pope's favor.[35] The basic difficulty in naming a successor was to find someone or something on which the kings of France and Spain could agree. Persons discussed the matter with the Pope in mid-September. Meanwhile, Cardinal Farnese appointed Frangipani vice-protector of the English nation. Frangipani now knew that Charnock protested to Borghese before passing into England, "excusing what he had done and lamenting the censure pronounced upon him."[36]

John Bennet, no less than Persons, was anxious to bridge the gap between contending parties or at least to ensure that the protesters remained a minority. Persons encouraged him, claiming that the latter had no motive for "the enkindling of new debates," seeing that the "treatise of schism" was never printed and "no further prosecuted" after the reconciliation. But this was precisely what the appellants disputed. Certainly, Bishop and Charnock did not help their cause in Rome by taking doctorates in Paris against orders. Charnock in England exercised priestly functions "against promise and oath." John Bennet and others sought to contain as closely as might be the divisive consequences of such private enterprise. Unfortunately, impartial spectators on the continent were led increasingly to see the English papists as suffering not for conscience but for their own love of troublemaking. Could persecution be so bad when they luxuriated thus in quarrels among themselves? Worst of all, it was now widely known that some had been "content to cooperate against their own brethren to the increase of their pressures both in prison and abroad."[37] It was therefore important to insist on the truth that the appellants were only a minority.

It is evident that Persons looked on the appellants by now as overgrown, recalcitrant students or mutinous soldiers who should be silenced by punishment and the heavy exercise of authority. One can understand his anxiety and that of his friends that the unity of the Catholic front should override all other considerations. The appellants, however, persuaded that a deal could be made even now with Elizabeth's government, but not while Jesuits were around, resented Blackwell's apparent refusal to reinstate their reputation as loyal Catholics. Colleton summed it up pithily as an estrangement starting "at Wisbech from Weston; the dissension now on foot from Fa Lister the author,

---

[35] RP to Frangipani, 16.ix.1600, Rome; (I) Anglia.A.VI, No. 31, contemporary Italian copy. Enclosed was a copy of Borghese's reply to Charnock. V. supra.

[36] Ibid.

[37] RP to John Bennet, 23/24.ix.1600, Rome; (I) Anglia.A.VI, No. 30, English contemp. copy.

from Fa Garnet the approver, from Fa Jones the increaser, from Fa Holtby the maintainer and from some other of the Society, the abettors of our most grievous wrongs and infamies."[38] Certainly, Blackwell saw the appellants as rebels who would not be quiet. Mutual distrust brought mutual hardening of attitudes. "How overlong and trouble-somely you have merchandised the crown and kingdom!" Thus Colleton to Persons.[39]

Since Blackwell refused to reopen the discussion on matters past, another appeal to Rome was inevitable. Persons reacted reason-ably, pointing out that "they must seek first their ordinary remedy by their immediate superiors there, and then if that satisfy not, to repair to the nuncio in Flanders who hath both the general authority of the protector for such affairs in those parts, as also special commission from his Holiness."[40] This would also ensure that, if their case went eventually to Rome, it would get the speedier settlement. Charnock's case would need to go to Rome, but the rest could be settled, one hoped, in England. John Bennet was Persons's point of contact with Colleton and Edward Bennet; but he was careful to send his letter open for the archpriest to read first, lest it "miscarry in the convey-ing"—or be misquoted and used to foment further strife. Persons was genuinely anxious that opportunity for intrigue and misunderstanding be reduced to a minimum. "Letters written abroad in such times, and in such causes as this, are often misconstrued by them as love not peace but seek matter of contention."[41]

Persons's carefulness was fully justified. The English govern-ment kept in tow a ragged, and not so ragged, army of spies and informers who fished constantly in troubled waters for a few crowns. Sir Thomas Parry, ambassador, reported from Paris on November 29, 1602, someone from Orleans who

> averred all he had delivered there, and added more a practice be-tween the priests and the Jesuits. . . . Further he charged Bagshaw the priest to have undertaken with his own hands to kill the Queen's Majesty; and when I confronted them together, maintained his asser-tion. But the next day after some private talk betwixt themselves apart,

the original party, again in Bagshaw's presence, told Parry a different tale. Bagshaw offered to go to England "to justify himself, holding this

---

[38] Colleton, *A just defence*, 32.

[39] Ibid., 176.

[40] RP to John Bennet, 23/24.ix.1600. V. supra.

[41] Ibid.

a Jesuitical practice by such sobornation to deface the secular priests."[42] Parry observed, "I told him it was possible that the Jesuits would return this as a device of the priests to disgrace their faction." Small wonder Elizabeth's government trusted and respected none of the priests, even if they made use of them.

Thomas James, "the English consul of Andalusia," shortly expected in Rome, was a man who had given Persons much valuable information.[43] John Cecil had done the same for the reigning Cecils for some ten years.[44] Persons, though not blissfully ignorant, rebuked John for not letting him see a copy of a letter answering his observations on the treatment of Bishop and his critique of Cecil's book against Crichton, before it was published to the whole world. Charnock claimed, however, that in a letter to Blackwell, Persons admitted that a Jesuit reply to the appellants was to be generally divulged before it came to the appellants' own hands. So the appellants were now replying in kind.[45] By this time the point had been reached where nothing that either side did could be accepted without sinister interpretation by the other. If one acted defensively, this was taken as aggressive malice. Persons sensibly refused to take the matter further with John Cecil unless he received "a friendly reply. . . . For I easily see the evil effect that can ensue of such writings."[46] All the same, he appealed to Cecil to see the iniquity of writing and publishing such matter, since it could only help "the common enemy." Surely Pope, protector, and archpriest in England were the authorities to decide disputed causes. "For God's sake let us remember that we are Catholic and priests, and that the making or feeding of division . . . must needs be a heinous sin in the sight of God, and most dishonourable before . . . wise and good men."[47] Even now Persons did not despair of reconciliation.

Sir Robert Cecil was, of course, much interested in European attempts to determine the coming succession crisis. Too intelligent to rely on the ordinary kind of spy for important information, he commissioned, it seems, an unnamed gentleman to deal with Sessa in Rome, who told Persons that Elizabeth's councillors, "especially the

---

[42] (VII) SP78/47, f.218, original dispatch.

[43] RP to John Bennet, ibid. For some account of T. James (1556-1613), see A. Loomier, S.J., (10) 11, 165–78.

[44] See Sir Francis Drake to the Privy Council, 5.ii.1593/4; (14) IV, 473f.

[45] See Charnock to Blackwell, 31.v.1600; (I) Anglia.A.II, No. 59, original(?), English.

[46] See RP to John Cecil, 14.xi.1600, Rome; (I) ibid., No. 63, contemporary copy, English.

[47] Ibid.

treasurer and secretary Cecil," were uncertain whom to support until they knew the Spanish king's mind. The choice lay, they agreed, between James VI and the infanta.[48] It is, of course, incredible that Cecil would have countenanced a Spanish and Catholic succession except as the last alternative to losing all power in the realm. If we doubt that he would rise or stoop to the duplicity implied in getting this kind of inside information, we may remind ourselves that some three years later all James's principal councillors were provided with substantial Spanish pensions on the implicit understanding that they passed over information and pursued policies acceptable to Spain. Meanwhile, the Cecilians stood in fear of what the Earl of Essex might have in mind; for although he was already under a cloud, it was one from which he could still reemerge into the sunlight of royal favor. Undoubtedly, he had a considerable following in the country and no ingrained hatred of Spain for all his Protestantism. Cecil's dealings with Rome could therefore be taken as a parallel to the secret correspondence with Scotland which began in April 1600. This eventually hobbled the Earl of Northumberland, yet another of the secretary's competitors.[49]

The unnamed gentleman in question asked that no initiative be taken until the Queen actually died. If the Spaniards accepted this, it would mean that all initiative would lie with the English government, since they would be the first to learn of her death. Significantly, Charles Howard of Effingham was to be excluded from these negotiations because he was a "simpleminded man and not very discreet"—in a word, too honest. Cecil and his friends were represented as wanting peace with Spain; and, indeed, it was only Her Majesty who kept them on the warpath, believing that the best guarantee of England's safety lay in continuing the war in the Low Countries. Cecil's negotiator wanted an early reply from the King of Spain, so that "a safe person" could be "sent to Persons" in the spring "to deal with other special points." This "safe person" might even "wear the habit of his Order." Persons, hardly gullible, but too ready at times to be carried away by

[48] RP to Duke of Sessa, 13.xi.1600, Rome, "avisos secretos de Inglaterra descifrada de la cifra particular"; (VIII) Estado 972, f.10, Spanish; (43) An.xxiv, fasc.47 (i–vi.1955), 32–34, English translation in full. See A. J. Loomie, "Sir Robert Cecil and the Spanish Embassy," (65) xlii, No. 105 (v.1969), 30–57.

[49] E. Goldsmid, ed., *The Secret Correspondence of Sir Robert Cecil with James VI of Scotland* (Edinburgh, 1887), passim. The correspondence was conducted between Henry Howard in London and Edward Bruce in Scotland, so that if knowledge of it came to light prematurely, Cecil could have repudiated it. The first publication of these letters was by Hales in 1766. See A. Collins, *Memorials*, II, 326. For the ninth earl, see Mark Nicholls, *Investigating the Gunpowder Plot* (Manchester, 1991) and "Politics and Percies," Cambridge Ph.D. thesis, 1985.

hope, described the proposals as coming from "a very reliable person."[50] Philip should make up his mind quickly. Wisely enough, he did not.

It was a nice irony that, if Cecil through remote control hoped to keep the King of Spain and Persons "in play," Persons intended no less with regard to King James. "I am . . . of opinion that it would be no bad thing to keep the King of Scotland in play also with polite words, and to feed his hopes, so as to see if he is willing to be converted, because in that case some trust could be placed in him." Persons foresaw one thing correctly. "They will all come to terms with the King of Scotland the moment they realise that his Majesty is relinquishing the claims of the Lady Infanta. Then the King of Scotland will not need his Majesty's support . . . to form a party in England large enough to ensure him the crown without notable opposition." Furthermore, "he would become so proud and cocksure in heresy that there would be no hope of his conversion." So Philip should inform the English privy council that he intended to support the infanta's claim energetically. This would at least oblige James, if he arrived at the English throne, to come to terms with Spain.[51] In all this, Persons was, in contemporary phrase, reckoning the bill without the host. But he must have had his doubts about Robert Cecil's true motives. Perhaps he reacted to the situation, not really believing that he would achieve anything this way, but on the principle that human affairs are always uncertain and some kind of happy outcome was long overdue. At long last the Lord in his merciful providence might intervene to bring the Catholics to that haven of peace which they had earned by so much suffering so patiently borne for so long. It was not to be.

---

[50] RP to Sessa, 13.xi.1600. V. supra.

[51] Ibid. See also A. J. Loomie, S.J., "Philip III and the Stuart Succession in England, 1600–1603," in *Revue belge de philologie et d'histoire* 43, No. 2, (1965): 492–514.

Chapter Eighteen

The Second Appeal
November 1600–September 1602

The final estrangement between Blackwell and the appellants occurred on October 17, 1600, when the archpriest suspended the faculties of John Mush and John Colleton. He had done it for the first time when they refused to acknowledge Blackwell's authority before the arrival of the papal brief of April 6, 1599. He did it the second time "because they defend their cause and require satisfaction &c [*sic*] and have sent divers letters full of contumelies and calumniations . . . against . . . ourselves [and] other superiors."[1] The clergy were informed by letter of October 17, so that they could warn the faithful against receiving the sacraments at their hands. This was followed on October 18 by what J. H. Pollen described as "the most extravagant of all his 'edicts.'"[2] The archpriest had ordered that there should be no "communications or meetings which could give ground for schism." The "unquiet" had ignored this, although he had urged them "in most conciliatory language" to conform. To preserve peace and unity, he then decreed "complete silence concerning the earlier dissension." However, any priest could absolve *in foro externo* from past censures after due submission. The decree also declared that Cajetan's original constitutive letters were binding as an authoritative act of the Holy See, and all who denied it had been rebels. Anyone who defended orally or in writing the "former disobedience" would be suspended if a priest and excommunicated if a layman. "Secret gatherings" (*conventiones*) had fostered schism, so these were forbidden except for "devotion" and "hospitality"; and even these were to be referred to Blackwell or his assistants. Most controversial: "We forbid under pain of suspension *a divinis* and the loss of all faculties any priests to go about in any way collecting votes in word or writing, or to give his name to any cause whatsoever unless it has been previously communicated to us or two of our assistants." His final appeal was against the calumnies going the round attacking himself and the Society of Jesus.[3]

---

[1] Colleton, *A just defence*, 226.

[2] J. H. Pollen, S.J., (46) 53.

[3] (XI) Series 238, vol.47, f.238, original; (XIV) 46/10/17.

Blackwell was undoubtedly sincere in his efforts to reestablish peace on the mission. But a simple act of oblivion would have put the appellants much more obviously in the wrong when they reopened the controversy. As it was, he seemed to make himself the last court of appeal, almost blocking recourse to Rome. Men like Colleton and Mush could only take this as a challenge to make a new appeal. On November 17, 1600, thirty-three priests—a small fraction of the total on the mission—signed an appeal to the Pope against all that they had "endured at the hands of the Fathers of the Society of Jesus" and from the archpriest. Colleton forwarded a copy to Blackwell with a covering letter of November 25. This was dignified and moderate in tone.[4] The appeal was much taken up with Lister's never-to-be-forgotten treatise. Admittedly, in his zeal to restore unity, Blackwell had followed the letter of his instructions but hardly the spirit. Aspiring to imitate Persons's firmness, perhaps, he only achieved heavy-handedness. Persons might well have attempted to silence the appellants but not before he listened to them. All the same, the archpriest had a near-impossible task. He was not dealing with students who could be sent away but with grown men who were there to stay and who, at least in Colleton's case, were better informed than he was in some areas.

As we have seen, the appellants' underlying grievance was not their reputation as schismatics but the very presence of the Jesuits in England, which interfered with their view of political necessities. As a principal ally of the Jesuits, nothing that Blackwell did could have won their approval. If he could not be opposed on this pretext, they would have found another. Too conciliatory an attitude would have been taken as weakness and an invitation to press even harder. As it was, his maladroitness almost turned the appellants into martyrs. The attention of some Catholics was distracted from the authority which was really making martyrs and bleeding the papists to death through a system of fines and persecution.

Undoubtedly, deprivation of faculties was a drastic step and should have been delayed. Writing to Charnock on June 17, 1600, Blackwell reminded him that it had never been the Pope's intention in the circumstances of the mission to resort "to the form of contentious court trials, especially in the revocation of faculties, the grant whereof, as also the continuance, is to be deemed merely voluntary." Delegated faculties such as those of Mush and Colleton could be revoked "without any crime committed at the only pleasure of the grantor or of one that hath authority from him."[5] Possibly, but this was marching behind

---

[4] (11) III, App. cxxxii–cxliv.

[5] Ibid., App. cxli. Quoted in the Appeal of 17.xi.1600.

a banner with hammer and sickle rather than lamb and flag. So it was that on November 17 the thirty-three priests, "fearing more grievous oppression in the time to come," demanded of Blackwell "instantly, more instantly and most instantly" dimissorial letters submitting their cause to the Pope. The letter was given as from Wisbech. Pope Clement issued a brief from St. Mark's in answer to this appeal on August 17, 1601.[6] Trying to please everyone, it pleased no one, since the two sides were now only agreed in their irreconcilability. Cajetan's institution of the archpriest was upheld and it was made clear that his authority extended to all the faithful. But Blackwell was rebuked, albeit in mild terms, for demanding apology for their previous stance before the priests could take advantage of the settlement offered by the brief of 1600. He was warned, "You would do well to remember that your whole authority is intended for the edification and not the destruction of souls. . . . You are not only the spiritual head of all the Catholics there but also their father." He should exercise patience and reflect before deciding. Books should not be published in his defence, since this could only further "contentions and rivalries." But the question was put to the priests who failed to obey the archpriest, "Why did you not give credence to the letters of Cardinal Henry, your Protector?" The past was best forgotten. "We did not defer to your appeal since we desire union and concord among you not dissension." Lister's treatise and any other writings in the same vein were declared suppressed by apostolic authority with excommunication ipso facto for those who wrote such things in future, circulated them, or even kept them. The word "schism" was not to be used. How was it that those who faced imprisonment, torture, and death could not find it in them to love one another?[7] At least part of the answer, no doubt, lay in the psychology of persecution.

In the autumn of 1601, Cajetan approached Persons, prompted by the Pope perhaps, for his views on the brief of August 17. After discussion with certain conationals, he fully endorsed the prohibition of another battle of books, but "all were agreed that it would be best to omit the penalty of excommunication" as too drastic. Certainly, prior leave of Pope or protector should be obtained before any such books

---

[6] Ibid., App. cxlix–cliv.

[7] See ibid. RP wrote to Blackwell on the subject of the brief on 17.x.1601, answering doubts about the papal excommunication and how it applied to the "treatise of schism," and the divulgation or retention of this and other works. Sadly, this letter is only known from a brief reference in (II) f.339, where Grene refers RP to the Protector of 17.xii.1601 (v. infra). "Very many other letters" to Colleton, Cecil, Bishop, Blackwell, and Garnet "concerning the said faction" Grene omitted, "they being very tedious, although there appears therein great patience, meekness, prudence, etc. [sic] of F. Persons."

were printed. However, excommunication was appropriate for "these intrigues with heretical officials by the disaffected to the prejudice of Catholics." The archpriest should have a faculty to confer the sacrament of confirmation, which would meet another complaint of those who wanted bishops. All of this called for another brief.[8]

From a letter from Garnet of August 16, Persons learned of his mother's death.[9] It was apparently unexpected, since Garnet had reported on January 14 that she was in good health and did not lack the ministrations of a priest.[10] She may have been keeping a house for the Jesuits at least from March 1598, for Garnet reported on March 18, 1601, that he had to leave her suddenly, although with "a maid or two to look after her," because of a descent by the pursuivants.[11] Persons also had to bear with the tale of his alleged illegitimacy, which was going the rounds in England, even in print.[12]

The brief of August 17, 1601, only reached Blackwell, it seems, in October.[13] Expecting a further brief if only to clarify the question of printing books,[14] he delayed promulgation until the end of the year. His opponents did not wait to organize a new appeal to Rome. This time they enlisted the support of French diplomacy to bolster their cause if only to counteract Spanish and also Jesuit influence. The French had expelled the Jesuits in 1594 for their alleged part—quite unjustly if one takes note of the evidence—in an attempt on the life of Henri IV. John Mush and Anthony Champney were now the leading lights of the movement. Mush wrote to "Mr Smith" from Paris on November 17, 1601, exactly six weeks after leaving England. They were still awaiting the arrival of "Mr Bluet etc." [sic]. Mush thought they had already lost their "whole cause through neglecting to follow it with speed." The nuncio, who was "wholly for the Jesuits," showed them a copy of "this late letter or Bull or I know not what of his Holiness. . . . And earnest he is that we go not to Rome. You see how his Holiness followeth Fr Persons's suggestions still, and will not admit of our appeal, but will have all controversies to cease without hearing us, or clearing us of the infamies, but rather condemning us of disobe-

---

[8] RP to Protector, 17.xii.1601, Rome; (I) Anglia.A.III, No. 34, Latin a.l.s.; (II) f.339.

[9] (II) f.553; see (1) 37 which gives earlier references to Christina.

[10] (II) f.546; (1) 37. These references to RP's mother are drawn from (II); all in (1) 36–38.

[11] (II) f.597.

[12] See chap. 1, 1–2.

[13] See (46) 65.

[14] RP to Protector, 17.xii. V. supra.

dience." However, he was not to be blamed and could be trusted to understand things better after he had heard the truth from their own mouths. The Jesuits' principal object was "to oppress our whole church and to subdue all to themselves and to the Spaniards." Ominously, "I think it behoveth her Majesty and Sir Robert [Cecil] to look to it, to favour and further us, their faithful servants, both in this great contention and in the practice of our mission at home." They knew that the appellants were "unjustly persecuted by their adversaries and ours, because we dislike and will not run their dangerous courses." If the government allowed them "liberty in practice of our religion which the old priests have, we might do them better services for preservation of her Majesty's state than they are advised of." Sir Robert should grant liberty of conscience provided "these spies be called out of the realm, peace be wrought in Ireland, and all Catholics pay XII pence in the pound. This letter or Bull is not much to be respected. Make your benefits thereby as ye can. Subscribe to nothing, and rest so till you hear from us at Rome where we hope to do good." More money was needed for the journey. Meanwhile, "Mr Doc. Cecil I find very sincere, faithful and honest. He hath suffered much by evil tongues."[15]

It is more than likely that the original inspiration for enlisting French support came from Sir Robert Cecil. If he did not suggest it, the appellants would certainly not have proceeded so far without his approval. At least vaguely aware that something was afoot, Persons wrote to William Bishop on December 24, 1601, and again on January 6, 1602, assuring him of his desire for peace and understanding. But Bishop took no direct part in this appeal.[16] While the nuncio in Paris, del Bufalo, was altogether discouraging towards the appellants, Frangipani in Brussels showed his customary lack of firmness. The French government was not as warm as the appellants could have wished, since negotiations were proceeding for the readmission of the Jesuits to France. However, Philippe de Béthune, French ambassador in Rome, was eventually instructed to protect and assist. This he did most effectively. Villeroy, secretary of state, was no doubt chiefly influenced by John Cecil, the ablest member of the deputation.

At Calais the appellants had divided into two groups. Thomas Bluet, Christopher Bagshaw, and Francis Barnby went to Brussels, while Mush and Champney moved to Paris, where they met up with

---

[15] John Mush to Nicholas(?) Smith, 7.ix.1601, Paris; (XII) Fairhurst MS 2006, ff.283r–84v. For the "old priests," see (73) passim; P. McGrath and Joy Rowe, "The Marian Priests under Elizabeth I," (10) 17, 103–20. This rejects C. Haigh's odd notion that RP was the main traducer of the Marian clergy (p. 103).

[16] The only record of this letter (II) f.489 (?).

John Cecil. The Paris group left for Rome about January 10.[17] They did not wait for the Brussels party to catch up with them, and there may have been some intention of giving them the slip. Bluet and Bagshaw, certainly, would not have found their place easily in a party of diplomats. Francis Barnby in a signed document of March 3, 1604, swore on oath to give up the practice of his priesthood.[18] In a letter to Mush, Bagshaw overflowed with indignation at being left behind. He referred to Mush's "fine architecture of a commonwealth" in which Bagshaw was not even to be admitted as a citizen.[19] Bluet eventually went on to Rome. Bagshaw stayed in Paris.

A detailed history of the appeal does not belong to a life of Persons, but he was much involved at least as a deus ex machina. On January 20, 1602, he petitioned the Pope for a third brief which would reject the appellant plea and uphold the archpriest.[20] It was on February 14 that the appellants arrived in Rome, but word of this did not reach Persons until Baynes met Mush in the Chiesa Nuova, apparently by accident, on February 20. On the twenty-first Persons, Haddock, and Baynes called on Borghese. So did the appellants. All were received with customary Roman urbanity. However, Borghese rebuked the "disobedience to the archpriest" even if he cleared them of schism. Significantly, it was through de Béthune that the appellants sought audience with the Pope. Here too, Persons had preceded them, telling the ambassador they were "factious and seditious" and ready to deal with heretics, with further home truths of the same kind.[21]

On February 28 a serious division appeared among the appellants. Bluet cut himself off from Cecil, Mush, and Champney and kept with Peres, Pearse, or Pierse, a priest who had lived in Paris and Brussels and now, seemingly, belonged to the French ambassador's household. The appellants by some means got hold of a letter from

---

[17] See J. Bossy, "Henri IV, the Appellants and the Jesuits," (10) 8, 80–122, especially 81: an excellent short account of the second appeal using the Fairhurst MSS in Lambeth Palace Library, including de Béthune's correspondence.

[18] See (XII) Fairhurst MS 2006, f.191r, a.l.s.

[19] C. Bagshaw to J. Mush, n.d. [ii/iii.1601/2] [Paris]; (XII) ibid., f.182r/v, a.l.s.

[20] "Petitio ad Suam Sanctitatem manu Personii scripta subscribenda ab Anglis pro tertio Brevi contra seditiosos," 20.i.1602; (II) 465. Grene entered here, "Variæ aliæ petitiones seu libelli supplices de eadem materia viz. contra seditiosos in Anglia presbyteros ab eodem Personio scripta servantur inter eius epistolas in Archivio: 2 et 23 Febr.1602. . . ."

[21] John Mush's diary, 1602; (42) II, 1–4, English. This diary is used here for the "Appeal," since it seems to be the only surviving document giving a spontaneous day-to-day account of proceedings in Rome. Other narratives in (42) II have the disadvantages of prepared and edited accounts incorporating, presumably, afterthoughts and appeals to memory to strengthen the appellant case.

Persons to Holt from Genoa, probably that of March 15, 1597, "touching state matters." They lent this to Mr. Pearse about February 20, but he refused to hand it back. He had evidently decided to use it to establish a personal interest in the controversy.[22] They found him "very heady and contentious and ready to fall out with us three," while apparently confiding in Bluet.[23] On March 2, Mush and his friends met Pearse and Bluet by chance at de Béthune's, who was trying to preserve some unity in the group. On March 4 they all had to endure another unwelcome chance meeting, this time with Persons and Smith at the Vatican. Persons was surprised they had not called at the college but expressed pleasure at their coming "for now all would be ended." Meanwhile, the archpriest's proctors were on their way to present their side of the case. On March 5 Persons and Smith spent two hours with Cardinal d'Ossat, who with de Béthune was the main prop of the appellants and lightning rod for any papal wrath at their coming. That night the appellants met the Pope in an hour-long audience at which he expressed frank disapproval of "their books, defence of heretics, denial of his deposing power," and disobedience to all authority. According to Mush, he was annoyed that "we named her queen whom the See Apostolic had deposed and excommunicated." Moreover, "a toleration or liberty of conscience in England . . . would do harm and make Catholics become heretics."[24]

But these were first reactions. Cardinals Aragon and Borghese were appointed exclusively to hear the appellants' case.[25] In the hope of spiking Persons's guns, the appellants delated to the Pope Robert Southwell's *A humble supplication to her Majestie*. This addressed the Queen in respectful terms; but Richard Walpole and Persons hastened to explain to the Pope that, while the language of appellants and Jesuits might be similar, their aims were very different.[26]

This delation was a clever device of John Cecil to draw fire away from the appellants' books. Not even Persons had seen the book, which had only circulated in manuscript; until this and other Jesuit

---

[22] (42) II, 4. See "Certe annotationi maligni del Dottor Perseo sopra la detta lettera del Padre Personio di 15 Marzo 1597 con le risposte," (III) Old Series VI, No. 20, holog.

[23] Ibid., p. 5.

[24] See "Discorso sopra la proposta che s'ha a fare, per quanto si dice, a Vostra Santità da alcuni sacerdoti Inglesi a nome della Regina di Inghilterra circa il dar libertà di coscienza ai Catholici in quel regno," (VI) Anglia 36.I, f.101r.

[25] J. Mush, *Diary*, p. 6.

[26] "Petitio ad Pontificem anno 1602, transcripta ex autographo: scripta a RP Personio vel potius Richard Walpolo (utriusque character similitudinem habet ad invicem)," (II) f.466.

books arrived, no judgment could be rendered on one side of the controversy. In the event, the examination was not completed before the final brief was ready, so the appellant books escaped censure.[27]

Persons, like most wicked animals when attacked, had a tendency to defend himself and, even more, his cause. Working with a copy of the appellants' main charges, he drew up an answer on March 12, 1602, which attempted to throw light on "the whole controversy about the matters of England."[28] On March 19, in spite of the papal prohibition, Mush and friends called on d'Ossat and the Cardinal of St. George. Persons was still preparing his broadside "out of many books."[29] There were frequent visits over the next few days to Aragon and Borghese and occasionally others. All, as the appellants admitted, wanted reconciliation.[30] Aragon at one point significantly dismissed both sides as *terribles*.[31] On April 30 Walpole or Persons gave Borghese their history of the appellant cause over the last few years. It broke no new ground, but the compiler was well aware of the importance of having the last word if possible.[32] The archpriest's procurators presented their report at the end of April, asking further that the appellants be obliged to sign all the documents they delivered to Pope and cardinals. Mush claimed that "this was but to protract time."[33]

Persons had realized for some time that not all the fault lay with the appellants. He was now aware that Pope and cardinals were

---

[27] See (46) p. 92.

[28] RP, "An answer to a seditious memorial," 12.iii.1601/2, Rome; (II) f.351. This "seditious memorial" was that drawn up by "Dr Pierce and Mr Constable," it seems; (45) No. 58.I, dated 12.iii.1601/2. RP's replies are included as comments in the margin and in the text. See ibid., No. 58. II.

[29] Ibid., p. 8.

[30] Ibid., pp. 10–12.

[31] Some of the appellants were charged with immorality. An unnamed to RP from England, 13.iii.1602, enclosed three letters, presumably intercepted, from the priest William Clark. One purported to be to his mistress. The husband in whose house Clark had lived apostatized in consequence. Clark had acted similarly in London. All of this was public knowledge; (II) f.456a. Mush has the laconic entry in his diary for 21.vii.1602, "I received my daughter's letter"; (42) II, p. 18.

[32] (I) Anglia.A.III,No. 11, "Aprilis 1602" [in margin of [f.1r]]; (11) III, clix–clxii. This incomplete document is in RP's hand. On 16.iv. RP sent an account of matters to date probably to the Spanish council of state(?), "Relacion breve de lo que ha pasado con 4 clerigos Yngleses llamados &c *[sic]* desde su venida a Roma que fue en 16 Febrero hasta los 16 de Abril en que esto se escrive 16.iv. 1602." It is more summary than Mush's but broadly agrees with it, though critical of the appellants. RP claims the only thing they begged so far from the Pope was to be declared guiltless of rebellion or schism; (II) ff.456b–58a; original was in RP's hand.

[33] (42) II, p. 13. Entry for 30.iv.1604.

reaching the same dangerous conclusion. Writing to Garnet on April 2, 1602, he warned "that the archpriest and ours be blamed for too much bitterness."[34] Garnet should restrain the Jesuits from excess in expressing disapproval of this further appeal. The Roman authorities were now fully cognizant of another side to the question. Persons was quick to catch their mood. At the end of April, he cautioned Garnet and Blackwell both, "nothing must be done there lite pendente. . . . We find that it doth no good but exasperateth more."[35] Persons did not expatiate, but he was obviously aware that the diplomatic protection of France made the appellants something more than a few rebel priests. "We must sail here according to the winds and weather, not respecting only what reason, equity and justice would require . . . but what the conditions of times and men both there and here do bear." The fact that the appellants had the support of the English government gave Rome the idea that a negotiated settlement with the persecuting power might still be possible. So even if the Vatican disliked the appellants' "actions and manner of proceeding," they could not be dismissed out of hand, especially since not all the bellicosity was theirs. Rome showed itself "consequently misliking and angry also when the least show of occasion or exasperation is given on our side."[36] Persons was now on the defensive.

Not only from expediency, we may suppose, Persons still tried to reach out to the appellants, especially to those who had received their training in colleges founded in partnership with Allen. In May 1602 he tried to contact John Bennet, who was now joined with Edward in the appeal, not so much a *volte face* as a conversion. A point of persecution was reached in the Nazi concentration camps when the persecuted began to identify with their persecutors. This curious effect seemed to show itself in some of the appellants. Persons refused to regard them as enemies, perhaps understanding something of their deeper motivation, when he addressed them "heartily as friends and old companions." He was not insincere, merely anxious to show goodwill—more realistic than his adversaries in assessing the overall situation, but certainly a man hoping hopelessly.[37]

A letter from Blackwell of April 6 made it clear he was not prepared to retreat from earlier positions. Evidently feeling that Per-

---

[34] (II) f.489.

[35] RP to Blackwell, 30.iv.1602, Rome; (II) f.344. The omission in the above is Grene's. Grene mistakenly dated the letter to 1601.

[36] Ibid.

[37] RP to John Bennet, 19.v.1602, Rome; (II) f.431. Grene wrongly dated it to 1601.

sons had let him down, he rejected his "overmuch mildness." Far from
the changing scene in Rome, he could not see the need to alter attitudes in England. Persons did his best to convince him.[38] "The eager
manner of proceeding of the Cust[omer=archpriest] in these times . . .
is not allowed by them." Rome insisted that authority was given *ad
ædificationem* and not *in destructionem*. If Blackwell had to endure "indignity" and "insolence" from the appellants, this was to be "borne or
dissembled rather than to drive men to so great breaches." There was
a fear that the appellants would be driven out of the Church altogether. Persons had tried to get Blackwell's case accepted without
reserve, but had been unsuccessful.[39]

Perhaps it was a pity that Persons had not tried to restrain the
archpriest before this time. But if he offered wisdom better late than
never, he did not sell out his own side. While giving the cardinals his
answer, which they passed to Mush on May 3, Persons and the procurators, Parker and Archer, denied that the gravamina of the other side
were true. French diplomacy continued to work strenuously for the
appellants, however. Nevertheless, when Champney and Mush paid
Borghese a visit on May 21, he refused to exclude the Jesuits Walpole
and Thomas Owen, already present, from hearing what they had to
say.[40] The appellants may have had a better reason than animosity for
not wanting the Jesuits on hand. Champney and Mush claimed to have
original letters but the Jesuits "would not acknowledge Mr Blackwell's
hand." They were accused of "prating and quarrelling at everything."
Persons tried later to get a meeting with Mush, assuring him that,
although everyone agreed he was the man "most injured" by Mush
and company "in their books and speeches," he was ready to forget the
past for the sake of the future. He asked Mush whether it was "the
spirit of Christ to contend in this sort . . . and to join with the persecutor himself to help out our passionate pretences against our own
brethren."[41]

Clearly, by this time the appellants no less than Persons were
committed to a total view of the situation from which they could not
return. Certainly, if Mush and the rest had gone back to England
reconciled to the Jesuits, they would soon have faced the terrors of

---

[38] RP to Blackwell, 30.iv.1602. V. supra.

[39] S. to s., 20.v.1601, Rome; (II) f.436. Referring to the archpriest in the third
person was a device to confuse interceptors and conceal the identity of correspondents.
The letter was only endorsed in the copy which Grene saw as by RP, and not in his
hand.

[40] *Diary*, p. 14.

[41] RP to J. Mush, 25.v.1602, Rome; (I) Anglia A.III, No. 121, contemporary
copy endd: in another hand. See (II) f.475.

Her Majesty's Tower. However, we could not justly suppose that they were concerned merely for their own comfort and safety. Persons's absence from this important meeting of May 21 was explained in a letter of May 25.[42] He had been obliged to make two courtesy visits to Civitavecchia, one to see off to Spain the Countess of Lemos, whose confessor he had been in Rome.

Nothing much was done in his absence in the appellant affair, nor until June 12, when Mush admitted the cardinals were growing "full weary . . . to see so great clamours raised upon so small grounds." The grounds seemed smaller still in view of the appellants' refusal to acknowledge any of their books save two in Latin. They were "highly offended" at the suggestion that they wished to get the Jesuits out of England, and only marveled that the Jesuits should be meddling "in this matter that appertained unto secular priests."[43] Although "the greatest subject of all their invectives is Father Persons," they were careful to keep his name out of writings consigned to the cardinals. The latter received yet another installment on June 12, and twenty sheets from Persons and Haydock shortly before.[44] Understandably, Borghese told Mush, "There should be no more writing," and refused to deliver Persons's latest to them lest it provoke yet another retort.

One person at least was pleased by all this. On June 20 Mush visited de Béthune to tell him, "the queen willed him . . . to thank him in Rome from her for his good offices" in connection with the appellants.[45] The Roman authorities now had their revenge on the men who seemed to be wasting so much of their time. On June 27 Borghese told Mush that the Pope had committed their affair and all the paper that went with it to the cardinals of the Holy Office. "Thus we were after five months to begin again," groaned Mush. Needless to say, it was all Persons's fault "or others of the Spanish faction."[46] But Mush was now beginning to get the message. The next time he met Persons at Borghese's he "had a few words with him." On June 23 Persons, doggedly ploughing his own furrow, wrote asking Sessa to use his influence with

---

[42] The writer is not indicated, although it is understood to be by RP on the last page, "Relation of the proceedings of the Appellants in Rome, 25 May 1602," (I) Anglia.A.III, No. 13. Tierney referred to this as "Persons's rough draft," but it is not in his hand: more likely Richard Walpole's. Another copy in (II) ff.450b–52a with the title, "A note about the proceedings of the English priests in Rome that call themselves Appellants."

[43] Ibid.

[44] (42) II, p. 15.

[45] Ibid.

[46] Ibid.

the Pope to see that the system of rule by the archpriest was maintained.[47]

A new round of negotiation now began with the cardinals of the Inquisition. Pinelli, with sunny Italian optimism and unaware of the sterner stuff from which Englishmen were made, thought it could all be settled over a good dinner. "We thanked him but refused to have any dealing with Fr Persons."[48] There was also de Béthune to consider, who would not have countenanced any rapprochement with the Spanish faction, as he dubbed the archpriest's party. Without French backing, the appellants would doubtless have foundered long before. On July 3 de Béthune gave Mush money for his expenses. Perhaps he also brought about a reconciliation with Bluet, who from now on was back with the main party. On July 20 Mush had 150 crowns from Borghese as from the Pope and on July 21 another 180 arrived from Paris. A rapprochement even seemed possible between the Churches of Rome and England. Persons was excluded from the secret negotiations, perhaps because of his condemnation of appellant connections with the Bishop of London.[49] However, Persons claimed "to conceal such matters as we can" of the appellants' delinquencies, lest any offence involved turn to the discredit of all.[50]

Persons knew that Blackwell could not but be discouraged by what was happening in Rome. The nuncio in Flanders was still a friend, and for that matter the Pope understood the situation when the appellants cried "for remedy of all." For the rest, "be of good cheer, and lose not heart, for God and all good men will stand with you, and seditious men in the end will come to naught."[51] But on July 20, 1602, the Congregation of the Inquisition issued a decree, later confirmed by the Pope, whereby the archpriest was "condemned for oppressing the said priests in often declaring them to have been schismatics, rebellious and disobedient and for this course forbade them the use of their faculties, and that they could not defend themselves from that infamy." He was also condemned "because he did not admit of the appeal."[52] All this represented a major tactical defeat for Persons and Blackwell both.

---

[47] (II) f.428a.

[48] (42) II, p. 17.

[49] See "Breve relatione di quanto si è trattato tra S. Santità ry il Rè d'Inghilterra"; (IV) Misc.Arm III, 44, ff.226–41 (viii.1603–12–12.i.1604).

[50] RP to Blackwell, 15.vii.1602, Rome; (II) f.460, English. See S. to Garnet, 14.vii., mainly in cipher; ibid. f.339.

[51] Ibid.

[52] (42), 193–94, Latin.

Perhaps the latter was already set on the road which led to the capitulation of 1607.

Persons was never a man to admit defeat or believe that enemies were irreconcilable. He tried once again to establish rapport with Mush in a letter of July 31. It repeated previous appeals and met, inevitably, with the same stony response.[53] On August 9, the terms of the definitive settlement were communicated to both parties. It pleased neither, and both met by chance at Borghese's to express their disappointment.[54] Lobbying continued and, according to Mush, "Persons and his trudged about to the cardinals," no doubt with Mush in hot pursuit.[55]

Perhaps it was with relief from the appeal that Persons turned to Sir James Lindsey, then in Rome as a spokesman for the claims of James VI at the Vatican. Persons was at pains in a letter to the King to remove misunderstanding of his attitude to the English accession. The only obstacle in the way of unreserved support on the part of Catholics was the King's religion. "Our hopes in the said principal point decaying . . . daily, your Majesty in his wisdom and equity cannot marvel if those zealous endeavours of Catholics for your Majesty become more cold for the time."[56] All this was accompanied by properly deferential expressions of affection.

The interlude in appellant affairs was brief. The Pope, "wearied, as he said, with the interpellations of both sides," told the cardinals of the Inquisition in effect to hurry it up. They obeyed willingly. There was another congregation on September 6.[57] On September 12 "matters were handled . . . before his Holiness very largely, and ended." Instructions were issued for a brief to be drawn up in secrecy.[58] Secrecy or no secrecy, the two sides still trudged about the cardinals.

---

[53] RP to J. Mush, 31.vii.1602, Rome; (II) f.472b, copy in Grene's hand.

[54] (42) II, 19f. Grene examined "many letters of these matters" in the VEC archives. He noted more particularly, "The coppy of a letter written by a Cath[olic] Englishman in Flanders to his friend in England about the affairs of the Appellant priests in Rome, and a niew book sett forth by John Collinton. 1o Aug.1602," (II) f.351a. See ibid., 339b, 465a. This reference includes a fourteen-sheet letter of RP "of all the whole proceedings unto that day" [1.viii.1602].

[55] (42) II, 22. See RP to Spinelli, 22.viii.1602; (III) Old Series VII, No. 56, Italian.

[56] RP to James VI, 18.viii.1602, Rome; (I) Anglia. A.III, No. 20, contemp. copy; (II) f.465b.

[57] RP to ?, 14.ix.1602; (I) ibid., No. 22, English, latter part in RP's hand, also ten corrections in the preceding text. The endorsement was partly covered in binding the MS. RP agrees with Mush on 12.ix. as the date of the final settlement.

[58] (42) II, 23. Entry for 14.ix.

On September 18 Mush met the archpriest's procurators by chance. They urged reconciliation. Mush's reply was an almost prophetic indication of the future course of English recusant history. "I told them that neither they nor the great calumniator Persons showed any sincere desire of peace . . . for still they laboured to injure us, and opposed themselves to everything they could learn we laboured for, however needful soever it were to our church." The Pope intended a reconciliation at an audience projected for October 3. Mush suspected "a plot laid by Persons and them, that before his Holiness we might be made friends and ask each other pardon." To avoid so great a calamity, Mush and supporters called on de Béthune two hours before the audience to get advice. An audience for both sides presented the appellants with a dilemma Mush defined well enough: "How to answer before his Holiness that we might neither offend by refusing to entertain friendship with Persons more than in Christian charity we were bound, nor displease the Christian King and our own state by condescending to what his Holiness would . . . move us unto." In the event, the Pope did not appear on the day appointed thanks to the pressure of other and doubtless more congenial business. So Persons "and his departed. All this," recalled Mush, "while we stood praying there might be no audience that day."[59] Prayers are sometimes curiously answered. After Mush's report to de Béthune on October 4, the ambassador effectively "altered his Holiness's mind about reconciliation" by telling him that he must choose between reconciliation and the intervention of Henri IV. If the priests made it up with Persons, de Béthune would have nothing more to do with them, and the king would make no approach to Elizabeth.[60] The Pope yielded, albeit reluctantly. Nevertheless, he told Thomas Fitzherbert and the procurators, "He would make us friends with them all before we should pass out at his chamberdoor."[61] Evidently, not a pronouncement involving infallibility!

In the spring of 1601, Persons became peripherally involved with yet another Elizabethan adventurer, Sir Anthony Shirley. His career reminds one of another, Thomas Stucley, who met a colorful end some twenty years previously.[62] Persons took Shirley's side of a quarrel which developed between him and a rival claimant to the office of Persian envoy at the Vatican.[63] Nearer to Persons's own interest was

---

[59] Ibid., 25.

[60] J. Bossy, "Henri IV, the Appellants and the Jesuits," (10) 8, 86.

[61] (42) II, 25.

[62] For the Shirleys, see Sir E. Denison Ross, *Sir Anthony Shirley and His Persian Adventures* (London, 1933); D. W. Davies, *Elizabethan Errant* . . . (Ithaca, N.Y.: Cornell University, 1967).

[63] "Risposte a certe calumnie publicate sotto nome d'un Memoriale a sua

a new problem involving relations with Protestants. Ecumenism was a word not yet invented, and the generally accepted view among Protestants and Catholics was that there could be no *communicatio in sacris.* "Church papists," however, tried to make the best of both worlds. The Jesuits were opposed to attendance at Protestant services but did not make it matter of heresy. However, Garnet felt it necessary to get Persons's advice about a letter he had seen making such attendance a *gran peccato d'heresia esterna e proprio schisma.*[64] Most believed that such was no more than

> a schismatical act, that is to say, tending to division among them of one faith, and a sin in respect of the scandal, of the perils of infection . . . but properly heresy or schism I never knew any man yet to hold it, for that to make heresy there must be obstinate error in not believing some point of faith; and to make schism there must be rebellion against the true head of the Church, which were hard to prove always in this case; and . . . we have had much ado here to persuade it to be always mortal sin, but only upon certain particular considerations of our state and country.[65]

Certainly, there was no foundation for the view that a Catholic should not have conference with any "heretical minister," although prudence might well prevent the unskilled from getting into arguments with a professional on the other side. It might, for obvious reasons, be a priest's duty to engage in such dialogue.

Thomas James, consul of the English nation in Spain, left Rome for Flanders in May 1601 to report to Alberto and Isabella on English affairs. Persons wrote to the consul in June to hope that Infanta Isabella, would one day become Elizabeth II of England. In case she were not aware of what her future duties might entail, Persons had thoughtfully written "a small book or memorial" in Spanish which he would be glad to give her. He had it ready while she was still in Spain but "lacked courage" at the time to offer it. Now it could be oppor-

---

Santità contro il Signor Don Antonio Ambasciatore del Re di Persia" ([April?], 1601); (II) f.470. The year 1601 is given in a brief mention in (II) f.339. The original used "3 sheets of paper."

[64] RP to H. Garnet, 30.iv.1601, Rome; (II) f.464, English. Much of this was in cipher undeciphered by Grene. He thought the date was 30.iv.1602; J. H. Pollen put it in 1601.

[65] The work was presumably RP's *A briefe discourse conteyning certayne reasons why catholiques refuse to goe to church* . . . , first printed at Greenstreet, East Ham, in 1580. Further editions were issued at Douai in 1599 and 1601. See BL catalogue under RP. Gregory Martin published *A treatise of schisme shewing that all Catholiques ought in any wise to abstaine altogether from heretical conventicles, to witt, their prayers, sermons &c[sic] devided into foure chapters* . . ." (Douai, 1578). Frontispiece printed in (18) facing p. 326. See (79) passim.

tune. "I have always secretly kept the book ready for whomsoever God should will to take in hand this great enterprise."[66]

Unlike Robert Charnock, William Bishop observed the Roman order not to go to England. But he was equally anxious to see his own country again. He enlisted Persons's support to get the cardinal protectors to rescind the "censure" against his return. Persons undertook in mid-May to help him "notwithstanding all matters past." In the present climate of Rome, a good word for an appellant could help Persons as well as Bishop. Persons complied and went further, trying "to procure the remove of the diffidency or scruple which is in many about your degree." Bishop had already approached the protectors; but, good appellant that he was, he saw Jesuits behind every decision made in Rome and was determined to tread warily. In fact, he had made a good impression. "When you come into England they mean both to honour you and to use you confidently in respect of the obedience you have showed in observing their sentence, far differently than Mr Charnock, as they say."[67]

To deal with every charge leveled against Persons and the Jesuits would need more than one book and perhaps fail to find even one interested reader. The charge to which Persons was especially sensitive was that a rift had been about to develop between Cardinal Allen and the Society, which was only prevented by the latter's death. Charnock developed this in *A reply to a notorious libel*.[68] Persons's letter of August 8, 1601, complained to John Sweet that this was "very dishonourable unto him" in view of all that he had done for Allen as well as the cause. A point made in the "libels" was "that the cardinal was weary of the Jesuits before he died, misliked the government of the seminaries, reported evil of Persons and his over-vehement nature, . . . kept down the Jesuits while he lived, and if he had lived on would have taken another course." All of which, as Persons justly observed, could be disproved out of the cardinal's writings and letters, including those to Paget, Throckmorton, Morgan, and others. These had op-

---

[66] RP to the Infanta, 10.vi.1601, Rome; (II) f.420, Spanish. The work in question was RP's *Memorial for the reformation of England* of 1596. V. supra. RP wrote to Lord Semple on 28.v.1601, expressing his hopes for a Catholic successor in England; (II) f.489.

[67] RP to William Bishop, 28.vii.1601, Rome; (II) f.467, English. RP also wrote to J. Cecil and "gave a cover to the packett to Mr Doctor Davison wherin there was also a letter to my Lord Semple." V. supra. The letter of 28.vii. included a copy of RP to Bishop of 30.vi. This covered much the same ground as the later letter but referred to the publication of the two books at Rouen by the "discontented priests," one book in Latin, the other in English, both a furtherance to "publique scandall."

[68] Charnock, *A reply* . . . , 78f. V. supra.

posed the Jesuits partly because they wanted the advancement of Owen Lewis rather than Allen to the cardinalate. The present crop of rumors was traced to John Mush. About six months before he died, Allen exhorted him and his friends to abandon "the faction then newly raised against the Fathers in England." Hesketh, using the name Allen, intended to write to Mush and others to add a living and more effective voice to the silent witness of documents in attic and archive. Some said, "Never so foul contumelious books were ever written by sober men as these be."[69]

---

[69] RP to John Sweet, 6.viii.1601, Rome; (II) ff.474b, 475a, English, from a contemporary copy endorsed, signed, and dated in RP's hand. See also T. Worthington to Hesketh/Allen, 18.xii.1601; (9) 396f.

Chapter Nineteen

End of the Appeal: October 1602–1603

Anew chapter in the archpriest controversy opened on October 5, 1602, when Mush was officially informed that a brief was ready for papal approval and seal. Even at this late hour, Persons, joined by Thomas Owen, Nicholas Smith, Richard Walpole, and three others, made a final appeal that appellant books, or at least unorthodox views expressed in them, be condemned. The Inquisition decree of July 20 had already condemned them as largely heretical.[1] Persons also hoped that the Pope would insist on reconciliation, but he was not sanguine about the final outcome.[2] Meanwhile, interested parties did their best to keep the wound open. "We heard that Persons and his bragged that the pope had kept us here so many months, and in the end had granted us nothing to the purpose."[3]

Copies of the brief were given to Mush and "Mr Persons man" on October 11. On the thirteenth, Mush and friends "carried the Brief to the ambassador." Dutifully, they refused to have anything to do with Persons. On the sixteenth, they had a cordial audience with the Pope, who tried to conquer by kindness. Mush was allowed "to communicate all [his] faculties to ten priests in England," while each appellant received fifty crowns viaticum.[4] Mush ended his diary on October 19. On the same day Persons broke the less-than-joyful news to Garnet. Like everyone else, "the Customer"—Blackwell—must have patience.[5] Persons concluded that "matters are where they were at the beginning." The archpriest's faculties could not have been enlarged "except

---

[1] Unsigned to Clement VIII, 6.x.1602; (II) f.428a, summary; (I) Anglia.A.III, No. 23, draft with alterations; (42) II, 25.

[2] RP to J. Creswell, 6.x.1602, Rome; (I) Anglia.A.VI, No. 35, contemp. copy: mainly taken up with replies to queries contained in JC's letters of 7 and 20.ix. concerning the colleges in Spain; many names in cipher undeciphered. The General insists that Frs. Warford and Blackfan may not be delayed beyond the spring before going to England.

[3] (42) II, 26. Entry for 10.x.1602.

[4] Ibid.

[5] RP to H. Garnet, 19.x.1602, Rome; (I) Anglia.A.III, No. 24, English, contemporary copy, answers HG's of 1.ix. Most of the names are in cipher, but the text usefully recounts recent events.

the contrary part should have been made desperate." But time might be on his side. As it was, many things were confirmed "and enlarged also." The archpriest could choose his assistants, the seminaries stood in statu quo antea, but with authority to give testimonial letters, while the Jesuits had been completely vindicated. The loss of faculties incurred by dealing with heretics would be "a great bridle to many." Much depended on "patience, silence and longanimity" and avoiding "new occasions of exasperations." The archpriest and his friends "must accommodate themselves or else do worse, and all the world will see where the fault lieth." Persons adopted a statesmanlike attitude which realized that the Roman authorities likewise had to practise the art of the possible. Blackwell's rule had been largely vindicated in spite of his "many sharp letters," which had made even his friends in Rome knit their brows.[6]

Fr. Robert now reacted to the strain of it all. He begged Garnet "to let him repose . . . at least for a year, for so he hath need."[7] He saw off the archpriest's procurators, who left Rome on October 18 also provided with a viaticum generous enough to sweeten the taste of seeming failure. John Bossy summed it up well. "There can be few simpler examples of the way in which international politics embittered personal relations among the English clergy."[8] On their return to England the appellants were almost immediately put unmistakably in their place by the Queen's government. A proclamation issued on November 5 (O.S.) banished all Jesuits and secular priests from the realm forthwith. Admitting that secular priests, or at least the appellants, were less obnoxious than Jesuits, it concluded that they all concurred "in apparent disobedience and disloyalty." They too recognized "our mortal enemy the pope." There could be no question of granting "toleration of two religions" in the realm. No Spaniard could have stated the case for persecution more simply or clearly.[9] Nevertheless, there was an element of self-preservation in all this. The end of the reign was clearly approaching and the next monarch might well entertain different beliefs. In December Persons reported to Possevino, the distinguished Jesuit diplomat, "By God's grace, the Catholic religion is spreading widely every day, more than could have been expected." This was why the government supported "the appellant priests and

---

[6] Brief of 5.x.1602; (11) III, clxxxi–clxxxiii. Tierney described it as "in favour of the Appellants."

[7] This letter of 19.x. includes many undeciphered references to individuals.

[8] J. Bossy, "Henri IV, the Appellants . . . ," 86.

[9] (3) III, 250–55. See "Edictum Reginæ impressum et promulgatum 15 Novembris [N.S.] 1602 contra catholicos . . . ," Latin translation from the English by RP; (II) f.351a; (I) Anglia.A.VI, No. 36, corrections in RP's hand.

allowed their books to be printed and spread through England." But if they did not obey the brief, the Catholics would shun them, knowing that "by treating with the heretics they thereby lost their faculties." Persons hoped that they would obey, thus ending the whole sorry business.[10]

There was no question of the Jesuits being called out of England. The Pope not only gave them "a most flattering testimonial" but forbade under pain of excommunication any who wrote against their Institute or even attacked particular members. They were in greater esteem than ever in the eyes of all "good Catholics" in England, even if efforts had been made to persuade the King of France they were only Spaniards in thin disguise. The colleges in Spain seemed to prove the point. But "we have never had as yet any grounds for believing that the King of Spain has any pretensions to the kingdom of England, or that English Catholics are minded to give it to him." They only wanted, claimed Persons, "a Catholic king whatever his nationality." Persons prayed for a happy issue, not "for one person rather than another." As for Henri IV, he only felt "love and respect" for him since he too wanted a Catholic succession in England.[11]

After the recent painful lesson of Kinsale, Spain and its allies were coming to accept the impossibility of a military solution to the English question. Beset by more pressing difficulties, Philip III decided to opt out of the succession stakes in any form. He wrote to assure the Pope—and perhaps a copy of the letter went to England—that he would countenance the accession of any eligible Catholic to the English throne "in case the King of Scotland would not be Catholic."[12] The Pope was content with this and the King of France, presumably, even more so.

The four principal appellants found their way to Paris to be ready for eventualities, and on January 1, 1603, Persons made another appeal for unity. De Béthune himself had made it clear to Persons, if he needed any clarification, that the appellants avoided him in Rome because Queen Elizabeth had committed their cause to Henri IV on the understanding that they would not contact her enemies in Rome. The November decree seemed a good reason for rapprochement. "Just as the heretics are making evil use of the quarrel between us for the

---

[10] RP to Antonio Possevino, 7.xii.1602, Rome; (I) Anglia.A.III, No. 25, contemp. Italian copy.

[11] The letter of 7.xii. above acknowledges receipt of the first parts of Possevino's "two volumes of the 'Bibliotheca Selecta'" which had been sent to Aquaviva by a Brother Jerome. The books were apparently by English authors but not yet printed.

[12] RP to A. Rivers, 6.vii.1603, Rome; (1) p. 214; (II) f.445.

ruin of our common cause, so we in turn should combine . . . to protect this same cause."[13] It was also important that the French king should not allow himself to be used as a wedge to be driven between the English Catholics by Elizabeth and her council. Persons unburdened himself to Possevino, hoping he would manage to convince the King that the Jesuits and nonappellants represented the majority of Catholics in England. Persons also wanted an agent of the archpriest to be allowed to reside in Paris, so that the King could hear the other side. Another in England might have access to his ambassador there. Persons now hoped that France and Spain would unite to promote another "neither French nor Spanish to the crown of England, which was the Prince of Parma." Undoubtedly, the Queen's edict had given offence in France.[14]

The King of France saw reason in all this. So much so that one of the appellants reported to Secretary Cecil that they "feared by Persons to be supplanted." The Jesuits were now back in favor, even as court preachers. A diplomatic revolution seemed imminent when the Admiral of Aragon was received in most friendly manner as he passed through France to Spain. The French ambassador enjoyed similar courtesy at Valladolid. Even the appellants' "best friends" now urged them to make at least a kind of peace. Small wonder if they felt hard-pressed. Persons in Rome cultivated not only the French ambassador but also the Cardinal d'Ossat, a politician more than ordinarily astute, who was aware of the veering wind from Paris. The death of Queen Elizabeth in March removed another obstacle. The appellants did their best to counter all this—hence their presence in Paris—where they had the full support of Sir Thomas Parry, English ambassador. Parry thought no better of them than Sir Robert Cecil but also realized their usefulness in causing division. The appellants continued to kiss the hand that whipped them. "We thought it . . . very expedient both for the discharge of our duties and the service . . . of his Majesty that he should understand by that which hath passed how to proceed . . . with

---

[13] RP to J. Cecil, J. Mush, A. Champney, T. Bluet, 1.i.1603, Rome; (XII) MS Fairhurst 2006, ff.208r–9v, Latin. See (II) ff.462b–63b. Grene recorded letters of 4.i., 19.ii., 17.iii., 4.v., 18.v., 21.v.1603 giving "the scandalous dealings of factious priests" inter alia. Grene admits, "I have not time nor stomack to reade them all, and much less to copy them." RP was now relying on others to copy and write at his dictation: "I am so ill of my eyes as that I could not write this with my own hand," letter of 17.iii. See (II) ff.421a,449a and 341b.

[14] RP to Possevino, 4.1.1603, Rome; Bibliothèque nationale, Paris, MS français 15578, f.3; (II) f.449a, brief summary; (XII) MS Fairhurst 2006, ff.206r–7v, English summary in Bluet's(?) hand probably intended for Sir Robert Cecil. See J. M. Prat, S.J., *Recherches historiques sur la compagnie de Jésus en France du temps du P. Coton, 1564–1623* (Lyons, 1876), Vol. 5, 184–90.

such cunning companions as Persons and his complices."[15] But King James no longer needed the papists, not even for information.

Persons now attempted to enlist the services of the poet and litterateur Henry Constable in the cause of reunion. In February 1603 he wrote to him in Paris by way of the French ambassador's diplomatic mail.[16] Parry, as was his duty, did his best to forestall any such calamity as reunion. He reported to his master on the twenty-second (N.S.) that Villeroy was urging John Cecil and Bagshaw to follow Persons's initiative. They had to agree among themselves before a successor to Elizabeth could be determined. Cecil and Bagshaw were now generally taken to be informers at least for the English government. In consequence, "Persons is more busy in these practices and more confident of success than at any time heretofore."[17] After the proclamation the appellants were well aware of the true motives of the English government in dealing with them while keeping them at arm's length. Bluet reported Bagshaw as saying they would "never get good by dealing with the Council; that Mr Secretary was very unconstant." Whatever his previous dealings with Spain, he was now "all Scottish," remarking further, "It was a special providence of God that the papists fell out, otherwise their party would have been too strong."[18] Bluet and Bagshaw both wished—separately—to go to England to make their reports to government on friend and foe. "Mr Secretary," understandably, was by no means eager to see them.[19]

The appellants pursued their own blend of policy and intrigue long after the accession of James I. In May 1603 Parry reported to Cecil a visit from Bagshaw to give him details of the latest plot of "Persons and his crew" to publish letters from Robert Cecil to them revealing his erstwhile intentions "for advancement of the Spanish pretensions." Pressed by Parry, Bagshaw could offer no proof. The same evening John Cecil visited Parry to disclaim Bagshaw and that "society of the priests" lately arrived from England. Mr. John wished to be the sole channel of information for King James on proceedings in Rome "and other secrets communicated to him by Mr. Villeroy with

---

[15] Bluet's(?) memorial; (XII) MS Fairhurst 2006, ff.206r–7v.

[16] See "The summe of a letter written to Mr Constable by Parsons under the name of Sweete from Rome the 24 of February 1603 sent by Eliott in the frenche embassa: pacquet," (XII) ibid., f.195v, Bluet's hand. A John Sweet was a secular priest. The original of this letter is lost. Parry refers to Bluet's letters and summaries in his letter to R. Cecil of 12/22.ii.1603. V. infra.

[17] Sir Thomas Parry to R. Cecil, 12/22.ii.1603; (VII) SP78/48, f.79r, signed dispatch.

[18] Notes in Bluet's hand, c.24.ii.1603; (XII) ibid., f.195v.

[19] C. Bagshaw to R. Cecil, 18/28.ii.1603, Paris; (VII) SP78/48, f.91r, a.l.s.

whom he hath great credit." Parry refused him a passport and warned him that if he went to England, "it would be at his own peril."[20]

As in any modern totalitarian state, it was sometimes relatives and friends in England who were made to pay for the sins of the exiles. Persons's sister died in sinister circumstances when "upon pretension of seeking for stolen geese" the pursuivants searched her house on Christmas night. Looking "in her boxes for other manner of geese," they found "agnus deis and beads and suchlike. She was so frighted of the knaves that she died on Innocents' Day." She had already been hunted out of another parish by the minister on account of her brother.[21] Of the other brothers, Richard and his wife had been living as Catholics for some seven years "but poorly in outward show." Thomas was emphatically not Catholic, "nor is there any hope."[22] John remained a minister of the Church by Law Established, while George, a Catholic, escaped persecution by living most of the time abroad.[23]

News reached Rome on April 18 of Queen Elizabeth's death. On April 26, *Litaniæ et preces recitandæ pro fide propaganda in Regnis Angliæ et Scotiæ* appeared in official print. Persons reported universal joy at Elizabeth's death but rejoicing only in a muted key for James. "The doubtfulness how this new king [would] proceed cast much water into the wine and held many men in suspense," Persons, no doubt, included.[24] The exiles were glad to see the two kingdoms united and thought in any case, "It cannot go so bad with them under this man as before under the queen." Elizabeth had shut herself off at least in her later years. However, a man "must needs go abroad sometimes" so that "books, memorials and the like" could be presented to him. Most thought that the "rigour of persecution" in Scotland had been due to "the barbarous tyranny of that puritanical presbytery which held the king himself also in awe" rather than to any preference of his own. But in July this year a bizarre brace of plots was almost certainly steered if not contrived by Sir Robert Cecil to make sure that James would become as secluded in his habits as her late Majesty. Apparent attempts on the King's life, known as the "main" and "by" plots, were used to convince James that he could not go among his people or meet anyone who had not first passed the filter of Cecil and his colleagues. The Queen was dead but *regnum cecilianum* lived on.

[20] Sir Thomas Parry to R. Cecil, 24.v./3.vi.1603, Paris; (VII) SP78/49, f.129r, signed dispatch.

[21] H. Garnet to RP, 16.iii.1603; (II) f.554; see (I)37.

[22] (6) 144; no source of the letter is given.

[23] (I) 38.

[24] See RP to ? at Padua, 26.iv.1603, Rome; (II) f.490.

Whatever their misgivings, Persons, the Italians, and most of the exiles hoped that James would follow "a moderate course" in religious matters.[25] With Spain and France acquiescent, he might even accede to the Empire! Although the Pope could not be happy about James's religion, "he will hardly be induced to do anything against him." The most serious threat to James could come from his own Scots, who might not know where to stop in taking advantage of the English. "The Scottish in this town do begin already to exasperate too much in speeches everywhere against the English." If this happened in England, one could expect "foul broils." A last word on the theme occurred in Persons's letter to Bagshaw in May. "God hath thought best to make him first king, and now we must hope and pray that He will make him also a Catholic."[26]

Yet another Elizabethan adventurer with whom Persons had contact at this time was Richard Hawkins, son of Sir John, who followed the paternal footsteps—or wake—in various expeditions against the Spanish dominions. He was captured and imprisoned in Lima from 1597 to 1602, when Persons's efforts to get him released finally bore fruit.[27] He wrote to Persons from Valladolid on November 2, 1602. In his reply the Jesuit hoped he would use his influence to bring about peace between England and Spain. When he got to England at the year's end, he apparently supported this view before the Privy Council. Spain was ready for peace, as Sessa admitted to Persons. Far from ready for peace with Persons, even now, was Dr. Bagshaw. A letter of January 1 to Paris received no reply, so Persons tried again in May. Bagshaw had been "grieved with a new report" in Rome that he had been in correspondence with the Privy Council since the papal prohibition. Persons reassured him that, whatever had been written about this before, he had been cleared "fully in that behalf" by a certain Percival and so all should be "wholly forgotten and forgiven."[28]

By the end of May, Persons had received and read King James's book *Basilikon doron*, "a princely gift and a princely work,"[29]

---

[25] Ibid.

[26] RP to C. Bagshaw, 18.v.1603, Rome; (I) Anglia.A.III, No. 34, a.l.s.

[27] See DNB and Michael Lewis, *The Hawkins Dynasty* (London, 1969), 168–220. Richard was knighted on his return to England in 1603. See RP to R. Hawkins, 4.v.1603, Rome; (I) Anglia.A.III, No. 33; see (II) f.421.

[28] RP to C. Bagshaw, 18.v.1603. V. supra. W. Persevall is noted in the VEC Pilgrim Book ((12) VI, 576) as of Somersetshire. He stayed at the VEC from 12.iv. for seventeen days, receiving six crowns at his departure. Nothing in the Douai Diary suggests he was received again.

[29] RP to "NT" (H. Garnet), 24.v.1603, Rome; (VII) SP14/1, No. 84, a.l.s., intercepted or handed over? The edition of James's book was that of London, 1603. See

which he passed on to the Pope and others in Rome after translation into Latin. Pope Clement "could scarce hold back tears for comfort to hear certain passages in favour of virtue and hatred of vice" which Persons read to him. Well aware that some of the priests as well as Protestants and Puritans were doing their best to discredit him with the King, Persons asked Garnet to procure "that some men not ungrateful to his Majesty" put his record straight with the monarch. Persons had already written two letters to the King in the Queen's lifetime: one by the Earl of Angus, which had been intercepted, and one by Sir James Lindsey. In both he reminded the King of his services to his mother and to himself in financial matters. If he still resented the *Book of Succession,* he should remember that Cardinal Allen and Sir Francis Englefield were the principal authors; but, if he were still not satisfied, he would make compensation "abundantly in other services hereafter."

On May 23 Persons had an audience with the Pope on English affairs. He urged him, and Aldobrandino likewise, to get someone sent to England to plead the cause of the Catholics. The ambassadors at King James's court should be urged to do likewise.[30] But it was already evident that pressure was being brought to bear on James to make him continue Elizabeth's policy of persecution. Since Henri IV's ambassador was a Huguenot, little could be looked for from him. The exiles in Flanders thought that if the Pope sent anyone it should be "secretly under some other pretext," such as attendance at the coronation. The envoy could be a layman "with secret letters" from the Pope. A point for emphasis was that Calvinists in France and Lutherans in Germany already enjoyed toleration. The only reason for not extending it to Catholics in England was the nameless fears of Protestant imagination.[31]

Persons's misgivings with regard to King James seemed fully justified by the summer of 1603.[32] The "poor, distressed and frightened Catholics" were no better off. The King's study of "a free and absolute monarchy" was now to hand, maintaining that "an absolute king is subject to no law but is absolute lord of all things." Moreover, "at his coronation he must swear to uphold the religion which he finds

---

also RP to Clement VIII, n.d.; (IV) F.B.IV,95, a.l.s.

[30] RP to Aldobrandino, 24.v.1603, Rome; (IV) F. Borg. III, 124.G.2, f.27, a.l.s., Italian; (II) f.324.

[31] RP to Clement VIII, 30.v.1603; (IV) F.Borgh. III, 124.G, f.29. See also s. to H. Garnet, 20.vi.; (VII) SP14/11, No. 6, copy(?), RP's credential for a gentleman visiting England.

[32] RP to Borghese, vii(?).1603; (IV) ibid., f.31r/v, a.l.s. Schondonck to RP, 14.vi. 1603; ibid., f.32r. This, or a copy, was enclosed in the letter to Borghese. Giles Schondonck was rector of St. Omers.

established in the kingdom." Persons offered the Pope a translation of
this small but "pestilential" book. With the wisdom of hindsight, he
now saw that the Spaniards, though good men and willing to help,
never had forces "answerable to their desires or ours." Hard pressed in
Europe, they were left to deal almost entirely alone with the Barbary
corsairs and other Mediterranean problems. For at least five years past,
he claimed to have been convinced that "it was not secure to adventure
upon any forcible attempts." There could be no short, swift answer to
England's problem. There would never be an empresa.[33] Persons in a
recriminatory mood thought that what he took to be his own candor
had made him suspect with the Spanish authorities for some two or
three years past. So he knew nothing of "Timothy his journey nor his
companion," that is, Thomas Wintour's trip to Spain in 1602, apparently to urge the Spaniards to be ready at the fateful hour of Elizabeth's death.[34]

Persons now blamed Philip II for procrastinating in the early
years of Elizabeth's reign "when he might have reformed all easily
which afterwards he paid for dearly." He should have done more to
push the cause of the infanta "while the state of France did permit
him," and also tried to win "this present King of England whilst he
might have done it in his minority." His successor's worst mistake was
to miss the moment of the Queen's death. The English Catholics were
not blameless. They should have made "some show of union among
themselves, and of their forces and numbers at the Queen's death."
They should not have protested against the Scottish king's entry but
only asked to know "with what conditions his Majesty would receive
them" after their treatment at the hands of the late queen "not like
subjects but slaves."[35] All this "I told you so" came from a man no little
embittered and frustrated at seeing a large part of his lifetime's work
wasted.

The Catholic community in England, unlike the Huguenots in
France, chose the way of nonviolence, which, in the event, led to
martyrdom and near extinction. This was justified from the highest
Christian standpoint, but not all Catholics, foreigners especially, saw
things from this lofty eminence. The Italians, according to Persons,
thought the English Catholics themselves should have done something
if they had any force or strength at all. Two things were now clear.

---

[33] RP to Anthony Rivers, 6.vii.1603, Rome; (II) f.444; (1) 215.

[34] See A. J. Loomie, *Guy Fawkes in Spain* . . . , IHR, special supplement 9,
xi.1971, 10.

[35] RP to A. Rivers, 6.vii.; (1) 215f. The Catholics were not as supine as RP
thought. See Ian D. Grosvenor, "Catholics and Politics: The Worcestershire election of
1604," (10) 14, 149–62.

King James was firmly seated on his throne and must be accepted by his fellow monarchs. At the same time, the English Catholics were a spent force which could be ignored by Scots, English, and everyone else. Diplomatic pressure could be exercised to relieve their lot, but this could be perfunctory. In any case, peace with Spain must come first. Perhaps it did not take the wit of Persons to reach another conclusion. "Their peace will be nothing worth. . . . The English will help the Hollanders underhand as they did for many years together of the late queen's reign, and as the French are said to do now."[36] Force had failed, so the "first and chief" remedy must now be prayer. The powder had proved to be damp but trust in God remained. The Vatican agreed. The year 1570 might have been a century away. The Catholics must trust in the ambassadors and keep their heads down. They must "take heed lest upon passion some break out and be oppressed . . . or cause more severity to others." Already the Pope had "ordained now sundry times . . . that all such rash attempts be avoided." Nothing could have helped the English government abroad as much as a gunpowder plot in any new campaign against the papists.

That the religious situation in England was not all that simple appeared in a letter to Persons at the end of September 1603. He speedily informed Aldobrandino. "Mr Anthony Standen, who was recently sent from the King of England to the house of Lorraine, the republic of Venice and to the grand duke, being a Catholic and an old friend of mine, wrote to me secretly from Florence telling me various things about the present king."[37] Renewing a request for someone of standing to be sent to James to discuss religion, Standen thought the Bishop of Evreux a suitable candidate. This choice would also please the King of France.[38] Persons's trust of Standen was suggested by three letters, or summaries of them, written in the latter part of 1603, it would seem. Persons saw Anne of Denmark, James's queen and reportedly a convert to Catholicism, "a newborn lamb set down among so many ravening wolves." She should be cultivated as a source of intelligence not least for Persons. Relics were to be sent to her by way of Florence. The King now seemed past hope. "So we must make it our aim, with the queen's help, to have the children, now of tender age, instructed in the Catholic faith." Standen knew of possible tutors "not

---

[36] RP to A. Rivers, 6.vii.1603. V. supra, 216f.

[37] RP to Aldobrandino, 28.ix.1603. Rome; (IV) F.Borgh. III.124.G.2, f.35r/v, a.l.s.

[38] An endorsement in the Pope's(?) hand on the above letter runs, "Perhaps it would not be amiss for Persons himself to say a word on the subject to the Duca di Vegli to see what he thinks about it, having regard to the jealousies there are in this affair." See also RP to A. Standen, 6.x.1603; (II) f.421.

reputed as Catholics but yet have obtained their doctor's degree here with great distinction."[39]

Until now, English Jesuits received training as novices in a foreign house of the Society, most commonly Sant'Andrea in Rome. A specifically English noviceship in exile was now proposed. In the autumn of 1604, Giles Schondonck, S.J., indicated the willingness of the bishop of St. Omer to assist. Persons urged Giles to go ahead, perhaps using the services of William Baldwin. But all should be kept secret until the project was fairly matured.[40] On October 12 Persons produced a letter of introduction for the son-in-law of the Lord Chief Justice of England. He had left England secretly and intended to become a Catholic. John Sweet accompanied him and vouched for his good faith.[41]

It seemed time to dare another approach to King James. As a "poor worm of the earth" Persons crawled to congratulate the king on his accession. He begged James not to spurn him for his "baseness" but rather to accept his "innocency and true loyal meaning before God and man." The twin harp strings of his earlier services to James and the essential good meaning of the *Book of Succession* were touched again. The readiness of Catholics to acknowledge his succession was sufficient proof of their loyalty.[42] Persons no longer appealed to the King to change his religion but only to allow "freedom of their conscience" to all whatever their "nation, faction or religion." Attempts to coerce could only cause "infinite inward disgust of heart"; and it was to be hoped the King would avoid Elizabeth's sorry precedent. True, "she was terrified by crafty persuasion . . . that except she showed herself an enemy to Catholic religion and to the pope . . . she could not be held for legitimate, for so much as the Church of Rome had disannulled her mother's marriage." Persons did not enlarge on this but pointed out that no kind of question could arise with regard to James's origins. Unlike Elizabeth, James's troubles had all arisen "from those that were

---

[39] (V) MS Barb.Lat.2190 (formerly Barb.XXX.75) f.3. According to (II) f.476, RP wrote "several letters . . . concerning" Standen in 1604, described as visiting "severall princes of Italy to informe them of his [James VI's] coming to the crowne and without or perhaps against his master's order came also to Rome to have the blessing of the Pope who gave him several things of devotion for the queene, for which cause he was put in prison in London, Feb. 1604." Letters of 10.ii., 12.iv. and 11.v. to the Pope are mentioned. The first two seem to be lost.

[40] RP to G. Schondonck, 5.x.1603, Rome; (XVI), Carton 31, Varia S.J.; (I) Cardwell transcripts III, f.209.

[41] RP to Aldobrandino, 12.x.1603, Rome; (IV) F.Borgh. III, 124.G.2, f.37r/v, Italian a.l.s.

[42] RP to James I, 18.x.1603, Rome; (I) Anglia.A.III, No. 36, contemp. copy.

of opposite religion."[43] So there was no need for James to alienate those of a religion shared with most of western Europe. True, there were those who "would not have princes to stand of themselves by the . . . goodwill of their subjects, but to lean on them, and reign by them, and their industry in making parts and factions." This was clearly a shrewd thrust at the ruling Cecils. But as the King would hardly have seen this before Mr. Secretary Cecil, perhaps Persons should have kept the thought to himself. The King would need the Catholics as a counterbalance to the "Protestants and Puritans" for it would be impossible to reconcile the latter. The only way to keep all in "love and service" was "to permit freedom of their consciences, which was wont to be also the common doctrine of Luther, Calvin and all other new doctors of our age." The writer ended with an apology for being "so long and tedious to so high and occupied a prince," with a further assurance of service even to the shedding of his blood.[44]

Persons used an opportunity about this time to prove not only his acceptance of James's accession but also his regard for his safety. In letters to the King dated October 18 and 25, both lost in the original— or perhaps destroyed for reasons of state—Persons warned him of an assassination attempt by a certain "Rollino."[45] Robert Cecil knew the name, since extant "notes" at Hatfield give his alias of Delfino Fleming. There was also an Andrew Ramires who, to confuse and cover his tracks, also used the name "Delfino." They were accomplices in whatever it was they had in mind.[46] The "notes" do not add much to our knowledge. Similar episodes suggest that Ramires and Delfino, well aware of the good market for such things, concocted a bogus scheme to assassinate James. They contacted unnamed Catholics in Flanders, including Jesuits, to lend themselves plausibility. Persons got word of it, perhaps by someone's design to help discredit him further with James. But neither the Jesuit nor his colleagues had time for such methods, and warned James in the letters. One wonders how far Persons believed in the plot. In any case, he knew that he was dealing with people who would not allow his reputation to be restored or even improved. At all events, armed with their "evidence" and collected names, the "assassins" went to London to reveal all for a reward. It was a dangerous game and could blow up in the faces of the players, as Verney and Mather discovered in 1572 and Edward Squire in 1598.

[43] Ibid. Elizabeth's illegitimacy was not a serious bar to papal recognition. See E. Cardwell, *Documentary annals . . . of the Church of England* (Oxford, 1844), 285.

[44] RP to James I, 18.x.1603. V. supra.

[45] See RP to H. Garnet, 26.ii.1604, Rome; (II) f.467.

[46] (14) XV, 397. Nuremberg was a center of fine craftsmanship practiced by such families as the Jamnitzers.

Certainly, Robert Cecil did not trust them and concluded from Persons's letters that it was a mere device to curry favor with the King. It is, of course, possible and even likely that Cecil used the pair in the first place as agents provocateurs to sound out Persons, and perhaps entrap him by his silence, as happened to the luckless Duke of Norfolk in 1572.[47] Needless to say, Persons's letters were not acknowledged.

This was not the end of the affair. By February 1604 Rollino was in Rome. He was imprisoned on suspicion for a time but the "common judges" and "the governor" decided he had committed no fault. His departure from England argues that his work had at least the tacit approval of Mr. Secretary, who was not the man to condone or ignore a villain even if there was only Persons's word for his delinquency. Rollino visited Persons and perhaps the Pope. Persons "imposed upon him a severe charge and commination under pain of excommunication ipso facto that he should not go forward in this or any other attempt upon his Majesty's person, but should seek [to] let [hinder] or discover the same, if any such matter were."[48] Persons hoped that a fair interpretation would be made of his solicitude for James, and also of the fact that prayers were ordered in Rome for the King's conversion. At least one of Persons's letters reached the royal presence, at which, "when the king had read through the letters, and in Cecil's presence, he burst out laughing."[49] This suggests, once again, that the whole thing was one of Cecil's well-known contrivances. Persons referred to the matter once more in a letter of May 1604 to the Pope, assuring him that he had told the king of "the precautions taken by your Holiness for his security"; also that he had nothing to fear from the English Catholics.[50] Well might King and secretary allow themselves a hearty laugh of derision. William Crichton was a man much chagrined by the turn events were taking under the new king. As one of James's erstwhile most ardent and optimistic supporters, he made no attempt to conceal his disappointment in a letter to Persons of September 20. Persons, who never lacked magnanimity, replied in encouraging terms and with never a hint of "I told you so!" On the contrary. "You must not so easily lose courage nor hope of our king. Sunt duodecim horæ diei." He endorsed Crichton's desire to go to

---

[47] For earlier plots, see (26) (43) 3–82, (45). *Guy Fawkes: The Real Story of the Gunpowder Plot?* (London, 1969). Martin Mume, *Treason and Plot,* 68, 188.

[48] RP to H. Garnet, 26.ii.1604, Rome. V. supra. "Let" here means "prevent."

[49] From an account of the death of Richard Blount, S.J., 1.vi.1638, London; (XVI) Carton 29, varia S.J., Latin. The present is taken from a transcript by J. Morris, S.J., in (1). The original covered eight pages.

[50] RP to Clement VIII, 11.v.1604, Rome; (IV) F.Borgh. III.124G.2, ff.45r–48v, Italian a.l.s.

England, where Garnet would be expecting him. The Pope was interested by the fact that Crichton had, reportedly, a passport from King
James. Typically, in spite of Crichton's former reaction to the *Book of
Succession,* Persons now asked him to send "in secret" to Paris to read
and comment on "somewhat in the preface of the three conversions of
England" which he had just completed.[51] The first treason trials in the
new reign took place at Winchester in mid-November 1603. On December 18 an unidentified correspondent in England sent Persons an
account of the "main" and "by" plots. All too short, it helped nevertheless to explain much that was not evident from official English sources.

> In the northern parts of the kingdom there were a number of men
> who were going about collecting names and signatures from various
> people to a memorial which they wished to present to the king, asking
> for liberty of conscience. It pleased the Bishop of Durham, however,
> who is a great enemy of the Catholics, to attempt to ingratiate himself
> still further with the king by making the affair seem altogether sus-
> pect. He hinted that its real purpose was to set on foot some kind of
> rebellion. In consequence, he further obtained a commission to seize
> and examine all persons found to have had some part in this memo-
> rial. The general feeling is that much will be made of the business."

Much was.[52]

Two secular priests were involved, William Watson and William Clark, who were executed at Winchester on December 9 in the
accustomed form for plebeian traitors. Watson, executed first, was
reported to have admitted that he was about "to die for the treason
. . . committed against the king and the realm. . . . He confessed
further that he had written a number of lying and scandalous books
against the Jesuits, of which he heartily repented"; also that he had
injured "many knights and gentlemen, for which he begged . . . pardon." He was allowed to hang until dead before being quartered,
probably a reward for his simple admission of guilt. With Clark the
case was otherwise. Using much the same words as Watson, he added
that "a book of his was in the hands of the councillors" which he
hoped would be printed, since "it was likely to benefit his country and
would injure no one." The book was never published. Clark, meanwhile, paid dear for his indiscretion. "There was such bad management
in the end that when he fell to the ground he had all his senses com-

[51] RP to Crichton, 21.x.1603, Rome; (VII) SP 78/50, No. 59, contemp. copy.
The letter was presumably intercepted, copied, and allowed to go on its way.

[52] RP's report on a letter from England, 18.xii.1603, NS; (VI) Anglia.31.I,
f.247. For an account of the execution, see (45) Doc. 537; (IV) F.Borgh. II, 448AB,
f.333r/v.

pletely, with the result that when the hangman cut out his heart, he uttered the words, Jesus help me!"

Some five weeks later, Persons broached the subject again. Watson and Clark were "among the most headstrong of all the seditious priests." Disdaining the archpriest and the Jesuits, they "wrote several scandalous books, and were in communication with the Bishop of London and other heretics." To improve their case with these men, "they accused the Jesuits and other more zealous Catholics of acts of treason against the King's Majesty and the state." For their sins "God permitted them to be the first Catholic priests to fall genuinely into the crime of treason." However, they died as Catholics and priests, "so we have said Masses for them." Certainly, to reassure the general public, some gesture against the papists seemed called for, because, in view of an approaching peace with Spain, they had been dealt with lightly and were raising their heads again. Someone wrote, "I witnessed a solemn Mass, with very good singing . . . within the walls of a private house; and there was a fair attendance. We hope the situation will further improve with every passing day."[53]

Persons now hoped that "controversy among the heretics themselves" would help the Catholics by wearying the King to the point where he would "gradually come to rely more on the Catholic party and eventually discover the truth of their religion." Certainly, there was no prospect of reconciliation or even compromise between Puritans and bishops. Persons gave Aldobrandino a copy of James's "new decrees," intended to meet if only to a limted extent some of the Puritans' demands. A letter of November 14 included the news that two Puritan preachers had been sentenced to death for preaching sedition. It was also reported that a million in gold had been offered in return for tolerating papists, to be paid after Elizabeth's penal code had been repealed. Someone in Flanders begged the Pope to consider the matter and put it to the King of Spain at least as a basis for further negotiation.[54]

The year 1603 witnessed another embarrassing development at Valladolid. As John Blackfan reported, the English Benedictines were eager to enter the mission field, especially as one of their men, Mark Barkworth, had been martyred there. "They secretly introduced into

---

[53] RP to Possevino, 24.i.1604, Rome; (VI) Anglia.31.I, f.246, Italian copy; another copy in (XVII) Fo.Mediceo, F.921, lettere di particolari f.319r, i.ii.1604, f.319r.

[54] RP to Aldobrandino, 24.xii.1603, Rome; (IV) F.Borgh. III.124.G.2, f.43, Italian a.l.s. The decree in question is presumably "A proclamation concerning such as seditiously seeke reformation in Church matters," from Wilton; (13) 60–63. See (II) f.474, Latin reference to two decrees of 24.x.1603 and of 15.iii.1604 seemingly put into Latin for the Pope.

the college agents to entice the students to join their own ranks, putting the rule of St. Benedict into the hands of a number of them, and adding glowing praises." When the students saw "how much they were sought after, their heads began to swell. . . . They neglected the rules of the house; indeed, came rather to despise them and slackened their efforts at prayer and study." Cliques formed. "Admonished for some fault, they insolently put themselves on their dignity and answered the superior back." The situation was uncannily like that which had plagued the college in Rome.[55] The Jesuits immediately confronted with the challenge were unable to cope. Gentle measures achieved nothing, nor did the light and virtually symbolic punishments available in the cloister. It all came to a head in a students' riot. At one point they greeted the rector and certain Fathers with "dreadful curses," crying out that they were "going at once to the nuncio." There are overtones here of hysteria and hypertension, arguing, perhaps, a regime which had been too tight. The rampage lasted a day, in the course of which the rector ordered all outside doors to be locked, lest "they broke out and gave rise to a scandal among the people." In fact, externs working in the college lost no time in spreading a piquant piece of gossip through the town. When the main force of the gale was spent, the rector gave the demonstrators leave to take themselves off. They hurried away to the royal monastery of St. Benedict. The abbot heard their case sympathetically but sent them back with orders to behave peaceably until remedy could be found. He went immediately to the nuncio, Ginnasio. Pedro Ruis, the Jesuit rector, also called on him that evening in the company of Joseph Creswell. Ginnasio, shortly afterwards created cardinal, saw in all this a providential means of taking the Jesuits down a peg. After hearing the abbot, he reportedly refused "to listen calmly to what our Fathers had to say." Not very tactfully, Ruis expressed his sorrow that Ginnasio "had not made his Holiness sufficiently careful for the peace of the English church when he accepted tumultuous spirits of this kind to be sent on the English mission."[56] Ginnasio showed proper diplomatic anger at this reflection on the wisdom of the Vatican. "'So indeed,' cried his Illustrious Lordship, 'he wished to teach his Holiness how to rule the Church! Bring shackles and let him be loaded with them and shut up in a narrow dungeon until it can be decided what to do with him!'" The rector fell suppliant to his knees and begged pardon for his offences, fervently seconded by Creswell. The operatic interlude ended for the moment

---

[55] Blackfan, *Annales Collegii S. Albani.* For details of MS and author, see introduction to the above by J. H. Pollen, S.J., 1–23; also 72.

[56] Ibid., 74. Details of those leaving to join the Order of St. Benedict in CRS 30, 60–79: ix and x.1603 were the peak months.

when the nuncio ordered Ruis to leave the city as soon as possible and find a substitute in his office.

Altogether twenty-five of the discontented students were admitted to the Order of St. Benedict over the next five months, including an initial group of a dozen. The effect on the college was all that its enemies could have wished. If the superior attempted to restrain any student, he threatened to depart at once for the Benedictines. All this had its effect on former benefactors in the locality. Whereas formerly it had not been difficult to maintain seventy-two, they could now "scarcely find bread" for the forty remaining. The year 1604 was quieter but with the calm of stagnation rather than recovery. "Studies languished; college discipline lay low." Worse still, those who departed for the Benedictines left with minds and memories soured towards the Jesuits, a factor which was to produce bitter fruit in the years to come.[57] But as a Benedictine authority wrote, "St Alban's at Valladolid . . . worried all those who were connected with it."[58] Blackfan did not enlarge on the point, but a large measure of blame lay with the Society. Creswell admitted "the prodigality and favouritism of the Spanish rectors." Persons had to agree. Creswell himself was not always easy to live with. After coming to Valladolid in 1601, he clashed with his conationals at times as well as with the Spaniards.

The Benedictines shared the English mission from 1603. This offered an alternative vocation to students distinct from seculars and Jesuits, whose example had not been uniformly inspiring. Dr. Lunn believes the summer riot of 1603 had nothing to do with the monks, in spite of propaganda and the rulebook of St. Benedict put in circulation by mysterious "agents." Undoubtedly, the English government took as much interest in the Spanish colleges as in the Roman.[59] They would have been helped at least unconsciously by students from Rome who complained of real or imaginary grievances or who thought that business could be done with Secretary Cecil or who were genuinely in search of a higher ideal not otherwise obviously to hand. Their experience of Spain after Persons's departure might not have attracted them to the Society of Jesus. The best evidence for this came not from any appellant, Protestant, or government agent but from Joseph Creswell, vice-prefect.[60]

---

[57] Ibid., 75.

[58] D. Lunn, *The English Benedictines 1540–1688* (London, 1980), 58; (74) 22–27.

[59] See Lunn, *The English Benedictines*, 59. (74) includes a short but very perceptive account of these times.

[60] See chap. 20.

Chapter Twenty

Approaches to James I: 1604

E arly in 1604 a strict watch was kept on couriers and posts at the English ports. All the same, Persons reported to the Pope early in February the arrival of a trusty messenger. One of his letters contained secret information for the Pope alone that certain English councillors had proposed to a Spanish envoy through a Jesuit that the Catholics might get toleration if they were prepared to pay for it. The Spanish ambassador and certain Catholics seemed favorable. Persons was an optimist but not a fool. "Consider the whole matter suspect. The councillors are merely out to get money and to make fools of the papists." However, it could do no harm to go along with them for a time. "Unless your Holiness has a better idea."[1]

The man who suffered most from the latest attempt to settle the archpriest problem was the archpriest. Put firmly in the wrong by the brief of October 5, 1602, with regard to the appellants' main protest, it was doubtless considered kind to let him go on and try again. With the easy wisdom of hindsight, it might have been kinder to have sent him into retirement or transferred him to some less exacting task. As it was, naked to his enemies, and exposed to the superior and merciless wit of his critics, he hardly knew which way to turn. The omniscient Jesuits, including Persons, did not after all know everything, and their influence in Rome was clearly limited. To confirm the point, *Venerunt nuper* of October 5 forbade him to deal with them in business arising from his office, even with the superior in order to get information. His authority was limited to seminary priests and declared null where the laity were concerned. He could not inflict censures, launch decrees, take any steps against the appellants or suspend any priests without the cardinal protector's approval.[2]

---

[1] RP to Clement VIII, 7.ii.[1604], Rome; (IV) F.Borgh. II.448AB, f.332r, a.l.s.; RP's suspicions were well founded. The technique of extracting money from the enemy was used successfully on the Spaniards for a time. See A. J. Loomie, "Sir Robert Cecil and the Spanish Embassy"; (65) XLII, 30–57; (75) 10–12. The Constable of Castile gave an intelligent overall appraisal of the religious situation in England in a memo of 22.xi.1604; ibid., 26–44, 58f. Pensions to the privy councilors; ibid., 61, 90, 147.

[2] See (11) III, App. clxxi.

A greater man than Blackwell could have wilted under these blows of fortune. Understanding his isolation, Persons urged the Pope early in 1604 to keep in touch with him "through a cardinal, the protector, Borghese, Bellarmine or the nuncio in Flanders."[3] The Pope should also define the prohibition more precisely so that Blackwell could consult the Jesuits in matters of doctrine and morals if not about allocation of priests and other affairs.[4]

The problem in Valladolid had by now reached the point where it was mooted that the college be moved elsewhere. In his letter to Creswell of April 6, Persons admitted that the Spanish Jesuits must bear some responsibility for an unhappy state of affairs. "Every day they make some fresh inroad into the rights of the seminary." The local Spanish procurator warned Persons that college affairs had been handled unfairly in the provincial congregation. It was much resented that Spanish ducats, ever in short supply, should go to nourish Englishmen, enemies of Spain whatever their faith. Undoubtedly, by this time many had heard of the anti-Spanish stance taken up by John Cecil and his friends. The Spanish procurator wished to draw up a financial agreement with Persons; but he, quite correctly, felt the matter should be handled by Creswell, the man on the spot.[5]

On February 22 (O.S.) James I issued a proclamation "commanding all Jesuits, Seminaries and priests to depart the realm by a day appointed." This was March 19.[6] On May 6 Persons sent Aldobrandino a letter and a copy of the edict translated, probably into Latin. The first of its kind in the new reign had been issued on October 24, 1603 (O.S.).[7] Persons tried to see the cardinal but wasted a whole day in waiting and was unwell in consequence.[8] Persons admitted in his letter that he knew he was accused of interfering and lobbying the great. But everyone did as much, if he could, and his only object was to pass on "reliable information" from English sources. Meanwhile, "daily prayers and penances" were offered in Rome for King James's conversion.[9]

---

[3] RP to Clement VIII, 7.ii.[1604]. V. supra.

[4] Ibid. RP acknowledged receipt of "the English book" sent him by the Pope by way of "Signor Marcello." This was presumably James I's *Basilikon doron*. RP thought it should be answered without offence to the author or state as far as might be.

[5] See J. Creswell, *Responsio ad calumnias*, (I) A.V.9, p. 260.

[6] (13) 71–73.

[7] Ibid., 60–63.

[8] RP to Aldobrandino, 6.v.1604, Rome; (IV) Fo. Borgh.III, 124.G.2, ff.49r–50v, Italian.

[9] Ibid.

On his return to England, Anthony Standen was imprisoned for a time in the Tower and on release kept under surveillance. Persons informed Pope Clement on May 11, "What they chiefly hold against him was that he revealed to the King of France, as soon as he left England, a secret proposal put to him by certain Huguenot leaders in Paris, in his capacity as the King of England's ambassador, that they could supply 60,000 men for any expedition he chose, provided he would declare himself head and captain-general of their religion." Henri IV was much incensed and swore that if he took arms against them, he would not leave one Huguenot in all France. Standen spoke of the matter too lightly in Venice and elsewhere, "as is proved from many letters written from those parts."[10] Unwilling to make the above the published reason for Standen's imprisonment, the English council claimed it was on account of the gifts sent from the Pope to Queen Anne. Persons apparently knew nothing about any of this, as he reminded the Pope, before he told him about it at Frascati, "when Standen was already in Paris."

Much ado was made in England about a letter allegedly from Persons found on Standen, and the Paris nuncio made this the cause of Standen's arrest. Persons admitted writing to Standen from Frascati in October, but at the Pope's order. It dealt only with Standen's proposal that Perron, bishop of Evreux, be sent to England. It contained nothing that James should not see. Indeed, the Jesuit hoped he would see it. In fact, the letter found on Standen was one of his own addressed to Persons, which came to the hands of the English ambassador in Paris. This was due to "the treachery . . . of one or other of the disaffected Englishmen residing in Paris who gave it out that it was a letter of [Persons's] in order to make him more odious, as if [he] had been the cause of Standen's imprisonment and peril."[11] Dr. Davison in Paris, a man "serious, sincerely pious and completely straightforward" gave Persons the full story. The nuncio gave Davison Persons's letter of October 1603, to be handed to Sir Anthony, and he carried out this request. Standen's reply only reached Davison some fifteen days after Standen's departure from Paris. It was brought to him by one of Persons's enemies in the English community and subsequently handed to "a certain Scot."[12] Persons solemnly, and altogether credibly, assured the Pope that he had never received this reply. "When the truth comes

---

[10] RP to Clement VIII, 11.v.1604; ibid., f.45 olim f.43. Rome; The "many letters" were possibly among the losses of 1773.

[11] Ibid.

[12] This person was given a copy by RP's instructions of his *The three conversions of England:* see Davison's letter. V. infra.

out, the nuncio, a very wise man, will know how far and whom he can trust among our people in Paris."[13]

This small episode throws light on the enormous difficulty the Vatican faced as it attempted to establish contact with James I and his government, especially because the King and his government had no particular motive or desire to foster such contact. The Jesuits were the obvious men for the Pope to trust; since these were distrusted by so many others, however, the Vatican could not lean on them too far without the appearance of partiality. In any case, the English in exile and at home who opposed the Jesuits had the better chance, however tenuous, of making contact with the persecutor. There was a serious attempt at Church reunion at this time, serious at any rate on the part of the Vatican, though it was obviously unable to accept the basic Protestant position. The Jesuits remained on the periphery. The first ecumenical attempts to circumvent the definitions of Trent were now in evidence. One of the "disaffected Englishmen" in Paris "is now beginning to talk of a free general council in conformity with the views of the King of England, saying further that the Council of Trent was free in name only and not in fact." As for Davison, already old and sick, he would be in "danger of death if it was known to the faction that he was passing information."[14]

Before mid-May, Persons had the text of the King's speech to Parliament, which opened on March 19 (O.S.), the first since the Parliament dissolved on December 19, 1601. Omitting "unseemly words used . . . against the Holy See," Persons translated or summarized, as the matter was relevant in the Roman context. The King seemed to be ready for "some relief for the Catholics," and negotiations were proceeding "through one of the privy councillors whose favour the Catholics bought secretly." But faith unfaithful might still keep them falsely true as they took their bribes and gave nothing in return. It was encouraging that no mention was made of Watson or Clark, or of the archpriest and Jesuits, "as the late queen was always wont to do." Less encouraging was the state of Persons's health. On July 17, excusing his absence from Aldobrandino's antechamber, he admitted, "I have now been in bed for more than two months with continuing bouts of fever which have finally resolved themselves into

---

[13] Ibid. RP also translates into Italian "part of the letter from Dr Davison, an Englishman in Paris" of 29.iii.1604. It acknowledged RP's letter of 7.ii. but was troubled that it made no mention of Davison's own of 25.i. "which went with one from Sir Anthony Standen for your reverence in reply to yours." Davison revealed that Standen's reply to RP had first been shown to the English ambassador before being "lost" on the way to Rome. But Davison did not know this loss for certain and wished to find out.

[14] Ibid.

triple quartan agues."[15] On September 12 he wrote to Creswell, significantly by the hand of Brother John Dilly, on the way to Tivoli "for change of air for so much as my ague still endureth."

William Weston, following the General's wish, was to stay on at Valladolid for at least another year. The General hoped that Weston, a man of more than ordinary spiritual gifts, might "help much the peace of the scholars and moderate their humour of being Benedictines." There and everywhere the adversary seemed to triumph. "His Holiness here is easy to hear complaints. . . . In fine, Father mine,"—Creswell—"you and I are most battered at for that we stand at the stern; and though by God's grace it diminisheth not my courage in God's cause, yet maketh me more circumspect."[16] He warned Creswell, who was much more choleric and less urbane than Persons, not to take part in factions against Fr. Peralta. He had been rector "some twelve years" and his experience and integrity were not to be lightly discarded. Creswell must also avoid any rift with the Spanish Jesuits, "which would be our ruin." Touching relations with the students, there was a difference between solicitude and overwatchfulness. "Absolutely the best way to quiet and hold peaceable our youth is to let them alone and be sparing in dealing with them, for the more solicitous and watchful we will seem to be . . . which they call jealousy, the worse they are." Nor should Creswell show displeasure towards those who wished to join the Order of St. Benedict.[17]

Creswell had put in hard work for the colleges in Spain since 1592. "He was not a diplomat, nor a great educator. Instead he worked tirelessly in the manifold details of somehow keeping the colleges going. His constant reports and reminders assured the royal grants and the approval of the Council of State and the Court; undoubtedly his work was essential to the survival of the colleges."[18] At the same time, he could not brook opposition or play a waiting game once he was convinced of the rightness of his cause. His relations with Francis de Peralta had begun well, but friction developed over questions of jurisdiction and authority. Differences of national temperament contributed much to a crisis in the relations between English and Spanish Jesuits by September 1604.[19] Persons's instincts were always on

---

[15] (IV) F.Borgh. III,124.G.2, f.51r/v, Italian, from the VEC, signed only(?).

[16] (II) f.458. Grene's summary seems inadequate, although it quotes from the original letter presumably destroyed in 1773. It answers Creswell's "soli" of 20.vii.1604.

[17] Ibid., f.340.

[18] A. J. Loomie, (59) 203f. There is nothing in this short life of Creswell (Chapter VI) on his relations with Peralta this year.

[19] See F. J. Price, S.J., to RP, 10 and 24.viii.1604, both letters mentioned in RP

the side of authority and especially on the side of those who could make or break the work of the English mission. He never lost sight of the essential fact that the Spaniards were hosting exiles who in the last resort were largely without resources save what the Spanish could spare for them from their own pressing needs.

John Price and Henry Tichborne shared Creswell's viewpoint regarding the Spanish scene. They wrote to Persons on August 10 and 24, and Persons replied to them on October 15 notwithstanding a fit of ague. He defended Peralta vigorously, referring to a "large Spanish letter of Fr Creswell" which seemed to go beyond "a plain invective," comparing this unfavorably with "the truly moderate writing of Fr Peralta himself" and of others.[20] Creswell aggravated the situation, Persons thought, by going to Malaga "in these heats"—seasonal or choleric?—although a very sick man, to get Peralta replaced. The contention had now fallen out so completely into the open that Aquaviva had to intervene. He agreed to the idea of changing the rector at Valladolid but insisted that it should be "done quietly." Peralta was ready to go but wanted his own side of the case, reasonably enough, to be heard first. It was, of course, important to keep the students out of this kind of contention. Creswell was therefore bidden to return to Valladolid and "treat the matter with more secrecy and less contentiousness." The General and Persons would then do their best to settle things according to his "liking and contentment."[21]

Aquaviva had no intention of interfering unnecessarily with the vice-prefect of the English Jesuits in Spain. "Principal and extraordinary matters" needing his attention included "the changes of persons of the Society from one seminary to another, or to any place out of the seminary and of their offices therein, as also principal contracts and buildings of moment." In urgent cases, the vice-prefect had full discretionary powers. Creswell was therefore by no means unfairly circumscribed in his office. However, he was urged to cooperate fully with the local provincial while being subject to rectors "in discipline and governing of the house." All was to be effected by "moderation and friendly conference."[22] It is remarkable, not that two races as proud and uncompromising as the Spanish and the English should have found it difficult to live together at all times, but that they should have managed it for any time at all. In any case, the conduct of a del Rio could

---

to Price, 11.x.1604, Tivoli; (I) Anglia.A.III, No. 45, in Bro. John Dilly's hand, signed by RP.

[20] (I) Anglia.A.III, No. 46, contemp. copy.

[21] Ibid.

[22] See "Rules for the English Mission" translated from H. More in (16) 298–307.

hardly be defended even by the Spaniards, and the fact that two able and well-balanced English Jesuits agreed with Creswell is significant.[23] Persons virtually admitted in a letter to Warford of October 15 that diplomacy largely determined his own stance. If all had been done through him and "reason alone" and in secrecy, "a change might have been made." As it was, he had to weigh "the honour of our nation against him who is presumed to have laboured many years faithfully for us in that place." Warford was further accused of increasing rather than allaying Creswell's misgivings, even suggesting that there was an estrangement between him and Persons. Certainly, the General held Creswell in high regard.[24]

Amid all the distractions, Persons the author managed to produce about this time *An instruction and direction for the spiritual helpe of such Inglish gentlewomen as desyre to lead a more retired and recollected life than the ordinarie in Ingland doth yeald.*[25] It was meant for ladies living in the world who wanted "a more grave, staid and retired kind of life" but could not embrace "the monastical life for the many lets which our country yieldeth against that holy purpose at this present." The book was based on the writer's experience of what he had seen abroad, especially in Italy and Spain, where many preferred to live a retired life at home rather than enter a convent.[26] He described a typical arrangement. Having assured themselves of their "temporal portions," a group came together "in some house of their own, or some part . . . of their friends' house." After "particular devotions" they met every morning for work with the needle or something "fit for their estates" to the accompaniment of spiritual reading and edifying conversation. In the afternoon they could be visited by friends and relatives, including "religious men," to discuss spiritual matters and hear exhortations, although this was usually left to their chaplain. The "more ancient among them" assumed the role of a quasi mother superior.

They only went out together and saw to it that companions were of like minds with themselves. They dressed like other women "but after the common sort with great modesty"; "matrons" tended to black, while the "younger sort" could adopt "more liberty of apparel." Some of them took vows on a personal not a community basis with the advice of their confessor. A vow of obedience could be made to "the

---

[23] See RP to Henry Tichbourne, 16.x.1604, Rome; (I) Anglia.A.III, No. 47, "soli." RP feared he had been drawn into the quarrel by others. Also s. to W. Warford, 15.x.1604; (II) f.421.

[24] Ibid.

[25] Contemp. copy of 30.x.1604; (I) Anglia.A.VI, No. 53, f.259.

[26] See (II) f.340, where the date 30.x. is given. The greater part of the document (No. 53 above) is missing.

ghostly father" and even the "spiritual mother," but only on a temporary basis with the possibility of renewal. A vow of chastity "virginal, vidual or matrimonial" could be taken, but the last only with the husband's consent. Married women, then, were not excluded. They might even take an attenuated vow of poverty, providing themselves only with necessities and giving the rest to God and the poor. The presence of such people in a house would not only bring God's blessing and give a good example but "greatly help also to the virtuous education of their young children." Such a way of life was more difficult in England but not impossible, since the divine "assistance is always greater where the impediments and hindrances be more strong." This information was supplied in answer to Garnet's inquiries and was probably based on Anne Vaux and her friends.[27]

About mid-November Persons moved to Naples *ex medicorum consilio*. Some said, according to inspired rumor, that he had been "commanded to depart Rome." Persons's friends took the trouble to deny this in a letter to England of February 26, 1605.[28] Thomas Owen acted as his vice-rector in Rome.[29] There was at this time a separation even more ominous. By the end of 1604, a rift no longer to be concealed developed between Persons and Creswell.

The Fifth General Congregation of 1593 brought victory to the General and those who wanted the continued unity of the Society, but it left many of the defeated in Spain nursing injured pride. Persons's contribution was not unknown, and there was something like closure in the Spanish ranks against the English strangers in their midst. This is evident from Creswell's letters and even from what can be read between the lines in Persons's letters while he was still in Spain. In an apologia written later consequent upon a foiled attempt to found a college in Madrid in 1613, Creswell described the demoralizing effect of Spanish lack of interest, as he took it, in the English foundations. The basic difficulty was that, as always in Church appointments as with others, there were not enough of the best to go round. Inevitably, the provincials kept their best men for Spanish appointments. The sec-

---

[27] Ibid.

[28] (II) f.340. This attestation was copied originally on f.785, in the portion of (II) that is lost. See (II) f.476: likewise "some other letters of no great moment this yeare 1604 kept in the archives of the English College." Letters of 6 and 9.xii. mentioned "Antony Copley, penitent, for having slandered F. Persons." Copley, involved in some way with the main and by plots still awaiting fuller investigation, was allowed to go abroad about this time, probably to spy for R. Cecil.

[29] Thomas Owen puts "V.R." after his signature, referring to himself in Copley's testimonial as "Collegii Anglorum de Urbe Vice Rector," (VI) Anglia 31.II, f.285.

ond—or third—best were all that could be spared for the English. An obvious way to improve the situation on paper was to discourage complaint. As Creswell described it, the English, and especially students, were inhibited from complaining against rectors, since they knew that their names and not merely their complaints were likely to be revealed to the superiors concerned. What followed might be not so much retribution as persecution. They could not even write to Rome, because when complaints came back to Spain they had to be attributed to the English, who were clearly doing their best to destroy the Spaniards' good name. So "they excused rather than corrected faults, and the greater they were the more they excused them to overcome any appearance of having defaulted."[30]

The extraordinary expansion of the Society of Jesus under Aquaviva had its adverse side. In Spain at least, men had been admitted who were far from corresponding to the elitist ideal of St. Ignatius. So great was the demand for Jesuits to meet the burgeoning needs of education and the Catholic Reformation generally that too little attention could be paid to quality, in order to ensure quantity. Creswell's comments may include the exaggerations of frustration, but they purvey some important truth. He claimed to live for years "between Scylla and Charybdis." If he left rectors to their own devices, there were almost daily incidents "unworthy of superiors and unacceptable to their subjects." This was the other side of John Cecil's coin and may help to account for his "defection." Others might persevere but leave with many tales to discredit their teachers. If Creswell brought pressure to bear, the rectors "stirred up the whole province" and turned the issue into one of race and national interest. Objections were raised against rectors wasting money on junketing and lavish entertainment of their friends. In the warmth of the protective fur of a state religion, the lice multiplied. Official visitors might protest, but after their departure all reverted to normality. The students were embittered at seeing money raised with difficulty for their own upkeep being thrown away. Local keepers of college accounts were not above suspicion of manipulating them to obscure the record of extravagance. The rector at Seville was reported at one time to defy not only the orders of the visitor but even of the General. Blood relatives had offices with or under him or were province consultors, so that redress was impossible.

At Valladolid the students were looking back to the halcyon days of Rodrigo de Cabredo. They now felt that the people who mattered took no interest in them. Once again they were forced to hear

---

[30] "Ex responsione ad calumnias contra P. Josephum Creswelum, scripta ab ipso P. Creswelo," (I) A.V.9, 239–69. See also "The later life and writings of Joseph Creswell, S.J., 1556–1623," (10) x.1979, 79–144; A. J. Loomie, (59) 182–229.

philosophy lectures at unsocial hours at another house of the Society to avoid a clash with the university. This involved a literally killing journey four times a day under a merciless sun. Many fell into fever. Nine died in one year. Cabredo had remedied this but his successors reverted to the original system. The teachers were also changed often, perhaps three or four times during the course, with resulting confusion of ideas. Sometimes the lecturers did not know Latin well enough to go beyond their script. Further attempts to explain more fully in Spanish hardly helped students in the first year, who for the most part thus lost the rudiments of logic and philosophy on which the rest depended. Worse still, "there were daily molestations" from some of these preceptors; and, if they were subsequently dismissed from the Society for loose morals, the damage had been done.

Creswell and his English confreres put up with all this for years for the sake of the seminary. The limit was reached when a man altogether unqualified for the task, Christopher Suarez, succeeded Cabredo. A conscientious visitor removed him, but only just in time to save the seminary from shipwreck. After his removal, Suarez initiated a campaign against Persons, the principal agent of his downfall, and then against Creswell, Persons's successor. The campaign included a "notorious little book . . . written against the English" and later published under the auspices of Christopher Suarez.

All of these misfortunes led Persons to draw up his rules for the mission. The General saved the English seminaries in Spain by adopting them. However, the rector at Valladolid could claim that the province had its own rights, since Spanish affairs, in accordance with papal decrees, were subject to local provincials and rectors. Creswell himself was partly responsible for this unhappy arrangement, for during his Roman stay in 1590 he not only procured but also composed the papal diplomas making these seminaries subject to the Society and seemingly on these terms. Some ambiguity in the wording led rectors to suppose that, while their appointment depended on the General, their subsequent activities were under the eye only of the Holy See or the provincial. Designed to protect the seminaries from arbitrary treatment by provincials, these arrangements did not envision that rector and provincial might combine on occasion against what appeared to be the best interests of the students. Persons tried to get the Valladolid foundation deed altered in Rome, but the only practicable solution was to put in a rector who would obey the General and through him the rules for the seminaries drawn up by Persons and Creswell. Small wonder if in all this some of the students turned hopefully to the Order of St. Benedict!

So obnoxious did the harassment of the students become that on April 9, 1604, Persons wrote to Creswell about transferring the Valladolid seminary to another place.[31] He concluded, "We think that some of our Spanish Fathers need a good penance for the very small humanity they show us, usurping every day something else in that seminary." Persons advised Creswell, meanwhile, to negotiate with the local procurator, and "grant him all that seemed just." The situation had not improved when Persons wrote to Pareces, the rector, on April 1, 1608.[32] But while Creswell and Persons agreed about Valladolid, a difference of view persisted with regard to Peralta, rector at Seville. Persons wished him to stay for all the good he had done in the past. Creswell wished him removed for all the good he was failing to do in the present. A difference of view became a rift.

---

[31] Letter quoted in (I) A.V.9. V. supra.

[32] See below, chap. 23.

Chapter Twenty-one

Year of Crisis: 1605

At the beginning of 1605, Persons was still preoccupied with the problems of the colleges in exile, notably Seville. On January 8 he rebuked Warford, Tichbourne, and Price "for their uncharitable factions against Fr Peralta, rector of Seville."[1] As for Creswell, his relations with him were near the breaking point. Indeed, the only chance of reestablishing mutual understanding lay in a visit to Rome, "you having entered into those apprehensions and suspicions of me." He hoped Creswell would not make difficulties over this.[2] Addressing himself to the students, including priests, at Seville, he regretted their "common letter" and one similar sent to the General. All the same, he was "much comforted" by their "modest and moderate manner of writing without any demonstration of spleen or passion, which . . . is the way to negotiate with superiors."[3] He saw the difficulty with regard to the aging Peralta, but held out no hope of immediate remedy. However, he would advise Walpole to persuade the rector to remove any unreasonable burdens if such had been imposed. Meanwhile, they must be "patient, humble and observant of rule and collegial discipline," letting "superiors dispose." They must always remember "we are banished men and live on alms, and must not expect to be so well accommodated in a strange country as in our own."

Anthony Copley was another who, excusing himself by the difficulty of the times, found it hard to settle in occupation or allegiance. Somewhere in the periphery of the main and by plots of 1603, he was imprisoned and released on pardon but on condition of going into exile.[4] This meant, in the context of the times, that he either had rendered services to the government or was about to for the future.

---

[1] RP to W. Warford, H. Tichbourne, and F. J. Price, 8.i.1605, Rome; (II) f.489.

[2] RP to Creswell, 8.i.1605, Naples; (II) f.423. Grene indicates several omissions in his own quotations.

[3] (II) f.298.

[4] Docquet, 18.viii.1604 (OS); (29) 1603–10, 143. He was described as of middle height, with a red beard, aged about 35, with a cyst near the right eye in the angle of nose and cheekbone. See T. Owen, S.J., to Borghese, 24.xi.1604, VEC; (I) Anglia.A.III, No. 48; copy endd. by RP.

He went to France, hoping to get from the authorities "letters of mediation to his Majesty for the pardoning of his banishment." He tried the same in Brussels. He also hoped for a Spanish pension but "found little encouragement therein."[5] He was in Rome by November 1604 visiting Borghese and, later, Thomas Owen in the English College on November 24. One of his self-appointed tasks was to ask pardon of Persons, "against whom he had written so many false and scandalous things"; but it had all been at Bagshaw's dictation, whom he took to be entirely trustworthy. After discovering his mistake, his first desire was to be reconciled to God and then to man. Owen as well as Copley knew that "those books of his and Watson's" and company, in which they wrote "many things against the pope's authority," were "still in the hands of the Inquisition." Copley hoped for the finalization of his pardon by the spring of 1605, so that he could return to England. Meanwhile, he proceeded to Naples to seek out Persons. Evidently, he had decided to wring all he could from the exiles in the way of money and information, and especially from the Jesuits, who had the reputation of wielding most of the modest influence which the exiles could command.

Copley found Persons in Naples early in December. Indulgent as always towards his fellow countrymen down on their luck, whatever their credibility, Persons wrote letters of recommendation dated December 6 and 9,[6] and gave him fifteen ducats. Wasting no time, he declared his intention of returning to Rome on the eleventh, but as a changed man. "By your good hand I am so moulded from my former fashion of a mistaken man; and so nox nocti indicavit scientiam. . . . I mean, nox tribulationis nocti erroris mei"; and finished by praising Fr. Robert's "singular endeavours in God's cause and our country . . . these many years."[7] Back in Rome in January 1605, Copley received from Thomas Owen a formal testimonial in Latin obligingly drawn up for him on the seventeenth, witnessing to a change of heart which included reconciliation with the archpriest and the Jesuits. Copley made the round of the churches, repudiated his books as "false and scandalous" and behaved generally like a reformed character.[8]

It is possible that at this stage Copley's change of heart was as sincere as might be in such a man. At all events, a writing in his hand

---

[5] Sir Thomas Edmondes to Earl of Salisbury, 10. 11.vii.1605 (O.S.); (XIII) Stowe MSS, 168, f.67r. See (VII) SP 77,7.1, f.200r.

[6] (II) f.476.

[7] A. Copley to RP, 10.xii.1604, Naples; (I) Anglia.A.III, No. 49, a.l.s.

[8] (VI) Anglia 31.II, ff.284r–85v. For Copley's books against the Jesuits, see STC, Nos. 5735, 5736. A signed and sealed copy of the testimonial was given to Copley for his own use.

dated March 2 and handed to the English ambassador in Venice set out "to exculpate Fr Persons."[9] The ambassador was neither pleased nor impressed, but he got a detailed account of Copley's dealings with Persons to forward to King James. Copley reported that Persons had never actively opposed James's title or succession, never said that the English nobility should be reduced in status, and knew of no money being taken out of England for the exclusive benefit of Jesuits. He never handled, even through agents, letters attacking third parties. He had never tried to bring about Bagshaw's death through the English government and had nothing to do with the alleged murder of Fisher, even if his death might be taken as a judgment on his shameless calumnies. Persons was not the executor of Englefield's last will and testament. Neither did he defraud Anthony Copley's eldest son of a legacy supposedly left him by Sir Francis.[10] The chief interest of all this and much else lies in the slanderous tales evidently going the rounds to make Persons the principal villain of the English piece. It seems fair to take Copley's present disclaimer as an indication of the value of such things. "In my . . . conference with Fr Persons and other his confreres I found the thought and conversation of all of them full of affection and loyalty towards his Majesty. . . . Spiteful tongues . . . in every part of Christendom" tried to promote hatred of the Jesuits, which in the event turned to "the disservice of his Majesty." Copley mentioned Watson's conversion in the face of death. He hoped, somewhat naively no doubt, that the ambassador would help to restore him to the King's good graces. If Copley hoped for fortune and favor in Rome, he was to be disappointed. The summer of 1605 saw him back in Brussels and trying his threadbare luck with another English ambassador, Sir Thomas Edmondes. Edmondes understood his instructions and the mind of the Earl of Salisbury well enough not to be forthcoming. On July 10/17, 1605, he reported Copley's coming to the earl. This time Copley said nothing about the Roman interlude and his reconciliation with the Jesuits. Even so, Edmondes rebuffed him without pity, refusing him not only a passport but reminding him of the consequences of returning without leave, which could mean "the forfeiting of his pardon." Another such adventurer also involved in the "main and by plots" was Sir Griffin Markham, who had likewise been pardoned

---

[9] "L'originale in francese di mano del detto Copleo con questo il quale a me egli diede, sicome in inglese haveva fatto all'Ambasciatore [inglese]"; (VI) ibid., ff.286r–87v, Italian. "Certaine principall poynts . . . ," the English document of which a copy was given to the English ambassador in Venice; (I) Anglia A.VII, No. 55. "Præcipua quædam capita de quibus in colloquio cum P. Personio Neapoli habito idem mihi satisfecit, ex qua satisfactione in conscientia me obligari ad pacem cum eo et Societate componendam judicavi . . . ," (I) Anglia.A.III, No. 50, signed "A.C."

[10] (I) Anglia.A.III, No. 50. V. supra.

conditionally, becoming, in effect, a spy in Europe.[11] After the latest repulse, Copley trailed back to Rome and the English College, where he stayed from January 24 until April 3, 1606.[12]

Another traveler who, rather against the probabilities, was allowed to return to Rome was Sir James Lindsay, who had brought letters from the Pope to James VI in 1602. Lindsay reached Rome early in 1605. "Doubtless exceeding his instructions, Lindsay gave Clement the impression that the king's conversion was imminent." Of course it was not, but Queen Anne was at least dallying with Catholicism at this time, and rumor was rife.[13] Sir Robert Cecil certainly stood in need of the Gunpowder Plot, which occurred most conveniently for him in November. Meanwhile, Lindsay was graciously received in the English College. With the former experience of the Anglo-Welsh problem still fresh in mind, Persons rejected his idea of uniting English and Scottish students in the same house. "I would be as glad to see both English and Scotch men and Irish also together in one house as any man living, and have equal affection to them all that be virtuous. Yet cannot but fear from divers and just causes that . . . then . . . there would be greater division between both nations than there now is."[14]

Successful English colonization in the New World began early in the seventeenth century. The first settlements of religious refugees were laid down by the Puritans in New England, which may be taken as dating from the Mayflower expedition of 1620. However, a project to found a settlement for English Catholic refugees in North America began about the same time as the commercially inspired Virginia scheme. Inevitably it came to Persons's attention. He produced a memorandum on the subject in March this year.[15] Not unsympathetic to "Mr Winslade's" project, he saw too many obstacles in the path. King James and his council would oppose it as being dishonorable and dangerous: "dishonourable" because they would be forcing "natural subjects to . . . abandon their own country in respect of persecution;

---

[11] From Brussels; (XIII) Stowe MS 168, f.67r; see (VII) SP 77/7/1, f.200r.

[12] (12), Vol. 7, *The Pilgrim Book* of the VEC, p. 580. Was Copley "a certain Englishman" who in 1605 "for some days received food and slept twice"? See ibid., p. 579.

[13] (15) 221.

[14] RP to ?, 1605; (II) f.437. This letter was among several more of 1605 now lost. RP to ?, 10.ii.1605; ibid., f.489. Thomas Pound's trouncing in the Star Chamber and unjust condemnation prompted RP to exclaim that there was "little hope of any good by King James."

[15] RP to "Mr Winslade," 18.iii.1605, Naples; (I) Anglia.A.III, No. 53. "My judgment about transferringe Englishe Catholiques to the northern partes for inhabitinge those partes and converting those barbarous people to Christianitie."

dangerous in that those men going abroad with averted mind might join together" and then come back for their kinsfolk. The King would oppose this, prevent any further development, and that would be the end of it. Even with persecution, the "better and richer" sort would not wish to leave England, while poorer men without their backing would be largely ineffective. Furthermore, any depletion in numbers of Catholics in England, especially of the more enterprising, could only weaken the whole movement and invite authority to tighten even further the screw of persecution, making the entry of priests and exit of students even more difficult.

Winslade's idea was to settle some thousand "husbandmen, labourers," and craftsmen, but where the beginning should be made was problematic. The King of Spain and his advisers were "jealous" that no stranger should set foot on Spanish soil in the Indies; and it was only with the greatest difficulty that an individual "could get licence once to go thither," and even then with great "sureties." So how would they react to a thousand? And members of a hostile nation, even though all of them were Catholic? The Spanish attitude was not simply dog-in-the-manger. The Spaniards knew they had the whole world ranged against them, and a colony of the kind projected could be a place where in time a hostile fleet might find shelter and support. With a long experience of piracy, French as well as English, they had lost no time in evicting the Frenchmen from Nova Francia. Initial costs would be prohibitive. And what of "those wild people, wild beasts, unexperienced air, [and] unprovided lands?" One aspect of the project pleased Persons, namely, the prospect of converting the heathen around them. Indeed, "I would desire myself to go in the journey, shutting my eyes to all other difficulties . . . but yet see that we do not deal here for ourselves only but for others also." In any case, the matter would need to be "broken" first in England and Spain—he could not undertake the latter—but then he would do what he could in Rome. "And this is all that I can say in this matter."[16]

By the end of March, Persons was beginning to chafe against exile. In two letters he begged Aquaviva's leave to return to Rome.[17] He was distressed to hear of the way matters were developing in the Spanish seminaries and of quarrels among the Jesuits. With scant justice he laid the blame on Creswell as "virtually the only cause." He should be summoned to Rome to give an account of himself. On April 1 Persons wrote to Creswell, making no attempt to conceal his disapproval. Creswell's letters over the past few months had doubled the

---

[16] Ibid. The new colony would have been called Florimbega.

[17] See 31.iii. and 1.iv.1605, Naples; (II) f.424.

effect of his fever and robbed him of sleep. He urged him to "reflect a little more" and see if what he wrote was really "true or false."[18] Creswell for his part resented Persons's failure to accept his view of the Spanish scene or to persuade the General to do likewise. Brutus seemed no longer to love his Cassius. Persons only admitted one of his numerous accusations, namely, that he procured his summons to Rome "without delay for consultation on some matters and to give [him] satisfaction in others which seemed impossible by letter."[19]

Persons's stay in Naples, with its celebrated thermal baths, would have been sufficiently justified on health grounds, but a letter of mid-April 1605 reveals more. Fr. Robert complained to the General "of the injury done him by Pope Clement in condemning him to exile— not judicially—without examining his case."[20] Persons's Jesuit colleagues were doing their best to scotch the idea that he had been sent from Rome in disgrace in 1604. Dom John Roberts, O.S.B., was doing his best to counteract this disclaimer, an indication of the poor relations between English Benedictines and Jesuits at this time. The Jesuit Anthony Hoskins in England interviewed Dom Anselm Beck on May 28, when he tried to correct what he took to be misinformation.[21] Since both were relying on outside sources and felt the need to defend their country right or wrong, as it were, the conversation ended, alas, in confrontation. Beck's parting shot was that there were two kinds of people, those who supported the Jesuits and those who supported the truth. Beck had been a student at the Venerable English College during the troubles and retained bitter memories. No Jesuit, thought Beck, could be believed since no Jesuit told the truth. Even the spiritual works of the Society, such as giving the Exercises of St. Ignatius, he regarded as highly suspect. Before there could be peace between the orders, the Jesuits must prove that they had never impeded a vocation to the Order of St. Benedict, that they had never opposed the setting up of a Benedictine mission in England, that they had never calumniated any Benedictine, and that they had never tried to get any Benedictine turned out of any house in England. There were more

---

[18] RP to J. Creswell, 1.iv.1605, Naples; (II) f.426. Acknowledges JC's of 19.ii. Grene leaves a space of two lines at this point, perhaps with the intention of adding later entries found undecipherable at the time.

[19] Ibid.

[20] RP to Aquaviva, 15.iv.1605, Naples; (II) f.494, English and Italian. Grene observed, "The letter should all be copyed—he understood this order of the pope by a letter of Fr General."

[21] A. Hoskins to H. Garnet, 29.vi.1605 (O.S.?); London; (VI) Anglia 31.II, ff.279r–80r, Latin. "On the abortive attempt to make peace with the Benedictine Fathers of the English nation."

general accusations against the Society, with a final threat to send a report of all complaints to Rome. Hoskins concluded that peace was impossible on the terms offered, "and we would make further attempts in vain. It is an old and incurable wound." By this time many English Benedictines had joined forces with the appellants, thinking with them that if the withdrawal of the Jesuits from the English scene could bring peace with the government, it was a small price to pay even if the Jesuits had been impeccable; and experience of the colleges abroad proved for many that they were not. The worsening relations between two significant orders was all the more tragic, since both were producing martyrs in England. Dom John Roberts, descendant of a princely house in Wales, was the first prior of the English Benedictine house at Douai; he crowned several periods of banishment with martyrdom at Tyburn on December 10, 1610. He was thirty-four years old.[22]

Misunderstanding continued likewise between Persons and Creswell, who wrote frequently with bitterness.[23] although on March 11, his letter was "more mild and friendly than many of [his] former."[24] Unfortunately, a gap in Creswell's known correspondence between 1598 and 1605 hides the detailed progress of the misunderstanding from us. There was no hint of disagreement before Persons left Spain for Rome in 1597. Creswell wrote always in generous and even glowing terms of Persons, as in a letter to Aldobrandino of January 23, 1597. Certainly, he felt the increased burden of work with Persons's departure. He must also have experienced a considerable change in the climate of the Spanish court with the death of Philip II in 1598. One can only speculate as to whether Persons could have improved on Creswell in dealing with the new king. Creswell was careful not to spread alarm and despondency unnecessarily, claiming that in the seminaries "peace and concord flourished." He was writing selectively rather than untruthfully, we may charitably suppose.[25] It

---

[22] See (35) V.

[23] We have to rely on Grene's summaries. He based his judgment on RP to Creswell, 9.iv and 23.iv.1605; (II) f.423. Unfortunately, Grene found the matter too "ungratefull" to purvey details.

[24] RP to Creswell, 23.iv. V. supra. Creswell seems to have been very sensitive to criticism or opposition, but there was no hint of rivalry in the correspondence between RP and JC from 1592–98; (IV) F.Borgh. III,124 and I.448. JC to Aldobrandino, 23.i.1597, Madrid; ibid., F.Borgh. III.G.2: "If he (RP) does not give your . . . Lordship all the satisfaction that can be desired from a responsible religious and faithful servant . . . of the Apostolic See, I do not wish [you] to give me any further credence." There is a gap in the known correspondence of JC and RP between 1598–1605, so the origin of the estrangement is unknown. Sir Charles Cornwallis, English ambassador in Spain, learned of it and informed R. Cecil; (64) II, 226; (59) 217f.

[25] (IV) F.Borgh. III, 124.G.2, f.103, Italian a.l.s.; ibid., JC's letters to Rome

must be remembered that before us are the relations between two hard-driven, conscientious men, coping with at least partial failure and disappointment and pushed to the point of exhaustion, not to say breakdown. On August 1, 1607, twenty-seven students put their names to a letter scarcely intended to bring Persons peace of mind. "General disgust" had been growing this year thanks to "diverse innovations." They complained in effect of overwork and too little free time or recreation. Health suffered; but, if any fell ill, "no sick man was looked unto unless his fellow scholar would play the infermero, and those who have died . . . are chiefly those which wholly abandoned their exercise." They appealed to Creswell, but the Jesuit staff, including Richard Walpole presumably, told them he "had nothing to do in it." Appeal to the provincial, of which Walpole disapproved, brought no redress. "We were circumvented and posted from one to another these two years." They seemed to blame Walpole mainly, "who is far from our sincere affection for this and diverse others his inventions, as they are from all sincere proceedings." Protest was taken as "sedition" with the threat of expulsion. They asked that "we may have recourse to Fr Rector or Fr Creswell in all things as heretofore, who now have their hands tied in the very smallest matters by your letters to Fr Richard." The plea was made in moderate terms, ending with an appeal for Persons's "accustomed kindness" towards them.[26]

In October Creswell was summoned to Rome for consultation.[27] However he fared with his fellow Jesuits, he had the consolation of a good relationship with the English ambassador, Sir Charles Cornwallis. But Creswell was soon to learn that the implacable Salisbury, anxious to convince the world that there was no such thing as a good Jesuit, bracketed him with other Jesuits and Hugh Owen, whom he later wished to implicate in the Gunpowder Plot.[28] Salisbury was not alone in his reservations concerning Jesuits. Replying to a letter of about April 20, Thomas Owen could give Persons "no consolation at all" regarding his return to Rome, so he was asked to bring the matter up once a week until Aquaviva took action. Persons wanted to know at least who was responsible for his banishment, "Spain, France, the pope etc. *[sic]*," how long he was required to stay away, and what he should say to inquirers. He knew well that he must abide by the General's decision. One cheering piece of news from Spain was that a certain

---

1594–98.

[26] See CRS 30(1930), 90f. Copy.

[27] (59) 218.

[28] See (64)II, 273, 283, quoted (59) 219. Creswell addressed a frank but courteous letter to Salisbury on 20.vi.1605, appealing for toleration for papists and giving assurances of political loyalty; (XIII) Cotton MS, Vespasian.C.XIII, ff.207r–8v, copy.

Donna Alvisa had offered a "donation for the use of the noviceship in Flanders." Not without a hint of pressure, Persons told Owen to "lay it together with other Spanish papers" until he came. Meanwhile, whatever else divided the English Fathers in Spain, they all agreed that Creswell should go to Rome as their spokesman.[29]

Clement VIII, the great obstacle to Persons's return to Rome, died on March 5. Persons had written to the cardinals Farnese and Zapata, pillars of the Spanish interest, who used their influence with the new pope, Paul V, elected on April 27. Persons was able to return to Rome two months earlier than his doctors could have wished, but he would brook no further delay in view of the "contradictory letters and relations from Spain." These, added to Creswell's "disgust and disunion" from Persons, were causing Aquaviva and Perez, the Spanish assistant, much perplexity. It was time for God to "see to the rest."[30]

Joseph Creswell shared none of Persons's enthusiasm for a journey Romewards, and to the impatient Persons showed signs of foot dragging. The latter considered it urgent that Creswell appear in Rome, because observers had begun to regard the disagreement between the Fathers as schism, a view that some traced back to Creswell.[31] Writing from the English College, Rome, on May 13, Persons, Owen, and Edward Coffin signed a letter asking the General "to remedy the scandalous faction."[32] Creswell resisted any visit to Rome; and in a significant move Aquaviva, while urging him to come, did not put him under formal obedience. In a letter of July, Creswell admitted he would have liked to be in Rome "for a few days" to honor the memory of Clement VIII, who recognized him as a "man of truth which he greatly loved himself." It is at least likely that Creswell's letters, added to what he heard from others, determined the Pope's attitude not only to Persons but to the whole Society of Jesus. Creswell did more than drop dark hints. "I believe I could have given [Clement] entire satisfaction concerning the Society's affairs, which were represented to him differently from the way they really are and . . . have been, in fact, since I left his Holiness."[33] Few men served God with a pure intention. Most were like the Indians of Peru "who, even

---

[29] RP to T. Owen, n.d., endd. "maggio 1605," Naples; (I) Anglia.A.III, No. 54, a.l.s. Grene's note: "F. Persons Tivoli." But there was nothing in the contents to suggest RP had left Naples. Or was Tivoli as close as he dared to come to Rome while awaiting a call to finish the journey?

[30] RP to Creswell, 9 and 23.iv.1605; (II) f.423.

[31] Ibid.

[32] (II) 489.

[33] J. Creswell to a cardinal unidentified, 8.vii.1605, Valladolid; (VI) Anglia 36, ff.231r–34v, Italian copy; (VII) 31/9 f.113 from (IV) F.Borgh. II.

after their conversion to our holy faith, continue to worship their little idol in secret." *Prudentia carnis* weighed too much. Creswell emerged as successful in his resistance to a Roman visit, and by mid-May it was agreed that Richard Walpole should make the visit instead.[34]

Garnet reported a good deal of malaise among the Catholics in England as the new reign promised to be too much like the last. The only slender hope of improvement seemed to lie with the Spanish ambassador, who would reside in England now that peace with Spain was reestablished. Persons approached Philip III on the subject. The ambassador should not let himself be "easily taken in by the flatteries and deceits of heretics and politicians." He should distribute pensions to the archpriest and his assistants as well as Garnet, who now had "forty religious in his charge," but not to layfolk save "in very exceptional cases," since this led to "jealousies, complaints, resentments and other evils."[35] In the event, it would be a matter of finding something left over from the Spanish distributions to James's privy council! In accordance with international convention, peace with Spain meant that Englishmen could now serve in its forces abroad. Catholic gentlemen, cut off from any adequate public career in England, could serve in the armies of the archduke in Flanders. Persons proposed a panel of six to eight priests there to act as chaplains and give religious instruction to recruits. They would, it was hoped, return to England as lay apostles. But in view of so many spies and informers, an adequate screening device was essential. The four seminaries in Spain and Flanders must also be kept operative, since "almost entirely from them . . . the spiritual welfare of England . . . had its source." St. Omers was in some respects the most important of these, for it housed "more than one hundred young sons of gentlemen who were very important in England" and was "the seedbed of other seminaries."

Financial difficulties were everywhere chronic. Douai received on paper two thousand ducats per annum in alms from Philip; but, as no particular source was specified for them, they went unpaid for years. Valladolid had a more precise endowment but was still some three thousand ducats in debt. The Seville foundation had no endowment at all. Nevertheless, without Philip's help they could scarcely survive—or so the King should be persuaded. Peace with Spain meant that English ambassadors in Spain and Flanders could use their influence against the seminaries. This was chiefly significant in Valladolid, which was now the Spanish capital. This might be one good reason for

---

[34] RP to Philip III, 16.v.1605, Rome; (IX) Serie II, Leg. 2, contemp. copy; (VIII) E.843, No. 12.

[35] Ibid. For the Spanish pensions, see (65).

transferring the seminary to Salamanca. The ambassador's retinue as mainly "heretics, or politicians and spies" could be expected to use every means to corrupt the students and turn them into informers. They could then "hit at their relatives in England by finding out their identity." But in the last resort Persons had to leave all to Philip's good judgment.[36] In the event, Persons's worst fears were not realized. At least, not immediately. Sir Charles Cornwallis proved to be a humane and civilized man, with whom Creswell had a good understanding for some time.

At the end of May Persons wrote to Creswell again to urge unity with the other English Jesuits there as well as with himself. This was all the more important since some were suggesting that the offices of prefect and vice-prefect be abolished and the English institutions placed completely under local superiors.[37] As we have seen, by this time the General accepted Creswell's reluctance to come to Rome and told him to stay where he was.[38]

Paul V, refusing to continue the estrangements of his predecessor, received Persons, an old acquaintance, in audience before the end of June. It is likely that the new papal attitude towards Persons accounted for Creswell's ever-increasing unwillingness to come to Rome. Paul was sufficiently impressed with Persons to ask him to draw up a short memorandum on what might be done to combat heresy in northern Europe. Persons's prospectus took in twelve countries, including Muscovy, and dealt with numerous fortified towns and city-states in Protestant hands. His reflections made no very original contribution to the discussion, perhaps, but it is notable that he now insisted on the validity of spiritual weapons alone. Many would be interested in mission work among these nations, but so far there were "few pontiffs whose thoughts . . . [were] concerned with them."[39] It was also time to reconstitute the Congregation for the Propagation of the Faith, "instituted long ago but not kept in being." This could be more effective than "a multitude of committees and discussions." Inevitably, he tried to focus attention on England, where "more than in other kingdoms" there was "a definite inclination to preserve and restore the Catholic religion." Diplomatic pressure should be brought to bear on King James to make him grant "some little liberty," which the blood of so

---

[36] Ibid.

[37] RP to Creswell, 31.v.1605, Rome; (II) f.427. Creswell was warned against Fixer "as being so united to Dr Cecil, the most opposite to the Society that we have."

[38] Ibid., f.424. Grene's brief summary indicates no reason for this.

[39] RP to Paul V, 30.vi.1605, Rome; (XVIII) *Raccolta Mongardino*, Vol. 61, No. 4, Latin.

many martyrs had surely earned. The Catholics were quite prepared to pay for the sorry privilege of not being persecuted, although not to the extent of the crushing fines initiated under Elizabeth and now reimposed.[40]

By August 21 Aquaviva thought again about letting Creswell pass up the Roman visit. Indeed, he hoped Creswell would put himself as speedily as possible on the road to where all roads proverbially led.[41] But resistance continued. Warford had now joined Creswell, who continued to rail bitterly against Walpole as well as against Peralta and Persons, so that "all [were] scandalised thereat."[42]

All of which presumably took further toll of Persons's health. At all events he fell ill again. In mid-December he wrote to Possevino to include the information that since his return from Naples he had not been well, and so, on medical advice which this time he took, he had "written very litle indeed to [his] friends except about urgent and essential matters."[43] From Possevino—not from Creswell—he had disquieting news of Sir Charles Cornwallis. His attitude had become more hostile thanks to two recent conversions to Catholicism, that of his nephew and also of his chaplain, James Wadsworth, although the latter eventually returned to the Anglican fold. A Spanish Father informed Persons from Spain that "the person with whom his nephew left his letters and manuscripts"—Persons asked that the fact be kept secret—"found one from the ambassador urging him very earnestly to stand firm in his religion, and not to put any trust in the follies and stupidities—these were his words—which he had perceived in our Catholic religion in Italy and Spain." Cornwallis, for all Persons's hopes, remained a convinced Calvinist of the Anglican reform.

Possevino had information on Edmund Thornhill, a canon of Vicenza and avowed enemy of the Jesuits—a man by report "restless, unreliable and headstrong." He waged a determined campaign against the Society in England and Paris as well as Italy. Possevino thought he might still be won over if he could be persuaded to do the Ignatian Spiritual Exercises; but even the optimistic Persons caviled at this. He took Thornhill to be much to blame in the affair of Anthony Standen "and brought him to ruin." Persons also suspected the canon of persuading Standen to keep his mission secret from him with consequences which, in the event, proved disastrous to Standen himself.

---

[40] Ibid.

[41] RP to Creswell, 22.viii.1605, Rome; (II) f.427.

[42] See RP to W. Warford, 18.x.1605, Rome; ibid.

[43] RP to A. Possevino, 17.xii.1605, Rome; (VI) Opp.NN.333, f.282, Italian copy; ibid., Gal.93, ff.282r–83v.

Standen's exile to Italy had been imposed as a punishment for his indiscretion and, although Persons did not say so, doubtless to atone for past misdeeds by present spying. The prospect in England was bleak. The persecution of Catholics was severe. "Every day the prospect of a blood-bath grows nearer."[44]

---

[44] Ibid. Thornhill is not mentioned by name, but the context makes it clear he is meant.

Chapter Twenty-two

The Gunpowder Plot ═══
and a New Appeal: 1606 ═══

N ews of the Gunpowder Plot of November 5, 1605, traveled appropriately with the speed of sound rather than light. Not until mid-March of 1606 could Persons send the General a translation of the royal proclamation against the Jesuits John Gerard, Henry Garnet, and Oswald Tesimond, alias Greenway, whom Salisbury was anxious to implicate. They were described accurately in the proclamation, so that details must have come "from members of our household." Persons never doubted their innocence. "They have tried by one means or another to involve them, but I doubt not that is going to make their innocence clear, either alive or dead."[1] But their guilt was insisted on in newsletters from London of April 8 and 14. By this time Henry Garnet, captured at the end of January, had been tried, inevitably found guilty by the current rules, and awaited execution.[2]

---

[1] RP to Aquaviva, 18.iii.1606, Rome; (II) f.428. Much contemporary or near-contemporary documentation in D. Bartoli's *Collections;* (VI) Anglia 38.I. The two longest contemporary narratives are by John Gerard, S.J.; (I) A.IV.1, *Collectania C:* and Oswald Tesimond, S.J. (I) MS A.IV.4. Gerard's was printed in John Morris, S.J., *The Condition of Catholics under James I . . . ,* 2nd ed. (London, 1872); Tesimond's in *The Gunpowder Plot* (London: The Folio Society, 1973), trans. and ed. from the Italian. A good general bibliography with some indication of MS sources in Mark Nicholls, *Investigating the Gunpowder Plot* (London, 1991). See also his "Sir Charles Percy"; (10) 18, 237–50; also "Politics and Percies," doctoral thesis, Cambridge, 1985. For the Spanish connection see A. J. Loomie, *Guy Fawkes in Spain,* Bulletin of the IHR, Special Supplement No. 9, xi.1971. There was a deliberate and largely successful attempt, presumably by English agents, to call in and destroy any surviving evidence of an English connection in 1601–3. This operated in Spain, as Loomie makes clear, and also in Flanders(?). See Archives du Royaume, Brussels, *Papers d'Etat et de l'audience, Négotiations d'Angleterre,* vol. 363, correspondence de 1600; vol. 364, correspondence de 1604. Any correspondence for the intervening years is missing at least from its proper place. M. Nicholls *Investigating the Gunpowder Plot* attempts to refute Edwards, *Guy Fawkes: The Real Story . . . ?* His main objections are answered in Edwards, "Still Investigating Gunpowder Plot," (10) 21, 305–46. <*Guy Fawkes: The Truer Story of the Gunpowder Plot* awaits publication. W. K. L. Webb, S.J., produced a large unpublished thesis preserved in B.P.A. Based on considerable research, this too rejects the standard thesis but does not provide a satisfactory alternative solution.

[2] See *Relatio persecutionis in Anglia etc [sic],* Latin memo, original in RP's hand;

Meanwhile, at long last, early in December 1605 Joseph Cres-well set out for Rome.[3] His visit had three important consequences: first, an attempt to define exactly the relations between superiors and subjects, indigenous and foreign, in the English stations abroad; sec-ond, Creswell had a chance to state his case and meet his critics; third, personal contact in Rome seems to have removed all misunderstanding between him and Persons. Certainly, when Creswell paid a second visit to Rome in 1617 and drew up a list of grievances against the Spanish Jesuits, his references to Persons were altogether kind.[4] Creswell re-turned to Spain in April 1606 to resume his difficult task. There is no further record of strained relations with Persons.

In mid-May, on the advice of Persons, Creswell, and others, Aquaviva drew up regulations for the English institutions in exile.[5] God "is afflicting us in so many ways that we need to stand closely united among ourselves." The prefect was thinking of Garnet's impending execution. "The worst they tell us is that he has admitted to some previous knowledge of the plot; and that is bad enough in all con-science." Oswald Tesimond, another wanted man, arrived safely in Flanders, but his fellow Jesuits soon moved him on to Italy. He had much to communicate which could only be by word of mouth. Persons had instructions for him left at Bologna or Loreto as to whether he should come to Rome, and whether openly or in secret.[6]

The appellant question now reemerged. Persons baldly in-formed Aquaviva in mid-May of the arrival in Rome of John Cecil and Anthony Champney, whose object was "to make trouble for the Society in England." Paul V consulted the Society and got "good advice." Persons urged Aquaviva to press the case for the English Jesuits, since its justice was "evident."[7] But there was a fresh threat in England. A new oath of allegiance was coming before Parliament to trap Catholic consciences. Dr. Harrison, the archpriest's procurator, had information

---

(II) f.428.

[3] (59) 218.

[4] (a) *Responsio ad calumnias contra P. Josephum Creswellum:* (b) *C. fuisse semper piæ memoriæ Patris Personii amicissimum, et nemini post RP Generali secundum:* Latin MSS brought from the Jesuit library at Liège. V. supra, Chap. 20.

[5] See (II) f.483. Grene gave only the Latin title, which does not correspond exactly to the preamble to the MS printed in More's *Historia . . .* , Lib. 6, 241–48. But the date 15.v. on p. 248 agrees with the date on RP's document. Grene claimed that the regulations were kept among RP's papers in the VEC, "and it seems altogether probable that Persons wrote them as also the preceding letter." For the text, see (16), 1981 edition, 298–307.

[6] RP to Aquaviva, 15.v.1606, Rome; (VI) Anglia 32.I, f.31r/v, a.l.s.

[7] Ibid.

which was passed to Cardinal Bellarmine as the expert in the field. Clement VIII had referred the matter to the Holy Office in 1602. "This pernicious oath" had been "drawn from the doctrine of the appellant priests as set out in their printed books." The archpriest's two procurators in Rome in 1602 had been assured that "this doctrine would be condemned." It was not, and so its propounders felt encouraged to believe it could not be "false and heretical," as the rest maintained. The "liberal" influence was growing. "The best ... way of rebutting this wretched oath, and of instructing the Catholics as to what they should do, would be to condemn the perverse doctrine drawn up in the adjoining syllabus."[8]

The two appellants should be obliged to "repudiate this oath, and witness the fact in writing for themselves and their companions in an official document." It should be brought to the notice of King James and his council. Persons assured Bellarmine that the Catholics wanted this decisive action.[9] Persons himself wrote *A Discourse against taking the oath in England.*[10] Unpublished, the work offered comment on more than the oath. Although the "sundry priests" who favored the oath did so out of compassion, they certainly did not carry "the consent of all." In fact only six others had been consulted, of whom three "did utterly disclaim from it as a thing no way allowable." Expediency could not justify taking an oath "evil in itself," since it admitted the King's supremacy in spiritual matters with a specific denial of any papal right to interfere. "It were a vain and frivolous thing to urge men with such violence to forswear a temporal authority which the pope never claimed nor Catholic ever acknowledged." The aim of the oath was spiritual not temporal. "In no other sense is there made mention in the whole oath either of authority to depose, excommunicate, dispose of kingdoms, discharge of subjects' obedience and allegiance, liberty to take arms, power to deprive or execute, power of absolution, pardons and dispensations from oaths etc. *[sic]*." One clause specifically excluded equivocation and mental reservation in taking the oath, so that various shifts used by Catholics to save their consciences were invalidated from the outset.[11]

---

[8] Memorial for Card. Bellarmine, 18.v.1606; (I) Anglia.A.III, No. 60, rough draft in RP's hand; (11) IV, App. cxxxv. The English given here corrects what appears to be some confusion in the Italian as to the writer's meaning. See Ann M. C. Forster, "The Oath Tendered," (10)14, 86–96, formulae for the oaths 1534–1829.

[9] (I) Anglia.A.III, No. 60. RP adds a note, "All the [printed] books to the number of 11 or 12 were handed in at the Holy Office." RP's "catalogo" or syllabus referred to them in the margin.

[10] (II) ff.161–74. Grene adds to the title, "written by F. Persons, 1606."

[11] See (5), 34f. See A. E. Mallock, "Fr. Henry Garnet's Treatise of Equivoca-

The treatise against the oath also included Persons's doctrine on equivocation, to which he would soon devote a whole book, a subject very relevant to strained Catholic consciences in the context of the oath. "If you ask them how they can equivocate, seeing they swear not to do it, they will answer that they will equivocate in that point also, and so still equivocate upon equivocation procedendo in infinitum." But, as Persons insisted, there were limits to the lawfulness of equivocation; "first in matters of faith, it is all one in effect to equivocate and deny if it be exacted; and this point of the pope's authority to depose princes, if it be not expressly defined as many learned men do hold, yet by all men's opinion it is so near unto faith that it cannot be denied without a notable error in faith. . . ." His main objection to the oath was that it allowed too much to the King and not enough to the Pope. All the same, "the pope cannot excommunicate, depose, or absolve the king unlawfully." But "a king hath no authority to make unjust laws, to take his subjects' goods wrongfully, to execute persons condemned unjustly." Some matters admitted no equivocation, and to add an oath made it "a thing most damnable." And even if one were only dealing with "matters of fact" rather than faith, "whensoever equivocation doth cause . . . unjust damage to our neighbour in soul, body or goods, there is no equivocation justifiable"; still less when the injury touched God or religion "or some public hurt for the gain of private lucre." In general, "the common position of all divines is that the pope hath authority to excommunicate or depose princes," though whether this power came directly or indirectly from God was disputed.

The present oath could not be taken, since it denied the papal deposing power, understanding the phrase "rebus sic stantibus" to be implicitly added. The oath denied the power itself, not merely its practical use. Nor could persecution justify taking it any more than it could justify any other betrayal of faith. For this an unjust government was to blame. "Such as love to sleep in their own misery" claimed "that the seminary priests . . . raised this persecution, and Pius V his proceeding against [Elizabeth] by excommunication was cause of our trouble, as some in their printed books . . . seem indiscreetly at the least to utter."[12] "Not every occasion unjustly taken is unjustly given to do evil." Otherwise, one could say that a magistrate did wrong in punishing an offender because he drove him thus to more serious offences. Persons had more difficulty in showing that, if a magistrate out of kindness to a papist assured him that the oath only meant that

tion," (10) 15, 387–95: and P. J. Holmes, "Elizabethan Casuistry," CRS 64 (1973), passim.

[12] Marginal reference here to "Mr Broughton." Richard Broughton, *A just and moderate answer to a most iniurious and seditious pamphlet intituled, An exact discovery of Romish doctrine in case of conspiracie and rebellion . . .* (1606); Scolar Reprint 93 (1972).

the Pope could not depose without good cause, even then he could not take it. But here there entered the danger of scandal. Nor was the situation materially altered because the Catholic had much to lose: property and even wife and children.

Persons analyzed the oath gobbet by gobbet, inexorably exposing its flaws and presuppositions. Even to swear that James was "lawful and rightful king" presumed something "hard or rather impossible for any man to know of any prince in the world." Certainly, the man in the English street could hardly be expected to have such certainty about James or about his right to "all other his dominions and countries." The good subject should simply assume the best or safest and "live in due obedience without swearing to anything he knoweth not nor is bound to know." The phrase added, "and the pope," could only be included to exclude his spiritual authority, since he had no more temporal authority against James than any other prince not mentioned by name. "To deny the pope's authority to depose the king is to deny the power of Christ given unto the pope over his Church, and exempting the king from his power is to acknowledge and swear the king's supremacy." There were further phrases in the oath referring to the Pope and having in view the same end of rejecting his authority.

The Pope in matters disputed could proceed by two ways:

> The one precisely as pope by way of the ecclesiastical censure, the other as a temporal prince . . . if an injury were offered to him as a temporal lord, and could not right himself but by violence; and to deny the pope's authority in either were a thing unlawful, the latter because it were against common justice, and the former because it were against religion also.

Furthermore, to say the Pope could not dissolve subjects from their allegiance would be "to prefer an unjust law of an English parliament of mere laymen before the lawful decree . . . of a general council of fathers and all Christian princes submitting themselves unto the same." The principle was established by the Third Lateran Council. Regarding deposition, "the pope as pope doth never execute his own sentence but rather to that effect doth *invocare auxilium brachii sæcularis.*" Once the papal sentence of excommunication and deposition was pronounced, its execution was left, without more formality, "unto the zeal, strength and discretion of him that is able to perform it."

Persons added a very important observation to all this. "A subject may lawfully omit or refuse the pope's censure against his prince, neither can he be proved thereunto by any censure." Thus Persons answered the common Protestant objection that, if a Pope excommunicated a monarch, his Catholic subjects must ipso facto become traitors.

In case the subjects of the king would remain loyal unto him, without prejudice of their religion and conscience, and should promise or swear the same as upon just reasons they might be induced to do, there is no cause why the king should persecute his own because of the pope's deposition; neither can such deposition be any just cause of that persecution.

If James's oath had merely demanded that, "notwithstanding any declaration or sentence of excommunication or deprivation," the subject promised allegiance, any Catholic could have taken it without a qualm of conscience. The King and his advisers must have known this, so that the real object was to make life impossible for the papists and drive them out of existence. It was an apostate priest and Jesuit, Christopher Perkins, dismissed from the Society on October 14, 1581, who was mainly instrumental in drawing up an oath designed deliberately to trip up his former coreligionists, one "so phrased as to give the appearance of orthodoxy."[13]

Persons grasped another nettle firmly: tyrannicide. The problem was an ancient one. Most recoil less from the concept of tyrannicide itself than from the definition of the tyrant. Paragraph three of James's oath described assassination of an excommunicated or deposed sovereign as "impious and heretical" and "damnable." But there was good biblical precedent for it. Persons mentioned Saul, Roboam, Ozias, Achab, "and others" in the Old Testament, which thereby

do seem to approve it. The General Council of Lateran by a decree declareth it. The practice of the Church and divers popes' proceedings have confirmed it. The uniform consent of learned divines and canonists do teach it. None but heretics, or inclining to heresy or disorder, disclaim from it. And must we Catholics only of all other needs swear that from our hearts we detest and abjure it as impious, heretical and damnable?

On the contrary, to deny that the pope could depose princes was "scandalous, temerarious and erroneous doctrine" even if it was not formally heretical. If equivocation could justify taking such an oath, then one could justify "the denying of Peter and the betraying of Judas and the condemnation of Pilate, and what other crime so ever you can imagine." Quite simply, "in faith matters it is not lawful to equivocate."

The fourth provision of the oath denied the right of the pope or anyone else to absolve or dispense from it once taken. But this would deny "that the pope hath authority to absolve one from an impious oath." Such an oath was "an execration of verity." Finally, the oath was to be taken "according to the express words" and plain

---

[13] (60) 189.

meaning "without any equivocation or mental evasion . . . whatsoever." This sealed off all retreat compatible with sincerity and integrity, so that the only course left for a papist was to refuse it. "What greater necessity is there to save a man's estate than to save his said truth and honesty?"

It was not to be expected that the above view, which was also the Roman and orthodox one, would pass unchallenged even by Catholics. Roger Widdrington, a Benedictine monk writing under the alias of Thomas Preston, produced between 1611 and 1619 nine works propounding a contrary view.[14] Inevitably he became "a diehard enemy of the Jesuits."[15] Certainly, the oath was more than a test of merely civil or temporal obedience. It was gratuitous to insist that Catholics be obliged to declare that the doctrine of the papal deposing power was heretical. As David Lunn put it, "most Catholics would have thought twice before calling the pope a heretic. Thus the oath was as contentious as Pius V's bull of excommunication."[16]

The brief of October 5, 1602, exhorted both sides in the appellant controversy to harmony and mutual charity, but it could not change the ground on which each side took its stand. So when John Cecil and Anthony Champney came to Rome in the spring of 1606, chorus and counter-chorus produced a cacophany heard already. About May 20 Persons drew up another of his memorials, one intended to anticipate the presumed fuller exposition of the archpriest's agents. By this time he had no illusions about John Cecil. Thomas Bluet, well-known to the Archbishop of Canterbury, died shortly after returning to England in 1601. John Mush and Francis Barnby were reconciled to the archpriest, although Barnby signed a statement giving up the practice of his priesthood.[17]

Cecil and Champney, the unblest pair of sirens now in Rome, carried on "this same dissension among the English, partly in France and partly in England," being "recognised as men of unruly and turbulent disposition." Champney, the younger man, might have been a scholar but abandoned his studies to pursue, as Persons saw it, politics and faction, including negotiations with heretical bishops. John Cecil was reserved for the darkest portrait. From Persons's viewpoint he had undoubtedly been guilty of gross betrayal. His intrigues "pro-

---

[14] For his works, see STC under Widdrington, Roger: also Ann M. C. Forster, "The Real Roger Widdrington," (10) 11, 196–205; W. K. L. Webb, S.J., "Thomas Preston alias Roger Widdrington, 1567–1640," ibid., 2, 216–68.

[15] D. Lunn, *The English Benedictines*, 18.

[16] Ibid., 39.

[17] See (XII) Fairhurst MS 2006, f.191r, a.l.s. of 3/13.iii.1603.

cured his expulsion from the English College"—so why did Persons trust him for so long?—"and then from Cardinal Allen's household." After serious gaffes in Spain, Allen sent him two or three times to England and Scotland. "In none of them did he give a good account of himself." In fact many Catholics concluded he was a spy. Claiming a family connection with Sir Robert, he was twice released after capture, and shortly thereafter followed a sharp persecution of persons apparently informed on. Moving to Paris to repair his broken bridges, John Cecil's great chance came with the appellants of 1601. He went with them to Rome in 1602 to help with his knowledge of Italian and experience, albeit limited, of the Roman Curia. Back in Paris, the appellants left an account of their doings with the English ambassador and Cecil to act as their agent. He continued to inform the ambassador on Roman affairs.[18] Returning to England after James's accession, he was arrested in connection with the alleged conspiracy of Clark and Watson, a timely reminder that no kind of papist was really welcome to the regime. Persons claimed further, "because he was short of real facts he invented many things supposedly negotiated and concluded in Rome, including apostolic briefs drawn up by his Holiness, and discussions held by cardinals, which were never . . . thought of."[19] He was the first of the spurious flies on the ceiling, perhaps initiating what was to become a tradition reaching to our own times. Cecil and Champney would repeat the performance of 1602, giving the English College a wide berth in spite of repeated invitations to visit. They had their eye mainly on relations with the Anglican hierarchy and the English government rather than on the good of the recusant cause. Their case should be committed to a third party and the truth sifted by inquiries conducted under oath.[20]

---

[18] RP, *Memorial against Cecil and Champney*, (I) Anglia.A.III, No. 73, rough draft in RP's hand; (11) V, app. xiv.

[19] Ibid. The present writer has never found such a document. Much was destroyed in the VEC at the Suppression.

[20] Ibid. A shorter memorial dated 26.v.1606 and covering much the same ground was submitted by the archpriest's agents. This too exists as a draft apparently in RP's hand; (I) Anglia. A.III, No. 61; (11) V, app. xiii. This was a covering letter or document for "two attached papers." The first was seemingly RP's memorial as described above; the second was a copy of J. Cecil's memo given to the English privy council. In this, cardinals, ambassadors, and "even princes themselves and the apostolic see" were "traduced, falsely calumniated, and brought into contempt before the king of England." The latest delegation was expected, as previously, to promote misunderstanding between the Holy See, the English Crown, and the Catholic exiles. J. Cecil should be obliged to give security not to leave Rome before he had "answered the accusations brought against him."

The execution of Henry Garnet on May 13 (N.S.) on a charge of complicity in the Gunpowder Plot greatly assisted the cause of the Society's enemies in Europe and especially Rome. It was as well that Paul V and not Clement VIII was now happily reigning, since the latter might have accepted the guilt of the Jesuits more readily and shown his displeasure more obviously. As it was, Persons had to endure the humiliation of news sheets and rumors circulating in Rome which brought the English Jesuits into considerable disrepute. Even Persons had not "sufficient courage" to approach the Pope. He could only hope that God and time would disperse the storm. While the Pope might not be too ready to believe it all, his vision was necessarily blurred by so much smoke. A letter received by Persons on May 23 made it clear that he was no longer the Pope's confidant in English affairs. It referred in oblique terms to "the negotiation" being carried out with the utmost secrecy involving James and the privy councillors. They made it clear that, if they had known what it was about, they would have prevented it.[21] Persons thought it might have had to do with an offer of money in return for toleration.

Writing on June 17 to comfort his brethren in England in their latest tribulation, Persons roundly condemned the Gunpowder Plot. "God pardon those gentlemen's souls. . . . Their attempt was pernicious and utterly misliked by all good men."[22] But he repudiated "the infamous rumours . . . spread abroad . . . against good Father Garnet." Consoled by his exemplary death, he awaited more details of his end. Aquaviva could only urge the English Jesuits to redouble their efforts to give "edification to all and no just offence to any."[23] Persons does not seem to have questioned the authenticity of the plot, although, knowing the Jesuits in England and their explicit orders not to resort to violence, it was inconceivable that they would have flouted the clear orders of Pope and General. His best information came from John Gerard, a Jesuit falsely accused, who "passed this way some months gone, but made little or no abode lest offence might be taken thereat." At all events, he stayed long enough to convince the well-disposed of his "rare virtue" and of his innocence of any part in the plot. Indeed, he himself insisted that the General examine him before witnesses and command him on oath and *in virtute sanctæ obedientiæ* to tell the truth. He actually submitted to this examination and protested

---

[21] RP to Paul V, vi.[1606], Rome; (IV) F.Borgh. III.131.C, f.120, a.l.s.

[22] (II) f.428. See R. Broughton, *A just and moderate answer*. V. supra.

[23] Ibid. For Garnet's death and popular disapproval, see (75) 82. In 1607 further executions were suspended as counterproductive; ibid., 99f.

his innocence, "which the rest of his behaviour doth easily make probable." [24]

Sir Thomas Shirley, swashbuckling elder brother of Sir Anthony, arrived in Rome in late June.[25] Persons had no time for him and warned Borghese that he might try to take advantage of him.[26] Hardly more welcome were Champney and Cecil, who arrived about mid-July. Persons wrote to them because, expecting his hostility, they had avoided the college, even refusing to "take part in the prayers said in our church." They had made no reply to Persons's letter of January 1, 1603, addressed to them in Paris, in which he made a strenuous appeal for reconciliation. On the contrary, he had been mocked with "ribald laughter" in letters sent to England. He still wanted rapprochement. "The king and those who advised him declared publicly that this disunion, so useful to the state, should be fostered in every way for our destruction. This was afterwards reprinted and published. I cannot think of a sharper spur to make us end this quarrel."[27] For the Jesuits in England, the only consolation could be spiritual, as he wrote to Richard Holtby, alias Duckett, on July 8 and again on July 29. Parliament's latest draconian laws meant that for the Catholics, "the greatest benefit that upon earth God can bestow upon his servants . . . is to suffer for him and with a short account to end all reckonings."[28]

Nothing succeeds like excess. Propaganda pushed by the English government against the papists after the Gunpowder Plot received a new impetus from the tale of another plot aimed at the King in the summer of 1606. Persons learned of it from a letter of July 19 from London to a gentleman in Florence. It concerned "Colonel Jacques's brother with a man called Ball," an Irishman, who intended the king's death.[29] This is yet another of the too numerous plots of

---

[24] RP to ?, 29.xii.1606, Rome; (II) f.447.

[25] See E. Denison Ross, *Anthony Shirley and His Persian Adventures;* Davies, *Elizabethan Errant.*

[26] RP to Borghese, 2.viii.1606, Rome; (IV) F.Borgh. II.448.AB, f.26, a.l.s.

[27] RP to J. Cecil and A. Champney, 16.vii.1606, Rome; (I) Anglia.A.III, No. 63, Latin copy; (11) V. app. xvii.

[28] RP to the Jesuits in England, 29.vii.1606; (I) Anglia.A.VI, No. 60, contemp. English copy, no endorsement; (II) f.430, Latin translation. For the persecution of the Catholics after the Gunpowder Plot, see (75) 83; for R. Cecil as the main inspiration, ibid., 86, n.2. The possibility of compounding for toleration receded, see ibid., 76,77. "Compounding," a common word in this context, means negotiating for more reasonable terms on the amount of fine to be paid. Persecution had never been so severe; ibid., 71, 95–97.

[29] See RP to Paul V, viii(?).1606; (IV) F.Borgh. III.7C, f.395, a.l.s. See A. J. Loomie, "Spain and the Jacobean Catholics," CRS 64 (1973): 78(n), 86f.

Regnum Cecilianum waiting to be unraveled. Some of the men of that generation were more critical than many of our own. "They are of opinion that it will all turn out to be a stratagem of Cecil's to put the king in fear that everyone is trying to kill him; as they did with the late queen. They also wish to increase his distrust of the archduke so that he will help the Dutch with larger forces."[30]

Certainly, the latest "plot" was used to justify the harsh repression accompanying the new oath imposed on Catholics. Someone wrote on July 27 about "the present afflictions of Catholic people there, not only in respect of the new statutes but by urging also the oath lately devised to afflict men's consciences."[31] A new division arose among the priests between those who thought the oath could conscientiously be taken and those who did not, a result foreseen and desired by James's government. When the oath appeared some five months before, "seven or eight of the learnedest divines" concluded that the former oath "was not so intolerable as this is now." No Catholic could take it without grave sin even to save all he possessed. They also thought "the pope's authority in chastising princes upon just cause is de fide," so that denial meant "denying our faith." Not even the pope could dispense in the matter since it was not about a de facto issue but concerned the papal power as such. There was no honorable way to escape persecution, since "we are bound to confess a truth simply, with what danger or loss soever."[32]

Persons sounded out Cardinal Bellarmine and others, who agreed that "the form of the oath as it lieth is heretical" and impossible for a Catholic to take with a good conscience. As for the Pope, when questioned he

> answered most resolutely that as for any actual use of censures against his majesty, he meant not, but rather to use all courtesy possible and convenient; but as for the authority of the See Apostolic in such affairs, he was so resolute in defence thereof as rather he would lose his head . . . than yield in the least jot thereof.

He even told Persons later that "he would not hold such priests for Catholic" who wavered in this. In any case, as Persons believed, if the Catholics gave way on this, their enemies would still think up new ways of entangling their consciences.

---

[30] Ibid. The "Ball plot" still awaits fuller critical investigation, but a cursory examination confirms the surmise of RP's friends.

[31] RP to (?), 26.viii.1606, Rome; (XIII) Add.MS 14,030, f.87, a.l.s.; (III) Old Series VIII, No. 4. For Catholic reactions to the oath, see (76) 160–63.

[32] RP to (?), 26.viii.1606. James I showed positive hatred to the Catholics after the plot. See (75) 95f.

Inevitably there were those who said that it was easy for Persons and his friends, living in safety if not ease, to take the rigorous view; but, if they had to live on the English scene, they might change their minds and tune. Persons did allow, nay insist, that Catholics should yield every kind of temporal obedience. That is,

> they acknowledge his Majesty for true lord and king over all his dominions, and to have all kingly authorities and power over his subjects as much as any king ever had within his realm, or as any other Catholic king in the world abroad. That they will never conspire against his person, state and dignity nor conceal other. That they will never procure, provoke or persuade an ecclesiastical censure against his Majesty or his heirs, but rather will dissuade and hinder the same what they can, and do verily hope and will still; desire that no such thing be done by the pope that now is or his successors.[33]

So much effort had its effect on Persons's health. "I am but weak at this time having been lately very sick."[34] Weak or not, on September 1 he penned another memorial to the Pope, asking for a brief against the oath, forbidding attendance at Anglican services, "and to repress the appellants then in Rome." With or without his prompting, a brief was produced this month.[35] By autumn the intimations of mortality became more insistent: pain in his "side and reins" now "more vehement . . . especially after exercise" and the appearance of "divers little red pimples" like "ringworm."[36]

By the end of the year, Persons became peripherally involved in a scandal surrounding Robert Dudley, the Earl of Leicester's son, who claimed and used the title "Earl of Warwick." Dudley came to Europe in January 1606, bringing with him "his kinswoman Mistress Southwell, in man's apparel." They went through a form of marriage at Lyons, but there had been two previous marriages, the partner of the second still surviving. Dudley and Captain Eliot, his agent, seem to

---

[33] RP to (?), 26.viii.1606. False reports were being spread to exacerbate relations between Rome and London. Early in 1606 the Venetian ambassador reported James as declaring, "I have dispatches from Rome informing me that the pope intends to excommunicate me; the catholics threaten to dethrone me and to take my life unless I grant them liberty of conscience. I shall most certainly be obliged to stain my hands with their blood, though sorely against my will," (15) 227. In fact the Pope refused to oblige James's subjects to obedience by formal instrument, although he urged them to do so in fact. See (75) 84.

[34] RP to (?), 26.viii.1606. Ending the letter, after RP's initials, comes a statement by Thomas Fitzherbert corroborating the fact of "his Holiness earnest speeches" to RP and himself "about the unlawfulness of the new oath."

[35] See (II) ff.483, 489. Aquaviva mentioned the brief in a letter of 28.ix.; see ibid. For the text of the brief of 22.ix., see (76) 157–60.

[36] See RP to Edward Coffin, 8.x.1606, VEC; (II) 437.

have behaved with less than candor, so that the Vatican found itself saddled with a charge tending to recur that it was too ready to accommodate persons of exalted rank in such matters.[37] At all events, the pair, settled in Florence, had remained faithful up to the present. Dudley was accomplished in several fields, including mathematics and naval architecture, so that Archduke Cosimo II appointed him chamberlain to his wife, Magdalen, and in 1620 secured his creation as Earl of Warwick in the Holy Roman Empire.[38]

The brief of October 5/15, 1602, while disentangling some aspects of the recusant situation in England, seemed to tie knots elsewhere. With the laudable intention of making it clear to all that Blackwell was not in the pocket of the Jesuits, the later brief of 1606, as we have seen, forbade him to discuss or even communicate matters concerning his office with the Jesuit superior in England. He therefore looked for advice and allies elsewhere. Some of these led him to believe that King James's oath could be taken by Catholics with a good conscience. Persons reacted by asking the Pope, in the name of William Singleton and the other assistants, for a revision of Clement VIII's brief which would allow contact as formerly between archpriest and Jesuits. Its absence had been "the principal cause of the archpriest having followed the advice of others and given his approval to this last oath."[39]

To give the screw of persecution another sharp turn, on July 10 a proclamation was issued ordering all Jesuits and other priests to depart the realm.[40] Within a fortnight some forty-seven priests were sent into exile, including William Singleton. He reached Rome by way of Douai on October 9.[41] He and his companions were well treated in Rome and sent back to Douai with a generous viaticum.[42]

The murder of Sir Thomas Crompton and the "deadly wounding in Lorraine" of a courier from Sir Henry Wotton, English ambassador in Venice, were a pretext even more than a reason for discouraging Englishmen from overseas excursions. Cecil's government was now "so loath to have young men of judgment to come abroad as they say

---

[37] For details, see RP to F. Bemondo [O. Tesimond, S.J.], 9/19.i.1607; (VII) SP85 (Italian States), bundle 3, f.109r: also T. Fitzherbert to T. Owen, ix.1606; (I) Anglia.A.,III, No. 67; (II) f.458.

[38] For his achievements see DNB.

[39] RP to Paul V, memorial, 10.xi.1606; (II) f.424.

[40] See (11) IV, app. cxxxii.

[41] Ibid., app. cxxxiv and (18) 318.

[42] RP to (?), 29.xii.1606, Rome; (II) f.447; (64) I, II, passim.

that licences are now as hard to be had as leases, and almost as dear as purchases."[43]

This year appeared Persons's *An answere to the fifth part of reportes lately set forth by Syr Edward Cooke, Knight, the Kinges attorney general, concerning the ancient and moderne municipall lawes of England which do appertayne to spirituell power and jurisdiction.* Written by "a Catholic divine" and published at St. Omers in 1606, this work aimed to show the continuity of Catholicism in England "from our first kings christened unto these days." Persons was coy about the authorship of this book. In the of December 29, he only admitted, "it is God's providence to permit that such books should come forth" to demonstrate "the truth as otherwise could not be done without importunity or offence. Would God the King may read it for that it most importeth both him and us. I understand that his Majesty was presented presently with the attorney's book. This will be a full antidotum."[44]

---

[43] Ibid. This was not Crompton, the Admiralty judge who held office till 1608; (14) xix.

[44] Ibid. Unfortunately, no English Jesuit catalogue survives for 1606. The 1610 catalogue gives names but not houses or employments. Mr. G. W. Kuehn of Boston is preparing a study of RP's "An answere. . . ." He noticed that RP admitted authorship on page 583 of his last book, *A quiet and sober reckoning* . . . (1609) "when in summarising the Catholic Devine's Answer . . . he inadvertently slips into the first person for several paragraphs."

P ersons's first preoccupation in 1607 was to comfort his brethren in a bleak time of increased persecution. To prayers he could add little more than words. He spared neither. An exhortation of early January urged the Jesuits to be faithful to their Institute especially in the matter of obedience.[1] "Above all, they must observe what had often been prescribed from Rome; hold aloof from politics and matters alien to the Institute even if lawful in themselves; . . . avoid any action which could offend the prince and disturb the commonwealth; and persuade others to do the same." They must preserve "mutual peace and charity," keep their nerve even when faced with death, and behave abstemiously lest they prove "grievous or burdensome" to their hosts. It was necessary to adopt disguise but the practice had its dangers, especially since the Jesuits usually adopted that of gentlemen. "Prodigality in the spending of money, which is sometimes indulged in by religious on the pretext of contempt for money, is to be absolutely avoided; as also unsuitable purchases and still more the buying of presents." Chastity could be at risk since, even in Catholic houses, conversation was often earthy and contact with women unavoidable—indeed, a priestly duty. "Dissimulation in the use of food, dress, conversation, games, or general behaviour" was only permissible in the presence of strangers. Otherwise, "attention [should be] paid to religious discipline as time and place allowed."

It was desirable that "not less than two Jesuits should live together in each residence," or at least close enough to "get mutual help, advice and consolation from one another." A more experienced Father in each locality should be "prefect of spritual matters," visiting houses where Jesuits stayed and giving advice, even by letter. Larger reunions should be avoided, but smaller groups might meet for renewal of vows and similar purposes. Everyone should have at least one spiritual book by him, to be supplied from St. Omer, Douai, or elsewhere, as well as the Summary of the Constitutions and rulebook. They should keep in touch not only with their local superior but also

---

[1] RP "Ad Patres Societatis Jesu in Anglicana vinea laborantes," 9.i.1607, Rome; (II) f.479 (see f.349); (16) f.350, with important variations from the MS, Latin.

with the prefect in Rome as far as they could. The superior and his consultors should write once a year and others as far as safety permitted.[2]

Surprisingly, persecution seems to have done nothing to diminish numbers in the English College, Rome. Early in January Persons reported to Greenway in Naples, "We are here many mouths . . . and a dozen scholars above the ordinary number, who upon occasion of the present persecution in England offering themselves, and being otherwise subjects of exceeding good parts, and some graduates and the most gentlemen, my heart served me not to refuse them." Practical as ever, the writer wanted Greenway to use his influence with the viceroy to see that a hundred butts of wine were duly delivered to the college.[3]

Persons was not the only writer among the Roman exiles. Thomas Fitzherbert was busy with "the second part of his book of religion and policy." From London *A true and perfect relation of the whole proceedings against the late most barbarous traitors, Garnet a Jesuit, and his confederates* . . . had reached Rome, presumably the Earl of Northampton's account published in 1606. The Inquisition was expected to censure it. Persons, assuming that this ambivalent man was a Catholic, thought that the earl's secret enemies had induced him to write it to destroy his reputation with Catholics. Persons had already given Greenway a copy of the answer to Sir Edward Coke's book.[4] A digest of the latest recusancy laws in England arrived from Germany, but Persons blocked a move to publish it in Italian translation, lest it provoke reaction. "It may be the king at length will reflect somewhat upon his violent course."[5] Persons also gave Greenway his opinion on William Barlow, bishop of Rochester's, book defending the institution of bishops in the Church.[6] "There was never good cause worse handled, and . . . if his fellow bishops . . . did no better defend their cause than he, or that the king's special favour and authority do not hold them up, they will fall, and the ministers will have the upper hand, which I should be sorry for." Not that the papists had much to hope

---

[2] Ibid.

[3] RP to Philippo Bemondo (Greenway/Tesimond), 19.i.1607; (VII) SP85, Bundle 3, f.109, letter intercepted or surrendered.

[4] Ibid.

[5] Ibid. They had appeared in print in Spain as *Las leyes nuevamente hechas en el Parlamento de Inglaterra este año de MDCVI contro los Catholicos ingleses, que llaman Recusantes, traduzidas de su original impresso en Ingles;* (VIII) E.2512 and 962. See (75) 110f.

[6] The full title ran, "One of the foure sermons/ preached before the king's majestie at Hampton Court/ in September last./ This concerning the antiquitie and superioritie of bishops," Sept. 21, 1606, London; see Catalogue of the McAlpin collection in the Union Theological Seminary, New York, Vol. 1, 1927, p. 193.

for from any of them. But at least James's establishment would leave
the cathedrals and churches intact, so that when the Catholics eventually prevailed, as they surely would after God's due "chastisement of
sin," they would "need nothing but exchange of incumbents for restoring God's truth again."[7]

Doubtless, it was at Persons's prompting that Aquaviva early
this year addressed a letter to his English subjects.[8] They should be
encouraged by what had happened elsewhere. "After a sharp storm"
the Jesuits had been restored in France. "We see the like in Japonia
and China where they were brought very lately to far greater straits
and extremities." Likewise in Poland. But the arm of the English
secretary of state was more than ordinarily long. Even in Naples,
Tesimond considered it politic to use the alias of Beaumont or Bemondo, and Persons agreed with him.[9] Hugh Owen and William Baldwin
in Flanders had suffered considerable molestation although they had
escaped extradition. Among the English community in Naples one
must presuppose the presence of spies and even assassins.

Undeniably, the slur cast on the Society by the Gunpowder
Plot forced even Persons to assume a defensive posture. But as time
passed the rest of the world, and no few even in England, grew increasingly doubtful that they knew the real truth behind this bizarre
nonevent. A curious phenomenon which influenced opinion in an age
more readily disposed to accept the miraculous was the appearance of
Garnet's head, as it was alleged, on an ear of wheat which had been
splashed with his blood at his execution. Perhaps it served the English
government right, since they lost no opportunity to assure the world of
extraordinary divine interventions from time to time to bolster the
regime. Witnesses far from friendly saw it and drawings of the object
survived, but not the original; so further comment would be superfluous. Joseph Creswell refused to believe it. Certainly, Persons knew by
now the lengths to which the opposition was prepared to go, and in
the name of religion, to bring himself and his Society into discredit.[10]

Fresh instructions, enlarging on Aquaviva's letter of January
9/10, were now addressed to the Jesuit superior and his men in England.[11] They exhorted Richard Holtby, Garnet's successor, to suavity,

---

[7] RP to Bemondo/Greenway, 19.i.1607, Rome; (VII) SP85. V. supra.

[8] See ibid.

[9] Ibid. See (30) 1st Series, London, 1872, 143–83.

[10] RP to Aquaviva, 30.i.1607, Rome; (II) f.429. See (75) 110f.

[11] "Instructiones quædam pro superiore missionis Anglicanæ, copied out of F.
Persons's own handwriting, and written in the General's name (doubtless to be subscribed by Fr. General) dated February 1607. The letter mentioned in the first line dated

and his subjects to obedience and fraternal union. He should move his men around frequently at least to keep them in the sense of being completely disposable. Lay hosts should accept the idea of fairly frequent change and not become overattached to individuals. "The source of the gravest evils and temptations" was idleness, so the superior should keep his men fully occupied "whether in literary and devotional pursuits, or in the assembling of arguments to confute the heretics . . . or in noting and recording facts for the history of the Church." Once a year or thereabouts someone should come to Rome "to give direct information by word of mouth concerning mission affairs." Although some "trustworthy travellers" did get through, closer watch was kept at the ports, "where they insist on seeing the letters carried by all carriers."[12]

A letter in cipher came to Persons about this time, describing a recent approach by some of the Privy Council to the Spanish ambassador. It again held out hope of "obtaining some degree of toleration for the Catholics in return for a sum of money." Some "persons of high position, nominally Catholic," gave it plausibility. Persons was dismissive. "I suspect that the councillors want to get more money out of the papists and make fools of them into the bargain." All the same, one could play them along to see what was aimed at. What the papists really needed was confirmation in their allegiance to Rome. One way to ensure this was to allow free communication between archpriest and Jesuits. The Pope had recently passed to Persons a book unnamed but probably the "King's Book" on the subject of the Gunpowder Plot, to which an answer was being prepared by André l'Heureux, a Cretan Jesuit. This was published in 1610. In the new attitude of caution towards the English state, the problem was to vindicate truth "without giving just offence to individuals or to the state as far as possible."[13] Persons had supplied a defence of Garnet in an appendix to his 1606 *Answere . . . to Coke,* entitled "An epistle dedicatory to Syr Edward Cooke, Knight."[14]

"George H" arrived in Venice in the spring of 1607. Robert Cecil would not have appointed an agent or informant without first vetting him, but as "George H" told his story to Persons, soon after he

---

4 Idus Januarii in (16) p. 350. Incipit, Facere non possum etc. *[sic]*, and likely may be also composed by F. Persons as his Instructiones certainly was" (II) f.349.

[12] RP to Paul V, 7.ii.1607, Rome; (IV) F.Borgh. II.448.AB, f.332.

[13] Ibid. Spain maintained diplomatic pressure for toleration even after the plot. See (75) passim; the French also, ibid., 101. <However, it now appeared that French influence had succeeded in getting RP sent away from Rome under Clement VIII; ibid., 104.

[14] See (70) 86–89. The Cretan Jesuit published under the name of Eudaemon Joannes, *Apologia pro H. Garnetto* at Cologne.

arrived in Venice, a letter was delivered to him "with great care and diligence . . . from a gentleman of my Lord Cecil . . . with a bountiful bill of exchange." The letter made an appeal "to be true, constant and continue in Rome, to send his honour with all speed Cardinal Bellarmine's answer to the King's book."[15] Other works were mentioned. The informant made no secret of his caliber. "I am a young and idle fellow . . . far unfit to perform an office of so great observation."[16] But others of the breed could be effective and dangerous. On April 24 Persons warned the Vatican about spies "commissioned by Secretary Cecil for Italy and chiefly for Rome."[17] Someone had already warned Persons to "beware of two Georges, E.C. and H.O., for both of them have salaries from England for serving in Italy and mainly in Rome." Salisbury was boasting that "he is excellently served, and has better reports on affairs in that quarter than anywhere else on earth." The truth of Cecil's claim was exaggerated, at least if he relied only on papers preserved at Hatfield and in the "Italian States" in the Public Record Office. Nevertheless, his intelligence could be startlingly good. "Before the last Brief came from the pope . . . there arrived from Rome another copy for the Archbishop of Canterbury to hand to the King." Those concerned should be careful whom they trusted!

On May 6 Persons sent the Pope a copy printed in Flanders of his "two short treatises" against going to Protestant services. He had written them "at the request of many Catholics to set at rest much doubt and controversy."[18] But Persons felt bound to recommend the suppression of a work by William Alabaster appearing at this time, although it had been approved by Flemish Jesuits. Alabaster accompanied Essex's expedition of 1596 as a chaplain, but in 1598 converted to Catholicism and trained in the English College, Rome.[19] Persons took the trouble to explain his disapproval in courteous terms to Alabaster himself.[20] Alabaster took it badly. He was subsequently reported as eccentric if not unstable and refusing to observe the discipline of the college, and this had its effect on his fellow students.[21] He was handled sympathetically and transfer recommended, as he desired, to read

---

[15] George H to RP, 14.iv.1607, Venice; (IV) F.Borgh. III, Vol. 43, f.15.

[16] Ibid. He hoped to receive RP's reply at Padua; or, if this could not be done safely—there was a large English community there—then "at Millen by Captayne Standlye's meanes."

[17] RP to Paul V, 22.iv.1607, Rome; (IV) F.Borgh. III, 43DE, f.16, a.l.s.

[18] (II) f.458.

[19] See William Alabaster, E. Leveson, W. Higham, et al to Paul V, 18.xii.1598; (IV) F.Borgh. III.124.G.1, f.30 r/v, signed application.

[20] RP to Alabaster, 12.v.1607, Rome; (II) f.340.

[21] See RP(?) to Aquaviva, [22.ix.1609 ?]; (II) f.485, a fragment only.

Greek or Hebrew in an Italian university as a prelude to medical studies. But in 1610 he decamped to Marseilles, inveighing bitterly against Rome and the Jesuits. Having seen the error of his ways, his intention now was "to live and die a protestant."[22] The future author of *Roxana* now applied an overfertile imagination to put about "many lies to the effect that Persons was not only aware of the Gunpowder Plot but was in fact its head. This was certain and indeed well-known, and all the English in Rome outside the college talked of it as such." He also claimed that Bellarmine approved of the death in 1610 of the King of France and the manner of it, and thought it time to do the same for the King of England. Cardinal Siripandi might well exclaim against "the lies and slander that poured from him over the years." Such a man could hardly fail to make a good career in contemporary England. Alabaster acquired a prebend in St. Paul's, London, and as a successful author, full of years if not honor, survived until 1640.[23]

The latter half of 1607 saw unrest everywhere in English Catholic communities, not excluding nuns. Worthington, president of Douai, informed Persons in a letter of May 28 that he was obliged to send away seven students. Persons hoped that it was not simply because they wished to become religious, since the Pope had "declared that the alumni of the seminaries may lawfully go into religion."[24] Friction now arose from the laudable efforts of the Benedictines to set up a mission in England with houses on the continent analogous to Jesuit foundations.[25] The English Benedictine revival came from two congregations, the Spanish and the Cassinese, the latter centered in Monte Cassino. It is taken to begin when Robert Sayers, a man of ability and learning, took the habit at Monte Cassino in 1588 as "Dom Gregory." English subjects of this congregation entered at Monte Cassino, Padua, and Venice. By 1595, 19 out of the 303 students who passed through the English College, Rome, had become Benedictines.[26] Allen fully recognized the legitimacy of such vocations, since the spirit

---

[22] See Siripandi, S.J., to RP, 21.vi.1610, Florence; (II) f.487.

[23] Grene notes references to Alabaster in (II), ff. 356, 549, 551, 485, 539, 487. There were further references up to f.800 but all has been lost after f.609. See also, R. V. Caro, S.J., "William Alabaster: rhetor, mediator, devotional poet," (10) 19, 62–80, 155–71.

[24] RP(?) to Worthington, 23.vi.1607; (II) f.341.

[25] See Frédéric Fabre, "The Settling of the English Benedictines at Douai: As Seen Chiefly Through . . . the Vatican Archives, 1607–1611," *Downside Review*, 52 (1934): 1–64, unpublished documents on 3, 54–64. D. Lunn, *The English Benedictines 1540–1688* (London, 1980), especially Chaps. 1–3.

[26] By this time, thirty-one had joined the Society of Jesus, fourteen the Dominicans, ten the Franciscans; in addition, there were ten Carmelites and four Carthusians.

bloweth where it listeth; but inevitably there were those who regarded this departure to the orders as a deflection from the real purpose of the seminaries, which was to produce missionaries for England. The strain and drain were felt chiefly at Valladolid and Seville.[27] The point was taken by the Benedictines in 1594 when the general chapter of the Cassinese Congregation petitioned the Pope to allow its English subjects to form an English mission. Hitherto the work had been shared by secular priests, Jesuits, and surviving Marian priests. The 1594 petition was followed by others from Owen Lewis and from English noblemen who hoped that the celebrated Benedictine *pax* might make itself felt in an area where it was much needed. On March 20, 1603, Clement VIII granted a faculty for a pioneering group of Benedictines to go to England. Meanwhile, vocations to the order increased, so that it seemed to be taking over from the Jesuits as the best and latest outlet for enthusiastic endeavor. The Jesuits' reputation after the Gunpowder Plot was not a little tarnished, and their failure to deal with student power and discontent was by this time chronic.

Soon after the decree of 1603, some English members of the Spanish Congregation set up a monastery in Douai, which had the advantages of being on Spanish territory, close to England, and already a center for exiles. It also possessed a university with important Benedictine foundations in or near Arras, Marchiennes, and Anchin. But many of the exiles, including the Jesuits, doubted if the resources would bear this further burden without collapsing. They feared the emergence of regional xenophobia which could resent, and reasonably, the limited resources of the state being poured out on the hungry nationals of a power by no means friendly, even now with peace of a kind declared. At all events, "in 1603, two of the Valladolid students who became Benedictines in the exodus of 1599 succeeded in gaining the help of the abbot of Arras . . . to forward the work of providing a separate monastery for the English monks."[28] In the event they acquitted themselves well, becoming professors in the college at Marchiennes and in the university.

At about the time of the Queen's death, Dom Augustine of the Valladolid, or Spanish, Congregation, arrived in England with two companions. In June 1603 Anselm Beech and Thomas Preston, of the Cassinese Congregation of St. Justin of Padua, set out from Rome to join them. In view of St. Ignatius's early connection with, and even debt to, the Order of St. Benedict, it could not be supposed that there was any inherent prejudice on the part of the Jesuits against the Bene-

---

[27] See (17) 217f.

[28] (17) 222.

dictines. Nevertheless, because many of the latter nursed some resentment or reaction against the Society as a result of their experience in the colleges, and because they became involved in the archpriest controversy on the side of the appellants, friction even in the short term was unavoidable.

With all the enthusiasm of the first wave of secular priests and Jesuits, inspired by their protomartyr, Mark Barkworth, and happy in having no recent history, the English Benedictine mission went from strength to strength. By 1607 it was well established. Like the secular priests and Jesuits, the monks produced strong and original characters and from the point of view of authority, sometimes enfants terribles. According to L. Hicks, S.J., trouble between the orders traced its origins to "the wholly imprudent means by which the enthusiastic young Benedictines, without experience of the English mission, and at a critical moment of renewed persecution, tried to set their work on foot. Their means were far from spiritual and involved a close alliance with a veteran intriguer, William Gifford, and with the persecuting politicians. Their leader, Augustine Bradshaw, had received consistent kindness from the Jesuits, on his own admission—from Garnet, Blackfan, and Oldcorne. Before the Douai project was raised at all, they had become involved in an intrigue to secure the withdrawal of the Jesuits from England at a moment of fierce persecution (January 1606)."[29] For his intrigues Gifford was expelled from the archduke's territories, for all the latter's Anglophilia.

The Benedictines denied the charges and countercharged the Jesuits with calumny. While the Privy Council could hardly rejoice at the appearance of yet another head of the hydra on English soil, they rightly judged that this too had a mouth which could be made to feed on the papist cause itself. Sir Thomas Edmondes, ambassador in Brussels, reported to Cecil early in 1607 the possibilities of sowing new discords. Dr. Worthington of Douai, "who is wholly the Jesuits' creature, hath been lately here to sue unto the archduke that . . . White [A. Bradshaw, O.S.B.] . . . may not be suffered to proceed to the creating of a college of English students of his order at Douai." Edmondes hinted at means by which Jesuits and Benedictines might be more closely embroiled. "The Jesuits will not allow of any seminaries but such as they may absolutely govern, and to have the means to choose out of them the best spirits to draw into their Society. And therefore

---

[29] See L. Hicks, S.J., "The exile of Dr William Gifford from Lille in 1606," (10) 7, 214–38; D. Lunn, "Chaplains to the English Regiment in Spanish Flanders, 1605–6," ibid., 11, 133–55.

Baldwin did interesse himself, and join with the president in prevent-
ing that suit."[30]

The English government was set in its determination to push
any advantage against the Jesuits offered by the Gunpowder Plot.
Edmundes discussed with "a confident friend" of the nuncio the possibility of getting Hugh Owen and William Baldwin, chaplain to the
English regiment in Flanders, extradited to England, both being falsely
accused of complicity. Bradshaw, alias White, was used by the nuncio
as a go-between for communications with Edmondes. White told him
"how earnestly" the nuncio wished to meet the ambassador to assure
him of "his master's and his own great detestation of the treason." The
nuncio was even prepared to put on lay dress for the occasion, but
Edmondes was quick to assure him by White that he desired no such
thing. He added craftily that he was sure the King could trust "the
pope for doing him right against those wicked conspirators in case
they were to be required of him." The Gunpowder Plot conveniently
excused the King from offering anything in return. White was to tell
the nuncio, "I durst not give ear to any further overtures [for the
papists] . . . considering what had lately fallen out in England." But he
could be sure there would be no "inhuman proceeding" against them.
The Benedictine came back next day with the nuncio's thanks and a
further offer: "whether if the pope, to gratify his Majesty for securing
him against his doubt of the practice of the Jesuits would yield to call
all the Jesuits out of England, his Majesty would likewise grant any . . .
liberty of conscience to the Catholics"? The Puritan Edmondes replied
tersely that such a remedy was "far from curing the disease whereof it
was question."[31]

At the end of February, Edmondes reported an interview with
the archduke in which he did his best to blacken the Jesuits and restore the reputation of William Gifford. He even suggested that Gifford's fall from grace had "made him resolve to go into England and
. . . cast himself into the hands of the state had he not been diverted
from the same." Gifford was far too useful a listening post for the
ambassador among the Flanders exiles to be lost in this way. The
archduke was not forthcoming. Edmondes reported White's strenuous
efforts to get a Benedictine foundation set up in Douai. President
Richardot claimed that this had been refused to avoid annoying King

---

[30] T. Edmondes to R. Cecil, 22.1/1.ii.1607; (VII) SP 77/8 part 1, f.235v, signed
dispatch; Fabre, "The Settling of the English Benedictines," 15–16, but footnote references seem in error.

[31] S. to s., 6/16.1.1606/7; (VII) SP 77/8, part 1, ff.6–10v, original dispatch; see
(14) XVIII, 8f. See F. Edwards, "The Attempt in 1608 on Hugh Owen, Intelligencer for
the Archdukes in Flanders," (10) XVII (1984), 140–57.

James. Edmondes parried this with malevolent skill. "But I told him that it was more to gratify the Jesuits." Baldwin was not extradited, but he was so discouraged by the slur of complicity that he no longer visited Richardot: another if minor victory for Salisbury.[32]

Augustine Bradshaw, Augustine of St. John, reported on March 26 to Nicholas Fitzherbert in Rome on the projected Douai foundation.[33] The latter was assured that Worthington was not only trying to get the Benedictines out of Douai but even out of England. In fact this was based on his interpretation of a Latin word in a letter from the nuncio. The latter informed Bradshaw he had an official announcement to make—"quod tibi denuntiandum erit." Innocently or otherwise, Bradshaw took *denuntiandum* to mean "threatening" or "menacing" instead of merely "announcing," so that Fitzherbert could assume that the Jesuits had launched an attack on them.[34] In truth, it was the Pope, no less, who had forbidden the Benedictines to erect a new house in Douai, but certainly not that they should be expelled from Flanders.[35] Bentivoglio reassured them on the point, and to soften the blow recommended neighboring abbots to go on giving them alms.[36]

To Worthington had fallen the unenviable task of reforming a college which had changed considerably in spirit if not in structure since the death of Allen. In his day Douai needed no rules, for it housed only mature students in the days of first fervor and the rift among the clergy had not yet occurred. By 1607, however, the rule of right reason was no longer a sufficient guide. Student discontent at new restrictions coming in with rules drove some to Rome or Spain. By September 1604 eight had left for Spain. Ralph Green followed them on September 6, "who a few days before had caused some disturbance, and persuaded a number of students to sign a petition for the upholding of certain customary liberties which they feared were about to be restricted."[37] Two more left in 1605, while in March 1607 seven

---

[32] T. Edmondes to R. Cecil, 18/28.ii.1606/47; ibid., part 2, ff.245r–7v, signed dispatch.

[33] See F. Fabre, "The Settling of the English Benedictines," 55f, letter in full.

[34] See Lewis and Short, *A Latin Dictionary*. The first meaning of *denuntiare* is "to give an official intimation" or "to make an official announcement of one's intentions by means of a messenger, herald etc *[sic]*." The standard of Latinity among the priests, especially the appellants and seminarians, was rarely high.

[35] Borghese to Bentivoglio, Rome; (V) Cod.Barb. 5919, f.277, Italian; F. Fabre, "The Settling of the English Benedictines," 56.

[36] (IV) F.Borgh. II, Vol. 100, f.180; Fabre, "The Settling of the English Benedictines," 56–57; his letter of 18.viii.; ibid., 56.

[37] Fabre, "The Settling of the English Benedictines," 13.

students asked permission to join the projected Benedictine house in Douai, which was formally opened by Augustine Bradshaw on May 12, 1607. They were officially dismissed on May 25.[38] Time alone would tell which vocations were genuine. With the disbanding of the English regiment in Flanders in May 1606—a signal triumph for Salisbury—Bradshaw, formerly a chaplain, was free to concentrate on Douai. Worthington, a friend of the Jesuits, and under constant attack from William Gifford since 1603, could not be enthusiastic about an institution which owed much to his avowed enemy. On January 20, 1607, Worthington sent a memorial on the subject to Rome through the Brussels nuncio, Decio Caraffa.[39]

While Creswell was in Rome, the situation at Valladolid deteriorated further. Twenty-seven students dated a protest to Persons on August 1, 1607, detailing unwelcome innovations since 1605.[40] The Spanish provincial's regime left them "not one day in the whole year free from lessons . . . except vineyard days which are very few by reason of so many Holy Days and High Masses, and oftentimes scarce one or two in a month if the weather be bad." Health had never been worse. Some died, chiefly those who had "wholly abandoned their exercise." The theology students were near to open rebellion. Creswell had done his best but had no real authority. Richard Walpole, caught between them all and forced back on diplomacy, followed less than "sincere proceedings." The only hope lay with Creswell and the Spanish rector, not the provincial, who, according to the book, had the last word.[41]

Persons with Blackfan at his elbow, the man with recent, firsthand experience, replied in mid-September. The authority of Creswell and Persons touched only "points concerning the English mission" and disposing of subjects. Matters of everyday routine were the province of local superiors, especially the provincial. Persons defended Walpole and repudiated the idea that he or anyone else was tied to his directives. His comfort for the students was decidedly cold. They should concentrate on union and giving good example, so that local people might be moved to open their purses to help them. On this they all depended. Many in England enduring the heat of persecu-

---

[38] See Lunn, *The English Benedictines,* Chaps. 3 and 4.

[39] See Fabre, "The Settling of the English Benedictines," 14, 54. Fabre claims the memorial was against the English Benedictines, but there is no evidence of this in Caraffa's letter. The memorial itself is seemingly lost.

[40] CRS 30, 90–91. Four students did not sign.

[41] Ibid.

tion would be happy to exchange it for their peace. Twelve disputations a year was nothing much to complain about.[42]

Writing to Creswell in the autumn, however, Persons made it clear that he knew the unrest at Valladolid had deeper causes than student petulance or boredom. "The great dissension" between Creswell and Walpole had caused "great disorder." Creswell was made responsible; but the General appointed Luis da Ponte, one of his most distinguished subjects, to make a formal visitation, very necessary since "the disorders were cause that many scholars went to the Benedictines."[43] Persons wrote to Pareces, rector at Valladolid, on April 1, 1608, telling him bluntly that the imminent ruin of the college was mainly due to contempt for the instructions and settlement drawn up at Rome. Why should the students respect authority when they saw it flouted by their Jesuit mentors and teachers? Much harm was being done in England by men who came back disgruntled, leading Holtby to think that "it would be a good thing if the seminary were disbanded." Notable patrons and supporters of the Society were being alienated by the tales going the rounds, which could not be brushed off as slander. If charity was lacking among some of the Jesuits, so was the spirit of poverty. Pareces was another del Rio, it seems, entertaining lavishly and keeping far more servants than necessary, while ruling like a despot and following the advice of strangers who knew nothing of the real problems. Creswell added his own burthen of grievances with regard to rectors who had a preference for conationals as servants, who wasted and stole the property of the house.[44] Meanwhile, the Benedictines at Douai continued to consolidate their position, assisted in no small degree by the support of Cardinal de Givry, Henri IV's agent at the Vatican.[45]

Compared with Valladolid, St. Omers at this time was the happy country without a history, but it did have financial problems. Persons, pressed by higher authority, had to order the zealous rector in the summer of 1607 to "admit no more boys than he [could] well maintain, and those of just age and capacity."[46] The college in Rome was likewise enjoying a period of relative calm, with all the scholars in

---

[42] RP to the Valladolid students, 18.ix.1607, Rome; (IX) Serie 2; CRS 30, 91–93.

[43] RP to Creswell, 15.x.1607, Rome; (II) f.490.

[44] *Responsio ad calumnias contra [Creswell]* . . . , V. supra; f.261. See Luis de la Puente, S.J., to Creswell, 30.vi.1608; (I) Anglia.A.III, No. 81.

[45] (V) Cod.Barb.Lat.5919,f.293; F. Fabre, "The Settling of the English Benedictines," 57. D. Lunn, *The English Benedictines*, 74–78.

[46] RP to Giles Schondonck, 7.vii.1607, Rome; (II) f.429.

good health. As for himself, he suffered in July from a pain in his left side but evidently not severe enough to take his mind off a new problem.

English ladies, no less than men, felt that national temperament might have to play its part in a religious vocation. But not even Jesuits always recognized that sauce for the goose went also with the gander. This summer Baldwin and Singleton reported from Flanders about "our nuns of Louvain meaning . . . to go forth of their monastery." Persons was discouraging about thus "imbarking themselves so far without biscuit."[47] The criticism was directed principally at Mary Ward, perhaps the most remarkable woman of her generation on the English international scene. She left England in 1606 with a firm intention to enter religion and carried letters of introduction to the Jesuits at St. Omers. The best they could find for her was a place as a lay sister in the Walloon convent of the Poor Clares. She stood it for a year before departing to found a convent for Poor Clares of her own nation. There was much unrest among English nuns in their dispersal centers on the continent. The Benedictine convent at Brussels, founded in 1598 by Lady Mary Percy, offered an example of what might be done by way of remedy. But not even Persons seems to have regarded Mary Ward's secession as more than an expression of obstinacy and idiosyncrasy. Women, like children, should be seen and not heard; and if they were nuns, not even seen. However, "so many young English ladies of high birth, remarkable alike for personal and mental gifts, had come to Saint Omer in . . . 1606 with the idea of entering religion" that the English Jesuits got a separate house set up for them. Ward's brief experience of the Walloon convent was long enough to convince her that English nuns needed confessors and spiritual directors of their own nation. The English Franciscans had no house of their own, while the Anglo-Benedictine foundation was still in its infancy, so the house was placed under the local Jesuits. Neither Franciscans nor Jesuits were pleased, since the provincial of the former thought all Poor Clares should be under his jurisdiction, and the latter objected that the Jesuit rule forbade them to manage religious houses of women. Eventually, Mary Ward succeeded in setting up a house for her Sisters at Gravelines, wisely deciding that another religious house at St. Omer would be one too many. While she was at St. Omer, the Jesuit Roger Lee became her spiritual director and confessor. She left the convent about Easter as a further step, conscious or otherwise, towards the flowering of her own extraordinary and painful vocation.[48]

---

[47] RP to T. Owen, vice-rector at the VEC, 29.vii.1607, Frascati; (II) f.337.

[48] See (17) 164–69. See Mathilde Köhler, *Mary Ward: ein Frauenschicksal des 17 Jarhunderts* (Munich, 1984).

Whatever Persons might have wished, the Jesuit involvement was not to end quickly.

News from England this year spoke only of harassment and positive persecution as the heavy fines for recusancy were extorted once again with full rigor. Many believed that Salisbury was spurring on the appellant priest Thomas Wright to preach the permissibility of the oath and of attendance at Protestant services.[49] The screw was turning on Persons's personal suffering. But in spite of a fifteen-day racking from sciatica, he wrote to the Pope in mid-August to report a strong rumor of Blackwell's arrest.[50] In fact he was arrested on June 24. Imprisoned in the Gatehouse, he publicly defended the oath before the Archbishop of Canterbury and then on July 7 took it himself. Soon after, he was removed to the Clink, in the liberty of the Bishop of Winchester, where life was tolerable and even comfortable. He was deposed as archpriest on February 1, 1608. Meanwhile, before the full scandal became known, Persons urged the Pope to send Blackwell a letter of encouragement, since the "rumour spread by rivals these past years that he was not greatly favoured at Rome" had left him "somewhat depressed and discouraged."

Directly connected with the problem presented by George Blackwell was that concerning the governance of the Catholic community in England. The appointment of bishops must now seem inopportune. But whatever the appellants might think or print, the solution did not lie with the Jesuits. Persons was instinctively ready to spring to the defence of papal decisions. Meanwhile, "as to creating bishops, I find the common opinion among Catholics . . . is . . . that in view of the difficulties of the times, it is a doubtful issue." Certainly, the presence of bishops would spur the persecutors to new efforts. They would be a further financial burden on an impoverished community; and, unless they were agreed among themselves, their presence would be another source of disunity.[51] Not for the first time, Persons was almost a prophet. One Blackwell was enough. His letter to the clergy of July 7/17 advised them to take the oath and tell their people to do the same. Rome was stung into action. On August 23 a second brief was issued condemning the oath.[52]

It fell to Persons to communicate this latest brief to his Jesuits. But timing was important, because he did not wish it even to appear

---

[49] ? to RP, 4/14.viii.1607, London; (II) f.490.

[50] RP to Paul V, 12.viii.1607, Frascati; (II) f.429 and 455, Italian.

[51] See (11) IV, app. xxviii. RP to Paul V, 12. viii.1607 for his views on bishops. V. supra.

[52] (11) IV, app. xxix.

that it had been engineered by the Jesuits. Edward Coffin in Rome was given a copy and a covering letter on September 6, with orders to make copies but not to tell anyone about the brief or send it away before further orders. The copies were to be sent sealed to Baldwin in Flanders. Meanwhile, the final exhortation was to speed and secrecy.[53]

Misunderstanding with the Benedictines and the aftermath of Blackwell's oath taking continued as the outstanding problems of 1607.[54] Inevitably, King, Council, and Church by Law Established enjoyed a field day at Blackwell's capitulation. A book published early in 1608 set out his reasons for taking the oath and included relevant documents.[55] George Birkhead, his successor as archpriest, while loyal to Rome, leaned decidedly towards the appellants and away from the Jesuits, a tendency which could only be strengthened by the news coming out of Valladolid.

Perhaps Persons's best contribution to the future this year was *A treatise tending to mitigation towards Catholicke subjects in England. Wherein is declared, That it is not impossible for Subjects of different religion (especially Catholickes and Protestantes) to live together in dutifull obedience and subjection under the government of his Majesty of Great Britany. . . .* It was directed primarily against Thomas Morton, royal chaplain and Dean of Gloucester from 1606, who attacked Catholic teaching, or alleged Catholic teaching, in *A Full Satisfaction concerning a double Romish Iniquitie: heinous rebellion, and more than heathenish Aequivocation . . . ,* published in 1606. Morton began the controversy with *An Exact Discoverie of Romish doctrine in the case of Conspiracie and Rebellion . . . ,* printed in 1605. He tried to show that "Romish schooles" were hotbeds of sedition and "popish priests" were rightly executed as traitors without more ado.[56]

In the course of his reply, Persons produced the first reasoned and sustained plea in the English language for religious toleration. J. Lecler admitted, "Although Persons did not treat this subject with great thoroughness, his arguments ad hominem are sometimes clever

[53] RP to Edward Coffin, 6.ix.1607, Frascati; (II) f.357, English.

[54] RP to Paul V, 22.xi.1607, Rome; (II) f.430.

[55] *A large examination taken / at Lambeth, according to his / Majestie's direction, point by point, / of M. George Blackwell made Arch/ priest of England by Pope Clement 8. / Upon occasion of a certaine answere of his, / without the privitie of the State, to a letter lately sent unto him from Cardinall Bellarmine blaming him for taking/ the oath of Allegiance . . . ,* Robert Barker (London, 1607 [1608]). It included Bellarmine to Blackwell, 28.ix.1607; Blackwell to Bellarmine, 13.xii.; his examination by Canterbury; and Blackwell to the English Catholics from the Clink, 20.i.1608.

[56] Quoted in (70) 82.

and rather interesting."[57] W. K. Jordan clearly resented the fact that Persons so far spoiled the image of a papist as to favor toleration at all. "In one of the amazing flights from orthodoxy of which he was occasionally guilty in order to drive his arguments home, Persons came close to holding that men should enjoy liberty of conscience as a natural right."[58] He not only came close, he arrived.

In the controversy concerning the government of the secular clergy in England, there were those who claimed that neither the Jesuits nor any other religious should concern themselves with the secular clergy. This was unrealistic, since they also had to work alongside the rest, preferably in harmony. Members of the orders were far inferior in numbers to the secular priests, but their work was important. Persons wanted a system of government which would at least not increase the difficulties of his own men, and the appointment of a leader one could see as a friend and not an enemy. While there is no precise or scientific way of measuring influence, undoubtedly someone who served the Church and his order with no kind of self-seeking, as Persons did, wielded influence. But there is no reason to suppose the Vatican failed to see the dangers of letting itself be led by Persons or any other Jesuit in solving this crucial issue. If there were objections against setting up bishops, there were as many difficulties in the way of making suitable appointments.

On July 10 Secretary of State Borghese instructed Caraffa, nuncio in Spain, to sound out the English for possible candidates.[59] He might consult Jesuits, but with reserve. Creswell was reported to be against setting up bishops. In August Maffeo Barberini, nuncio in France, was also approached. His main difficulty was to think of candidates with the confidence of all parties. He agreed, appellants as well as Jesuits should be consulted.[60] Christopher Bagshaw headed his list as "born of honourable father and mother, a doctor in theology, very erudite and literate," and as having spent many years in prison for the faith. However, he was "extremely hostile to the Jesuits, not well-affected towards the apostolic see, and of too vehement, not to say arrogant, temperament." John Cecil followed: "Well born, doctor in theology, very eloquent and shows prudence and experience in affairs, but he is noted for his unstable temperament and for seeking his own.

---

[57] J. Lecler, *Toleration and the Reformation* 2 (London, 1960): 445.

[58] W. K. Jordan, *The Development of Religious Toleration in England I, 1603–40* (London, 1936), 502. Pages 500–505 fairly completely misjudge and misunderstand the position of RP and the Catholics at this time.

[59] (IV) F.Borgh. II.23–24, ff.224r–41v.

[60] See L. Hicks, "Letters of Thomas Fitzherbert 1608–1610," CRS 41 (1948), 14–15, n.4.

Formerly he liked the Jesuits little but now favours them, it is supposed for the use he can make of them." Richard Smith received scant praise. "Anyone who talks with him once or twice, for all he is a doctor of theology, will conclude he is quite unsuitable for the office." Champney and Charnock were rejected as too hostile to the Jesuits. Wothington, Martin Array, Singleton, George Birkhead, and others were mentioned only to be rejected as "too addicted to the Jesuits." Those most acceptable to all parties included Arthur Pitts, the Cardinal of Lorraine's chancellor, three Capuchins including Fr. Archangel (Barlow), and Matthew Kellison at Rheims.[61] In the event, Birkhead was chosen to follow Blackwell, and only as an archpriest. If Persons had anything to do with it, hoping for someone who would follow his suggestions willingly if not meekly, he was to be bitterly disappointed.

---

[61] This document was almost certainly (IV) Segreteria di Stato, Inghilterra, 19, ff.35r–6r.

I n 1603, Blaise, Franciscan bishop of St. Omer, gave the Jesuits a property at Watten for an English novitiate. Philip III confirmed the gift in 1604 and Paul V allowed its purpose in 1607. Edmondes, the English ambassador in Flanders, however, made it his business to foil the enterprise. The proximity of the site to England had been a reason for the gift in the first place, but this was also a reason for official English opposition.[1] The project eventually materialized but not until long after the death of Persons as well as Archduke Albert. The latter was inevitably overawed by a country which could do him damage at least economically. Persons included a complaint in a letter of February 6, writing about "the difficulties and delays . . . in respect of reasons of state." The obstacles did not all come from the English side. The house was large and imposing and would be noticed by travelers to and from England who would find out about "the people which should dwell there." Thence would arise "many molestations and dangers both from English heretics and also from the state of Flanders calling us into suspicion for resort of Englishmen thither." Trouble could come from a future bishop and from the "monks of that Order." All in all, a more modest beginning was more appropriate.[2] Persons favored a house at St. Omer, though not adjoining the existing seminary, "lest we should seem to allure those youths, or to live of them or upon their rents." However, the rector of the seminary could direct it with English Fathers as master of novices and procurator, keeping funds carefully separate. The General could lay down "convenient rules." Some novices, by the General's dispensation even while still novices, could go on to "humanity or positive divinity" at St. Omers, or philosophy or "school divinity" in the English College, Douai. The General was ready to allow up to twenty to go on to Rome. The bishop's support, moral and financial, and the favor of the Flemish Jesuit province were essential.[3]

---

[1] See (17) 149. RP tried to convince Philip III of the need in 1604. See (75) 18.

[2] RP to a Jesuit at Valladolid, 6.ii.1608; (IX) Serie 2, Leg. 2, contemporary copy.

[3] Ibid.

Persons's health was now edging him towards the exit. He wrote to Matthew Kellison, chancellor of Rheims University, in the spring, "I have experience, I thank God, of continual almost indisposition which admonisheth me also to prepare myself for . . . eternity."[4] His weariness to the point of exasperation with the endless dissensions or at least points of difference among his brethren becomes increasingly evident. A writer himself, he managed to encourage others. He told Kellison, regarding a forthcoming book, "I doubt not but that it will do much good. The more soldiers to the battery the better."[5] Even now he did not despair of reconciliation with enemies and critics. Referring optimistically to William Gifford, he wrote, "Tell him that we have been old friends and must be again or else we shall never dwell together in the next life, which God forbid."[6]

On March 15 George Birkhead acknowledged receipt of the brief of February 1 appointing him successor to Blackwell, whom it also deposed. Persons was the vehicle of communication between the Vatican and Birkhead, something the latter did not find reassuring. As good politics added to the demands of Christian virtue, Persons did not allow himself to become emotionally overcommitted either to people or their differences and quarrels. He did not bear grudges and was always ready for reconciliation, cherishing the conviction that, as right reason prevailed in a man, so he must come to agree with him. But the English mission of the early seventeenth century was no longer that of the late sixteenth. The divisions induced by the archpriest controversy in its totality, which involved opposite views on the role of Spain and of the English government in the survival of Catholicism, could not be solved on the evidence generally available in Persons's day. His position, even if proved correct by subsequent historical revelation, was not patently obvious to his own generation. There was room for good men to differ. The declared appellants were still a minority in 1608, but they had many sympathizers; anyone at the head of the Catholic community must take them into account. At least for these, the Society of Jesus was now well established as a whipping boy for all that went wrong or seemed unacceptable coming from Rome. It was therefore seen by many as unfortunate that Paul V should reverse the policy of Clement VIII to the point of making Persons the point of contact between himself and the secular clergy. Persons, rightly convinced of the purity of his intentions towards the whole mission, could

---

[4] RP to M. Kellison, 26.iv.1608, Rome; (X) No. 3. For Kellison see (18).

[5] The book was presumably *A reply to Sotcliffe's answer to the survey of the new religion, in which his insufficient answers and manifest follies are discovered* (Rheims, 1608). See (19) 79/[210].

[6] RP to Kellison, 26.iv.1608. V. supra.

not see the tactical disadvantages of clinging to a role which belonged already to an earlier age. The Pope, aware of his loyalty to the Holy See and devotion to the cause, did not see it either. Birkhead was clearly embarrassed that he should be expected to become another early Blackwell in his relations with Persons. He soon made it clear that he had no intention of doing so. In mid-May Persons reported the safe arrival of Birkhead's letters at the Vatican. Paul V was doubtless relieved to know that his rejection of the oath and recantation demanded from those who took it had been "received and obeyed also so dutifully" by the new archpriest "notwithstanding all difficulties and dangers." Birkhead had done his best to avoid the new responsibility, as he made clear to Persons in a letter of March 2. Persons consoled him, "You must think God hath chosen you to bear the brunt and there is no remedy but to put your shoulders under it." It was a high compliment that he should be chosen to amend the fault of his erring predecessor. But Blackwell should be prayed for so that he "return to his old peace of mind and union with his friends." For the rest, Persons and Birkhead agreed that "charity towards all must be the first direction" and also peace if it might be "procured without prejudice of the common cause." Otherwise, "patience, fortitude, humility and magnanimity must remedy all."[7]

Birkhead saw his main task as the avoidance of controversy and the reuniting of a confused and divided body. Undeniably, the Jesuits were a center of controversy, even if the same had to be said of their opponents. This made it difficult to side with Jesuits even though they were so obviously on the side of Roman orthodoxy. Persons saw in the archpriest's reserve towards him simply an unfortunate echo of a recent past, which he hoped would die away. Only malice could interpret all his efforts to help the mission as Jesuitical manipulation and interference. But another event, in itself trivial, from the recent past now seemed to confirm the worst suspicions of some who could not be easily dismissed as merely malicious.

Anthony Browne, Viscount Montague of Cowdray, allowed his house to be used as the archpriest's headquarters, so that his feelings and susceptibilities were an important factor in the recusant scene. Writing to Birkhead on May 18, Persons admitted that he had withheld a letter from Montague to the Roman authorities. This was well in the past, but Persons had only explained his action, or inaction, to Montague "not long ago." Moved only by "a desire to serve him," he had done what he "presumed himself would have commanded . . . if

---

[7] RP to Chamberlayne *vere* Birkhead, 18.v.1608, Rome; (X) No. 4. See (11) V, xxvii and IV, note on pp. 76–79. NB Tierney/Dodd extracts often omit important matter.

he had been present," following the advice of "most secret friends that most loved and honoured the party." The letter, apparently written in the latter half of 1605, had urged the appointment of bishops in England. It was probably connected with the appeal which Cecil and Champney brought to Rome in 1606. Knowing the casualness, not to say negligence, of Roman officials dealing with matters which were supposed to be confidential, Persons, after due consultation, gave the Pope merely a summary of Browne's letter, though admitting his identity. Part of his intention was to protect Browne, who, as a recusant, had been in serious conflict with the law of England on a number of occasions.[8]

It was an indication of general feeling by this time that Montague could resent this exercise of discretion. He now wanted the letter back. In a letter of July 5, which revealed Thomas Fitzherbert as his principal adviser, and wisely making Birkhead his intermediary, Persons offered to deliver the original letter if the viscount so wished.[9] Apparently he did not, and the letter was returned by way of Birkhead, with due acknowledgement of his mediation, in a letter of August 21.[10]

Birkhead made it clear in a letter of April 14 to Persons that he was working under great difficulties. The latter assured him of Jesuit support, stressing that the clause in the brief of October 5, 1602, limiting contact between archpriest and Jesuits had been deliberately dropped in the latest brief. Had Blackwell been able to consult the Jesuits, his unfortunate fall from grace would not have occurred. Persons was glad that Birkhead was doing his best to reconcile those who opposed his office if not himself. All the same, he must not surrender too much even for the sake of peace. Someone mentioned by Birkhead as the "mouth of the rest" advised him to cut loose from Thomas Fitzherbert. Persons was dismayed. "Before you leave him for their sakes," let them find someone as "fit, able and willing as he is to further the common cause."[11] Birkhead thought he had found such a man.

---

[8] See (20) 5f, n.6.

[9] RP to Birkhead, 5.vii.1608, Rome; (X) No. 7, a.l.s.

[10] S. to s., 21.viii.1608, Rome; (X) No. 8, a.l.s. See (20) p. 6, No. 8. Concerning the return of the letter, see ibid., 31, 33.

[11] S. to s., 31.v.1608, Rome; (X) No. 5. See (20) 8–13. Fitzherbert's wife died in 1588. Probably in 1601 he went to Rome and was ordained priest on 24.iii.1602, and appointed clergy-agent. On 15.viii.1606 he made a private vow to join the Society of Jesus, but did so only in 1615. He died in 1640 aged 88. See (35).

In an effort to restore equilibrium by pleasing both sides, and for "quietness sake," Birkhead toyed with the idea of appointing an appellant as his agent in Rome. Persons's reaction was foreseeable. Fitzherbert would be glad to have someone at his side to lighten his labor; but, unless he could see eye to eye with Persons and his friends, he "would be a great cause of trouble and confusion here, and would be able to do you no pleasure at all." As for the English in Rome, Persons doubted if four out of a hundred agreed with the appellants and to have one of these as agent "would seem a strange thing." They enjoyed little credit with Paul V, who, as Cardinal Borghese, had witnessed the earlier troubles at close hand.[12] But as an exponent of the art of the possible, Persons was ready to see some of the appellants appointed assistants to Birkhead if this would keep them quiet. The names of Bishop, Colleton, "the two Benets," and Smith were mentioned, if without enthusiasm. Dr. Smith, at any rate, had no record of being "discontented."[13]

The Pope, Edward Cardinal Farnese, and his *substitutus*, Innocenzio de Bubalis, all wanted to hear from Birkhead. Not that the archpriest had been behindhand in his reports. Persons found them all "very well written" and worthy of "signore Paul's" immediate attention. Like another Paul admonishing Timothy, Persons warned Birkhead to keep his brethren in their place. He must not leave his "old tried friends for their brickle friendship."

He had another important point to make.

> As for the desire of bishops, none of them can be more earnest therein with order and modesty than we have been here both for many years past, and now of late, and at this present, and we have his Hol[iness] in a very good disposition to grant it, if he might be persuaded that it would cut off factions and confirm union among us; but he feareth that if the parties be not well chosen, they will be capita factionum.

If Birkhead could find three or four fit men apart from himself, Rome would give him "all assistance for obtaining the same." Persons was never opposed to the appointment of bishops.[14]

By June, friction between English Jesuits and Benedictines which had developed at Valladolid and Douai reached top-level atten-

---

[12] Ibid. The appellants too easily assumed the role of spokesmen for all the English clergy and have been accepted as such too uncritically by some historians. See (20), 10.

[13] RP to Birkhead, 31.v.1608. V. supra. Printed with misleading omissions in (11) V, xxix.

[14] Ibid.

tion in both orders. Neither side at this level, foreseeably, was anxious for collision. Luis de la Puente, native of Valladolid and foremost Jesuit and spiritual writer of his day, was called on to practice his preaching. At an interview with the Benedictine Father General at Valladolid, he did his best to satisfy him with documentary material supplied by Persons. The Benedictine informed de la Puente that aspirants to his order in the college at Valladolid had "already been placed under the orders of his monks in Flanders, and by his command had gone to throw themselves at the feet of the Fathers of the Society to unite themselves with them and refer their complaints to them." Dom Anselmo, who had been supporting the students, was not a member of the General's congregation and therefore not part of his concern. Persons already knew this.[15] "John Broughton and others . . . put in serious complaints here to the prior and other monks because [the Jesuits] expelled them from the college only because they wanted to be monks."[16] De la Puente was able to satisfy the prior and also the Benedictine general, at least regarding general goodwill, using a paper supplied by Persons. "Although he had his doubts," the Benedictine general decided to adopt its suggestions "as the best way of dealing . . . sincerely with all concerned, and especially with me, because he is very friendly to the Society." He was "much troubled" that not only the aspirants themselves had been dismissed but also those who had tried to persuade others, and even those who confided their vocation to another.

There can be little doubt that at the height of the student unrest the Jesuits at Valladolid had overreacted. At all events, de la Puente was not prepared to defend what he took to be undue rigor. He told Persons that he was advising "our Father"—Creswell?—to revise standing orders to make it clear that Jesuits did not oppose entry into other orders. Nor should the students be forbidden to discuss such matters among themselves. In any case, fewer were coming to a seminary which seemed to be dying. Nor was the dying a metaphor. In 1607 "some kind of epidemic . . . invaded the student body towards the end of the year." Many died. The survivors were left prostrate for months and incapable of serious study. "In fact the college seemed more like a hospital than an academy,"[17] a resemblance

[15] "Epistola Ludovici de Ponte ad Personium, Romam, ex autographo," 6.vi.1608, Valladolid; (II) f.178b, 179a, in margin, "De alumnis Sem. Vallisol. petentibus Ord. Benedictinorum," Spanish. For Dom Anselm, see (17) passim.

[16] The Spanish copy gives "Juan Boton." There was no "Button" among the protesting students at Valladolid at this time (?). The name given comes closest to a name given in CRS 30, 91.

[17] Blackfan, *Annales*. . . . , 81, 83.

continuing well into 1608. Lay externs brought in to help with nursing and running the house were inadequately supervised and damaged and stole so much of the property that it looked as if an army had completed a sack. Persons seems not to have grasped the gravity of the situation.

Birkhead's letter to Persons of April 24 raised a subject likely to recur, that of "faculties." The Pope assured him through Persons that he had "all the faculties that his predecessor had," thus seeming to admit that he was not quite sure himself. Much had been granted orally. If they did not seem sufficient, the Pope would reconsider. Persons had to admit that he would need to look for "copies of the old faculties. Some let is the absence of our protector who, as I remember, gave him all his faculties, yet I cannot tell till he come." Birkhead's main queries concerned consecrating chalices and reading heretical books. As far as Persons knew, the former was limited to "some three or four over the realm." It was "esteemed here episcopal" and Birkhead should reserve it to himself. He should receive permission for reading forbidden books but use it "with much discretion." Although health was troubling him—he had been forced to answer "by another man's hand . . . and that briefly"—Persons had taken the trouble to get an interview with "Paul" to get the answers to the archpriest's queries.[18]

Because he was not the agent for the secular clergy in Rome, Persons's claim that he had nothing, at least directly, to do with granting or withholding faculties is plausible. He was essentially a passer of messages between the General and his Jesuit subjects, and between Pope and protector and the secular clergy. He was entitled and obliged by duty to advise, but for good or ill his advice was by no means always followed. Faculties were given or withheld at the discretion of the donor. But inevitably the man in the middle and with undeniable influence became the whipping boy for the aggrieved, a role by now well established in the wider context.

On the vexed question of bishops for England, Birkhead had to be reassured that there was no fixed objection in Rome to the idea. But the Pope was not pleased to hear that some wished to come to Rome "to solicit that and other matters, for he saith that he knoweth what may be said in pro, but would be glad to hear the solution of the difficulties in contra."[19] Persons was aware of his role as scapegoat. "As

[18] RP to Birkhead alias Salvin, 21.vi.1608, Rome; (III) Old Series, VIII, No. 62, a.l.s.; (11) V, xxxi, with omissions. See (20) 13–18.

[19] Ibid. See (20) 14 and n.4. Birkhead's faculties are given in (III) ibid., No. 82. See (20) 29 and n.7.

for them that lay all upon your friend here, they do him much wrong, for that he abstaineth from dealing in their affairs whatsoever he can, but only to pray for them. Yet being in the place he is, when he is asked his opinion, he cannot but speak it with his reasons for the same." He had, after all, "as much interest as another to speak his mind." Having, worked for it for so long, he was convinced that he knew what was for the good of the mission as well as another. If this annoyed some people, "he may not leave to do good for not offending them that would let or hinder the same."[20]

At this stage Birkhead was ready to take Persons into his confidence, writing frequently and candidly about his problems. On May 7 he described the effect of nerves frayed from relentless persecution. Persons kept his comfort on a high spiritual plane. Where else could it be found? God had brought the Church through worse and would do as much for Birkhead unless he gave him "a more excellent crown by martyrdom, which was the highest happiness of all."[21] The Jesuit disclaimed any responsibility for Birkhead's appointment. He merely gave the Pope "a list of the Assistants with a relation of their ages and abilities to perform the office." Nor was Persons's the only advice asked for and given. Birkhead's was the second name on Persons's list, the first being passed over as too old; and he should see in this "rather God Almighty his lot than any negotiation at all" and feel stronger in consequence. Persons did not wish him to be partisan. "You do exceeding well in seeking by all good and lawful means to content all parties, or rather to procure that there be no parties."

Thomas Fitzherbert, of a distinguished Staffordshire family, gave all his attention to the Catholic cause after his wife's death in 1588. He was ordained in the English College, Rome, on March 24, 1602, and soon after appointed agent for the clergy. Any influence that Persons had would have helped to promote a kindred spirit—so kindred that on August 15, 1606, he vowed to join the Jesuits, though this was delayed in the event until 1613.[22] But in 1608 he was already far too close to the Society and to Persons to please many in England.

The issue of episcopal appointment was to become a wedge driven ever deeper between the archpriest and Persons. Persons insisted that in Rome the idea was "much desired," while he himself "was never averted from it but always did see many reasons for it." He had

[20] RP to Birkhead, 21.vi. V. supra.

[21] S to s., 5.vii.1608, Rome; (X) No. 6, a.l.s.; (11) V, xxxii with many omissions. In spite of persecution, the Catholics showed remarkable fidelity, crowding the Masses in the Spanish embassy chapel, for example. See (75) 116, 118, 123.

[22] See (20) 19–21.

offered several "petitions and motions" himself since Allen's death and more recently supported John Sweet.[23] Most recently, he had persuaded the Pope to have the protector investigate the difficulties and set up a commission to select four or five names from which he could choose the fittest. Persons now advised Birkhead to discuss it all with his friends and then petition Rome. "And as for me, you may assure them that they shall not only find me not contrary but as desirous as any man to have it go forward."[24] One thing needed emphasis. "His Holiness said to me expressly that he would not have any sent hither for the suit of bishops." All should be done by letter. Furthermore, Persons wanted no mention of his own name. "For I know it will be evil taken, and so will anything else that shall fall out otherwise than they desire, though I have no part therein."[25] In fact, the Pope would rely ultimately on the cardinals of the Inquisition, who were thorough in their methods, "all very wise, and of different humours," who would decide, as one could believe, "without passion or particular affection to any man or matter." It had been their idea to follow Blackwell with another archpriest rather than bishops.

The appellants concluded, however, that in spite of their voluminous correspondence with Rome, they still had no real influence at the highest level. From mid-April it was clear they intended to get Fitzherbert replaced as their agent.[26] Fitzherbert admitted that he could be well content to relinquish a task which brought with it much labor and no thanks, but he feared the damage that might be done if the wrong person succeeded him. The appellants, for all their large pretensions, still only represented a minority, however vociferous; and some had "intelligence with heretics," so that nothing that Rome wished to keep secret would be withheld from King James and his council.[27]

The Vatican made no change of policy towards the King in spite of continuing persecution. Neither was there any surrender of principle in the matter of the oath. Birkhead informed Persons on May 17 that the order to all priests to retract and seek reconciliation within two months under pain of losing their faculties was likely to bring waverers and wanderers back to the fold, except the "late archpriest and two or three others under arrest with him in London, and [who]

---

[23] Ibid., 14, n.4.

[24] Fatigued(?), RP ended the letter by another hand.

[25] T.F. to Salvin (Birkhead), 13.vi.1608, Rome; (20) 17.

[26] S. to s., 31.v.1608, Rome; (20) 9, 21.

[27] Ibid.; (20) 6, 21.

were in constant touch with the pseudo-archbishop of Canterbury."[28]
. But the "unquiet" were pressing harder than ever for bishops, demanding another deputation to Rome and refusing to "be still until
they obtain[ed] it." About this time Persons gave the protector a summary of "arguments on either side," as had been requested. Along with
this were a list of remedies for various "difficulties," not all of which
had been aired in England for fear of irritating the appellants rather
than stirring them to reflection.

About the time when William Alabaster was looking for the
exit, two rather more distinguished Englishmen were looking for the
way in.[29] One was the grandson of the Earl of Exeter, Robert Cecil's
elder half-brother, the Baron de Roos.[30] The other unnamed, heir to
one of "the greatest houses in England," was probably Thomas Cecil
Croftes, Baron Wentworth, who succeeded to his peerage on August
13, 1603. Persons the optimist saw this as the promise of dawn. Certainly, it seemed to prove that those making recusant history at this
time provided their contemporaries with more than a sorry tale of
internal feuding and disedifying quarrelsomeness. Persons observed
that, if "this Lord Cecil" returned to England a staunch Catholic, he
could greatly influence young Prince Henry. "If God has elected a
member of the house of Cecil, which has brought religion to ruin in
England, to restore it thus, it would be a wonderful sign of Divine
Providence." There was news also of Sir Toby Matthew, a "very tal-
ented" man of letters, who had converted to Catholicism about a year
previously. After ten months in prison in England, by repute for
refusing the oath, he was sent into exile out of consideration for his
father, the Archbishop of York.[31] James lately had sent an agent to
reside in Florence whom the grand duke should "speed on his way
quickly for he [would] be there only as a spy." Meanwhile, English
youth of the ruling classes felt "this universal attraction to the Catholic
faith," so that the Privy Council was "afraid to let them travel to Italy
or other Catholic countries." Evidently they were not deterred by the

---

[28] RP to Paul V, 6.vii.1608, Rome; (IV) F.Borgh. IV.86, f.30, a.l.s.

[29] For the danger to noblemen from their servants, see Edwards, *The Marvellous
Chance,* passim; CRS 21, 43–44.

[30] He died without issue at Naples on 27.vi.1618. See S. R. Gardiner, *History of
England . . . 1603–1642,* III; (15) 395–96; HMC Guides to the reports 1870–1911 and
1911–57.

[31] Adverse public reaction to the executions of Thomas Garnet, S.J., and
George Gervaise, O.S.B., brought some relaxation in the more extreme forms of persecution. Some mitigation of the law was promised. When the justices went on circuit, they
were told not to hang Catholics but to settle for what they could afford. Even a revision
of the oath was mooted; (75) 118, 120.

internal dissensions of the Catholic community. Or perhaps relatively little of this appeared on the outside.

Persons had to tell the Pope in July, "Fresh complaints have come from . . . Douai, Valladolid, England and Flanders about the disagreements with the English Benedictine Fathers." A cardinal of the Holy Office should be appointed to make an impartial examination of the causes and propose a remedy. Farnese, the protector, had received more memorials on the subject, which would go to the Pope.[32] Bianchetti was directed to adjudicate and a papal decree of December 10 was deemed to have closed the affair.[33] Meanwhile, Birkhead informed Persons on July 10 that the "majority of priests" who had upheld the oath had now made their submission in writing. Only Blackwell, Charnock, Tempest, Warmington, and Hebburn, still in prison, refused to comply. Presumably with a view to putting the controversy back on its feet, the Privy Council was reported to be ready to modify the oath in some of its more offensive passages. A new form of words acceptable to Catholics had been submitted to it.[34]

John Mush now led the movement in England for the appointment of bishops. Persons thought Cardinal Bianchetti should forthwith take up the matter with the Pope.[35] The question was the main subject of Birkhead's letter of June 21 and of Persons's reply two months later. Aware of the pressure on the archpriest to avoid negotiation through himself, Persons assured him he would be very ready to relinquish the burden if Birkhead could be otherwise "provided and furnished." All the same, he would always be ready to help, if only because it was "grateful to his Holiness and other superiors here."[36] To vindicate once again his own readiness for an episcopate, he called to mind his memorandum of 1597, submitted shortly after coming from Spain. He was not blind to the objections, especially that bishops, if they were recruited from the appellants, would probably unite against the religious orders working on the mission. He warned, "So long as your friends there stand out with such acerbity of spirit . . . against those that never offended them, and do labour with them in the same cause . . . I have little hope of any good to succeed." New agents to replace "Mr Swyn-

---

[32] RP to Paul V, 6.vii.1608 (v. supra). The new memorial mentioned by RP was probably Dom Anselm's "convincing answers to the 8 objections brought against the Benedictines by their opponents." This reached the Pope.

[33] T. Fitzherbert to T. Worthington, president of Douai, 2.viii.1608, Rome; (20), pp. 25–27. See (17) 224.

[34] RP to Paul V, after 10.vii.1608, Rome; (II) f.454. See also (75) 122.

[35] Ibid.; (II) f.454.

[36] RP to Birkhead, 21.viii.1608; (X) No. 8, a.l.s. See (11) V, xxxvii.

erton"—Fitzherbert—might be welcome. "But if they come with the spirit of opposition against all religious and their friends, as by that which hath been written to his Holiness may be gathered, neither his Holiness, I presume, will anyway like thereof. Nor can we." Convinced that he always advised impartially and equally convinced that appellant representatives could not, he foresaw the necessity of "religious men" also having their agent to counter the others. This would mean division and contradiction, making it impossible for Rome to decide or act. "This animosity . . . without cause is odious both to God and man, and will overthrow all but especially the authors; and I say it is without cause for that I know no religious man desirous to meddle in their affairs."[37]

The appellants tried to justify their aloofness from Persons and the Jesuits by the papal brief of 1602. Persons hastened to knock away this prop. Clement VIII had not prohibited all dealing with Jesuits "as though we were excommunicate," but only that Blackwell should not discuss matters of his government with Jesuits. Paul V had further defined and broadened this restriction so that "the prohibition was to be understood only of treating together matters of state, or that might justly offend the state." Nor was Fitzherbert dependent on Persons. "He dependeth upon no man but upon his Holiness and the King of Spain from whom he hath an honourable pension." As a man of "known wisdom and efficiency," he was trusted and respected by the Pope; and any new agent should tread warily in his regard. In spite of all, Persons still believed that any attitude of hostility to himself or the Society came only from a small minority. But however much Persons may have denied it, and truthfully, and however much Birkhead was inclined to believe him, and reasonably, the conviction was growing under appellant influence that Persons was the main obstacle to the appointment of bishops. The Vatican itself would never have withheld so obvious a blessing. Birkhead, clearly, had to perform a very delicate balancing act. The appellants by now had more influence than Persons cared to admit; but Birkhead had to maintain good relations not only with them but also with the Jesuits, since these obviously were trusted by the Pope. In England the Jesuits, orthodox in religion, could easily be presented, especially under pressure from government, as less than "loyal" to the civil power. In the past they had openly supported foreign invasion. Would they do so still?

The appellants answered in effect that, whether they would or would not, it was better for the sake of the future to have no contact with an organization which stirred such bad past memories in a Privy

---

[37] Ibid.

Council which was not going to forget and with which they still hoped desperately to do a deal. Persons was perhaps too old to understand the dilemma or to think out a new position. As he saw it, Birkhead's problem was mainly to stand firm. "Otherwise you will be carried down the river . . . and so grow into great diffidence with others who, in our judgments and that of his Holiness . . . seem the better and quieter part." By now "many hundred priests" going peacefully about their daily round pointed up the gratuitous quarrelsomeness of those who even wanted to make an issue out of Persons's failure, for good reasons, to deliver Lord Montague's letter to the Pope some years before.[38] The archpriest seemed to agree with the prefect that it was absurd that "some learned persons" considered it "a crime of diverting things from the Apostolic fountain" and were so "highly scandalised therewith" that they would rather "suffer death than permit it." Hyperbole of this kind may have amused the privy council but could not help in the more objective atmosphere of Rome.

Persons now had before him "the form sent hither of a new oath set down in divers fashions." With it came "an English memorial to the heads of the Council" in the name not only of Birkhead and his assistants but also of "the provincial of the Benedictines, Franciscans and Jesuits"—the first welcome sign of unity in the English Catholic clerical community? Even before he had studied it in detail, Persons was apprehensive. He was sure His Holiness would dislike "any forwardness . . . showed to such oaths wherein either tacit or expressed his authority is impugned by the adversary." The Inquisition cardinals would need to mull it over; and no more than the Pope would they welcome an oath "wherein any reference to religion is implied." The oath should only promise "such and so much civil obedience as any Catholic subject can or doth owe to his temporal prince." In any case, Birkhead should "be always the last in these matters," asking the Pope for "particular direction, wherein here we shall assist you what we may." He was complimented for his care so far to consult Rome on more important issues.[39]

The papal decision on the three projected forms of oath was known by the end of September. "He disalloweth them all." The Pope also commended Birkhead for being "backward" in what touched the apostolic authority. Paul V found appellant books repellant; and, if anyone was known by name to have had a part in them, he would

[38] S. to s., 23.viii.1608, Rome; (X) No. 10, first parag. and postscript in RP's hand, initialed by him. No. 11 is a copy of No. 10, also initialed. Addressed to "Mr Salvin"; (20) 6, n.8. See RP to same, 4.ix.1608. V. infra.

[39] S. to s., 23.viii. V. supra. Postscript also dated 23.viii. See Swinnerton/Fitzherbert to Birkhead, 23.viii.; (20) 28–33. By now de Bubalis was no longer vice-protector.

certainly be required to make "the canonical purgation."[40] The Pope did not wish for new clergy agents. Birkhead was also now advised "to stand firm against pressure for bishops."[41]

John Mush was unshakably convinced that the final decision on the episcopal question really lay with Persons. He broke a long silence to plead with him to do what he was already trying to do, although Mush would not believe it. Persons, exasperated at Mush's "strange manner of writing," tried to persuade Birkhead to use his influence to convince him. "I have concurred and do concur with him and his in the general suit if they may be gotten." But those anxious for yet another deputation to Rome should remember "Rome is a long stable wherein a horse may outlabour himself in kicking and winching without striking others that will keep themselves far enough from him"—a metaphor surfacing from childhood memories of the farm?[42]

John Colleton, Mush's close colleague, also wrote to Persons at this time, likewise urging him to push the episcopal cause. The letter was intercepted. Persons's failure to reply was taken as a further affront.[43] Colleton did not deny Blackwell's fall from grace in taking the oath; but, as formerly Blackwell's substitute, he refused to regard his fall from grace as affecting his own position.[44] He had discussed with Birkhead why "many ancient priests stood estranged from the Jesuits" and suggested remedies. He appealed to Persons, "If your Society, especially yourself, who (as most believe) hath the greatest hand in the aggrievances, should now effectually join with the priests in their suit for bishops," leaving them to nominate candidates or at least to have the last word in their choice, all misunderstanding would be removed. He hoped to come to Rome with a fresh deputation when he could debate "all matters thoroughly" with Persons.[45] Not that "I thought myself able to reason matters with you or to any other end more vain." He covered this offensive aside with a feeble apology, asking "pardon of whatsoever passed amiss" in their relations during

---

[40] RP to Birkhead, 4.ix.1608, Rome; (X) No. 12, a.l.s. The first line of this letter is damaged. See (11) V, xlii.

[41] S.to s., 13.ix.1608, Rome; (X) No. 13, a.l.s. This answered Birkhead's of 10.vii. See (11) V, xliv.

[42] Ibid. RP was willing that "your best patron and myne"—Montague?—should be allowed to see RP's letter to Mush if Birkhead thought it "expedient."

[43] J. Colleton to RP, 20.ix.1608, London; (VII) SP 14, Vol. 36, No. 24, a.l.s.(?); (11) V, xlv. A later endorsement, "30 September," indicates that the letter is probably O.S.

[44] Written "Horbey" and presumed to be "Holtby," superior of the English Jesuit mission.

[45] J. Colleton to RP, 20.ix.1608. V. supra.

"the late controversy," even if his conscience did not accuse him of "any great matter." The offer of reconciliation was thus backhanded, with no prospect of a negotiated peace.

Although Persons never received Colleton's letter of September 20, its main points repeated so faithfully the convictions—and could one say the prejudices?—of his party that when Persons wrote to Birkhead in early October, it seemed like a reply. He was anxious to satisfy Birkhead and his brethren. "I do neither meddle with their affairs nor desire it, nor did ever pretend to have the least authority over the least priest in England." He had "expressly admonished" his Jesuits "to attend to their own affairs in God's service, et pacem habere cum omnibus quantum fieri potest." He was quite ready to receive "any confident friend" of Birkhead's as his agent in Rome.[46] Where the Pope was concerned, Persons spoke only when he was spoken to, and his critics could hardly expect him to deny answer. The latest decision on bishops and on the oath had come from the Pope through Cardinal Bianchetti, based presumably on information from the nuncios in Paris and Brussels. Persons, anxious to avoid further misunderstanding, asked Bianchetti to request the Pope and the Inquisition cardinals "from whom the order came" to appoint someone else to communicate it to the archpriest. "Albeit I might write it to our Fathers of whom I have charge, yet I desire him to pardon me for writing it to [the archpriest] for that it might offend others." A new order was given for the message to be sent through the nuncios. Fitzherbert would write to Birkhead, asking him not to send anything to Rome by Persons which could be sent some other way.

There was a certain pathos in Persons's realization that for many Catholics now as well as Protestants he could do no right and was the source of all that went wrong. "I am writing to take away . . . these misconcepts . . . and the more to satisfy . . . you my old friends . . . but how to do it is the difficulty, especially in the last point, about sending of some hither, wherein you have now understood his Holiness' resolute answer to the contrary."[47] Inevitably, the Pope preferred Persons's attitude toward himself and his authority to the cavalier approach of the appellants, especially towards his *Breves*. Hard-pressed by the threat and often the fact of persecution, the appellants were more concerned to appease an English government which could do

---

[46] RP to Birkhead, 4.x.1608, Rome; (X) No. 14, a.l.s.; (11) V, xlix, partly printed. Grene notes, "other letters might be transcribed if tyme did permit, namely that of October 4 to Toby Matthew, and many others," including one to Mush of 13.ix.; (II) f.344.

[47] RP to Birkhead, 12.x.1608; (X) No. 15, a.l.s. Also another copy with signature and last two lines of the postscript in RP's hand.

them harm than placate a distant pope who could do them little tangible good. As Fitzherbert bluntly informed Birkhead, "His Holiness, having seen that not only his Breves but also Cardinal Bellarmine's letter to the old archpriest"—of September 28, 1607—"have been so scanned, cavilled, calumniated and finally published in print"—needless to say without permission—"is resolved for the present neither to send any more Breves nor answers in writing, nor to permit any cardinal to do it."[48] Fitzherbert's letter to Birkhead of September 6 this year underlined the fact that the Pope wanted no more agents and procurators in Rome from whichever side they were sent.

Birkhead accepted the papal decision in the matter of sending agents. But Persons's letter of October 12 refers for the first time to "Mr Dr Smith," whom the archpriest had wished to represent him. Persons was sorry he could not come, because he might have seen for himself how matters lay, and that he was not the man who decided all in Rome. Indeed, Persons was so anxious to remove the impression of his responsibility for the papal prohibition that he now suggested a way round it! Smith should come to Rome "to see this city for his private devotions, or otherwise that may not contradict his Holiness's order . . . and afterward when Mr Dr Smith should have been here some time . . . you might send him a commission, and in the mean space he might both create and speak in matters that shall occur as a man experienced and your confident friend." In due course, the Pope might himself raise the issue of bishops with him. Smith could attempt the journey even in winter, since he was still young and men traveled to Rome in all seasons.[49]

There were now in England more priests than places to receive them. This did not mean that too many were being ordained so much as that the policy of relentless persecution and anti-papist propaganda after the Gunpowder Plot was beginning to pay off. Fewer Catholics were now able or willing to play hosts to their clergy. Nor could the priests always be trusted, notably those with appellant sympathies, not to betray their hosts, knowingly or otherwise, to the government. How many might follow the example of John Cecil? Birkhead suggested more priests should be kept abroad for further studies. This was reasonable, but Persons pointed out the problems associated with finance and accommodation. Once the students had "ended their courses . . . they must give room to others. When they depart . . . they have no place else to go unto but to your parts." The disadvantage of having specifically English houses abroad was that the end product

---

[48] T. Fitzherbert to Birkhead, 6.ix.1608, Rome; (20) 34–35 and nn.4–6.

[49] RP to Birkhead, 12.x.1608. V. supra.

could not be absorbed easily or at all into work on the continent among foreigners.

No consolation came with news from Valladolid. Walter Morgan, S.J., recounted a tale of woe to which Persons replied at the end of August.[50] He was moved to "exceeding great grief" especially on account of the "irreparable hurt both spiritual and temporal" to which the students were exposed.[51] The latter wrote a common letter to Persons on August 8, who responded by sending John Blackfan with two students from Rome to put the house in order. He arrived at Valladolid on November 2.[52] Blackfan's report convinced Persons that the students had not been exaggerating in describing their plight. The few seminarians left were "either prostrate on their beds or else so pale and emaciated in their squalor that they looked more like corpses than men." The two English Fathers were so close to death themselves that one died soon after Blackfan's arrival. "The only healthy person in the house was the rector. He was on the verge of collapse from the strain of so much disaster."[53] When the students wrote again to Persons in August, they could only report fresh discontent. Most had been "of very good natures and dispositions," driven to "scandalous tumultuation and disobedient carriage" only as a result of desperation. The Pope had been informed; but he, knowing no more than Persons and no doubt influenced by the latter's original assumption, simply ordered Bianchetti, in charge of English affairs, to get them "all dismissed and put out of the house." It seemed that at his life's end one of Persons's main efforts had been wasted. "You know the labours I took there to erect those seminaries."[54] Blackfan knew more than most about them. The latter now set to work to restore the stricken community. The arrival of twelve students from Flanders, arranged while he was still in Rome, provided the fresh blood needed. The Spanish rector was encouraged to meet the challenge. Just in time, perhaps, the situation was saved. Blackfan was justly triumphalist. "The whole aspect of the college was renewed and its earlier discipline began to grow again from the hidden seed. By God's mercy the epidemic which had raged for so long" subsided. Studies revived. But the new tranquility was to be short-lived.[55]

---

[50] This was quite probably an alias of William Warford, S.J., who died at Valladolid on 3.xi.1608. See (12) VII, 815 and CRS 30, 94.

[51] RP to Walter Morgan, S.J., 29.viii.1608, Rome; (IX) Serie II, leg.2, a.l.s.

[52] See CRS 30, xxii.

[53] Blackfan, *Annales* . . . , 84.

[54] RP to Morgan, 29.viii. V. supra.

[55] Blackfan, *Annales Collegii Sancti Albani*, 84.

Towards the end of November, Persons replied to a letter from Birkhead dated September 24 giving him a full account of the English scene. Continuing persecution stretched nerves to the breaking point and could put a rough edge on conversation even among the persecuted. If Birkhead spoke truth, the Jesuits were not immune from the prevailing tensions. Persons took his point, writing to Holtby to get his men to see about "repressing all hard speeches and exasperating words, if any have passed, and to have all matters past abolished, if they see correspondence on the other side."[56] This was, of course, a condition, however reasonable, which might make rapprochement very difficult, if not impossible. Fitzherbert felt bound to remind Birkhead on October 4 that the appellants were a minority. "It seemeth that you hold those men to be the body of our clergy (or at least they will seem to be)." Their agent could only hope in God that he had "not yet deserved of the whole clergy of England as to have such deep exceptions taken unto me by the whole body, yea, or by the tenth part thereof."[57]

Like the ache of a decayed tooth, the affair of Lord Montague's letter went on nagging. Even by the end of November, the letter had not yet reached him. Satisfied at first with the explanation of the original non-delivery, he began once again to feel resentment thanks to the opposition of some English Jesuits in Flanders to his project for setting up a convent of Clarissas in the Low Countries. This opposition also caused considerable annoyance to the Jesuit general and Persons. The latter suspected, no doubt with reason, that the appellants had poured oil rather than water on a quarrel which had almost been extinguished. Nor was the influence of the recalcitrants in the Clink extinguished. "It must needs recreate both Cant[erbury] and Lon[don] and the whole crew to see them so obstinate. God forgive them!"[58]

By this time, Montague's ill-fated letter had not got beyond Cardinal Bellarmine's worktable. Unaware of the deeper implications, he had failed to treat it as a matter of urgency. Persons begged him on December 6 to return it to him, so that he could send it off "today, by the courier, if possible. Otherwise he will be very upset since he has asked for it with much insistence for his greater security."[59]

Perhaps the most satisfactory feature of a not particularly auspicious year was the decree issued by the Holy Office on December

---

[56] RP to Birkhead, 26.xi.1608, Rome; (X) No. 17, a.l.s.

[57] T. Fitherbert to Birkhead, 4.x.1608, Rome; (20) 39–43. For a criticism of the larger appellant claims, see ibid., p. 10, n.4.

[58] RP to Birkhead, 26.xi. V. supra.

[59] See also (11) V, app. vii–viii, x.

10 which promised to end a long misunderstanding by regularizing relations between Benedictines and Jesuits on the English mission field.[60] The decree, signed by the Pope, was an expression of his own mind. Its striving for impartiality and fairness was evident. The Jesuits were forbidden under pain of excommunication to prevent students from becoming Benedictines; and, although it was under no such heavy penalty, the Benedictines were forbidden to solicit students to join their order. Hasty admission of candidates to either order was ruled out. Familiarity with heretics and approval of the forbidden oath were also frowned on. But these were Benedictine, hardly Jesuit, tendencies, no doubt with the intention of pushing *pax* to the limits of the possible. All were discouraged from engaging in political activity. Anselm Beech and Robert Persons were forbidden by name to return to England.[61] Persons at this late stage would hardly have been tempted.

---

[60] *Regulæ observandæ a Patribus Ordinis Sancti Benedicti et Patribus Societatis Jesu ad eam quae inter religiosos esse oportet concordiam conservandam ad cultus divini et fidei catholicæ in regno Angliæ propagationem a S.mo Domino N.ro Paulo Papa V in Sacro Inquisitionis Congregatione ordinatæ . . .* 10.xii.1608; (17) 224; CRS 30, xxii.

[61] See Lunn, *The English Benedictines,* 81–82.

Father Robert began this year by hoping that it would be "better than some former have been." The Vatican had heard by way of Paris of a prospect of rapprochement between the appellants and their critics, including the Jesuits. At all events, they were talking to one another. They were also discussing the form of an oath of allegiance which all papists might take with a good conscience and the State might be prepared to accept.[1] Persons assured the archpriest in his letter of January 3 that he and his friends were anxious for peace, no less than was the Pope, of course. However, the Paris nuncio's reports seemed to throw the blame for lack of it on the Jesuits, not the first indication of the superior skill of the appellants in managing their propaganda. Reporting to Rome on November 11, 1608, Ubaldini seemed to imply that Persons was the main obstacle to progress towards reconciliation. "The good offices of his Holiness" with the Jesuit would be "very useful so that he can get the Jesuit party to smooth the way."

The shadow of Lord Montague still loomed in connection with the nuns in Flanders. "As for the Clarisses, I desire all good unto them if only for the sake of pleasing their patron, Lord Montague." Thus Persons to Birkhead on January 3, assuring him that he had instructed the English Jesuits in Flanders to follow Montague's wishes closely. In this he was fully supported by Aquaviva.[2] While anxious not to put obstacles in the way of setting up religious houses for women, Persons insisted that his men should not "meddle further therein than to help them afar off what they can."[3] Their spiritual directors should be, as far as possible, members of their own order. Another house was about

---

[1] Ubaldini to Borghese, 24.vi.1608, Paris; (IV) Segreteria di Stato, Francia 53, f.70r/v, register copies. S. to s., 19.viii.; ibid., f.97v. S. to s., 11.xi.; ibid., f.133v. RP to Birkhead, 3.i.1609; (X) No. 18, a.l.s.

[2] See (20) 6.

[3] See Mary C. E. Chambers, I.B.V.M., *The Life of Mary Ward 1585–1645* 1 (London, 1882): 107–25; and M. Köhler, *Mary Ward*, passim.

to open in Portugal. "I am very glad," rejoiced Persons, "that the young ladies are arrived at Lisbon. Christ Jesus bless them!"[4]

As another tap to the end of a familiar wedge, Persons conceded to Birkhead that it might be useful to send someone in his name, as the new incumbent, to inform the Pope on affairs and problems as he saw them. But all should be done "so as no great noise come before him (as of new stirs) by letter either of the two nuncios of Paris or Brussels (as needeth not) or others."[5] To ease matters further, Montague's fateful letter had now been retrieved from Bellarmine's office and sent by "a safe passage" to England via Flanders. For Montague his letter had by this time become Desdemona's handkerchief for Othello.[6] Montague, Benedictines, and appellants took up the practiced chorus against Jesuits and Persons in particular for what in Rome had gone against them. It was to be expected that the exclusion of Anselm Beech from the English scene would be taken as a piece of Jesuit maneuvering, although in fact it had been Cardinal Lanfranco's "poliza" or memorandum which did most to bring this about. The Pope had left the matter to the Inquisition. "Some will try to use it to reinforce the bad opinion they already have of us, that we will not accept other people to work with us. God knows this is not like us!"[7] None of this helped to promote the cause of Persons's health. He reported to Birkhead on August 23, "The pains of my stomach . . . grow upon me," pains severe enough to prevent him writing by his own hand.[8]

On January 30 the Pope summoned "two Fathers of the Benedictines and two of the Society," making "a final peace between them under severe commandment to observe the same. The chief points were that one part speak well of the other, forget all things past; that the one part hinder not any scholars of seminaries that will be of any approved religion, nor the other allure unto them any by indirect means; that none be sent into England as of the mission but after the novitiate ended; that the rules of the seminaries have their force and be observed . . . and some other like points."[9] Thus ended a quarrel

---

[4] RP to Birkhead, 3.i.1609. V. supra.

[5] S. to s., 14.ii.1609; (x) No. 19, a.l.s. This answers Birkhead's letters of 8.xi and 8.xii.1608.

[6] Ibid. and (20) 5, n.8. RP commented that he had received no word of "Mr Collington's letter," presumably already intercepted. V. supra. See also s. to s., 14.iii.-1609. V. infra.

[7] RP to Bellarmine, 6.xii.1608, Rome; (I) Anglia.A.VI, No. 70, f.317, Italian, signed and endd. by RP. See Lunn, *The English Benedictines*, 95–97.

[8] RP to Birkhead, 23.viii.1608. V. supra.

[9] S. to s., 14.ii.1609. Postscript. V. supra.

which should never have begun and presumably would not have without outside intervention. It was reported to Thomas Fitzherbert that "all these broils" between the Benedictines and the English College at Douai had originated with "my Lord of Salisbury."[10] Likely enough.

The correspondence between Persons and Fitzherbert leaves no room for doubt that they did their best to promote the main object of the appellants. About mid-March, the Pope sent a "resolution" into England concerning bishops. After getting information he would decide according to what had been "proposed unto him and desired." All seemed to augur well.[11] Some information came by Montague's agent, "Mr Fletcher," who went to Rome after installing two ladies in a convent in Flanders. Blackwell, meanwhile, "with his company," had received twenty pounds apiece from the Archbishop of Canterbury, he himself being allowed "to go abroad at his pleasure." Persons thought the Pope should be informed, although Birkhead chivalrously preferred to shelter his late colleague from any further storm. But Birkhead should declare "the loss of his faculties" incurred ipso facto. Rome liked to know what was going on; and gratitude for information received, although Persons did not explicitly say so, might have its effect on the episcopal question.[12] The protector, Bianchetti, and others, "great men, expect great gratitude for the countenance they show, and are ready to be discontented if they be not often by letters saluted of their friends."

Birkhead's letter to Persons of January 20 makes it clear that the appellants were still harping on the one string, blaming the Jesuit for imaginary complaints which caused their not being "suffered to write, speak, nor come unto [the Pope] to declare their pitiful case or to purge themselves of such complaints." Persons dismissed this typical effusion with the simple observation that no complaints had been made, and that anyone who wished could write or come to Rome in person. But the Pope had literally no time for further deputations with the specific object of procuring bishops.[13] At all events, Birkhead now felt that he could bow to appellant pressure with a good conscience and appointed Dr. Richard Smith as his Roman agent. Envisaged from the beginning of March, the appointment was put into effect at the end.[14]

---

[10] T. Fitzherbert to W. Worthington, 7.iii.1609, Rome; (20) 47.

[11] RP to Birkhead, 14.iii.1609, Rome; (X) No. 20.

[12] For the "Clinkers," see (20) 54, n.9.

[13] RP to Birkhead, 14.iii.1609. V. supra.

[14] See (20) 118, n.1, and 135, para. 2, Smith's "instructions" are in English on

British Protestants, least of all King James, did not take it kindly when replies were printed to their published attacks on Catholic doctrine. Some Catholics also felt that it was better to let taunts go unanswered rather than attempt even a courteous retort if it provoked more persecution. Persons wanted Birkhead's opinion, which, he hoped, would animate "these people here," including the Pope.[15] Paul V expressly commissioned Bellarmine to write a reply to James's *Triplici nodo . . . An apologie for the oath of allegiance, against the two breves of Paulus Quintus, and the late letter of Cardinal Bellarmine to G. Blackwell,* published in Latin and English in 1607. Bellarmine published a reply at Cologne in 1608 under the name of his chaplain, Matteo Torti.[16] James replied with a new edition of his own work in 1609 and further commissioned a reply from Lancelot Andrewes, bishop of Chichester.

On March 28 Fr. Robert Jones was appointed to succeed Richard Holtby as superior of the English Jesuit mission, with Richard Blount as his "socius." Living apart to avoid danger, they should consult often together. Richard Holtby would continue as a consultor, with William Wright, Anthony Hoskins, and Michael Walpole. Other "graver Fathers" could also be asked for advice. Holtby's appointment of "spiritual directors" through the country had worked well. These received the renewal of vows by their confreres every six months, whenever they might dare to meet together for this purpose. Then the Summary of the Constitutions and Common Rules would be read, "together with the instructions contained in the fourteen points which we wrote here in Rome on January 9, 1607."[17] Every Jesuit was bound to read the Constitutions and rules privately at least twice a year. The superior must see that this was done. In acccordance with their vow of poverty, all must give at least an approximate account of income and expenditure over the previous six months. Once a year the superior had to send a report to Rome on the state of the mission, spiritual and temporal.[18] The orders and notices contained in the *acta* of the latest general congregation, the Sixth, would be sent as soon as available in print.[19]

135–37.

[15] RP to Birkhead, 14.iii. RP to Bro. Thomas Howard, 5.iii., dismissing him from the Society of Jesus; (IX) Serie II, Leg. 2, a.l.s.

[16] (70) 91–93.

[17] RP, "Ad Patres Soc.tis Jesu in Anglicana vinea laborantes," 9.i.1607. V. supra, chap. 23.

[18] RP to R. Jones, 28.iii.1609, Rome; (VI) Anglia 36.I, f.2r/v.

[19] The congregation lasted from 21.ii. until 29.iii.1608: decrees in *Institutum Societatis Iesu* I (Rome, 1869), 267–89.

When Persons answered Birkhead's letter of February 27 at the beginning of May, Smith was already reported to have landed "on this side of the sea." He was careful not to publicize his journey southwards, although there were those who interpreted it ill that while staying at St. Omers he visited neither nuncio nor the college at Douai. There were various surmises as to his intentions in visiting less tranquil spirits on the way to Rome, but Persons was optimistic. "Yet do I interpret all to be done to quiet better men's humours and form them to a general peace."[20]

Persons's much-exercised patience was now sorely tried by the prospect of yet another round of misunderstanding with the Benedictines—this time not with the sons but the daughters of St. Benedict. By an irony not relished by the wiser concerned, a situation arose in the monastery of the English Benedictine nuns in Brussels which put the Jesuits in much the same position that the Benedictines had occupied vis-à-vis the English students at Valladolid. An internal dissension arose in which certain English Jesuits of the locality supported a breakaway movement among some of the nuns, who went off to found their own establishment at Louvain. In view of the delicacy of relations with the Order of St. Benedict after a quarrel which had only just been healed, Persons was understandably exasperated at the prospect of a fresh collision. The trouble centered in the Abbey of the Glorious Assumption of Our Lady at Brussels, the first foundation of English Benedictine nuns in Europe, set up in 1598 by Lady Mary Percy, daughter of the seventh Earl of Northumberland. An unusual feature was that the spiritual direction was not entrusted to Benedictine monks. The convent grew rapidly from its original dozen or so Sisters, recruiting from distinguished recusant families. William Holt and Robert Persons had both been involved in the foundation. Persons's niece, Mary Persons, was one of the nuns. In 1599 the Archbishop of Mechlin appointed a secular priest, Robert Chambers, as the first confessor and spiritual director. Since his direction did not suit all tastes, the abbess allowed the nuns to have recourse to a Jesuit. A difference between two approaches to spirituality soon assumed the appearance of the all-too-familiar rivalry between Jesuits and appellants. In consequence, a group of nuns who felt that life was made intolerable for them through their adherence to the Jesuits, decided to set up their own convent in Louvain.[21]

---

[20] RP to Birkhead, 2.v.1609, Rome; (X) No. 21, a.l.s. See (11) V, lviii.

[21] See (17) 256–60. The 1609 project was seemingly abortive. The permanent settlement dates from 1624.

Persons was by no means sympathetic, for he feared a new flare-up with the Benedictines. A letter of May 16 to Fr. Thomas Talbot asked for more information especially from William Baldwin. Persons complained of the latter's failure to be forthcoming, although his "manner of short writing" was "sufficiently known" to him.

Persons was chiefly put out by the fact that the whole transaction had not been properly referred to himself or anyone else in Rome. This would have mattered less if the Order of St. Benedict had not been involved. As it was, the ramifications of the question were more than local. Persons did not doubt the good intentions of all concerned, but before going so far they should have consulted the center. "You say if I had been there I would have proceeded no otherwise, but by your leave, I would have consulted it better, and . . . not . . . yielded to an actual separation of the nuns without . . . the approbation of others, and assurance of going forward." The consequence was, "our best friends write against it, and so do the greater part of all the monastery." Most serious, the archbishop had not given his approval, nor was it easy for him now to do so.[22] Persons and, more seriously, the rest of Rome had been left in the dark or at best twilight. He had been "fed with other pretences and no word of the true cause set down." Talbot had told Persons that Hugh Owen favored the scheme, but Persons knew from the latter's confidential letters that this was untrue. Since the abbess, Chambers, and "principal persons of the monastery" were opposed, the "common bruit" was already claiming that "ours have divided an united house, and carried away such as would follow them. . . . And if the Benedictines and other adversaries would enter with the monastery upon this occasion, what a stir shall we have?" There was even the appalling prospect of another battle of books. Persons could only hope that all would be settled before the General got to hear of it. Meanwhile, he wanted "the names, qualities and number of those discontented nuns . . . and how they proceed now."[23] On June 13 Persons wrote directly to Hugh Owen, urging him to circumvent the project and head off the dissension. The secession was prevented at least at that time.[24]

Dr. Richard Smith arrived in Rome on May 11. Persons extended to him and his companion, "Mr Moor"—Thomas More—the "most kindest entertainment" he could in the English College. The college was crowded, and the normal period for a guest's stay was

---

[22] RP to Thomas Talbot, 16.v.1609; (I) Anglia. A.III, No. 94, copy. RP sent Baldwin "by this post" copies of "three lardge letters" written to RP on the subject.

[23] Ibid.

[24] (II) f.469. Grene asks if this was the real beginning of the Ghent foundation.

eight days, but they were allowed to stay on indefinitely. Smith showed Persons his commission and instructions from Birkhead. The first point was that the archpriest "be bound not to deal" with the Jesuits, or the latter with the archpriest, in matters of government. Smith was "very earnest" to have Persons's consent.[25] The latter kept matters at a clinical and unemotional level according to one account, agreeing that, if this was what the archpriest wanted, he would go along with it; but the Pope and the General were also interested. The best thing would be for Smith and Fitzherbert to discuss the matter with the Pope at their first audience and accept his decision. Fitzherbert was ready to accept this arrangement, Smith was not; indeed, he revealed from the outset an attitude of suspicion and mistrust which was to sour the whole negotiation. He insisted on first seeing the Pope himself with More alone. Persons, no doubt accurately discerning Smith's mood, went along with this request. So did the General. In the event, the Pope did little more than repeat what Paul V told Blackwell through Cardinal Farnese. The latest brief forbade consultation with Jesuits on administrative matters, not questions of doctrine and moral theology. Without implying that he expected Smith to report on him in glowing terms, Persons reassured Birkhead that nothing said so far had led him to change his mind about helping Smith. However, they should work with Fitzherbert, a man "learned, pious and wise and of very good credit and experience in this court." They seemed too inclined "to discard him, or use him only for a cipher." If they did, they would "find him no child."[26] Persons urged Birkhead to impress this point on his agents "without showing to have received advertisement" from himself. At one point Smith assured Persons that he had seen one of his letters to Birkhead affirming "that his Holiness neither would have any more reasons, neither have anything written, nor any man sent about the affairs of England." Persons had never, as he reasonably claimed, written anything as crude as this. When he was asked for the "clause together with the date of the letter," Smith, not surprisingly, could not oblige. But Persons was determined not to quarrel. He described their relations as "very friendly." The agents were invited to spend a day at the villa house and sing Mass on Trinity Sunday. "Nor shall any office of courtesy on our part be wanting, God willing." The main points of Smith's explicit instructions concerned keeping the Holy See fully informed, improving educational and other opportunities for young priests, excluding from the mission "illiterate and un-

---

[25] RP to Birkhead, 6.vi.1609, Rome; (X) No. 22, a.l.s. See (11) V, lxii; and (20) 48, n.1. Instructions; ibid., 102–5, 135–37.

[26] S. to s., 6.vi. V. supra.

trained priests," and the problem of finding places for priests on a mission which was shrinking under persecution.

The program was shown to Persons and Fitzherbert, together with Birkhead's "declaration . . . of intention." This claimed that "the sending of the agent is not for the purpose of renewing our earlier petition for bishops nor for stirring up of disputes, past or present, but is an act of friendship and trust, and intended for no other purpose than to establish peace and quiet among us all."[27] The "declaration" directed Smith "to establish peace and concord more firmly" with Persons and deal with him as the Pope directed on clergy affairs. He should also cooperate with Fitzherbert, who was expected to put into Smith's hands "the greater part of the whole business" while remaining "always ready to give help and advice for the benefit of our common cause." But beneath the surface rippling brightly in a charitable sun ran a cold undercurrent of suspicion. "Lest he try to give one impression to the pope and another entirely different to my agent about us, I insist that my agent shall consult very frequently and amicably with [Persons] about our concerns, so that in their reports to the pope there may be no discrepancy or inconsistency."[28] Birkhead stated baldly that he did not want Persons to "interfere with any claim to authority" in matters concerning his "charge and government." He fully endorsed the Jesuit's own allowance that there should be no "subordination" of Smith to him. Smith should "treat him as the best of friends and a trusty assistant," in view of his "very long experience and skill in affairs." His "influence with the Holy See" could further the "cause and honour of all the clergy."

Persons undoubtedly felt that Birkhead had given way to Smith's tendency to dominate and even domineer. This trait was to be the cause of much future trouble. All the same, Persons decided to risk taking Birkhead fully into his confidence in his second letter of June 6, the first being clearly intended for general circulation. This second letter revealed a Persons wounded to the quick by the clear distrust and scarcely veiled dislike not only from the appellants in general but even from the man who now led the ragged army of Catholic survivors in England. Birkhead was warned at the outset that the letter contained matter to be kept secret and, if he did not wish this, he should "not read the same but presently burn the letter." It was only to be discussed with the Jesuit superior or with such as he indicated. After which Persons proceeded to shred some of the original propositions, although he assumed charitably that Birkhead had been under some

---

[27] (20) 137.

[28] (20) 102, 136: also 103–4 137.

pressure when he wrote it. Persons had no desire to lord it over Smith—"dominando occupari." Fitzherbert was asked to leave the prominent role to Smith—"maximam ei totius partem"—but Birkhead's commission and letter to the Pope gave them joint authority. Notwithstanding, Persons and Fitzherbert wished to remain "old fast friends . . . ready to concur with any reasonable means you can think upon for the peace so much desired."[29]

Persons strained every nerve, as he plausibly claimed, to remove "all matter of complaint" from Smith and More. "I have borne myself . . . as though I had been the scholar and they brought me up, and not I them, and as if they were ancient men in this court and knew all things . . . and I were young and knew nothing; which was needful if any peace were to be held." But it cost him dear. "Truly . . . I never dealt with any men in my life more heady and resolute in their opinions than is the doctor whom the other in all things secondeth." Fitzherbert likewise at a recent interview "found himself so overlaid . . . with words" that he had to throw up his hands in protest before "he got some audience and leave to speak." Persons attributed Smith's studentesque cocksureness to "lack of experience"; but harmony could not continue on this basis. The blest or unblest pair of sirens presumed to talk for the "priests and clergy of England" even if their conclusions were unlikely to be "the common judgment of all" or even of the majority. "We do not think," concluded Persons, "that you could easily have sent two others more passionately addicted that way," that is, the way of the appellants.

Smith, rather acting out God's Englishman abroad, seems to have used no more tact in dealing with Pope and cardinals than with the Jesuit. He was brash enough in a "large oration to his Holiness" to contrast "priests and religious men and their labours in England . . . gloriously advancing the one above the other," so that he managed to displease "all that heard it." The Pope, having his worst fears confirmed, inquired about Birkhead from Fitzherbert, who "took occasion thereby to speak honourably of him." Neither agent "spake anything in [his] praise." Persons wondered what they would do if the archpriest refused to "give them contentment in all other demands." When Bianchetti had an answer ready for the archpriest, Smith tried to forestall Fitzherbert by getting it for himself alone. The cardinal, however, knew "that they were jointly in commission" and called Fitzherbert first as the senior man. He passed it to the agents; but they "demanded a copy" from the cardinal himself, who denied it since what was "written by superior to superior" in Rome was not supplied

---

[29] RP to Birkhead, 6.vi.1609, Rome; (X) No. 23, second letter; (11) V, lxvi.

in copy. All the same, the cardinal, in the event, "told them the effect by word of mouth."[30]

Whatever the inner feelings of the men concerned, the exterior courtesies were carefully observed. There was mutual visiting and shared occasions sacred and profane. Persons and the General swallowed the bulky pill that forbade the archpriest to consult the Jesuits in matters of government, although they would have preferred that he be free to consult whom he wished "as other prelates do." When the Pope learned of their acquiescence, he made no further difficulty. But from a letter of John Cecil's from Paris, it is evident "that he was weary of English contentions."[31] So not necessarily for the pleasure of his company or because he valued his advice, Smith sought out Persons on June 24 to discuss two projects: a writers' house to produce antiheretical literature, and the "revocation of the Brief about making of doctors." Persons made no difficulty about the first, although he knew from experience the less endearing traits of literary men. He wondered "whether fit men to write would so easily be found that would be content to live in subordination." The second plea he rejected. The Pope had handled the matter as vice-protector, and the restriction on getting doctorates too easily had been imposed on the advice "of all the chief English in Rome at that time." And "no man here could safely imagine what interest or utility could arise" by revocation. In any case, it was always in the archpriest's power to recommend anyone to "have the grace."

Unbeknown to Fitzherbert, the agents obtained an interview with Bianchetti on June 26, where they aired the same two points. After referring the matter to "the whole Inquisition," the Pope decided against a house of writers for the present, although "he would not hinder or forbid it" and would even contribute to the printing costs of books genuinely defending the faith. He deferred the question of higher degrees. Bianchetti summoned Fitzherbert as well as the other agents to hear the papal decison. Afterwards they all came to the college to inform Persons, "and we live very good friends." This was the expurgated account of affairs written in one letter of July 4. Persons wrote another the same day, this one to be kept secret.[32] Smith had defended his colleagues in the Clink and was opposed to any papal gesture to reduce "the scandal and contempt" arising from their example. Smith was against depriving the recalcitrant priests of their

---

[30] Ibid.

[31] S. to s. 4.vii.1609, Rome; (X) No. 24, a.l.s. (11) V, lxxii, partly printed.

[32] S. to s., 4.vii.1609, Rome; (X) No. 25, 2nd letter, RP's hand unsigned; (11) V, lxxii.

faculties, lest they be driven to worse. Perhaps they might have been. Persons, however, thought that if they were pressed further, God would "give them grace to obey." Smith was not only dissatisfied with "the present state of things" but he and his friends took "every least occasion" to urge their case "with very shallow reasons oftentimes, as to us they seem." Worse still, they would "scarce with patience" listen to objections. Worst of all was "the inward and settled difference of judgment and affections . . . from those with whom they ought to join." Persons did his best to be patient, but it is unlikely that every Jesuit on the mission reacted with similar restraint to what they could take as calculated provocation. Birkhead alluded to this in one of his letters. Persons urged him to lodge any complaint he might have in this connection with the Jesuit superior, who would take disciplinary action. But Persons knew there was no path for himself open to reconciliation. He was too good and obvious a villain for his enemies to lose.[33]

The failure of the appellants, for all their compliance, to win any change in the attitude of the civil power was sufficiently proved when "the king's Latin book dedicated to all princes against the pope" appeared.[34] It was cause for marvel that the King made no secret of his authorship. Persons feared he might "draw answers from some princes' subjects with less respect than were convenient." He hoped that his own subjects would "wholly abstain or proceed with dutiful respects" not so much out of love for James, presumably, as out of fear that his resentment might increase persecution. On July 23 the Holy Office replied negatively to the petitions of the archpriest's agents. However, those who proved themselves in the seminaries might proceed to the doctorate after the usual four years' further study. All the same, the protector was not allowed to give formal approbation to this method of circumventing the original ban. Inevitably, the agents refused to believe that Persons was only reflecting the general attitude of Roman authority. Persons, on the other hand, assured Birkhead he had only discussed matters with Bianchetti and Bellarmine when he urged them not to make any difficulties about the demand for doctorates. The rectors of the colleges should be left to make their judgment in such cases, as was normal. For the rest, Persons was sorry that there was not

---

[33] Ibid.

[34] S. to s., 25.vii.1609, Rome; (X) No. 26, a.l.s. (11) V, lxxiii. The book was *An apologie for the oath of allegiance . . .* , published at the same time as a Latin translation, both new editions of his previous work now openly published under his own name. See (70) 92. Also (75) 127, 129.

more "familiarity and confidence and more communication in affairs."[35]

Early in August, with Bianchetti's approval, Persons approached the Archbishop of Malines with a respectful plea for "our English nuns at Brussels." Prompted by the advice of English correspondents in the city, he asked the archbishop, who was drawing up rules for the convent, to allow the nuns to elect or reelect their abbess every three years. This was not to be taken as a reflection on the present incumbent, but only to recommend a system of government successfully introduced by the Patriarch of Lisbon for the English Bridgettine convent there. Its success had won approval and confirmation from Rome, and there was question of applying it to all Benedictine convents of nuns. Anticipating the charge of interference, Persons pointed out that he was prompted by voices in the locality and by the fact that the issue affected the Jesuit order generally in its relations with the Order of St. Benedict.[36]

Even Persons's more open letter to Birkhead of mid-September did not conceal the "diffident dealing" of the archpriest's agents with the men at the English College. Nor had they bothered to conceal their mistrust at the very first meeting with Pope Paul. Suspicion is contagious. Pope and cardinals soon came to suspect the real intentions of the agents. This became clear at a meeting on September 2. "Nihil esse innovandum" was to be the rule for England for the time being. It was arguable that the agents had been their own worst enemy; but they could still see no fault in themselves, only in Persons.[37] In his "secret letter" of September 15, Persons tried to enlighten Birkhead on the reasons for Smith's failure. For one thing, he had been "over liberal in talk here to divers," claiming that it was not *de fide quod papa ullam habeat authoritatem deponendi principes*. Whatever the pros and cons of an issue controvertible even in that day, it was unfortunate that Smith saw fit to air a controversy which had no bearing on his own causes and could only confuse the issue.

In his "open letter" to Birkhead of September 15, Persons took up the charge that the Jesuits were interfering in the internal affairs of Douai College with disastrous consequences, even going so far as to manage it secretly. Birkhead suggested that as "a great mean of peace"

---

[35] S. to s., 25.vii. V. supra. For the doctorate question, see (20) 53, n.5.

[36] RP to Archbishop of Malines, 8.viii.1609, Rome; (I) Anglia.A.III, No. 96.

[37] RP to Birkhead, 16.ix.1609, Rome; (X) No. 28, a.l.s.; (11) V, lxxvii–lxxviii, partly printed. This "open letter" acknowledges B's letters of 6.vi. and 22.vii., and referred to two of his own of 8 and 22.viii. The "secret letter" was dated 15.ix.; ibid., No. 27; (11) V, lxxxv–lxxxvi, partly printed.

some of his colleagues should be appointed to Douai to institute reform and "unite against heretics," and also that they should be allowed to choose their president. Persons was in entire agreement. It had always been run by secular priests, "and so is like to be still" if the Jesuits had anything to do with it. Its government had been urged upon the Society in Allen's day and more recently, but the Society had avoided the compliment. However, the priests in control should be "moderate men . . . that will agree with others, and with such religious as of necessity they must have correspondence withal" in work for the common cause.[38] This did not mean that the college should come under the archpriest's jurisdiction, although, for obvious reasons, the appellants wanted this. Persons took care to put in a good word for Dr. Worthington, the president and an old friend. He was not helped by the fact that the Spanish subsidy remained unpaid. Even so, the nuncio Bentivoglio visited the college in May and commented favorably on what he found.

The most extraordinary attack on Persons and the Society at this time with regard to Douai came from John Mush. He wrote to Worthington on June 22, as Persons not unfairly claimed, "to put a dislike between us." Mush accused the Jesuits of "wicked and horrible partiality"—his own words—"ejecting readers, receiving boys, refusing university men" and all who did not "bring commendation from a Jesuit." All of this, especially the last, Persons claimed, was quite false. Everything that went wrong in the college, claimed Mush, was the fault of Jesuits. Although they had procured the promise of a pension from Spain many years before, the blame for its nonpayment must lie at their door. In fact St. Omers was suffering equally in this. Persons, as he convincingly claimed by appealing to the account books, procured during his eight or nine years in Spain some twenty thousand crowns for Douai alone. When Mush had procured half that sum, he might "ruffle" against him and his colleagues. "Priestly modesty might then also stay him somewhat from this manner of writing." All of this Persons offered as evidence that appellants should not be allowed to control Douai, since they would use it as a fortress from which to make forays against the Jesuits who were running other seminaries, thus spreading strife.[39]

Mush's unhappy letter reached the Pope, as Persons guessed, through Bentivoglio. It came at the worst possible time for the appellants, since it coincided with the appearance of King James's latest book attacking the papacy. Dr. William Barlow, bishop of Lincoln,

---

[38] S. to s., 16.ix.1609, postscript. V. supra. See (20) 58, n.5.

[39] S. to s., 16.ix. V. supra.

threw a little oil of his own on the fire by proclaiming in another book that "the secular priests that were agents in Rome . . . did at their return describe unto them Cardinal Burghesius, now pope, that he was a Tiberius Gracchus."[40] The Pope's general disgust with the English and their squabbles was likely to affect Jesuits as well, so that Persons had a powerful additional motive in his "secret letter" to Birkhead of September 15, urging him to act as a point of reconciliation for them all—something even more necessary in view of a new controversy swirling round Smith's answer to several books by Thomas Bell appearing from 1593 onwards. In 1593 Bell apostatized from the Catholic faith and priesthood. His books, not notably significant, were answered by Philip Woodward in 1605, and by Richard Smith in 1605 at Douai.[41] Smith too pointedly avoided any attempt to refute Bell's contention that the pope had no power to depose princes. In fact, Bell founded his own opinion on passages from the "secular priestes' bookes." Smith's *An answer to Thomas Bel's challenge* . . . was delated to the Roman Inquisition about the end of 1609. It is not clear that Persons had anything directly to do with this, although the existence of a *censura* in his hand shows that his opinion was sought. At all events, revenge seemed in order. Dr. Alabaster, then staying at the English College, "helped by Smith and his companions, made charges against Persons," including complicity in the Gunpowder Plot, and delated to the Inquisition his *Judgment of a Catholic Englishman* . . . , published anonymously in 1608.[42]

Persons had proceeded hitherto on the assumption that Birkhead like Blackwell before him was substantially in agreement with him. Any disagreement arose from appellant pressure rather than from his own conviction. He was rudely awakened by Birkhead's letter

---

[40] *An answer to a catholike Englishman* . . . (London, 1609). See STC (1948 ed.) (34); BL catalogue; (70) 110, No. 365.

[41] See (70) 147–48.

[42] (20) 122–23, n.26. See also *Censura brevis de quibusdam quæ hoc capite primo libri Domini Ricardi Smithei contra Belum hæreticum continentur,* (I) Anglia.A.VII, No. 24. This MS is endorsed, "(1) By Parsons—censura in caput primum D. Ricardi. (2) Originale." Manello Solinardi, the "assessore" of the Holy Office, apparently sent Barlow's book to RP with a covering letter of 20.x.1609, "a ciò alla lo veda et facci quello conoscera espediente per difessa della Santa Sede Catolica." He also wanted to know if a certain "Thomasso inglese" was staying in the college. See (I) Anglia.A.III, No. 97, a.l.s. See also *A discussion of the answer of Mr Barlow to the book intitled The judgment of a Catholick concerning the Apology of the new oath of allegiance, written by F. Persons but published after his death,* 1612, 4.to. Edward Coffin wrote the extensive preface laying open "the ignorance, lyes and impudent rayling of Mr Barlow," vindicating RP "from many calumnies," (II) f.356. Smith's correspondence for 1608–10 is in (III) Old Series, Vols. 8 and 9, passim. His memorial to Paul V on the causes of and remedies for discord are in the Old Brotherhood Archives, Oscott.

of July 22. This urged Persons "not to rub so much upon the name of the appellants." Persons replied with fervor if not heat. "I would the name were no more in memory, but here men cannot be understood except they use that name of distinction, for to use the words of secular priests in general, as Barlow, Bell and other heretics do, is too injurious to the residue of that order that have no part with them in the opposition which they make." Nor could they be described as "the English clergy," since many of these and the religious orders disagreed with them. "Appellants" was the word used by Pope and curia and would continue so until they "would cease from disunion." If Birkhead was surprised that Persons had foreseen so clearly the antagonism that Smith would arouse in Rome, the Jesuit insisted that Smith's characteristics left room for no other conclusion.[43] Delay in the arrival of letters could prolong the agony of misunderstanding, giving time for minor annoyances to grow like weeds neglected. Not until October 19 could Birkhead reply to Persons's letters of July 4 and 25. Birkhead had been away and the Jesuit's letters had only found him two months after their arrival in England.

Birkhead's reply of October 19 was cold but correct. His agents had admitted Persons's "charitable entertainment," while the archpriest wanted only peace. All the same, he was glad that the Pope had forbidden dealings with the Jesuits in matters of government.[44] Faced with the dilemma of choosing between the diverse views of Persons and Smith, Birkhead came down firmly on the side of his agents. He had the right to an agent who would "propose our suits according to my direction." Birkhead was ready to believe that Persons had not "crossed [him] with any of the cardinals," but some had their doubts. Smith had expressed no discontentment, wanted peace, and had shown "all humble obedience to his Holiness." Birkhead wanted no more confidential asides. "Good Father, I beseech you not to commit such things to me in secret any more. [Dr. Smith] is now my agent, and I repose a confidence and trust in his fidelity." He would not find him "guilty" until he were "convicted of falsity." He believed that, if Smith's mission had not gone well in Rome, it was the fault of Persons, who should have "condescended to join with [him]" in the matters proposed. Had all gone well, Birkhead would have "promised . . . all love and peace on our parts." As it was, they must simply be patient until somehow they could win Persons over. Meanwhile, "I will leave

---

[43] RP to Birkhead, 16.ix.1609. V. supra.
[44] Birkhead to RP, 19.x.1609, London(?); (11) V, lxxxii.

no stone unturned to keep mine in the best order I can towards all your company."[45]

If Birkhead felt at one with Smith, Fitzherbert was no less united to Persons. Indeed, Birkhead told Fitzherbert that "the brethren took him for a Jesuit" and asked for "satisfaction" or apology. The latter replied with spirit that he was glad they took him "for so honest a man." He spoke of those "who make all Jesuits that will not be enemies to Jesuits," and he was not the only one so labeled. Appellant exasperation at their failure should not conceal the fact that their weakness was in "the matters propounded" and not because of "any man's labour against" Smith. He had enjoyed ample opportunity to explain his case, which was considered by "many cardinals." Nevertheless, Fitzherbert was ready to go on helping them all he could.[46]

Knowing the strength of feeling against him and aware that Birkhead identified with the appellants, a less dogged man than Persons would have been tempted to give up. In any case, he had only a few more months to live. It would be excessively melodramatic, no doubt, to talk of a broken heart, but he could have felt no great desire to prolong an existence which promised so much less than eternity. All the same, he was a fighting man and remained so until his death. There could be no question of laying down a command unless it was taken from him. Neither the Vatican nor the General showed any desire to replace him, certainly not after having had closer contact with his critics from England. He understood perfectly the ways of both and enjoyed their complete confidence. He continued even now to fight for a bridgehead giving access to the new regime in England. Before he received Birkhead's letter of October 19, he wrote to reassure him of his and Fitzherbert's support of Smith while in Rome. They followed Birkhead's directions to let Smith "propose what he would," reserving only the right to express an opinion if asked—which, inevitably, they were. There were only differences "in some points," and it was a whole congregation of cardinals which made the final decisions. Smith's resentment at the rejection of his proposals and his determination to lay all the blame on the Society could only "cause marvel to them as have known our proceedings towards you."[47]

---

[45] Ibid. On 14.x.1609, RP wrote to tell Creswell of "Count Robert Shirley's" visit to the college. He was taking Paul Washington to the Spanish court as his chaplain, "a good, grave, learned and honest priest." Washington would then proceed to San Lucar to work in the English Jesuit house; (IX) Series II, Leg. 2.

[46] T. Fitzherbert to Birkhead, 19.x.1609, Rome; (20) 57–60. Regarding the independence of Rome's judgment, see (20) 70–73, n.3.

[47] RP to Birkhead, 30.x.1609, Rome; (X) No. 29, a.l.s.; (11) V, lxxxv. See Fitzherbert to Birkhead, 31.x.1609; (20) 60–63.

The picture of Smith that emerges from the correspondence of Persons and Fitzherbert is of a man obstinate, convinced of a knowledge and experience superior to all others, and unable to see himself in the wrong. His later history appears to confirm this. But it is fair to record that Creswell wrote to him on May 9, assuring him of his esteem for "a man of peace and of a quiet, sincere spirit, free from all turbulency and faction."[48] Likely enough, Creswell was indulging in harmless flattery to promote peace and "to disappoint the secret subtleties of our common enemies who do hope to undo us by private dissensions among ourselves, and in the meanwhile . . . laugh us to scorn."

Mush wrote to encourage Smith on June 19, urging him to be "secret . . . wise" and "stout" in his proceedings. "Once get credit with Paul and you may obtain all things necessary for our country."[49] Mush certainly contributed to appellant difficulties in getting their own way. He wrote to Cardinal Arrigone to urge that Jesuits have no dealings "in our affairs," warning him that he was dealing "with two of great cunning and long experience." Douai was on the edge of ruin thanks to "Worthington whom Persons placed."[50] Even Birkhead had to rebuke Smith mildly on September 17 for bringing up the Douai affair so soon and so maladroitly. Worthington was left "staggering," whereas with a little more subtlety he might have been drawn to the appellant view of things.[51] "Good old Dr Bavant" was the man who had opposed any "rough dealing" especially against Worthington. In any case, Birkhead had to admit that any immediate solution of Douai's problems was beyond him. Perhaps Persons was right in thinking that the Jesuits still had a contribution to make to the mission especially with regard to the seminaries. Meanwhile, if Persons was supplying Birkhead with a candid commentary on Smith, the latter was rendering the same service with regard to Persons.[52] In this tale of tangled relations, the marvel is not that Catholicism failed to flourish in England but that it survived at all. Perhaps without persecution it would not have done so.

---

[48] Creswell to Smith, 9.v.1609; (III) Old Series VIII, No. 107, p. 501. Contemporary but presumably not by Creswell, because according to a postscript he was too indisposed to write by his own hand. For Smith's latter career, see A. F. Allison, "Richard Smith's Gallican Backers and Jesuit Opponents . . . ," (10) 18, 329–401 with extensive references to sources.

[49] Mush to Smith, 19.vi.1609; (III) Old Series VIII, No. 120, p. 533, signed "J.Ra.", autog.

[50] Ibid. Mush to Arigone, 30.i.1609, London; ibid., No. 88, pp. 447–51, a.l.s., Latin.

[51] Birkhead to Baker (Smith), 17.ix.1609; ibid., No. 152, p. 617, a.l.s.

[52] Ibid.

Chapter Twenty-six

The Closing Scenes: 1609–1610

B irkhead seemed anxious to begin the new year well. But the first letter to Persons, while reiterating his desire for friendship with the Jesuits, reemphasized his dislike of any criticism of Smith. If Persons felt he had reason to complain, it should be to "those that can correct him." If "their highnesses" passed on such complaint to Birkhead, he would deal with Smith as they saw fit "to command and direct him."[1] Birkhead's loyalty to his agent had something admirable about it, but it could be regarded as given to the wrong man. To vindicate Smith it seemed necessary to imply that Persons was guilty of malice and calumny. "If you object against my agent things that are true, I . . . take it in good part, but if you . . . oppress him by false informations, I must bend myself, in all due respect to your gravity and years, to defend him as well as I can, if he give no cause to the contrary."

The archpriest strove to avoid an open breach between Smith and Persons. Replying to letters of October 16 and November 7, 1609, Smith was exhorted to patience in dealing with Birkhead's "old friend," and warned "to give them no offence." Persons had reported that Smith had failed to visit the college and had criticized both it and the Society. "This I trust you will not practise, howsoever you be moved in particular against him and Swinerton."[2]

In their letters of October 31, 1609, Persons and Fitzherbert told Birkhead that matters were "concluded in the Congregation of the Inquisition," although Smith made no mention of it in his letter of November 7.[3] Birkhead warned Smith against any counterdemonstration; but he would not give up, expecting "some . . . better success

---

[1] Birkhead to RP, 8.i.1610, London(?); (11) V, lxxxix–xci.

[2] Birkhead to Smith, 8.i.1610 (O.S.?); (III) Old Series, IX, No. 2, holog. A long letter of the spy John Reynolds to R. Cecil of 26.i.1610 describes his alleged experiences with the Jesuits, especially RP and Coffin in the V.E.C.; (VII) SP 85, vol. 3, ff.145r–50v, a.l.s. Reynolds was apparently befriended by Alabaster while in Rome. This interesting detail occurs. "The Coledge sends all their letters (or the most part) for England by way of Doway, and the post departeth heer hence the saterdaie." RP and Coffin, discerning his true role, denounced him to the Inquisition, which imprisoned him.

[3] Birkhead to Smith, 8.i.1610 (OS?); (III) Old Series, IX, No. 2, holog.

when we prefer any sent again." Time was on their side. Meanwhile, Persons and his friends must be borne with. It would not be for long. Having no inkling of the restraint which the archpriest was endeavoring to exercise on Smith, Persons felt only the pain of estrangement from an almost exact contemporary. This was sufficiently proved by Birkhead's all too literal interpretation of the papal injunction against dealing with Jesuits "in matters of government." Birkhead found that Persons's broader interpretation almost amounted to indifference; and so he complained to Smith, asking him to get "some new admonition to keep the order strictly . . . barring us to deal with the Fathers in matters belonging to our government, and yet . . . to use them friendly and well."[4]

Inwardly, Birkhead was probably much relieved by the decisions against a college of writers and against appointing bishops, at least at that time. "You will not believe what a trouble it is to gather men's voices" and then to nominate those they wished. Nor were the assistants greatly helpful in this. Birkhead felt with Persons that stronger measures might have been adopted against the "Clinkers"; but he saw the point that Rome preferred all the suffering and persecution undergone by the recusants to come from the secular state. In any case, there was a marked difference between feelings in the rarified upper atmosphere of Church politics and those of the workers at ground level. The implacable John Mush might send Birkhead letters "so brief and plain" that they could not be passed on before being "better tempered." However, "those of the Society here with us do outwardly bear themselves well and with good respect," although their friends might "sometimes show their fervent affection in terms not tending to peace." In general, "mine behave themselves well to them so that we are in much peace in regard of former times, though not with such alacrity on all sides as would be required."[5]

Early in March, Persons sent word of the Pope's decisions on English affairs "by two ways" so that the message should arrive safely by at least one channel. Persons hoped it would "work the quiet and peace between us which . . . all good men desire." He further reported Smith's compliance with Birkhead's exhortations. "Your agent hath been here of late with me, and we have treated friendly of all matters, and renewed our old friendship; and as I never to my knowledge gave him cause of alienation . . . so was the reconciliation easy."[6]

---

[4] Ibid.

[5] Ibid.

[6] RP to Birkhead, 6.iii.1610, Rome; (X) No. 30, a.l.s. See (11) V, xcvi. RP received B's letter of 18.x.1609 on 9.i.1610, replying on 20.iii.

A few weeks later and with the arrival of another letter, it was evident that most of the smiling had been with the teeth. Birkhead's clear and cold defence of his agent against any attempt by Persons to criticize him even in an aside brought the parties back to square one. On March 20 Persons expostulated strongly against Smith as a tainted channel of information. "As by seeing through a glass, the colour must appear such as the glass hath in it, and the water must needs taste of the scent wherewith the channel is imbued by which it passeth," so Smith had left characteristic marks of untruthfulness on the news he gave the archpriest. "It was both our and your evil hap when you lighted upon such a mediator who showeth himself so passionate and captious as even in private talk he will often mistake a man's word so as presently he is bound to justify himself, and much more afterward will misrepresent or misconstrue them." Persons was sorry to have to say it, but say it he must. He had heard others "complain of the same."[7] Smith was a man who listened to no one but himself.

It is evident that what really galled Persons was the fact that Smith would take no share of the blame for anything that had gone wrong. Worse still, "whatsoever he should not effectuate to his will, he would ascribe to [Jesuit] contradiction and thereby excuse himself." As for Birkhead's suggestion that Persons only complain to their superiors in Rome, "superiors are wise enough to note such things of themselves." They well knew that Persons had "not complained of him, nor made contradiction against him nor his affairs as he imagineth and hath informed you." Birkhead wanted peace and friendship with the Jesuits if it could be had. But what more could they do? They had never opposed appointing bishops nor did they wish to interfere in the archpriest's government. What stung most was the accusation of giving false information about Smith. "After so many years of religion," he never thought to be so accused. He well knew "what a great sin it is to misrepresent any man" and could never do so deliberately. Undoubtedly, he was living in a relatively distant past when the secular clergy without exception had looked up to the Jesuits as teachers, guides, and mentors. For many by this time, the Society was no longer a symbol of success but an obstacle in the way of progress. Bad mistakes had been made in the handling of the seminaries and adherence to the policies of Spain had proved disastrous. The wrong horse had won. It did not require the limited genius of Smith to understand this. On the other hand, Persons and his colleagues, while aware of past mistakes, could not see themselves made into general scapegoats without resentment, or understand why they could not be accepted fully, in view of past

---

[7] S. to s., 20.iii.1610, Rome; (X) No. 31, a.l.s.; (11) V, xcvii.

work and experience, as coworkers for any future which Catholicism might have in England. A sense of rejection and ingratitude could sometimes make the less long-suffering react sharply. Birkhead was well aware of the changed climate even since the days of Blackwell. He could not afford to appear as the cat's-paw of Persons and his Society, however much confidence they might continue to enjoy in Rome. But it was surely unnecessary to suggest that the "Clinkers" defended their action by something they found in Persons's writings.[8] Even in Rome, where more balanced views prevailed, perhaps, the Jesuits were not allowed to dominate the English scene. This was undoubtedly wise.

The above letter to Birkhead seems to have been the last of Persons's "business" letters. From now on his thoughts were taken up with a future life rather than with what was left on earth. The closing month or so was recorded in considerable detail by Edward Coffin. It reads like the passing of a saint. This may seem incongruous if not incredible, coming at the end of a life seemingly absorbed in politics— one concerned with worldly causes where they touched material even more than spiritual where they touched worldly, as it must often seem. But perhaps it is necessary at this point to correct a wrong impression which might have been left by this attempt at biography. Persons the priest, and also the man, tried to live consistently against the backdrop of his own Spiritual Directory. His life in the spirit has to lie beyond the scope of an account which can only be based on externals. He left no spiritual diary, or if he did, it has not survived. Nevertheless, this inner spirit comes through all his letters, even those most preoccupied with material causes. It is therefore fitting that this essential theme of his life be allowed to sound at the end like the closing bars of a symphony or the final chorus of an oratorio. However we assess the achievement of the ecclesiastic, he saw himself, and so did his friends, as a man who had fought a good fight and kept the faith, even if one cannot travel without getting dusty or fight without coming away with a few scars.

Whether or not his end was hastened by the latest disillusionment in his relations with Birkhead and the realization that the initiative in recusant affairs had passed to the appellants, he had a clear premonition before the middle of April that his end was near. He prepared a letter in English signed by himself and in the copies to the archpriest and the secular clergy. "Being now, as I hope, very shortly to end this mortal life and go to my Saviour, I could not forget in my greatest agonies to take my leave of you, your assistants and all your other subjects by this my last farewell, in testimony of the charity and

---

[8] Ibid.

perfect love and affection which I do bear and always have borne
yourself together with them all in Christ Jesus." His last desire was for
peace and union among all the clergy, secular and religious. He repudiated even the "least desire or imagination of superiority" over the
rest, desiring only "friendly concurrence" between his and theirs.[9]
Similar letters were addressed to the Jesuits, with an appeal for prayers
in his last crisis and an exhortation to mutual charity.[10]

Persons wrote to the General, "I cannot long survive being
subject to such intense pain. And therefore I pray the God of mercies
. . . to shorten my time that I may the sooner be dissolved and be with
him." Schooled to endure pain from his earliest youth, the habit did
not desert him now. He had practical advice for the General. Fr.
Thomas Owen was recommended to succeed as prefect with Silisdon as
his socius. He wanted Owen to direct the English College, since he had
"been working in it successfully for many years." An Englishman
should be minister. "I am afraid that if the students were under anyone else, they would soon relapse into their former unruliness." For
the rest, Aquaviva was exhorted to keep English affairs close to his
heart, as he had done hitherto. He wrote "with some reserve" of Fr.
Coffin, but recognized that he had "excellently carried out his duties as
confessor" and so should continue.[11] Distracted with pain and more
urgent business, Persons still remembered Bishop Blaise of St. Omer, a
good friend of the English Catholic cause, and his conational Fr.
Schondonck.[12]

Death might be near but peace still lay some distance away.
The eccentric Alabaster, as it was reported, "accused Persons of twelve
articles of unsound doctrine collected partly out of his published
writings, and partly out of a book not yet come to light whereof the
said party had by close means gotten a view." He was again accused of
complicity in the powder treason along with Tesimond, who was then
a penitentiary in St. Peter's.[13] Alabaster imparted his suspicions to the
English ambassador in Venice so that "his Majesty should know it, and
withal his zeal towards his country." Wotton assured Cecil he would
fan the flame. "And it will be the more easy because he is kindled with

---

[9] S. to s., 10.iv.1610, Rome; (X) No. 32, signed: No. 33 is another copy unsigned, "out of my bed, this Easter Eve, 1610."

[10] RP "ad nostros," 10.iv.1610; (II) f.342, copy. S. to the Valladolid superior
and community; (IX) Serie II, Leg. 2, copy endd. in J. Creswell's hand, (16) 363.

[11] RP to Aquaviva, 12.iv.1610; (II) f.343, Latin copy. The original was in
Coffin's hand and presumably signed by RP.

[12] RP to the Bishop of St. Omer, 13.iv.1610; (II) f.343, note only. Text in (16) 387.

[13] Sir Henry Wotton to R. Cecil, 13/23.iv.1610, Venice; (VII) SP Venice,99, No. 29.

spite, the Jesuits at Rome having first accused a late book of his, and having besides, which is the more sensible point, reduced his pension from the pope of twenty-five crowns the month to fifteen." The Vatican was now aware of Alabaster's open apostasy and flight to Marseilles, where he could hardly find words bad enough to describe Rome, Jesuits, and Inquisition. By now he had learned the error of his ways and wished only to live and die a Protestant, "telling a thousand lies and inventing a thousand calumnies"— mainly aimed at the Holy Office. He returned to England to enjoy a sufficient share of the fleshpots until his death in 1640.[14]

As Persons passed rapidly beyond the reach of friends and enemies alike, the last few days were described in loving detail by his faithful secretary and amanuensis, Edward Coffin.[15] "On Tuesday of Holy Week, April 6, Fr. Persons first complained of feeling unwell. Although he had written much in the morning, after dinner he ceased from writing but got on with dispatching a great deal of other business as if he felt no pain." After receiving a couple of visitors in the evening, he insisted on taking supper in the refectory with the students, "as he had done for the whole of Lent." Against the urging of the doctors, Persons insisted on making do with the sparse Lenten fare provided for the rest—no meat or eggs. His office work increased during the appellants' visit, but he made himself go through "his ordinary exercises of devotion in the chapel, saying the Office, meditation, and the daily visitation of all the altars of our church . . . to gain the station indulgences." After he had taken a modest supper, the pains in his chest and side which he had endured for three years past returned with greater intensity, so that he was unable to get any rest that night. He bore it all with singular patience and fortitude.

By morning the pain had eased sufficiently for him to sleep for a few hours. "After dinner, he asked for some of the Fathers and students to spend the time of recreation with him, and he spoke to me, who was the first to help him, with such cheerful countenance that there seemed to be nothing wrong with him." Indeed, he spoke of the futility of Barlow's book and regretted the time spent in answering it, which would have been better laid out on the second and third parts of the *Book of Resolution,* a work much desired in England. The choice had not been his. Barlow's book had been delated to the Inquisition, which ordered Persons to answer it. This he had done in four months,

[14] G. Siripandi to RP, 21.vi.1610, Florence; (II) f.487.

[15] (VI) Anglia 38.I, formerly "Fragmenta." See H. Foley, passim, and Hist.Angl. Suppl.II, IX, pp. 149–62. Pages 124a–166 of this collection are annotated "continet materias et notas Patris Bartoli pro continuanda sua historia D'Inghilterra." This present document is an extract from Coffin's work.

a remarkable achievement for a man so busy and in bad health. Even so, he was not able to complete his answer to the third part.

In spite of the optimism of doctors and the recession of the worst symptoms for a time, Persons was convinced he would be the next in the house to die and made no secret of his conviction. His improvement was short-lived. During the night of Wednesday, the fierce pain of the previous night returned. Again there was improvement early next morning; but at 1 P.M. an attack of fever began which lasted nine hours. He bore it with patience but at the end was so worn out that he could talk to nobody, although he did not lose consciousness. There was an attack on the morning of Maundy Thursday but not as severe as the previous one. Indeed, after the midday meal, "all the students were called together and he recreated with them in an atmosphere of relaxation." This was followed by another attack; but, because he remained fully conscious and rational throughout, it was difficult to foresee an early death even now. Vitelleschi, the Italian Assistant, came to see him, and so did many others that same evening as word of his condition got round among friends in the city.

The dying man was well aware of the significance of the time and season. He felt himself to be participating during these last days of Holy Week in the passion of Christ.

> He took note of the hours throughout the day, saying now is the third hour when Christ endured such and such. Now is the sixth hour when He suffered other things, and so on. He repeated frequently a verse of the psalm which had often been on his lips when he was well. "God have mercy on us and give us His blessing. Let the light of his countenance shine upon us and may He show us his mercy." By this time, representatives of cardinals, and not only of Farnese, Bianchetti, Bandino, and Bellarmine, came to pay their respects. They and other bishops and prelates would have come in person but were discouraged by the Fathers themselves, as was the Spanish ambassador, who sent small gifts as well as commiseration.

"That night—Good Friday—he managed to get some rest." Indeed, after receiving Viaticum he seemed so recovered that many thought the danger of death had passed. He himself knew better. A "double attack" of fever now caused him to summon the Jesuits in the college to his bedside. After telling them his time was at hand, he dismissed them to go on to write letters to the Bishop of St. Omer, Birkhead and his clergy, and to various Jesuits. Fr. Fabio de Fabiis, who had been Persons's first rector and his master of novices, now arrived with nine English novices from Sant'Andrea. On their knees they begged his blessing and received a short exhortation and a personal embrace. After them three assistants arrived successively, those of France, Spain, and Portugal. They stayed until dinner time. Aquaviva came after dinner, although not feeling very well himself, to ask for any last messages and advice. He was followed by a number of Jesuits and many priests and noblemen from the city. Some indulged in excessive and excessively formal speeches. Not surprisingly, all this brought on an attack of fever that night worse than anything preceding, so that the Fathers refused to let anyone else see him next day. Not even Bellarmine or the Commissary of the Inquisition were admitted. When the Pope heard from Farnese of Persons's condition, he sent him "his blessing with all the indulgences in amplissima forma which were usually given to dying cardinals. This brought the Father much consolation."

Once again, the dying man rallied. "On Easter Day itself, the illness seemed somewhat to have lifted." The students received "this happy news" with much joy, "for they all deplored his loss as something beyond ordinary misfortune." They had prayed much and carried out various devotions for his recovery, "making it clear that no preceding superior in this house had ever been more beloved, or his passing deemed more bitter." Since no other superior had been loved at all, if previous records are to be believed, this could well be true. Man is an emotional animal, and Coffin's account may not be simply the effort of someone trying to be edifying. There probably was a reaction in favor of Persons and even of the Society, at least in the college, in the highly emotional atmosphere surrounding the death of anyone and especially him.

The patient lingered on until Easter Wednesday. By this time "his first reply to any question always gave satisfaction, although when he continued to speak he might begin to ramble." The General was among the last to visit him. Calling the English Fathers together in an adjoining room, he declared, "Truly, I see him as a martyr. I have known him for thirty-five years and have always held him for a saint." Permission was given for the body "of so great a man" to be buried not in the professed house but in the college which he had endeavored so strenuously to serve for a lifetime. Instruction was also given that his body should be "embalmed, placed in a casket and so committed to the earth." Even now, after the General's departure, others came to see Fr. Robert for the last time, and he did his best to acknowledge their presence. His last speech was with the students while psalms were read to him, which he repeated until his voice failed completely. He died about 2 A.M. on Thursday morning at the age of sixty-four, thirty-four of which had been lived in the Society. He left his friends the memory of a man who lived out his motto fully, acting in all things *suaviter et fortiter*.

The body was brought into the chapel next morning. "Many came to kiss his hand," especially Jesuits. Adulatory phrases flow on such occasions, but the sense of loss seems to have been widely felt. The brethren delayed the embalming operation by some hours, wanting confirmation from the General, since Jesuit corpses were not usually so treated. When the surgeon arrived the same evening, he made some difficulty about the operation.[16] The weather was hot, and "the body being in process of decay, would give off a stench with risk of infection" after so much delay. However, he complied, being "the college surgeon and well-disposed towards the deceased." In any case, "he subsequently received a reward for his labours rather larger than he expected." In fact, apart from his liver "and another organ," the body proved to be in good condition. The cadaver, duly casketed, was "buried before the high altar to the right of Cardinal Allen, while the Bishop of Cassano lay on the left."

The epitaph on the stone capping the grave recorded his death on April 15. He was described as "a most learned and upright priest" and an "excellent director" of the English College. His share in other foundations was also indicated. Even the appellants could hardly have denied that "he enjoyed no part of the peace he tried to reestablish, and never refused a contest in defence of truth." It was, of course, the truth as he saw it. But there is no other kind of truth for anyone.[17]

Persons's death was often noticed in the larger world beyond Rome with more relief than sorrow perhaps. Positive hatred did not spring from Protestant bosoms alone. The process of belittling him began almost before the body was cold. Anthony Champney reported from Paris he heard from someone in the nuncio's train that when the Pope heard of his demise, he merely observed that "now Fr Persons is dead matters of England would go better."[18] Grounds for vindication or criticism of our subject are sufficiently provided, it is hoped, in the text. An attempt at a last word from the biographer seems therefore superfluous. A last word from the man who knew him well, however, and who was with him at the end, may not be out of place. He observed "the change of heart in the college where the increase in observance was so great that he seemed to be our Elias. . . . With his mantle, he bequeathed to each and all of the students a double share of his spirit. Hence the general peace of mind which followed him and . . . caused astonishment in all." The General came to the college the

---

[16] The word used is "obesum," which could mean swollen or obese. See Lewis and Short dictionary.

[17] Latin epitaph in the VEC. Transcript in (XIV), 46/12/7.

[18] M. Kellison to R. Smith, 18.vi.1610, Rheims; (III) Old Series IX, No. 44.

Saturday after Persons's death to exhort them to stay in their present peace. Even the less critical spirits often felt that nothing in life became him quite so much as his manner of leaving it. Professor J. B. Black summed him up as "a subtle and complex character. Gifted with a trenchant personality, he had all the qualities—resourcefulness, perseverance, foresight—that show the man of action rather than the saint or the pastor. His mind never ran on small things."[19] But the large thing on which he had set his mind and to which he gave his whole life was something that the culture not only of his own country but of the whole English-speaking world was to see as increasingly alien. This was nothing less than the final triumph of the Church—Holy, Roman, Catholic, and Apostolic. Attitudes are changing, and it may be that they will eventually change far enough for all to see that he had a point. As Pasternak observed, history is a process without end, and Persons's tale is only a small ripple in a mighty flood still rolling onwards. But if any general reappraisal of his life still lies far in the future, perhaps he could already be regarded as deserving of a place in the calendar of warrior saints. Certainly his cause never had a doughtier fighter or a supporter more single-minded in his devotion.

---

[19] J. Black, *The Reign of Elizabeth, 1558–1603* (Oxford, 1959), 2nd ed., n, 179f.

Index

Monsi, Archdeacon Michael de, 57, 58, 60
Montague, Viscount. *See* **Browne**
Montecassino, 338
Mora, Domenico(?), 206
More, Thomas, 374, 375, 377
Morgan, Thomas, 53, 80, 81, 87, 91, 96, 97, 100, 109, 111, 118, 183, 190, 214, 276
Morgan, Walter, 366
Morone, Cardinal Giovanni, 15, 16, 18, 19, 21, 22, 26
Morton, Thomas, dean of Gloucester, 347
Morton, Earl of, 69, 103, 122
Munck, Levinus, 226
Munday, Anthony, 18 n.29
Murray, secular priest(?), 248
Mush, John, 1, 2, 93, 232, 238, 261, 262, 264-268, 270-274, 277, 278, 325, 360, 363, 381, 385, 387, 388
Music, 126, 152

Nau, Claude, French secretary to Mary, Queen of Scots, 81
Navarre, Henry of. *See also* **Henri IV,** 127, 140
Nether Stowey, 1, 2, 8
Neville, Sir Henry, 228
Nichols, John, 52, 53, 62
Norris, John, 138, 182, 183
Norris, Sylvester, 201, 205, 207, 210
Northampton, Earl of, 334
Northumberland:
7th Earl of, 373
8th Earl of, 53, 90, 91, 101, 102, 104, 229, 235, 259
Norton, Dr Nicholas, 27
Novitiate, 288, 314
Nuns, 345, 369, 373, 374, 380

Obedience, temporal, to James I, 330, 333
Ogilvie, Pury, 163
Oldcorne, Edward, 340
Olivares, Count, Spanish ambassador in Rome, 12, 26, 125, 127, 128, 132, 221

Olivier, Bernard, S.J., 220
Orange, William of, 106, 113
Orton, Henry, 35
Osborne, Edward, 67
Owen, Christopher, 19
Owen, Hugh, 61, 105, 114, 193, 194, 206, 218, 210, 313, 335, 341, 374
Owen, Thomas, S.J., 214, 270, 278, 302, 307, 313, 314, 390
Oxford, 3-13, 49, 94

Padilla, Antonio de, S.J., 139, 181
Padilla, Don Martin de, admiral of Castile, 194, 197
Padua, 11, 12
Paget, Charles, 53, 80, 81, 87-93, 96, 97, 100, 101, 111, 114, 118, 183, 190, 194, 201, 214-219, 226-230, 239, 240, 245, 255, 276
Paget, Lord, 35, 53, 87, 88, 93, 101, 113
Paliotti, Cardinal Gabriele, 26, 29
Papacy, loyalty to its prerogative, 51
Paravicini, Cardinal Basilio, 210
Pareces/Parraces(?), Pedro de, S.J., rector at Valladolid, 305, 313, 344
Parker, Richard, 270, 274, 279
Parlement, of Paris, 185
Parliament, of England, 47, 115, 125, 182, 183, 298
Parma, Prince of, 88, 89, 98, 101, 104, 105, 108, 113, 117, 118, 123, 126-128, 193, 281
Parry, Sir Thomas, English ambassador in France, 257, 258, 281-283, 297-326
Parry, William, 87, 96, 97, 99, 108, 227
Paschal/Pasquale, John, 27 n.19, 52
Pasquier, Etienne, 91, 92
Paul V, Pope, 314, 316, 320, 327, 329, 339, 342, 346, 350-354, 356, 358, 360, 362-366, 368, 370, 371, 375-378, 380-383, 385, 387, 393
Payne, John, 67
Peña, Dr Francesco de, official of the Rota, 207, 209, 210, 225